Fromm

Thailand

Here's what the critics say about Frommer's:

"Amazingly easy to use. Very portable, very complete."
—*Booklist*

♦

"The only mainstream guide to list specific prices. The Walter Cronkite of guidebooks—with all that implies."
—*Travel & Leisure*

♦

"Complete, concise, and filled with useful information."
—*New York Daily News*

♦

"Hotel information is close to encyclopedic."
—*Des Moines Sunday Register*

♦

"Detailed, accurate and easy-to-read information for all price ranges."
—*Glamour Magazine*

Other Great Guides for Your Trip:

Frommer's Australia

Frommer's China

Frommer's Hong Kong

Frommer's Nepal

Frommer's New Zealand

Frommer's Singapore & Malaysia

Frommer's Southeast Asia

Frommer's ®

4th Edition

Thailand

by Jennifer Eveland

IDG Books Worldwide, Inc.
An International Data Group Company
Foster City, CA • Chicago, IL • Indianapolis, IN • New York, NY

ABOUT THE AUTHOR

Jennifer Eveland's passion for Southeast Asia runs deep, having lived as a child in Singapore, vacationing in Malaysia and Thailand with her family. After completing *Frommer's Singapore and Malaysia*, 1st Edition, and chapters in *Frommer's Southeast Asia*, 1st Edition, last year, she gave up her apartment in New York City for a life of travel writing in the region. She lived for 8 months in Bangkok, from where she traveled the country compiling the information for this book. These days she divides her time between temporary homes throughout the region. If you see her creeping through jungles, gobbling savories from a hawker stall, or propping up a bar somewhere, make sure you say *sawatdee*.

IDG BOOKS WORLDWIDE, INC.

An International Data Group Company
919 E. Hillsdale Blvd.
Suite 400
Foster City, CA 94404

Find us online at **www.frommers.com**

ISBN 0-02-862889-6
ISSN 1055-5412

Editor: Claudia Kirschhoch
Production Editor: Scott Barnes
Photo Editor: Richard Fox
Design by Michele Laseau
Staff Cartographers: John Decamillis and Roberta Stockwell
Page Creation by: Natalie Hollifield, Heather Pope, Linda Quigley, and Julie Trippetti

SPECIAL SALES

For general information on IDG Books Worldwide's books in the U.S., please call our Consumer Customer Service department at 1-800-762-2974. For reseller information, including discounts, bulk sales, customized editions, and premium sales, please call our Reseller Customer Service department at 1-800-434-3422.

Manufactured in the United States of America

5 4 3 2 1

Contents

List of Maps

ACKNOWLEDGMENTS

My gratitude to Charubhong Pangsapa at the Tourism Authority of Thailand in Bangkok and all the great TAT staff around the country who supplied me with invaluable information. I am indebted to Methinee Noke Pratoomsuvarn, my friend and research assistant in Bangkok. For their great insights, I'd also like to thank Tom Kasper and Janewit Sithiwongs. Special acknowledgment goes to Andrew Chan and Thavee Ploogsawat, who held down the fort in Bangkok while I was out gallivanting about the countryside. To all the brilliant locals, expatriates, and travelers who let me pick their brains for the best and latest information—a big fat *kop khun ka* to every one. Finally, for additional inspiration, a special thank-you to Karn Tor Sawetjinda.

Previous editions of this volume were composed by John Bozeman, Kyle McCarthy, and John Levy, whose careful work made my job that much more enjoyable. Last but not least, Matt Hannafin gave me this great opportunity. I owe him a whole brewery.

AN INVITATION TO THE READER

In researching this book, we discovered many wonderful places—hotels, restaurants, shops, and more. We're sure you'll find others. Please tell us about them, so we can share the information with your fellow travelers in upcoming editions. If you were disappointed with a recommendation, we'd love to know that, too. Please write to:

Frommer's Thailand, 4th Edition
IDG Travel
1633 Broadway
New York, NY 10019

AN ADDITIONAL NOTE

Please be advised that travel information is subject to change at any time—and this is especially true of prices. We therefore suggest that you write or call ahead for confirmation when making your travel plans. The authors, editors, and publisher cannot be held responsible for the experiences of readers while traveling. Your safety is important to us, however, so we encourage you to stay alert and be aware of your surroundings. Keep a close eye on cameras, purses, and wallets, all favorite targets of thieves and pickpockets.

WHAT THE SYMBOLS MEAN

✪ Frommer's Favorites

Our favorite places and experiences—outstanding for quality, value, or both.

The following abbreviations are used for credit cards:

AE	American Express	EURO	Eurocard
CB	Carte Blanche	JCB	Japan Credit Bank
DC	Diners Club	MC	MasterCard
DISC	Discover	V	Visa
ER	EnRoute		

FIND FROMMER'S ONLINE

www.frommers.com offers pages of up-to-the-minute listings on almost 200 cities around the globe—including the latest bargains and candid, personal articles updated daily by Arthur Frommer himself. No other Web site offers such comprehensive and timely coverage of the world of travel.

The Best of Thailand

Thailand's allure is pure Oriental fantasy—a dream world of royal palaces with delicately peaked roofs, glittering temples that pierce the skyline, and serene images of the Buddha radiating peace and divine knowledge. It is the bustle of Bangkok, with its simple canal- and river-side communities, a sprawling Chinatown, and outdoor markets nestled in its modern cityscape—where a walk down any street is a heady combination of incense and jasmine, chile and garlic. And then there's the exquisite countryside—flat plains carpeted with rice paddies and dotted with tiny villages, mountains of luxuriant teak forests where elephants once roamed wild, and acres of coconut palms worked by deft monkeys. Thailand is a tapestry of ancient civilizations—with each one's exquisite arts and beliefs melded permanently into the national psyche. Behind every warm Thai smile there lies a mystique inherited from ancient cultures, and mysterious superstitions we can only surmise.

In Thailand you'll find adventure of all kinds—extreme sports both on land and off, trekking journeys to tribal villages, and motorcycle trips to border town curiosities. Gorgeous tropical islands are home to long, sandy postcard-perfect stretches of beach, where you'll find everything from laid-back bungalow guesthouses to posh Thai-styled five-star resorts. The cuisine is equally captivating, with its sweet, sour, and salty notes heated by a unique, fiery spice many have come to crave.

I've combined research and observations for this volume—relevant travel advice, up-to-date information, the best restaurant and hotel recommendations, and information on all there is to see and do in the Kingdom. So come to The Land of Smiles and see the very best of what it has in store for you.

1 The Best Cultural Experiences

- **Celebrate Songkran:** April 13th marks the first day of *Songkran,* the Thai New Year. In traditional times, Thais would wash Buddha images in local temples, and then sprinkle water on the hands of their elders as a show of filial piety. These days, however, *Songkran* has escalated into a nation-wide water fight. Khao San Road in Bangkok is a mob scene, stuffed to the gills with dancing people, smeared from head to toe with talc paste. You will be joyously exhausted, wet to the bone, caked with chunks of powder, and aching from laughter. See chapters 2 and 11.

- **Take a Different Kind of Sunday Drive:** Make the overland journey from Chiang Mai, Thailand's northern capital, to Mae Hong Son, buried in the foothills of the Himalayas. The oft-described treacherous trip—narrow roads, crumbling cliffs, insane drivers swerving at unnerving rates, and maybe a wandering armed rebel or two—is not. Though the hairpins may be wicked, the biggest challenge awaiting you will be bobbing chickens, and the occasional water buffalo herd. At Pai, mountains give way to rice paddy–carpeted valleys dotted with quaint wooden farmhouses, then wooden houses turn into surreal bamboo shacks. Then the jungle gives way to spectacular blue skies and mountain ranges, rolling hills green with lush jungle, and jutting limestone cliffs. Somewhere, not far from here, the Burmese border looms in the distance. See chapters 12 and 13.

- **Make merit:** While many Thai people will "make merit" on a daily basis, it's possible for visitors to participate in this age-old tradition as well. This custom—gestures that secure a better life after this one—can be performed in any number of ways: offer pails filled with necessary daily objects like soaps, foods, robes, and a small donation to the Abbott of a monastery; contribute to a monk's morning meal with offerings of food; or, purchase a caged bird at one of the temple complexes and set them free (a fabulous photo op as well). It's best to consult a Thai about formalities and customs beforehand in order to understand complex matters of etiquette. And remember, always thank the receiving monk—he will never thank you. He never begs; only offers you the opportunity to better your life.

- **Pet an Elephant:** No matter how often you see it, it will never fail to amaze: elephants lumbering along Bangkok city streets, peeking in doors and greeting strangers. The huge creatures are at first daunting, but to spend a little time around them is to learn how docile, graceful and majestic these beasts are—truly a magnificent symbol of Thailand. It is a pity to see them wandering in traffic, begging to tourists for 20B bunches of sugar cane (sold by accompanying trainers) and although some argue that purchasing the sugar cane encourages streetwalking, until an organization finds other arrangements for these animals, those 20B treats are a surefire way to brighten your evening.

- **Discover Spirit Houses:** Take the time to notice one of Thailand's delightful curiosities—spirit houses. These dainty shrines, some of them quite elaborate, sit atop a post in every yard to house spirits—family spirits or spirits of former dwellers. Each day the household will place offerings of flowers, drinks and food to care for the spirits and keep them happy. The spirit house is erected shortly after a new occupant enters a home.

  Each municipality also has a "city shrine," a larger spirit house maintained for the entire town. These will always be well tended, draped with colorful garlands and offerings from residents. Thais rarely neglect the shrines, their ancestors or the spirit world—a tradition that is as alive today as it has been for centuries.

- **Watch the Royal Barges:** Find out when launchings of the Royal Barges are scheduled and head for lunch at **Ton Pho**, overlooking the Chao Phraya River (43 Phra-Athit Road, Banglamphu ☎ 02/280-0452) (see chapter 4 for a full review). Watch as the long slender gondolas twinkle in the sun, their bows curved with the shape of swans' heads, their sides low, almost touching the water as they glide gracefully in regal splendor. The Royal Barges are set afloat on state occasions, usually once or twice a month, and can be seen up-close and personal at The Royal Barges museum. The Tourism Authority of Thailand (TAT) has the latest calendar of launchings. See chapter 5 for more details.

- **Surrender to Fate:** In Thailand, fate works in strange ways—a broken down bus, nobody who speaks English for miles, disconnected phone service. When it changes your plans it can ruin your day. Or it can make your whole experience. Repeat this phrase often: *mai pen rai*—never mind—and you will enjoy Thailand all the more.

2 The Best Resorts

- **Marriott Royal Garden Riverside Hotel Bangkok** (Bangkok; ☎ 02/ 476-0021): After a day of crazy Bangkok traffic and exhausting sightseeing, you'll be relieved to hop aboard the ferryboat that'll take you to this sanctuary on the other side of the river. A city hotel that looks like a resort, the Marriott is simultaneously convenient and remote. See chapter 4.
- **Banyan Tree Phuket** (Phuket; ☎ 076/324-374): With private villas that are pure romantic luxury, Banyan Tree has become a favorite for honeymooners. But don't just come for the romance—options for dining and holiday activities are endless. See chapter 8.
- **Le Royal Meridien Phuket Yacht Club** (Phuket; ☎ 076/381-156): If you're traveling with your family, you'll love Le Meridien's many fun activities, excellent holiday day-care center, beach lifeguards, and great dining options. Moms and Dads can have the perfect vacation, and the kids won't want to leave. See chapter 8.
- **Royal Garden Village Hua Hin** (Pattaya; ☎ 038/412-120): Smack in the middle of the Pattaya Beach shopping, dining and nightlife strip, Royal Garden is set back in gardens, with a sense of peace and serenity. See chapter 6.
- **Chiva-Som International Health Resort** (Hua Hin; ☎ 032/536-536): Exquisite luxury and personalized care keep international celebrities on their list of regulars. After experiencing Chiva Som's masterful collection of beauty and health treatments, you'll know how the rich and famous stay so gorgeous. See chapter 7.
- **Laem Set Inn** (Ko Samui; ☎ 077/424-393): Heralded in glossy overseas publications, Laem Set is quite a shining star. And for good reason—the quiet isolated location and charming local decor make for the ideal Samui getaway. See chapter 7.
- **The Regent Chiang Mai** (Chiang Mai; ☎ 053/298181): Luxurious Thai-style suites, excellent restaurants, a multitude of activities and the most amazing swimming pool you've ever seen await you at The Regent Chiang Mai. Don't forget to meet their resident water buffalo family—they work the resort's private rice paddies. See chapter 12.

3 The Best Luxury Hotels

- **The Sukhothai** (Bangkok; ☎ 02/287-022): Steeped in Asian mystique and contemporary luxury, Sukhothai's bold architectural expression successfully combines the best of old and new. See chapter 4.
- **Hotel Sofitel Central** (Hua Hin; ☎ 032/512-021): Recent renovations and additions haven't altered this historic hotel's rich heritage, impeccable service and fantastic grounds. See chapter 7.
- **The Oriental** (Bangkok; ☎ 02/236-0400): One of the world's premier hotels, the Oriental has its roots in the days of romantic steamship travel. On the Chao Phraya River, ferries and long-tail boats stop at the pier regularly, making trips to old Bangkok incredibly simple and fun. See chapter 4.

- **The Westin Chiang Mai** (Chiang Mai; ☎ 053/275-300): This is *the* address in Chiang Mai. The northern capital's best new luxury hotel has spacious, attractive rooms with city views, and fine service. See chapter 12.

4 The Best Hotels with Character

- **Felix Phra-Nang Inn** (Krabi; ☎ 075/637-130): From its rustic Thai-style log cabin exterior, to guest rooms with Chinese tiled floors, stucco walls pressed with tiny shells, canopy beds with seashell garlands, and odd slate tiled bathrooms, the Felix never fails to delight. See chapter 7.
- **The Princess Village** (Ko Samui; ☎ 077/422-216): Ko Samui's Chaweng Beach has a slew of choices, but none as exotic as Princess Village. Thai-style houses on stilts surround lily ponds and gardens. While other places are definitely more modern, here you'll feel surrounded by exotic Thailand night and day. See chapter 7.
- **River Ping Palace** (Chiang Mai; ☎ 053/274-932): Not only is River Ping affordable, but quite lovely as well. Dripping with cozy old-world charm, this renovated Thai-style teak mansion induces fantasies of travelers' tales of yesterday. See chapter 12.
- **The Golden Triangle Inn** (Chiang Rai; ☎ 053/711-339): One of the older choices in Chiang Rai, Golden Triangle keeps it simple and personalized. Preserving gardens and maintaining quaint guestrooms, the staff goes out of their way to make your stay enjoyable. See chapter 13.
- **First Hotel** (Mae Sot; ☎ 055/531-233): My pick for the oddest hotel in Thailand, this place is still the best choice in town. Behind a shoddy facade dwells a wild masterpiece of carved wood ceilings and beams, with marble throughout— from the lobby through the halls to the guest rooms. All this, and low prices, too. See chapter 9.

5 The Best Party Beaches

- **Patong Beach** (Phuket): Is it famous or infamous? It's the best place for shopping, but prices are inflated; the best for nightlife, but it can get very seedy; and the best for water sports activities, but it can get crowded. Still, for better or worse, everyone ends up on Patong eventually. See chapter 8.
- **Chaweng Beach** (Ko Samui): If you like the beach, but don't want to feel like you're marooned, then Chaweng has all the life you're looking for. With countless dining options, shopping, nightlife, and activities (and tourists), Chaweng gets bashed by beach purists, but in truth it's sort of a gas, and the beach is still great. See chapter 7.
- **Haad Rin** (Ko Phangan): What started as a faint buzz among backpackers has exploded into a phenomenon. The famous Full-Moon Parties at Haad Rin are very real. Plan ahead—the party draws thousands. Stay away if you're with the Drug Enforcement Agency, or want to avoid being busted by increasing police raids. See chapter 7.

6 The Best Secluded Beaches

- **Ko Samet:** Pick any beach on this island. While it's not far from Bangkok, most people choose the more established island resorts instead—so Ko Samet remains underdeveloped, rustic, and easygoing. See chapter 6.

- **Nai Yang** (Phuket): As one of the most famous island resorts in the world, it would seem impossible to find a place on Phuket without the tourist hassle. Nai Yang developed as a wildlife preserve, has one of the most isolated beaches, and fantastic snorkeling. See chapter 8.
- **Mae Nam** (Ko Samui): Chose this small bay if you'd like a more intimate experience with a beach. Quiet and calm, the water is deep for the best swimming around, and visitors tend to be more mature and relaxed. See chapter 7.

7 The Best Outdoor Adventures

- **Rock climbing at Rai Ley Beach** (Krabi): According to experienced climbers, the seaside cliffs are a thrill, and one of the top 10 rock climbing destinations in the world. But you don't have to be an expert. Beginners are welcome to enjoy the challenge and the breathtaking views as well. See chapter 7.
- **Scuba diving** (Phuket): Scuba operators are a dime a dozen on Phuket, but one firm has taken the activity to new heights. Dive Master's Eco-Dive 2000 is developed by marine biologists and environmental experts to teach divers about the delicate ocean ecology while exploring remote and unspoiled underwater worlds. See chapter 8.
- **Snorkeling just about anywhere**: With huge living reefs and other odd creatures close to the water's surface, snorkeling in both the Andaman Sea and the Gulf of Thailand opens up under-the-sea wonders to anybody who can swim. Check out Phuket's bays, Ko Phi Phi, areas around Krabi, Ko Samui and islands along the eastern seaboard. See chapters 7, 8, and 9.
- **White-Water Rafting** (Pai): Paddle past protected forests, through canyons and along fossilized walls over wild rapids and calm waters. Thai Adventure Rafting spares no effort to ensure your safety—they're probably the most organized adventure outfit in the country. See chapter 13.

8 The Best of Natural Thailand

- **Phang-Nga Bay** (near Phuket): Imagine yourself in a Chinese scroll painting. Above you are hundreds of towering cliffs, jagged limestone towers peppered with lonely trees—each one an island in a peaceful bay. You won't believe your eyes. See chapter 8.
- **Route 1095 from Chiang Mai to Mae Hong Son:** The overland route to this Burmese border town leads you through the foothills of the Himalayas. Mountaintops open onto views of the misty hills all the way to Burma, while valleys are filled with peasant farms. See chapter 13.
- **Khao Yai National Park** (Northeast): Thailand's oldest and most visited park still throbs with wildlife, from elephants to tigers to more than 300 species of birds. Hike along nature trails, or camp out to watch the excitement from watchtowers at night, the best time to see them in action. See chapter 10.

9 The Best Offbeat Vacation Activities

- *Manhora Song* (Bangkok): Few things capture the allure of old Bangkok like this old renovated rice barge turned luxury cruiser. Let your imagination run wild as you gaze out at life along the Chao Phraya River—if you can pull your eyes away from the beauty of the boat itself. See chapter 5.

- **Northern Thailand by Motorcycle:** With safe roads, plenty of petrol stations and rest stops, and friendly folks along the way to lend a hand, touring the kingdom by motorcycle is as uncomplicated as it is exhilarating. Some of the most adventurous trips are in the northern mountains, especially along the Mae Khong River. For the best scenery, however, in Isan the Mae Khong wanders through breathtaking river scenes—the road winds through many small villages and towns, and there are so many interesting temples, natural wonders and quaint villages to visit. See chapters 10 and 13.
- **Cooking Classes:** Love the food, but can't make heads or tails of a produce market? Thailand's best hotels have put together some great morning classes, with hands-on practice and lesson on traditional culture and local ingredients. See chapters 5, 8, and 12.
- **Thai Boxing School:** What are you, chicken? Go on, give it a try. One of the most famous schools in Thailand invites foreigners for training in English, from beginner to master training. If you love the sport and value the culture, plan your vacation around the 10-day course. See chapter 8.
- **Novice monk and meditation programs:** Almost every Thai man enters the *sangha,* or monkhood, for some period of time, usually 2 weeks, and the more learned monks practice one or more of the 40 Buddhist meditations. Many monasteries have opened their doors to foreign laypeople for novice monk programs, for a more intimate experience with Theravada Buddhism, and for meditation courses. See chapters 8 and 12.

10 The Best Shopping

- **Chatuchak Weekend Market** (Bangkok): A tourist attraction in its own right, Thailand's largest market is a never-ending village of bargains—from fighting cocks to clothing, tools, antiques and so much more. Don't get lost. See chapter 5.
- **Night Market** (Chiang Mai): Tribal crafts and locally produced items line Chang Klan Road and the giant market building—find bags, clothes, jewelry, and trinkets plus cheap knock-offs. Don't forget to bargain. See chapter 12.
- **Sankamphaeng Road** (Chiang Mai): This 5.5-mile stretch of highway is home to shops, showrooms, and factories with Thailand's best handicrafts—bronze and silver, furniture, ceramics, antiques, umbrellas, silks and cottons, and paper goods. See chapter 12.

11 The Most Intriguing Archaeological Sights

- **Ayutthaya:** The former capital of Siam was one of the world's largest and most sophisticated cities before it was sacked by the Burmese in 1756. Today it remains one of Thailand's greatest historical treasures, with abundant evidence of its former grandeur. It's easily reached in a day trip from Bangkok. See chapter 5.
- **Sukhothai:** Founded in 1238, Sukhothai (The Dawn of Happiness) was a capital of an early Thai kingdom. Many of the ruins of this religious and cultural center are faithfully preserved and well maintained in an idyllic setting. See chapter 9.
- **Phimai:** Thailand's most famous and best restored Khmer sanctuary was built nearly 1,000 years ago to honor the Hindu god Shiva—it is believed that Phimai predates the great Angkor Wat, and even influenced its style. Later, Phimai was converted into a Buddhist temple. An especially fine museum highlighting its treasures is nearby. See chapter 10.

- **Ban Chiang World Heritage Center** (Ban Chiang): The most complete and fascinating site in Thailand, possibly even Southeast Asia, this exhibit of artifacts and skeletons dating from 12,000 to 5,000 B.C. toured the world before settling at the original excavation site in Ban Chiang. See chapter 10.

12 The Best Museums

- **The National Museum** (Bangkok): Simply the biggest and best repository of the nation's treasures. Objects from throughout Thailand's long and various history include beautiful stone carvings of Hindu deities, exquisite Buddha images, gold jewelry, ceramics, royal costumes, wood carvings, musical instruments, and more. See chapter 5.
- **Phimai National Museum:** This handsome modern building houses a well-presented collection of treasures from Khmer-era Thailand, including stone carvings and jewelry. See chapter 10.
- **The Institute for Southern Thai Studies:** The history of Thailand's southern regions, and its Malay influenced cultures are catalogued and displayed in this sprawling exhibit. Give yourself at least 3 hours. See chapter 7.

13 The Best Small Towns

- **Pai:** Not your typical tiny mountain-valley farming village, Pai has become a little known favorite for travelers who want a little small-town relaxation. The scenery is gorgeous, bungalows are cheap, food is good—and the nightlife is surprisingly fun. You will want to stay longer than you planned. See chapter 13.
- **Mae Sot:** A charming little border town—you can jump over to Burma on a day pass, or stay and shop for Burmese trinkets in the market on the Thailand side of the river. Small and friendly, this town is very accessible to foreigners. See chapter 9.
- **Songkhla:** On the seaside in the south of Thailand, past the beaches of Samui and the bustle of Nakhon Si Thammarat, Songkhla gets few big reports in the tourist trade. Still the place has history, great museums, a nice beach, and good hotels and restaurants (thanks to the small but significant European and American expatriate community working here). See chapter 7.
- **Si Chiang Mai** (Isan): For a quiet getaway, breathtaking Mae Khong River scenery, and natural wonders easily accessible by bike or motorcycle ride, you could relax in this small friendly place for days and still not see and do everything. See chapter 10.

14 The Best First-Class Restaurants

- **The Normandie Grill** (Oriental Hotel, Bangkok; ☎ 02/236-0400): The formal service and setting are a bit formidable, the prices are steep, but the food at The Normandie is to die for. See chapter 4.
- **The Spice Market** (The Regent Bangkok, Bangkok; ☎ 02/251-6127): The atmosphere lives up to its name, the service brisk and friendly, and the food is authentically spiced and attractively presented. See chapter 4.
- **Le Coq d'Or** (Chiang Mai; ☎ 053/282-024): Have your French cuisine in a delightful old British country house in northern Thailand. Coq d'Or's menu may be somewhat limited, but each offering is perfection. See chapter 12.

- **The Boathouse** (Boathouse Inn, Phuket; ☎ 076/330-557): While there are other more formal dining experiences on the island, the Boathouse Inn has First-Class cuisine—so delicious, travelers enroll in their cookery school to learn their secrets. Wine lovers appreciate their fine selection of labels. See chapter 8.

15 The Best Small Restaurants

- **Ta-Krite** (Chiang Mai; ☎ 053/278-298): This little cafe provides a lovely resting spot for visitors ambling around the Old City. Hidden behind cooling houseplants, the charming cafe also has incredibly affordable lunches—true value for money. See chapter 12.
- **Ka Jok See** (Phuket Town; ☎ 076/217-903): This is one of my favorites—for smart decor and chic and friendly attitude, plus some very, very good Thai food. See chapter 8.
- **PIC Kitchen** (Pattaya; ☎ 038/428-374): Little Thai pavilions sit amid this overgrown garden, where Thai dishes are not only inexpensive, but scrumptious as well. I love the nightly live jazz. See chapter 6.
- **The Golden Triangle International Cafe** (Chiang Rai; ☎ 053/711-339): The Thai menu here tops the list—a virtual book with a full explanation of Thai menus and dishes. A great meal, plus an education. See chapter 13.
- **Comme** (Bangkok; ☎ 02/280-0647): On the chic Pra-Athit Road strip, this place has become one of my favorites for hanging out. You can eat great Thai cooking till you drop and be shocked at how low the check is. But I go for the artsy atmosphere. See chapter 4.

16 The Most Fascinating Temples

- **Wat Phra Kaeo** (Bangkok): With its flamboyant colors and rich details, this shrine is a magnificent setting for Thailand's most revered image, the Emerald Buddha. Inside the main temple building, a profusion of offerings surrounds the pedestal that supports the tiny image. See chapter 5.
- **Wat Arun** (Thonburi/Bangkok): The golden Temple of Dawn shimmers in the sunrise across the Chao Phraya River from Bangkok, but the sunset is even better still. As you climb its steep central *prang* (tower), you get a close view of the porcelain pieces that make its floral design. See chapter 5.
- **Wat Yai** (Phitsanulok): One of the most holy temples in the country, Wat Yai is home to the Phra Buddha Chinarat image, cast in bronze. One of the few remaining Sukhothai images, this one is the prototype for many replicas today. Outside, the temple complex hums with activity. See chapter 9.
- **Wat Mahathat** (Nakhon Si Thammarat): The city is the center of southern Buddhism in Thailand—the first Thai capital to convert to Theravada Buddhism, and a major influence on the kingdoms to follow. The main chedi contains a relic of the Buddha brought from Sri Lanka more than a millennium ago. See chapter 7.
- **Wat Ko Keo Suttharam** (Phetchaburi): The walls of the main hall were painted in the 1730s, during the Kingdom of Ayutthaya, and while the murals are fading, you can still make out the images of the earliest Westerners to come to the country. See chapter 7.

Planning a Trip to Thailand 2

Reading this chapter before you set out can save you money, time, and headaches. Here's where you'll find travel know-how, such as when to visit, what documents you'll need, and where to get more information. These basics can make the difference between a smooth ride and a bumpy one.

1 The Regions in Brief

The Thais often compare their land to the shape of an elephant's head, seen in profile, facing right. Thailand is located roughly equidistant from China and India; centuries of migration from southern China and trade contacts with India brought tremendous influences from each of these Asian centers. Located in the center of Southeast Asia, Thailand borders Burma (Myanmar) to the north and west, Laos to the northeast, Cambodia (Kampuchea) to the east, and Malaysia to the south. Its southwestern coast stretches along the Andaman Sea, and its southern and southeastern coastlines border the Gulf of Thailand. Thailand covers roughly 180,000 square miles and is divided into six major geographic zones.

Western Thailand   On the opposite side of the country, west of Bangkok, are mountains and valleys carved by the Kwai River, the site of the infamous World War II "Death Railway," named for the 12,000 prisoners of war who died in Japanese labor camps during its construction. A bridge over the river near Kanchanaburi was made famous by the film *Bridge on the River Kwai,* and is a stop on the lists of many travelers who come to learn about this story in the war's history, witness the site, and pay respects to those whose lives were lost. Just to the north of Bangkok (which is in every way the center of the country, along the Chao Phraya River banks) is Ayutthaya, Thailand's capital after Sukhothai.

The Southeastern Coast   The southeastern coast is lined with seaside resorts, such as Pattaya and the islands Ko Samet and Ko Chang. Farther east, in the mountains, is Thailand's greatest concentration of sapphire and ruby mines. Recently, natural gas deposits were discovered off the southeastern coast, and the government has constructed two new deep water ports that will soon be accessible by rail, easing some of the industrial pressure on Bangkok. This area has also been in the papers lately as a gateway for ancient artifacts being transported out of Cambodia. Although Thailand is trying to crack down on the illicit trade of antiquities such as temple carvings and Buddha images from the Khmer dynasty, the border has proven quite difficult to patrol.

The Southern Peninsula   A long, narrow peninsula (the elephant's trunk), extends south to the Malaysian border, with the Andaman Sea on the west and the Gulf of Thailand on the east. The eastern coastline along the gulf extends more than 1,125 miles; the western shoreline runs 445 miles along the Andaman Sea. This region is the most tropical in the country, with heavy rainfall during the monsoons. (The northeast monsoon, roughly from November to April, brings clear weather and calm seas to the west coast; the southwest monsoon, March to October, brings similar conditions to the east coast.) There are glamorous beach resorts here (people visit them even during the rainy season; it doesn't rain all day), such as the western islands of Phuket and nearby Ko Pi Pi, Krabi, and Ko Tarutao. Ko Samui, off the east coast, is a bit more relaxed and not yet as expensive. The south is also interesting as the home of the majority of Thailand's Muslim minority, who have put quite a stamp on the southernmost provinces. The primary industries in this region are tin mining, rubber production, coconut and oil palm plantations, fishing, and of course, tourism.

The Central Plain   In contrast to the poor soil of Isan, Thailand's central plain is an extremely fertile region, providing the country and the world with much of its abundant rice crop. The main city of the central plain is Phitsanulok, northeast of which are the impressive remains of Sukhothai, Thailand's first capital, and the ancient city of Si Satchanalai; to the south is Lopburi, an ancient Mon/Khmer settlement.

Isan   The broad and relatively infertile northeast plateau (the ear of the elephant), Isan is the least developed region in Thailand, bordered by the Mekong River (*Mae Nam Khong* in Thai). One of the country's four great rivers, the Mekong separates the country from neighboring Laos on the north and northeast boundaries. The people of Isan share a cultural similarity with Laos, but you needn't travel to Isan to meet them. Many young Isan people find their way to the capital city for work. Chances are your taxi driver in Bangkok is from this region. Isan is dusty in the cool winter and muddy during the summer monsoon, but it contains the most ancient Bronze Age village in the country (if not the world), more than 5,600 years old, at Ban Chiang. There are also major Khmer ruins at Phimai, outside Khorat, and outside Surin and Buriram. Other than potash mining and subsistence farming, the region has little economic development, though recently there has been some growth of industry in and around Khorat and Khon Kaen.

Northern Thailand   The north (the forehead of the elephant) is a relatively cool mountainous region at the foothills of the Himalayas, where elephants have traditionally provided the heavy labor needed to harvest teak and other hardwoods. In the past, this region was under control of the powerful and influential Lanna Kingdom. Today it is largely populated by Tai Yai people, the original Thai people who migrated from southern China in the first centuries of the millennium, yet the region is more famous for the colorful hill tribe people who dwell in the jungles high in the mountains. Like most of Thailand, the cool hills in the north are well suited for farming, particularly for strawberries, asparagus, peaches, litchis, and other fruits. At higher elevations many hill-tribe farmers cultivate opium poppies, though an agricultural program recently advanced by Thailand's king is introducing more productive crops. (The people who grow addictive crops rarely profit in the trade and like everyone else they are often ruined by them.) The cooler temperatures also make the north a favorite destination for Thais on holiday, especially from March to May, when the rest of the country is scorching. The major cities in the north are Chiang Mai, Chiang Rai, Lamphun, Lampang, and Mae Hong Son.

Thailand

Chiang Saen
Chiang Rai
Chiang Khong
Fang
GOLDEN TRIANGLE
Pai
Mae Hong Son
NORTHERN HILLS
Chiang Mai
Nan
Lamphun
Lampang
Mae Sariang
Phrae
Wang
Yom
Si Satchanalai
Uttaradit
Loei
Sukhothai
Tak
MAE KHONG VALLEY
Chi
Mae Sot
CENTRAL PLAINS
Phitsanulok
Kamphaeng Phet
Phetchabun
Ping
Nong Khai
Udon Thani
Ban Chiang
Nakhon Phanom
Khon Kaen
ISAN
VIENTIANE
LAOS
VIETNAM

BURMA (MYANMAR)

Nakhon Sawan
Khwae Noi
Chao Phraya
WESTERN THAILAND
Lopburi
Phimai
Mun
Ubon Ratchathani
Nakhon Ratchasima (Khorat)
Surin
Sam Rong
Nam Tok
Kanchanaburi
Ayutthaya
Nakhon Pathom
★ BANGKOK
Chon Buri
Bangsaen
CAMBODIA (KAMPUCHEA)
Andaman Sea
Phetchaburi
Cha-Am
Hua Hin
Pattaya
Rayong
Ban Phe
Chanthaburi
Ko Samet
CHANTHABURI PROVINCE
SOUTHEASTERN COAST
Prachuap Khiri Khan
Ko Chang
Ko Mak
Trat
Chumphon
Ko Tao
Ko Kut
Phnom Penh
Ranong
Ko Phangngan
Ko Surin (Surin National Marine Park)
Surat Thani
Ko Samui
Gulf of Thailand
(Gulf of Siam)
Khanom
Phangnga
SOUTHERN PENINSULA
Nakhon Si Thammarat
VIETNAM
Phuket
Krabi
Ko Pi Pi
Andaman Sea
Songkhla
Hat Yai
Pattani
Ko Tarutao (Tarutao National Park)
Narathiwat
MALAYSIA
Sungai Kolok

0   100 mi
0   100 km
N

Legend
Railway ++++++

11

2 Visitor Information, Entry Requirements & Money

VISITOR INFORMATION

A major source of free and excellent information is the **Tourist Authority of Thailand (TAT),** with 22 offices throughout the country and more abroad. Consult the TAT on travel plans, hotels, transportation options, and current schedules for festivals and holidays. They produce and distribute countless colorful and informative brochures on regions and activities in the country—plus special tips for travelers. A multilingual **Tourist Police** force is part of the TAT in all major tourist areas within Thailand. They are helpful in emergencies (such as filing police reports for theft) and can provide local information.

In North America, there are **TAT offices** at 3440 Wilshire Blvd., Suite 1100, Los Angeles, CA 90010 (☎ **213/382-2353,** fax 213/389-7544); 303 East Wacker Dr., Suite 400, Chicago, IL 60601 (☎ **312/819-3990,** fax 312/565-0359); and 5 World Trade Center, Suite 3443, New York, NY 10048 (☎ **212/432-0433,** fax 212/912-0920). The office in Chicago is responsible for TAT activities in Canada.

In **Australia,** you'll find a **TAT office** in the National Australia Bank House 255, Level 2, George Street, Sydney 2000 N.S.W. (☎ **02/9247-7549,** fax 02/9251-2465). This office also covers TAT business in New Zealand.

In the **United Kingdom,** the **TAT office** is at 49 Albemarle St., London WIX 3FE (☎ **071/499-7679,** fax 071/629-5519).

ON THE INTERNET   The Internet has become an invaluable source for travel information, and Thailand has been quick to have its say in the ranks of travel-related Web sites. The following sites provide current travel information, and will give you a good prep course before your visit. www.asiatravel.com; www.bangkoknet.com; and www.thailine.com/thailand/english are the best places to start your Web search. Business travelers will be delighted to find Thailand's brand new Web site, the latest rage with business information, legal details, visa issues, travel particulars and a complete directory of links to related Web sites. Check out www.ethailand.com.

ENTRY REQUIREMENTS

PASSPORTS & VISAS   All visitors to Thailand must carry a valid **passport** with **proof of onward passage** (either a return or through ticket). Visa applications are not required if you are staying less than 30 days and are a national of one of 41 designated countries, including Australia, Canada, Ireland, New Zealand, the United Kingdom, and the United States (New Zealanders may stay up to 3 months).

Entry and departure must be through one of the four major airports (Don Muang in Bangkok, Chiang Mai, Phuket, and Hat Yai) or via train from Malaysia. While it is possible to enter the Kingdom through other ports of entry, your best bet is to check with the Thai consulate or embassy in your country if you plan to enter Thailand via an exotic port. If you wish to extend your stay beyond 30 days, report to the **Immigration Division** of the **Royal Thai Police Department** at 507 Soi Suan Phu (off Sathorn Road) (☎ **02/281-7171**). A 30-day extension will cost 500B ($13.15). If you overstay your visa you will be charged 200B ($5.25) per day, which may not sound like much of a penalty, but if your cumulative daily penalties amount to over 20,000B, the authorities may consider tossing you in the immigration jail.

THAI EMBASSIES OVERSEAS   In the **United States** contact the **Royal Thai Embassy,** 1024 Wisconsin Ave., NW, Suite 401, Washington, DC 20007 (☎ **202/944-3600,** fax 202/944-3611); **The Permanent Mission of Thailand** to the United Nations, 351 E. 52nd St., New York, New York 10022 (☎ **212/754-2230,** fax

212/754-2535); the **Royal Thai Consulate-General,** 801 N. La Brea Ave., Los Angeles, CA 90038 (☎ **213/937-1894,** fax 213/937-5987); the **Royal Thai Consulate General,** 35 E. Wacker Dr., Suite 1834, Chicago, IL 60601 (☎ **312/ 236-2447,** fax 312/236-1906). In **Canada** contact the **Royal Thai Embassy,** 180 Island Park Dr., Ottawa, Ontario K1Y OA2 (☎ **613/722-4444,** fax 613/722-6624); the **Royal Thai Embassy,** 106-736 Granville St., Vancouver, BC V6Z 1G4 (☎ **604/ 687-1143,** fax 604/687-4434). In **Australia** contact the **Royal Thai Embassy,** 111 Empire Circuit Yarralumla, ACT 2600 Canberra (☎ **06/273-1149,** fax 06/ 273-1518); **Royal Thai Consulate General,** 2nd floor, 75-77 Pitt St., Sydney, NSW 2000 (☎ **02/9241-2120,** fax 02/9247-8312). In **New Zealand** contact the **Royal Thai Embassy,** 2 Cook St., Karori, P.O. Box 17226, Wellington (☎ **644/476-8618,** fax 644/476-3677). In the **United Kingdom** contact the **Royal Thai Embassy,** 1-3 Yorkshire House, Grosvenor Crescent, London SWIX7EBP (☎ **171/259-5051,** fax 171/235-9808).

MEDICAL REQUIREMENTS   No inoculations or vaccinations are required unless you are coming from or passing through areas infected with yellow fever. Yellow fever certificates are required for those coming from 14 African and South American countries. Check at the consulate or embassy for up-to-date information about health certificates that may be required for entry.

CUSTOMS REGULATIONS   It is prohibited by law to bring the following items into Thailand: narcotics, pornography, firearms and ammunition, and agricultural products. Tourists are allowed to enter the country with one liter of alcohol and 200 cigarettes (or 250 grams of cigars or smoking tobacco) per adult, duty free. Photographic equipment (one still, video, or movie camera, plus five rolls of still film or three rolls of 8mm or 16mm motion-picture film), and "professional instruments" (typewriter, personal computer, and so on) are allowed, provided they are taken out of the country on departure. (The film rule is not strictly enforced.) Tourists are permitted to take gold out of the country without export duty, unless you are dealing in import/export related business.

EXPORT OF ANTIQUES OR ART FROM THAILAND   The government wants to keep track of all pieces of art and antiquity that leave the Kingdom, and so special permission is required for removing these items from the country. Buddha images, Bodhisattva images, or fragments thereof are forbidden to be taken from the country. Exceptions are made for practicing Buddhists who will use the image for worship, cultural exchange, or study purposes. To remove these items, special permission must be granted from the Department of Fine Arts.

You will be required to submit the object, two 5-by-7-inch photographs of the front view of the object, your passport, and a photocopy of your passport notarized by your home Embassy. The authorization process takes 8 days.

For further details contact the **Bureau of Archaeology and National Museum** (☎ **02/281-6766** or 02/528-5032); the **Chiang Mai National Museum** (☎ **053/221-308**); or the **Songkhla National Museum** (☎ **074/311-728**).

Please note—this is only an issue if the object in question is an antique, especially one that has been removed from a temple or palace, or a piece that has particular historic value to the kingdom. If you purchase a small Buddha image, or, say, an amulet, you can just ship it or pack it in your bag. These are mostly modern reproductions. Any antique dealer will be able to notify you about which images require special permission.

On a cultural note—while you may not have to ask for government permission, Thais believe you must ask permission from the Buddha image itself before moving or

The Baht, the U.S. Dollar, the Australian Dollar & the British Pound

Thai B	US $	Australian $	British £
1	.03	.04	.02
2	.05	.10	.03
3	.08	.12	.05
4	.11	.16	.07
5	.14	.20	.08
6	.16	.24	.10
7	.18	.28	.12
8	.22	.32	.13
9	.24	.36	.15
10	.27	.40	.17
20	.54	.80	.33
50	1.35	2.00	.83
100	2.70	4.00	.67
500	13.51	20.00	8.33
1,000	27.03	40.00	16.67
5,000	135.14	200.00	83.33
10,000	270.27	400.00	166.67

washing it. Images are believed to have personalities of their own (separate from the Buddha they represent), so out of respect, Thais always ask the image first.

MONEY

CURRENCY   The Thai unit of currency is the **baht** (written B) divided into 100 **satang** (though you'll rarely see a satang coin). Copper-colored coins represent 25 and 50 satang; silver-colored coins are 1B, 2B, and 5B (*Note:* The 1B and old 5B coins are the same size); and the new 10B coin is silver and copper. Bank notes come in denominations of 10B (brown), 20B (green), 50B (blue), 100B (red), 500B (purple), and 1,000B (khaki).

CURRENCY REQUIREMENTS   There are no restrictions on the import of foreign currencies or traveler's checks, but you cannot export foreign currency in excess of 50,000B ($1,315.80) per person or 500,000B ($13,157.90) if exiting to a neighboring country. Checks and drafts other than travelers checks must be sold to a bank within 15 days of arrival.

CURRENCY EXCHANGE RATES   Before the currency crisis in July 1997, one U.S. dollar could buy you 25 Thai baht. During the worst of the crisis, the value was 55 baht to the U.S. dollar. At the time of writing, it remained low at around 36 or 37 baht to the U.S. dollar, but had been relatively stable for months. I've used an approximate average of recent rates for the conversions in the above table, as well as for amounts listed throughout the book: US$1 = 38B. I can't guarantee the rates will remain constant until the time you travel, but they may still serve as a useful guideline.

ATM NETWORKS   Automated-teller machines (ATMs) are by far the most convenient way to access cash in Thailand—they give the best currency exchange rates

What Things Cost in Bangkok	U.S. $
Taxi from the airport to the city center including expressway toll	6.60
Local telephone call (private pay phone) per minute	.08
Double at The Oriental (very expensive)	220–270
Double at Bossotel Inn (moderate)	21.05
Double at Peachy Guesthouse (inexpensive)	5.25
Dinner for one, without wine, at Sala Thip (moderate)	15.80
Dinner for one, without wine, at Cabbages & Condoms (inexpensive)	9.20
Dinner for one, without wine, at Suda Restaurant (inexpensive)	5.25
Pint of beer at a hotel bar	6.60
Pint of beer at a local bar	3.15
Coca-Cola	0.30
Cup of coffee	1.30–1.85
Roll of ASA 100 Kodacolor film, 36 exposures	3.15
Admission to the National Museum	0.55
Movie ticket	3.15

(usually the rate of the day), and make traveler's checks almost obsolete, except for when you're traveling to remote destinations. Be aware that most ATMs charge about $1 to $2 for each withdrawal. Most major banks have them, both in Bangkok and in cities and towns nationwide. Check with your bank before leaving home to find out if your debit card is linked into either the MasterCard/Cirrus or the Visa/PLUS networks. These will give you local currency, instantly debiting your account, and maybe even provide you with an account of current balances available on your slip. **Cirrus** (☎ **800/424-7787;** www.mastercard.com/atm/) and **Plus** (☎ **800/843-7587;** www.visa.com/atms) are the two most popular networks; check the back of your ATM card to see which network your bank belongs to. Use the 800 numbers to locate ATMs in your destination. If you're traveling abroad, ask your bank for a list of overseas ATMs. Be sure to check the daily withdrawal limit before you depart, and ask whether you need a new personal ID number.

While not all banks are part of the network, I always have luck with Bangkok Bank, Thai Farmers Bank, Siam Commercial Bank, or Bank of Ayudhya. These major banks have branches in every city and many small towns. I've cited major bank locations in each town's "Fast Facts" listing.

TRAVELER'S CHECKS & CREDIT CARDS   Traveler's checks are negotiable in most banks, hotels, restaurants, and tourist-oriented shops, but you'll receive a better rate by cashing them at commercial banks.

Nearly all international hotels and larger businesses accept major credit cards, but few accept personal checks. Despite protest from credit-card companies, many establishments add a 3% to 5% surcharge for payment by credit card, but this can be refunded if you report it. Use discretion in using your card and in questionable establishments, don't let your card out of your sight, even for a moment, and be sure to keep all receipts. Never leave your cards with others for safekeeping (such as during a trek). If you don't want to carry them, put them in a hotel safe. There have been numerous reports of charges having been made while cards were left at guest houses, or small shops running extra slips against your card. So traveler's checks might be the safest bet. In smaller towns and remote provinces, the baht will be the only acceptable currency.

To report a lost or stolen credit card, you can call these service lines: **American Express** (☎ 02/273-0033); **Diners Club** (☎ 02/238-3660); **JCB** (Japanese Credit Bank) (☎ 02/631-1938); **MasterCard** (☎ 02/260-8572); and **Visa** (☎ 02/256-7326).

3 When to Go

THE CLIMATE In the **northern and central areas** of the country there are three distinct seasons. The hot season lasts from March to May, with temperatures averaging in the upper 90s Fahrenheit (mid-30s Celsius); April is the hottest month. During this period there is very little rain, if any at all. The rainy season begins in June and lasts until October; the average temperature is 84°F (29°C) with 90% humidity. While the rainy season brings frequent showers, it's rare for them to last for a whole day or for days on end. Daily showers will come in torrents, usually in the late afternoon or evening for a brief time—maybe 3 or 4 hours—only to clear up. The cool season, from November through February, has temperatures from the high 70s to low 80s Fahrenheit (26°C), with moderate and infrequent rain showers. In the north during the cool season, day temperatures can be as low as 60°F (16°C) in Chiang Mai and 41°F (5°C) in the hills.

The **southern half of the country,** particularly the southern Malay Peninsula, has intermittent showers year-round, and daily ones during the rainy season (temperatures average in the low 80s/30°C). If you're traveling to Phuket or Ko Samui, it will be helpful to note that the high season is from November to May, when the weather is best, although the low season is seeing an increase in visitation, possibly due to discounted rates. However, Thailand's monsoon isn't as imposing as in other Asian countries—it's rare for it to rain for days and you can actually travel around the country in some comfort.

HOLIDAYS Many holidays are based on the Thai lunar calendar, falling on the full moon of each month; check with TAT for the current year's schedule. Chapter 11 includes a list of festivals and events specific to the north.

On national holidays government offices are closed, as well as some shops and services—though not all. All transportation modes will still be in operation, as well as many restaurants and nightlife establishments with the exception of Buddhist Lent in July, and the King's Birthday in December when almost all bars stop serving alcohol for the day.

In **January** Thailand celebrates New Year's Day same as the rest of the world (nursing a hangover). In **late February or early March** (depending on the lunar cycle) is Makha Bucha Day, when temples celebrate the day 1,250 disciples spontaneously gathered to hear the Buddha preach his doctrine. **April** brings two holidays: Chakri Memorial Day (April 6) and Songkran (April 13 to 15). Chakri Memorial Day commemorates the founding of the Chakri dynasty (the reigning dynasty) while Songkran is the official New Year according to the Thai calendar. While the official New Year is on the 13th, Songkran festivals last from 3 to 10 days—with the most exciting celebration happening in Chiang Mai. After honoring local abbots and family elders, folks hit the streets for massive water fights. Be warned—foreigners are the Thais' favorite targets. Water guns are available at all markets—arm thyself and have a blast!

May brings many public holidays—National Labor Day falls on the 1st, Coronation Day (celebrating the coronation of H. M. King Bhumibol in 1950) is on the 5th, while the 14th is Royal Ploughing Day, the first day of the rice-planting cycle celebrated with a traditional Brahman parade. Visakha Bucha Day, marking the birth, enlightenment and death of the Buddha) will fall in mid-May depending on the lunar calendar. In **mid-July** Thais celebrate the Buddhist Lent immediately following Asarnha Bucha Day signaling the beginning of the Rains' Retreat and the 3-month period of meditation for all Buddhist monks—this was the day that the Buddha delivered his First Sermon to the first five disciples. **August** 12 honors the birthday of Her Majesty the Queen and also Mother's Day.

On **October** 23, Chulalongkorn Day, the country's favorite king, Rama V, is remembered. Loy Krathong, in early **November,** is one of Thailand's greatest holidays, honoring the water spirit and serving as a day to wash away sins committed during the previous year. The most spectacular celebrations are in Ayutthaya, Sukhothai and Chiang Mai. **December** 5th marks H. M. King Bhumibol's birthday and Father's Day. And finally, December 10, Constitution Day, recognizes Thailand's first constitution in 1932.

There are many more holidays celebrated by local people of various regions; check with TAT or see specific chapters for regional information and local schedules.

Thai Calendar of Events

January/February
- **Chinese New Year,** Bangkok. Head for Chinatown to celebrate the New Year with a Chingay parade—complete with Lion Dance (January or early February).

February
- **Flower Festival,** Chiang Mai. When all of the north is in bloom, Chiang Mai springs to life with parades, floats decorated with flowers, and beauty contests (first weekend).

March/April
- **Poi Sang Long,** Mae Hong Son. Offerings for monks are paraded through the streets to celebrate the ordination of young monks.

April
- **Pattaya Festival,** Pattaya. Parades and fireworks accompany a food festival and lots of partying (first week).
- **International Kite Festival,** Bangkok. The place to see this national pastime, with contests and displays (third week).

June/July
- **Phi Ta Khon,** Loei. This Buddhist festival features a procession of masked dancers and recitations from monks.

September/October
- **Boat Races,** Phitsanulok, Narathiwat. Races, country fairs, parades to mark the end of the rains (first week of each month).

October
- **Vegetarian Festival,** Phuket. Chinese religious festival with parades, temple ceremonies, athletic competitions (second week for nine days).

November
- **Elephant Roundup,** Surin. Elephant parades, demonstrations, and cultural performances (third weekend).

December
- **King's Cup Regatta,** Phuket. Global competitors race yachts in this international event (December 7–13).

4 The Active Vacation Planner

Today's traveler demands more from a vacation than ever before. While for some the ideal holiday is time spent lazing on a beach sucking back juicy cocktails, others want to push themselves to the limit, seeking thrills and adventure. Amazing Thailand's well-developed tourism industry has not overlooked this element of travel. Routes have opened up nature's wild side to those who would dare, and many operators have jockeyed into place providing adventure travel options that are professional, well planned and safe for everyone, from beginners to experts. The following section will give you an overview of the many options, but for planning details refer to the specific destination.

The first thing many people consider for an active vacation is **scuba diving** or **snorkeling.** Living coral reefs grace the waters of the Andaman Sea, off Thailand's southwest coast, and the Gulf of Thailand. More than 80 species of coral have been discovered in the Gulf, while the deeper and more saline Andaman has more than 210. Marine life includes hundreds of species of fish, plus numerous varieties of crustaceans and sea turtles. With the aid of underwater breathing apparatus, divers can get an up close and personal view of this undersea universe. For those without scuba certification, many reefs close to the surface are still vibrant.

From Phuket (see chapter 8), you can organize **long-term scuba trips** on live-aboard boats or you can take a day trip that includes two or three dives. From Ko Phi Phi, Krabi, Ko Samui, Hua Hin, Chumphon, and Pattaya (see chapters 6, 7, and 8), many operators schedule frequent trips. All are staffed with certified PADI dive masters, provide quality gear and decent boats, and are licensed by the Tourism Authority. Many offer scuba training and certification packages, and can have you ready to dive in 5 days. Pretty much every beach has independent operators or guesthouses that rent snorkels, masks, and fins for the day. A few boat operators take snorkelers to reefs off neighboring islands—especially at Ko Phi Phi, Krabi, Ko Samui, and Pattaya.

Thailand's mountainous jungle terrain in the north has become a haven for **trekkers,** particularly those who wish to visit remote villages inhabited by the tribal people who live there. While the average trek lasts 3 days and 2 nights, some like to go out into the wilds for up to 10 days or more. Trekking usually involves no more than 3 to 4 hours of straight walking on jungle paths. All tours provide local guides to accompany groups, and the guides will keep the pace steady but comfortable for all trekkers involved. Some trips break up the monotonous walking treks on elephant-back, in four-wheel-drive Jeeps or light rafting on flat bamboo rafts. Chiang Mai (see chapter 12) has the most trekking firms, while Chiang Rai, Pai, and Mae Hong Son (see chapter 13) also have their share of trekking companies.

Thailand's been working to preserve the nature and wildlife of its many different ecological zones, from swamp jungles in the south, to mountain forests in the north, to underwater marine parks in the Gulf of Thailand and the Andaman Sea. In more than 80 national parks, the kingdom also tries to teach visitors about not only the local wildlife species in residence, but also the delicate balance of each habitat. Many parks have clearly displayed informational exhibits at their visitor centers, trails with bridges and catwalks, and markers explaining the important elements of the environment and its inhabitants. Others provide rudimentary bungalow accommodations, or can rent tents and supplies for campers. For more complete information, get in touch with the **National Park Division,** Natural Resources Conservation Office, Royal Forest Department, 61 Phaholyothin Rd., Chatuchak, Bangkok 10900, ☎ 02/579-7223.

River rafting in rubber rafts and kayaks is also becoming increasingly popular in Thailand, with operators in Pai (see chapter 13) and Mae Sot (see chapter 9), taking small groups down local rivers. Winding through dense jungles, past rock formations and local villages, these trips include camping and sometimes trekking. Rapids are rarely extreme, but are big enough to be loads of fun, and safety measures are taken seriously. If you're a true enthusiast, talk to Thai Adventure Rafting in Pai about accompanying a group in your own kayak or canoe (see chapter 13).

A few lucky folks know that Thailand is home to one of the top 10 climbing walls in the world. **Rock climbing** at Rai Ley beach in Krabi (see chapter 7) is attracting lovers of the sport, who come to have a go at these challenging cliffs. Views are breathtaking—truly amazing scenery out into the Andaman and surrounding islands. A few small outfits accept beginners for training, or will organize climbs for more specialized experts, providing all equipment necessary.

There are all kinds of adventure travel operators in Thailand, but the best in the business by reputation is **The Wild Planet,** No. 9 Thonglor Soi 25, Sukhumvit 55, Prakanong, Bangkok 10110, Thailand (☎ **02/233-0997;** fax 02/712-8748; www.wild-planet.co.th; e-mail: omk@lox2.loxinfo.co.th). They plan scuba trips, trekking, rafting, and more, and will work with you to tailor make your itinerary.

5 Health & Insurance

STAYING HEALTHY

You probably won't develop any health problems in Thailand; however, it's best to be aware of potential problems associated with travel to exotic lands. I've found doctors in the United States have very little realistic information about health problems specific to the region—you may find this to be true in your country as well. Still, you may wish to get Hepatitis A, Hepatitis B, and tetanus vaccines before traveling.

SOME HEALTH TIPS

The most common illness in these parts is diarrhea. Don't be surprised if the change in climate and diet bring on an uncomfortable bout. My advice is to bring with you a good antidiarrhea medicine like Immodium, an electrolyte supplement to mix in plenty of water (to prevent dehydration and loss of energy), and, above all, a roll of toilet paper or packet of tissues for while you're away from your hotel. Don't count on public toilets having any. Some cases are caused by bacteria or viruses in either food or drinking water. Bottled water is sold everywhere, including popular Western brand names. But even the Thai bottled water is potable. If you're boiling your own, it must be boiled for at least 10 minutes before it's considered clean. While food in most restaurants is perfectly safe, be wary of street food. If you eat from a hawker stall, check out the ingredients very carefully for freshness and cleanliness. Watch them prepare it before you, and never eat anything that looks like it's been sitting around. Don't ever eat anything raw—vegetables included—from vendors. If your condition lasts for more than 24 hours, chances are you've picked something up and should find a doctor for possible antibiotic treatment.

Hepatitis A can be avoided using the same precautions for diarrhea. Most Asians are immune through exposure, but people from the West are very susceptible. Talk to your doctor about receiving a vaccine before your trip.

Major tourist areas such as Bangkok, Phuket, Ko Samui, and Chiang Mai are **malaria** free. However, malaria is still a problem in rural parts, particularly territories in the mountains to the north and near borders. Don't even bother with prophylactic tablets like chloroquine. They don't work here. The only solution is to cover up with long pants and sleeves after dark, stay indoors, sleep with mosquito netting, and use repellents. Make sure your repellent is specially made for the tropics. DEET works well, but it is a toxic chemical, so you may want to find one with smaller concentrations. OFF! Skintastic has only 6.65% DEET and works great. Also available in stores throughout the country is Autan, in spray, liquid and lotion, but it's got a 15% DEET concentration. If, despite these precautions, you develop a fever within 2 weeks of entering a high-risk area, be sure to consult a physician.

Dengue fever is a problem throughout Southeast Asia. Similar to malaria, the virus is spread through mosquito bites, but the mosquitoes that carry the virus only bite during the day. They are most commonly found in neighborhood areas, so make sure you wear repellent if you're visiting friends during the day. There is no existing prophylactic, so like malaria your best bet is to not be bit at all. Symptoms include fever, a skin rash, and severe headaches. Seek medical attention. For foreign visitors, the disease is rarely fatal, but for people who are native of endemic areas, the internal hemorrhaging caused by the virus often kills.

Thailand is not without its fair share of stray dogs. They're everywhere—sleeping on the side of the road, limping through hawker markets, hanging around temple complexes. Occasionally a **rabid** one makes its way into the mix. Stay clear of strange dogs, and find a doctor fast if you've been bitten. The sooner you receive treatment, the better.

Japanese encephalitis made the news in 1999. Malaysia claimed more than 200 deaths in the first half of the year as a result of the virus, and shot more than 200,000 pigs that were accused of spreading it. The Centers for Disease Control (CDC) in Atlanta discovered later that the virus responsible was not Japanese encephalitis, but something new. Still, Malaysia has strict bans on the export of pig food products, so the pork you get in Thailand is perfectly safe to eat. Meanwhile, the CDC is working on a remedy for the mysterious illness. Japanese encephalitis is a viral infection that attacks the brain, and it's actually spread by mosquito bite. Like malaria and dengue, you should try to avoid being bitten.

Don't swim in **freshwater streams or pools** (other than chlorinated hotel pools), as they are frequently contaminated. Avoid the ocean near the outlets of sewage pipes and freshwater streams, because of contaminated water (especially around Pattaya)—poisonous sea snakes often inhabit these areas. Be especially careful of coral reefs (such as those along Phuket), jellyfish, and sea urchins, and treat all cuts or stings immediately by washing with soap and water and applying an antimicrobal preparation. Antihistamines can help with allergic responses. Ear infections are a common problem; those prone to ear infections can use mild boric acid or vinegar solutions to prevent or combat them.

Avoid **sunstroke** or **heat exhaustion** by exercising caution about physical activity. Thailand's slower pace of life is dictated by the hot and humid weather. Drink lots of liquid to avoid dehydration; bottled water is inexpensive and widely available. Avoid excessive exposure to the sun, use a strong sunscreen, and wear a hat for protection. Restricting alcohol consumption and eating lightly will help you to acclimate.

SEX FOR SALE

Every day you're in Thailand, in any part of the country, you will see foreigners enjoying the company of Thai women and men. Although prostitution is illegal, it's as much a part of the tourism industry as superb hotels and stunning beaches.

In poor, uneducated, rural families, where sons are counted on as farm labor, sex has become an income-earning occupation for daughters who have few other job alternatives. It's true that most of the urban sex workers earn more income than their families back home, sending savings home each month to support younger siblings and older parents. Yet girls sent to the big cities as CSWs (the official term is "commercial sex worker") can sometimes quietly retire, return to their villages, and even get married. Growth in tourist arrivals has meant a tremendous increase in new clientele, and the economic crisis in 1997 saw a lot of companies close or lay off employees—many office workers or otherwise-employed women and men found themselves turning to prostitution to make ends meet. Thai society tends to ignore the men employed as CSWs. In fact, many straight men entertain gay clientele just for the income-earning opportunity. Transvestite entertainment is common and even popular in the larger cities and resorts.

With a legacy of royal patronage and social acceptance, the oldest profession has been part of Thailand's economy for centuries. Today this burgeoning industry is still publicly ignored, and since the subject is controversial, the number of CSWs fluctuates depending on whom you talk to. Some groups will say only 80,000, while others will put the number as high as 800,000.

Some clients are insisting on younger and younger CSWs in the foolhardy belief that children will be AIDS-free. As a result, Thailand currently has the world's largest child sex industry. Many traders go to the countryside promising children they will have urban employment opportunities, such as domestic service, dishwashing, or housekeeping work. With negligence on one hand, and complicity on the other, they then enslave male and female children in sex clubs and massage parlors.

Thailand has aggressively developed research and education programs on the subject of **AIDS.** The largest nongovernmental organization in Thailand, the PCDA, led by the courageous and innovative public health crusader Meechai Viravaidya, has enlarged the scope of its rural development programs from family planning and cottage-industry schemes, to distributing condoms and running seminars for CSWs. Even the royal family is in on it: Her Royal Highness, Princess Chulaporn Walailuke, founder of the Chulaporn Research Institute and an internationally known activist, sponsored the 1990 International Global AIDS Conference in Bangkok, and continues to be active.

These recent efforts must be working somewhat, as an increasing number of women and men refuse clients who won't wear a condom. According to the Thai government's Department of Communicable Diseases, AIDS Divisions, in July 1999 it was estimated as many as 119,259 carry the AIDS virus, but the Population & Community Development Association claims that more than one million is a more accurate account. In 1998, 32,935 Thais died of AIDS-related illnesses, and that number is expected to double in the next decade.

Western embassies report numerous cases of tourists who are drugged in their hotel rooms by the girl of the night, waking 2 days later to find all their valuables gone. There are a shocking number of stories about young Western travelers found dead in their hotel rooms from unexplained causes. Exercise caution in your dealings with strangers. If you use the services of commercial sex workers, take proper precautions; men should wear a latex condom.

INSURANCE

Check your insurance policy before departure to make sure that overseas medical treatment, hospitalization, and medical evaluation are fully covered. However, most make you pay the bills up front at the time of care, and you'll get a refund after you've returned and filed all the paperwork. Members of **Blue Cross/Blue Shield** can now use their cards at select hospitals in most major cities worldwide (☎ 800/810-BLUE, or www.bluecares.com/blue/bluecard/wwn for a list of hospitals). For independent travel health-insurance providers, see below. Your homeowner's insurance should cover stolen luggage. The airlines are responsible for $1,250 on domestic flights if they lose your luggage; if you plan to carry anything more valuable than that, keep it in your carry-on bag.

If you do require additional insurance, try one of the companies listed below. But don't pay for more than you need. For example, if you need only trip cancellation insurance, don't purchase coverage for lost or stolen property. Trip cancellation insurance costs approximately 6% to 8% of the total value of your vacation.

Among the reputable issuers of travel insurance are:

Access America (☎ 800/284-8300); **Travel Guard International** (☎ 800/826-1300); **Travel Insured International** (☎ 800/243-3174); **Columbus Travel Insurance** (☎ 0171/375-0011 in London; www2.columbusdirect.com/columbusdirect); **International SOS Assistance** (☎ 800/523-8930), strictly an assistance company; **Travelex Insurance Services** (☎ 800/228-9792).

Companies specializing in accident and medical care include:

MEDEX International (☎ 888/MEDEX-00 or 410/453-6300; fax 410/453-6301; www.medexassist.com); **Travel Assistance International** (Worldwide Assistance Services) (☎ 800/821-2828 or 202/828-5894; fax 202/828-5896); **The Divers Alert Network** (DAN) (☎ 800/446-2671 or 919/684-2948) insures scuba divers.

6 Getting There

BY PLANE

When you plan your trip, consider that Thailand has more than one international airport. While most international flights arrive in Bangkok, flights from Kuala Lumpur take you direct to Phuket, Hat Yai, and Chiang Mai, while flights from Singapore fly to Phuket, Hat Yai, Chiang Mai, and Ko Samui. Laos, Burma (Myanmar), and Southern China are also connected by regular flights to Chiang Mai. Specific details are provided in chapter 7 for Ko Samui and Hat Yai, chapter 8 for Phuket, and chapter 12 for Chiang Mai.

FLIGHTS FROM NORTH AMERICA   Thai Airways International (☎ 800/426-5204) in conjunction with United Airlines flies daily to Bangkok from Los Angeles. **United Airlines** (☎ 800/241-6522; www.ual.com) and **Northwest Airlines** (☎ 800/447-4747; www.nwa.com) can connect pretty much any airport in North America to Bangkok via daily flights. **Canadian Airlines International** (☎ 800/661-2227) flies to Bangkok from Vancouver via Hong Kong 4 days a week.

FLIGHTS FROM AUSTRALIA   Thai Airways (☎ toll free within Australia 300/651-960 or ☎ Brisbane 7/3215-4700; ☎ Perth 8/9322-7522) services Bangkok from Sydney daily and from Brisbane, Melbourne, and Perth three times a week. From Perth, two of the flights stop in Phuket before flying on to Bangkok. **Qantas** (☎ toll-free within Australia 131211; www.quantas.com) has, in addition to dailies from Sydney, direct flights to Bangkok from Brisbane and Melbourne three times a week. **British Airways** (☎ 2/8904-8800 in Sydney; ☎ 7/3223-3123 in Brisbane; ☎ 8/9425-7711; www.british-airways.com) flies daily from Sydney.

FLIGHTS FROM THE UNITED KINGDOM   Daily, nonstop flights from London to Bangkok are offered by **British Airways (☎ 0345/22-21-11 from anywhere within the United Kingdom; www.british-airways.com).

FLYING FOR LESS: TIPS FOR GETTING THE BEST AIRFARES

Passengers within the same airplane cabin are rarely paying the same fare for their seats. Business travelers who need to purchase tickets at the last minute, change their itinerary at a moment's notice, or get home before the weekend pay the premium rate, known as the full fare. Passengers who can book their ticket long in advance, who don't mind staying over Saturday night, or who are willing to travel on a Tuesday, Wednesday, or Thursday after 7pm, will pay a fraction of the full fare. On most flights, even the shortest hops, the full fare is close to $1,000 or more, but a 7-day or 14-day advance purchase ticket is closer to $200–$300. Here are a few other easy ways to save.

1. Periodically airlines lower prices on their most popular routes. Check your newspaper for advertised discounts or call the airlines directly and ask if any **promotional rates** or special fares are available. You'll almost never see a sale during the peak summer vacation months of July and August, or during the Thanksgiving or Christmas seasons; but in periods of low-volume travel, you should pay no more than $400 for a cross-country flight. If your schedule is flexible, ask if you can secure a cheaper fare by staying an extra day or by flying midweek. (Many airlines won't volunteer this information.) If you already hold a ticket when a sale breaks, it may even pay to exchange your ticket, which usually incurs a $50 to $75 charge.

    Note, however, that the lowest-priced fares are often nonrefundable, require advance purchase of 1 to 3 weeks and a certain length of stay, and carry penalties for changing dates of travel.

2. **Consolidators,** also known as bucket shops, are a good place to find low fares. Consolidators buy seats in bulk from the airlines and then sell them back to the public at prices below even the airlines' discounted rates. Their small boxed ads usually run in the Sunday travel section at the bottom of the page. Before you pay, however, ask for a confirmation number from the consolidator and then call the airline itself to confirm your seat. Be prepared to book your ticket with a different consolidator—there are many to choose from—if the airline can't confirm your reservation. Also be aware that bucket shop tickets are usually nonrefundable or rigged with stiff cancellation penalties, often as high as 50% to 75% of the ticket price.

    Council Travel (☎ 800/226-8624; www.counciltravel.com) and **STA Travel** (☎ 800/781-4040; www.sta.travel.com) cater especially to young travelers, but their bargain basement prices are available to people of all ages. **Travel Bargains** (☎ 800/AIR-FARE; www.1800airfare.com) was formerly owned by TWA but now offers the deepest discounts on many other airlines, with a 4-day advance purchase. Other reliable consolidators include **1-800-FLY-CHEAP** (www.1800flycheap.com); **TFI Tours International** (☎ 800/745-8000 or 212/736-1140), which serves as a clearinghouse for unused seats; or "rebators" such as **Travel Avenue** (☎ 800/333-3335 or 312/876-1116) and the **Smart Traveller** (☎ 800/448-3338 in the U.S., or 305/448-3338), which rebate part of their commissions to you.

3. Book a seat on a **charter flight.** Discounted fares have pared the number available, but they can still be found. Most charter operators advertise and sell their seats through travel agents, thus making these local professionals your best source of information for available flights. Before deciding to take a charter flight, however, check the restrictions on the ticket: You may be asked to purchase a tour package, to pay in advance, to be amenable if the day of departure is changed, to pay a service charge, to fly on an airline you're not familiar with (this usually is not the case), and to pay harsh penalties if you cancel—but be understanding if the charter doesn't fill up and is canceled up to 10 days before departure. Summer charters fill up more quickly than others and are almost sure to fly, but if you decide on a charter flight, seriously consider cancellation and baggage insurance.

Cyberdeals for Net Surfers

It's possible to get some great deals on airfare, hotels, and car rentals via the Internet. Grab your mouse and surf before you take off—you could save a bundle on your trip. The Web sites highlighted below are worth checking out, especially since all services are free. Always check the lowest published fare, however, before you shop for flights on-line.

Arthur Frommer's Budget Travel (www.frommers.com)   Home of the Encyclopedia of Travel and *Arthur Frommer's Budget Travel* magazine and daily newsletter, this site offers detailed information on 200 cities and islands around the world, and up-to-the-minute ways to save dramatically on flights, hotels, car reservations, and cruises. Book an entire vacation on line and research your destination before you leave. Consult the message board to set up "hospitality exchanges" in other countries, to talk with other travelers who have visited a hotel you're considering, or to direct travel questions to Arthur Frommer himself. The newsletter is updated daily to keep you abreast of the latest breaking ways to save, to publicize new hot spots and best buys, and to present veteran readers with fresh, ever-changing approaches to travel.

Microsoft Expedia (www.expedia.com)   The best part of this multipurpose travel site is the "Fare Tracker": You fill out a form on the screen indicating that you're interested in cheap flights from your hometown, and, once a week, they'll e-mail you the best airfare deals on up to three destinations. The site's "Travel Agent" will steer you to bargains on hotels and car rentals, and with the help of hotel and airline seat pinpointers, you can book everything right on line. This site is even useful once you're booked. Before you depart, log on to Expedia for maps and up-to-date travel information, including weather reports and foreign exchange rates.

Travelocity (www.travelocity.com)   This is one of the best travel sites out there, especially for finding cheap airfare. In addition to its "Personal Fare Watcher," which notifies you via e-mail of the lowest airfares for up to five different destinations, Travelocity will track the three lowest fares for any routes on any dates in minutes. You can book a flight right then and there, and if you need a rental car or hotel, Travelocity will find you the best deal via the SABRE computer reservations system (another huge travel agent database). Click on "Last Minute Deals" for the latest travel bargains, including a link to "H.O.T. Coupons" (www.hotcoupons.com), where you can print out electronic coupons for travel in the United States and Canada.

4. Look into **courier flights.** Companies that hire couriers use your luggage allowance for their business baggage; in return, you get a deeply discounted ticket. Flights are often offered at the last minute, and you may have to arrange a pretrip interview to make sure you're right for the job. **Now Voyager** (☎ 212/431-1616) flies from New York. Now Voyager also offers noncourier discounted fares, so call the company even if you don't want to fly as a courier.

5. Join a travel club such as **Moment's Notice** (☎ 718/234-6295) or **Sears Discount Travel Club** (☎ 800/433-9383, or 800/255-1487 to join), which supply unsold tickets at discounted prices. You pay an annual membership fee to get the club's hotline number. Of course, you're limited to what's available, so you have to be flexible.

The Trip (www.thetrip.com) This site is really geared toward the business traveler, but vacationers-to-be can also use The Trip's exceptionally powerful fare-finding engine, which will e-mail you every week with the best city-to-city airfare deals for as many as 10 routes. The Trip uses the Internet Travel Network, another reputable travel agent database, to book hotels and restaurants.

E-Savers Programs Several major airlines offer a free e-mail service known as E-Savers, via which they'll send you their best bargain airfares on a regular basis. Here's how it works: Once a week (usually Wednesday), or whenever a sale fare comes up, subscribers receive a list of discounted flights to and from various destinations, both international and domestic. Here's the catch: These fares are usually only available if you leave the very next Saturday (or sometimes Friday night) and return on the following Monday or Tuesday. It's really a service for the spontaneously inclined and travelers looking for a quick getaway. But the fares are cheap, so it's worth taking a look. If you have a preference for certain airlines (in other words, the ones you fly most frequently), sign up with them first.

Here's a partial list of airlines and their Web sites, where you can not only get on the e-mailing lists, but also book flights directly:

- **American Airlines:** www.aa.com
- **British Airways:** www.british-airways.com
- **Canadian Airlines International:** www.cdnair.ca
- **Continental Airlines:** www.flycontiental.com
- **Northwest Airlines:** www.nwa.com
- **TWA:** www.twa.com
- **US Airways:** www.usairways.com
- **United Airlines:** www.ual.com
- **Virgin Airways:** www.virgin.com

One caveat: You'll get frequent-flier miles if you purchase one of these fares, but you can't use miles to buy the ticket.

Smarter Living (www.smarterliving.com) If the thought of all that surfing and comparison shopping gives you a headache, then head right for Smarter Living. Sign up for their newsletter service, and every week you'll get a customized e-mail summarizing the discount fares available from your departure city. Smarter Living tracks more than 15 different airlines, so it's a worthwhile time-saver.

BY TRAIN

Thailand is accessible via train from Singapore and peninsular Malaysia. Malaysia's **Keretapi Tanah Melayu Berhad (KTM)** begins in Singapore (☎ 65/222-5165), stopping in Kuala Lumpur (☎ 603/273-8000) and Butterworth (Penang) (☎ 604/323-7962) before heading for Thailand, where it joins service with the State Railway of Thailand. Bangkok's Hua Lamphong Railway Station is centrally located on Krung Kassem Road (☎ 02/223-7010 or 02/223-7020). Taxis, tuk-tuks (motorized three-wheeled vehicles), and public buses are just outside the station.

The *Eastern & Oriental Express,* sister to the Venice Simplon-Orient-Express, runs once a week between Singapore and Bangkok in exquisite luxury, with occasional departures between Bangkok and Chiang Mai. For reservations from the United States and Canada call ☎ 800/524-2420; from Australia ☎ 3/9699-9766; from New Zealand ☎ 9/379-3708; and from the United Kingdom ☎ 171/805-5100. From Singapore, Malaysia, and Thailand contact E&O in Singapore at ☎ 65/392-3500.

BY BUS

There is limited private bus transportation linking Singapore and Malaysia with Hat Yai in southern Thailand. In Singapore, call the **Singapore Tourism Board** at ☎ 800/334-1335, and in Malaysia call the **Malaysia Tourism Board** (☎ 603/293-5188) for more information. From Lao, regular buses can carry you over the border from Vientiane. The number to call for **Tourist Information in Vientiane** is ☎ 856-21/212-248.

BY SHIP

Sun Cruises is the biggest name in cruising for the region. Stopping in Singapore, Malacca, and Penang in Malaysia, and Phuket, their floating resort has six restaurants, four Jacuzzis, pool, fitness center, spa, deck games, and seven bars and lounges. For details contact **Pacific Leisure** (Thailand), 156/13 Phang Nga Rd., Phuket, 83000 (☎ 076/232-511, fax 076/232-510, www.pacific-leisure.com).

7 Getting Around

Transportation within Thailand is accessible, efficient, and inexpensive. If your time is short, fly. But if you have the time to take in the countryside, travel by bus, train, or private car.

BY PLANE

Bangkok's **Don Muang International Airport** may not be as glitzy as its neighbors' newer airports, but it works—services and gates are easy to find, many airport staff speak English, there's convenient transportation to town, and it's relatively safe. Airports in other cities usually tend to have money changing facilities, information counters, and waiting ground transportation. In the very small places, you'll have to arrange airport pick-up either through your hotel or the airline.

Most domestic flights are on **Thai Airways,** part of Thai Airways International, 89 Vibhavadi Rangsit Rd., Bangkok (☎ 02/232-8000), with Bangkok as its hub. Flights connect Bangkok and 27 domestic cities, including Chiang Mai, Chiang Rai, Mae Hong Son, Phitsanulok, Loei, Surat Thani, and Phuket. There are also connecting flights between many of these cities.

Bangkok Airways, 60 Queen Sirikit Convention Center, New Ratchadaphisek Road, Bangkok (☎ 02/229-3456), or Pacific Place Building, 140 Sukhumvit Rd. (☎ 02/253-4014 or 02/229-3465), has a very convenient flight that links Phuket with Ko Samui directly. It also flies to Ranong, U Tapao (near Pattaya), Sukhothai, Chiang Mai, with international flights from Singapore and Phnom Penh. Angel Air, the newest airline on the scene, has an interesting timetable with direct flights from Bangkok to Chiang Rai; Chiang Mai to Udon Thani; Bangkok to Phuket, and international flights from Kunming in China and Singapore. Their reservation line is ☎ 02/953-2260 (Monday to Friday, 8:30am to 5:30pm) or 02/535-6287 (Saturday and Sunday, 8:30am to 6pm). Find their head office at 499/7 Vibhavadi Rangsit Rd., Chatuchak, Bangkok.

BY TRAIN

Renovations that began in 1998 are now completed, and Bangkok's once crowded and cumbersome **Hua Lampong Railway Station** now makes train travel even more convenient. Clear signs point the way to public toilets, coin phones, the food court, and baggage check area. A Post & Telegraph Office, Information Counter, police box, ATMs and money-changing facilities, convenience shops, baggage check, and restaurants surround a large open seating area.

From this hub, the State Railway of Thailand provides regular service to destinations north as far as Chiang Mai, northeast to Udon Thani, east to Pattaya and south to Thailand's southern border, where it connects with Malaysia's *Keretapi Tanah Melayu Berhad* (KTM) with service to Penang (Butterworth), Kuala Lumpur, and Singapore. Complete schedules and fare information can be obtained at any railway station, or by calling **Hua Lampong Railway** Station directly at ☎ **02/223-7010** or 02/223-7020. Advance bookings can be made by calling ☎ **02/223-3762** or 02/224-7788.

Fares are a bit tricky to figure out at first because they use a double charge system. The first charge depends on the distance you travel between stations, for example a trip from Bangkok to Hua Hin (229km) is 202B ($5.30) for first-class travel, 102B ($2.70) for second class, and 44B ($1.15) for third class. From Bangkok to Chiang Mai (751km) the rates are something more like 593B ($15.60) for first class, 281B ($7.40) for second class, and 121B ($3.20) for third class.

The second, or "supplementary," charge is relative to the speed at which you travel and the comfort level you desire. There are more than a few different trains, each running at a different speed. The fastest is the Special Express, which is used primarily for long-distance hauls. These trains cut travel time by as much as 60%, and have sleeper cars, which are a must for the really long trips. Supplementary charges range from 40B ($1.05) for Rapid Train to 120B ($3.15) for Special Express with catering service. Sleeping berth supplementary charges are from 100B ($2.65) for a second-class upper berth on a Rapid Train to 520B ($13.70) per person for a double first-class cabin.

Warning: On trains, pay close attention to your possessions. Thievery is common on overnight trips.

BY BUS

Thailand has a very efficient and inexpensive bus system, highly recommended for budget travelers and short-haul trips. Buses are the cheapest transportation to the farthest and most remote destinations in the country. Options abound, but the major choices are public or private, air-conditioned or nonair-conditioned. Most travelers use the private, air-conditioned buses. Ideally, buses are best for short excursions; expect to pay a minimum of 50B ($1.30) for a one-way ticket. Longer-haul buses are an excellent value (usually less than $1 per hour of travel), but their slowness can be a real liability.

Warning: When traveling by long-distance bus, pay close attention to your possessions. Thievery is common, particularly on overnight buses when valuables are left in overhead racks.

BY TAXI

The more expensive, private cars affiliated with hotels and travel agents post their rates, but you'll have to negotiate with public sedan taxis, sometimes even metered taxis, and tuk-tuk (motorized three-wheel trishaw/pedicab) drivers. If you don't know the correct fare, ask a shop owner, hotelier, or restaurateur what you should expect to pay for your destination and negotiate accordingly. Most taxi fares will average from 50B ($1.30) in provincial towns, to 125B ($3.30) within Bangkok, depending on route, distance, traffic, condition of the car, and mood of the driver. Tuk-tuks cost about 35% less, though bargaining can sometimes be more difficult. In many provincial areas and some resorts, small pickup trucks called *songtao* cruise the main streets offering group-ride taxi service at cheap, set fees. With taxis, tuk-tuks, or songtaos, always remember to agree on your fare before engaging a driver or you will almost certainly overpay. Tipping is not expected.

BY CAR

Renting a car is a snap in Thailand, although I don't recommend driving yourself in Bangkok. One-way streets, construction projects and traffic jams are frequent and frustrating. Outside the city, it's an option, though Thai drivers are quite reckless, and American drivers must reorient themselves to driving on the left side of the road.

Among the many car-rental agencies, **Avis** has offices around the country with representatives in Bangkok at 2/12 Wireless Rd. (☎ 02/255-5300) and the major destinations.

You can rent a car with or without a driver. All drivers are required to have an international driver's license. At the time of writing, self-drive rates started at 1,600B ($42.10) per day for a Suzuki Caribian (a four-wheel-drive sport vehicle; yes, that's how they spell it), Toyota Corolla or Nissan Sunny, plus modest drop-off fees for one-way trips. A Volvo 740 GL with driver cost over 6,300B ($165.80) per day. There's also a living allowance charge for the driver on overnight trips.

Local tour operators in larger destinations like Chiang Mai, Phuket, or Ko Samui will rent cars for considerably cheaper than the larger, more well-known agencies. Sometimes the savings are up to 50%. These companies also rarely require international driver licenses, but will accept your local license from back home as proof you know how to drive. Always ask if you will still be covered by their insurance policy—if you are taken to court for an accident, you may be found guilty for not being properly licensed. Make sure you're covered before you sign.

Gas stations are conveniently located along highways an in towns and cities. Esso, Shell, Caltex, and ptt all have competitive rates. Expect to pay about 400B ($10.53) each time you fill your tank.

PACKAGE TOURS

Several tour operators within Thailand offer package tours originating in Bangkok and including many resort, cultural, or historical destinations. **World Travel Service Ltd.,** 1053 Charoen Krung Rd., 10500 Bangkok (☎ 02/233-5900), is one of the oldest. **Turismo Thai,** 511 Sriayutthaya Rd., Soi 6, Payathai, 10400 Bangkok (☎ 02/ 245-1551) has a wonderful reputation.

Both can arrange individualized itineraries depending on particular destinations you'd prefer (these agencies can also get very favorable flight and hotel bargains!), or can place you on an even less expensive coach tour, if you don't mind sharing your experience with other travelers. Agencies like these are particularly helpful if you are short on time, and would like to fit in as many activities as possible.

8 Tips on Shopping

Anyone who travels to a strange land is always wary of being overcharged for services or overpaying for items when they're out shopping simply because they're a "tourist." In Thailand, it's a special torture because many times prices are not firmly stated and in markets prices are not tagged. One way we gauge whether or not we're overspending is to translate any amount into our native currencies and consider how much we'd pay for a similar item or service back home. My advice is to get yourself out of this habit as quickly as possible, because here it's a faulty indicator.

For example, in Patong Beach a lady tried to charge me 380B for a short batik skirt. In my native currency, that's about 10 bucks. Well, if I went to a street market in New

Driving Rules & Tips

Always drive on the left side of the road. Maximum speed limit for cars inside a city limit is 60kmph (36 mph); outside a city limit, 80kmph (48 mph). Give the right-of-way to vehicles coming from main roads. There is no turning on a red light. Slow down through school zones and around hospitals. If involved in a traffic accident that causes injury or property damage, notify the police. Never operate a vehicle if under the influence of drugs or alcohol.

Take care when passing. Thai drivers pass on blind corners and hills all the time, and motorcycles tooling along the side of the road present possible traffic problems. You'll need your best defensive driving sensibilities.

York City, I'd probably pay that much for the same skirt. The thinking follows that if I can bargain the price down to 250B to 300B ($6.60 to $7.90), I'm making out like a bandit. Until I realize that same skirt is sold in Bangkok for 100B ($2.65)! Even if I paid less for it than I would have back home, the real value of the skirt is far less. Now, you can't be expected to just walk off the plane, sniff the air, and miraculously know the true value of everything you see. So I suggest employing a little bit of inquiry and observation before you commit to your purchases. One piece of sound advice: The more tourists you see, the higher the prices will be.

In department stores and shopping malls, prices are accepted as marked. Credit cards are widely accepted in shops, but watch your card carefully to make sure double plates aren't run off your card for a single purchase. Most shops are open daily from 9am or 10am to anywhere between 6pm to 9pm. Markets open early, maybe about 6am, for produce, flowers and meats, with the exception of night markets (usually beginning at 6pm and lasting until 10pm or 11pm).

9 Tips on Accommodations

Thailand has countless hotels, with the well-traveled areas in Bangkok, Phuket, Chiang Mai, Pattaya and Ko Samui offering up the widest assortment. International chains like Sheraton, Marriott, Westin, Le Meridien, and Holiday Inn have some of the finest hotels and resorts in the country, while the Thai-owned and operated Dusit hotels group has gorgeous properties that can compete with the best. Five-star hotels and resorts spare no detail for the business or leisure traveler, providing designer toiletries, plush robes, in-room stereo systems, in-house videos, and many other creature comforts that will fill your life with luxury. Some of the best restaurants are operated by hotels, with some places offering up to five or six different restaurants from which to choose. With more facilities, better activity options and services, and well-trained staff, you'll have the time of your life, but plan to spend more than 10,000B ($263.15) a night for a double room. In this book I list these places under the "Very Expensive" category. Many hotels in this category have started quoting prices in U.S. dollars to buffer the effects of the recent currency devaluation—the price will be converted to Thai baht according to the rate at the time of check-in. At these hotels the price in baht is not listed.

Most hotels that fall into the "Expensive" category have less deluxe accommodations—the many amenities will not be designer brands; silk bathrobes, personal stereos and in-house movies are gone, and room design and furnishings become less luxurious. However, most rooms are handsome and well maintained, and facilities tend to be good quality. Expect to pay around 5,000B ($131.60) per night.

You can find a good selection of "Moderate" hotels and resorts that can put you up in major cities all over the country. In Bangkok and major tourist centers, where prices tend to be higher (in the 3,000B/$78.95 range), these modern facilities provide good value for money, most have swimming pools, good restaurants, toiletries in the room, satellite television with movie channels, in-room safes, and International Direct Dialing from your room. In smaller cities and towns, this category is about the best you can do, but some of these moderately priced options can have facilities and rooms of surprising quality. And prices are discounted greatly. In someplace like Phitsanulok or Nakhon Si Thammarat, you'll pay between 1,000B and 1,500B ($26.30 and $39.45) for a double room for the night. Sometimes special packages lower prices as low as 700B ($18.40) per night—truly a deal.

It's possible to stay in Thailand on a shoestring—a huge number of guest houses pop up each year, many operated by moms and pops or by foreigners who want a piece of the action. If you go really inexpensive, expect to rough it. Cold-water showers, fan-cooled rooms, and dormitories are the norm. But sometimes you find inexpensive accommodations that stand out from the pack—quaint beachside bungalow villages, city hotels with good locations, or small guesthouses with excellent staff. For this guidebook, I've been very picky about the inexpensive places I've listed, recommending only places where I feel anyone will feel comfortable. For these places you can expect to pay about 700B to 900B ($18.40 to $23.70) in Bangkok, Phuket, and Chiang Mai, and between 300B and 500B ($ 7.90 and $13.15) elsewhere.

Expensive and moderately priced hotels add a 10% service charge plus 7% government tax, also called value added tax (VAT), with the exception of special offers that are mostly inclusive of these fees. Almost all inexpensive places include tax and gratuity in the quoted rate.

Fast Facts: Thailand

American Express The American Express agent in Thailand is **Sea Tours Company,** with offices in Bangkok, Phuket, and Chiang Mai. In Bangkok the Sea Tours office is at 88-92 Phayathai Plaza Building, 8th floor, 128 Phayathai Rd. (☎ **02/216-5783,** fax 02/216-5757). See "Fast Facts" in chapters 8 and 9 for branch contacts in Phuket and Chiang Mai.

ATM Networks Most major banks throughout the country have automated teller machines. In general you can get cash with your debit card at any Bangkok Bank, Thai Farmers Bank, Siam Commercial Bank, Bank of Ayudhya—provided your card is hooked into the MasterCard/Cirrus or Visa/PLUS network. See the "Money" section earlier in this chapter.

Banks Most hotels will change foreign currency, but banks and money changers offer better rates. Official banking hours are Monday to Friday 8:30am to 3:30pm. Major cities have foreign-exchange banks and money changers, which are open daily until as late as 10pm for exchange.

All charge a commission (usually 5B/13¢) and government stamp tax (3B/8¢) per traveler's check. It's essential to have your passport for cashing traveler's checks, as a photocopy will often not suffice. Carry baht and some cash dollars when traveling to more remote areas.

Business Hours Government offices (including branch post offices) are open Monday to Friday 8:30am to 4:30pm, with a lunch break between noon and 1pm. Businesses are generally open 8am to 5pm. Shops often stay open from

8am until 7pm or later, seven days a week. Department stores are generally open 10am to 7pm.

Car Rentals   See "Getting Around," above in this chapter.

Climate   See "When to Go," above in this chapter.

Currency   See "Money," above in this chapter.

Customs   See "Customs" above in this chapter. All items must be declared. Firearms and ammunition can only be brought in with a permit from the police department or local registration office.

Documents Required   See "Visitor Information & Entry Requirements," above in this chapter.

Driving Rules   See "Getting Around," above in this chapter.

Drugstores   Throughout the country, there are excellent drugstores stocked with many brand-name medications and toiletries, plus less expensive local brands. Pharmacists often speak some English, and a surprising number of drugs that require a prescription elsewhere can be dispensed at their discretion.

Electricity   All outlets—except in some luxury hotels—are 220 volts AC (50 cycles). Outlets have two flat-pronged holes, so you may need an adapter. If you use a 110-volt hair dryer, electric shaver, or battery charger for a computer, bring a transformer and adapter.

Embassies & Consulates   While most countries have consular representation in Bangkok, the United States, Australia, Canada, and the United Kingdom also have consulates in Chiang Mai. See chapters 3 and 12 for details. Most embassies will deal with emergency situations on a 24-hour basis, though visas are often issued only in the morning. If you are seriously injured or ill, do not hesitate to call your embassy for assistance.

Emergencies   Throughout the country, the emergency number is ☎ **191** for police or medical assistance, or ☎ **1699** for the Tourist Police. Don't expect many English speakers at these numbers outside the major tourist areas. (Ambulances must be summoned from hospitals rather than through a central service.) You should also contact your embassy or consulate, the Tourist Police, or the local Tourist Authority of Thailand (TAT) office.

Etiquette   See "Etiquette" in Appendix A.

Holidays   See "When to Go," above in this chapter.

Information   See "Visitor Information," above in this chapter.

Language   Central (often called Bangkok) Thai is the official language. English is spoken in the major cities at most hotels, restaurants, and shops, and is the second language of the professional class, as well as the international business language. (For more information on the Thai language see "The Language" in Appendix A)

Mail   You can use *poste restante* as an address anywhere in the country. For those unfamiliar with this service, it is comparable to General Delivery in the United States, whereby you can receive mail addressed to you, care of Poste Restante, GPO, Name of City. You need either a valid passport or ID card, must sign a receipt, and pay 1B (3¢) per letter received. Hours of operation are the same as the post office. Airmail postcards to the United States cost 12B to 15B (32¢ to 39¢), depending on the size of the card; first-class letters cost 19B (5¢) per 5 grams (rates to Europe are about the same). Airmail delivery usually takes 7 days.

Air parcel post costs 606B ($15.95) per kilogram. Surface or sea parcel post costs 215B ($5.65) for 1 kilogram (3 or 4 months for delivery). International Express Mail (EMS) costs 440B ($11.60) from 1 to 250 grams, with delivery guaranteed within 4 days. See individual chapters for local post offices and their hours.

Shipping by air freight is expensive. Two major international delivery services have their main dispatching offices in Bangkok, though they deliver throughout the country; these are **DHL Thailand,** Grand Amarin Tower Building, Phetchaburi Road (☎ **02/207-0600**), and **Federal Express,** at Rama IV Road (☎ **02/367-3222**). **UPS Parcel Delivery Service,** with a main branch in Bangkok at 16/1 Soi 44/1 Sukhumvit Road (☎ **02/712-3300**), also has branches elsewhere in Thailand. Many businesses will also package and mail merchandise for a reasonable price.

Maps The TAT gives out excellent regional and city maps at their information offices, and there are a number of good privately produced maps, usually free, available at most hotels and many businesses. For specific map recommendations, see "Visitor Information" in each region.

Newspapers & Magazines The major domestic English-language dailies are the *Bangkok Post* and the *Nation,* distributed in the morning in the capital and later in the day around the country. They cover the domestic political scene, as well as international news from AP, UPI, and Reuters wire services, and cost 20B (55¢). Both the *Asian Wall Street Journal* and *International Herald Tribune* are available Monday to Friday on their day of publication in Bangkok (in the provinces a day or two later). *Time, Newsweek,* the *Economist, Asiaweek,* and the *Far Eastern Economic Review* are sold at newsstands in the international hotels, as well as in bookstores in all the major cities.

Police The Tourist Police (☎ **1699**), with offices in every city (see specific chapters), speak English (and other foreign languages) and are open 24 hours. You should call them in an emergency rather than the regular police at ☎ **191** because there is no guarantee that the regular police operator will speak English.

Tourist Police who patrol nightclub areas, especially where go-go bars are present, are incredibly efficient. If you should run into any troubles in these areas, do not hesitate to contact them. They will take the most minor offence seriously and will work hard until the crime is solved.

Radio & TV International television is supplied by the Star Broadcasting network, sending American, British and Australian television shows, CNN or BBC news channels, ESPN sports, movie channels like HBO and CINEMAX, and Asian MTV via satellite to subscribers. Expensive and moderate hotels usually carry a few of these channels, otherwise you're stuck with local programming which never has foreign language subtitles. In Bangkok, FMX (95.5 FM) has American and British pop hits, plus regular local and international news updates in English. News from Radio Thailand News Relay is delivered at 7am, 12:30pm, 7pm, and 8pm. In the evenings, from 9:30 to midnight, Chula-longkorn University's radio station (101.5 FM) plays a variety of classical music.

Rest Rooms Many restaurants and all hotels above the budget level will have Western toilets. Shops and budget hotels will have an Asian toilet, what I like to call a "squatty potty," a hole in the ground with foot pads on either side. Near the toilet is a water bucket or sink with a small ladle. The water is for flushing and cleaning the toilet. Don't count on these places having toilet paper. Some shopping malls have dispensers outside the rest room—3B (8¢) for some paper.

Dispose of it in the wastebasket provided, as it will clog up rudimentary sewage systems.

Safety   Serious crime in Thailand is rare; petty crime such as purse snatching or pickpocketing is common. Particular care should be taken by those traveling over land (especially on overnight buses and trains) in remote parts of the country and near the Burmese and Laotian borders, as local bandits or rebel groups sometimes rob travelers.

Beware of credit-card scams; carry a minimum of cards, don't allow them out of your sight, and keep all receipts. Never leave your cards with others for safe-keeping (such as during a trek). If you don't want to carry them, put them in a hotel safe. Don't carry unnecessary valuables, and keep those you do carry in your hotel's safe. Pay particular attention to your things, especially purses and wallets, on public transportation.

A special warning: Be wary of strangers who offer to guide you (particularly in Bangkok), take you to any shop (especially jewelry shops), or buy you food or drink. This is most likely to occur near a tourist sight. Be warned that this kind of forward behavior is simply not normal for the average Thai. There are rare exceptions, but most likely these new "friends" will try to swindle you in some way. This often takes the form of trying to persuade you to buy "high quality" jewelry or gems (usually worthless) at "bargain" prices. Also, beware of anyone inviting you to his or her home, then offering to show you a famous Thai card game or engage you in any sort of gambling. You *will* lose. If you are approached about such schemes, call the Tourist Police immediately.

For those who contemplate bringing a prostitute to their hotel room, be advised of the danger of food or drink laced with sleeping potions. There are many incidents with victims waking up 2 days later to find their valuables gone. Women who work at go-go bars are more likely to be trustworthy—you know where they work.

Taxes & Service Charges   Hotels charge a 7% government value added tax (VAT) and typically add a 10% service charge; hotel restaurants add 8.25% government tax. Smaller hotels quote the price inclusive of these charges.

Telephone, Telex & Fax   Major hotels in Bangkok, Pattaya, Phuket, Chiang Mai, and the provincial capitals have international direct-dial (IDD), long-distance service, and in-house fax transmission. Hotels charge a surcharge on local and long-distance calls, which can add up to 50% in some cases. Credit-card or collect calls are a much better value, but most hotels also add a hefty service charge for them to your bill.

Most major post offices, have special booths for overseas calls, as well as fax and telex service, usually open 7am to 11pm. There are Overseas Telegraph and Telephone offices (also called OCO or Overseas Call Office) open 24 hours throughout the country for long-distance international calls and telex and fax service. In addition, several guest houses and travel agents in tourist areas offer long-distance calling on their private line. Local calls can be made from any red public pay telephone. Calls cost 1B for 3 minutes, with additional 1B coins needed after hearing multiple beeps on the line. Blue public phones are for long-distance calls within Thailand. Card phones can be found in most airports, in many public buildings, and in larger shopping centers. Cards can be purchased in several denominations at Telephone Organization of Thailand offices.

For more dialing information see "Telephone Tips" on the inside back cover. All numbers listed in this book are preceded by the appropriate local area code.

Time Zone Bangkok and all of Thailand are 7 hours ahead of GMT (Greenwich mean time). During winter months, this means that Bangkok is exactly 7 hours ahead of London, 12 hours ahead of New York, 15 hours ahead of Los Angeles. Daylight saving time will add 1 hour to these figures.

Tipping If a service charge is not added to your restaurant check, a 10% to 15% tip is appropriate. In small noodle shops, a 10B tip may be given if the service is particularly good. Airport or hotel porters expect tips of 20B (55¢) per bag (in very expensive hotels, I'll double it to 40B or 50B per bag ($1.05 or $1.30). The gracious hostesses who show you to your room in the better hotels usually do not expect a tip, but you should feel free to reward good service wherever you find it. Tipping taxi drivers is not expected. Carry small bills, as many cab drivers either don't have (or won't admit having) small change.

Water Don't drink the tap water, even in the major hotels. Most hotels provide bottled water in or near the minibar or in the bathroom; use it for brushing your teeth as well as drinking. Most restaurants serve bottled or boiled water and ice made from boiled water, but always ask to be sure.

Introducing Bangkok 3

Bangkok is an ancient and a modern city, where a network of *klongs* (canals) offset staggering automobile traffic, giant outdoor markets compete with glittering shopping malls, and modern buildings rise in the city that grew around the Grand Palace and the Temple of the Emerald Buddha. It's the financial capital of one of the fastest-growing economies in the world, despite economic setbacks in 1997, and some of the worst air and water pollution on earth. Outside this core are new high-rise neighborhoods, more Wild West boom towns than manicured suburbs, where most of the city's ten million (the figure is unofficial, but generally believed true) inhabitants reside. Though not exactly a microcosm of all of Southeast Asia, Bangkok is definitely the region's most exotic and, at the same time, out-of-control capital city. For many first-time visitors, it's an assault on the senses.

Bangkok has probably the greatest concentration of luxury hotels of any city in the world, and, as the capital of sumptuous Thai cuisine, some of the best dining options. Even in a city choked by cars and pollution, frenetic building, and a pace that rivals that of New York, you'll likely encounter the uniquely Thai tradition of fine, friendly service. And with the exception of Chiang Mai, Bangkok offers unrivaled shopping for Southeast Asian handicrafts, antiques, silk, and jewels. For nightlife, there are no exceptions—the disco hit from the '80s "One Night in Bangkok" still delivers.

1 Orientation

ARRIVING

The capital's central location makes it both the region's and the country's major transportation hub. Bangkok has a huge modern airport (which may not be the most modern facility, but is one of the most efficient in Asia), three bus terminals, and a centrally located train station. Within the city, taxis and tuk-tuks (three-wheeled motorized trishaws/pedicabs) cruise the broad avenues and provide inexpensive, reliable transportation. The brand-new elevated rail line (opening in late 1999) has limited service now, but with future lines scheduled to open, will reach many parts of the city.

BY PLANE

Bangkok is a major hub for air travel in Southeast Asia, with more than 70 airlines providing service. Almost all international and domestic

Bangkok at a Glance

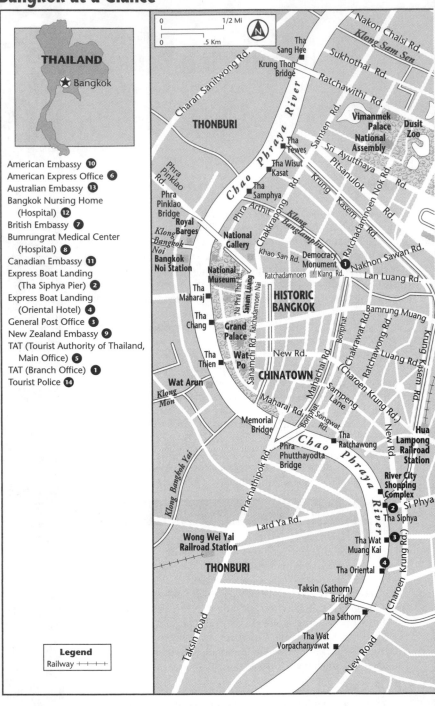

THAILAND

★ Bangkok

American Embassy ⑩
American Express Office ⑥
Australian Embassy ⑬
Bangkok Nursing Home
  (Hospital) ⑫
British Embassy ⑦
Bumrungrat Medical Center
  (Hospital) ⑧
Canadian Embassy ⑪
Express Boat Landing
  (Tha Siphya Pier) ②
Express Boat Landing
  (Oriental Hotel) ④
General Post Office ③
New Zealand Embassy ⑨
TAT (Tourist Authority of Thailand,
  Main Office) ⑤
TAT (Branch Office) ①
Tourist Police ⑭

Legend
Railway +‑+‑+‑+

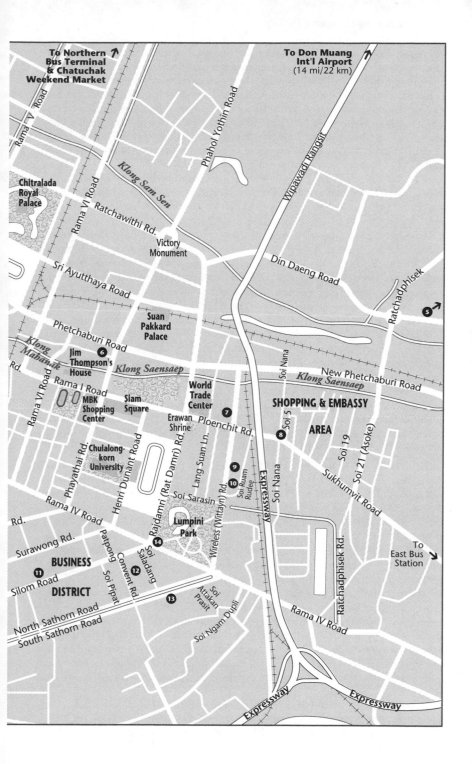

To Northern ↑
Bus Terminal
& Chatuchak
Weekend Market

To Don Muang
Int'l Airport
(14 mi/22 km) ↗

Rama V Road

Phahol Yothin Road

Klong Sam Sen

Wipawadi Rangsit

Chitralada
Royal
Palace

Rama VI Road

Ratchawithi Rd.

Victory
Monument

Din Daeng Road

Ratchadphisek

5 ↗

Sri Ayutthaya Road

Phetchaburi Road

Suan
Pakkard
Palace

Klong
Mahanak
Rd.

Jim
Thompson's
House

6

Klong Saensaep

Soi Nana

New Phetchaburi Road

Klong Saensaep

Rama VI Road

Rama I Road

MBK
Shopping
Center

Siam
Square

World
Trade
Center

7

SHOPPING & EMBASSY

Soi 5

8

AREA

Erawan
Shrine

Ploenchit Rd.

Soi 19

Soi 21 (Asoke)

Phayathai Rd.

Chulalong-
korn
University

Henri Dunant Road

Rajdamri (Rat Damri) Rd.

Lang Suan Ln.

9

10

Soi Ruam
Rudee

Soi Nana

Sukhumvit Road

Rama IV Road

Soi Sarasin

Wireless (Wittayu) Rd.

Expressway

Surawong Rd.

BUSINESS

11

Silom Road

DISTRICT

Patpong

Convent Rd.

Soi Pipat

Soi
Saladang

12

14

Lumpini
Park

Ratchadphisek Rd.

To
East Bus
Station ↗

North Sathorn Road

South Sathorn Road

13

Soi
Attakan
Prasit

Soi Ngam Dupli

Rama IV Road

Expressway

Expressway

37

flights come and go from **Don Muang International Airport,** which is 22km (14 miles) north of the heart of the city. International and domestic flights arrive at different terminals, a short 1km (⁶/₁₀ mile) walk or a free shuttle ride apart.

Travelers arriving at the international terminal will find a wide range of services awaiting them, available 24 hours unless otherwise noted: free luggage carts at the arrival gates; luggage storage for 25B (65¢) per day with a 3-month maximum; currency exchange banks with the same rates as in-town banks; a post office with overseas telephone service; an **Airport Information Booth** and a **Tourist Authority of Thailand (TAT)** booth, open 8:30am to 4:30pm (☎ 02/523-8972); a Thai Hotel Association desk, which will assist you in finding available accommodations; restaurants, serving both Thai and international food; a minimarket; and the first-class Amari Airport Hotel (see "Accommodations" in chapter 4), a short walk or free shuttle ride away.

The domestic terminal offers most of these services, though on a more limited schedule: luggage storage, for 25B (65¢) a day, 14-day limit, open 6am to 11pm; a post office in the departure wing with overseas telephone service, a foreign exchange bank, and the Hotel Association desk, open 24 hours; and a cafeteria-style coffee shop.

The airport provides free shuttle service between the international and domestic terminals, with buses every 15 minutes. If you have light luggage, you might find it more enjoyable (and sometimes faster) to walk. For general airport information, call ☎ **02/535-1111;** 02/535-1254 for departures; or 02/535-1301 for arrivals. Passengers on domestic flights pay 30B (80¢) departure tax, which is paid for when you purchase your ticket, while those on international flights must purchase a 500B ($13.15) departure tax ticket from either vending machines or sales booths just after check-in before you enter immigration. Make sure you have adequate funds, there aren't any ATMs once you reach this point. Children under 2 years are exempt.

The **Lost and Found Counter** (☎ **02/535-2811** or 02/535-1254) is in the arrival lounge and manned around the clock. (If you leave something on an aircraft or airline bus, contact the airline as soon as possible.)

GETTING TO & FROM THE AIRPORT   Though the airport is just north of the city, it can seem maddeningly far (half an hour late at night, with a bus taking as long as 2 hours during rush hours). Plan on an hour-long taxi ride from the airport into the city, and at least that long from one end of the city to the other. Most of the larger hotels will pick up guests from the airport if requested in advance, at a typical charge of 650B ($17.10), or you can hail a cab and pay metered fare (about 250B to 350B/$6.60 to $9.20). You can easily arrange for an air-conditioned minibus, taxi, or limousine to your hotel; these are found outside the arrival hall of both the international and domestic terminals (ground floor level).

Taxis are hailed outside the arrival halls at both the domestic and international terminals. They're usually lined up in a long queue. Charges will be according to the meter, plus a 50B ($1.30) service charge for airport service. The driver will almost always ask if you would like to take the expressway. **Chalerm Mahanakhon Expressway** connects the airport with downtown Bangkok, and is a true relief during rush hour traffic. If you agree (which you should) he'll ask for 40B ($1.05) once you reach the toll booth, so make sure you get change ("small money") before leaving the airport.

Private **limousine** services have air-conditioned sedans for hire from booths in the arrival halls of both international and domestic airports. Trips to town start from 650B ($17.10). For advanced booking call ☎ **02/535-5931** for international arrival and ☎ **02/535-1894** for domestic arrival.

The **Airport Bus** is a convenient and inexpensive alternative. With 24-hour service, stopping regularly at international and domestic terminals, three bus routes serve the city's various well-traveled points—Silom and Chaoren Krung Road near the river and in the business district, Khao San Road in the historic district, Sukhumvit in the shopping/Embassy area, and many other destinations. At the stops outside the arrival halls, helpful staff wait to advise travelers. Tell them your hotel and they'll direct you to the correct bus. Pay onboard 70B ($1.85).

Public buses no. A4 (through Historic Bangkok and the Business District), 16B (40¢); A10 (to the Northern Bus Terminal, Dusit area and Southern Bus Terminal), 16B (40¢); A13 (Sukhumvit Road in the Shopping/Embassy Area to the Eastern Bus Terminal), 16B (40¢); and A20 (to Siam Square in the Shopping/Embassy Area, and the Hua Lamphong Railway Station), 16B (40¢) are the most relevant lines. If you're a die-hard budgeter, turn right outside the terminal and find the bus stop about 50 meters away on the highway, but be warned that city buses become very crowded and there is very little room for luggage, as well as ample opportunity for thieves.

The **Airport Express Train** runs between the Don Muang station near the airport and the central Hua Lampong Rail Station four times a day Monday to Friday only in each direction. If your destination in Bangkok is near Hua Lampong Station, consider taking the train there; for 10B (25¢) you can save lots of time and hassle (trip time: 1 hour). Standard train service is somewhat erratic—approximately every half hour during the day—but if you're traveling light during the day or early evening and in no great hurry, you can take the elevated footbridge between Don Muang Station and the airport terminal and make the trip for as little as 5B (15¢) third-class, 10B (25¢) second-class. Tickets can be purchased at the station.

BY TRAIN

The Thai rail network is extremely well organized, connecting Bangkok with major cities throughout the country. (You can also travel by train to Bangkok from Singapore, via Kuala Lumpur and Butterworth, Malaysia.)

All trains to and from the capital stop at **Hua Lampong Railroad Station** (☎ **02/223-7010** or 02/223-7020), east of Chinatown, at the intersection of Rama IV and Krung Kasem roads. Inside the station clear signs point the way to public toilets, coin phones, the food court, and baggage check area. A Post & Telegraph Office, Information Counter, police box, ATMs and money-changing facilities, convenience shops, baggage check, and restaurants surround a large open seating area.

One shocker for first-timers to the station are the nice people who will approach you in the station offering help—directing you to trains, ticket booths, and ground transportation. Although you might be suspicious, relax; these people are official representatives, with badges to prove it, and do provide helpful information—no touts.

As the station is centrally located, a metered taxi will cost no more than 100B ($2.65) to most hotels; a tuk-tuk should be no more than 70B ($1.85). Both are located directly outside the terminal.

BY BUS

Bangkok has three major bus stations, each serving a different part of the country. All air-conditioned public buses to the west and the southern peninsula arrive and depart from the **Southern Bus Terminal** (☎ **02/435-1199**) on Charan Sanitwong Road (near Bangkok Noi Station), west of the river over the Phra Pinklao Bridge from the Democracy Monument; nonair-conditioned buses to the south and west arrive and leave from a separate terminal (☎ **02/411-0061**) on Phra Pinklao Road at Highway 338. Service to the east coast (including Pattaya) arrives and departs from the **Eastern**

Bus Terminal (☎ 02/390-1230), on Sukhumvit Road opposite Soi 63 (Ekamai Road). Buses to the north, northeast, and northwest arrive and leave from the **Northern Bus Terminal** (☎ 02/272-5761), Phahonyothin Road, just west of the airport freeway near the Chatuchak Weekend Market. Some private companies have buses arriving and departing from their offices in town; other companies, at the terminals.

VISITOR INFORMATION

The **Tourist Authority of Thailand (TAT)** offers thorough and accurate information and assistance about all aspects of traveling in Thailand. If you haven't already visited one of their offices overseas, you can stop by their counter in the international terminal of Don Muang airport when you arrive (☎ 02/523-8972), open daily 8:30am to 4:30pm. Their main office, at Le Concorde Building, Ratchadaphisek Road (☎ 02/694-1222), doesn't make for an easy stop-off for information—Ratchadaphisek can be far from most traveler's routes within the city. Far more convenient, the branch office at Ratchadamnoen Nok Avenue (☎ 02/282-9773) provides excellent information not far from the Grand Palace and other sites in historic Bangkok. And if you're heading out to the Chatuchak Weekend Market, you can stop by their information booth there (☎ 02/272-7448).

USEFUL PUBLICATIONS   The TAT produces an enormous amount of glossy tourist brochures on every destination in the country, including Bangkok. Bangkok also has a ton of free magazines, most of which are available for free in hotel lobbies throughout the city. Look for the slim *Thaiways,* produced bimonthly with maps, tips, and facts (about Pattaya, Chiang Mai, and Phuket as well) plus articles on Thai culture. *Bangkok Dining & Entertainment,* another slim volume, specializes mostly in restaurant write-ups and nightlife coverage. On sale in bookstores (see listings in chapter 6 under "Shopping"), pick up a copy of *Metro Magazine* (100B/$2.65) for the best nightlife and restaurant listings, what's happening, plus funny and fascinating social commentary. For a peek into the lives of Thailand's high-brow hobnobbers, *Thailand Tattler* covers the charity ball and art gala set in between Madison Avenue adverts (80B/$2.10).

CITY LAYOUT

Vintage 19th-century photographs of Bangkok show vivid images of life on the **Chao Phraya River,** bustling with bobbing vessels that ranged from the humblest rowboat to elaborate royal barges. This was the original gateway to Krung Thep, or Bangkok, as it was known to early outsiders, who arrived via boat traveling upriver from the Gulf of Siam. Rama I, upon moving the capital city from Thonburi on the west bank to Bangkok on the East, dug a series of canals fanning out from the S-shaped river. For strategical reasons, the canals replicated the moat system used at Ayutthaya, Siam's former kingdom, bolstering the city from invasion. For significant spiritual reasons, these waters represented the primordial oceans that surrounded the Buddhist heavens. A small artificial island cut into the land along the riverbank became the site for the Grand Palace, Wat Phra Kaeo (the Temple of the Emerald Buddha) and Wat Po. To this day the island is still known as **Rattanakosin.** This is the historical center of the city, perhaps the most visited part of the city by travelers. It's the best starting point for getting your bearings in Bangkok.

Klongs continued to span eastward as the city's population grew. Chinese and Indian merchants formed settlements alongside the river, southeast of Rattanakosin. The **Chinatown** of today still bustles with commerce, culture, and energy along all its narrow streets and back alleys. The main thoroughfare through Chinatown, Charoen Krung Road (sometimes called by its former name, New Road) snakes southward, following the shape of the river. On the eastern edge of Chinatown, **Hua Lamphong Railway Station,** the hub for rail travel in the country, is centrally located but adds to the local congestion.

Just beyond Chinatown along the river bank, in an area called **Bangrak,** foreign diplomats built European-style buildings to house their embassies. The Oriental Hotel, the grande dame of Bangkok's plush hotels, was suitably placed on the river in this cosmopolitan neighborhood. Bangrak's main thoroughfares, Suriwong Road, Silom Road, and Sathorn Road originate at Charoen Krung and run parallel all the way to Rama IV Road. Within Bangrak you'll find many embassy buildings, fine hotels, and high-rise office buildings, restaurants and pubs, plus the Patpong night-time entertainment hub and market.

Back to Rattanakosin, as you head north upriver in the other direction from Chinatown, you'll hit **Banglamphu,** home to Bangkok's National Museum, Wat Suthat, and The Giant Swing and Klong Phu Khao Thong (Golden Mount). The centerpoint, the huge Democracy Monument, marks the traffic circle where the wide Ratchadamnoen Klong Road intersects Dinso Road. But Banglamphu's biggest claim to fame these days is Khao San Road, a small street that, over the years, has become the main congregation center for backpackers—with budget accommodations, inexpensive restaurants, numerous travel agents, and lots of nightlife.

Further north of Banglamphu, the area known as **Dusit** is home to Wat Benchamabophit, Vinmarnmek Palace, the Dusit Zoo, and many parks.

As Bangkok began to sprawl, **Thonburi,** the brief site of the former capital across the river from the Grand Palace, continued in relative isolation. Many temples here pre-date those of Bangkok, and the area remained mostly residential. In the twentieth century, automobiles replaced boats, and as a result, paved roads replaced klongs. Bangkok was quick to fill in most canals. Luckily many in Thonburi survived. A long-tail boat ride through back canals is a high point of a trip here. Thai riverside houses, both traditional and new, and neighborhood businesses, some of them floating, reveal glimpses of life as it might have been 200 years ago. On dry land, you'll have to cross the Phra Pin Klao Bridge from Banglamphu to reach Bangkok's **Southern Bus Terminal** in this area.

Meanwhile back on the other side of the river, Bangkok was thriving. Over the two centuries since its founding, the city fanned eastward. From Rattanakosin, beyond Banglamphu and Bangrak, the area called Pathumwan became home to many residences, the most famous of which is Jim Thompson's house, a stunning Thai style house open to visitors. Nowadays this area is better known as **Siam Square,** named for the huge shopping malls that draw locals and visitors day and night. The area's hotels, cafes, and nightclubs glitter with modern style—many come here to stroll along Rama I and Ratchadamri Roads to see and be seen.

Beyond Pathumwan, **Wireless (Witthayu) Road** runs north to south between Rama IV (at the edge of Bangrak) to Rama I Road (at the edge of Pathumwan). Here, huge embassy complexes and exclusive hotels cater to diplomats, business people, and well-heeled travelers.

At this point Rama I Road (running west to east) turns into Ploenchit Road, and after two blocks, **Sukhumvit Road.** Sukhumvit's fame today is its huge expatriate population. Many foreign workers choose to live in the streets that branch from this long road, bringing with them demand for good restaurants, entertainment spots, shopping and services. Along Sukhumvit, you'll find luxury hotels alongside inexpensive accommodations, fine dining and cheap local eats, first-rate shopping malls and street-side bazaars. While Bangkok's major attractions are elsewhere in the city (travel between this area and the sights of historical Bangkok can take up to an hour), Sukhumvit's accommodations and dining options make it a good choice for your temporary home. However, be warned, Sukhumvit is very long—it leads all the way beyond Pattaya along the east coast. If you continue beyond Sukhumvit Soi 24, you'll feel like you're in Siberia. Bangkok's **Eastern Bus Terminal,** at Soi Ekkamai, is at Sukhumvit Soi 63.

Most visitors arrive via **Don Muang International Airport,** a 40-minute drive north of the city center off the Chalerm Mahanakhon Expressway. Nearby, the Chatuchak weekend market and Bangkok's **Northern Bus Terminal** provide another good excuse for visitors to venture here.

FINDING AN ADDRESS   Street numbers follow Western conventions, to a point, in that even-numbered addresses are on one side of the street and odd-numbered on the opposite side. Most addresses are subdivided by a "/" symbol, as in 123/4 Silom Rd., which is a variation on sequential numbering that accounts for new construction. Be aware that 123 and 124 Silom Rd. will be on opposite sides of the street, but not necessarily close to each other. You'll find the term *Soi* frequently in addresses. A soi is a small lane off a major street. So, 45 Soi 23 Sukhumvit (sometimes written 45 Soi Sukhumvit 23), is found at number 45 on Soi 23, a lane that runs perpendicular to Sukhumvit Road. Even-numbered sois will be on the north side, and odd-numbered on the south side, though Soi 21 and Soi 20 may be far apart.

It's a good idea to ask the staff at your hotel to write the address of your destination in Thai, to assist taxi drivers. Many drivers do not speak English, or if they do, may not understand your pronunciation of a street address. Even more are unfamiliar with following directions from a map. Most hotels have a "taxi card" with their address in Thai to assist guests.

STREET MAPS   There are three excellent Bangkok maps. The first is "Latest Tour's Guide to Bangkok and Thailand"—affectionately called "The Bus Map." It costs 60B ($1.60) and is available at most hotels and bookstores, though the TAT sells it for 35B (90¢) at their main office. The "Bangkok Thailand Guide Map," by Discovery Map, is a slightly more up-to-date version of the Bus Map and also costs 60B ($1.60). The third map I enthusiastically recommend is Nancy Chandler's "Map of Bangkok"—also known as "The Market Map and Much More." Nancy, a graphic designer who lived in Bangkok for 19 years, uses her keen eye for quality and value (not to mention the bizarre) to fashion a colorful guide focused on Bangkok's rich markets, shopping opportunities, and sightseeing highlights. The map costs 120B ($3.15) and is available at most bookstores.

Most hotels will provide Bangkok guides with simple maps to their guests free for the asking. The "Thaiways Map of Bangkok" is one of the better ones, and it includes detailed maps of the more important areas.

NEIGHBORHOODS IN BRIEF

For this book, hotels, restaurants, and attractions have been subdivided into four main regions within the city to help you make smart choices about where to stay and dine, and what there is to see and do.

On the River   Though the Chao Phraya River runs far beyond the city limits of Bangkok, this area roughly contains Bangkok's grand riverside hotels. I've also included a few other hotels in this area, as well as the River City Shopping Complex, and some other smaller shopping malls.

Historic Bangkok, Near the Grand Palace   This area, the site of the original Bangkok capital, lays within the confines of **Rattanakosin** Island, created as a defense measure by King Rama I. A *klong* (canal), now called Klong Ong Ang, was dug from a point at a bend in the Chao Phraya River (near what is now the Memorial Bridge), running north, then turning east near Wat Saket, where it became Klong Banglamphu, and rejoined the river north of the Phra Pinklao Bridge. The area includes a majority of the tourist sites, beginning with Wat Po, the Grand Palace and Wat Phra Kaeo, then continuing north to the **Dusit** Zoo and Vimanmek Palace Museum. There are numerous historic wats, the National Museum, and the National Theater and Library. There are only a handful of first-class and moderate hotels in this area, but their proximity to the sites makes it an attractive area to stay in. Low-budget travelers will find guest houses and cheap hotels east of the Democracy Monument and north of Ratchadamnoen Klang Road, especially along Khao San Road.

The Business District   The Business District, the area known locally as **Bangrak,** is bounded by Rama IV Road on the east, Chinatown on the north, Chaoren Krung Road (or New Road, near the river) on the west, and South Sathorn Road on the south. Silom Road and Surawong Road run east-west through the center. As its name implies, many banks, businesses and embassies have offices in this area, but it's also a good choice for vacation travelers with its many shops and malls, good restaurants, high-quality hotels, and the famous Patpong nightlife area.

The Shopping/Embassy Area   This includes the neighborhoods on either side of the thoroughfare called Rama I Road on its western end, then Ploenchit Road as it runs east and crosses Ratchadamri Road, and finally, Sukhumvit Road as it crosses under the airport freeway. Here are several deluxe hotels, many first-class and moderate hotels, numerous shopping complexes, the newer office buildings, most of the Western embassies, and a large concentration of the expatriate community. Although this book refers to the area as "Shopping/Embassy," it's centrally located with access to all of Bangkok's activities—the name is merely a title for reference.

2 Getting Around

You'll be happy to know Bangkok's legendary traffic has eased up a bit since its heyday in the early '90s. Time was it took over 2 hours for a taxi to get from one side of town to the other during rush hour, but these days the same trip might take just over an hour. Possible reasons include the government's actions to build expressways and a commuter rail system, and the economic downturn's effects on expensive personal driving habits. Still, traffic can be frustrating—especially weekday mornings between 8am and 10am and the afternoon rush between 4pm and 7pm. Take notice of weather conditions, as rainstorms can bring traffic to a halt for hours during heavy downpours.

A fabulous alternative that is largely overlooked is water travel, either on the Chao Phraya River or the remaining klongs that branch from it. Almost all sites and tourist services are located near the river and are easily reached from other river points by the excellent and inexpensive Chao Phraya Express Boat system. Taxis are still a relative bargain and the best alternative on land. Open-air tuk-tuks are recommended only for short trips, as they expose you to heavy doses of auto fumes, and you will have to bargain hard for a fair fare.

BY FERRY & LONG-TAIL BOAT   Travel on the river is as much a mode of transportation as it is an attraction in itself. While efficient, it's a fairly tranquil way to get around and provides a remarkable window to local life, as well as good views of the city. Branching off from the river is the ancient network of klongs, most of which are serviced by the basic long-tail boats (*hang yao*).

The **Chao Phraya Express Company** (☎ 02/222-5330) operates a system of ferries that run up and down the river, stopping at the many piers (*tha* in Thai) on both sides of the river (the piers are marked on almost every Bangkok map). Cross-river ferries carry passengers back and forth across the river from almost every express-boat pier, though often from a separate landing. Most tourists will board the express boats near the Oriental Hotel, at the pier just south of the hotel, or at the Tha Siphya Pier, just south of the Royal Orchid Sheraton. There are numerous other piers (many of which charge a 1B (5¢) entrance fee), though most are hard to find from the road: Ask your hotel desk for guidance, ask on the street, or look for small signs pointing the way to express-boat piers. Other major piers include Tha Ratchawong (in Chinatown off Ratchawong Road), Tha Thien (near Wat Po), Tha Chang (near the Temple of the Emerald Buddha), and Tha Maharaj (near Wat Mahathat).

Express boats are long white boats with a pointed bow and a large number near the front. They carry the Chao Phraya Express logo on the side, and have bench seats and open sides. Don't confuse these with the smaller, cross-river ferries, distinguished by their squatter shape and rounded bow.

Boats pull up and pause for a fleeting moment, so boarding passengers must step lively. Fares are based on distance. The onboard ticket taker will ask your destination and charge between 5B and 10B (15¢ and 25¢) for the trip, the best deal in town. To exit, move to the back of the boat and be ready to hop off. As on any public conveyance in Bangkok, keep a close hold on your belongings. Cross-river ferries will usually cost 2B to 4B (5¢ to 10¢). Both express boats and ferries operate daily between 6am and 6pm, with boats arriving every 10 minutes or so.

Long-tail boats—slender, noisy, motorized gondolas—provide ferrylike transportation through the inland klongs on the Thonburi side, leaving when full from the Tha Ratchawong, Tha Thien, Tha Chang, and Tha Maharaj piers. Allow an hour to ride on one, just to see the fascinating neighborhoods across the river. The fare should be 5B to 10B (15¢ to 25¢). Get off at any stop and take another boat back.

You can also charter your own long-tail boat for about 300B per hour for a private tour at the Boat Tour Center near the River City Complex or at Tha Chang.

Those looking for adventure or those staying in the Shopping/Embassy Area should try the system of long-tail boat taxis operating on Klong Mahanak, which runs parallel to and between Phetchaburi Road and Rama I/Ploenchit/Sukhumvit Road. You can board at most major cross-streets (such as Ratchadamri, Wireless, or Soi Asoke no. 21) and ride to the western end, near Wat Saket and the Democracy Monument. The government has joined what began as a private venture, adding new, larger "River Buses" that ply the length of Klong Mahanak, a major east-west klong. These are known as *Saensaep,* or "deep pain," but the name doesn't reflect the service, which is efficient and much easier and faster than taxis. If you're heading all the way west to Wat Saket, you will have to transfer from the river bus to a smaller, shallow-draft boat at the Krung Kasem Road intersection. Fares run from 8B to 20B (20¢ to 55¢), depending on the distance, and include transfers. This is definitely an adventure, as the klong's appearance and odor are questionable, especially in the hot season. But it's cheap, quick, fun, and a surefire way to meet people.

BY PUBLIC BUS   Unfortunately, the very cheap, frequent, and fairly fast public bus system must be used with care because of pickpockets, purse slashers, and other petty criminals who take advantage of the densely crowded conditions. A word of advice: Take the less crowded air-conditioned ones for a few baht extra; keep your possessions in front of you, carry only what you can afford to lose, and stay away from the back door where most thieves lurk. The Bus Map (Latest Tour's *Guide to Bangkok*) provides route information. The most practical air-conditioned routes are: A1 (looping from the Grand Palace area to Rama IV Road, Siam Square, then east down Ploenchit and Sukhumvit Roads); A2 (running a loop through the Business District (Bangrak) area along Silom and Surawong Roads); A3 (connecting the Dusit area near the zoo and Khao San Road before crossing the Chao Phraya); and A8 (running the length of Rama I, Ploenchit and Sukhumvit Roads). Fares are collected onboard—even for air-conditioned routes fares are barely over 10B (25¢). Try to have exact change or "small money."

BY TAXI   Since the government revolutionized the taxi industry by requiring drivers to have and use meters, traveling around Bangkok is much easier. Those with "Taxi-Meter" signs on the roof are small but comfortable, mostly air-conditioned, and surprisingly cheap: 35B (90¢) for the first 3km and approximately 5B (15¢) per kilometer thereafter, depending on the pace of traffic. (Of course some drivers tamper with their meters, but even their fares are still far less than fares in Western cities.) You can hail taxis along any road at any time, or join queues in front of hotels and shopping malls. It's a cold day in hell when you find a cabbie that speaks English; many drivers are immigrants from rural areas, mostly Isan, and they often don't know Bangkok very well. Be patient and keep hailing until one understands and accepts your destination. (Remember that having someone write it in Thai beforehand will be helpful.) At night, especially around Patpong, taxis will try to barter a flat fare (usually much higher than what the metered fare would be). Insist he use the meter, or get out and find an honest cab. While tipping is not expected, many cab drivers will pretend they have no change for you. It's true that most don't have cash available to break even a 1000B or 500B note. But you should be able to get exact change from 100B notes. Don't wait around for change under 5B (15¢)—it's always appreciated.

Certain hotels offer private luxury cars, like Mercedes-Benz, if you request a "taxi" from the concierge. Rates run approximately double the taxi fare, or about 500B per hour.

BY CAR & DRIVER   Once you get a look at Bangkok's city plan, traffic situation, and crazy driving rules, you'd have to be a sadist to try to drive yourself around these streets. Still, a private car is by far the most convenient and comfortable way to get around to all the sights, especially if you have limited time in the capital. Your best bet is to hire a car with a driver. Reputable companies provide sedans with drivers who know the city well, some of whom speak English. They also offer the option of an accompanying tour guide—professionals or students who can take you around each sight. The best, and most expensive, cars for hire are provided at the major hotels. These will be high-profile cars, like Volvos or high-end Japanese cars, the drivers will speak English, and the price will start at 250B ($6.60) for almost any trip. They can be hired with driver by the hour for about 500B ($13.15) per hour with a 3-hour minimum. The day rate will range from 2,000B to 3,000B ($52.65 to $78.95) for a 9-hour day, with 200km (120 miles) included. You can arrange this through your hotel's transportation desk or through a travel agent.

Sea Tours (☎ 02/251-4862) and **World Travel** (☎ 02/233-5900) are two companies that can also arrange English-speaking guides to lead you on a customized tour at similar rates. **Avis,** 2/12 Wireless Rd. (☎ 02/255-5300), and **Hertz** (☎ 02/253-6251) also offer chauffeured cars, but at the highest rates. Expect to pay 6,300B ($165.80) per day for a car with a driver—they'll provide you with a Volvo for your money.

BY TUK-TUK　Truly a national mascot, the tuk-tuk, a small three-wheeled open-sided vehicle powered by a motorcycle engine, is noisy and smoky, but good fun. Most drivers are certified kamikazes, whipping around city traffic like a bat out of hell. Note tuk-tuk decor: bright colors, gilded ornamentation, and flashing lights. I don't recommend using these beasts for longer trips or during rush hour jams—if you get stuck behind a bus or truck, you'll be coughing up exhaust fumes for days to follow. But for short trips, or off-peak hours they're quite user-friendly.

All tuk-tuk fares are negotiated, and drivers are skilled at getting the highest prices from visitors. Bargain between 40B ($1.05) for short trips, and 150B ($3.95) for longer ones. Either way, you'll always end up paying more than a local.

One word of warning: Tuk-tuk drivers are notorious for trying to talk travelers into shopping trips (if you're a woman) and massage jaunts (if you're a man). Touts are always a scam, as drivers get commission for bringing people into certain establishments. Insist they take you where you want to go via the most direct route.

BY MOTORCYCLE TAXI　On every street corner, packs of drivers in colored vests wait, motorcycles nearby, to shuttle passengers around the city. These guys have their advantages and disadvantages. They get you around fast when you're in a hurry (weaving through traffic jams and speeding down straightaways) but they're also incredibly unsafe. Most don't have helmets for passengers, and some take all sorts of strategic risks on the road a la Evil Kneivel. Use them only in a pinch, and strictly for short distances. They'll charge you from 5B (15¢) for a few blocks to 60B ($1.60) for greater distances. Hold on tight and keep your knees tucked in.

ON FOOT　It's easy and safe to walk around Bangkok, though you'll find the traffic congestion generates so much air pollution that you'll limit your walking to certain neighborhoods and smaller streets. Bangkok sidewalks—all buckled tiles, loose coverings, and tangled wires—make you wonder how the latest style of platform shoe hasn't put more women in the broken ankle ward. When crossing streets, a tip is to find Thais who are also crossing and follow them when they head out into traffic. Otherwise you could be left standing on the corner forever, not sure when to jump out. (For a few great walking tours, see chapter 5).

Fast Facts: Bangkok

Airport　See "Arriving" above in this chapter.

American Express　The **American Express** agent in Bangkok is Sea Tours Company, 88-92 8th floor, Phayathai Plaza Building, 128 Phayathai Road, Ratchavethi, Bangkok 10400 ☎ **02/216-5783,** fax 02/216-5757. Hours are Monday to Friday 8:30am to 4:30pm; Saturday 8:30am to 11:30pm. You must bring your passport for all transactions. American Express will let you write a personal check in an emergency for up to $1,000 received in traveler's checks (once every 21 days). Another neat thing they do is mail forwarding from your home address to any of their agents worldwide. Or you can speak with them before your trip and arrange to have large vacation charges split into smaller monthly payments. Chat them up (call your other credit card companies, too) to find out about all the benefits, assistance and opportunities that come with the card. If you're unfortunate enough to lose your card, call the American Express hot line at ☎ **02/273-0033.**

ATMs　See "Fast Facts: Thailand" in chapter 2.

Banks　Many international banks maintain offices in Bangkok, including **Bank of America,** next door to the Hilton at 2/2 Wireless Rd. (☎ 02/255-0396);

Bank of California, 183 Ratchadamri Road (☎02/251-5310); **Bank of New York,** Sino-Thai Tower, Sukhumvit 21 Road ☎02/261-4374); **Chase Manhattan Bank,** Siam Shopping Center, 965 Rama I Road (☎02/252-1141); **Citibank,** 82 North Sathorn Road (☎02/232-2000); **National Australia Bank,** 90 North Sathorn Road, (☎02/236-6017); and **Standard Chartered Bank,** 990 Rama IV Road (☎02/636-1000). However, a customer of one of these banks cannot use these as branches of their domestic bank; accessing personal funds from a foreign account will require special arrangements before leaving home.

Bookstores   You'll find a number of bookstores offering a wide variety of English-language books. One of the best for an extensive selection of books on Thailand and Asia is **Asia Books,** with stores at 21 Sukhumvit Rd. (between Soi 15 and 17, ☎ 02/651-0428); on the ground and third floor of the Landmark Plaza Building (☎ 02/252-5839) on Sukhumvit Road at Soi 4; on the third floor of Thaniya Plaza (☎ 02/231-2106) off Silom Road; second floor of Times Square on Sukhumvit Road between Soi 12 & 14 (☎ 02/255-6209); and in the Peninsula Plaza mall near the Regent Hotel on Ratchadamri Road, south of Rama I Road (☎ 02/253-9786). All are open daily from 10am to 8 or 9pm. You'll find a good selection of English-language paperbacks at **Bookazine,** in Patpong on the 1st floor at CP Tower, 313 Silom Rd. (☎ 02/231-0016); in Ploenchit on the 3rd floor at Amarin Plaza 494–502 Ploenchit Rd. (☎ 02/256-9304); and Siam Square, 286 Siam Square opposite Siam Center, Rama I Road (☎ 02/255-3778). Another large and gorgeous bookstore, **Books Kinokuniya** has shops in Pathumwan at Isetan Department Store, 6th floor, World Trade Center, Ratchadamri Road (☎ 02/255-9834), and on Sukhumvit at Emporium Shopping Complex, 3rd floor, 622 Sukhumvit Road Soi 24 (☎ 02/664-8554). For secondhand books, visit **Global Used Books,** 762 Sukhumvit Rd. between Soi 30 & 32 (☎ 02/261-4422). Almost every international-class hotel has a newsstand, with papers and a few books.

Business Hours   Government offices (including branch post offices) are open Monday to Friday 8:30am to 4:30pm, with a lunch break between noon and 1pm. Businesses are generally open 8am to 5pm. Shops often stay open from 8am until 7pm or later, 7 days a week. Department stores are generally open 10am to 7pm.

Car Rentals   See "Getting Around: By Car & Driver," above in this chapter.

Climate   See "When to Go," in chapter 2.

Currency Exchange   Most banks will exchange foreign currency Monday to Friday 8:30am to 3:30pm. Exchange booths affiliated with the major banks are found in all tourist areas, open daily from as early as 7am to as late as 9pm.

Dentists & Doctors   Thailand has an excellent medical care system. Most medical personnel speak English and many were trained overseas. Most of the better hotels have doctors and/or nurses on staff or on call who can treat minor maladies. Check first with your concierge for assistance, then contact your country's consulate if you need further help.

Embassies & Consulates   Your home embassy in Thailand can help you in emergencies—medical and legal (legal, to an extent), and is the place to contact if you've lost your travel documents and need them replaced. The following is a list of major foreign representatives in Bangkok: Embassy of the United States of America, 120-22 Wireless Rd., ☎ 02/205-4000; Canada Embassy, 138 Silom Rd., ☎ 02/238-3001; Australian Embassy, 37 South Sathorn Rd., ☎ 02/

287-2680; New Zealand Embassy, 93 Wireless Rd., ☎ **02/254-3865;** and the British Embassy, 1031 Wireless Rd., ☎ **02/253-0191.**

Emergencies   In any emergency, first call Bangkok's Tourist Police—dial ☎ **1155** or 02/694-1222, ext. 1. Someone there will speak English. In case of fire, call ☎ **199** or 02/246-0199. Ambulance service is handled by private hospitals; see "Hospitals" below, or call your hotel's front desk. For medical evacuation and ambulance service call ☎ **02/255-1133.** For operator assisted overseas calls dial 100.

Eyeglass Repair   You'll find optical shops in all the major shopping areas of the city, most of which can provide replacement glasses within 24 hours at reasonable prices. For eye problems, try the **Rutnin Eye Hospital** at 80 Sukhumvit Soi 21 (Soi Asoke), ☎ **02/258-0442.**

Hospitals   All hospitals listed here offer 24-hour emergency room care and ambulance service. Be advised that you may need your passport and a deposit of up to 20,000B ($526.30) before you are admitted. Bills must be settled before you leave. Your domestic medical insurance policy will probably not be accepted for payment, though major credit cards are. Among the best hospitals with English-speaking staff are Bumrungrat Medical Center and Hospital, 33 Soi 3, Sukhumvit Rd. (☎ **02/253-0250**); and Bangkok Nursing Home, 9 Convent Rd., between Silom and Sathorn roads, south of Rama IV Road (☎ **02/233-2610**). The Bangkok General Hospital is off New Phetchaburi Road, at 2 Soi Soonvijai 7 (☎ **02/318-0066**). The public and busy Chulalongkorn Hospital, 1873 Rama IV Road (☎ **02/252-8181**) and Ramathibodi University Hospital, 270 Rama IV Road (☎ **02/246-0024**) are leading teaching and research facilities. The former carries snakebite serum.

All medical facilities will provide blood screening services to detect HIV antibodies, as well as syphilis and Hepatitis B. Results are available within a week, and costs are usually under 1,000B. The tests are accurate beyond 3 months after initial exposure to these sexually transmitted diseases.

Hot Lines   The **Community Services of Bangkok,** 15/1 Sukhumvit Soi 33 (☎ **02/258-4998**), provides long- and short-term counseling, which may or may not be helpful for vacation travelers, but is highly recommended for those spending longer periods of time in Thailand and suffer stress associated with adjustment. Also call CSB if you'd like to keep up with your Alcoholics Anonymous or Narcotics Anonymous meetings while in Bangkok.

Information   See "Visitor Information & Entry Requirements," above in this chapter.

Internet Cafes   Demand from busy travelers has increased the number of Internet cafes both in Bangkok and upcountry. The highest concentration of cafes are around Khao San Road and in Patpong. Prices range from as low as 2.5B (5¢) per minute to 300B ($7.90) per hour (usually in the more swanky cafes, where they also serve coffee and sandwiches), so make sure you check beforehand. Most guest houses and shopping malls have usage areas, and these charges are always more affordable than using the business center in your hotel.

Lost Property   If you have lost anything or had your valuables stolen, call the **Tourist Police,** Crime Suppression Division, Vorachak Road (☎ **02/513-3844**). Believe it or not, there have been several reports of lost items being returned to the appropriate consulate by taxi drivers or bus attendants. Call the consular services section of your embassy to check.

Luggage Storage   Both the domestic and international terminals of Don Muang airport offer luggage storage for 25B a day—7am to 10pm in the domestic terminal, 24 hours a day in the international terminal. Most hotels will allow you to store luggage while away on trips in the countryside.

Mail   See "Fast Facts: Thailand" in chapter 2 for rates. If shipping a parcel from Bangkok, take advantage of the Packing Service offered by the GPO; open Monday to Friday 8am to 4:30pm, Saturday to Sunday and holidays 9am to noon. Small cardboard packing cartons cost 5B to 17B (15¢ to 45¢); they pack things for you for 5B (15¢)!

Maps   See "Visitor Information," above in this chapter.

Newspapers & Magazines   *Metro Magazine,* 80B ($2.10) at many better hotels and the bookstores recommended above, is the best single source of current information about what's happening in Bangkok, especially the entertainment and social scene. *Where* and *Look East* are slick monthly English-language magazines distributed free. Both emphasize events and features about Bangkok, with lesser coverage of other Thai cities and provinces. See "Fast Facts: Thailand" in chapter 2 for more information.

Pharmacies   Bangkok has a great many pharmacies, though the drugs dispensed may differ widely in quality. Among the better outlets is the British Dispensary, on the corner of Charoen Krung Road (New Road) and Oriental Lane (☎ 02/234-1910).

Police   Call the Tourist Police (☎ 1155 or 02/694-1222 ext. 1), open 24 hours, for assistance.

Post Office   The General Post Office (GPO) is on Charoen Krung Road (New Road), between the Oriental and Sheraton Royal Orchid hotels (☎ 02/233-1050). Telegraph and telephone service are available in the north end of the building. GPO hours are Monday to Friday 8am to 8pm, Saturday to Sunday and holidays 8am to 1pm.

Radio & TV   See "Fast Facts: Thailand" in chapter 2 for more information. Television channels include 3, 5, 7, 9, and 11, which offer some English-language programming. Check the *Bangkok Post* or the *Nation* for listings. It's a rare hotel that doesn't offer in-house cable TV (VDO in Thai) and English-language movies.

Safety   In general, Bangkok is a safe city, but the Bangkok public buses are infamous for skilled and ingenious pickpockets. Don't seek out trouble—avoid public disagreements or hostility (especially with a Thai), and steer clear of gambling activities. Rely on your gut instincts—if you get the creepy feeling that something illicit is happening in the midst, chances are you're right. Remove yourself from the scene to avoid getting caught up in someone else's drama.

Taxes   See "Fast Facts: Thailand" in chapter 2.

Taxis   See "Getting Around," above in this chapter.

Telephone, Telegrams & Telex   The main government telephone office occupies a separate building on the grounds of the GPO (General Post Office) on Charoen Krung Road (New Road) between the Oriental and Royal Orchid Sheraton Hotels and is open daily 24 hours. This office is for international calls. The procedure for making a call is as follows: Book your call by filling out a form at one of the desks, specifying the telephone number you wish to call and an approximate length of your call; take the form to the cashier and pay; wait until you are called to a booth. Beware of the hotel surcharges on international calls, usually 25% to 40% (check with the operator before dialing). A credit-card or collect call placed from your room also carries a service charge. See "Fast Facts: Thailand" in chapter 2 for additional information.

There are also blue or the newer silver long-distance telephones in strategic places throughout Bangkok (such as the airport), used for domestic long-distance calls, at rates from 6B to 18B (15¢ to 45¢) per minute. You will need a pile of 5B coins and can observe your running total on the meter, putting in more coins as needed. For information within the Bangkok metropolitan area, dial ☎ **13,** or find an English-language copy of the *Greater Bangkok Business Listing;* for the provinces dial ☎ **183.**

Telegraph services, including fax service and telegram restante service, are offered in the telephone and telegraph office of the GPO, open daily 24 hours. The same services (except for telegram restante) are offered at the telephone and telegraph offices at Don Muang airport. A fax to the United States costs about 400B ($10.55) and must be prepared on the official form. Every hotel offers normal fax service as well.

Where to Stay & Dine in Bangkok

4

If you checked the annual surveys of the world's great hotels, you'd certainly find Bangkok well represented. Fortunately, the capital offers a rich variety of choices in all price categories, and, compared to similar facilities in Europe, even the most expensive, truly grand hotels are good value. Dining is one of the country's greatest attractions, and in Bangkok visitors will find everything from a superb Thai banquet to noodle shops, from gourmet French fare to pizza.

1 Accommodations

As a result of the economic downturn in 1997, there have been a few changes in the Bangkok hotel industry (changes that are also seen in major tourist centers around the country). For starters, a lot of the larger international five-star hotels have been quoting room rates in American dollars. (See chapter 2, "Tips on Accommodations.") The rate remains steady, to be converted at the daily rate during your stay. While it prevents these places from losing their shirts in the face of currency value fluctuations, there's not much of a savings for you in terms of taking advantage of your foreign cash. Still, chat up these places for special discount packages, or whatever extras they can throw in with the rate they're charging you—free breakfasts, airport transfers, laundry, or local calls. You're more likely to get favorable packages from moderately priced hotels, which depend on the tourist industry rather than business travelers with fat corporate accounts. For the lowest rates in town, make your booking through a travel agent at home—major hotels guarantee agents rock bottom prices in return for filling rooms.

In the high season (December through February), you must make reservations well in advance for the very expensive and expensive hotels, and even for the popular guest houses, or you may find yourself with no room at the inn. Unless otherwise noted, the prices listed are subject to 7% government tax and 10% service charge.

ON THE RIVER

This is one of the most convenient and picturesque parts of the city. The river hotels have the priceless view of, and easy access to, the fascinating Chao Phraya River. View and access don't come cheaply, and you'll pay the highest prices at the three centrally located facilities. For less money, you can go up or downriver, and with the future opening

Bangkok Accommodations

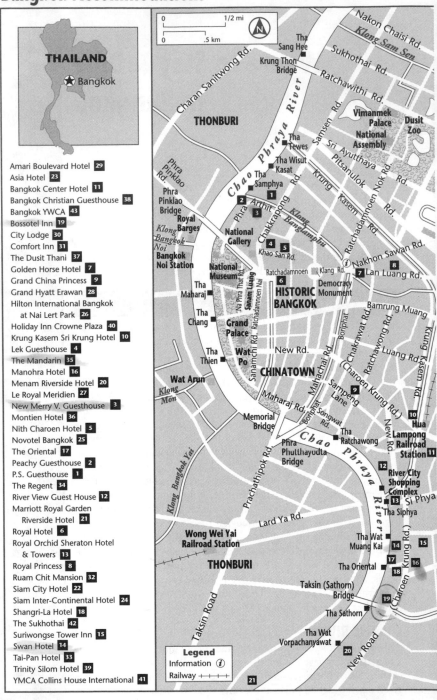

Amari Boulevard Hotel **29**
Asia Hotel **23**
Bangkok Center Hotel **11**
Bangkok Christian Guesthouse **38**
Bangkok YWCA **43**
Bossotel Inn **19**
City Lodge **30**
Comfort Inn **31**
The Dusit Thani **37**
Golden Horse Hotel **7**
Grand China Princess **9**
Grand Hyatt Erawan **28**
Hilton International Bangkok
    at Nai Lert Park **26**
Holiday Inn Crowne Plaza **40**
Krung Kasem Sri Krung Hotel **10**
Lek Guesthouse **4**
The Mandarin **35**
Manohra Hotel **16**
Menam Riverside Hotel **20**
Le Royal Meridien **27**
New Merry V. Guesthouse **3**
Montien Hotel **36**
Nith Charoen Hotel **5**
Novotel Bangkok **25**
The Oriental **17**
Peachy Guesthouse **2**
P.S. Guesthouse **1**
The Regent **34**
River View Guest House **12**
Marriott Royal Garden
    Riverside Hotel **21**
Royal Hotel **6**
Royal Orchid Sheraton Hotel
    & Towers **13**
Royal Princess **8**
Ruam Chit Mansion **32**
Siam City Hotel **22**
Siam Inter-Continental Hotel **24**
Shangri-La Hotel **18**
The Sukhothai **42**
Suriwongse Tower Inn **15**
Swan Hotel **14**
Tai-Pan Hotel **33**
Trinity Silom Hotel **39**
YMCA Collins House International **41**

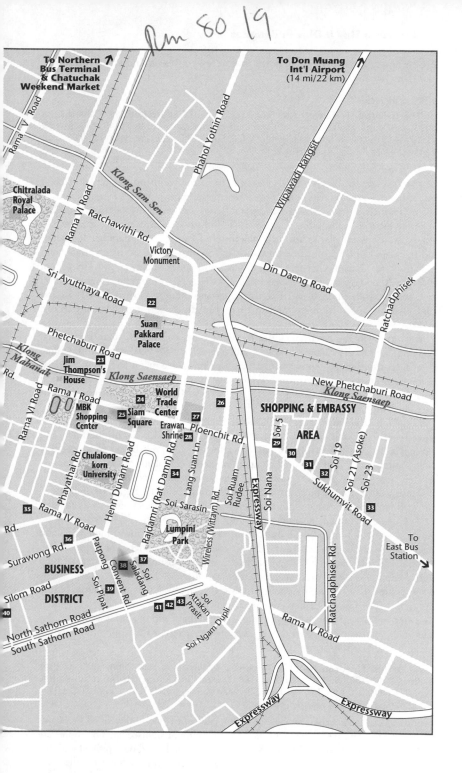

Rm 80 19

To Northern
Bus Terminal
& Chatuchak
Weekend Market

To Don Muang
Int'l Airport
(14 mi/22 km)

Rama V Road

Phahol Yothin Road

Wipawadi Rangsit

Klong Sam Sen

Chitralada
Royal
Palace

Rama VI Road

Ratchawithi Rd.

Victory
Monument

Din Daeng Road

Ratchadphisek

Sri Ayutthaya Road

22

Phetchaburi Road

Suan
Pakkard
Palace

Klong
Mahanak

Rd.

Jim
Thompson's
House

23

Klong Saensaep

New Phetchaburi Road

Klong Saensaep

Rama I Road

Rama VI Road

MBK
Shopping
Center

24

25 Siam
Square

World
Trade
Center

26

SHOPPING & EMBASSY

Soi 5

AREA

27

Erawan
Shrine

28

Ploenchit Rd.

29

30

Soi 19

Soi 21 (Asoke)

Soi 23

Chulalong-
korn
University

Phayathai Rd.

Henri Dunant Road

Rajdamri (Rat Damri) Rd.

Lang Suan Ln.

34

Soi Ruam
Rudee

31

32

Sukhumvit Road

33

35

Rama IV Road

Soi Sarasin

Wireless (Wittayu) Rd.

Soi Nana

Expressway

To
East Bus
Station

Rd.

36

Lumpini
Park

Surawong Rd.

BUSINESS

Silom Road

DISTRICT

Patpong

Convent Rd.

Soi Pipat

39

Soi
Saladang

37

38

41 **42** **43**

Soi
Attakan
Prasit

Ratchadphisek Rd.

40

North Sathorn Road

South Sathorn Road

Soi Ngam Dupli

Rama IV Road

Expressway

Expressway

53

of some new hotels across river, to hotels that are less convenient but provide their own boat transportation.

VERY EXPENSIVE

✪ **The Oriental.** 48 Oriental Ave., Bangkok 10500. ☎ **800/526-6566** in the U.S., or 02/236-0400. Fax 02/236-1937. www.mandarin-oriental.com. 396 units. A/C MINIBAR TV TEL. $250–$310 double; from $380 suite. AE, DC, EURO, MC, V. On the riverfront off Charoen Krung Rd. (New Rd.).

Cited in publications too numerous to list and favored by everyone from honeymooners to CEOs, the Oriental has long been in the pantheon of the world's best hotels. Its history dates from the 1860s when the original hotel, no longer standing, was established by two Danish sea captains soon after King Mongkut (Rama IV) reopened Siam to world trade. The hotel has withstood occupation by Japanese and American troops and played host to a long roster of Thai and international dignitaries and celebrities, most famousl writers such as Joseph Conrad, Somerset Maugham, Noel Coward, Graham Greene, John Le Carré, and James Michener. Jim Thompson, of Thai silk trade fame, even served briefly as the hotel's proprietor. New buildings have been added—the first in 1876, the larger and more modern pair in 1958 and 1976—so that today it's more modern than colonial, though it retains considerable charm.

In addition to the usual amenities found at other top hotels, there is the Thai Cooking School; the *Oriental Queen I* and *II* making daily river runs up the Chao Phraya; an exquisite spa center; the nearby shopping arcade that offers a fine selection of shops; in-house restaurants with a wide range of quality options; a nightly classical Thai dance concert; and daily cultural programs with lectures and demonstrations covering a wide range of Thai culture.

It's the level and range of service, however, that distinguishes the Oriental from the other riverfront hotels. It's probably a more practical choice for businessmen and diplomats than for tourists, but if you can afford it, you probably won't come away disappointed. Even with increased competition and a complaint or two, the Oriental remains very popular, so make a reservation as far in advance as possible.

Dining/Diversions: The Normandie (see "Dining" below) is highly recommended for the finest in Continental dining, and high tea in the Author's Lounge is a romantic treat. TehCihna House is a wonderful building with a fantastically expensive (by no means universally admired) Cantonese menu. Equally regarded for its high prices and less than perfect food is Lord Jim's, the Oriental's seafood outlet. The Bamboo Bar, however, is one of Bangkok's finest jazz venues, while SalaRim Naam has great evening cultural performances to accompany excellent cuisine.

Amenities: Two swimming pools, fitness center, tennis and squash courts, beauty and health spa, business center, cooking school, beauty salon and barbershop, shopping arcade, tour boat for daily excursions to Ayyutahaya and the Summer Palace, 24-hour room service, concierge, butler service, limousine service, helicopter transfers, car rental, tour desk, baby-sitting, laundry service.

Royal Orchid Sheraton Hotel & Towers. 2 Captain Bush Lane, Siphya Rd., Bangkok 10500. ☎ **800/325-3535**, or 02/266-0123. Fax 02/236-8320. www.royalorchidsheraton. com. 772 units. A/C MINIBAR TV TEL. $220–$276 double; from $300 suite. AE, DC, EURO, MC, V. Next to River City Mall.

The Royal Orchid has the best view of the magnificent Chao Phraya of all the major riverfront inns, and it's an excellent base for shopping or sightseeing. The rooms are spacious, pastel hued, and trimmed with warm teakwood, lending a refined and distinctly Thai ambience. The Sheraton Towers, a hotel within a hotel on the 26th through 28th floors (with its own check-in desk and express elevator), offers more ornate decor and a higher level of service for a premium; Tower suites, for example, have personal fax machines in the sitting room, and all rooms are manned by 24-hour butlers.

Dining/Diversions: The Royal Orchid boasts five major food outlets, including such cuisine as Japanese, grill, Italian, Thai, and generic Western. The Thara Thong Thai restaurant has a fabulous riverside cultural show with traditional dance and costumes, and the restaurant itself is quite elegant.

Amenities: Two outdoor swimming pools, fitness center, sauna, tennis courts, business center, beauty salon and barbershop, shopping arcade, 24-hour room service, concierge, limousine service, massage, baby-sitting, laundry service.

Shangri-La Hotel. 89 Soi Wat Suan Plu, Charoen Krung Rd. (New Rd.), Bangkok 10500. ☎ **800/942-5050** in the U.S., or 02/236-7777. Fax 02/236-8579. www.shangri-la.com. 850 units. A/C MINIBAR TV TEL. $200–$300 double; from $340 suite. AE, DC, MC, V. Adjacent to Sathorn Bridge, with access off Chaoren Krung Rd. (New Rd.) at south end of Silom Rd.

The opulent but thoroughly modern Shangri-La, on the banks of the Chao Phraya, boasts acres of polished marble, a jungle of tropical plants and flowers, and two towers with breathtaking views of the river. All rooms have a view of the river, are decorated with lush carpeting and teak furniture, and have marble bathrooms; amenities include flowers, slippers, hair dryer, safe, and a tea- and coffeemaker. The views are terrific from the higher floor, deluxe rooms, and most have either a balcony or a small sitting room, making them closer to junior suites and a particularly good value for on-the-river upscale accommodations. For such an enormous place, the level of service and facilities is surprisingly good.

The superluxurious Krung Thep Wing adds another 17-story, river-view tower to the grounds, as well as a restaurant, riverside swimming pool, and breakfast lounge. Deluxe features include a separate shower stall, twin sinks, and bidets in the especially large marble bathrooms. Small balconies overlook the Sathorn Bridge and busy Chao Phraya River. The livelier main building is a better value for holiday travelers and families, while the quieter Krung Thep Wing is recommended for those seeking respite from bustling Bangkok or a sojourn in luxury.

Dining/Diversions: Extravagance here means nine separate dining choices, including the riverside Coffee Garden and Menam Terrace (which offers a huge international buffet dinner); popular Shang Palace for Chinese food; and one of Bangkok's prettiest settings for Thai cuisine, Sala Thip (see "Dining," below). Angelini and Edogin round out international restaurants with Italian and Japanese cuisine, respectively. The hotel's river cruiser, the *Ayutthaya Princess,* motors up the Chao Phraya to Ayutthaya daily and makes a 3-hour dinner cruise.

Amenities: Two outdoor swimming pools, two Jacuzzis, fitness center, tennis courts, squash courts, business center, beauty salon and barbershop, shopping arcade, concierge, 24-hour room service, limousine service, helicopter transfer, yacht charter, massage, baby-sitting, laundry service.

EXPENSIVE

✪ **Marriott Royal Garden Riverside Hotel.** 257/1–3 Charoen Nakhorn Rd., Thonburi, Bangkok 10600. ☎ **800/344-1212** in the U.S., or 02/476-0021. Fax 02/476-1120. 420 units. A/C MINIBAR TV TEL. $125–$145 double; $175–$225 suite. AE, DC, MC, V. On the Thonburi (east) side of the Chao Phraya River, north of the Krung Thep Bridge, 15 min. by boat from River City.

This luxuriously sprawling complex on the banks of the Chao Phraya is across the river and a few miles downstream from the heart of Bangkok. As you board the hotel's long tailed boat and make the short trip down river, you will feel the crazy city release you from its grip. Once at the hotel, you'll think you're at a resort, the three wings of the hotel surrounding a large landscaped pool area with lily ponds and fountains, and a wonderful spa for a very uniquely calming Bangkok experience. Marriott Royal Garden also has tennis courts and a shopping arcade. Rooms are comfortable and modern, tastefully decorated in cool shades and fully equipped with all the amenities. Boats go to and from River City shopping mall every half hour, from early to late. Choose the Royal Garden Riverside if you want to enjoy Bangkok, but can't stand the insanity of big city life.

Dining/Diversions: They go for the big international names—Trader Vic's Polynesian Restaurant and Benihana Japanese-American Steakhouse, as well as their own Garden Cafe (Thai and International Cuisine), the Rice Mill Chinese Restaurant, and the Riverside Terrace for beef and seafood. They also operate an evening dinner cruise aboard the Manhora, a beautifully restored rice barge.

Amenities: Outdoor swimming pool and Jacuzzi, tennis courts, fitness center, business center, beauty salon and barbershop, shopping arcade, 24-hour room service, concierge, limousine service, tour desk, massage, baby-sitting (arranged with advanced notice), laundry service.

Menam Riverside Hotel. 2074 Charoen Krung Rd. (New Rd.), Yannawa, Bangkok 10120. ☎ 02/289-1148. Fax 02/291-9400. www.menam-hotel.com. 711 units. A/C MINIBAR TV TEL. 3,600B–3,900B ($94.75–$102.65) double; from 6,000B ($157.90) suite. AE, DC, MC, V. 3km (1.8 miles) south of Sathorn Bridge.

Here's a special value. In the previous edition, Menam was listed under "Very Expensive" hotels, but discounted rates now give you the same facility for less money. For a large hotel, the place offers a fair amount of charm with an unpretentious, comfortable air. It's downriver, a lengthy bus or taxi trip from most of the major tourist attractions, but if you're adventurous enough to try the riverboats (and we recommend that you do), the location can work to your advantage. The hotel offers hourly shuttle boats to either the Oriental Hotel or River City Shopping Center, or you can walk a block up New Road and hop on the Chao Phraya Express Boats to go almost anywhere on the river. The hotel is popular with tour groups, drawn by its very reasonable prices. Deluxe river-view rooms are nicely appointed, with colorful Chinese murals and marble-tiled bathrooms. The style and view set them well apart from the less appealing (but 10% cheaper) city-view standard rooms, which look a bit worn down by the steady stream of tour groups. The pool is large, though screened from the river by the Riverview Terrace Barbecue. As with any major hotel, you must book at least one month in advance for high-season travel.

Dining: The Chinese luncheon buffet at Menam Tien is very popular, and there is an evening seafood buffet at the Riverside Terrace Barbecue. In addition to the Chainam coffee shop (which has a Japanese Corner with an open kitchen), there's also a bakery at the lobby level.

Amenities: Swimming pool, fitness center, business center, beauty salon and barbershop, shopping arcade, 24-hour room service, concierge, limousine service, shuttle boat service, tour counter, massage, baby-sitting, laundry service.

MODERATE

✪ **Bossotel Inn.** 55/12–14 Soi Charoen Krung 42/1, Bangrak, Bangkok 10500. ☎ 02/630-6120. Fax 02/237-3225. 46 units. A/C MINIBAR TV TEL. 800B ($21.05) double. AE, MC, V. Off Charoen Krung Rd., on Soi 42, near Shangri-La Hotel.

The Bossotel has clean rooms and fantastic location—just a quick walk to Chao Phraya River. You'd be hard pressed to find this kind of location for the price. Many

Superior #38⁰⁰ BOSSBK @ B

other guests agree, as the inn hosts mainly long-term visitors. Make sure you request a larger corner room when booking—guest room sizes vary greatly. The western and Thai lobby coffee shop changed management recently—a much needed improvement to food quality, but room service still stops at around 10:30pm. They also have HBO and CNN in the guest rooms, as well as laundry service and a small business center. Check out the traditional Thai massage on the 2nd floor—hotel guests can get a high-quality 2-hour massage for only 240B ($6.30). Unbelievable.

INEXPENSIVE

River View Guest House. 768 Soi Panurangsri, Songwat Rd., Sanjao Tosuekong, Taladnoi, Bangkok 10100. ☎ 02/234-5429. Fax 02/237-5428. 44 units. 690B ($18.15) double with AC; 450B ($11.85) double with fan. Rates include tax and service. MC, V. 500m southeast of railroad station, between the intersection of Songwat and Chaoren Krung rds. and the river.

As you might gather from the address, this special place deep in the heart of China-town, only 5 minutes from the railroad station, and a stone's throw from the river, is difficult to find, but the views of the river and a neighboring Chinese temple make it worth the effort. Half of this guest house's appeal is that you wander through the neighboring sois, lanes, and labyrinthine alleys—somewhat grubby but safe—looking for signs and asking people, who smile and point the way. There's a lot of variety in the quality, upkeep, and views from each room, so look first if you're lucky enough to arrive when there's more than one room open. Breakfast with the international clientele in the eighth floor restaurant, overlooking temples and the busy Chao Phraya, is a truly special experience. How can you find it? Let the airport taxi desk arrange your trip in, or have someone write out the address for you in Thai. Then, as soon as you get there, grab a business card and keep it with you when you venture out to show passersby when asking directions back to the hotel.

Swan Hotel. 31 Soi Charoen Krung 36, New Rd., Bangkok 10500. ☎ 02/234-8594. 72 units. TEL. 775B ($21.05) double with A/C; 550B ($14.45) double with fan. Rates include tax and service. No credit cards. Off New Rd.

Many budget travelers have discovered the Swan, on the banks of the Chao Phraya River in the shadow of the aristocratic Oriental in the middle of Bangkok's Gold Coast. The pool is large, there's a left luggage and laundry service, and most rooms are air-conditioned—all have toilets and showers, but with limited hot-water hours. Some rooms are clean but dark, worn, and shabby. Look before committing to a room, and check out the rear wing.

HISTORIC BANGKOK—NEAR THE GRAND PALACE

Most of the major tourist sights are located here, making sightseeing on foot a plea-sure and taxi rides mercifully short. You'll find fewer restaurant choices than in other areas, but enough. For budget travelers, the widest range of low-price accommoda-tions are found in this area in Banglamphu, around Khao San Road.

EXPENSIVE

Grand China Princess. 215 Yaowarat Rd., Samphantawong, Bangkok 10100. ☎ 02/224-9977. Fax 02/224-7999. www.grandchina.com. 155 units. A/C MINIBAR TV TEL. 3,200B–3,500B ($84.20–$92.10) double; from 7,000B ($184.20) suite. AE, DC, MC, V. Corner of Ratchawong Rd., just south of Charoen Krung (New Rd.).

Luxurious yet affordable—close to many attractions, and only a 5-minute walk from Ratchawong pier and the Chao Phraya ferry system, amid the bustling shop houses and businesses of colorful Chinatown—the Grand China Princess begins 10 stories above a shopping arcade and Chinese restaurant. Rooms are modern, yet gracefully

Oriental and very comfortable, with amenities typically found in much more expensive hotels. The suites are especially roomy, and decorated in muted tones of rose and gray. The 25th floor features Bangkok's first revolving lounge, with spectacular views over the city and Chao Phraya River.

Dining/Diversions: For Japanese try Sukura Tei, for Chinese try Siang Ping Loh (with a great dim sum lunch), or have Western and Thai favorites at the coffee shop—they have a good buffet lunch special for 150B ($3.95) per person. The Club Lounge is the only rooftop revolving lounge in Bangkok, with views of neighboring Chinatown.

Amenities: Fitness center with Jacuzzi, business center, room service, concierge, limousine service, massage, laundry service.

✪ **Royal Princess.** 269 Larn Luang Rd., Pomprab, Bangkok 10100. ☎ **02/281-3088.** Fax 02/280-1314. www.royalprincess.com. 170 units. A/C MINIBAR TV TEL. 3,600B–4,300B ($94.75–$113.15) double; from 6,500B ($171.05) suite. AE, DC, MC, V. East of Wat Saket.

This first-class hotel near the Grand Palace in the Ratanakosin Island area more than lives up to the high standards of the Thai-owned Dusit Thani Hotels and Resorts family. Completed in 1989, its proximity to government offices brings a steady flow of official visitors (including major movers and shakers on lunch break), but is also recommended highly to leisure travelers interested in the sights of old Bangkok. Public spaces are wall-to-wall marble, and bustle with activity, yet the scale is intimate. Rooms are very tastefully appointed in muted blues and grays; marble bathrooms are fully stocked with amenities. Higher-priced deluxe rooms have balconies overlooking the tropically landscaped pool, while the superior rooms of the same style look out over the neighborhood. It's a 10-minute taxi ride to either the Grand Palace or Vimanmek Palace, and though the area lacks diverse dining, the authentic flavor of this old neighborhood more than compensates.

Dining: The Empress Restaurant (see "Dining," below) serves superb Cantonese cuisine; the Mikado offers fine Japanese cuisine in a garden setting; and Piccolo provides Italian specialties. The Princess Café serves both Asian and Western food, with a sumptuous Thai buffet available at lunch.

Amenities: Swimming pool, business center, exercise room, 24-hour room service, concierge, limousine service, tour desk, massage, baby-sitting, laundry.

MODERATE

Golden Horse Hotel. 5/1–2 Damrongrok Rd., Bangkok 10100. ☎ **02/280-1920.** Fax 02/280-3404. 130 units. A/C MINIBAR TV TEL. 600B–1,800B ($15.80–$47.35) double. MC, V. North side of Klong Mahanak near Wat Saket.

This small hotel is conveniently located just 1 block from the main Thai Airways International office and near the city's major tourist attractions. Because of its popularity with economy-minded tourists and small groups, the busy staff is helpful and ready to answer any questions. Rooms are simply furnished but well maintained and comfortable. Higher-floor, south-facing rooms even have a view of nearby Wat Saket, the golden chedi on the mount.

The attractive marble lobby has seating areas and newspapers for guests, as well as a large restaurant serving moderately priced Thai food, some Chinese and continental favorites.

Royal Hotel. 2 Ratchadamnoen Rd., Bangkok 10200. ☎ **02/222-9111.** Fax 02/224-1909. 130 units. A/C MINIBAR TV TEL. 800B ($21.05) double. AE, MC, V. 2 blocks east of National Museum.

The venerable Royal, near Thammasat University and a 5-minute walk from the Royal Palace, is perfect for budget-minded sightseers. The glitzy lobby, with polished marble floors, chandeliers, and massive modern white Corinthian columns, was a field hospital during the May 1991 Democracy demonstrations. Now it's again abuzz with guests from around the world. The simpler old wing's large staircase and other architectural details date from the art deco era. Other aspects of the Royal date from the 1950s, so that the overall effect is an architectural pastiche. Clean, kitschy (pink, ruffled polyester Chinese bedspreads) doubles in the old wing have high ceilings and are quite spacious. Request a room that faces away from the noisy street.

The nondescript new wing has comfortable, already-worn rooms that are usually presold to group tours. Many overlook the small pool. Other facilities include a multinational cuisine restaurant, an inexpensive 24-hour coffee shop, a tour desk, and several shops. The reception desk will arrange baby-sitters.

INEXPENSIVE

The budget accommodations in historic Bangkok are clustered together on and near Khao San Road in the Banglamphu neighborhood, which has become a center for Western shoestring travelers and lost much of its authenticity. (The street has become a virtual bazaar, with jewelry, clothing, wood carvings, and cassette tapes at moderate prices.) There are several dozen guest houses in the area, and if the ones suggested here arc full you'll probably soon find another. Reservations may be lost or irrelevant, so arrive as early in the day as possible. If the Khao San scene is too generic or intense for you, head toward the river for lower-key possibilities.

Lek Guesthouse. 125–127 Khao San Rd., Banglamphu, Bangkok 10200. ☎ **02/281-2775.** 20 units. 150B ($3.95) double. Rates include tax and service. No credit cards. Near Chakkra Phong Rd.

What distinguishes the Lek from the others in a row of guest houses is that it's slightly more dependable than its neighbors. The accommodations are as basic as can be—small partitions, all with fans—but most guests who've stayed here felt that the proprietor and family work hard to make guests feel at home. The house has a safe for storing valuables, a simple roof terrace, free luggage storage for guests that have checked out, laundry facilities, and a few balconies. For a quieter night, request a room away from the street.

New Merry V. Guesthouse. 18–20 Phra Athit Rd., Banglamphu, Bangkok 10200. ☎ **02/280-3315.** 70 units. 380B ($10) double with A/C; 250B ($6.60) double with fan. No credit cards. Across from the Phra Athit boat pier.

A good traveler's center, where young and old come for simplicity and proximity to the river. There's a laundry facility, storage lockers, bulletin board, internet cafe, and a basic cafe with tables in a courtyard. Prices listed are for rooms with attached bathrooms—cheaper rooms are available with shared toilets. Not to be confused with the older Merry V. Guesthouse around the corner—this newer facility is far superior.

Nith Charoen Hotel. 183 Khao San Rd., Banglamphu, Bangkok 10200. ☎ **02/281-9872.** 25 units. 300B ($7.90) double with fan. Rates include tax and service. No credit cards. Between Chakkra Phong and Tanao rds.

Set back from busy Khao San Road, this well-maintained guest house is a good choice if you're willing to pay a higher price for a quieter and cleaner place. Staff is friendly, and all rooms have a simple cold-water Asian bath, as well as a toilet and shower, and there's a 24-hour guard.

P.S. Guesthouse. 9 Phra Sumeru Rd., Chanasongkram Pranakorn, Bangkok 10200. ☎ **02/282-3932.** 50 units. 190B ($5) double; 250B ($6.60) triple. Rates include tax and service. No credit cards. 2 blocks north of the Phra Arthit ferry pier; turn right on Phra Sumeru.

Another in the "Spartan but clean" category. The small rooms barely give you walking space around the twin beds, but there are fans, screened windows, and washed linens for each, as well as scrubbed-clean toilets and cold showers down the hall. Rooms start on the second floor, above the simple Evergreen Restaurant. You'll find the higher floors quieter. Security is good, but make sure you request a window if it's important—they have plenty of rooms without (at 10% discount).

Peachy Guesthouse. 10 Phra Arthit Rd., Banglamphu, Bangkok 10200. ☎ **02/281-6471.** 35 units. 200B ($5.25) double with fan. Rates include tax and service. No credit cards. 1 block from Phra Arthit Express Boat pier.

This large, comfortable guest house is tops for the price. Rooms are stacked in a U-shaped block around a courtyard where breakfast and snacks are served. Large, bright rooms are Spartan but clean, most with ceiling fans. Communal toilets and cold-water showers on each floor are kept very clean. Peachy also has a funky lounge on each floor where fellow travelers can hang out. This place is popular with a budget crowd more mature than that found in the Khao San Road guest houses—Peace Corps and UNICEF workers, as well as families.

THE BUSINESS DISTRICT

Sure, this area is convenient for business travelers whose appointments are concentrated in nearby office buildings and banks, but if you're here on leisure, don't be put off by the "Business District" name, which is merely to distinguish this are from the others. There is a wide range of choices in the upper- and middle-price categories as well as some good values in the inexpensive range. It's an easy taxi ride to the river area and a 30-minute trip to the Palace area (depending on the time of day).

VERY EXPENSIVE

The Dusit Thani. Rama IV Rd., Bangkok 10500. ☎ **212/697-8600** in the U.S., or 02/236-0450. Fax 02/236-6400. www.dusit.com. 530 units. A/C MINIBAR TV TEL. $120 double; from $150 suite. AE, DC, JCB, MC, V. At corner of Silom and Rama IV rds. opposite Lumpini Park.

"The Dusit" continues to be a favorite meeting place for locals, the expatriate community, and visiting celebrities, as after over 3 decades of operation, it retains its legendary reputation as one of Bangkok's premier hotels. Too bad about the overhead pass that cuts so close to the front entrance—the government has been trying to squeak every last millimeter from the hotel to build a stop for its commuter rail service—testimony to the Dusit's fabulous location, but disastrous for the appearance of the grounds. The lobby, while grand, is not the same marble and mirror disaster as some of the newer hotels in Asia. Splashing lobby fountains, exotic flower displays, and a poolside waterfall cascading through dense foliage make it a welcome retreat at the end of a day's sightseeing. Unfortunately, the old gal could stand some renovations; some of the guest rooms look a little too well worn. Superior rooms in the Executive Wing are newly redone (1996), and far fresher. Make sure you ask about special discount rates here—as low as $50 per night in summer months.

   Dining/Diversions: Of the hotel's eight restaurants, the Mayflower (Chinese) and the Benjarong (Thai) are ranked among the finest in Bangkok (see "Dining," below). The top-floor California/Asian fusion cuisine Tiara Restaurant has a sensational view over the city. The popular Pavilion Coffeeshop (open 24 hours), and Chinatown Restaurant are relatively less expensive choices. There is also a steakhouse and an excellent Vietnamese restaurant, as well as Japanese eateries, the latter two especially popular with businesspeople.

   Amenities: Business center, spa and fitness center, tennis and squash courts, outdoor swimming pool, driving range, shopping arcade, barbershop and beauty salon,

24-hour room service, butler service, in-room VCRs, concierge, limousine service, massage, baby-sitting, laundry/valet.

✪ **The Sukhothai.** 13/3 South Sathorn Rd., Bangkok 10120. **800/637-7200** in the U.S., or 02/287-0222. Fax 02/287-4980. 226 units. A/C MINIBAR TV TEL. $230–$270 double; from $320 suite. AE, DC, MC, V. South of Lumpini Park, near intersection of Rama IV and Wireless rds., next to the YMCA.

The elegant new Sukhothai, a property of the prestigious Beaufort Group from Singapore, brings sensual luxury to a noisy, busy locale better known for the neighboring low-budget YWCA and YMCA hostels. Inside the Sukhothai's five white pavilions, visitors find a welcome, if studied, serenity. Broad, colonnaded public spaces feature redbrick stupas, black-tiled wading pools, and sculpture with harmonious mud- and olive-toned silk panels and dull-black metalwork. Terra-cotta friezes, stupa-shaped wall sconces, and celadon ceramics and tiles evoke the ancient kingdom of Sukhothai.

Guest-room pavilions overlook lotus ponds inspired by the gardens of the Sukhothai era. Teak and cinnabar-accented rooms strive for the latest in luxury: reclining chaises, butler service, two full-size teak closets, separate shower stall in granite bathrooms, personal fax machines on request, and terraces with the Garden Suites. Though elegant design is the Sukhothai's most obvious attribute, guests commend its excellent service and assured sense of privacy.

Dining/Diversions: Among the several stylish dining venues, the less formal Colonnade Coffee Shop is most popular at Sunday brunch, when local jazz bands play while guests cruise the deluxe international buffet. Formal French fare is dished up at lunch (Monday to Friday only) or dinner (nightly) in La Noppamas's elegant silver and beige dining room. Celadon is the gourmet Thai restaurant, housed in a pavilion perched above a water garden.

Amenities: Olympic-size swimming pool, fitness center, two squash courts, tennis court, business center, Guerlain beauty salon, upscale shopping arcade, room service, 24-hour butler service, concierge, limousine service, massage, baby-sitting, laundry.

EXPENSIVE

Holiday Inn Crowne Plaza. 981 Silom Rd., Bangkok 10500. ☎ **800/465-4329** in the U.S., or 02/238-4300. Fax 02/238-5289. 726 units. A/C MINIBAR TV TEL. $159–$189 double; from $259 suite. AE, DC, MC, V. On Silom Rd. 1 block above (east of) Charoen Krung Rd.

Crowne Plaza, Holiday Inn's upmarket chain of hotels, provides high quality service and a level of luxury unexpected by those familiar with standard Holiday Inn accommodations in the United States. The top choice for families traveling to Bangkok; while there is a 500B charge for an extra bed, there's no charge for children under 19 years of age accompanying parents. Their very comfortable guest rooms are lovely, with masculine striped fabrics offsetting floral prints for a soft and homelike appeal. Rooms in the Plaza Tower are an especially good value, though smaller than those in the Crowne Tower, with high ceilings that give a spacious feel and oversized porthole windows, framed by heavy drapery, overlooking the city. The location is very convenient, near the expressway, a short walk from the river (and the Shangri-La and Oriental), in the middle of the gem-trade district. The huge lobby seating areas are always humming with travelers who are either resting from a day's adventure, or waiting to begin a new one.

Dining: The Window on Silom Restaurant serves one of Bangkok's better breakfast buffets. In the afternoon, the hotel serves a fine high tea in the Orchid Lounge. The Thai Pavillion and the Mogul-cuisine Tandoor serve lunch and dinner.

Amenities: Swimming pool, health club, tennis court, business center, beauty salon and barbershop, shopping arcade, 24-hour room service, concierge, limousine service, baby-sitting, laundry service.

The Mandarin. 662 Rama IV Rd., Bangkok 10500. ☎ **02/238-0230.** Fax 02/237-1620. 400 units. A/C MINIBAR TV TEL. 2,900B–3,300B ($76.30–$86.85) double; from 5,500B ($144.75) suite. AE, DC, MC, V. West of intersection of Rama IV and Si Phraya rds.

The Mandarin, a property of the Dutch Golden Tulip Hotels Group, is a glitzy, full-service hotel, perhaps better known in Bangkok for its nightclub (wildly popular with locals on weekends) than for its rooms. The lively lobby combines velvet-upholstered reproductions of Asian and European antiques with polished-brass doors and glittering chandeliers. All accommodations are clean, modern, and spacious. Rates vary with size and decor, but all rooms are good value. The pool is small, often shrouded in shade, and noisy from the nearby traffic. However, double-pane windows cut down on street noise inside the hotel and make its convenient location bearable.

Dining/Diversions: The Mandarin hosts the queen of Bangkok cocktail lounges, with a disco next door. These clubs and the 24-hour Coffee Shop (also with live bands!) are open nightly, but the real action takes place on the weekends.

Amenities: Small outdoor swimming pool, business center, beauty salon and barbershop, shopping arcade, 24-hour room service, concierge, limousine service, tour desk, baby-sitting (with some notice), laundry service.

Montien Hotel. 54 Surawong Rd., Bangkok 10500. ☎ **02/233-7060.** Fax 02/236-5218. www.montien.com. 475 units. A/C MINIBAR TV TEL. 4,400B–6,000B ($115.80–$157.90) double; from 8,000B ($210.55) suite. AE, DC, MC, V. Near Patpong.

Like many of the first-class tourist hotels that are attempting to break into the business market in Bangkok, the Montien is really two facilities in one. The first is directed at its traditional market, mainly Australian groups, who occupy the lower floors of one of the Montien's two wings with their dark teak hallways and bright, pleasant rooms. The other wing has been thoroughly upgraded and renamed the Executive Club. In this part of the hotel, dark teak has given way to bleached wood, granite, and matching gray carpet. The elegantly furnished Executive Club commons, adjoining the business center, serves complimentary continental breakfast and, in the evening, free drinks. The third-floor outdoor pool has an adjacent fitness center with sauna..

Dining: The Montien has an in-house bakery and good French and Chinese restaurants. The Jade Garden Cantonese Restaurant is excellent but very expensive.

Amenities: Outdoor swimming pool, fitness center, business center, beauty salon and barbershop, shopping arcade, 24-hour room service, concierge, limousine service, tour desk, massage, baby-sitting, laundry service, fortune-telling.

MODERATE

Manohra Hotel. 412 Surawong Rd., Bangkok 10500. ☎ **02/234-5070.** Fax 02/237-7662. 250 units. A/C MINIBAR TV TEL. 2,825B ($74.35) double; from 7,062B ($185.85) suite. AE, DC, JCB, MC, V. Between Charoesn Krung (New Rd.) and Mahesak Rd.

This bright, modern, and fetching hotel, a 5-minute walk from the river and the Oriental Hotel, is a quiet oasis. The glitzy glass-and-stone-sheathed lobby faces a small indoor swimming pool. Guest rooms are rather dimly lit and smaller than those in other first-class hotels, but they have a full range of amenities. Often booked by European tours. Its pleasant coffee shop overlooks the busy street.

Trinity Silom Hotel. 425/15 Silom Soi 5, Bangkok 10500. ☎ **02/231-5333.** Fax 02/ 231-5417. 104 units. A/C MINIBAR TV TEL. 1,694B ($44.60) double; 7,600B ($200) suite. Rates include American breakfast. AE, MC, V. Behind Bangkok Bank, 2 short blocks south of Silom Rd. on Soi 5, near Patpong.

At the quiet end of "Can't Keep Your Money" Lane (famous among Bangkokians for its many and various bargains), you'll find the most pleasant small midpriced hotel in the area. It has the marble lobby and tastefully furnished rooms of a large hotel, with the intimacy of a smaller European establishment. The staff is charming, friendly, and helpful. The coffee shop has good food and service at reasonable prices; there's a super-market a few doors up and plenty of nearby restaurants. The rooftop swimming pool in an adjacent tower, fitness center, beauty shop, massage and sauna, and easy access to both the Silom Road business-and-shopping activity and the river make this top of the class for both comfort and convenience.

INEXPENSIVE

Bangkok Christian Guesthouse. 123 Saladaeng, Soi 2, Convent Rd., Bangkok 10500. ☎ **02/233-6303.** Fax 02/237-1742. 30 units. A/C TEL. 1,000B ($26.30) double. No credit cards. 1 block south of Silom Rd. off the corner of Convent Rd.

This tranquil two-story guest house, originally a Presbyterian missionary residence, was converted into a lodge in the late 1960s, and is now operated by the Church of Christ in Thailand (as a result, you'll find a Christian atmosphere here). Large recently refurbished rooms are simple but spotless. The nicest rooms are on the second floor overlooking the large lawn with its sitting area, goldfish pond, and teak pavilion. There's a grandma-style lounge and library, a cheap restaurant, and a friendly young staff.

Bangkok YWCA. 13 Sathorn Tai Rd., Bangkok 10120. ☎ **02/286-3310.** 46 units (10 with shared bathroom). A/C. 880B ($23.15) double. Rates include tax and service. No credit cards. A short walk south of intersection of Rama IV and Wireless rds.

The venerable YWCA offers clean, simple rooms to women, men, and couples. It would be hard, if not impossible, to top this Y for value. There's a nice pool, beauty salon, tour desk, common TV lounge, a canteen/snack bar, and a very popular full-service restaurant where two can dine for less than 250B. There's also the YWCA Cooking School and the Sri Pattana Thai Language School.

Suriwongse Tower Inn. Executive House Building, 410/3–4 Suriwong Rd., Bangrak, Bangkok 10500. ☎ **02/235-1206.** Fax 02/237-1482. 80 units. A/C MINIBAR TV TEL. 1,350B ($35.55) double. AE, MC, V. Between Charoen Krung (New Rd.) and Mahesak Rd.

This establishment is difficult to find because it's on the 14th to 18th floors of the modern Executive House condominium tower, in a cul-de-sac off noisy Suriwong Road. It's a good value for families who will appreciate its oversized rooms (formerly apartments) with small balconies, some with great river views, well-kept bathrooms, and simple, eclectic international modern furnishings. Though it's well maintained, with a nice staff and a small coffee shop on the ground floor, some of the rooms are a bit bleak, so check yours out before accepting it.

✪ **YMCA Collins House International.** 27 S. Sathorn Tai Rd., Bangkok 10120. ☎ **02/287-1900.** Fax 02/286-1996. 258 units. A/C TV TEL. 1,400B ($36.85) double. AE, MC, V. A short walk south of intersection of Rama IV and Wireless rds.

This modern, nine-story hotel with sparkling, homey rooms with private showers, and a 75-foot swimming pool, is tucked into a quiet lane off South Sathorn Road near Lumphini Park. A good value in the moderate price range, with no compromise in comfort. Both staff and clientele are very friendly and the Y's front desk offers copy, fax, telex, and secretarial services. Several people have claimed that the Rossukon Restaurant has the most delicious and varied buffet (multiethnic cuisine) in town, at a bargain price.

A new wing contains a gym and second restaurant, as well as 120 more deluxe rooms featuring TV, minibar, and full bathtubs, at higher prices. Families should note that this YMCA even has suites—a Bangkok best buy.

THE SHOPPING/EMBASSY AREA

This is a wide-ranging area, covering the hotels on either side of Sukhumvit/ Ploenchit/Rama I Road. Many of the major shopping centers and stores are here, as well as the Sukhumvit shopping area, which is popular with the expatriate community. Many businesses have spread into office towers in the area, so business travelers may also find it convenient. Luxury hotels, such as the new Amari Atrium, a Radisson, and a Sheraton, are rising up like mushrooms along Sukhumvit, and the glut should help you negotiate a lower rate. Moderate and inexpensive accommodations, on the other hand, are disappearing or becoming so problematic that many can't even be recommended. Budget-minded travelers interested in the sights should stay nearer the river, which isn't so far away on the map, but the taxi ride to the Palace area can be well over an hour at peak traffic times.

VERY EXPENSIVE

Grand Hyatt Erawan. 494 Ratchadamri Rd., Bangkok 10330. ☎ **800/233-1234** in the U.S., or 02/254-1234. Fax 02/254-6308. www.hyatt.com. 400 units. A/C MINIBAR TV TEL. $250–$300 double; from $350 suite. AE, DC, MC, V. Corner of Rama I Rd.

Hyatt has replaced the old Erawan Hotel near Bangkok's famed Erawan shrine, the bustling, open-air temple dedicated to the four-headed Brahma, Tan Thao Mahaprom. The lobby entrance is guarded by two bronze Erawans, and inside dozens of banyan trees dapple the light pouring into a four-story atrium—the air filled with the sounds of waterfalls and gurgling goldfish ponds.

The works of dozens of contemporary Thai artists grace hallways and spacious rooms, where earth-toned silks, celadon accessories, antique-finish furnishings, parquet floors, oriental rugs, large bathrooms, and city views abound. In addition to the facilities one expects from a five-star hotel, there is a delightful fifth-floor pool terrace, where a waterfall tumbles down a rocky wall into a full-size hot tub.

Dining/Diversions: The pleasant lobby restaurant features a grand buffet at breakfast, lunch, and dinner, as well as a continental à la carte menu and high tea. Spasso is the Hyatt's trendy Italian bistro-cum-jazz bar, a popular local hangout. The stunning high-style Deco Chinese Restaurant is a gourmet's delight and worth a special trip. The basement shopping arcade features a pastry and cappuccino parlor.

Amenities: Rooftop swimming pool, large health club with jogging track and spa, grass tennis and squash courts, business center, beauty salon and barbershop, rooftop heliport, shopping arcade, 24-hour room service, concierge, limousine service, helicopter transfers, tour desk, massage, baby-sitting, laundry.

✪ **Hilton International Bangkok at Nai Lert Park.** 2 Wireless Rd., Bangkok 10330. ☎ **800/HILTONS** in the U.S., or 02/253-0123. Fax 02/253-6509. www.hilton.com. 338 units. A/C MINIBAR TV TEL. $185–$205 double; from $368 suite. AE, DC, JCB, MC, V. Between Ploenchit Rd. and New Phetchaburi Rd.

Set in lushly landscaped Nai Lert Park, near the British and American embassies, this tropical paradise is something of a mixed blessing—you will sleep far from the madding crowd, but you may find the taxi ride to the river or tourist sights a minor nuisance (though the adventurous will ride the convenient klong boat to the Grand Palace Area). However, after a long day of business or sightseeing, returning to the peaceful tranquility of the Hilton has the very comfortable feeling of returning home. The airy atrium lobby, with its classic teak pavilion and open garden views, ranks as one of the great public spaces in Bangkok. And the gorgeous free form pool in landscaped gardens is a total resort experience. The spacious guest rooms all have bougainvillea-draped balconies; the most preferred (and expensive) rooms overlook the pool. Other facilities include a fitness center with tennis and squash courts, and an exclusive shopping arcade.

Hilton offers many year-round packages to draw not only businesspeople, but leisure travelers as well. Special deals can be as low as $99 a night—expensive for some, but especially attractive for those who demand the finest facilities.

Dining/Diversions: Food service is outstanding and a very good value. The "coffee shop," Suan Saranrom, is a grand dining area overlooking the garden; it has for many years been voted the best Thai restaurant in a Bangkok hotel. The elegant Ma Maison offers excellent French cuisine (see "Dining," below). Genji, the Japanese Restaurant, a cozy lobby bar, and an evening poolside grill are other possibilities.

Amenities: World-class outdoor swimming pool, fitness center with tennis and squash courts, business center, beauty salon and barbershop, shopping arcade, 24-hour room service, concierge, limousine service, car rental. Tour desk, mobile telephone rental, massage, baby-sitting, laundry service.

Le Royal Meridien. 971, 973 Ploenchit Rd., Lumphini, Pathumwan, Bangkok 10330. ☎ 800/225-5843 in the U.S., or 02/656-0444. Fax 02/656-0555. www.lemeridien.com. 381 units. A/C MINIBAR TV TEL. $250–$275 double; from $330 suite. AE, DC, MC, V. Near intersection of Rama I and Ratchadamri rds.

Also named Le Meridien President for the President Tower Complex that houses the hotel, this group-tour-oriented place has undergone extensive renovation, and the gray marble lobby now has a welcoming and homey ambience, unlike too many Bangkok hotels that are impressive but cold. Rooms are compact but attractive, with pale paneling, tasteful pastel furnishings, and the usual luxury amenities. The newer suites are more sumptuously appointed.

Dining/Diversions: The Fireplace Grill is considered one of Bangkok's best Western dining rooms. Cappuccino is one of Bangkok's better coffee shops; desserts are excellent. In addition you have Thai, Japanese, and Chinese restaurants to choose from.

Amenities: Two swimming pools, two fitness centers, business center, beauty salon and barbershop, shopping arcade, 24-hour room service, concierge, limousine service, car rentals, tour desk, massage, baby-sitting, laundry service.

Novotel Bangkok. Siam Square Soi 6, Bangkok 10330. ☎ 02/255-6888. Fax 02/254-1328. 465 units. A/C MINIBAR TV TEL. 6,474B–7,415B ($170.35–$195.15) double; from 8,476B ($223.05) suite. AE, DC, JCB, MC, V. In Siam Square off Rama I Rd.

This elegant and opulent high-rise hotel in the Siam Square shopping area is one of this French chain's best inns. The grand marble, granite, and glass entrance leads into an expansive gray stone interior that is complemented by soft leather-upholstered sofas and chairs. Pastel tones carry over into guest quarters, where the rooms are spacious and fully equipped. Facilities include the 18th-floor no-smoking suites, a fully equipped business center that overlooks the hotel's kidney-shaped pool, and a sleek chrome-and-mirror fitness center.

The location isn't too bad for visiting Bangkok's traditional tourist sites, but if you're in town on business or prefer one of Bangkok's better shopping areas, the Novotel is a fine choice. The hotel just celebrated its 10-year anniversary in grand style, so ask if any special promotions are still available.

Dining/Diversions: The Pastel Lounge serves a delicious continental breakfast and afternoon tea, and in the evening there's an oh-so-elegant string quartet. Chinese, Thai, seafood, and Western food are available in the hotel's other dining outlets.

Amenities: No-smoking floor, swimming pool, health club, business center, bakery, beauty salon, barbershop, 24-hour room service, concierge, limousine service, baby-sitting, laundry service.

✪ **The Regent.** 155 Ratchadamri Rd., Bangkok 10330. ☎ **800/545-4000** in the U.S., or 02/251-6127. Fax 02/253-9195. www.regenthotels.com. 356 units. A/C MINIBAR TV TEL. $200–$245 double; $315 cabana; from $300 suite. AE, DC, MC, V. South of Rama I Rd.

The Regent is a modern palace. From your first entrance through the massive lobby you'll be captured by the grand staircase, huge and gorgeous Thai murals, and gold sunbursts on the vaulted ceiling. The impeccable service begins at the front desk, where guests are greeted, then escorted to their room to complete check-in and enjoy the waiting fruit basket and box of chocolates. The air of luxury pervades each room; traditional style Thai murals, handsome color schemes, and a plush carpeted dressing area off the tiled bath. The more expensive rooms have a view of the Royal Bangkok Sport Club and racetrack.

Cabana rooms and suites face the large pool and terrace area which is filled with palms and lotus pools, and all sorts of tropical greenery. Regent also has one of the finest hotel spas in Bangkok. The secluded Clinique La Prarie guides guests through individually tailored beauty programs and treatments.

Dining: The informal Spice Market is one of the finest Thai restaurants in the city (see "Dining," below). At Shintaro you can enjoy Japanese cuisine in a contemporary setting, while their new Italian-American restaurant serves up some hearty pastas.

Amenities: Pool and health club with sauna, business center, beauty salon and barbershop, gourmet bakery and deli, shopping arcade, 24-hour room service, concierge, health clinic, limousine service, baby-sitting, laundry/valet. Business service goes above and beyond the call of duty: dual phone lines, Internet access through TV, and 24-hour business services.

Siam Inter-Continental Hotel. 967 Rama I Rd., Bangkok 10330. ☎ **02/253-0355.** Fax 02/254-5474. 400 units. A/C MINIBAR TV TEL. $132–$156 double; from $257 suite. AE, DC, JCB, MC, V. Opposite Siam Square.

Set in 26 acres of parkland—part of the Srapatum Royal Palace estate—the Siam Inter-Continental is an island of calm in frenetic Bangkok. A graceful driveway leads to the sprawling ranch-style complex with a spacious lobby overlooking the well-landscaped grounds, which offer some of the best outdoor sports facilities in Bangkok: groomed jogging trails, lit tennis courts, a golf minicourse and driving range. A small playground is also popular with children.

Pastel carpets and dark Chinese-style furniture provide a rich, pleasing ambience. The Club Inter-Continental Wing is the two-story equivalent of an "executive" floor, with slightly smarter furnishings and free breakfast and drinks in the private lounge.

Dining/Diversions: The all-you-can-eat buffet lunch at Similan, the Inter-Continental's Thai and sometimes seafood restaurant, is an excellent value.

Amenities: Swimming pool, sports center, business center, beauty salon, barbershop, shopping arcade, bakery, 24-hour room-service, concierge, limousine service, baby-sitting, laundry.

EXPENSIVE

Amari Boulevard Hotel. 2 Soi 5, Sukhumvit Rd., Bangkok 10110. ☎ **02/255-2930.** Fax 02/255-2950. www.amari.com. 315 units. A/C MINIBAR TV TEL. $127–$221 double; from $318 suite. AE, DC, MC, V. North of Sukhumvit Rd., on Soi 5.

Since the completion of a glass-and-steel tower that seems to lean back against the original hotel, the modern Boulevard appears more elegant than ever. The newer Krung Thep Wing has spacious rooms in contemporary muted tones, featuring full-granite bathrooms and terrific city views. The larger corner deluxe rooms are especially striking, with separate shower stalls, two seating areas, and a desk. The original wing has mahogany-paneled hallways and attractive balconied rooms that are a better value. When rooms are discounted 40% to 60% in the low season, this hotel is a very good value. A rooftop swimming pool shelters you somewhat from Sukhumvit's smog, and the health club is quite popular with locals who have outside membership.

Dining/Diversions: The Peppermill Restaurant serves an array of international cuisine, including Thai, Japanese, and vegetarian dishes. In addition, there is a 24-hour bar serving snacks.

Amenities: Outdoor swimming pool, fitness center, business center, beauty salon and barbershop, 24-hour room service, concierge, limousine service, tour desk, baby-sitting, massage, laundry.

Siam City Hotel. 477 Si Ayuthaya Rd., Bangkok 10400. ☎ **02/247-0120.** Fax 02/247-0178. 515 units. A/C MINIBAR TV TEL. 2,999B ($78.90) double; from 3,777B ($99.40) suite. AE, DC, JCB, MC, V. Near intersection with Phaya Thai Rd., across from Suan Pakkard Palace.

This excellent hotel offers luxury without pretension and a good location—near Chitralada Palace, the Royal Turf Club, the Marble Wat, and Dusit Zoo, yet convenient to the business, government, and shopping districts, as well as the expressway to the airport. Rooms are large, comfortable, and tastefully decorated in muted colors—for a restful retreat after a demanding day of sightseeing or business. Executive suites feature a living room or an in-room office with fax and computer connections, spacious bathrooms with separate showers, and butler service.

Dining/Diversions: The lobby Patummat Restaurant serves international and Thai cuisine, as well as a sumptuous buffet breakfast. The Primavera Restaurant specializes in Mediterranean cuisine, and there's Chinese cuisine at the Lin-Fa, Japanese at the Nishimura, Asian at the Asian Cafe, and snacks at the Pink Elephant Ice-Cream Parlor and City Shoppe and Bakery.

Amenities: Swimming pool, health club, business center, beauty salon, shopping arcade, 24-hour room service, concierge, limousine service, tour/travel/car rental desk, baby-sitting, laundry and dry cleaning.

Tai-Pan Hotel. 25 Sukhumvit Soi 23, Bangkok 10110. ☎ **02/260-9888.** Fax 02/259-7908. www.tai-pan.com. 150 units. A/C MINIBAR TV TEL. 2,825B ($74.35) double; from 6,000B ($157.90) suite. AE, DC, MC, V. 1 block north of Sukhumvit Rd. on Soi 23.

Opened in 1991, this modern white tower rises above a quiet soi in a neighborhood that's perfect for shoppers, decorators, and those in the fashion industry. Shops, dining, and entertainment catering to foreign residents make it convenient in one aspect, but the distance from major attractions can be a little daunting. However, the attentive staff and the bright, carpeted rooms with comfortable sitting areas and city views and all the facilities you'd expect from a more expensive hotel guarantee a pleasant stay and make it a good value. The excellent coffee shop has bargain buffet breakfasts and lunches. If a good swimming pool and exercise room are important, look elsewhere.

Dining: Excellent coffee shop with bargain buffet breakfasts and lunches. Great Thai and continental food.

Amenities: Small swimming pool, exercise room, business center, 24-hour room service, limousine service, baby-sitting, laundry.

MODERATE

Asia Hotel. 296 Phayathai Rd., Bangkok 10400. ☎ **02/215-0808**. Fax 02/215-4360. www.asiahotel.co.th. 650 units. A/C MINIBAR TV TEL. 3,200B–3,600B ($84.20–$94.75) double; from 5,000B ($131.60) suite. AE, MC, V. Between Petchaburi and Rama I rds.

Location and affordability add to the attractiveness of Asia Hotel. Near the main shopping boulevard housing Bangkok's best and largest shopping malls, Asia's also not too far from historic attractions. The lobby's got some nice Thai decorative touches, but the rooms are like motel rooms—a little busy looking, but clean and well maintained. Five restaurants serve up everything from standard Chinese to Vietnamese—even Brazilian. But you're so close to the cafe's of Rama I, you probably won't hang around the hotel too much.

INEXPENSIVE

✪ **City Lodge.** 137/1–3 Sukhumvit Soi 9, Bangkok 10110. ☎ **02/253-7705.** Fax 02/255-4667. 28 units. A/C MINIBAR TV TEL. 910B ($23.95) double. MC, V. Corner of Sukhumvit and Soi 9.

Budget watchers will appreciate the two small, spiffy City Lodges. Both the newer lodge on Soi 9, and its nearby cousin, the older, 35-room City Lodge on Soi 19 (☎ **02/254-4783,** fax 02/255-7340), provide clean, compact rooms with simple, modern decor. Each has a pleasant coffee shop (facing the bustle on Sukhumvit Road at Soi 9; serving Italian fare on Soi 19), a small but friendly staff, and privileges at the rooftop swimming pool at the more deluxe Amari Boulevard Hotel on Soi 5. All three belong to the Amari Hotels and Resorts Group. No frills here, but still a lot of comfort for your money.

Comfort Inn. 153/11 Soi 11, Sukhumvit Rd., Bangkok 10110. ☎ **02/251-0745.** Fax 02/254-3562. 36 units. A/C MINIBAR TV TEL. 700B ($18.40) double. MC, V. North of Sukhumvit Rd. opposite Swiss Park Hotel.

This small hotel has clean, compact rooms, very simply furnished but with a warm, homey feel. The friendly staff and quiet but convenient location on Soi Chaiyod make it a good value. A 5% discount is offered for stays of a week or longer, 10% for a month or more.

Ruam Chit Mansion. 1–15 Soi 15, Sukhumvit Rd., Bangkok 10110. ☎ **02/254-2228.** Fax 02/253-2406. 16 units. A/C TV. 1,350B ($35.55) double. MC, V. North of Sukhumvit near Ambassador Hotel.

This basic place is over a supermarket, so at least provisions are nearby (there's a convenient empty fridge in each room), and it has a good solid reputation, as well as hot water. Guests are allowed to use the kitchen and refrigerator. Monthly rates are available.

THE AIRPORT AREA

Don Muang International Airport is so far from the center of Bangkok that it makes sense to stay in the area only if you have connecting flights and want to avoid the time and expense of a taxi to a city hotel.

Amari Airport Hotel. 333 Chert Wudthakas Rd., Don Muang, Bangkok 10210. ☎ **02/566-1020.** Fax 02/566-1941. www.amari.com. 434 units. A/C MINIBAR TV TEL. $175–$212; from $350 suite. AE, MC, V. Just west of international terminal, connected by an elevated footbridge.

This is the fanciest, the closest, and, if budget is not a concern, the best of all choices near the airport. It's connected by an overpass to the international terminal, from which you can take a free shuttle to the domestic terminal about half a mile away. It's a short walk to the Don Muang railroad station, where many, but not all, trains to and from the north stop en route to and from Bangkok's Hua Lampong station. For those wanting to pop into the city, there's a shuttle bus that runs regularly to Ploenchit Road in the heart of Bangkok's shopping district.

The Airport Hotel has all the facilities you'd expect from a first-class hotel, including the Cockpit Lounge, Le Bel-Air Grill, Airbridge Café, and Zeppelin Coffee

Shop (open 24 hours). Flight arrival and departure information scrolls across monitors in the lobby (ask about discount rates for ministay packages, if you have a short layover and want to shower and relax). Spacious deluxe rooms are decorated in soothing pastel colors and, best yet, the windows are soundproof. Although expensive, this hotel tries to give you your money's worth, especially on the new premium-rate Executive Floor.

Golden Dragon Hotel. 20/21 Ngarm Wongwan Rd., Bangkok 11000. ☎ **02/589-0130.** Fax 02/589-8305. 120 units. A/C TV TEL. 900B ($23.70) double. Rates include tax and service. AE, MC, V. 10km (6 miles) or 15 min. south of Don Muang International Airport.

For travelers in transit, this is the best, relatively inexpensive alternative in the area. Rooms are simple but clean, though this establishment is in the running for the Hardest-Mattress-in-Thailand Award. There's a pool and basic restaurant.

Quality Suites Airport. 99/401–485 Soi Benjamitr, Chaeng Wattana Rd., Bangkok 10210. ☎ **02/982-2022.** Fax 02/982-2036. 80 units. A/C MINIBAR TV TEL. From 1,700B ($44.75) suite. AE, MC, V. 3km (15 min.) north of airport.

These roomy, well-furnished, comfortable deluxe suites are particularly recommended for families, especially those with tight flight schedules. Most amenities are available, including swimming pool, fitness center, restaurant and bar, convenience store, satellite TV, laundry, baby-sitting, and free shuttle bus to the airport any time. Like Amari Airport Hotel, they also offer short-stay packages for folks with shorter in-transit times.

THE RAILROAD STATION AREA
As in most cities, the area around the train station is not what you'd call idyllic. If you're in Bangkok for more than 1 night, take a tuk-tuk or taxi to a recommended hotel in another part of town, or contact the information booth in the terminal (open Monday through Friday from 8:30am to 6pm; to noon all other days and holidays) for advice.

Bangkok Center Hotel. 328 Rama IV Rd., Bangkok 10500. ☎ **02/238-4848.** Fax 02/235-1780. 250 units. A/C MINIBAR TV TEL. 1,000B ($26.30) double. AE, DC, MC, V. Two blocks east of the Hua Lampong Railroad Station.

It's a basic businessperson's hotel—plain, functional, and set back from the busy, clamorous thoroughfare. Rooms are simple, clean, and comfortable. There's a lunchtime buffet in the scenic rooftop ballroom and a popular Chinese restaurant (open daily 11am to 2pm and 6 to 10pm) downstairs.

Krung Kasem Sri Krung Hotel. 1860 Krung Kasem Rd., Bangkok 10100. ☎ **02/225-0132.** Fax 02/225-4702. 129 units. A/C TV TEL. 550B ($14.45) double. Rates include tax and service. No credit cards. One block west of Hua Lampong Railroad Station.

Turn right from the front of the station and cross the klong (canal) to find this best nearby budget choice for cross-country train travelers. Rooms have air-conditioning, private toilet and shower, as well as a high standard of cleanliness. The quieter, back-facing rooms have small balconies and a city view. Each of its seven floors has a luggage locker, handy for storage during an upcountry expedition. Business travelers and neighborhood vendors like the Valentine Coffee Shop's inexpensive Thai/Chinese fare.

2 Dining

Thai food is among the finest cuisine in Southeast Asia, and some would argue, in the world. Bangkok offers a delightful variety of Thai restaurants, ranging from simple noodle stands to elegant dining rooms offering "royal" cuisine. It's so reasonably priced

Bangkok Dining

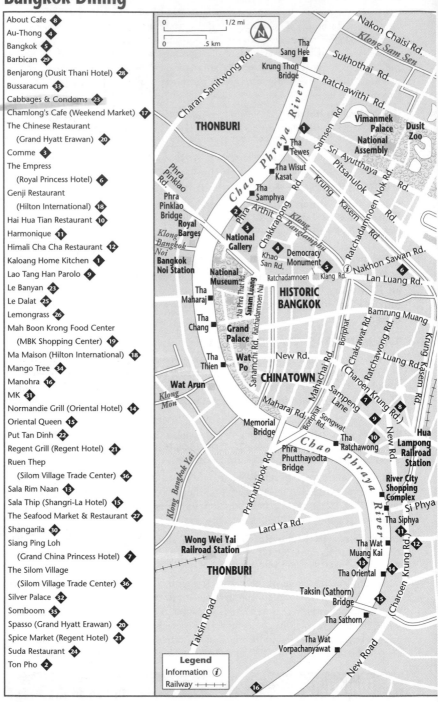

About Cafe **8**
Au-Thong **4**
Bangkok **5**
Barbican **29**
Benjarong (Dusit Thani Hotel) **28**
Bussaracum **33**
Cabbages & Condoms **23**
Chamlong's Cafe (Weekend Market) **17**
The Chinese Restaurant
   (Grand Hyatt Erawan) **20**
Comme **3**
The Empress
   (Royal Princess Hotel) **6**
Genji Restaurant
   (Hilton International) **18**
Hai Hua Tian Restaurant **10**
Harmonique **11**
Himali Cha Cha Restaurant **12**
Kaloang Home Kitchen **1**
Lao Tang Han Parolo **9**
Le Banyan **23**
Le Dalat **25**
Lemongrass **26**
Mah Boon Krong Food Center
   (MBK Shopping Center) **19**
Ma Maison (Hilton International) **18**
Mango Tree **34**
Manohra **16**
MK **31**
Normandie Grill (Oriental Hotel) **14**
Oriental Queen **15**
Put Tan Dinh **22**
Regent Grill (Regent Hotel) **21**
Ruen Thep
   (Silom Village Trade Center) **36**
Sala Rim Naan **13**
Sala Thip (Shangri-La Hotel) **15**
The Seafood Market & Restaurant **27**
Shangarila **30**
Siang Ping Loh
   (Grand China Princess Hotel) **7**
The Silom Village
   (Silom Village Trade Center) **36**
Silver Palace **32**
Somboom **35**
Spasso (Grand Hyatt Erawan) **20**
Spice Market (Regent Hotel) **21**
Suda Restaurant **24**
Ton Pho **2**

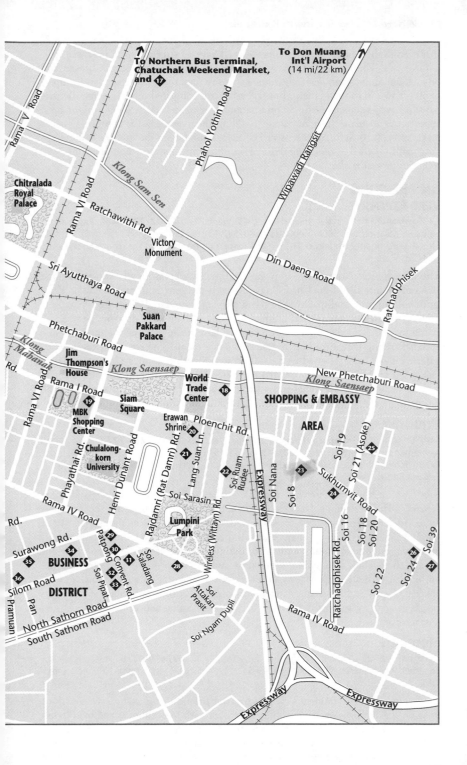

that even in the fanciest Thai restaurant, you'll have a hard time spending more than $40 for two! The city also offers a spectacular array of fine European, Chinese, and other Asian dining spots, generally more expensive than those catering to locals (up to $150 for two in the top hotels), but still a bargain compared to back home. Be prepared for ever-changing menus, as internationally renowned chefs are known for guest appearances in many finer restaurants, adding their own masterful touches to the dishes offered. You'll find inexpensive Thai-style fast food, on the street or in the shopping malls. *Metro Magazine* contains reviews of recently opened restaurants plus short recaps of proven establishments.

ON THE RIVER
VERY EXPENSIVE

✪ **Normandie Grill.** In the Oriental Hotel, 48 Oriental Ave. ☎ **02/236-0400.** Reservations required. Main courses 600B–1,600B ($15.80–$42.10); set dinner 3,500B ($92.10). AE, DC, MC, V. Daily noon–2pm and 7–11pm. Off Charoen Krung (New Rd.), overlooking the river. FRENCH.

The ultra-elegant Normandie, atop the renowned Oriental Hotel, with panoramic views of Thonburi and the Chao Phraya River, is the apex in formal dining in Thailand, both in price and quality. The room glistens in gold and silver, from place settings to chandeliers, and the warm tones of golden silks impart a delicious glow. Some of the highest rated master chefs from France have made guest appearances at Normandie, adding their own unique touches to the menu. The set menu begins with panfried goose liver, followed by a panfried turbot with potato and leek in a parsley sauce. The beef fillet main course, in a red wine sauce, is a stroll through heaven. The set also includes cheese, coffee and a sinful dessert. Reservations are a must, as the dining room is relatively small, and a jacket and tie are required.

EXPENSIVE

Sala Thip. In the Shangri-La Hotel, 89 Soi Wat Suan Plu. ☎ **02/236-7777.** Reservations recommended. Main courses 200B–450B ($5.25–$11.85). AE, DC, MC, V. Mon–Sat 6–10:30pm; high-season Sun buffet dinner 6–10:30pm. Overlooking Chao Phraya River, near Sathorn Bridge. THAI.

Sala Thip, on the river terrace of the Shangri-La Hotel, is arguably Bangkok's most romantic Thai restaurant. Classical music and traditional cuisine are superbly presented under one of two aged, carved teak pavilions perched over a lotus pond or at outdoor tables overlooking the river. (For those who crave a less humid environment, grab a table in one of the air-conditioned dining rooms.) Although the food may not inspire aficionados, it is skillfully prepared and nicely served. Set menus help the uninitiated with ordering: Many courses include Thai spring rolls, pomelo salad with chicken, a spicy seafood soup, snapper with chile sauce, and your choice of Thai curries. Keep your eyes peeled for masked dancers performing between the tables at various intervals.

MODERATE

Harmonique. 22 Chaoren Krung (New Rd.) Soi 34. ☎ **02/630-6270.** Reservations not accepted. Main courses 70B–200B ($1.85–$5.25). Mon–Sat 11am–10pm. No credit cards. THAI.

A nice little find, Harmonique's special character practically oozes from the courtyard walls of this old mansion. Small dining rooms set with cozy antiques and marble-top tables are inviting and friendly. While the cuisine here is Thai, it's not exactly authentic—much of it leans toward Western tastes, and there's a big Chinese influence here. But it's all still very good—the tom yam with fish was moderately spicy with enormous chunks of fish, and the sizzling grilled seafood platter is nice and garlicky (chiles on the side). They also feature good Thai salads. The service is far better during the week than on weekends.

INEXPENSIVE

Himali Cha Cha Restaurant. 1229/11 Charoen Krung Rd. ☎ **02/235-1569.** Main courses 75B–250B ($1.95–$6.60). AE, DC, MC, V. Daily 11am–3:30pm and 6–11:30pm. On a side street off Charoen Krung (New Rd.), corner of Surawong. INDIAN.

Cha Cha, the graying chef and proprietor, was on Lord Mountbatten's staff in India. Then he went on to cook for the diplomatic corps in Laos; after that country's fall, he came to Bangkok to open this restaurant in 1980. House specialties include a mutton barbecue, chicken tikka and chicken masala. The Indian *thali* plates are great, especially for lunch. Some complain that Himali Cha Cha, and its sister restaurant at 2 Sukhumit Soi 35 (☎ 02/258-8843) have become a bit too commercial and bland, but I found it to be quite nice for the price.

HISTORIC BANGKOK—NEAR THE GRAND PALACE
EXPENSIVE

✪ **The Empress.** Royal Princess Hotel, 269 Larn Luang Rd. ☎ **02/281-3088.** Reservations recommended. Main courses 120B–1,600B ($3.15–$42.10). AE, DC, MC, V. Daily 11:30am–2:30pm and 6–10pm. West of Krung Kasem Rd. CHINESE.

This elegant hotel restaurant specializes in dim sum and gourmet Cantonese cuisine, without MSG. The high-style mint and jade green padded banquettes are jammed at lunch with government officials, upscale tourists, and local businesspeople, all savoring a selection from the 20 or so dim sum choices. The fresh steamed, fried, and boiled morsels (mostly seafood) provide an inexpensive midday break. Cantonese specialties include a tart abalone salad, whole steamed fish, and bird's-nest soup. Even the lesser priced fare is delicious and artfully presented. Try the tender tea-leaf smoked duck, steamed bean curd stuffed with minced prawns, and sautéed seasonal vegetables with crabmeat sauce. And how can you resist a dish called "the escaping eunuch"? Packed with chunks of sea cucumber, abalone, shark's fin, dried scallops, black chicken, and mushrooms—this soup is delicious.

MODERATE

✪ **Bangkok Bar and Restaurant.** 591 Phra Sumen Rd. ☎ **02/281-6237.** Reservations recommended for weekends. Main courses 70B–150B ($1.85–$3.95). Daily 6am–2am. No credit cards. North of Democracy Monument. THAI.

A brand-new entry on the capital's dining scene, Bangkok is fresh and bold—a great alternative to places with more hype than taste. In a renovated 150-year-old mansion alongside Klong Banglamphu, all your senses are visited with local contemporary art on the walls (don't forget to walk upstairs for more exhibit space), deep jazz and funk rhythms wafting through the air, and sensational Thai food—but be warned, it's spicy. After scraping half the green chiles off my sea bass—steamed with lemon, garlic, and chile—it was no longer atomic, but delectable. But there are plenty of dishes that are not so spicy—the chicken wrapped in pandanus leaves is crispy and savory, and the coconut milk soup has a great creamy texture and sweet flavor. With a full bar and interesting cocktails, this place will be a success for years to come.

✪ **Kaloang Home Kitchen.** 2 Soi Wat Thevarajkunchorn, Si Ayutthaya Rd. ☎ **02/281-9228.** Reservations required for boat tables only. Main courses 70B–200B ($1.85–$5.25). AE, MC, V. Daily 11am–11pm. Behind the National Library. Go down Sri Ayuttaya Rd., cross Samsen Road, hang a left then a right to the river. THAI.

Tips on Dining

While Thai food reigns supreme in the kingdom, international cuisine like Italian, French, German, and American are served up in everything from elegant venues to small cafes. In many cases, continental cuisine is combined with local fare—mixing Asian and Western ingredients, preparation styles and serving preferences for what is called "Fusion Food" or "East-Meets-West." While some gourmet purists may resent the bastardization, many times the result is quite a thrill.

Hotels will oftentimes house the finer restaurants, with most moderate choices scattered around town. Naturally, places like Bangkok, Phuket, Chiang Mai, Ko Samui, and Pattaya have the largest selection of restaurants. A lot of these places are downright chic, catering to a more cosmopolitan Thai and international clientele. In very small towns, I recommend eating at your hotel in some instances. Expensive and moderate restaurants almost always accept some form of credit card payment.

Cheap eats are abundant throughout Thailand. Night bazaars and hawker stalls tempt passers-by with the smell of garlic, chile, and barbecued meats. If you decide to go for it, pick a stall that looks clean. Check all ingredients for freshness, from meats to oils, and watch them prepare the dish before your eyes. Don't eat anything raw. Thais have a better natural immunity to common bacterium—but these wee-beasties can wreck an otherwise brilliant holiday. I've found most small coffee shops and local restaurants to be fairly clean and compliant with basic health standards.

Tipping is not the custom here, where in some instances a 10% gratuity is included in your bill. Still, most Thais will leave the coins or a 20B (55¢) note from their change. There have been a few cases where I've dined in a better establishment and noticed that 10% has not been added to my bill. In these cases I've at times slipped the amount to the server. While it's not absolutely necessary, as an American I still have a hard time getting out of the habit. But basically you needn't sweat the tip.

For ambience alone, the Kaloang Home Kitchen is a favorite. This riverside cafe, overlooking the Royal Yacht Pier and adjoining a lovely residential neighborhood, is as authentically Thai as any you'll find in the capital. The huge portions alone are well worth the trip. Make sure you ask about their daily specials, which don't appear on the menu, or try house specialties like *yam paduk fu,* a salad of roasted catfish whipped into a foam and crisply (and deliciously) fried, *sam lee* fish with mango, and marinated chicken.

There are two separate dining areas: a covered wooden pier set with simple outdoor furniture and a retired wooden boat that holds about 10 small tables. It may require patience to hunt this one down, but you'll be rewarded with a memorable off-the-beaten-tourist-track experience. The restaurant sometimes requires men to wear a sport coat.

Ton Pho Restaurant. 43 Phra-Athit Rd., Banglamphu. ☎ **02/280-0452.** Reservations recommended on weekends. Main courses 50B–260B ($1.30–$6.85). Daily 11am–10pm. JCB, MC, V. One block north of Phra-Athit ferry pier. THAI.

Another great choice for dining along the Chao Phraya River, Ton Pho is closer and easier to find, plus you still have a lovely riverside venue. I was lucky one day to have my lunch while watching the Royal Barges, the delicate gilt boats that parade the royal family through the city on special occasions, practice on the river. Their extensive menu has a large selection of seafood specials, plus chicken and beef dishes (although the beef here was a bit too tough for my taste)—and their soups are lovely. Call the TAT to find out about Royal Barges practice, then make your reservations for some great lunch entertainment.

INEXPENSIVE

Au-Thong. 78 Rambutri Rd. behind Khao San Rd. ☎ **02/629-2172.** Reservations not necessary. Entrees 70B–180B ($1.85–$4.75). No credit cards. Daily noon–10:30pm. THAI.

In a nice little wooden house situated off the main road, Au-Thong serves up some spicy traditional Thai cuisine in a peaceful setting (you can sit outside in the courtyard garden on cooler evenings). The food is Thai, but they also feature dishes from Isan— spicy sausages and fried river fish delicacies. If you're staying in the Khao San Road area, this place is recommended if you'd like to get off the main tourist thoroughfares and away from the din of backpacker consumerism.

Commé. Phra-Athit Rd. ☎ **02/280-0647.** Reservations not accepted. Entrees 50B–120B ($1.32–$3.16). Tues–Sun 6pm–2am. No credit cards. Opposite Ton Pho, 1 block north of Phra-Athit ferry pier. THAI.

Phra-Athit Road has enjoyed a recent spark of trendy new restaurants and cafe openings in the past year. Quite the place to hang out, it had the double joy of being hip and affordable at the same time. Of all the places here, I like Commé. Small and brightly lit, the staff is laid back and good-humored, the art will always give you something to talk about, and the menu (although somewhat limited) is quite good—and surprisingly inexpensive for the quality. Beer is served, but if you prefer wine or spirits, you'll have to bring your own.

THE BUSINESS DISTRICT

The touristy Silom Village Trade Center, 286 Silom Rd., at Soi 24, has a number of good dining venues. **The Silom Village** serves Thai and other Asian dishes, specializing in fresh seafood, sold by weight. **The Ruen Thep** offers more elegant fare with classical Thai dance in the evenings.

EXPENSIVE

Benjarong. The Dusit Thani, Rama IV Rd. ☎ **02/236-0450,** ext. 2699. Reservations recommended. Main courses 180B–600B ($4.75–$15.80). AE, DC, JCB, MC, V. Daily 11:30am–2pm and 6:30–10pm. Closed for lunch Sat–Sun. Corner of Silom Rd. and Rama IV Rd. THAI.

You'll want to get dressed up for this elegant dining room, named for the exquisite five-color pottery once reserved exclusively for the use of royalty. Benjarong prides itself on offering the five basic flavors of Thai cuisine (salty, bitter, hot, sweet, and sour) in traditional "royal" dishes. While their à la carte menu is extensive, the most popular dishes are the sweet red curry crab claws, and the exotic grilled fish with black beans in banana leaves. The illustrated menu will help you navigate your way through the choices and whet your appetite. For after-dinner treats, the *kong wan* is an ornate selection of typical Thai desserts—distinctive, light, and not too sweet.

MODERATE

The Barbican. 9/4–5 Soi Thaniya, Silom Rd. ☎ **02/233-4141.** Reservations not necessary. Main courses 120B–540B ($3.16–$14.21). AE, DC, MC, V. Daily 11:30am–2:30pm and 6pm–12:30am. One block east of Patpong between Silom and Surawong rds. INTERNATIONAL.

Having spent my share of nights at Barbican's happening bar, I was surprised to discover how wonderful their food was. More than just your typical bar food (yes, they do have good tapas, and fabulous fried brie), entrees include great pasta dishes with an Asian twist—the mushroom goulash is incredible. Pretty much everything on the menu is superb. Choose from the lively happy hour atmosphere downstairs, or the smaller, less rowdy dining room upstairs. Both have Barbican's signature slate and polished steel look, but upstairs is a bit more warm in feel, with wood accents.

Bussaracum. 139 Sathiwon Building, Pan Rd. off Silom Rd. ☎ **02/226-6312.** Reservations recommended. Main courses 110B–280B ($2.90–$7.35). AE, DC, MC, V. Daily 11:30am–2pm and 5:30–10:30pm. Between Silom and Sathorn rds. THAI.

This is a traditional favorite for Thais hosting foreigners because of the fine food and the classical royal decor.

At this tranquil, teak-paneled sanctuary with linen tablecloths, the menu changes monthly. Their *rhoom* (minced pork and shrimp in egg-net wrapping) was the favorite appetizer of King Rama II. The *saengwa* (cold shrimp salad served in a squash gourd) is an unusual dish that complements their noteworthy *tom yam* soup and *gaeng kari gai hang* (special chicken curry). Allow the helpful staff to make suggestions, and finish the meal with *bauloy sarm see*, a dessert of taro and pumpkin in coconut milk.

Shangarila. 58/4–9 Thaniya Rd., in Thaniya Plaza, off Silom Rd. ☎ **02/234-0861.** Reservations recommended. Main courses 80B–350B ($2.10–$9.20). AE, DC, MC, V. West of Patpong. CHINESE.

The decor is bright and splashy, with a carp pond taking up part of the downstairs room and chandeliers everywhere. The fine food is inexpensive, well prepared, and more interesting than at many casual Chinese eateries. The traditional beggar's chicken is stuffed with mushrooms and baked in a thick clay coating. Peking duck, peppery Shanghai dumpling soup, and the fresh seafood dishes (especially crab) are among our favorites. The crisp mille-feuille-style Shanghai spring rolls are light as air. Dishes come in three sizes—which is perfect if you want to sample the options. The place is almost always packed, though, so come early.

Silver Palace. 5 Soi Pipat, Silom Rd., 7th floor. ☎ **02/235-5118.** Reservations recommended. Main courses 120B–280B ($3.15–$7.35). AE, DC, MC, V. Dim sum daily 11am–2pm; dinner daily 6–11pm. Across Silom Rd. from Patpong, near Bangkok Bank. CHINESE.

Edith Tai's Silver Palace, in newer and larger quarters, is still one of Bangkok's best and most attractive Cantonese restaurants. Its warm, elegant dining room is furnished with lovely Chinese bentwood chairs. The basic menu is diverse and imaginative, with exotic seasonal specials changing often. The duck, seafood, and shark's-fin choices are extensive and delicious. Try the drunken prawns (marinated live in wine and steamed at your table) and the fabulous Peking duck. Other favorites include braised duck with *eight-jewel* (vegetables and condiments) rice, a large and truly succulent whole roast pig (sometimes devoured by as few as three diners), subtly flavored prawns, asparagus with crabmeat in a light sauce, and tender fried duck in steamed ginger. Some complex dishes, such as the superb Peking duck, *phu thew chang*, and other shark's-fin specialties, require advance notice.

Somboon Seafood. 169/7–11 Surawong Rd. ☎ **02/233-3104.** Reservations not necessary. Seafood at market prices (about 800B/$21.05 for two). No credit cards. Daily 4–11pm. Just across from the Peugeot building. SEAFOOD.

This one's for those who would sacrifice atmosphere for excellent food. Packed nightly, you'll still be able to find a table (the place is huge). The staff is extremely friendly—between them and the picture menu you'll be able to order the best dishes and have the finest recommendations. Peruse the large aquariums outside to see all the live seafood options like prawn, fishes, lobsters, and crabs (guaranteed freshness). The house specialty chili crab is especially excellent, as is the *tom yang goong* (they'll be glad to tone down the spice for any of the dishes here).

INEXPENSIVE

MK. Ground Floor, Silom Complex. ☎ **02/231-3106.** Reservations not required. Suki for two about 200B–300B ($5.25–$7.90). MC, V. Daily 10:30am–10pm. Basement level of shopping mall. SUKIYAKI.

If you've never tried suki, it's a fantastic light meal. From the menu, select any number of fresh vegetables, fishballs, meats, noodles, wontons and the like, pop them into the boiling water and, presto—you have a delicious, healthy meal. At MK, all ingredients are incredibly fresh, and the accompanying dipping sauce is sweet and only mildly spicy. MK also has other locations around the city. Visit them on the ground floor at the World Trade Center (☎ **02/255-9728**), the 2nd Floor at Mah Boon Krong shopping mall (☎ **02/217-9246**), or on Sukhumvit Soi 39 (☎ **02/260-1988**).

The Mango Tree. 37 Soi Anumarn Ratchathon. ☎ **02/236-2820.** Reservations recommended. Main courses 90B–350B ($2.35–$9.20). AE, DC, MC, V. Daily 10am–2pm and 6–10pm. Off west end of Surawong Rd., across from Tawana Ramada Hotel. THAI.

Reader John D. Connelly of Chicago brought this excellent classical Thai restaurant to Frommer's attention. A lovely 80-year-old Siamese restaurant house with its own tropical garden, it offers a quiet retreat from the hectic business district. Live traditional music and classical Thai decorative touches fill the house with charm, and the attentive staff serve well-prepared dishes from all regions of the country. Their mild green chicken curry and their crispy spring rolls are both excellent—but the menu is extensive, so feel free to experiment. Only trouble is, the food isn't exactly authentic. Yet although it's been toned down for foreign palates, it's still quite decent.

THE SHOPPING/EMBASSY AREA

EXPENSIVE

The Chinese Restaurant. Grand Hyatt Erawan, 494 Ratchadamri Rd. ☎ **02/254-1234.** Reservations recommended. Main courses 150B–900B ($3.95–$23.70). AE, DC, MC, V. Daily 11:30am–2:30pm and 6:30–11pm. Corner of Ploenchit Rd. CHINESE.

Style and substance are harmoniously blended in this ultra-elegant gourmet Cantonese restaurant. We also recommend their exceptionally light dim sum, including some imaginative vegetable and seafood combinations wrapped in seaweed, instead of the typical rice flour pastry. Their shark's fin, the highlight of any respectable Chinese restaurant, is very good. A delightful gastronomic experience in a high-style Shanghai deco-inspired dining room.

✪ **Genji Restaurant.** Hilton International Bangkok at Nai Lert Park, 2 Wireless Rd. ☎ **02/253-0123.** Reservations recommended; required for a tatami room. Main courses 100B–1,200B ($2.65–$31.60); set dinners 850B–2,000B ($22.35–$52.65). AE, DC, MC, V. Daily noon–2:30pm and 6:30–10:30pm. In Nai Lert Park, north of Ploenchit Rd. JAPANESE.

One of the best Japanese restaurants in Bangkok is located in a great hotel that caters to a large Japanese clientele. If you go to Genji for lunch you'll likely discover a room full of Japanese businesspeople, a good sign for sushi eaters. Lunch served from the set menu is not only delicious but also an excellent value. At dinner there are both set menus and an enormous selection of à la carte dishes, including excellent sushi, sashimi (1,800B/$47.35 for sushi imported from Japan and 350B/$9.20 for the local selections), and *makizushi,* a rich hot-pot concoction, plus a variety of fish and seafood, as well as Kobe beef.

○ Le Banyan. 59 Sukhumvit Soi 8. ☎ **02/253-5556.** Reservations recommended. Main courses 350B–1,500B ($9.20–$39.45). AE, DC, MC, V. Mon–Sat 6–10pm. One block south of Sukhumvit Rd. FRENCH.

In the same league as the top hotel French restaurants, this local favorite serves fine classic French cuisine with Thai touches. A spreading banyan tree on the edge of the gardenlike grounds, on a quiet Sukhumvit soi, inspires the name. Dining rooms are warmly furnished, with sisal matting and white clapboard walls adorned with Thai carvings, old photos, and prints of early Bangkok.

The most popular house special is pressed duck for two: Baked duck is carved and pressed to yield juices that are combined with goose liver, shallots, wine, and Armagnac or calvados to make the sauce. The sliced meat is lightly sautéed, and when bathed in the sauce, creates a sensational dish. Other fine choices include a rack of lamb à la Provençale and salmon with lemongrass. All are served with seasonal vegetables and can be enjoyed with one of their reasonably priced wines. A friendly and capable staff help make this a memorable dining experience.

✪ Ma Maison. In Hilton International Bangkok at Nai Lert Park, 2 Wireless Rd. ☎ **02/253-0123.** Reservations recommended at lunch; required at dinner. Set dinners from 1,000B to 1,700B ($26.30–$44.75); set lunch 490B ($12.90). AE, DC, MC, V. Daily 11:30am–2pm; 6:30–10pm. In Nai Lert Park, north of Ploenchit Rd. CONTINENTAL.

The food is superb, the service attentive and unpretentious, and the pastel and bleached wood decor soothing and gracious. The king and queen, who rarely dine in public except at state ceremonies, have graced the restaurant with their royal presence, as have many other dignitaries. If you're on a budget and want to try Ma Maison, go for the fixed-price lunch, three courses at a very reasonable price.

Though the menu changes occasionally, it remains basically French. You can enjoy a classic, succulent sliced breast of duck with panfried reinette apples or oven-baked rack of lamb with rosemary sauce, among other highly imaginative dishes. For dessert there are several excellent fruit pastries, as well as the usual tempting creamy sweets. A fine wine list rounds out the menu, but be careful: The French varieties, in particular, are very expensive.

The Regent Grill. The Regent, 155 Ratchadamri Rd. ☎ **02/251-6127.** Reservations recommended. Main courses 350B–1,000B ($9.20–$26.30). AE, DC, MC, V. Mon–Fri noon–2:30pm and 6:30–11pm. South of Rama I Rd. CONTINENTAL.

The Regent Grill is a delightfully bright, cheerful space, with an equally colorful menu. Daily specials often combine Thai ingredients with those from Mexico or Italy, lending a certain "California" quality to the Grill's inventive menu. Lunch might include a vegetable salad with a tart coriander dressing, creamy corn bisque with rock lobster, and grilled *plakapong* with caper mayonnaise. Dinner delights include lobster cream soup with lemongrass, angel hair pasta with Thai basil and tomato, and surf and turf (U.S. prime rib with a tiger prawn).

As with almost all first-class Bangkok restaurants, watch out for surprisingly high wine prices—a bottle of average quality runs about 1,000B ($26.30).

MODERATE

Lemongrass. 5/1 Sukhumvit Soi 24. ☎ **02/258-8637.** Reservations highly recommended. Main courses 120B–550B ($3.15–$14.45). AE, DC, MC, V. Daily 11am–2pm and 6–11pm. South of Sukhumvit Rd. on Soi 24. THAI.

Nouvelle Thai cuisine, somewhat tailored to the western tastes of its predominantly expatriate customers, is the specialty of this pleasant restaurant in an old Thai mansion handsomely converted and furnished with antiques. There are occasional complaints about small portions and slow service, but most of the waiters speak some English and will help guide you through the menu, which contains a full spectrum of Thai cuisine, including fiery southern dishes.

Try house favorites pomelo salad or chicken satay. Also excellent is the *tom yang kung* (a spicy sweet-and-sour prawn soup with ginger shoots), and the tender and juicy lemongrass chicken.

Seafood Market & Restaurant. 89 Sukhumvit Soi 24 (Soi Kasame). ☎ **02/261-2071.** Reservations suggested for weekend dinner. Market prices, see below. Daily 11:30am–midnight. AE, DC, JCB, MC, V. SEAFOOD.

Chances are you've never had a dining experience like this before, and if you're a seafood fan, you'll love it. After you've been seated, look over the list of preparation styles, then walk to the back and take a shopping cart. Peruse the no fewer than 40 different creatures of the sea, either live or on ice, all priced by the kilo. Pay for it all at the cashier, then cart it back to the table. Waiters are skilled at making perfect suggestions for your catch, and what comes out of the kitchen is divine. I had the most tender squid broiled in butter and the meatiest grouper I've ever imagined, deep-fried with chiles. Cooking charges and corkage are paid separately at the end of the meal. The seafood is market price, the fish ranging from 195B to 625B ($5.15 to $16.45) per kilo, with imported Alaskan king crab weighing in at a high 1,800B per/kilo ($47.35) and cuttlefish at only 245B per kilo ($6.45). Cooking charges range from 60B to 120B ($1.60 to $3.15).

Spasso. Grand Hyatt Erawan, 494 Ratchadamri Rd. ☎ **02/254-1234.** Reservations recommended for dinner. Main courses 220B–600B ($5.80–$15.80). AE, DC, MC, V. Daily noon–2:30am (kitchen closes 10:30pm). Corner of Ploenchit Rd. ITALIAN.

Spasso is as well known as a nightlife spot as it is for Italian cuisine. A hip and classy place, the bar is mobbed and there's a jovial crowd waiting outside to get inside this arty modern trattoria with fabulous decor. The food is a treat, from an authentic caponata (eggplant salad served with goat cheese) or minestrone, followed by the gnocchi with pesto sauce or the Thai-style fusilli with chiles and shrimp. Thin-crust pizza fans will find a dozen combos, all made with fresh ingredients and baked in a brick oven. Local bands start at around 9:30pm, and the dancing makes it hard to concentrate on food.

✪ **Spice Market.** The Regent, 155 Ratchadamri Rd. ☎ **02/251-6127.** Reservations recommended. Main courses 150B–600B ($3.95–$15.80) (set menus 690B–960B/ $18.15–$25.25). AE, DC, MC, V. Daily 11:30am–2:30pm and 6–11pm. South of Rama I Rd. THAI.

Many contend that the Spice Market is the city's finest pure Thai restaurant. The theatrical decor reflects the name: burlap spice sacks, ceramic pots, and glass jars set in dark-wood cabinets around the dining area playfully re-create the mercantile feel of a traditional Thai shop house. The food is artfully presented, authentically spiced, and extraordinarily delicious, with featured regional specialties for a great way to sample dishes from places you may or may not be traveling to in the kingdom. House specialties include *nam prik ong*, crispy rice cakes with minced pork dip; *nua phad bai kapraow,* fried beef with chile and fresh basil; and *siew ngap*, red curry with roasted duck in coconut milk. The menu's "chile rating" guarantees that spices are tempered to your palate.

Tan Dinh. Ruam Rudee Village, 20/6–7 Soi Ruam Rudee, Ploenchit Rd. ☎ **02/650-8986.** Reservations not necessary. Main courses 150B–250B ($3.95–$6.60). AE, DC, MC, V. Daily 11am–2:30pm and 6pm–11pm. One block south of Ploenchit Rd. VIETNAMESE.

Street Food—Caveat Emptor

Lovers of traditional street food should note that on almost every corner in Bangkok, you'll find a food stand serving simple and inexpensive fare. You must be careful of what you eat and make your own judgment about the freshness of the food and the hygiene of the stand. Check over all ingredients carefully for freshness—everything from cooking oils to meats—and watch them prepare the dish in front of you. Noodle soups, stir-fry, and satay generally tend to be fine in terms of hygiene. And lunchtime is the best time to try these hawker stalls—food hasn't had a chance to sit out all day in the heat. Some things not to eat: anything raw (including vegetables), anything that looks undercooked, or drinks with ice (most places buy ice made from bottled water, only to drag the ice bags along the filthy sidewalks!).

Other notes: Look for the snack stands that sell all sorts of fried insects. Grasshoppers, beetles (that look like cockroaches), scorpions, ants, and grubs are a favorite snack for the Isan people who come from the northeast to work in Bangkok. Although I'll eat pretty much anything, so I can comment on a wide range of local cuisine, I had to draw a line at the bugs. But a dear friend assured me they taste just like chicken. If you do go for this or any other "street snack," a note on etiquette—Thais don't walk down the street munching away, but will sit to eat or take away to some other location.

While foreigners have been known to come down with diarrhea after eating Thai food, if symptoms persist more than 24 hours or become painful, have yourself checked out for bacterial or viral infection from food or water contamination.

Contemporary and comfortable with a friendly and helpful staff, Tan Dinh is a great choice for Vietnamese. The appetizers could be main dishes themselves—spring rolls either steamed or fried, and (my favorite) a sumptuous duck ravioli. For entrees you can go for light shrimp wrapped around sugar cane or the heartier leg of lamb skewers. Be careful when ordering, however. For two or three people the dishes are just right, but for larger groups, they'll double each plate you order—so your eyes may pop out when you get the bill. Be sure to go over your order well with the waiter! Wines and mixed drinks are also available.

INEXPENSIVE

Cabbages & Condoms. 10 Sukhumvit Soi 12. ☎ **02/229-4610.** Reservations recommended. 70B–200B ($1.85–$5.25). Daily 11am–10pm. AE, DC, MC, V. THAI.

Here's a theme restaurant with a purpose. Opened by local hero Mechai Viravaidya, founder of the Population & Community Development Association, the restaurant helps fund population control, AIDS awareness, and a host of rural development programs. Set in a large compound, the two-story restaurant has air-conditioned indoor dining—but if you sit on the garden terrace, you're in a fairy land of twinkling lights in romantic greenery. The house recommends the *sam lee dad deao*, which is a huge deep-fried cotton fish with chile and mango on the side. Another great dish is the *kai hor bai teoy*, fried boneless chicken wrapped in pandan leaves with a dark sweet soy sauce for dipping. There's also a large selection of vegetable and bean curd entrees.

Before you leave, be sure to check out the gift shop's whimsical condom-related merchandise. The restaurant apologizes for not providing after-dinner mints, but feel free to help yourself to a free condom instead.

✪ **Le Dalat.** 14 Sukhumvit Soi 23. ☎ **02/661-7967.** Reservations recommended at dinner. Main courses 130B–180B ($3.40–$4.75). AE, MC, V. Daily 11:30am–2:30pm and 6–10pm. Just north of Sukhumvit Rd. VIETNAMESE/FRENCH.

Le Dalat's fine food and lovely garden setting make for a charming evening. The restaurant is casual and understatedly elegant, housed in an old Thai house done up in Vietnamese and Chinese antiques. The excellent food is prepared by Vietnamese-trained Thai chefs. Go for the *bi guon* (spring rolls with herbs and pork), *chao tom* (pounded shrimp laced on ground sugarcane in a basket of fresh noodles), and *cha ra* (fresh fillet of grilled fish). In nice weather, you'll enjoy dining in the gracefully land-scaped outdoor garden. A very highly recommended restaurant.

Suda Restaurant. 6-6/1 Soi 14, Sukhumvit Rd. ☎ **02/252-2597.** Main courses 40B–180B ($1.05–$4.75). No credit cards. Daily 11am–midnight. One block south of Sukhumvit Rd. THAI.

This is one of those basic restaurants where good food makes up for a lack of style. The plain open-air, high-ceilinged room with overhead fans cooling the local crowd (mostly Thais and expatriates) spills out onto the sidewalk. The food is good, solid, well-prepared Thai cuisine with Chinese overtones. Recommended dishes include the *tom yam kai* (coconut-milk soup with chicken), grilled yellowfin tuna with cashew nuts and roasted curry paste, fried squid with vegetables over rice, and the fried fish with three-flavor sauce. Cheap and good.

CHINATOWN

There are few, if any, large Chinese restaurants in the Chinatown area other than in the hotels. Locals eat at small food stalls or tiny hole-in-the-wall eateries.

INEXPENSIVE

About Café. 402–8 Matreejit Rd., Pomprab (near the railway station). ☎ **02/623-1742.** Reservations not necessary. Main courses 60B–120B ($1.60–$3.15). No credit cards. Open Mon–Sat 7pm–midnight. VEGETARIAN.

About Café is not exactly a restaurant, per se. While they do have some fine vegetarian dishes and assorted herbal teas, most come for the atmosphere. About Café and About Gallery is especially loved for its contribution to the local contemporary arts scene. As one of the first cutting-edge galleries in town, it's really become quite a hangout—and comes highly recommended for anyone who likes to learn about other cultures through the arts they produce. Check out local papers and *Metro Magazine* for special exhibits and performances.

Hai Hua Tian Restaurant. 113 Songsawat Rd. ☎ **02/222-3029.** Reservations not necessary. Main courses 70B–150B ($1.85–$3.95). No credit cards. Daily 11am–11pm. CHINESE.

For a simple Chinatown restaurant, Hai Hua Tian is basic but good. Best known for shark's fin dishes, the menu has a large assortment of other well-prepared dishes like crab claws in curry pastes (which is particularly tasty), plus other fish and fowl spe-cialties. Be prepared to trek through the kitchen to reach the dining room just behind.

Lao Tang Han Paloh. 467/1 Yaowarat Rd. No phone. Main courses 50B–300B ($1.30–$7.90). No credit cards. Daily 9am–2pm. Opposite China Town Hotel. CHINESE.

Here's one of those stalls with the obligatory Peking Duck hanging in the window, but what brings people here is the goose—stewed in red soy sauce, it's tender and juicy even more so than duck. At about 300B ($7.90) for half a bird, you can also order accompanying innards and clear soup, served with a variety of sauces for dipping and flavor. Lunchtime gets packed, both outside in the coffee shop area and behind in the air-conditioned dining room. A very special place in Chinatown for authentic delicacies.

DINNER WITH THAI DANCE

Sala Rim Naan. On the Thonburi side of the Chao Phraya River, opposite the Oriental Hotel. ☎ 02/437-6211. Reservations required. Buffet lunch 400B ($10.55); fixed-price dinner 1,100B ($28.95) adult, 900B ($23.70) children. AE, MC, V. Daily noon–2pm; dinner 7pm, performance 8:30pm. Take the free shuttle boat from the Oriental Hotel pier. THAI.

As you would expect from the Oriental, this Thai restaurant is one of Bangkok's special places. Guests sit on pillows at low tables in the glittering, bronze-trimmed, teak and marble main hall, and dine on finely crafted Thai dishes. (Readers occasionally complain about the food, but everyone loves the ambience.) In the evening, classical dancers from Bangkok's Department of Fine Arts perform a 1-hour show of royal dances of the Sukhothai and Ayutthaya periods, as well as various folk dances.

Lunch is served buffet-style, with no dance performance, while dinner is a full-service affair. You can take the free shuttle from the dock behind the Authors' Wing of the Oriental Hotel, or ferry pick-ups can be arranged from other hotels. Check with your concierge.

DINNER & LUNCH CRUISES ON THE CHAO PHRAYA

While there are a number of tour operators who offer dinner cruises along the Chao Phraya, if you want to eat decent food I only have one solid recommendation. The *Manohra,* a reconverted antique rice barge, cruises the river nightly serving a six course Thai dinner that's delicious (and not overly spicy). The quality of the food is excellent, especially considering most other dinner cruises serve lukewarm indescribables. The set menu is 900B ($23.70) per person, and *Manohra* sets sail at 7:30pm (but you can pick it up at the Oriental pier, where it stops at about 7:40pm). Be sure to book in advance to make sure the boat isn't rented out for a private party. Call the Marriott Royal Garden Riverside Hotel (☎ 02/476-0021).

Another fine choice is the *Oriental Queen,* which runs up and down the river each day. The lunch cruise to Ayutthaya is great—you can see a lot more during the day than you would during a dinner cruise. Managed by The Oriental, you can definitely expect the finest of everything; however, the Oriental Queen is a modern air-conditioned luxury cruiser, so it lacks a little of the romantic atmosphere of the rice-barge. Call The Oriental (☎ 02/236-0400, ext. 3133) for bookings. The lunch buffet costs 1,900B ($50) per adult and 1,500B ($39.45) per child.

What to See & Do in Bangkok

5

If the sights and smells of Bangkok's crazy city streets haven't started your heart racing, the sheer multitude of wonders in the Big Mango will surely perplex. How will you possibly begin to see everything you want to see and take in all the amazing experiences you want to have? To be honest, you could spend weeks here and still feel like you've only scratched the surface. In this chapter, I've presented the best and most exciting attractions in the city, so you won't feel like you've missed out on anything. To help you plan, we've divided this chapter into the following subcategories. **Bangkok's Waterways** gives you the ins and outs of the city's waterways, and the pleasures of traveling along the canals. **Bangkok's Historical Treasures** covers magnificent palaces, rich antique homes, and fascinating museums packed with the nation's treasures. Bangkok's endless supply of gorgeous religious complexes are laid out in **The Wats,** followed by a couple of **Bangkok Walking Tours,** which will help you navigate through some interesting streets while taking in the city's sights. **Cultural Pursuits** lets you in on unique cultural experiences like Thai boxing, traditional massage, kite flying, cock fighting and other unusual activities. **Staying Active** is for sports people—both participants and observers—who'd like a little relaxation and fun during their stay. Sport-shoppers will be in heaven after reading the low-down on the scene in **Shopping,** and **Bangkok After Dark** will give you all the details of evening arts and cultural performances, the nightclub scene and the city's risqué counterculture. The end of the chapter explains the many day trips from the capital.

1 Bangkok's Waterways

The history of Bangkok was written on its waterways, which until recent years were the essential focus of the city's life. When the 18th-century capital was moved from Ayutthaya to Thonburi, and then across the river to Bangkok, King Rama I built a canal (now called Klong Ong Ang and Klong Banglamphu), which created Ratanakosin Island out of the large bend in the river, to strengthen the defensive position of the Grand Palace. Other canals (klongs) were added, which became the boulevards and avenues of the city. Boats were the primary means of transportation, with horse-drawn travel reserved for royalty.

As Ayutthaya was before it, Bangkok came to be known as the "Venice of the East," but sadly, many of these klongs have been paved

Bangkok Attractions

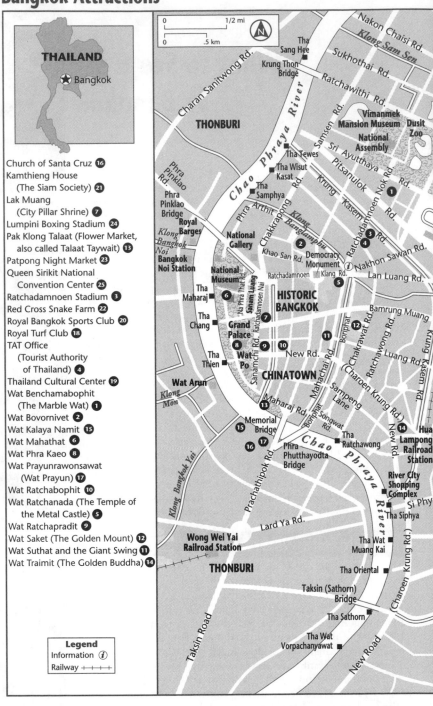

Legend
Information (i)
Railway ++++

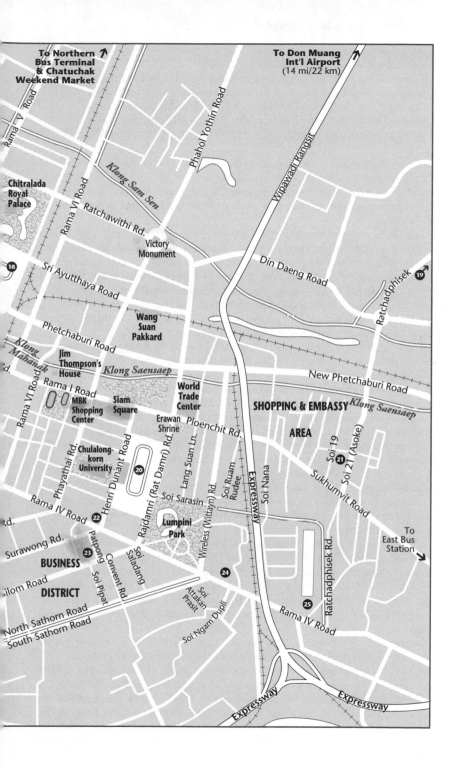

Bangkok's Must-See Sights

If you have a limited amount of time in Bangkok, there are some major attractions where you should concentrate your attentions first. The Grand Palace, Wat Phra Kaeo, Wat Po, The National Museum, and Wat Arun are the main points to hit. If you can fit these into your agenda, you've seen the major highlights.

over in the last decade or so. The magnificent **Chao Phraya River** ("the River of Kings"), however, continues to cut through the heart of the city, separating the early capital of Thonburi from today's Bangkok. On the Thonburi side, the klongs still branch off into a network of arteries that are relatively unchanged as the centers of neighborhood life.

Boats of all sizes and shapes ply the Chao Phraya River day and night. Ferries run up, down, and across the river, carrying commuters to work, kids to school, and saffron-robed monks to temple. Strangely elegant rice barges pull mountains of rice, gravel, sand, lumber, vegetables, and the countless families who make them their homes. The **Royal Barges**—long, graceful, gilt crafts—usually seen on display in museums only, make appearances en parade once or twice each month to celebrate the arrival of visiting dignitaries or other special events. Call the TAT (☎ **1155**), to see if any upcoming dates coincide with your stay. They're splendid.

The strangest, most frequently seen boat on the river is the *hang yao,* or long-tailed water taxi, a long, thin, graceful vessel, powered by an automobile engine connected by a long, exposed shaft (tail) to the propeller. The exposed engine is balanced on a fulcrum mount, and muscular boatmen move the entire motor and shaft assembly to steer the boat—an amazing feat of strength and balance, especially at 30 knots. These water taxis carry passengers throughout the maze of klongs and are vital in transporting fresh food from upriver farms and fresh fish from coastal villages to Bangkok.

For an intimate glimpse of traditional Thai life, schedule a few hours to explore the waterways. You'll see people using the river to bathe, wash their clothes, and even brush their teeth at water's edge (a practice not recommended to tourists). Floating kitchens in sampans serve rice and noodles to customers in other boats. Men dance across carpets of logs floating to lumber mills. Wooden houses on stilts spread back from the banks of the river and klongs, each with its own spirit house perfumed with incense and decked out with flowers and other offerings.

There are several approaches to tour the klongs. Both **Sea Tours,** suite no. 88–92, 8th floor, Payathai Plaza Rajthavee (☎ **02/216-5783**), and **World Travel,** 1053 Charoen Krung (New Road) (☎ **02/5900**), offer standard group tours: The basic canal tour is organized around a so-called "Floating Market" in Thonburi, but it has become very touristy and crowded (the trip lasts from 8:30am to noon, and costs about 800B/$21.05). Instead, take either a rice barge cruise or another type of canal tour.

Better yet, charter a long-tail *hang yao* for about 300B ($7.90) an hour—expect to negotiate the price, and be sure to agree on the charge *before* you get in the boat. You'll find boats for hire at the Tha Chang ferry pier near Wat Phra Kaeo, the pier at River City Shopping Complex, or you can organize it through your hotel concierge. Beware of independent boat operators who offer to take you to the nearby Thonburi Floating Market or to souvenir or gem shops. Take your time and explore Klong Bangkok Noi and Klong Bangkok Yai, with a stop at the Royal Barges Museum on the way back (see "Bangkok's Historical Treasures" in the next section for information on the Royal Barges Museum).

A more leisurely way to see the klongs is to travel on the local long-tail taxis that depart from almost every Chao Phraya Express Boat pier. Try the Ratchawong (also spelled Rajawongse) Pier in Chinatown, where you can climb into any long-tail boat that is filling up and ride up Klong Bangkok Yai, across the river in Thonburi. The fare is a paltry 5B (13¢) and you can ride until you want to turn back, then get off and catch the next boat back.

If you've got the time, take a day to visit the more authentic floating market at Damnoen Saduak, about 80km (48 miles) southwest of Bangkok in Ratchaburi Province (see "Side Trips from Bangkok," below.)

2 Bangkok's Historical Treasures

The intertwining of Thailand's many cultural influences manifests itself in everything from the architectural splendor of ornate palaces and temples to the delicate lines of ancient arts. Indian, Khmer, Chinese, European, and Thai histories collide in the design of the Grand Palace, Wat Phra Kaeo, and Wat Po, as well as the unbelievable collection of priceless items on display at the National Museum. Jim Thompson's House, filled with grand antiques and objets d'art, offers a peek into the life of one of Thailand's most famous expatriate entrepreneurs.

✪ **The Grand Palace.** Near the river on Na Phra Lan Rd. near Sanam Luang. ☎ **02/222-0094.** Admission 125B ($3.30). Price includes Wat Phra Kaeo and the Coin Pavilion inside the Grand Palace grounds, as well as admission to the Vimanmek Palace (near the National Assembly). Daily 8:30am–11:30am and 1–3:30pm; most individual buildings are closed to the public except on special days proclaimed by the king. Take the Chao Phraya Express Boat to the Tha Chang Pier, then walk east and south.

One of King Rama I's earliest accomplishments was to move the capital from Thonburi to a more defensible site on the opposite bank of the Chao Phraya. He chose the center of the Chinese community, which was then moved south to Sampeng, the current Chinatown. He intended to reproduce the destroyed capital of Ayutthaya. The construction of the Grand Palace and Wat Phra Kaeo were the first phase of his grand goal, though both were added to and rebuilt in subsequent reigns.

The palace as it appears today was greatly influenced by Western architecture, including colonial and Victorian motifs. Anna—tutor to the son of Rama IV and the central figure in the story *The King and I*—lived here. The royal family moved to Chitralada Palace after the death of King Ananda in 1946, but it was here, in 1981, that General Chitpatima attempted to overthrow the government in an unsuccessful coup.

As you enter the palace gate, built in the 1780s, you'll see the **Pavilion for Holy Water,** where priests swore loyalty to the royal family and purified themselves with water from Thailand's four main rivers. Nearby is a lacquered-wood structure called the **Arporn Phimok Prasad (Disrobing Pavilion),** built so the king could conveniently mount his palanquin for royal elephant precessions. (Most of the time it served as a kind of elephant parking lot.)

Also nearby is the Chakri Maha Prasad, designed by Western architects as a royal residence for Rama IV to commemorate the centennial of the Chakri dynasty. The king's advisors urged him to use Thai motifs to demonstrate his independence from growing Western influence: The Thai, temple-style roof rests physically and symbolically on top of an imperial Victorian building. This Thai-Victorian building contains the ashes of royal family members on the third floor, the throne room and reception hall on the main floor, and a collection of weapons on the ground floor.

The whitewashed stone building nearby now serves as the **Funeral Hall,** though it was originally the residence of Rama I and Rama II. The corpse of a deceased royal figure is kept in this building for a year before it is cremated in a nearby field. On each of the four corners of the roof is a **garuda** (the half-human, half-bird "steed" of Rama, an avatar of the Hindu god Vishnu), symbolizing the king, who is considered a reincarnation of Rama. The palace garden was rebuilt under Rama IV in the 1860s, and the highlight here is a section that reproduces the landscape of a Thai mountain-and-woods fable. This structure was used as a ceremonial place for Thai princes to cut their topknot in a coming-of-age ritual.

The Grand Palace also has a harem, the **Forbidden Quarters** (no one other than the king was allowed to enter), where the king's wives lived (King Bhumibol Adulyadej ended the age-old tradition of polygamy and has only one wife, Queen Sirikit). Close by is the **Amarin Vinichai Prasad,** or Coronation Hall, built by Rama I and added to by subsequent kings. Today this building is used, like the palace in general, for royal coronations, weddings, and state events only, and it is here that the king makes his grandest appearances.

✪ **Wat Phra Kaeo.** In the Grand Palace complex. ☎ **02/222-0094.** Admission included in the Grand Palace fee, 125B ($3.30). Daily 8:30–11:30am and 1–3:30pm. Take the Chao Phraya Express Boat to Tha Chang Pier, then walk east and south.

The Wat Phra Kaeo ("Temple of the Holy Jewel Image"), or as it is commonly known, the Temple of the Emerald Buddha, is the royal chapel and probably the shrine most revered by the Thai people. It sits within the grounds of the Grand Palace, surrounded by walls more than a mile long, and contains some of the finest examples of Buddhist sculpture, architecture, painting, and decorative craft in the country.

Central to the wat is the **Emerald Buddha** itself, a rather small, dark statue, a little more than 2 feet high, made of green jasper or perhaps jadeite ("emerald" in Thai refers to intense green color, not the specific stone) that sits atop a huge gold altar. Legend says it came from Sri Lanka, but most art historians believe that it was sculpted in the 14th century in northern Thailand, as it is in the Chiang Saen (Lanna Thai) style. (Part of its mystery arises because no one is allowed near it, save the king.) This much venerated image is said to have once been covered with plaster and gold leaf and kept inside a *chedi* (stupas or mounds) in Chiang Rai. After the monument was damaged in a storm in 1434, the image needed to be moved to another location. As it was being transported, it was dropped and the plaster broke away. The reigning king of Chiang Mai, at the time the most powerful state in the north, tried to bring the Buddha to his city, but on three separate occasions the elephant that was to transport the statue stopped at the same spot at a crossroads in Lampang. Not one to offend the spirit of the Buddha, the king built a monumental wat at that spot in Lampang, where it remained for 32 years.

A more determined monarch, King Tiloka, insisted that the Emerald Buddha be brought to Chiang Mai, where it was housed in the Wat Chedi Luang until 1552, when Laotian invaders took the image back to Luang Prabang. Twelve years later, the statue was moved again, this time to Vientiane, Laos, where it stayed for 214 years, until General Chakri (later King Rama I) brought it back to the capital at Thonburi

---

Impressions

The royal Wat is not a wat but a city of wats; ... there are structures made of tiles and encrusted with strange tile flowers ... and small ones, rows of them, that look like the prizes in a shooting gallery at a village fair in the country of the gods.
—Somerset Maugham, *The Gentleman in the Parlour,* 1930

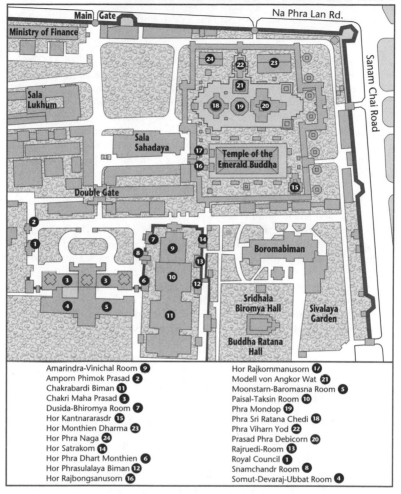

The Grand Palace & Wat Phra Kaeo

Main Gate

Na Phra Lan Rd.

Ministry of Finance

Sanam Chai Road

Sala Lukhum

Sala Sahadaya

24
22
23
21
18 19 20

Temple of the Emerald Buddha

17
16

15

Double Gate

2
1
7
14
8
9
13
3 3
6
10
12
4 5
11

Boromabiman

Sridhala Biromya Hall

Sivalaya Garden

Buddha Ratana Hall

Amarindra-Vinichal Room 9	Hor Rajkornmanusorn 17
Amporn Phimok Prasad 2	Modell von Angkor Wat 21
Chakrabardi Biman 11	Moonstarn-Baromasna Room 5
Chakri Maha Prasad 3	Paisal-Taksin Room 10
Dusida-Bhiromya Room 7	Phra Mondop 19
Hor Kantnararasdr 15	Phra Sri Ratana Chedi 18
Hor Monthien Dharma 23	Phra Viharn Yod 22
Hor Phra Naga 24	Prasad Phra Debicorn 20
Hor Satrakom 14	Rajruedi-Room 13
Hor Phra Dhart Monthien 6	Royal Council 1
Hor Phrasulalaya Biman 12	Snamchandr Room 8
Hor Rajbongsanusorn 16	Somut-Devaraj-Ubbat Room 4

after his successful campaign in Laos. In 1784, when he moved the capital across the river to Bangkok, Rama I installed the precious figure in its present shrine, where it has remained, a tangible symbol of the Thai nation. It's feared that removal of the image from Bangkok will signify the end of the Chakri dynasty.

The Buddha, like many others in Thailand, is covered in a seasonal cloak, changed three times a year to correspond to the summer, winter, and rainy months. The changing of the robes is an important ritual, performed by the king, who also sprinkles water over the monks and well-wishers to bring good fortune during the upcoming season.

The Emerald Buddha is housed in an equally magnificent *bot* (the central shrine in a Buddhist temple), used by monks for important religious rituals. The interior walls are decorated with late Ayutthaya-style murals depicting the life of the Buddha, steps to enlightenment, and the Buddhist cosmology of the Worlds of Desire, Being, and Illusion. The cycle begins with the birth of the Buddha, which can be seen in the middle of the left wall as you enter the sanctuary, and the story continues counterclockwise. Also note the exquisite inlaid mother-of-pearl work on the door panels.

The surrounding portico of the bot is an example of masterful Thai craftsmanship. On the perimeter are 12 open pavilions, built during the reign of Rama I. The inside walls of the compound are decorated with murals depicting the entire *Ramakien,* the Thai national epic, painted during the reign of Rama I and last restored in 1982, in 178 scenes beginning at the north gate and continuing clockwise.

Subsequent kings built more monuments and restored or embellished existing structures. Among the most interesting of these are the three pagodas to the immediate north of the *ubosoth,* representing the changing centers of Buddhist influence: The first, to the west, is **Phra Si Ratana Chedi,** a 19th-century Sri Lankan–style stupa housing ashes of the Buddha; second, in the middle is the library, or **Phra Mondop,** built in Thai style by Rama I, known for its excellently crafted Ayutthaya-style mother-of-pearl doors, bookcases containing the *Tripitaka* (sacred Buddhist manuscripts), human- and dragon-headed *nagas* (snakes), and statues of Chakri kings; and third, to the east, is the **Royal Pantheon,** built in Khmer style during the 19th century—it's open to the public in October for 1 day to commemorate the founding of the Chakri dynasty. To the immediate north of the library is a model of Angkor Wat, the most sacred of all Cambodian shrines, the model constructed by King Mongkut as a reminder that the neighboring state was under the dominion of Thailand. To the west of the bot, near the entry gate, is a black stone statue of a hermit, considered a patron of medicine, before which relatives of the ill and infirm pay homage and make offerings of joss sticks, fruit, flowers, and candles.

Scattered around the complex are statues of elephants, thought to represent independence and power. Thai kings went to battle atop elephants, and it is customary for parents to walk their children around an elephant three times to bring them strength. You can rub the head of an elephant statue for good luck, and notice how smooth it is from the touch of millions.

✪ **The National Museum.** Na Phra That Rd. ☎ **02/224-1333.** Admission 20B (55¢). Wed–Sun 9am–4pm. Free English-language tours: Buddhism culture, Wed 9:30am; art, culture, religion, Thurs 9:30am; call the museum or check a newspaper for more details and current schedule. About a half mile north of the Grand Palace.

The National Museum, a short (15-minute) walk north of the Grand Palace and the Temple of the Emerald Buddha, is the country's central treasury of art and archaeology (32 branches are located throughout the provinces). Some of the buildings are themselves works of art.

The current museum—the largest in Southeast Asia—was built as part of the Grand Palace complex when the capital of Siam was moved from Thonburi to Bangkok in 1782. Originally the palace of Rama I's brother, the deputy king and appointed successor, it was called the Wang Na ("Palace at the Front"). The position of princely successor was eventually abolished, and Rama V had the palace converted into a museum in 1884. Thammasat University, the College of Dramatic Arts, and the National Theater were also built on the royal grounds, along with additional museum buildings.

To see the entire collection (highly recommended), plan to spend at least 3 hours, starting with the **Thai History and the Prehistoric Galleries** in the first building. If you're rushed, go straight to the **Red House** behind it, a traditional 18th-century Thai building that was originally the living quarters of Princess Sri Sudarak, sister of King Rama I. It's furnished in period style, with many pieces originally owned by the princess.

Another essential stop is the **Phuttaisawan (Buddhaisawan) Chapel,** built in 1787 to house the Phra Phut Sihing, one of Thailand's most revered Buddha images, brought here from its original home in Chiang Mai. The chapel an exquisite example of Buddhist temple architecture.

From the chapel, work your way back through the main building of the royal palace to see the gold jewelry, some from the royal collections, and the Thai ceramics, including many pieces in the five-color bencharong style. The **Old Transportation Room** contains ivory carvings, elephant chairs, and royal palanquins. There are also rooms of royal emblems and insignia, stone carvings, wood carvings, costumes, textiles, musical instruments, and Buddhist religious artifacts.

Fine art and sculpture are found in the newer galleries at the rear of the museum compound. Gallery after gallery is filled with both Thai and pre-Thai sculpture (including some excellent Mon work) and Hindu and Buddhist images from the provinces.

The Royal Barges. On Klong Bangkok Noi, north of the Phra Pinklao Bridge, Thonburi. ☎ **02/424-0004.** Admission 30B (80¢) adults, children free. Daily 8:30am–5pm. Take a taxi over the Phra Pinklao Bridge or take a ferry to Tha Rot Fai ("Railway Landing"), walk west along the street parallel to and between the tracks and the klong until you come to a bridge over the klong, cross the bridge and follow the wooden walkway.

If you've hired a long-tail boat on the Chao Phraya, stop by this unique museum housing the royal barges. These elaborately decorated sailing vessels, the largest over 50 yards long and rowed by up to 60 men, are used by the royal family on state occasions or for high religious ceremonies. The king's barge, the *Suphanahong,* is decorated with red-and-gold carvings of fearsome mythological beasts, like the Garuda or the dragon on the bow and stern. (If you can't make it to the royal barges, there is a smaller display of barges at the National Museum, near Wat Phra Kaeo.)

Wang Suan Pakkard. 352 Si Ayutthaya Rd. ☎ **02/245-4934.** Admission 80B ($2.10) adults, 50B ($1.30) children, including material for a self-guided tour of grounds and collections. Open daily 9am–4pm. Between Phyathai and Ratchaprarop rds.

Wang Suan Pakkard ("Palace of the Lettuce Garden") is one of Bangkok's most delightful retreats. This peaceful oasis was the home of Princess Chumbhot of Nakhon Sawan. Five 19th-century teak houses were moved from Chiang Mai in 1952 and rebuilt in a beautifully landscaped garden on a private klong, separated by a high wall from the tumult of Bangkok's streets. The **Lacquer Pavilion** (actually an Ayutthaya house, moved here in 1958) was a birthday present from the prince to the princess.

Princess Chumbnot was an avid art collector and one of the country's most dedicated archaeologists—credited with having partly financed the excavations at Ban Chiang I in 1967. There is an entire room of objects from that site, including pottery and jewelry, surpassed only by the prehistoric findings exhibited at the National Museum. The balance of the collection is diverse, with Khmer sculpture, ivory boxes, perfume bottles, nielloware, marvelous prints by European artists depicting their image of Siamese people before the country opened to the Western world, a superb Buddha head from Ayutthaya, and a royal barge. Be sure to ask to see the pavilion housing the princess's collection of Thai and Chinese ceramics—it's exquisite.

The gift shop at Wang Suan Pakkard offers ceramics, some genuine and some reproductions, and prices are quite reasonable.

Vimanmek Mansion Museum. 193/2 Ratchavitee Rd., Dusit Palace grounds. ☎ **02/ 281-8166.** Admission 50B ($1.30); free if you already have a 125B ticket to the Grand Palace and Wat Phra Kaeo. Daily 9:30am–4pm. Opposite the Dusit Zoo, north of the National Assembly Building.

Built in 1901 by King Chulalongkorn the Great (Rama V) as the Celestial Residence, this large, beautiful, golden teakwood mansion was restored in 1982 for Bangkok's bicentennial and reopened by Queen Sirikit as a private museum with a collection of the royal family's memorabilia. An intriguing and informative hour-long tour takes you through a series of apartments and rooms (81 in all) in what is said to be the largest teak building in the world— the thought of all that gorgeous teakwood employed is staggering. The original Abhisek Dusit Throne Hall houses a display of Thai handicrafts, and nine other buildings north of the mansion display photographs, clocks, fabrics, royal carriages, and other regalia. Classical Thai dance, folk dance, and martial art demonstrations are given daily at 10:30am and 2pm.

Kamthieng House (The Siam Society). 131 Soi Asoke. ☎ **02/661-6470.** Admission 100B ($2.65) adults, 50B ($1.30) children. Tues–Sat 9am–noon and 1–5pm. North of Sukhumvit on Soi 21.

The 19th-century Kamthieng House, on the grounds of the Siam Society Headquarters, is a rice farmer's teak house transplanted from the banks of Chiang Mai's Ping River. Its collection, organized with financial help from the Asia and Rockefeller foundations, is oriented toward ethnographic objects illustrating the culture of everyday life.

Many agricultural and domestic items, including woven fish baskets and terra-cotta pots, are on display, but we were drawn most to the exhibit about the Chao Vieng, or city dwellers from the northern Lanna Thai Kingdom. If you plan to trek through that area, you will particularly enjoy this small but informative collection. We also enjoyed walking through the grounds, which are landscaped like a northern Thai garden.

The Siam Society also supports an excellent library and gallery, with information on nearly every aspect of Thai society, concentrating on regional culture. They also publish scholarly texts on Thai culture, which can be purchased.

Jim Thompson's House. Soi Kasemsan 2. ☎ **02/215-0122.** Admission 100B ($2.65). Mon–Sat 9am–5pm. On a small soi off Rama I Rd., opposite the National Stadium.

Jim Thompson was a New York architect who served in the OSS (Office of Strategic Services, now the CIA) in Thailand during World War II and afterward settled in Bangkok. Almost single-handedly he revived Thailand's silk industry, employing Thai Muslims as skilled silk weavers and building up a thriving industry. After expanding his sales to international markets, Mr. Thompson mysteriously disappeared in 1967 while vacationing in the Cameron Highlands of Malaysia. Despite extensive investigations, his disappearance has never been resolved. (The most recent theory, for which some evidence apparently exists, is that he was accidentally struck by a truck and his body hidden to prevent repercussions.)

Thompson's legacy is substantial, as both an entrepreneur and a collector, and his Thai house contains a splendid collection of Khmer sculpture, Chinese porcelain, Burmese carving (especially a 17th-century teak Buddha), and antique Thai scroll paintings.

Thompson's training as an architect paid off handsomely, if his house is any measure of his skill. It's composed of six linked teak and theng (harder than teak) wood houses from central Thailand that were rebuilt according to Thai architectural principles, but with Western additions (such as a staircase and window screens). In some rooms the floor is made of Italian marble, but the wall panels are pegged teak. The house slopes toward the center to help stabilize the structure (the original houses were built on stilts without foundations). The busy nearby Klong San Sap and landscaped garden make a lovely spot, especially on a hot day.

You can buy silk from the Jim Thompson Company retail shop at the intersection of Surawong and Rama IV roads (see "Shopping," below).

3 The Wats

There are so many temples in Bangkok, each one unique and inspiring in its own architecture, history, and spiritual importance. If you can only see a few, check out the ones with stars—these are the most revered and culturally significant (Wat Phra Kaeo is listed in the above section due to its location within the Grand Palace Compound). Unless otherwise stated, the best times to visit temples is in the early morning. The air is cool, monks busy themselves with morning activities, and the complexes are generally less crowded. Monks awake between 4am and 6am and eat breakfast by 7am, after which all are welcome to come for a visit.

During the morning hours, feel free to make a contribution to the sangha, the monkhood. Thais make regular offerings to monasteries as an act of merit-making. Supporting the monkhood brings one closer to Buddhist ideals, and increases the likelihood of a better life beyond this one. Many shops near temples sell saffron-colored pails filled with everyday supplies such as toothbrushes, soap, and other common necessities (starting at 150B/$3.95). Pick one up to bring to the temple, ask to see the abbot, and present him with your gift. Women should take care to place the gift on the saffron cloth he lays before him (never make physical contact with him). Put a small monetary contribution (about 100B/$2.65 is fine, but the amount is really up to you), and place it on top of the pail. You will be blessed with a sprinkle of jasmine water and prayers. Follow the actions of those around you. Wai (bow with your hands together) deeply, with your hands pressed together at forehead level (a show of great respect), and do not expect the abbot to wai in return—monks do not participate in this ritual. Also, do not expect him to say thank-you—it is you who must thank him for giving you the opportunity to make merit.

✪ **Wat Po.** Maharat Rd., near the river. ☎ 02/222-0933. 20B (55¢) donation. Daily 8am–5pm; massages offered until 6pm. About a half mile south of the Grand Palace.

Wat Po (Wat Phra Chetuphon), the Temple of the Reclining Buddha, was built by Rama I in the 16th century and is the oldest and largest Buddhist temple in Bangkok. The compound, divided into two sections by Chetuphon Road, is a 15-minute walk south of the Grand Palace entrance. The northern area contains the most important monuments, and the southern portion is where resident monks live.

Most people go straight to the enormous Reclining Buddha in the northern section. It's more than 140 feet long and 50 feet high, and was built during the mid-19th-century reign of Rama III. The statue is brick, covered with layers of plaster, and always-flaking gold leaf; the feet are inlaid with mother-of-pearl illustrations of 108 auspicious *laksanas* (characteristics) of the Buddha.

Outside, the grounds contain 91 *chedis* (stupas or mounds), four *wihaans* (halls), and a *bot* (the central shrine in a Buddhist temple). Most impressive, aside from the Reclining Buddha, are the four main chedis dedicated to the first four Chakri kings and, nearby, the library. Wat Po is among the most photogenic of all the wats in Bangkok.

Of all the major temples in Bangkok, this is one of the most active. The temple is considered Thailand's first public university, because many of its monuments and artworks explain principles of religion, science, and literature. Visitors still drop 1-satang coins in 108 bronze bowls—corresponding to the 108 auspicious characteristics of the Buddha—for good fortune and to help the monks keep up the wat.

The Deer & the Dhamma

Buddhism, as with any world religion, has its own set of universal symbols that are recognizable to followers, but aren't as easily grasped by outsiders. After you've visited your share of Buddhist temples, some of these objects and images appear familiar, but their significance can't be readily implied. These symbols developed after the Buddha's death 2,500 years ago—a time when it was forbidden to create an image of the Buddha. Followers developed these objects to remind followers of his doctrine and of his life—as the path to happiness. Most have sprung from the important episodes in his life; his birth, enlightenment, preaching, and death. Over the centuries, different countries and sects have adopted certain symbols, neglecting others that fail to have cultural meaning to local followers. The following symbols are used frequently throughout Thai Buddhism and are present in most temples. Some scholars disagree about the nature and origins of specific symbols, but I've captured the main messages of each, as understood widely by Thai Buddhists.

The **lotus,** a water flower, represents the birth of the Buddha. With its roots buried in the mud and its bloom reaching up toward the sky, petals outstretched, it is the beginning of the life of the Great Sage, who while on this earth would rise above the common experience to achieve divine knowledge. The lotus, as a symbol of the purity of the doctrine, cradles many seated Buddha images, while some devotees place closed buds on the altar before him.

Many temple complexes have a **fig tree** within the compound, which is usually wrapped in saffron or colored cloth. Underneath it's typical to find Buddha images and burning incense. This bodhi tree, or sacred fig tree, is believed to be the original under which the Buddha meditated and gained enlightenment. In India, followers brought seedlings from the original tree to plant inside temples. Seedlings from those trees eventually made their way to Ceylon—and from there more seedlings were brought to Siam with visiting monks. The distinct shape of the leaves of this tree—wide and spadelike—is replicated in temple carvings in stone and wood and in temple mural art. Actual leaves are also dried and sometimes gilt, and bear painted portraits of Thai kings or great monks. Sometimes a throne is used to show this episode in his life.

There are several primary religious symbols to mark the Buddha's preaching of his noble truth. Upon enlightenment, he went to Deer Park, where he delivered his first sermon to five disciples. This event in his life is called "Setting the Wheel of Law in Motion." The **Wheel of Law** is the Buddha's dhamma, or doctrine, the roundness of the wheel signifying the never-ending cycle of life, perfection that has no beginning and no end. The Buddha, in preaching his knowledge, set the wheel into motion, and thus the cycle of life, of rebirth, of eternity. Another symbol used to identify this episode is the **deer,** a reference to Deer Park itself.

The death of the Buddha is directly related to the **chedi,** or stupa. The most distinguishing feature of a temple complex, the chedi is a descendent of the death mound—the raised earth that covers a corpse buried beneath. The Buddha allowed his bodily relics to be spread throughout the world by his believers, who placed them under burial mounds. Over time these mounds developed into elaborate structures—in Thailand the most common of which is the bell-shaped chedi following Sri Lankan style. In Thailand, not all chedis contain sacred relics (wats honored with the name "Mahathat" are believed to contain actual relics) but usually cover a sacred Buddha image, or the ashes of a noble figure or pious monk.

You can learn about traditional Thai massage and medicine at the Traditional Medical Practitioners Association Center and even receive a restorative medical massage in the afternoon for about 180B ($4.75) an hour—but be advised that therapy massage is a serious discipline and rather rigorous. (True Thai massage, in contrast to the services offered at most "massage parlors," involves chiropractic manipulation and acupressure, as well as stretching, stroking, and kneading, and is something to be endured for its sensational salubrious effects. Massage courses of 7 to 10 days are also available.)

You can hire a well-informed and entertaining English-speaking guide; he will find you and offer his services for about 200B to 400B ($5.25 to $10.55), depending on the number in the party. There are also a few astrologers and palm readers available for consultation. For a small donation you can receive a blessing from a monk and a bracelet of braided colored string to commemorate the occasion. (Donations go toward upkeep and renovations.)

Wat Mahathat (Temple of the Great Relic). Na Phra That Rd. ☎ **02/221-5999.** 20B (55¢) donation. Daily 9am–5pm. Na Prathat Rd., near Sanam Luang Park, between the Grand Palace and the National Museum.

Built to house a relic of the Buddha, Wat Mahathat is one of Bangkok's oldest shrines and the headquarters for Thailand's largest monastic order. Also the home of the Center for Vipassana Meditation at Buddhist University, the most important center for the study of Buddhism and meditation, Wat Mahathat offers some programs in English. (See "Bangkok's Cultural Thrills" later in this chapter for more information about courses.)

Adjacent to it, between Maharat Road and the river, is the city's biggest amulet market, where a fantastic array of religious amulets, charms, talismans, and traditional medicine is sold. Each Sunday hundreds of worshipers squat on the ground studying tiny images of the Buddha with magnifying glasses, hoping to find one that will bring good fortune or ward off evil. Each amulet brings a specific kind of luck—to get the girl, to pass your exams, for a good harvest, or to ward off your mother-in-law—so if you buy one, choose carefully. (The newer amulet market is part of Wat Ratchanada, off the intersection of Mahachai Road and Ratchadamnoen Klang Road, across from the Golden Mount at Wat Saket.)

✪ Wat Arun (Temple of Dawn). West bank of the Chao Phraya, opposite Tha Thien Pier. ☎ **02/465-5640.** 20B donation (55¢). Daily 8am–5:30pm. Take a water taxi from Tha Tien Pier (near Wat Po) or cross the Phra Pinklao Bridge and follow the river south on Arun Amarin Rd (2B/5¢).

The 260-foot-high, Khmer-inspired tower, the centerpiece of the "Temple of Dawn," rises majestically from the banks of the Chao Phraya, across from Wat Po. This religious complex served as the royal chapel during King Taksin's reign (1809–24), when Thonburi was the capital of Thailand.

The original tower was only 50 feet high, but was expanded during the rule of Rama III (1824–51) to its current height. The exterior is decorated with flower and decorative motifs made of ceramic shards donated to the monastery by local people, at the request of Rama III. At the base of the complex are Chinese stone statues, once used as ballast in trading ships, gifts from Chinese merchants.

You can climb the central prang, but be warned: The steps are treacherously tall, narrow, and steep—and even more precarious coming down. If you go up, notice the caryatids and the Hindu gods atop the three-headed elephants. The view of the river, Wat Po, and Grand Palace is well worth the climb. Be sure to walk to the back of the tower to the monk's living quarters, a tranquil world far from the bustle of Bangkok's busy streets. Wat Arun is a sight to behold shimmering with the sunrise, but despite its name, a late afternoon visit is better so that you can enjoy the sunset.

Appreciating the Buddha Image

The Buddha is ever-present in Thailand, where small images grace everything from auto dashboards to amulet necklaces (believed to make the bearer invulnerable). Every Thai town has a prominent City Pillar shrine, to pay homage to the Buddha, honor the city's heroes, and appease town spirits, while every Thai Buddhist home has a well maintained altar devoted to his teachings. Unlike Christians, who honor Christ as a martyr and saint, Buddhists do not worship the Buddha as a god, but use his image as a reminder of his teachings. The Buddha is merely the human form for the doctrine he preached.

The Buddha as a subject of sculpture didn't come around until well after his death, the first ones appearing in India some 2,000 years ago. Because no images of him were created during his lifetime, artists relied on descriptions in scriptures to produce his likeness. Pali religious texts relayed 108 auspicious signs for recognizing a Buddha, which included wedged-shaped heels, fingers, and toes of equal length, thick rounded arms extending to the knees, a head shaped like an egg, hair like scorpion stingers, and a nose like a parrot's beak. Later artists added elongated earlobes in reference to Siddhattha's royal lineage—as a boy he would have worn heavy gold earrings. Many Thais will explain that the long earlobes symbolize his great wisdom. Almost everyone will tell you the most striking feature of almost every Buddha image is the pure serenity and deep joy in his facial expression. His face is relaxed, eyes half closed, and his lips form a whisper of a smile.

The tradition of Buddha sculpture places him in four primary positions. In the most common position he is seated with legs crossed as he was in his victory over Mara. Other famous poses include standing, walking (which is rare but sometimes beautifully rich with motion) and reclining (depicting the Buddha at his time of death). Thai temples will have many images placed throughout, with one primary Buddha image on the center altar. In many Thai temples you'll find a small row of seven similar sculptures, each depicting a different position corresponding with events in his life, one for each day of the week. Thais place great importance on the day of the week on which they were born, and have assigned positions for each day.

The Buddha is also portrayed with many different hand gestures, each of which symbolize an "attitude" of the Buddha. In the *vitarka mudra* position, where both hands are placed with palms flat outward in front of him, the Buddha

Wat Benchamabophit (the Marble Wat). Si Ayutthaya Rd. ☎ **02/281-2501.** 20B (55¢) donation. Daily 8am–5pm. South of the Assembly Building near Chitralada Palace.

Wat Benchamabophit, which tourists call the Marble Wat because of the white Carrara marble of which it's constructed, is an early 20th-century temple designed by Prince Narai, the half brother of Rama V. It's the most modern and one of the most beautiful of Bangkok's royal wats. Unlike the older complexes, there's no truly monumental wihaan or chedi dominating the grounds. Many smaller buildings reflect a melding of European materials and designs with traditional Thai religious architecture. Even the courtyards are paved with polished white marble. Walk inside the compound, beyond the main bot, to view the many Buddhas that represent various regional styles. During the early mornings, monks chant in the main chapel, sometimes so intensely that it seems as if the temple is going to lift off.

is teaching. The *varada mudra,* when the Buddha has his hands to his sides, palms facing to the front, is charity. In the *abhaya mudra* attitude the Buddha has one or two arms bent at his waist, palms flat forward for the viewer to see in an act of dispelling fear or stopping arguments. The most common hand gesture is the *bhumispara mudra.* In this attitude he is seated with his right hand on his knee pointed downward to show how the earth will bear witness to his enlightenment.

Thailand's most exquisite works of fine art are in the form of Buddha images, either carved from stone, forged from metals, or constructed in brick and mortar. In fact, most of these images can't even be seen, having been created only to be buried deep within chedis or larger works.

The kingdom of Sukhothai is heralded for its fine artwork, especially its Buddha sculptures, which are the epitome of Thai artistic genius. Created between the 13th through 15th centuries A.D., these images, mostly in bronze, depict the Buddha in an incredibly light, fluid, and ethereal state, with eyes and lips that seem to vaporize in a heavenly wisp at the corners. Simultaneously, in the northern Lanna Kingdom (13th through 16th centuries A.D.), the standing Buddha image was preferred, identified by his round face and fat hair curls. Images from Ayutthaya (1350–1767), in contrast to Sukhothai, became more simplified and serious, oftentimes cold and impersonal, concentrating more on the artistic style of the image and less on the spiritual meaning that radiates from it.

While each period of Thailand's history presents sculptures with unique details and character, many of these images, having been revered through time, have been moved from temple to temple and region to region making it quite difficult to identify the period and origin of a sculpture simply based upon its location. For example, the great Emerald Buddha that rests in Bangkok's Wat Phra Kaeo was the creation of northern Lop Buri artists in pre-Khmer times. When admiring an image in a temple, be sure not to walk between the Buddha and someone in prayer. Also, be careful not to sit with your feet pointed at the Buddha, a sign of great disrespect. Many Thais will purchase incense sticks at temples in sets of three—one each for the Buddha, the *Dhamma,* and the *Sangha* to light and bow with before the Buddha. Many others offer lotus buds; jasmine, orchid, and carnation garlands; and fruits, much the same as the Buddha's followers did when they came to pay last respects to their teacher after his death at the Sala Grove 2,500 years ago.

Wat Bovornivet. Phra Sumein Rd. Free admission. 8am–5pm. 20B (55¢) donation. North of Ratchadamnoen Klang Rd. near the Democracy Monument.

Although few visitors bother to come to this quiet retreat opposite the old town wall, it has its rewards. You can wander along the paths between the monks' quarters and the waterways, used by the king for water purification experiments. Several kings and princes have been monks here, including King Bhumibhol, the present king, and his son Crown Prince Vajiralongkorn. Prince Mongkut, later King Rama IV, served as abbot here for 14 years and founded the Thammayut order, for which the wat is the national headquarters. Of the two Buddha images inside the bot, the smaller one in front was cast in bronze in Sukhothai in 1257 to celebrate the country's liberation from Khmer rule. Several murals depict *farangs* (foreigners) in Thailand—the English at a horse race, American missionaries, Germans prospecting for minerals.

Wat Saket (The Golden Mount). Ratchadamnoen Klang and Boripihat rds. Entrance to wat is free; admission to the chedi, chedi 20B (55¢) donation. Open 9am–5pm.

Wat Saket is easily recognized by its golden chedi atop a fortresslike hill near the pier for Bangkok's east-west klong ferry. The wat was restored by King Rama I, and 30,000 bodies were brought here during a plague in the reign of Rama II. The hill, which is almost 80 meters high, is an artificial construction begun during the reign of Rama III. Rama IV brought in 1,000 teak logs to shore it up because it was sinking into the swampy ground. Rama V built the golden chedi to house a relic of Buddha, said to be from India or Nepal, given to him by the British. The concrete walls were added during World War II to keep the structure from collapsing.

The Golden Mount, a short but breathtaking climb that's best made in the morning, is most interesting for its vista of old Rattanakosin Island and the rooftops of Bangkok. Every late October to mid-November (for 9 days around the full moon) Wat Sakhet hosts Bangkok's most important temple fair, when the Golden Mount is wrapped with red cloth and a carnival erupts around it, with food and trinket stalls, theatrical performances, freak shows, animal circuses, and other monkey business.

Wat Suthat and the Giant Swing. Sao Chingcha Sq. ☎ **02/222-0280.** 20B (55¢) donation. Daily 9am–5pm. Near the intersection of Bamrung Muang Rd. and Ti Thong Rd.

This temple is among the oldest and largest in Bangkok, and Somerset Maugham declared its roofline the most beautiful. It was begun by Rama I and finished by Rama III; Rama II carved the panels for the wihaan's doors. It houses the beautiful 14th-century Phra Buddha Shakyamuni, a Buddha image that was brought from Sukhothai, and the ashes of King Rama VIII, Ananda Mahidol, brother of the current king, are contained in its base. The wall paintings for which it is known were done during Rama III's reign.

Outside the wihaan stand many Chinese pagodas, bronze horses, and figures of Chinese soldiers. The most important religious association, however, is with the Brahman priests who officiate at important state ceremonies, and there are two Hindu shrines nearby. To the northwest across the street is the Deva Sathan, which contains images of Shiva and Ganesh, and to the east, the smaller Saan Jao Phitsanu is dedicated to Vishnu.

The huge teak arch—also carved by Rama II—in front is all that remains of an original giant swing, which was used until 1932 to celebrate and thank Shiva for a bountiful rice harvest and to ask for the god's blessing on the next. The minister of rice, accompanied by hundreds of Brahman court astrologers, would lead a parade around the city walls to the temple precinct. Teams of men would ride the swing on arcs as high as 82 feet in the air, trying to grab a bag of silver coins with their teeth. Due to injuries and deaths, the dangerous swing ceremony has been discontinued, but the thanksgiving festival is still celebrated in mid-December after the rice harvest.

Wat Traimit (The Golden Buddha). Traimit Rd. 20B (55¢) donation. Daily 9am–5pm. West of Hua Lampong Station, just west of the intersection of Krung Kasem and Rama IV rds.; walk southwest on Traimit Rd. and look for a school on the right with a playground. The wat is up a flight of stairs overlooking the school.

Wat Traimit, which is thought to date from the 13th century, would hardly rate a second glance if not for its astonishing Buddha, which is nearly 10 feet high, weighs over 5 tons, and is believed to be cast of solid gold. It was discovered by accident in 1957 when an old stucco Buddha was being moved from a storeroom by a crane, which dropped it and shattered the plaster shell, revealing the shining gold beneath. This powerful image has such a bright, reflective surface that its edges seem to disappear, and it is truly dazzling. The graceful seated statue is thought to have been cast during the Sukhothai period and later covered with plaster to hide it from the Burmese or other invaders. Pieces of the stucco are on display in a case to the left.

4 Bangkok Walking Tours

Following are two interesting walking tours that avoid some of Bangkok's noise, traffic, and pollution problems and explore older neighborhoods via smaller back streets (*sois*).

Even though any walking trip will become a hot experience, keep in mind that you'll be entering religious buildings and will need to dress modestly—no tank tops or shorts. Also, carry bottled water and small baht bills or change to use for contributions at the wats (20B/55¢ is appropriate).

The directions for these routes are sometimes complicated, but don't hesitate to ask the locals if you lose your way.

Walking Tour—What's Wat?

Start: Wat Saket.
Finish: Wat Mahathat.
Time: Approximately 2 hours, not including tours of Wat Po, the Grand Palace complex, shopping, or snack stops.
Best Times: Weekend or weekdays in the cooler early morning.
Worst Times: During the midday heat and late afternoon (the Grand Palace closes at 3:30pm).

Our What's Wat tour is designed to serve as an introduction to many of Bangkok's best-known Buddhist shrines. The walk is centered in Rattanakosin or "old Bangkok," that is, the original part of the city, although many of the buildings and neighborhoods are anything but old. What you'll find is a view, some shopping, excellent sightseeing, a dose of exercise, and, if you're up for it, a traditional herbal massage.

If you're staying in the Sukhumvit Road area, I recommend getting to the starting point via klong (canal) transit, for extra adventure and an escape from rush hour traffic. Your hotel's front desk can tell you where the nearest pier is along Klong Mahanak, which runs parallel to Sukhumvit, Ploenchit and Rama I Roads all the way to Wat Saket. Hop on board the boat heading west and tell them "Pratunam" (fare will be between 5B to 10B (15¢ to 25¢). Pratunam is where you'll have to hop off the boat, cross over the klong on the overpass and hop on another one. Show your ticket stub from the first trip so you don't have to pay again. Relax, watch morning canal commuters, and take in the sights along the edges of the water. (We apologize in advance for the smell.)

The tour begins at:

1. **Wat Saket on Boriphat Road.** The stairs at this temple (also known as the Golden Mount) wind around the base of the massive structure and lead up to the top. There is a 5B (15¢) admission fee, ostensibly for a chance to look out over the city (the relics inside are of little aesthetic importance) and, to map out the balance of the walking tour. Proceed to the windows on your left as you enter the observatory room. Immediately in front and below is Wat Ratchanada; to the right are the four pillars of the Democracy Monument; farther away and to the left are Wat Suthat and the Giant Swing; and even more distant are the spires of the Grand Palace and Wat Po.

After descending the winding staircase and ramp, find your way back out to Thanon Boriphat and turn right. On Boriphat Road, have a look at some of the woodworking shops and lumber yards that line the road. Wood-carvers and craftspeople fashion intricately worked architectural elements—the lacelike eaves on those lovely Thai style wooden houses, carves doors, moldings for doorways and window openings.

Just before you cross over Klong Mahanak, if you're interested, you can buy all sorts of Chinese fireworks from some shops there. I don't recommend trying to clear them through customs, however. As you cross the bridge you can see the boats coming in for landing at the east-west ferry that shuttles people to the far eastern reaches of the city from this point. After the bridge, veer left, then turn left over yet another bridge, to proceed straight to:

2. Wat Ratchanada (The Temple of the Metal Castle). It's a big modern complex, but don't dawdle here, as there are many more (and more interesting) wats to discover.

Walk west (left) as you exit the wat on:

3. Ratchadamnoen Road, the Champs-Elysées of Bangkok (patterned after Paris' most famous boulevard). The buildings along this long stretch of road, built in the 1920s and '30s, were the first major integration of contemporary European city planning and architecture in Bangkok, a previously haphazard sprawl of klongs, bridges, and roads; you can be the judge of which system works better. During holidays and state events, this avenue is lined with decorations, royal emblems and bigger than life pictures of the king and queen. In the center, at an enormous traffic circle, pay a visit to the:

4. Democracy Monument, built to honor the establishment of the modern Thai form of parliamentary monarchy (which these days is under some strain). We like this spot for picture taking; if there's a group of visiting school kids check out the shutter-bug scene.

At the southern side of the traffic circle, Dinso Road, in contrast to Ratchadamnoen Road, is a narrow, shop-lined lane, shaded by old trees. Here you'll pass little novelty shops, gold vendors, discount audio and video tapes, food stalls, bakeries, and other assorted peddlers. We found a man making the cutest toy crickets out of bamboo leaves and ladies chatting in the shade while stringing fragrant jasmine garlands. After a few short blocks Dinso Road becomes Ti Thong Road. When you reach the intersection of Ti Thong and Bamrung Muang Road, you'll find the:

5. Giant Swing, which is now just a stand—the actual swing has been removed. It's interesting to note the lines of the almost fragile-looking structure. If you've spent any time at Jim Thompson's house (see "Bangkok's Historical Treasures," above) or wandering through an antiques shop, you'll recognize the Thai technique to build bases wider than tops, so objects grow narrow as they rise for balance and strength. You'll see it in houses, chests, cabinets, even swings. Before entering Wat Suthat (see below), I recommend a little side step onto Bamrung Muang Road (at the end of Ti Thong Road, once you reach the swing, hang a right).

This section of Bamrung Muang is lined with shops making Buddha images. Follow the stray glittering gold leaf stuck to the pavement on the road outside the shops. Inside you can watch the decorative processes—lacquering and gilding of the images—some of them huge, most of them in the Sukhothai style.

Back across the street, take some time to explore:

6. Wat Suthat, built over a 27-year period during the reign of Rama III (1824–51); the complex is a wonderful and typical cacophony of colors, smells, shapes, and textures found in the city's most intriguing temple grounds.

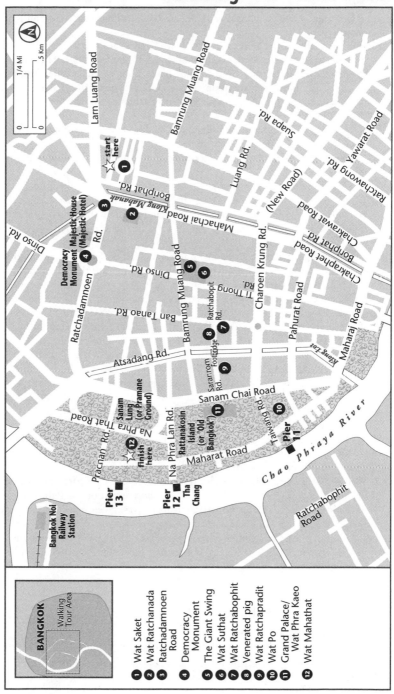

BANGKOK

Walking Tour Area

1 Wat Saket
2 Wat Ratchanada
3 Ratchadamnoen Road
4 Democracy Monument
5 The Giant Swing
6 Wat Suthat
7 Wat Ratchabophit
8 Venerated pig
9 Wat Ratchapradit
10 Wat Po
11 Grand Palace/Wat Phra Kaeo
12 Wat Mahathat

Continue several blocks along Ti Thong Road, making a right turn on Ratch-abophit Road to:

7. Wat Ratchabophit. The road leading down to the wat, with a noisy school and a legion of uniformed students, is another good one for shops. The temple is elaborately decorated and nicely maintained: Walk in and explore the inner sanctum. Pay particular attention to the mother-of-pearl inlaid door and the hand-painted tiles in this European-influenced complex. (It may remind some of the Marble Wat.)

Continue along Ratchabophit Road until it dead-ends into a klong. Cross over the footbridge, and on your right is a:

8. venerated pig (sculpture, that is) occupying a prominent position atop a rock tableau.

The street opposite this porcine beauty is Saranrom Road; take it to:

9. Wat Ratchapradit, which will be on your left, behind a fairly discreet gate. This certainly isn't a well-known place, but you can be among the wat cognoscenti in saying that you've been here, too: Check it out! It's full of neighborhood life, and kids play wild games of Ping-Pong.

After demonstrating your paddle proficiency, exit on Saranrom and turn left, continuing for a few blocks; this will cleverly deposit you at the rear of the Grand Palace on Sanam Chai Road. But that's for later; your goal is Wat Po, so turn left on Sanam Chai, continuing for several blocks, make a right on Chetuphon Road, and, voilà, you'll be at:

10. Wat Po, about 15 minutes from Wat Ratchapradit. This is the stop for those in need of a good herbal massage, Thai style (open daily 8am to 5pm; 100B/$2.65 per half hour). Don't miss the bottoms of the feet of the reclining Buddha.

After exiting Wat Po, work your way to Maharat Road, running parallel to the Chao Phraya, turn right and, if you have time, enter the gates to the Grand Palace. Allocate a good 2 hours to the:

11. Grand Palace/Wat Phra Kaeo complex. See "Beijing's Historical Treasures," above, for complete details.

Continue north along Maharat Road to Bangkok's most thriving street market for amulets and other tchotchkes; check out the Tha Chang fruit and vegetable market on the pier of the same name. Our final stop is:

12. Wat Mahathat, located on the Phra That Road, which runs parallel to Maharat. To find it, turn right on Na Phra Lan Road and veer left on Na Phra That; Wat Mahathat will be a little farther on, abutting the vast green known as the Sanam Luang or Pramane Ground (at the right time of year, April or so, you may see some mean kite flying/fighting here). This is one of Bangkok's oldest wats and of vast educational significance, as it contains the country's leading Buddhist teaching center.

Walking Tour—Thonburi

Start: Tha Saphan Phut Express Boat Pier.
Finish: Tha Tien Express Pier, opposite Wat Arun, near Wat Po.
Time: Allow approximately 2½ hours, not including an exploration of Wat Arun.
Best Times: Early morning or late afternoon.
Worst Times: Midday.

This tour starts with a walk over the river to a fascinating wat, circles a Portuguese Catholic church, continues through an old local neighborhood into an impressive wat

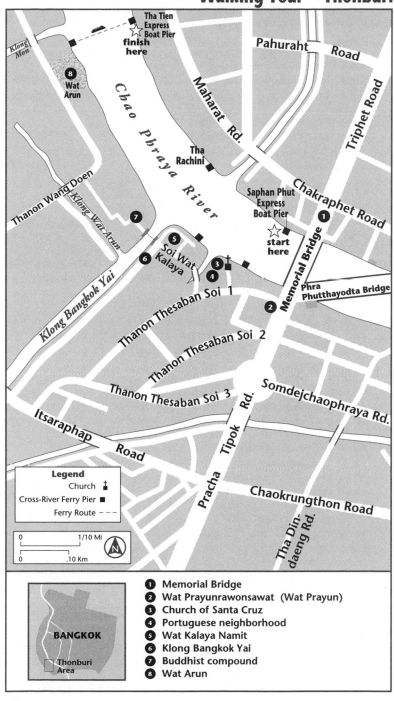

Walking Tour— Thonburi

Tha Tien Express Boat Pier

finish here

Klong Mon

8 Wat Arun

Chao Phraya River

Pahuraht Road

Triphet Road

Maharat Rd.

Tha Rachini

Chakraphet Road

Saphan Phut Express Boat Pier

1

start here

Memorial Bridge

Thanon Wang Doen

Klong Wat Arun

7

5

6

Soi Wat Kalaya

3

1

Klong Bangkok Yai

Thanon Thesaban Soi 1

2

Phra Phutthayodta Bridge

Thanon Thesaban Soi 2

Thanon Thesaban Soi 3

Somdejchaophraya Rd.

Itsaraphap Road

Pracha Tipok Rd.

Chaokrungthon Road

Tha Din-daeng Rd.

Legend
Church †
Cross-River Ferry Pier ■
Ferry Route – – –

0   1/10 Mi
0   .10 Km

N

BANGKOK

Thonburi Area

1 Memorial Bridge
2 Wat Prayunrawonsawat (Wat Prayun)
3 Church of Santa Cruz
4 Portuguese neighborhood
5 Wat Kalaya Namit
6 Klong Bangkok Yai
7 Buddhist compound
8 Wat Arun

complex, across a klong by small boat, and ends at the soaring Wat Arun, Temple of Dawn.

From the Tha Saphan Express Boat Pier, near the Pak Klong Talaat Market in Chinatown, walk over the upriver side of the:

1. Memorial Bridge. Pause in the middle and look upriver (northwest), where you will see the "high" points of your journey—the soaring points of chedis, the elegant peaks of temple rooftops, and the cross of the Church of Santa Cruz.

At the far side of the bridge, walk down the steps and continue to the right on the curved drive, past several food shops, across one small lane (Thanon Thesaban Soi 1), and then after another short walk, turn right into:

2. Wat Prayunrawonsawat (Wat Prayun), a complex of temples and buildings built during the reign of Rama III by a powerful local family. The complex is totally dominated by the immense (55-foot) chedi, but look first to your right as you enter to find Turtle Mount, a gnarled grotto of small shrines and stupas that rises out of the small pond. As you circle the mount (Buddhists go clockwise) you'll see the hundreds of turtles that give this grotto its name. You can buy bread or papaya to feed the critters, but don't forget to get a stick to put the food on, as the turtles have developed a taste for tourists' fingers. Enter the temples reverently, after removing your shoes. Near the temple shop, you can leave a donation toward a new temple roof.

Continue straight through the temple complex, past the giant chedi on your right, then turn right as you pass through the gate, after passing a small graveyard on your left. Turn left onto the small street (Thanon Thesaban Soi 1), then cross the street and turn right into a small walkway past the parking lot and walk toward the:

3. Church of Santa Cruz, also known as the Temple of Chinese Monk's Quarters, for reasons unknown. The original church was established on this site by the Portuguese community during the reign of King Taksin (1767–82) and was named after a crosslike piece of wood that washed ashore at the site. The first Portuguese came to Thailand in the 16th century as part of their exploration effort in Southeast Asia. Eventually, a minor colony developed here, though there is little Portuguese presence today. The present church was built in the early 20th century with an interior incorporating both Western and Chinese elements. Unfortunately, the doors are only open for daily masses (only delivered in Thai). Sunday masses are held at 6am, 8:30am, and 5pm; other days at 6am and 7pm.

Explore the labyrinth of walks through the:

4. Portuguese neighborhood adjacent to the church and admire the fine wooden houses there. Please respect the privacy of the residents, who are not accustomed to tourists in their neighborhoods. Most of the paths here end at a small klong, but there is a route that will lead back to a small street from which you can continue the tour. Kudos to those who find it, but most will want to retrace their steps to the church and then to Thanon Thesaban Soi 1, where you turn right onto that street and right again on the first street, Soi Wat Kalaya, and continue until you come to:

5. Wat Kalaya Namit. This is a complex of decaying buildings, the largest of which contains a huge (90-foot) seated Buddha image in the subduing Mara pose. The statue is sometimes lit only by a feeble fluorescent light, but wait for your eyes to adjust and you'll find it very impressive. You can purchase candles for the altar from the desk on the right. As always, remove your shoes and show proper reverence for the worshipers. Beggars outside the door will approach you as you enter and exit.

Organized Tours

There are numerous travel agencies offering local tours. Two of the largest are **Sea Tours** (☎ **02/251-4862**) and **World Travel Service** (☎ **02/233-5900**); both have branch offices in nearly every international hotel and can arrange daily standard package tours to all the major sights for discounted prices. You can also hire your own car and driver, with guide and interpreter for about 1,500B ($39.45) for a whole day—you design the agenda, where you want to go, and what you're interested in doing. It's great for shoppers. I recommend making a list of the places you'd like to visit, then present it to the agent when you book your car.

Walk to the river and inspect the rice barges that are home to the people who work them. For a short detour, turn right on the walkway, and you'll come to another interesting neighborhood and a cross-river ferry dock. To continue the tour, turn left at the river and walk until it turns through a series of homes and shops that specialize in recycling cooking-oil cans. Next to these shops runs:

6. Klong Bangkok Yai, where you'll soon come to a small dock where you can hail a small long-tail boat to cross the klong. You'll be charged 5B. (You can also reach the dock by returning to the street from Wat Kalaya Namit and walking until it dead-ends at the klong.)

After crossing the klong, you'll find a:

7. Buddhist compound. Turn left before the temples and walk past the school buildings up to the main road. Novice monks may try to practice English with you as you pass their quarters. Turn right past the school, then left at a white wall (behind which sits Vichai Prasit Fortress), then right again at the Klong Wat Arun. Walk until this small lane joins the larger street, Thanon Wang Doen, and follow it as it curves to the right and leads to the walls of:

8. Wat Arun, with its recognizable mosaicked chedi. Turn right into the Wat Arun complex and make your way past monks' quarters to the river, for refreshments and the main entrance to the wat.

The cross-river ferry dock is found on the upriver side of Wat Arun, where you can connect to the Tha Thien Express Boat stop. Cross over and return to your hotel, or walk from Tha Thien Pier inland to Wat Po and the Grand Palace. If you're going straight to the Grand Palace, take an upriver boat to Tha Chang Pier, one stop away.

5 Cultural Pursuits

Anyone can tell you that cultural curiosities don't merely exist in the structures of buildings or cloistered in special collections. Daily activities, festivals and ceremonies, and cultural events expose elements of civilization, both modern and ancient, that are fascinating to the outside observer. Try to plan your time to include some of the following activities, which offer a peek into the lives of the Thai people.

Begin your travel plans by asking the Tourism Authority about upcoming **traditional festivals** and ceremonies. Chapter 2 outlines major holidays, but the TAT (Ratchadamnoen Nok Avenue, ☎ **02/282-9773**) has up-to-date information about celebration dates and locations, and encourages all visitors to attend even the smallest events. Some of my fondest experiences have been the times when I've come to these occasions out of curiosity only to find myself an active participant, welcomed and encouraged by friendly Thai hosts. By joining these events, even as a passive observer, you'll find yourself feeling less like a voyeur and more connected to the city and its people. Also inquire about events upcountry before you leave the capital to explore other cities and regions. There's always something going on. See "When to Go" in chapter 2, and the "Songkran" box on in chapter 11.

Muay thai, or **Thai Boxing,** stretches beyond the boundaries of spectator sport in its presentation of Thai mores evident in pre-bout rituals, live musical performances, and the wild gambling antics of the audience. For details about the sport, its rites and cultural meaning, flip to the box on muay thai in chapter 8. In Bangkok, catch up to 15 bouts nightly at either of two stadiums. The **Ratchadamnoen Stadium** (Ratchadamnoen Nok Avenue ☎ 02/281-4205) hosts bouts every Monday, Wednesday, Thursday, and Sunday while the **Lumphini Staduim** (Rama IV Road, ☎ 02/251-4303) has bouts on Tuesdays, Fridays, and Saturdays. Tickets are 1,000B ($26.30) for ringside seats, 440B ($11.60) standing room only, and 220B ($5.80) if you don't mind crowding in the cage at the back. Shows start at 6:30pm or 7:30pm, depending on the stadium.

Okay, so it's not exactly culture, but you'll have a hard time getting out of Thailand without encountering some kind of snake show. Bangkok's biggest venue is at the **Red Cross Snake Farm,** 1871 Rama IV Rd. (☎ 02/252-0161). Located in the heart of Bangkok opposite the Montien Hotel, this institute for the study of venomous snakes, established in 1923, was the second facility of its type in the world (the first was in Brazil). There are slide shows and snake-handling demonstrations weekdays at 10:30am and 2pm; on weekends and holidays at 10:30am. You can also watch the handlers work with deadly cobras and equally poisonous banded kraits and green pit vipers, with demonstrations of venom milking. The venom is later gradually injected into horses, which produce antivenom for the treatment of snakebites. The Thai Red Cross sells medical guides and will also inoculate you against such maladies as typhoid, cholera, and smallpox in their clinic. The farm is open daily Monday to Friday 8:30am to 4pm, Saturday and Sunday 8:30am to noon; admission is 70B ($1.85). It's at the corner of Rama IV Road and Henri Dunant.

A good **traditional Thai massage** is one of life's true joys. A head-to-toe extravaganza of stretching muscles and kneading hands, a Thai massage starts your vacation off right—the perfect transition from everyday life back home to relaxing vacation mode. Whether you're involved in sporting activities or spending all day on your dogs touring the sights, make time during your trip to work out the kinks. And before you leave, have one more for the road. When you get home you'll be loose as a goose. Talk to your hotel's concierge—all hotels can arrange massages for you, sometimes in your room. If your hotel doesn't have massage facilities, sometimes they have discount programs with neighboring businesses.

In the city there are countless massage places, and many of them are quite good. Be aware that many "massage parlors" cater to gentlemen, with services beyond standard massage expectations. You can differentiate between the two different styles by looking for a sign specifically stating that the massage is "Traditional." Some upstanding places have blatant signs indicating the place is hanky-panky free. Try **Po Thong Thai Massage,** in the basement of the Fortuna Hotel, Sukhumvit Soi 5 (☎ 02/255-1045); (300B/$7.90 per hour), or **Arima Onsen,** 37/10-11 Soi Surawong Plaza, Surawong Road (☎ 02/235-2142; 200B/$5.25 per hour). The home of Thai massage, **Wat Po** is school to almost every masseuse in Bangkok, and has good cheap massages in an open-air pavilion within the temple complex—a very interesting experience (Chetuphon Road, ☎ 02/221-2974; 180B/$4.75 per hour). According to the experts, 2 hours is the minimum to experience the full benefits of Thai massage, but many will do it for 1 hour upon request. These places will also perform foot massages, which are equally divine.

Fancy a chance to learn cooking techniques from the pros? **Thai cooking classes** are extremely popular and fabulously presented, with hands-on practice in some of the most famous kitchens of Bangkok. Classes teach you all you need to know about Thai herbs, spices, and main ingredients—you'll never look at a produce market the same again. Lectures on Thai regional cuisine, cooking techniques, and menu planning complement classroom exercises to prepare all your favorite dishes. The best part is after, when you get to eat them! Classes are typically held in the mornings from 8am or 9am until noon, with lunch after. Oriental Hotel's program offers 4-day programs, but you can join in for 1 or 2 days only, if you'd like. The cost is $120 per person. Very expensive, but their chef is tops. Call them at ☎ **02/437-6211** for booking and information.

If you're traveling through Bangkok during February through April you can't beat the fantastic sights of the **kite-fighting** competitions held at Lumphini Park in the center of the city. Elaborate creations in vivid colors vie for prizes, and "fighting," a team spectator sport complete with sponsors, thrills onlookers. The TAT will have all the information you need about exact dates, or you can check the local papers or travel publications.

For Thais, **cockfighting** is a tradition as old as the hills. Country farmers raise cocks to be fighters, for the hope of bringing in a good one and making a small fortune. In markets, fighting cocks are kept under dome basket cages—in the animal section of Chatuchak Weekend Market (see below) you can see the birds up close. At the north end of the market you might catch a demonstration or an actual fight. The sport is legal in Thailand (so is the gambling involved). Be forewarned: Animal lovers will find this awful. Even though they've outlawed putting razors on the birds' wings, the fights get gory.

Wat Mahathat serves as one of Thailand's two Buddhist universities. As such, it has become a popular center for **meditation lessons and practice,** with English-speaking monks overseeing the technique—Vipassana, also called Insight Meditation. If you haven't been around to Wat Mahathat (Temple of the Great Relic) during your trips out into the city, you'll find it at Na Phra That Road near Sanam Luang Park, between the Grand Palace and the National Museum, or you can call **Wat Mahathat** in the mornings at ☎ **02/623-6337** or in the afternoons at ☎ **02/623-6326,** ext. 132. Classes are held daily from 7am to 10am, 1 to 4pm, and again from 6pm to 8pm. The length of time needed for practice and the results obtained will vary from individual to individual. While these short term lessons will teach you about the technique, those who are seeking a deeper learning may wish to look into the 26-day intensive Vipassana program at Wat Rampoeng in Chiang Mai (see chapter 12).

6 Staying Active

Golf enthusiasts will be happy to know you don't have to go out to the country to enjoy some of Thailand's best courses. Located within the city, or close by, some excellent courses, a few of them championship, lure enthusiasts, many of whom come to this country just to play the game. **Pinehurst Golf & Country Club,** 73 Paholyothin Rd., Klong Luang, Pathum Thani (☎ **02/516-8679,** fax 02/516-2000), sports three nine-hole courses at par 27 each. This prestigious club served as the venue for the 1992 Johnnie Walker Classic (greens fees: 1,500B/$39.45 weekdays, 2,000B/$52.65 weekends). **Rose Garden Golf Club,** 53/1 Moo 4, Petchkasem Highway, Sam Phran, Nakhon Pathom (☎ **02/253-0295-7,** fax 034/322-769-71), an esteemed par-72 course offers a pretty game, with scenery enhanced by wooded surrounds (greens fees: weekdays 700B/$18.40; weekends 1,300B/$34.20). **Unico Golf Club,** 47 Moo 7,

Krungthep Kretha Road, Prawet, Bangkok (☎ **02/377-9038,** fax 02/379-3780), is a well-established city course with many challenging holes (greens fees: weekdays 365B/$9.60; weekends 730B/19.20). **Winsan Golf Club** (National Park) 100 Moo 7, Riak Klong Song Road, Minburi, Bangkok (☎ **02/914-1930,** fax 02/914-1970), designed by American pro Jack Nicklaus, proves a tough course with many difficult shots and water hazards (greens fees: weekdays 1,400B/$36.85; weekends 2,200B/$57.90). You can also try the **Royal Thai Army Golf Club,** 459 Ram Indra Rd., Bang Kaen, Bangkok (☎ **02/521-1530,** fax 02/521-3391), which has both an old course and a new course to choose from. This well-maintained course was host to the Thai Open (greens fees: weekdays 600B/$15.80; weekends 800B/$21.05).

Few other cities in the world offer easier access to **horse racing.** There are two elegant tracks in the heart of town, with racing starting each Sunday at 12:10pm on an alternating schedule. The private **Royal Bangkok Sports Club** occupies a prime spot on Henri Dunant Road, opposite Chulalongkorn University, north of Rama IV Road (☎ **02/251-0181**). The **Royal Turf Club** is located just south of Chitralada Royal Palace on Phitsanulok Road (☎ **02/280-0020**). Admission to either is 150B ($3.95) and betting begins at 50B ($1.30) on a win-place basis only.

7 Shopping

It may not have Hong Kong's or Singapore's reputation for shopping, but Bangkok will dazzle you with every type of shop ranging from street shacks to ultrachic boutiques. Even the most world-weary shopper will find unusual, high-quality goods at very reasonable prices. The TAT publishes the *Thailand Shopping Guide,* which offers sound advice on what to purchase and which markets to visit. A commission reviews a vast number of shops in Bangkok and only recognizes those that operate on a high standard with fair trading practices. If you do encounter problems with merchants, you can contact the **Tourist Police** (☎ **02/694-1222,** ext. 1).

GREAT SHOPPING AREAS & MARKETS

There are many shopping areas in Bangkok, so plan your itinerary with a map. Serious shoppers will die for Nancy Chandler's *The Market Map and Much More*—you can pick it up at bookstores and magazine stands throughout the city once you arrive. One of the main considerations in planning your shopping routes is traffic. Try to concentrate on one area and spend your day exploring those streets, leaving another area for another day.

Most major hotels have shopping arcades, in many cases with respectable, quality shops, though their prices are often much higher than those in less upscale neighborhoods. The finest arcades are those at the Oriental and Regent hotels, filled with antiques and haute couture. Similarly priced quality goods can be found at the high-end malls, particularly at **River City,** next to the Royal Orchid Sheraton. **The World Trade Center, Sogo, Siam Discovery Center,** and **Central** (a nationwide chain of department stores) are the city's leading malls; all of these are centrally located in Bangkok's shopping district.

Specific streets or areas are also known for excellent shopping. Among these are the **Chinatown streets,** off and on Sampeng Lane, where you'll find the so-called Thieves Market, the Pahurat cloth market, and a thousand and one notions stands; the compact and general **Bangrak Market,** behind the Shangri-La Hotel; **Pratunam Market,** at the intersection of Phetchaburi and Ratchaprarop roads, the wholesale and retail ready-to-wear center, with a vast array of inexpensive clothing; **Sukhumvit Road,** with its upscale antiques and handicrafts shops as well as bookstores; **Silom and**

Shopping Along Sukhumvit Road

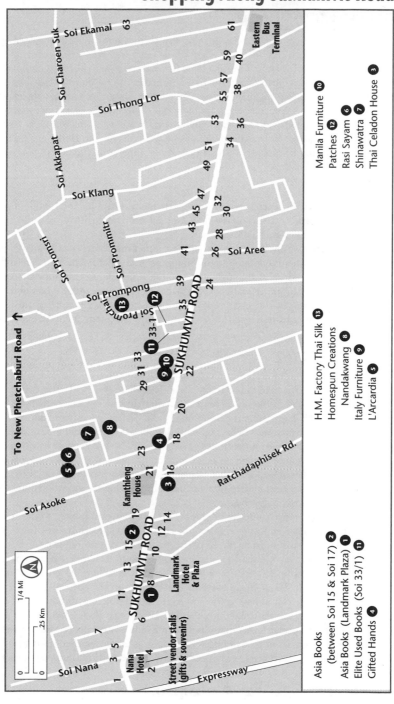

The Art of Bargaining

Nearly all shops will negotiate, so don't be shy. (If they don't want to haggle, they'll politely inform you that their prices are fixed—and even that ain't necessarily so.) Shop around a little first to develop a sense of what things should cost. Let the seller make the first offer, then counter with a reasonable offer somewhat less than you expect to pay. Always maintain a sense of humor; Thais resist unpleasant tactics. Take your time. (A companion may politely express disinterest or a desire to leave.) Once you've decided on an object, let your attention wander so that the seller doesn't know you're hooked. If there are several objects that interest you, work out a package deal. If you find something unusual that really appeals to you, don't pass it by hoping to find it cheaper later.

Surawong roads, with general merchandise, between the Oriental Hotel and Lumpini Park; **Thewet Market,** the wholesale flower outlet off Samsen Road; and the huge weekend market at **Chatuchak Park.**

Charoen Krung (New Road) and the smaller outlet roads near the Oriental Hotel were once lined with antique shops (see "Shopping A to Z," below). There are still a few in this congested area, although some of the finest shops have moved to the notable **River City shopping mall,** creating Bangkok's greatest concentration of high-end antique galleries. In this great sampling of Thai antiques, you're certain to find something to your taste; however, the River City shops are among the most expensive in the city.

SHOPPING A TO Z
ANTIQUES

Buying antiques in Thailand can be tricky. First of all, there's very little here that's considered antique in the European sense of the term. Most pieces that remain are less than 200 years old, dating from the beginning of the Chakri Dynasty in Bangkok. It's real easy for furniture builders to beat up reproductions to make them look authentic. Many collectors even doubt "Certificates of Authenticity" that accompany such items. Basically, if you've found something that's too good to be true, chances are it is too good to be true. Older items are either archeological finds or sacred objects. The Thai government has an interest in keeping these items in the country, and will require special permission for export (see below).

Buddha images, either complete or parts of an image, are prohibited from export, except for religious or educational purposes, and even in these instances you'll still have to obtain permission from the Department of Fine Arts to remove them from Thailand. Many dealers will tell you not to worry—and to be honest I've seen people stow Buddha images up to a foot high in their suitcases and have no problems at all leaving the country. Still, if you're nervous, check with the Department—they really only want to ensure you haven't fallen into some sacred object with national or historical importance (like, say, something that has been stolen from a temple and sold illegally, or a truly ancient image that was hidden inside a larger plaster one). If you're talking about an amulet or a small image that could fit in your pocket, don't sweat it. Details on how to contact the Department of Fine Arts and file for permission is provided in chapter 2.

L'Arcadia. 12/2 Soi Sukhumvit 23. ☎ **02/259-1517.**

This is a little gem of a shop with very good antique furniture (mostly from Myanmar/Burma), crafts, carved teak architectural ornaments, and older folk-art pieces.

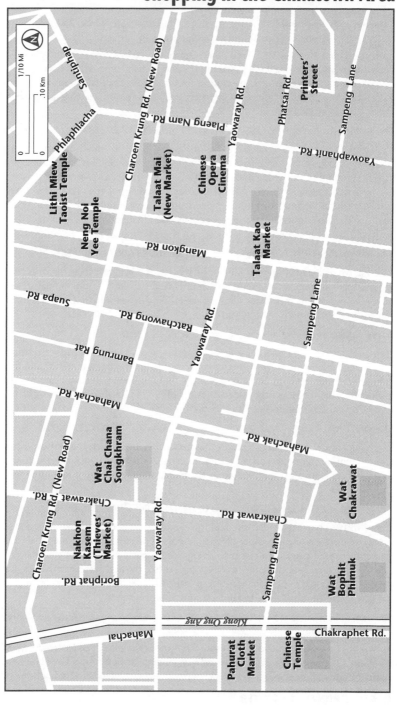

The Fine Arts. Sukhothai Hotel, Shop no. 4, 13/3 S. Sathorn Rd. ☎ **02/287-0222.**

An expensive but fine collection of terra-cotta pieces, Buddhist statuary, woven fabrics from the region, and one-of-a-kind objects grace the shelves of this small boutique in the ultrastylish Sukhothai Hotel. Among the shop's distinctive offerings are a collection of folk-art religious posters on cloth from Cambodia, terra-cotta reproductions of Sukhothai-era art, and architectural elements created by decorators to grace the hotel. Open daily 10am to 6pm.

The Golden Triangle. Room 301, River City, 23 Yotha Rd. ☎ **02/237-0077.**

This shop is quite unlike anything else in River City, if not in all of Bangkok, and is chiefly known for its excellent quality hill-tribe artifacts. This simply decorated gallery carries antique textiles and hill-tribe clothing and jewelry, reminding us more of the fine shops in Chiang Mai than most outlets in Bangkok. Silver jewelry from 20 to 100 years old, clothing made from authentic hill-tribe textiles, trading beads, and various musical instruments are among the highlights. Open daily 11am to 7pm.

The Height. Suite 354, River City, 23 Yotha Rd. ☎ **02/237-0077,** ext. 354.

Also known as Piak Padungsiriseth (for its owner), the Height is best for its excellent old mutmee silk, pottery, and statuary. Khun Piak also makes intricate miniature boats to order. For good quality, older silk, you can't do much better than this specialty boutique. Open daily 10am to 6:30pm.

Neold Collection. 149/2-3 Surawong Rd. ☎ **02/235-8352.**

A fine selection of new and old objects, including recently made paintings, shell hill-tribe belts, 19th-century Chinese puppets, and a small offering of furniture and finely crafted silver boxes. Open Monday to Friday 10am to 8pm, Saturday 10am to 4pm.

Branch showroom at the Regent Bangkok, 155 Ratchadamri Rd. (☎ **02/250-0737**) open 10am to 7pm.

The Old Time. River City Mall, 23 Yotha Rd., Suite 404–405. ☎ **02/237-0077.**

The Old Time is one of those places that gets better the longer you browse. Khmer stone sculptures, antique baskets, exquisite early 20th-century musical instruments, and betel-nut sets are found mixed with impressive 18th-century furniture. Open daily 10:30am to 7pm.

Peng Seng. 942/1–4 Rama IV Rd., corner of Surawong Rd. ☎ **02/236-8010.**

Those in the know swear that the sculptures and pottery sold at Peng Seng are genuine antiques. Among the more affordable objects were a series of Burmese carved wooden temple figures, two feet high. Peng Seng exports nearly all of the objects for sale, and can usually arrange the necessary papers (see the beginning of this section for details) for antiques. Not to be overlooked is the store's excellent selection of art books for sale. Open Monday to Saturday 9am to 6:30pm.

Saowthai Ikat. Room 438–440, The River City Shopping Complex, Yotha Rd. ☎ **02/237-0077,** ext. 438.

Saowthai Ikat is recommended for those who prize examples of older woven fabrics, especially their great selection of Lao and Cambodian "antique" silk. They also have a store in Room 308 at the Thaniya Plaza, 52 Silom Road. Open daily 10:30am to 7pm.

BRASS, BRONZE & PEWTER

Most of the major handicrafts, silk, or jewelry shops also carry brass or bronze flatware. Brass is an alloy mainly of copper and zinc, and bronze is copper and tin, but

Thais often make no distinction. The handmade quality and weight of Thai-designed bronzeware sets are lovely, but be warned that they will tarnish. Bronze and nickel alloy tarnishes less but costs a little more. Decorative pieces can be coated with silicon. Attractive decorative items are also available in pewter, an alloy of tin and lead.

Siam Bronze Factory. 1250 New Rd. ☎ **02/234-9436.**

This is one of Bangkok's larger outlets for complete bronzeware table settings. Be sure to inquire whether they'll pack and ship merchandise before buying as it may add up to $80, depending on the style and number of place settings you buy.

Thai Home Industries. 35 Oriental Lane, near Oriental Plaza. ☎ **02/234-1736.**

This is one of the better outlets for Thai souvenirs and especially bronzeware, though the sales staff could be a little friendlier. There are many different sets available, but be aware that they weigh up to 50 pounds and will have to be shipped home; expect to pay an additional $80 for shipping.

CERAMICS

The most popular Thai ceramics is the ornate *bencharong*, which was originally reserved for use by royalty, with colors restricted to red, green, blue, yellow, and white. (If gold is used for background or outline, it may be called *lai nam thong*, though the distinction is made less and less.) Celadon is much subtler but, to many, a more attractive ceramic. The traditional glaze is pale green (an approximation of jade) made from paddy silt and wood ash, though there are now blue, mauve, and other pastel colors. Unfortunately, celadon is increasingly difficult to find in Bangkok, though it is still produced in Chiang Mai. Chinese cobalt blue and white porcelain is very common and occasionally quite elegant.

Prasart Collection. Peninsula Plaza, 2nd floor, 153 Ratchadamri Rd. ☎ **02/253-9772.**

This boutique features copies of antique items from the collection at their museum. Lots of bencharong porcelain here, plus blue and white porcelain and other less garish color combinations. Open Monday to Saturday 1pm to 6pm.

Thai Celadon House. 8/6–8 Ratchadaphisek Rd., near Sukhumvit Rd., off Soi Asoke (16). ☎ **02/229-4383.** Fax 02/229-4346.

The Thai Celadon House displays and sells some of the most attractive celadon ceramics in the city, specializing in tableware. The factory is in Chiang Mai, but you can order at this showroom, and there's a seconds shop with slightly imperfect goods. Open Monday to Saturday 9am to 5pm.

CRAFTS

If you shop carefully, you'll find that Bangkok has a full selection of Thailand's best crafts, equal to anything found in the far-flung regions of the country and at prices that are comparable to such places as Surin, Chiang Mai, and Chiang Rai.

Chitralada Shop. Chitralada Palace. ☎ **02/281-1111.**

The royal family, in its ongoing effort to encourage production of Thai handicrafts, sponsors several stores in Bangkok under the name of the Chitralada Support Foundation. The Chitralada Shop, as well as the Hill Tribe Foundation at the Srapatum Palace, sells standard-quality Thai and hill-tribe crafts at reasonable prices. Open Monday to Friday 9am to 4pm. There is also a branch in the Oriental Plaza.

Gifted Hands. 172/18 Sukhumvit Soi 23. ☎ **02/258-4010.**

It's difficult to find but well worth the search. Gifted Hands is the shop of Cholada Hoover, a former art teacher who wanted to find a way to help her village. What she has done is to take traditional village silver jewelry design and her own glass beads and incorporate them with a more modern aesthetic. Gifted Hands also carries the nicest nielloware jewelry (with semiprecious stones) around. You'll find Gifted Hands on the same soi as Shinawatra; approaching from the south, it's the third 172 block on the right. Gifted Hands publishes a catalog and will ship. Open daily 8am to 6pm.

Homespun Creations Nandakwang. 108/3 Sukhumvit Soi 23 (Soi Prasanmitr). ☎ 02/258-1962.

This is the place for textured cotton housewares and "soft goods." Homespun features beautifully hand-spun and woven cotton napkins and place mats in a gorgeous array of colors. Open daily 9am to 6pm.

Lotus. Parichart Court, The Bangkok Regent Hotel, 155–157 Ratchadamri Rd. ☎ 02/250-0732.

This shop, perhaps more than any other in Bangkok, reflects the best of both Asian and European design sensibilities. With branches at Bangkok's Sukhothai and the Amanpuri in Phuket, Lotus is a favorite of upscale tourists from America, Europe, and Asia who are attracted to the new and old objects d'art collected by its European owners from Thailand, Burma, Indonesia, Tibet, and India. The exquisite, one-of-a-kind jewels and decorative objects are attractive, but prices are extremely high. Open Monday to Friday 10:30am to 8pm.

Narayana Phand. 127 Ratchadamri Rd., Pratumwan north of Gaysorn. ☎ 02/252-4670.

That this enormous handicraft emporium, partially funded by the government, is the ideal spot to work down that long list of souvenirs you need to buy before returning home. Not only is the breadth of goods impressive, but the quality/price relationship is at a very acceptable level. Open daily 10am to 8pm.

Patches. 591/16 Sukhumvit Soi 33/1. ☎ 02/258-5057.

Patches is the retail outlet for a women's self-help project started in the slums of Klong-toey by Catholic missionaries. Custom-made quilts of a decidedly non-Asian design (they look like what you might find in a rural American church sale!) are crafted by women from low-income families. There are a few Hmong-style products, but the main line of quilts, pillows, and table linens are of the early American variety. It generally takes about 6 weeks to finish a quilt, and they ship to the United States. Prices are extremely reasonable. Open Monday to Saturday 10am to 5pm.

✪ **Rasi Sayam.** 32 Sukhumvit Rd., Soi 23. ☎ 02/258-4195.

Jonathan Hayssen, a North American, has located some of the country's best craftspeople and encourages them to continue creating decorative and folk art by giving them an outlet for their work. To describe the crafts available for sale is to make an inventory of Thailand's best contemporarily produced work: Baskets, loom parts, bows, ceramics, lacquer ware, bells, wood carvings, textiles, and myriad one-of-a-kind pieces are on display in the attractively designed shops. If you're in a rush and can only get to a couple of shops, keep this one at the top of your list. Rasi Sayam is reliable, and will ship by UPS air. Open Monday to Saturday 9am to 5:30pm.

DEPARTMENT STORES & SHOPPING PLAZAS

Bangkok supports a mushrooming number of department store chains. The **Central** is the largest; its most accessible branches are on lower Silom Road, Ploenchit Road near the Le Méridien Président, and off the highway near the airport, next to the Hyatt. Similar to the Central chain is **Robinson's** (the most convenient branch is at the intersection of Rama IV and Silom), which, like Central, is best for buying staples such as socks, underwear, and other basics.

A real trip is browsing in the perpetually crowded **Thai Tokyu department store** in the Mah Boon Krong Center (where you'll also find Bangkok's best food court); this is better for the spectacle of "how Bangkok shops" than for the merchandise. The Tokyo based **Sogo Shopping Center,** just up the road from the Regent, is one of Bangkok's most upscale emporiums; it features merchandise from both European and Asian fashion houses.

Among the city's many shopping arcades, malls, and plazas, the most interesting are the huge **World Trade Center** (corner of Rama I and Ratchadamri Roads), **Phanthip Plaza** (a mall dedicated to computer dealers, especially bootleg software and games—on Phetchaburi Road behind the World Trade Center), the **River City** antiques mall, **Thaniya Plaza** (Soi Thaniya, Silom Road), the **Regent Hotel** shopping arcade, the nearby **Peninsula Plaza** arcade, and the venerable **Oriental Hotel** arcade.

DOLLS

Bangkok Dolls. 85 Soi Ratchatapan (Soi Mohleng), Makkasan. ☎ 02/245-3008.

The *New York Times* reported on this far out-of-the-way "factory" where intricately detailed figures are crafted. Traditional Thai dancers, hill-tribe figures, and playful images are the main products made and sold. It's best to call ahead, both to make sure that they're open and also for directions; plan on 45 to 60 minutes from the center of Bangkok. The shop is open Monday to Saturday 8am to 5pm; the factory, Monday to Saturday 8am to 5pm.

FASHION

Bangkok is internationally known for its designer look-alike fashions, counterfeit clothing bearing the famous labels "knocked off" at substantially lower prices than the original. Less known are the small, independent designers with their own Thai fashions that look good in Asia and back home. Quality of construction can vary from shoddy to outstanding, so give a careful once over to seams and material. If you only want to buy lengths of silk or cotton, see "Silk & Cotton," below in this section.

Art's Tailor. 62/15–16 Thaniya, Silom Rd. ☎ 02/233-3662.

This well-regarded tailor shop is primarily for men and carries a full line of wool and cotton fabrics for suits, pants, and shirts. It typically takes about three weeks for a suit to be fitted and finished. (There's a second location at 39 Ratchaprasong Shopping Center.) Open Monday to Saturday 8:30am to 5pm.

Choisy. 9/25 Surawong Rd. ☎ 02/233-7794.

This small French-owned and -operated boutique, next door to Jim Thompson Thai Silk Company, features ready-to-wear and custom clothing and is popular within the expatriate/diplomatic community. Its fashions tend to appeal to an older, more conservative clientele. Choisy's selections of silk clothing are made with thinner, less stiff fabrics than found in most Bangkok shops. There is a thriving tailoring business upstairs with well-made custom clothing. Open Monday to Saturday 10am to 6:30pm.

Julie Thai Cotton and Silk. 1279 New Rd. (Charoen Krung Rd.), near Silom Center. ☎ 02/237-6592.

This shop caters mainly to ladies' fashions with exceptionally well tailored silk dresses and linen suits. Open Monday to Saturday 9am to 6:30pm.

Perry's Thai Silk Co., Ltd. 60/2 Silom Rd. ☎ 02/233-9236.

This is a popular ready-to-wear as well as custom clothing boutique. Most bespoke outfits take a minimum of two to three days, and Perry's maintains a large inventory of both English and Italian fabrics. They also carry a line of silk products, including attractive appliqué pillows. Open Monday to Saturday 9am to 8pm.

River Mark. Suite 238 and 246, River City, 23 Yotha Rd. ☎ **02/237-0077,** ext. 238.

This and the Mark Collection (in suite 246) are among the best outlets in Bangkok for made-to-order linen clothing. It typically takes two to three days to custom-make a dress or suit, but you can expect good quality tailoring and fine materials. River Mark also carries a big selection of cotton, silk, and wool, but their linen inventory is especially large. Open Monday to Saturday 10:30am to 8pm.

FURNITURE

It may not be practical for a few small pieces, but some sophisticated shoppers buy rooms full of well-crafted antique and newly made furniture and have it shipped back home. Teak and other hardwoods as well as wicker and rattan are the most popular materials. The biggest concentration of furniture shops is along Sukhumvit between Sois 43 and 47.

Italy Furniture. 527–9 Sukhumvit Rd., between Sois 29 and 31. ☎ **02/258-4643.**

This design and manufacturing outlet of quality wicker and rattan furniture sells and ships to all parts of the world. Open Monday to Saturday 10am to 6pm.

Manila Furniture. 521 Sukhumvit Rd., near Soi 29. ☎ **02/258-2608.**

Just down the street from and very similar to Italy Furniture (see above), Manila also sells a complete line of rattan. You can pick styles from either the floor or from their photo book. It typically takes about three weeks to complete an order and a minimum of 1 month (count on three or four months) to ship. Open daily 8am to 7pm.

GIFTS/SOUVENIRS

Street vendors are hardly the most reliable purveyors of goods, but you can almost always count on them for delightful souvenirs—and if you're a good bargainer, you'll get the lowest price in Bangkok. The best stalls are along Silom Road, near the Silom Village, along Sukhumvit Road beginning at Soi 4, and in Chinatown. For many, the bustling Night Market in Patpong represents the best shopping for "counterfeit" goods in the city. Although I can't condone the purchase of counterfeit brand goods, a huge number of travelers head here to buy pirated audiotapes, CDs, and VDO-CDs.

JEWELRY

Sapphires, rubies, garnets, turquoise, and zircons are mined in Thailand, and nearly every other stone you can think of is imported and cut. You'll find jewelry and loose gems available nearly everywhere in Thailand, but most of it isn't exactly the real thing. (The previous authors of this book once bought a beautiful "pink diamond" in Chiang Mai, knowing of course it wasn't, but it was demonstrably quite hard and turned out to be a tourmaline worth a great deal more than the $5 they paid.) In general, however, if the offer seems too good to be true, it probably is. Any genuine stones offered to you in smaller shops will probably have noticeable flaws. The flawless ones are probably synthetic.

Rubies and sapphires are both corundum, which in its natural state comes in a broad spectrum of colors determined by trace elements and is valued according to the clarity and intensity of color. Synthetics are just as hard, clearer, and available in just about any color. Stones can also have their color enhanced by diffusion, a process of packing those with inferior color in the appropriate trace elements—titanium and iron oxides to get sapphire blue—and applying tremendous amounts of heat; the color won't wear or wash off, but it can be changed by high heat, and many a stone has faded when an unaware jeweler put his torch to it in mounting. (Again, there's nothing wrong with a diffused stone, as long as you know what you're buying, pay a fair price, and inform anyone working with it of its actual quality.)

Thai artisans are among the most skillful in the world, and their work in gold and silver is generally of high quality at very good value. If you're interested in a custom setting, bring a photo or drawing of what you'd like along and discuss your ideas at length.

If you're in town to explore the wholesale market, similar to New York's West 47th Street, head to Mahesak Road, just off Silom. Here you'll find Thai, Chinese, Iranian, Israeli, and Indian dealers, most of whom are engaged in the import and export of colored cut stones.

Nielloware, a distinctively Thai art form, may also catch your attention. Silver is plated with a mixture of silver, copper, lead, and sulfur, then fired for oxidation; the dark, shining, hematitelike surface that results is then incised with floral, flamelike, and other Thai designs.

Nearly all jewelers who display their work in the best hotel shopping arcades produce fine-quality pieces at fair prices. Nearly all jewelry shops, even the most exclusive, negotiate, so be prepared to ask for a "special discount" on the quoted price.

Asian Institute of Gemological Sciences. 484 Ratchadaphisek Rd. ☎ **02/267-4315.**

A number of quality gem and jewelry dealers offer a certificate of identification prepared by the AIGS, a professional agency that specializes in categorizing cut stones. A typical analysis takes 1 to 2 days and includes information about the cut, color, mineral content, and size of the free (unmounted) stones. Value is not assessed. If you intend to purchase expensive gems, and have the time, attend their three-hour course or take advantage of this service. There is a branch at the Jewelry Trade Center.

Thai law states that cost depends on negotiation between buyer and seller; sellers are not required to properly identify what they sell, and guarantees are frequently not honored. You can call TAT to inquire if there have been complaints against any shop from which you're considering making a purchase. Your credit card company may be able to help you in a dispute, if you have a detailed receipt, but don't count on it.

Bee Bijour. Grand Hyatt 1st Floor, No. 2, 494 Ratchadamri Rd. ☎ **02/252-1571.**

This is one of the better manufacturers of fashionable costume jewelry made with semiprecious stones. Although their main business is tailored to the export market, this boutique displays lines sold to the local and tourist markets as well. Open daily 10am to 7:30pm.

Bualaad Joaillier. 106–107 Peninsula Plaza, 153 Ratchadamri Rd. ☎ **02/253-9760.**

Fantastic stones (especially the Thai and Burmese rubies) and jewelry are on display at this decidedly upmarket jewelry design house. The quality is superb and, unlike most of the jewelry stores in Bangkok, this one eschews the current trends, preferring to base its designs on traditional motifs. Open Monday to Saturday 1 to 6pm.

Cabochon. Oriental Hotel Arcade, Oriental Ave. ☎ **02/236-6607.**

This well-established reputable boutique displays brilliant sapphire pendants and quality ruby rings accented with diamonds. As with the best shops, all of Cabochon's pieces are sold with certificates of authorization by AGIS gemologists with an offer of a refund. There's a branch in the Dusit Thani Hotel, ground floor, Rama IV Road (☎ **02/233-4371**). Both are open Monday to Friday 10am to 8pm, Sat 10am to 6pm, and the Oriental Branch is also open Sundays 10am to 6pm.

Tok Kwang. 224/6 Silom Rd. ☎ **02/233-0658.**

As soon as you enter you'll know you've come to a major jewelry store with quality and prices to match. Tok Kwang has been in business since 1946 and has built a solid reputation for the best pearls in town. Most of their pearls come from Japan, but an increasing number are imported from Burma and Australia. Tok Kwang also sells fine watches, diamonds, and gems. Open daily 9:30am to 5:30pm. There is a second branch at the Regent Bangkok, 155 Rajdamri Road (☎ **02/250-0735**). Open daily 10:30am to 6:30pm.

Uthai's Gems. 28/7 Soi Ruam Rudee, Phoenchit Rd. ☎ **02/253-8582.**

Uthai Daengrasmisopon is one of the most reliable jewelers in Bangkok. You'll be amazed at the number of Americans who stream in and out of his store and the number of repeat shoppers who make Uthai's their first stop on the Bangkok buying trail. Uthai has an enormous inventory of extremely well-priced, conservatively styled jewelry, but also offers custom work and repair. (Allow 2 to 3 days for simple items, longer for more complex work.) The quality and value of Uthai's gold chains, handcrafted in 22-karat gold, are impressive. Uthai also runs a mail-order business and has a good collection of bronzeware. Open Monday through Saturday daily 10am to 6pm.

✪ **Yves Joaillier.** Charn Issara Tower, 3rd Floor, 942/83 Rama IV Rd. ☎ **02/233-3292.**

This boutique, among the most elegant in Bangkok, has exquisite designs and exceptional quality. Yves Bernardeau's best designs incorporate contemporary European style with ancient Mediterranean motifs. Yves is brilliant at made-to-order jewelry; expect three days for a ring, one to two weeks for a necklace. His prices are competitive with the local market and bargains compared to American boutiques. All locally made jewelry with gems comes with AIGS certificates. Open Monday through Saturday 10am to 5:30pm.

LEATHER GOODS, SHOES & BOOTS

Many people leave Bangkok wearing shoes and cowboy boots made from ostrich, elephant, snake, alligator, or other exotic leathers. Before planning to purchase any goods made from these skins, consult your home embassy's customs office for a list of prohibited goods (endangered species and the like) or they could be confiscated upon your return. There are many shops along Charoen Krung (New Road) near the Oriental Hotel and in and around Patpong that also carry leather clothing, wallets, and purses.

Chao Phraya Bootery. 116/3 Silom Soi 4. ☎ **02/234-1226.**

This is an excellent outlet for shoes, boots, and a full range of leather accessories. In addition to having a large inventory, they do efficient custom work (cowboy boots only); expect to have a pair made within 4 to 5 days. Open daily 10am to 9pm.

MARKETS

Pak Klong Talaat. Along the Chao Phraya on Luk Luang.

Pak Klong Talaat (also called the Talaat Taywait) is home to Bangkok's cut-flower market. Huge bushels of cut flowers and vegetables arrive nightly; buyers from around the city shop in the very early morning hours. If you're wandering around the city after midnight looking for an offbeat attraction, stop by and choose from baskets of orchids, lotus, jasmine, marigolds, and many more. You can also watch the flower vendors threading garlands and assembling the huge, colorful, intricately patterned funeral wreaths. Open 24 hours. The market is located near the Memorial Bridge, on Chakrapatch Road.

Patpong Night Market. Patpong Soi 1, between Silom and Suriwong rds.

Patpong has been famous for its bars, neon lights, girls, sex shows, girls, massage parlors, and girls since the Vietnam War, but in the last 10 years it's become a major shopping attraction. The bustling Night Market features vendors of nearly everything faux: pirated CDs and tapes, designer knockoffs (many of which will actually survive a washing), copy watches (including "Rolexes" that should still be running when you get them through customs), leather goods stamped with desirable logos (sure to hold up better than cardboard)—not especially cheap, but lively and fun, especially if you enjoy crowds and the challenge of con artists. Open daily after sundown.

Weekend Market. Chatuchak Park.

If you're in Bangkok on a weekend, don't miss the Weekend Market, off the Airport Highway (about forty minutes away in traffic). It covers a vast area with rows of stalls selling everything—souvenirs, "antiques," fresh and dried seafood, vegetables and condiments, blue and white pottery, live fish that are scooped from tanks, pets of every sort (including a few endangered species), orchids and other exotic plants, clothing, and a host of strange exotic items you may not recognize. It's a great way to introduce yourself to the exotic sights, flavors, and colors of Thai life, as well as a good place to visit at the end of your trip for items you wish you'd bought elsewhere. There's some organization: Toward the front left you'll find plants, including orchids (which can also be found on the street just north of the market); toward the center it's crowded with blue jeans and T-shirts; live animals are found toward the right rear; minerals to the far right; ceramics, jewelry, counterfeit antiques, and so on, toward the left rear. (Nancy Chandler's illustrated *Market Map* has a color-coded insert.) Open on Saturdays and Sundays (also Wednesday evenings). Try to get there early in the morning before the sun bakes everything under the plastic tarps—including you.

SILK & COTTON

Besides those places listed below, there are also very good silk outlets in the international hotel shopping arcades. If you're looking for ready-to-wear or custom clothing, see "Fashion," above. Synthetics are frequently sold as silk (be wary of anything called "Japanese silk," which is really polyester), and if you're in doubt about a particular piece, select a thread and burn it; silk should smell like singed hair or feathers. Sometimes only the warp (lengthwise threads) is synthetic because it's more uniform and easier to work with, but as this isn't seen or felt, it's a less important consideration.

Design Thai. 304 Silom Rd. ☎ **02/235-1553.**

Design Thai is a deliberate imitation of Jim Thompson, in both style and merchandise (even the building is similar). Like Thompson's, they stock a wide range of fabrics and accessories including silk slippers, jewelry boxes, a good selection of purses, and a fuddy-duddy selection of ready-to-wear clothes. Open daily 9am to 7pm.

H. M. Factory Thai Silk. 45 Promchai, Sukhumvit 39. ☎ **02/258-8766.**

This is a lovely place to visit and a good place to watch mutmee silk in the weaving stage. Silk weavers buy raw material from Isan and spin and weave clothing and upholstery-grade fabric in the private garden/home. The majority of plain, patterned, and mutmee silk is available for sale by lengths, and there's a modest selection of clothing. This workshop may be hard to find, so keep your eye out for a sign (it's located on a side street off the soi). Open Monday through Saturday 8:30am to 6pm.

Shinawatra. 94 Sukhumvit Rd., Soi 23. ☎ **02/258-0295.**

The largest of this chain's stores is supplied by its own factory and has an enormous selection of both silk and cotton (particularly in wonderful solid colors), rivaling even

Jim Thompson for variety. Shinawatra also stocks a small line of handicrafts including dolls, crocodile purses, and teak accessories, as well as some jewelry. Open Monday to Saturday 8:30am to 5:30pm.

Jim Thompson Thai Silk Company. 9 Surawong Rd. ☎ **02/234-4900.**

It's nearly impossible to mention silk in Thailand without referring in some way to Jim Thompson (see Jim Thompson's House in "Bangkok's Historical Treasures" Traditional Architecture," above), the legendary American who reestablished the modern Thai industry of silk weaving. Even if you don't visit his company's elegant shop, most competitors will compare their workmanship and prices with his goods. For top-drawer goods, including finely woven cotton, Thompson's is the place—but expect to pay for the quality and know that the styles are ultraconservative. They sell silk or cotton by the yard and well-designed and crafted jewelry from India, Indonesia, and Thailand. Open daily 9am to 9pm.

SILVER
Chai Lai. Floor 1, Peninsula Plaza, Ratchadamri Rd. ☎ **02/252-1538.**

This is a great store for hill-tribe and older Thai jewelry at reasonable to high prices. One of the nicest selections outside of Chiang Mai. Open Monday to Saturday 11am to 6pm.

Chartered Gems Ltd. 92 Silom Soi 24. ☎ **02/233-9320.**

In addition to jewelry, this place has a great selection of nicely made silverware products. Open Monday to Saturday 9:30am to 7:30pm.

8 Bangkok After Dark

Bangkok is one of Asia's wildest nightlife scenes, with a huge range of cultural and hedonistic activities that should satisfy just about anyone. Artistic and cultural performances light up Bangkok evenings, after which countless discos and bars for all tastes keep you going until the wee hours. Most visitors won't leave without a stroll around Patpong, the famous sex strip and Night Market, with myriad vendors and blocks of bars and clubs.

For the hippest nightlife update, check out *Metro Magazine* (100B/$2.65) available at bookstores. Featuring monthly listings of art events (by both foreign and local artists), theater performances (including local theater companies performing modern Thai plays), and the club scene (very up to date), it's the best single source of information about entertainment in the Big Mango and a must-buy for those serious about exploring Bangkok culture. Both the *Bangkok Post* and *The Nation* offer daily listings of cultural events and performance schedules. The TAT (in Bangkok ☎ 1155) will also provide schedule information. Your hotel concierge should also be able to guide you toward the evening of your choice.

THE PERFORMING ARTS
Although the large shopping malls and international hotels often sponsor a cultural show, most travelers experience the Thai classical performing arts at a commercially staged dance show accompanying a Thai banquet; several hotels and restaurants offer this program. Generally there's a fixed-menu dinner of Thai favorites accompanied by a small orchestra, followed by a dance performance. Combined, you won't get the best food or the best dance. (See "Dinner with Thai Dance" in chapter 4 for specific recommendations.)

For a different experience, visit the **Erawan Shrine,** at the corner of Ratchadamri and Ploenchit roads (near the Grand Hyatt Erawan Bangkok and Sogo Department Store). In front of the large, white marble altar to Brahma, the Hindu god of creation, and Erawan, his three-headed elephant—you'll often find musicians and beautifully costumed dancers commissioned to amuse Brahma by a grateful or hopeful worshiper.

There are two major theaters for Thai and international performances, the National Theater and the Thai Cultural Center. The **National Theater,** 1 Na Phra That Road (☎ 02/224-1342), presents demonstrations of Thai classical dancing and music by performers from the School of Music and Dance in Bangkok, which are generally superior to those at the tourist restaurants and hotels. There are also performances by visiting ballet and theatrical companies. Call the TAT or the box office for the current schedule.

The **Thailand Cultural Center,** Thiem Ruammit Road off Ratchadaphisek Road, Huai Khwang (☎ 02/247-0028), is the newest and largest performance center in town, offering a wide variety of programs. The Bangkok Symphony performs here during its short summer season. Other local and visiting companies also present theater and dance at the center. If you're to see the *Ramayana* performed in Bangkok, this is probably the place you'll see it. Call for the current schedule.

For a bit of tongue-in-cheek theater, a couple of Cabaret shows in Bangkok feature *katoeys* (aka "Lady-Boys") in 6-inch heels and feather boas performing to pop hits. Many times these shows are hilarious—the best to try is **Calypso Cabaret,** Asia Hotel, 296 Phayathai Rd. (☎ 02/261-6355). Calypso enjoys a certain amount of fame in Bangkok, with some performances that are more creative than the standard drag parades at cabarets in Phuket or Pattaya. (Shows nightly at 8:15pm and 9:45pm; tickets 700B/$18.40). A more typical show for Thailand, featuring much of the same routine as at the resorts, is **Mambo,** Washington Square, Sukhumvit Soi 22 (☎ 02/259-5128), with shows nightly 8:30 and 10pm; tickets 800B ($21.05).

THE CLUB & BAR SCENE

Bangkok is huge, offering an endless selection of nighttime amusements. Most night places seem clustered around certain areas within the city, so I've broken down nightlife into the more popular areas—within each you can find all sorts of different entertainment. Drink prices will range from about 80B ($2.10) for a bottle of beer or a one-shot cocktail at a local bar, to double that at a hotel. If you'd just like to unwind with an evening cocktail, check out what's happening at your hotel's lobby bar; many set up jazzy live music to entertain folks. For the best lobby bar atmosphere head for **The Bamboo Bar** at the Oriental Hotel, Oriental Lane off Charoen Krung Road (☎ 02/236-0400), with classy live jazz—some of the best in the city, or **The Colonnade** at the Sukhothai Hotel, 13/3 Sathorn Rd. (☎ 02/287-0222), to enjoy the Sukhothai's sophisticated decor. For the infamous Bangkok sex show scene, check out "Patpong" below. Bars and discos are all over the city, with the bigger ones in the areas I've covered, plus an interesting local disco scene out on Ratchadaphisek Road. If you're looking for Bangkok's gay scene, start at Silom Soi 4 (see "Patpong" below).

PATPONG

The Patpong scene is centered around Soi Patpong 1 and Soi Patpong 2 between Surawong and Silom roads. Most people know Patpong for its reputation as the home of Bangkok's sex shows, but even if you're not exactly interested in risqué entertainment you'll probably find yourself there to explore this spot's large Night Market or array of interesting bars and discos. The market packs in stalls full of cheap knock-off goods, pirate recordings, and all sorts of souvenirs—a great browse but be prepared for some crowding.

Along the sides of the streets, men will try to lure you in to see a show. Take a peek at their menu boards to see what shows the girls will perform—it's definitely more circus spectacle than erotic dance. If you'd like to check out a show, be careful about the places you enter. Some add steep charges to your bill and threaten you if you can't pay the whole thing. If this (or anything else horrible) happens to you in one of these places, feel free to visit the Tourist Police booth on Surawong Road. The Tourist Police here are a force to be reckoned with, and have helped many a traveler out of just such a scam (see "The Sex Scene," below). For a decent place, go to **Fire Cat**—you won't find any cover charge or hidden costs, drinks are reasonably priced, and the girls are less assertive than other places in terms of buying them drinks. If you're tipping, keep it limited to 20B notes, otherwise you'll be mobbed by a million girls. Another fun place is **King's Castle,** for basic go-go—but guess which women are really women?

Despite its rap, Patpong also serves up some pretty great bars and discos. For the bar scene, you can always count on the scene at **O'Reilly's Irish Pub,** 62 Silom Rd., on the corner of Soi Thaniya just east of Patpong (☎ 02/632-7515), a lively watering hole, or **The Barbican,** 9/4–5 Soi Thaniya off Silom Road (☎ 02/234-3590), for stylish hanging out (and great food) plus the best jukebox this side of the Pacific Ocean. **Delaney's,** across from Patpong on Convent Road (next to Silom Complex), 1/5–6 Sivadon Building (☎ 02/266-7160), caters to Bangkok yuppies and foreign expatriates with Irish pub style and live music after office working hours. For good dancing, try out **King's Corner** or the more techno **Lucifer's,** both within the Patpong area. There's also **Legends** in the Dusit Thani Hotel, at the corner of Silom Road and Rama IV Road (☎ 02/236-0450), for a more upscale and fashionable place to see and be seen. I like heading to Silom Soi 4 (between Patpong 2 and Soi Thaniya off Silom Road), where you'll find small home-grown clubs spinning great music in a more intimate atmosphere. Silom Soi 4 is also where you'll find a lot of gay clubs. The most popular of which are **Telephone Bar** and **The Balcony** (both on Silom Soi 4).

SIAM SQUARE

Siam Square, on Rama I Road between Henri Dunant Road and Phayathai Road, houses quite a few popular joints. Here's where you'll find Bangkok's **Hard Rock Café,** featuring good live bands, 424/3–6 Siam Square Soi 11 (☎ 02/254-0830), and **Planet Hollywood,** Gaysorn Plaza, at the corner of Ploenchit Road and Ratchadamri Road (☎ 02/656-1358), also with live entertainment, plus decent food. At the **Hartmannsdorfer Brauhaus,** 2nd floor, Siam Discovery Center, Rama I Road (☎ 02/658-0223), you'll find home brews in a nice atmosphere—with special beer discounts on Sundays.

A great disco, **Concept CM²** has live bands (one night there was a jazzy bebop band—great if you can remember how to jitterbug) with DJ dance music in between—very popular place, Novotel Siam, Siam Square Soi 6 (☎ 02/255-6888). **Spasso,** Grand Hyatt Erewan Hotel, 494 Ratchadamri Road (☎ 02/254-1234), a fabulous Italian restaurant, turns into an equally fabulous, upscale club featuring live music—superb decor and atmosphere.

If you must find the best karaoke in Bangkok, try **Sensations,** Novotel Siam, Siam Square Soi 6 (☎ 02/255-6888). A huge selection of songs and excellent equipment. Ask about group discounts.

A little bit north of this area (a short cab ride away), near the Victory Monument, check out live "jazz" (more blues than jazz, but still good) at **Saxophone Pub and Restaurant.** They're at Phayathai Road just across from the traffic circle (☎ 02/246-5472).

KHAO SAN ROAD

Over on Rattanakosin Island in Old Bangkok the backpackers on Khao San Road have created quite a scene. Start at **Gulliver's** on the corner of Khao San and Chakrabongse roads to prime yourself, then explore the back lanes off Khao San for small dance clubs (some the size of broom closets) and hang outs. You'll find plenty of other travelers here, and the atmosphere is always laid-back and anything goes.

SUKHUMVIT ROAD

Along the long stretch of Sukhumvit Road, expatriate and locals have created an assortment of great places to check out—but most are not within walking distance of each other. Most will require a short hop by taxi or tuk-tuk in between.

The **Bull's Head,** Sukhumvit Soi 33/1 (☎ 02/259-444), a fun local pub, draws crowds with frequent theme parties and a clubhouse attitude. A few microbreweries draw crowds out to this area. **Bruahaus Bangkok,** President Park, Sukhumvit Soi 24 at the end of the soi (☎ 02/661-1111), and **Taurus Brew House,** Sukhumvit Soi 26 (☎ 02/661-2207), pack them in—especially on weekends—for home brews and live pop music. **Taurus** also boasts one of the better discos in the Sukhumvit area, just across from the Brew House, this hip and huge "complex" has live music, a giant disco, and good food. For the best live music, however, head for **Riva's,** Sheraton Grande Sukhumvit Hotel, 250 Sukhumvit Road (☎ 02/653-0333), with international bands and lots of dancing.

Similar to the Patpong sex show scene, two other areas out on Sukhumvit have go-go bars but without the hype. Check out **Nana Plaza** just South of Sukhumvit Road on Sukhumvit Soi 4 or **Soi Cowboy** (the oldest go-go scene, dating from Vietnam War days) between Soi Asoke (Sukhumvit Soi 21) and Sukhumvit Soi 23.

RCA (ROYAL CITY AVENUE)

This once booming nightclub center has gone through periods of popularity and slumps regularly, but lately it seems to be on an upswing again. Theme bars are easy to find, featuring theme architecture—it's perhaps more fun to walk along the avenue checking out the funky buildings than actually to hang out inside any of them. The RCA is off Soi Soonvijai between Rama IX and New Phetchaburi Roads.

High points at RCA include **Oleng,** 29/78-81 RCA, Block 5 (☎ 02/203-0972), with a fabulously laid-back opium den feel, and **Café Kept,** 29/82 RCA, Block 5 (no telephone,) is an attractive hang out where you can talk and actually hear your voice. **Route 66,** 29/37 RCA, Block 5 (☎ 02/203-0407), is a packed, loud and crazy disco—if you can't get in try **Interstate** next door. And check out wacky theme bars like **Raan Tad Phom** (barber shop), **Night Dive** (for aquanauts), or **Bond Street** (the London Underground).

RATCHADAPHISEK ROAD

Huge discos reign supreme at Ratchadaphisek—and it has a good, local feel. The area attracts mostly young urban Thais; you'll find fewer foreigners here than you will at other places. **Dance Fever** (☎ 02/247-4295) and **Hollywood** (☎ 02/246-4311) opposite Oscar Palace, are big and cavernous, with DJs spinning thumping Western hits and popular Thai songs. I also like **Sparks,** in the Emerald Hotel (☎ 02/276-4774), for a local disco experience—the people are friendly and welcoming, and in many ways more open to meeting new people than people at other hangout places.

"MODERN" OR "PHYSICAL" MASSAGE PARLORS

This is not *exactly* traditional Thai massage. Bangkok has hundreds of "modern" or "physical" massage parlors, which are heavily advertised, and offer something quite

---

Travel Tip

If you enter a club other than the ones listed in this book, ask up front about charges—cover charges, drink charges, show charges—these places can really try to rip you off. If you are presented with an exorbitant bill, your only logical recourse is to pay up and then call the Tourist Police (☎ **02/694-1222,** ext. 1) after the incident to try to reclaim your money. The Tourist Police can be very helpful in situations like these—they know how to deal with problems, and they take it very seriously. If you try to argue with club managers yourself, you may be met with violence, so use caution.

---

different from traditional Thai massage. Physical massage usually involves the masseuse using her entire body, thoroughly oiled to massage the customer, a "body-body" massage. If one wishes, a "sandwich," with two masseuses, can also be ordered.

Nearly all massage parlors are organized along the same lines. Guests enter the lobby where there's a coffee shop/bar and several waiting rooms where young Thai women wearing numbers pinned to their blouses sit on bleachers. Guests examine the women through a window and select their masseuse. Both guest and masseuse take a room in the building and typically spend between 1 and 2 hours on a massage. Rates for a physical massage start at about 600B ($15.80).

THE SEX SCENE

Although the 1985 hit song "One Night in Bangkok" was actually about chess (from the musical *Chess*), the song celebrated the naughtiest aspect of life in Bangkok. Since the 1960s—and particularly since the Vietnam War—Bangkok has served as the sin capital of Asia, with sex clubs, bars, massage parlors, and prostitutes concentrated in the Patpong, Nana Plaza, and Soi Cowboy districts. Recent acknowledgments by the Thai government of the startling increase in HIV-positive cases have toned down somewhat the sex-club scene, while some vendors have shifted their focus to younger and younger women. Prostitutes these days will insist their clients use a condom.

In the "Patpong" section above I've included a few suggestions where anyone can see a "Bangkok Sex Show" without being hassled by extra charges and seedy goings on—the places I've recommended are basically on the up and up and women are welcome, as are couples. To be honest, in all of these clubs the girls look bored, with most of the acts being performed with studied routine. In addition to go-go bars and sex shows, you'll also find gay go-go bars in Patpong, small clubs with sex on the menu and rooms upstairs, and some bars where oral sex is performed en bar (in all three districts).

Let's be perfectly frank: The men and women in the clubs are all available to take out of the bar. You'll be required to pay a "bar fine" (about 350B to 500B/$9.20 to $13.15) and you can take the companion of your choice out to other clubs, or to someplace more private. Some men buy girls out of bars just to go to the movies. If you're interested in having sex, you'll negotiate directly with him or her, and pay in cash. If this is your scene, stick with folks from the go-go bars and established clubs—these women and men are less likely to slip you drugs (which happens), rob your hotel room while you're sleeping (which happens), or get you mixed up with illegal activities (which happens). If you stick with club employees, you can always return to the club the next night to find them if something goes amiss. Also, know that many "gay" men working the scene are not really gay, but just in the business for the money.

If you're staying in a very expensive up-market hotel, many times you will not be allowed to bring prostitutes through the lobby. As an alternative, ask your new friend to recommend a cheap alternative hotel room nearby.

While prostitution is technically illegal in Thailand, this law is never enforced. International reports about poor farmers selling their children into prostitution are true—many children are held in brothels against their will. However, the majority of sex workers are adults who enter the industry of their own free will, for basic economic necessity. While most have an open-minded attitude toward the industry in general, there are some things going on in the scene that can be very upsetting for Western visitors. Child prostitution and pornography, slavery, and violence against sex workers all exist. In fact, Thai law can get serious about statutory rape—the legal age of consent is 15, and a few foreigners have served jail time for ignoring this law. If you encounter any of these activities, you can report them to either the **Tourist Police** (☎ 02/694-1222, ext. 1), the **Center for the Protection of Children's Rights (CPCR)** (☎ 02/412-1196), the **Friends of Women Foundation** (☎ 02/279-7158), the **Task Force to Fight Against Child Exploitation (FACE)** (☎ 02/509-5782), or the **Thailand National Commission on Women's Affairs (NCWA)** (☎ 02/512-0606).

9 Side Trips from Bangkok

There are plenty of easy day trips from Bangkok. Favorites include various cruises along the Chao Phraya to the more distant klongs and to the ancient capital of Ayutthaya, north of Bangkok, with a stop at the Bang Pa-In Summer Palace. There's also a floating market south of Bangkok that is still a bit more authentic than the one in town. Culture buffs should explore the Thailand-in-miniature Ancient City, the Rose Garden's performance arts show, and the world's tallest chedi at Nakhon Pathom. For those interested in a good wildlife show, there's the Samutprakarn Crocodile Farm and the Elephant Grounds. Kids will enjoy most of these, but if they are restless, head for one of the splashy, nearby water parks.

Ayutthaya, the Kingdom of Siam's second capital (after Sukhothai but before Bangkok), is a historical site that's commonly visited as a day trip, but may entice history, art, and architecture buffs into an overnight stay. Kanchanaburi is a jungle-clad village on the banks of the famous River Kwai, which can be seen on a long day trip, but is better enjoyed as an overnight excursion. Lopburi is an ancient Buddhist city with a few interesting sites, often visited as an overnight stop on the way to touring the Northeast.

EASY 1-DAY EXCURSIONS
RIVER DAY TRIPS

Several river tours venture outside Bangkok. The *Oriental Queen,* a luxurious cruise boat operated by the Oriental Hotel (☎ **02/236-0400**), leaves the Oriental Pier every day at 8am for Ayutthaya (see "Ayutthaya & Bang Pa-In," below, for more information about Ayutthaya). Buses meet the boat in Ayutthaya for tours of the city ruins and the lovely Bang Pa-In Summer Palace. At 5pm, the buses leave for the 2-hour return trip to Bangkok. You can also travel up by bus and return by boat. Cost is 1,900B ($50) per person, including lunch, tour, and full transportation.

A less expensive excursion to Ayutthaya is offered by the **Chao Phraya Express Company** (☎ 02/222-5330). Boats leave the Maharaj Pier (off Maharat Road, north of the Grand Palace) every Sunday at 8am. This tour covers the Thai Folk Arts and Handicraft Center, the Bang Pa-In Summer Palace in Ayutthaya, and the Pai Lom Temple, a sanctuary for open-bill storks (the best time to visit is from December to

June). The unguided, all-day excursion is very popular with locals and costs 300B ($7.90) per person, meals not included.

For a shorter and easier river trip, take the Chao Phraya Express Boats (you can catch one at the Thai Chang Pier) all the way up to Nonthaburi, about a half hour beyond the northern edge of Bangkok. You'll get the feeling of a smaller town, with its markets and gardens, and you can tour the colorful Klong Om.

FLOATING MARKET AT DAMNOEN

The Floating Market at Damnoen Saduak, Ratchaburi, is about 40 minutes south of Nakhon Pathom, so you can either combine the two sites into a 1-day trip or stop at Nakhon Pathom en route to Kanchanaburi (River Kwai). Some tours combine the Floating Market with a visit to the Rose Garden or with the River Kwai sights (see below for more on each). If you choose to go via organized tour, such as **World Travel Service** (☎ **02/233-5900**), expect to pay about 1,430B ($37.65) for the 1-day trip combo with the Rose Garden, or 1,320B ($34.75) for the 1-day trip combo with Kanchanaburi.

At a real floating market, food vendors sell their goods from small boats to local folk in other boats or in klong-side homes. There are some floating markets in Bangkok that have become so commercialized and touristy, they're beyond the point of interest. Some will tout the Damnoen market as more "authentic" than that in Bangkok. This version is about as precise a duplicate as you could imagine; it's fine for photographers, and you'll enjoy it as long as you resist the urge to buy anything. Goods are sold at this pressurized souvenir supermarket at up to five or six times their normal Bangkok prices!

To do it on your own, take a bus to Damnoen Saduak from the Southern Bus Terminal on Charansanitwong Road (☎ **02/435-1199**) (trip time: 2 hours; 55B/$1.45). Buses leave every 30 minutes starting at 4:30am. Leave early, since market activity peaks between 8am and 10am. From the Damnoen Saduak station, walk along the canal or take a water taxi for 20B (55¢) to the floating market. You can also rent a nonmotorized wooden boat for about 150B ($3.95) per half hour and explore it more fully. As always, negotiate the price (and do it with gusto; this can be a rip-off activity) with the driver before you leave.

THE ANCIENT CITY (MUANG BORAN)

This remarkable museum is a giant scale model of Thailand, with the country's major landmarks built full-scale or in miniature and spread over 200 acres. It has been built over the last 20 years by a local millionaire who has played out on a grand scale his obsession with Thai history.

Because it's far from the heart of Bangkok, the Ancient City is best visited by organized tour, though you can certainly go on your own. It's at kilometer 33 on the old Sukhumvit Highway in Samut Prakan Province (there's an extra 50B/$1.30 parking fee). For more information, contact the **Ancient City Co.,** on Ratchadamnoen Road in Bangkok (☎ **02/226-1936**); ask them for public bus route information.

All travel agents offer package tours that combine the Rose Garden with other attractions in the area, such as the Crocodile Farm or the huge Buddhist chedi in nearby Nakhon Pathom.

Admission to the Ancient City is 50B ($1.30) for adults and 25B (65¢) for children under 12. It's open daily from 9am to 5pm.

A CROCODILE FARM

Only 3km (2 miles) from the Ancient City you'll find the Samutprakan Crocodile Farm and Zoo, at kilometer 30 on the Old Sukhumvit Highway (☎ **02/703-5144**). The world's largest, it has more than 40,000 snappers, both fresh- and saltwater.

At the hourly show, handlers wrestle the crocs in murky ponds. A great outing for families!

Admission is 300B ($7.90) for adults, 250B ($6.60) for children. It's open daily from 8am to 6pm; feedings take place every hour.

ROSE GARDEN COUNTRY RESORT

Besides its rose garden, this attractive if somewhat touristy resort is known for its all-in-one show of Thai culture that includes Thai classical and folk dancing, Thai boxing, sword fighting, and cock fighting—a convenient way for visitors with limited time to digest some canned Thai culture. It's located 32km (20 miles) west of Bangkok on the way to Nakhon Pathom on Highway 4 (☎ 02/295-3261).

Surprisingly, the resort's restaurant is very appealing and not expensive. It overlooks the Nakhon Chaisri River, dotted with islands of water hyacinth. The *tom yam kung* and the green curry will set your taste buds afire. The pad thai noodles are good, as is the strange-looking but very tasty, spicy *pla krob salad* (dried fish with tamarind sauce).

Admission is 10B (25¢) for the grounds; 300B ($7.90) for the show. It's open daily from 8am to 6pm; the cultural show is at 2:45pm. Buses depart from the Southern Bus Terminal (☎ 02/435-1199) (only about 20B/55¢).

SAMPHRAN ELEPHANT GROUNDS & ZOO

Located 1km (⁶/₁₀ miles) north of the Rose Garden Country Resort in Yannowa (30km from the city), the Samphran Elephant Grounds and Zoo (☎ 02/284-1873) is a lush 22-acre garden complex offering an entertaining elephant show, plus thousands of crocodiles, including the world's largest white crocodile.

Admission is 300B ($7.90) for adults, 200B ($5.25) for children. The zoo is open daily from 9am to 6pm; crocodile wrestling shows—12:45 and 2:20pm; elephant show times—1:45 and 3:30pm; additional shows on Saturday, Sunday, and holidays at 10:30am.

NAKHON PATHOM

En route to Kanchanaburi—about 60km (37 miles) west of Bangkok—the chedi of Nakhon Pathom's Phra Pathom soars like a golden bell into the sky (it's actually made of orange tiles brought from China). It's the world's tallest Buddhist monument (413 ft.), and marks the spot where Buddhism was introduced to Thailand 2,300 years ago, making it one of the holiest shrines in the country. It was rebuilt at least twice: during the Khmer era, and in the 19th century by King Mongkut, who visited the site when he was studying Buddhism. Take the walk all the way around the central chedi and observe the many smaller shrines and their reclining and seated Buddha images.

Air-conditioned buses leave every ten minutes for Nakhon Pathom beginning at 5am from the Southern Bus Terminal (☎ 02/435-1199) (trip time: 1 hour; 27B/70¢). You can also combine a day trip to Nakhon Pathom (through any tour operator) with an early morning stop at the Damnoen Saduak Floating Market, or with a visit to the nearby Rose Garden and Samphran Elephant Grounds.

WATER PARKS

If the heat and the kids have gotten to you, consider a trip to one of two water parks. The closest is **Suan Siam (Siam Park)**, 101 Sukhapibarn 2 Rd., Bangkapi (☎ 02/919-7200), a 30-minute drive east of town (or an hour on bus no. 26 or 27 from the Victory Monument). It's a large complex of water slides (try the Super Spiral—about ¼ mile long), enormous swimming pools with artificial surf, waterfalls, landscaped gardens, playgrounds, beer garden, and more. There is a fishing farm on the way, which the kids might also enjoy.

Admission is 400B ($10.55) adults, 300B ($7.90) children, including rides. Siam Park is open daily 10am to 6pm.

AYUTTHAYA & BANG PA-IN
76km (47 miles) NW of Bangkok

AYUTTHAYA
Ayutthaya is one of Thailand's great historical highlights. Most people take the day tour from Bangkok and are allowed about 3 hours at the sites, but if you relish visiting archaeological ruins, Ayutthaya justifies an overnight stay.

From its establishment in 1350 by King U-Thong (Ramathibodi I) until its fall to the Burmese in 1767, Ayutthaya was Thailand's capital and home to 33 kings of various dynasties. At its zenith and until the mid–18th century, Ayutthaya was a vast, majestic city with three palaces and 400 splendid temples on an island threaded with 35 miles of canals—a city that mightily impressed European visitors (for a depiction of Westerners in the ancient city, see the Ayutthaya-era murals in Phetchaburi).

Traces of two major foreign settlements can still be seen. Religious objects, coins, porcelain, clay pipes, and skeletons of the Portuguese (who arrived in 1511) are displayed at the Settlement's memorial building. The Japanese memorial is a recently erected inscribed stone and a hall and gate.

There is something hauntingly sad about Ayutthaya. In 1767, after a 15-month siege, it was destroyed by the Burmese; today every temple testifies to the hatred that drives humans to rampant and wanton destruction. Here stands a row of headless Buddhas, there a head lies caught in the roots of a tree. Some temples are still being rescued from the jungle, and more are undergoing careful excavation.

The architecture of Ayutthaya is fascinating, especially if you've traveled around Thailand and absorbed the many important foreign influences. Those who have traveled to the Northeast will recognize the Khmer influence in the design of many of the ancient wats in Ayutthaya, particularly the cactus-shaped prang (tower). Those who have visited Sukhothai are certain to notice the similarity of buildings from that magnificent site. If you've just arrived and have confined your stay to Bangkok, you might note similarities with the riverside Wat Arun, an 18th-century structure that was built in the so-called Ayutthaya style, which is a melding of Sukhothai Buddhist influences with Hindu-inspired Khmer style.

There's a small TAT office at Si Sanphet Road opposite the National Museum (☎ 035/246-076). Stop by for maps and other information.

Essentials
GETTING THERE   By Train   Trains depart 9 times daily from Bangkok's Hua Lampong Railway Station (☎ 02/223-7010) starting at 7:45am (trip time: 1½ hours; about 15B/40¢ third class).

By Bus   Buses leave every 20 minutes from the Northern Bus Terminal in Bangkok (☎ 02/272-5761) beginning at 5:40am (trip time: 1½ hours; 40B/$1.05).

By Boat   Tours to Ayutthaya leave from the Oriental Hotel (☎ 02/236-0400), Shangri-La Hotel (☎ 02/236-7777), or River City pier daily at approximately 8am (and include a stop at Bang Pa-In). Day trips include a cruise on the Chao Phraya, tour of the ancient city and return by air-conditioned coach or vice versa (trip time: all day; 1,900B/$50).

✪ If you really want to turn your trip to Ayutthaya into an adventure, travel aboard the *Manhora Song*. This authentic 60-year old rice barge was rebuilt from its solid teak hull to meet international yacht-class standards. Four state rooms, with en suite

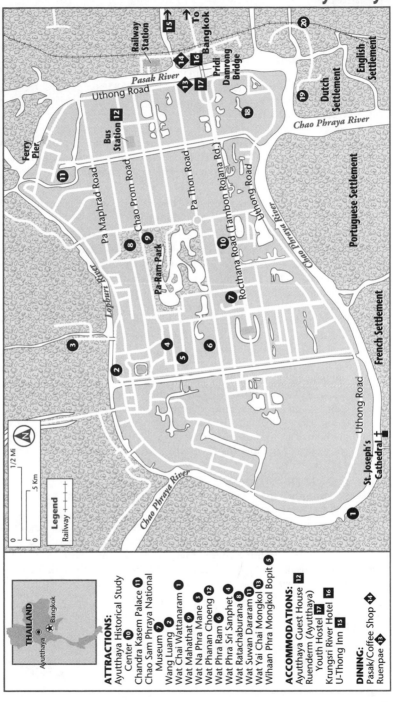

Ayutthaya

ATTRACTIONS:
Ayutthaya Historical Study
Center 🔟
Chandra Kasem Palace ⓫
Chao Sam Phraya National
Museum 🅖
Wang Luang ❷
Wat Chai Wattanaram ❶
Wat Mahathat ❾
Wat Na Phra Mane ❸
Wat Phanan Choeng ⓬
Wat Phra Ram ❻
Wat Phra Sri Sanphet ❹
Wat Ratachaburana ❽
Wat Suwan Dararam ⓫
Wat Yai Chai Mongkol ⓭
Wihaan Phra Mongkol Bopit ❺

ACCOMMODATIONS:
Ayutthaya Guest House ⓬
Ruenderm (Ayutthaya)
Youth Hostel ⓱
Krungsri River Hotel ⓰
U-Thong Inn ⓯

DINING:
Pasak/Coffee Shop ⓮
Ruenpae ⓭

bathrooms, are lavished in warm teak and mahogany, Thai silks, and regional arts and sculpture. The ship's crew serves cocktails, snacks, and delicious Thai meals on deck, which is luxuriously designed with both European and Thai touches, with a forward sundeck lounge area. The overnight trip includes a stop at Wat Bang Na, where ship's staff will accompany you to make merit to the abbot, if you so desire. The trip, inclusive of all meals, tours and transfers, runs between 12,882 and 14,706B ($339 and $387) per person, double occupancy, depending on the season. For reservations, telephone ☎ 02/476-0021; fax 02/476-1805.

A much cheaper, self-guided boat trip can be arranged through the **Chao Phraya Express Co.** (☎ 02/222-5330), which offers service on Sundays at 8am from the Maharat Pier to Ayutthaya. Return is via Bang Pa-In, where you can have lunch. The unguided, all-day excursion is very popular with locals and costs 300B ($7.90) per person, meals not included.

SPECIAL EVENTS   There is a week-long festival at the end of January, including elephant-training demonstrations and handicrafts fair.

ORIENTATION   The town is encircled by water with the perimeters defined by the Chao Phraya on the southern and western sides, the Lopburi River to the north, and the Pasak to the east. The main ferry pier is located on the east side of town, just opposite the train station. The Bangkok bus makes its last stop at the station adjacent to the Siam Commercial Bank Building, off Chao Prom Road in the downtown area (there is another stop before this that lets travelers off near the bridge). Buses from Phitsanulok stop 5km (3 miles) north of town; you'll need to take a 10B (25¢) local bus into the center.

GETTING AROUND   Once at Ayutthaya, a minibus or songtao from the train station into town will cost about 30B (80¢), but you may prefer to avoid the hustle and walk about 50 meters further to the river ferry, which will take you to city-island for 3B (10¢). You can hire a minibus for about 800B per day, and there are a few *samlors* (bicycle cabs) still available for those who prefer them and can bargain effectively. Better yet, hire a long-tail or other boat to see the city the leisurely way for about 100B ($2.65) per hour. There is regular minibus service between Ayutthaya and Bang Pa-In, departing from Chao Prom Market on the road of the same name (trip time: 50 minutes; 75B/$1.95).

What to See & Do

Ayutthaya Historical Study Center. Rojana Rd. ☎ **035/245-123.** Admission 100B ($2.65). Wed–Fri 9am–4:30pm, Sat–Sun 9am–5pm.

Established in 1990 to serve as an educational resource for students, scholars, and the public, the center presents displays of the ancient city including models of the palace and the port area and reconstructions of ships and architectural elements, as well as a fine selection of historical objects. There's an interesting section about the presence of foreigners in Ayutthaya. Start here for an overview of the area.

Chao Sam Phraya National Museum. Rojana Rd. ☎ **035/241-587.** Admission 30B (80¢). Wed–Sun 9am–noon, 1–4pm. 1½ blocks west of the center near the junction of Sri Sanphet Rd.

Thailand's second largest museum houses impressive antique bronze Buddha images, carved panels, religious objects, and other local artifacts. It's the first of two branches of the National Museum in Ayutthaya.

Chandra Kasem Palace. Northeast part of old city. Admission 20B (55¢). Wed–Sun 9am–noon, 1–4pm.

The other branch of the National Museum, the splendid Chandra Kasem Palace, was built in 1577 by King Maha Thamaraja (the 17th Ayutthaya monarch) for his son, who became King Naresuan. It was destroyed but later restored by King Mongkut, who stayed there whenever he visited Ayutthaya. On display are exquisite gold artifacts, jewelry, carvings, Buddha images, and domestic and religious objects from the 13th through 17th centuries.

Wihaan Phra Mongkol Bopit.

Wihaan Phra Mongkol Bopit, 7 blocks west of the Chandra Kasem Palace, is home to Thailand's largest seated bronze Buddha. It's housed in a somewhat cramped *wihaan,* built in 1956 in the style of the original, which was destroyed in 1767. This Buddha was either brought from Sukhothai or copied from a Sukhothai Buddha and was erected here in 1615 by King Ekatosarot, in honor of his brother Naresuan, who drove the Burmese from Sukhothai.

Wang Luang.

Wang Luang, the old royal palace, located in the northwestern end of the ancient city overlooking the Lopburi River, was destroyed by the Burmese. The foundations of the three main buildings can still be made out, and the size of the compound is impressive.

THE WATS   Near the old royal palace stands **Wat Phra Sri Sanphet,** originally built in 1448 as the king's private chapel (the equivalent of the Wat Phra Kaeo, Temple of the Emerald Buddha, in Bangkok) and renovated in the 16th and 17th centuries. The 55-foot bronze standing Buddha was originally cast in 1500 during the reign of the ninth king, Ramathipodi, and covered with gold. In 1767, the Burmese tried to melt the gold, causing a fire that destroyed the image and the temple; the one you see today is a replica. Nearby are three Sri Lankan-style chedis, built during the 15th century to enshrine the ashes of three Ayutthaya kings.

To the east of the royal palace, the prang of **Wat Phra Ram** soars into the sky. Originally built in 1369 by King Ramesuen (second King of Ayutthaya), the complex is in ruins.

Opposite **Wat Mahathat** (ca. 1384) stands **Wat Ratachaburana,** built in 1424 and splendidly restored—the prangs and chedis have even retained some of their original stucco. In the two crypts, excavators have found bronze Buddha images and votive tablets, as well as golden objects and jewelry, many of which are displayed in the Chao Sam Phraya Museum. There are also murals, rows of seated Buddhas, standing disciples, and Jataka (tales from the Buddha's former lives) scenes in the four niches, as well as a frieze of heavenly beings and some Chinese scenes. Both wats remain severely damaged despite restoration.

Wat Phanan Choeng was built in 1324, 26 years before King U-Thong founded Ayutthaya. The impressive Buddha image is 62 feet high and more than 45 feet from knee to knee. Adjacent to it is a small Chinese temple, a memorial to a princess betrothed to the king of Thailand, who committed suicide when he failed to attend her arrival.

Wat Suwan Dararam, across the river, is visited by the present royal couple when they come to Ayutthaya. It was built by Rama I. The murals and door panels depict stories from the *Ramakien.*

Wat Na Phra Mane, on the Lopburi side of the river, survived Ayutthaya's destruction and is worth visiting to see the black stone Buddha dating from the Mon (Dvaravati) period, as well as the principal Buddha fully decorated in regal attire.

Back on the main site on the other side of the river, one chedi serves as a moving reminder of the role women have often played in Thai history (in a country where they were expected to serve alongside men in war). Only a chedi and statue remain of a temple built to commemorate Queen Suriyothai, who was killed when she intervened in a duel (fought on the backs of elephants) between her husband and a Burmese general.

Don't miss **Wat Yai Chai Mongkol,** a few minutes' walk southeast of ancient Ayutthaya. (Cross the Pridi Damrong Bridge and the railroad, turn right at the first major intersection, pass through the commercial area, and find it on the left.) This well-tended temple was founded by King U-Thong in 1357 as a center for monks returning from study in Sri Lanka. The recently restored white reclining Buddha near the entrance was built by King Naresuan. The massive pagoda was also built by King Naresuan to celebrate his defeat of the Burmese at Suphanburi in 1593 by killing their crown prince in a single-handed combat on elephants.

A short distance from the other main temple sites (on the other side of the Chao Phraya, west of the royal palace is **Wat Chai Wattanaram,** which is still being restored. Roots and branches straggle around the many chedis and prangs. The overgrown complex has that haunted sense of tragedy about it—the essence of Ayutthaya.

Where to Stay

Ayutthaya Guest House. 16/2 Chao Prom Rd., Ayutthaya 13000. ☎ **035/232-658.** 10 units. 500B ($13.15) double with A/C, 160B ($4.20) double with fan. No credit cards. A short walk north of the in-town bus station.

Mr. Hong and family offer some of the best low-budget beds in Ayutthaya. There are bikes for rent, as well as a small inexpensive garden restaurant attached to the guest house.

Krungsri River Hotel. 27/2 Rojana Rd., Ayutthaya 13000. ☎ **035/244-333.** Fax 035/243-777. 202 units. A/C MINIBAR TV TEL. 1,650B ($43.40) double; 3,500B ($92.10) suite. AE, DC, MC, V. Northeast side of Pridi Damrong Bridge.

This handsome luxury hotel, within walking distance of the train station, opened in 1993. The marble-floored and high-columned lobby is cool and spacious, with furniture arranged on oriental rugs. Rooms are ample, clean, and comfortable, with good-sized gray granite bathrooms—some with superb views of the river and sites. (A number are reserved for nonsmokers.) The staff is professional and friendly, and there's 24-hour room service, a pool, health club with sauna, snooker room, small bowling alley, beauty salon, pub with live entertainment, and Cantonese and Japanese restaurants, as well as the excellent Pasak Coffee Shop (see "Where to Dine," below).

Ruenderm (Ayutthaya) Youth Hostel. 48 Moo 2, U-Thong Rd., Ayutthaya 13000. ☎ **035/241-978.** 250B ($6.60) per person, with shared cold-water shower. No credit cards. West bank of Pasak River north of Pridi Damron Bridge.

A beautiful teak house has been converted into comfortable guest quarters. The large, high-ceilinged rooms are furnished with antique tables and chairs and low futon-style beds that give a very traditional feel. A good restaurant sprawls on several decks at various heights, with one table on an old boat that juts out over the river.

U-Thong Inn. 210 Rojana Rd., Ayutthaya 13000. ☎ **035/242-236.** Fax 035/242-235. 100 units. A/C MINIBAR. 858B ($22.60) double; 1,488B ($39.15) junior suite. AE, DC, MC, V. 2km east of Pridi Damrong Bridge.

The U-Thong Inn is among the best of a modest selection. It has neat, clean, carpeted rooms and a pool. The front-desk personnel are accommodating, and the hotel provides laundry service. There's also a restaurant attached.

Where to Dine

For real budget dining, try the small food shops near the Hua-Raw and the Chao Prom markets or the informal restaurants across from the entrance to Wat Mahathat. For a different experience try the following:

Pasak Coffee Shop. In the Krungsri River Hotel. ☎ **035/244-333.** Main courses 120B–250B ($3.15–$6.60). AE, DC, MC, V. Daily 5am–11pm. Northeast side of Pridi Damrong Bridge. THAI/CONTINENTAL.

On the first floor of the area's best hotel, this bright and airy place has marble floors and seating on the riverside terrace, with a menu more varied than that found in most coffee shops. Standard Thai dishes are carefully prepared (and not too spicy!), and Western entrees include the popular cheeseburger.

Ruenpae. 44 Moo 2, U-Thong Rd. ☎ **035/251-807.** Main courses 75B–150B ($1.95–$3.95). Daily 11am–10pm. West bank of Pasak River north of Pridi Damrong Bridge. THAI/CHINESE.

Ruenpae is a simple floating riverfront restaurant. It offers a typical Thai/Chinese menu, with such dishes as steamed fish in plum sauce, roast chicken with salt, Nanking soy cake, grilled prawns, and beef with chile. A good place to enjoy a pretty good meal after a long day of sightseeing.

BANG PA-IN

Only 61km (38 miles) north of Bangkok, this royal palace is usually combined with Ayutthaya in a 1-day tour. Much of the palace isn't open to the public, so if given the choice, you may want to save your time to explore Ayutthaya fully.

The 17th-century temple and palace at Bang Pa-In were originally built by Ayutthaya's King Prasat Thong. They were abandoned when Bangkok became the capital until King Mongkut returned occasionally in the mid–19th century. His son King Chulalongkorn constructed the **royal palace** as it is seen today.

The architectural style mixes Thai with strong European influences. The building in the middle of the lake is the **Phra Thinang Aisawan Thippa-At,** an excellent example of classic Thai style. Behind it, in Versailles style, are the former **king's apartments,** which today serve as a hall for state ceremonies. The **Phra Thinang Wehat Chamrun,** also noteworthy, is a Chinese-style building (open to the public) where court members generally lived during the rainy and cool seasons. Also worth visiting is the **Phra Thinang Withun Thatsuna,** an observatory on a small island that affords a fine view of the countryside.

While you're across the Chao Phraya, the Gothic-style **Wat Nivet Thamaprawat** (built during King Chulalongkorn's reign), south of the palace grounds, is worth seeing. Buses leave regularly for Bang Pa-In from Bangkok's Northern Bus Terminal (☎ **02/272-5761**) and Ayutthaya's Chao Prom Market (Chao Prom Road), beginning at 6am. Admission to the palace is 40B ($1.05). Open daily 8:30am to 3pm.

KANCHANABURI

128km (79 miles) W of Bangkok; 65km (40 miles) W of Nakhon Pathom

Kanchanaburi stands at the junction where two tributaries—the Kwai Noi and the Kwai Yai—meet to form the Mae Khlong River. For most visitors, the town is indelibly marked by its famous bridge, spanning the Kwai River. A visit to this site is, for some, an emotional pilgrimage to honor the suffering and heroism of those who perished (and the few who survived) under their brutal Japanese overseers during World War II. However, previous Frommer's writers put it best when they wrote, "As moving as the story is, we find the actual site a good bit less inspiring and would recommend it only for those who are really passionate about this chapter of World War II history."

The city, near the bridge over the Kwai, is surrounded by some spectacular scenery, particularly to the north and west of town. Mountains rise in misty haze along the river; waterfalls abound as the jungle stretches away. You'll drive past fields of tapioca, tobacco, sugarcane, tamarind, mango, papaya, banana, and palm trees.

Kanchanaburi is a fine base for jumping off if you have a taste for exploring Thailand's natural areas, while the town itself is pretty dull and overly commercial. In other words, come to Kanchanaburi for an overnight stay to explore the area's diverse scenery or to delve into River Kwai lore. As a day trip, it's not so thrilling even when combined with stops at the Damnoen Saduak floating market or the giant stupa at Nakhon Pathom.

ESSENTIALS

GETTING THERE   By Train   Trains to Kanchanaburi depart from the Bangkok Noi/Thonburi Railway Station, just across the Chao Phraya River from Bangkok. If you're traveling by taxi you'll cross the Phra Pin Klao Bridge, just north of the historical district. The station is a short ride from there on Banphak Rotfai Road. If you're close to the Chao Phraya River, you can hop on a ferry to the Thonburi Railway Station Ferry Pier.

One morning train and one afternoon train link Thonburi to Kanchanaburi town (trip time: 3 hours; 25B/65¢), with two trains daily making the return. The train also continues to the River Kwai Bridge, and an additional six-minute trip (2B/5¢). If you're heading out on the weekend or a public holiday, the **State Railway of Thailand** has additional trains. Call them at ☎ 02/223-7010 for current scheduling. In Kanchanaburi, the railway station can be contacted at ☎ 034/561-052.

By Bus   Buses leave every 20 minutes from Bangkok's Southern Bus Station (☎ 02/435-1199). Trip time: 3 hours; 68B/$1.80.

By Car   Take Route 4 West from Bangkok.

VISITOR INFORMATION   The **TAT** office is on Saeng Chuto Road (☎ 034/511-200); open daily 8:30am to 4:30pm.

SPECIAL EVENTS   Beginning at the end of November, the River Kwai Bridge Festival is a sound and light demonstration (with fireworks donated by the Japanese government), cultural shows, special period train rides, historical displays, and a symbolic bombing of the bridge (twice weekly, Saturday and Wednesday).

WHAT TO SEE & DO

Before going to see the bridge itself (the main attraction) stop at the **JEATH War Museum,** adjacent to Wat Chaichumpol in town. Constructed of thatch and bamboo to resemble prisoners' barracks, it provides a sobering display of the suffering of the prisoners of war who built the bridge and the railroad.

JEATH stands for Japanese, English, American, Australian, Thai, and Hollanders, the nationalities that built the railway. It was constructed as a supply and communication link for the Japanese army in Burma, replacing the sea route (via the Strait of Malacca) that had been closed by the Allies.

The museum is filled with photographs, personal mementos, and newspaper accounts of the lives of the prisoners of war, recording the tortures the Japanese inflicted upon them—malnutrition, disease, and despair.

The Japanese originally calculated that it would take 5 to 6 years to complete the 425km (264 miles) track, but they reduced that figure to 18 months for the POWs.

It was finished in a year. Some 16,000 Allied prisoners, mostly British, Australian, and American, died. Even more brutal was the fate of another 100,000 Burmese, Chinese, Indians, Indonesians, Malays, and Thais who were also killed under forced labor and buried in unmarked graves where they dropped. Open daily 8:30am to 5pm; admission 25B (65¢).

You can also stop by the **Kanchanaburi War Cemetery,** on Saeng Chuto Road in town, near the railroad station, where every stone tells a story of a lost life. Many of the 6,982 graves are those of young men who died in their 20s and 30s far from home. Another cemetery, a few miles out of town, contains close to 2,000 graves. Another 1,750 POWs lie buried at the **Chon-Kai War Cemetery,** once the site of a POW camp, and now a tranquil place on the banks of the Kwai Noi about 2km (1.2 miles) south of town.

The **Bridge over the River Kwai** is about 4½ km (2½ miles) north of the town center. The steel bridge was brought from Java and assembled by POWs. It was bombed several times and rebuilt after the war, but the curved spans are the originals. You can walk across it, looking toward the mountains of Myanmar as you go. For some it's a nerve-racking experience: Rickety railroad ties laid on an open grid allow you to see the water below. If you visit during the River Kwai Bridge Week (usually the end of November or the beginning of December), you can also see a son et lumière spectacle.

Natural Sites & Adventure Tours

The area surrounding Kanchanaburi is widely known for its natural sites, especially the **Erawan Waterfall and National Park, Sai-Yok National Park,** and **La Wa Cave.** The best time to visit is during the rainy season (August to October) when the waterfalls are in full flood. There's bus service to most excursion destinations in the area. However, we recommend hiring a van with a driver from **B. T. Travel** (☎ 034/ 511-967), on Saeng Chuto Road, Kanchanaburi town, for about 1,800B ($47.35) per day. It's easier and more direct—you'll spend more time enjoying the sights than getting round to them.

Since **adventure tours** have become popular, this scenic area has begun capitalizing on its natural assets. The **RSP Travel Center,** 271/1 Saeng Chuto Rd., Kanchanaburi town (☎ 034/512-280), organizes local jungle treks and river-rafting trips to nearby national parks, with an overnight in a Karen Village. If you can't get up north to Chiang Mai for hill tribe trekking, this overnight trip will be the next best thing. The cost is 3,100B ($81.60) per person, everything included.

The **La Wa Cave** is about 75km (45 miles) from Kanchanaburi town, along Route 323; **Sai-Yok National Park** is about 104km (62 miles) along the same route; its focal point is its waterfall, Sai Yok Yai, often celebrated in Thai song and verse. You can take a private boat to these two places from Pak Saeng Pier at Tam-Bon Tha-Saow. The round-trip takes about 4 hours and costs about 950B ($25). Buses to Sai Yok take about 2 hours and cost 36B (95¢).

Just off Route 323, but further away from Kanchanaburi town, are **Dawadung Cave** (110km/68 miles), the **Hin Dat Hot Springs** (130km/80 miles), and the remote three-tiered waterfall **Pha Tat.**

The most popular attraction is **Erawan Waterfall and National Park,** about 65km (40 miles) along Route 3199. The waterfall is 1¼ miles long and drops down seven tiers, creating a series of ponds and streams. It's a great bird and butterfly sanctuary and a popular camping spot for locals. Buses leave for Erawan from the bus terminal in Kanchanaburi town on Saeng Chuto Road (☎ 034/511-182) every 50 minutes from 8am to 4pm. The trip takes about 1½ hours and, with guide, costs 110B ($2.90).

Buses to Sai Yok take about 2 hours and cost 70B ($1.85). The last bus returns to Kanchanaburi early, so check the schedule.

Along Route 3086 (31 miles north of Kanchanaburi town) in the Bo Phloi area, you can watch **sapphire mining.** From the roadside you'll spy the wooden framework of a winch and people filling wheelbarrows with hard lumps of earth. After washing through the mud, they may find—if they're lucky—blue or black sapphires and earn a day's living. Travel another 50km (30 miles) or so north along the same route and you'll come to the 300-meter-long **Than Lot Noi Cave** and **Traitrung Waterfall** in **Than Lot National Park.**

WHERE TO STAY

There are plenty of riverside guest houses and raft houses, but those along Song Kwai Road nearer the JEATH War Museum tend to be noisier. Those further north along Soi Rong Heeb and Maenam Kwai Road are more pleasant. The best place to stay is at a resort outside of town (shuttles provided), but for in-town accommodations, try:

Jolly Frog Backpacker's. Mae Nam Kwai Rd., Kanchanaburi 71000. ☎ **034/514-579.** 150B ($3.95) double. No credit cards.

The Jolly Frog has remained a clean and friendly place, located in the tourist center of town. Some rooms have toilet facilities; all are fan cooled. The well-informed staff can arrange treks and tours.

Nearby Places to Stay

Felix River Kwai Resort. 9/1 Moo 3 Thamakham, Kanchanaburi 71000. ☎ **034/515-061.** Fax 034/515-095. 235 units. A/C MINIBAR TV TEL. 1,700–1,900B ($44.75–$50) double; from 3,500B ($92.10) suite. Peak season surcharge (Dec 20–Jan 20) and during River Kwai Week 400B ($10.55), with compulsory gala meals. AE, DC, MC, V. On the banks of the River Kwai.

Built for but no longer managed by the Sheraton chain, the Felix is a long, low resort tucked into the dense undergrowth surrounding the river. Rooms are spacious and filled with amenities, offering mountain and river views. Some are reserved for nonsmokers; three others have been modified for travelers with disabilities. This is the most luxurious way to experience the River Kwai, and one sure to appeal to World War II veterans' groups looking for the comforts of home.

Dining/Diversions: The "fern bar" coffee shop offers good continental, and some Thai dishes, in a very pleasant setting. The more formal Guilin Restaurant is for Chinese fare. There's also a relaxing piano bar and a Karaoke bar.

Amenities: Two swimming pools, workout room, business center, 24-hour room service, concierge, car rental, doctor on call, Thai massage, baby-sitting, laundry.

River Kwai Jungle House. 378 Tharua, Thamaka, Kanchanaburi. ☎ **034/561-052.** Fax 034/561-429. 15 units. 800B–1,000B ($21.05–$26.30) per person. V. Pick up from the Kanchanaburi train station can be arranged.

The "Ban Rim Kwae," about 25 miles west along the river from Kanchanaburi, is in a forest of mango, bamboo, and bougainvillea; turkeys and chickens peck at the dust; a couple of pet monkeys hang around for company. This primitive "hotel" is a traditional, floating resort. Rattan bungalows with fans and Asian toilets float on the river, overlooking a stretch of the famed railway. The hotel conducts cave exploration at Tamka Sae, local treks, and rafting trips. You'll need a sense of adventure and flashlights as the grounds are poorly lit.

WHERE TO DINE

Most of the floating restaurants are there for the tour groups, overpriced and mediocre at best. If you're out touring the bridge at lunchtime, try the **River Kwai Restaurant**

(☎ 034/512540) or **Sai Yok** (☎ 034/512702), both nearby, which serve Thai and some Chinese dishes. Special mention goes out to the **Aree Bakery** (no phone), at 90–02 Pakpraek Rd., 2 blocks from the riverside. Sgt. Maj. Tanom Lonmasuarapan and wife run this American-style ice-cream shop that also serves breakfast and home-made fruit pies and cakes, until they run out of delicious treats in the afternoon.

Pae-Bann Noue. Song Kwai Rd. ☎ 034/512-326. Main courses 40B–90B ($1.05–$2.35). MC, V. Daily 10am–midnight. THAI.

Highlights at this riverside eatery in town are shrimp with lemongrass, steamed whole fish on lemongrass and salted prunes, beef with shredded eggplant and hot pepper, and rice noodles fried with pork, dried shrimp, and tomato sauce. Try the *kwai tiao pad thai,* a local variation on the famous noodle dish.

Tongnate (Thong Nathee). Song Kwai Rd. ☎ 034/512-944. Main courses 70B–180B ($1.85–$4.75). Daily 11am–midnight. MC, V. THAI/SEAFOOD.

The Tongnate is a riverside restaurant with a floating dining pavilion. During the evening there's an entertaining floor show featuring a bevy of local singers. Although the food isn't great, we can suggest rice with chicken, garlic, and fresh pepper and fresh river-poached fish in tomato sauce.

LOPBURI

153km (95 miles) N of Bangkok; 98km (61 miles) NE of Ayutthaya

From the 10th through the mid–13th century, Lopburi served as a satellite capital of the Khmer empire. With the rise of the Thai nation in Chiang Mai, and later in Sukhothai, the Khmer were driven out of Lopburi and the ancient city was reestablished as a second capital under the suzerainty of Ayutthaya. King Narai, who was the first Thai monarch to open the country to the West, collaborated with French architects in the 1660s to rebuild the city in a Thai-European mode. Today, Lopburi's few sites reflect these many presences: Hindu influenced Khmer-era temples, Buddhist influenced Sukhothai-Ayutthaya structures, and Jesuit-influenced European buildings. Many travelers make Lopburi their first overnight stop en route to exploring the Northeast (try to time it with the annual October Banana Festival).

Like Ayutthaya, the old town of Lopburi is surrounded by water, principally the Lopburi River on the southern and western perimeters. Just opposite the town gate, on the south side, is the train station. Most major tourist sites are located within the old city.

ESSENTIALS

GETTING THERE   By Train   Frequent train service operates from Bangkok (trip time: 2½ hours; 64B/$1.70 for a second-class seat).

By Bus   Buses depart every 15 minutes from Bangkok's Northern Bus Terminal (☎ 02/272-5761) between 4:30am and 8pm; trip time: 2½ hours; 67B/$1.75).

By Car   Take the main highway, Route 1, north past Ayutthaya on Route 32, to Singburi, and turn southeast to Lopburi.

WHAT TO SEE & DO

Phra Narai Ratchanivet Palace and **Somdet Phra Narai National Museum** are located on Sorasak Road, between Ratchadamnoen Road and Pratu Chai Road. The palace was built in 12 years during King Narai's reign, beginning in 1666. It was renovated by King Mongkut. Finds from the area and objects from the buildings in this complex are on display in the National Museum of Lopburi (also known as the Somdet Phra Narai National Museum). The palace grounds served as a reception area for Thai and European emissaries, and the buildings reflect both a local and Western sensibility. The Chantara Phisan Pavilion, built as a residence and reception hall for the King, is designed in Thai style, while the Dusit Sawan Thanya Maha Prasat Building is an audience hall (where King Narai is thought to have received Chevalier de Chaumont, Louis XIV's ambassador) that incorporates both Thai and French architectural styles. It contains a fine throne and antique mirrors imported from France. The Phiman Mongkut Pavilion was King Mongkut's Lopburi residence, designed by a Frenchman in a popular 19th-century European style, and used today to house archaeological finds from the area. His harem (so to speak) was housed in the nearby Phra Pratiep, where Thai folk arts are currently on view. The palace grounds are filled with fascinating structures, most in ruins, worth devoting a few hours to explore. Open Wednesday to Sunday 8:30am to 4:30pm; admission 10B (25¢).

Vichayen House was built as a residence for Chevalier de Chaumont (see paragraph above) by King Narai. The estate is largely in ruins, though there is still evidence of a Catholic chapel, several residences for the ambassador and his entourage, as well as water tanks and other outbuildings. Open daily 8:30am to 4:30pm; admission 25B (65¢).

Wat Phra Sri Maha That, a shrine located one block behind the train station, was probably built in the early 1300s, during the Khmer period. It was later rebuilt in the Sukhothai style, with additions made during the Ayutthaya era. One prang, Prang Prathan, is very finely decorated.

WHERE TO STAY & DINE

Lop Buri Inn. 28/9 Narai Maharat Rd., Lopburi 15000. ☎ **036/412300.** Fax 036/412-457. 134 units. A/C MINIBAR TEL. 600B ($15.80) double. MC, V. In the center of the Ancient City.

The largest hotel in Lopburi is also its most fully equipped and comfortable. Like most provincial hotels in popular stops, the Lop Buri Inn is often used by tour groups and suffers from wear and less-than-perfect upkeep. Its location, however, is central to both sites and restaurants, and the price is right.

The Eastern Seaboard 6

Thailand's beaches along the Gulf of Thailand are world renowned for their white sand, palm groves, and warm water. Today, most areas are served by tourism infrastructure, sometimes with indulgent accommodations. Although no sandy crescent is free from some sort of tourism intrusion, there are still areas that are relatively undeveloped.

Pattaya, the oldest and most decadent of Thailand's resort areas, lures people seeking a break from the big city because of its proximity to Bangkok (3 hours by bus). This complex beach resort has many faces. Big well-planned retreats lure families—moms shop, kids play, and dads golf. Weekenders from the Big Mango come to party all night in bars and discos, take in the water-sports action, and relax the days away lounging on the beaches. Men from all over the world come to live it up in Pattaya's sleazy side—you'll see countless go-go bars with macho (rented) choppers parked outside. Pattaya has received endless bad publicity for its terrible environmental pollution, skyrocketing AIDS cases, and reports of international mob ties. The local government has been cleaning up Pattaya Bay and enacting strict new waste management guidelines, even as development continues—yet despite all, I have found that my trips to this crazy place are always worth it.

Ko Samet is the star of Rayong Province: a small island (somewhat protected as a national park) whose makeshift bungalows create a very different feel from Pattaya's swinging hotels. It's easily reached by a 45-minute ferry ride from the tiny port of Ban Phe (4½ hours from Bangkok by bus); though isolated, it often gets crowded on the weekend due to its popularity with foreign low-budget tourists and Thais, especially during holidays. East of Ban Phe, along the coast of the South China Sea, are several new resorts in Rayong Province. Several high-end Thai hoteliers have invested in beachfront property, expecting Rayong to be the next "hot" resort, but public transport remains rudimentary. The provincial capital of Chanthaburi is a commercial hub for the East Coast, with not much happening, and is usually only visited en route to Ko Chang.

Ko Chang has earned a cult following among young budget travelers because its remote location has kept development to a minimum. Ninety-eight percent of the 600 or so rooms on this big island—Thailand's third largest—are coconut-wood bungalows with thatch roofs and shared toilets. It's quite far from Bangkok to the nondescript port of Trat (5 to 6 hours by bus), then another long ferry (2½ to 4 hours) to your desired port. But once there, it's easy to see what all the excitement is about.

1 En Route to Pattaya: Chonburi Province

Driving on Coastal Highway 3 eastbound from Bangkok is one of the fastest ways to get to the eastern beaches, though it's not particularly scenic. In between smoke-belching fish-canning factories and local manufacturing plants are salt fields, where spindly metallic windmills pump seawater from the Gulf of Thailand for processing. In this province, salt "mining" is beginning to overtake prawn farming as the most lucrative use of former family-held rice paddies, since rice cultivation is no longer profitable (due to water pollution and rising costs).

About 5km (3 miles) east from Chonburi town (or Amphur Muang) is **Angsila,** a fishing village best known for another industry—**bronze Buddha casting.** Mr. Pinit Tonerat owns one factory, well off the left side of the road just before you enter the village, where very large bronzes are cast using the lost-wax process. (Visitors are wel-come. To find it, ask at one of the stone souvenir stands—there's no sign.) In a com-plex ritual to welcome the newborn image—after offerings, chanting, and prayers by monks—the figure is heated, the wax discarded, and the molten bronze is poured in through the hollow base. Completed Buddhas may only be "rented" to their clients as the image is too sacred to have any material value.

Another point of interest for Thai tourists is **Si Racha,** a seaside resort 24km (15 miles) south of Chonburi, where fresh seafood and locally grown pineapple are popular souvenirs. There is daily ferry service (between 8:30am and 3pm, 50B/$1.30 one-way) to the island **Ko Si Chang,** an elegant 19th-century summer resort for the Thai elite. Pedicabs wait at the ferry pier to offer round-the-island 1-hour tours (about 125B/$3.30).

2 Pattaya

147km (91 miles) E of Bangkok

You'll hear Pattaya called anything from "Asia's premier resort" to "one big open-air brothel"—its legacy as Thailand's R&R capital for Vietnam-weary American troops—because of its several hundred beer bars, discos with scantily clad Thai teens, massage parlors, and transvestite clubs all jammed together along a beachfront strip. But it has another more elegant and sophisticated side seen in its big international resorts, retreats set in sprawling, manicured seaside gardens. It remains a popular destination with tour groups and independent travelers with little time—mostly male but plenty of families, too—and still the most favored weekend destination of Bangkok residents. For those who desire a more tranquil beach environment, I recommend heading south to Hua Hin/Cha-Am.

ESSENTIALS

GETTING THERE   By Plane   There's no airport in Pattaya, the nearest being in U Tapao, an hour east of the resort. Served by **Bangkok Airways** with a daily flight from Ko Samui (trip time: 1 hour). Make reservations through their offices at Bangkok (☎ 02/229-3456) and Ko Samui (☎ 077/425-012). They have an office in Pattaya at Royal Garden Plaza, 218 Beach Rd., 2d floor (☎ 038/411-965). To get to and from the airport to Pattaya, Bangkok Airways provides free shuttle service.

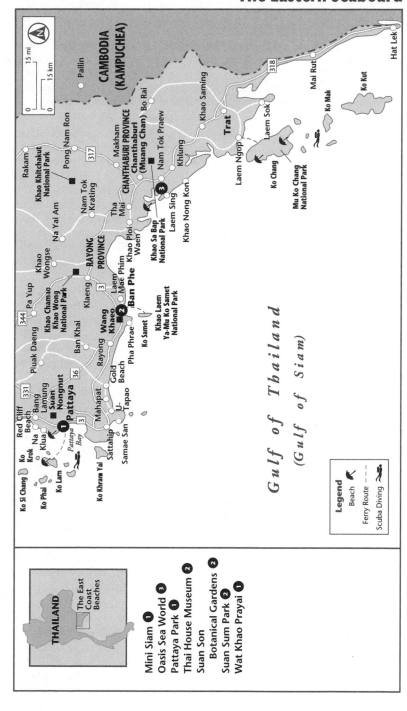

THAILAND

The East Coast Beaches

Mini Siam **1**
Oasis Sea World **3**
Pattaya Park **1**
Thai House Museum **2**
Suan Son
Botanical Gardens **2**
Suan Sum Park **2**
Wat Khao Prayai **1**

Legend

Beach
Ferry Route
Scuba Diving

By Train   Once-a-day train service leaves from Bangkok's Hua Lampong station at 6:55am and returns from Pattaya at 2:50pm. The 3-hour trip through the countryside is much more pleasant than that via the highway and costs only 31B (80¢). Call Hua Lampong in Bangkok at ☎ **02/223-7010** or the train station in Pattaya at ☎ **038/429285**. The train station is east of the resort strip off Sukhumvit Road near the intersection with North Pattaya Road. Outside you can catch a shared-ride songtao (minitruck) to the main beach (they'll drop you off anywhere along the main drag for about 20B/55¢).

By Public Bus   The most common and practical form of transportation to Pattaya is the bus. Buses depart from Bangkok's Eastern Bus Terminal on Sukhumvit Road opposite Soi 63, Ekamai Road (☎ **02/390-1230**), every half-hour beginning from 5am until 11pm every day. For air-conditioned coach the fare is 77B ($2.05). There's also regular bus service from Bangkok's Northern Bus Terminal (☎ **02/272-5761**), which can be a convenient way to avoid Bangkok rush-hour traffic if you're trying to get out during those hours (from central Bangkok you can take advantage of the less-congested expressway). The bus station in Pattaya for air-conditioned buses to and from Bangkok is on North Pattaya Road (☎ **038/429-877**). From there, catch a shared ride on a songtao that will stop anywhere you like along the main Beach Road (20B/55¢).

By Private Bus   Major hotels or travel agencies in Bangkok often operate their own transportation or can recommend private buses. Rung Reung Tour (☎ **02/429-877**), has air-conditioned bus service for 200B ($5.25), three times daily (9am, 1pm, and 5pm; trip time is 3 hours) to and from Bangkok's Don Muang airport. Minibuses leave all times of day from Khao San Road—there are a million travel agencies that can help you out—each will be happy to arrange accommodations, and many times the discounts are quite nice.

By Taxi   You can arrange a taxi at the desk in either terminal of Don Muang Airport for 1,250B ($32.90), or your hotel concierge can negotiate with a metered taxi driver to take you to a Pattaya resort, door to door, for about 1,500B ($39.45).

By Car   Take Highway 3 east from Bangkok. Companies such as **Avis** (☎ **02/ 255-5300**) offer chauffeur-driven limousine service for about 2,000B ($52.65).

VISITOR INFORMATION   I was disappointed to learn that the previously conveniently located TAT office (once in the center of Beach Road) has lost the battle with increasing rents and moved to a location south of Pattaya City, up the mountain on the road between Pattaya and neighboring resort Jomtien. You can hop any of the Jomtien-bound songtao and they'll drop you off at the office for 20B (55¢). The address is 609 Thappraya Rd. (☎ **038/429-113**).

A couple of free publications, *What's On Pattaya* and *Explore Pattaya and the East Coast*, are widely distributed to hotels and guest houses. They each contain good maps.

ORIENTATION   Pattaya is basically a long strip of hotels, bars, restaurants, travel agencies, and shops along Pattaya Beach Road, opposite a narrow beach overlooking Pattaya Bay. Roads and small lanes branch out from this main thoroughfare and connect to Pattaya 2 and Pattaya 3 roads, which run parallel to Beach Road. Of these lanes, North Pattaya Road, Central Pattaya Road, and South Pattaya Road are the main streets. At both the far northern (Dusit Resort) and southern (Royal Cliff Beach Resort) ends of the strip are two bluffs. Due south is condo-lined Jomtien Beach, a 15-minute ride from town.

GETTING AROUND   By Minibus or Songtao   *Songtao* (also called baht buses), pickups with two wooden benches in their bed, cruise the major streets for passengers

Pattaya

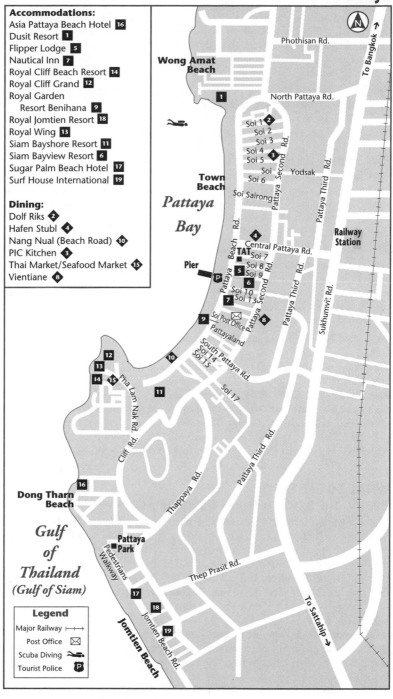

Accommodations:
Asia Pattaya Beach Hotel **16**
Dusit Resort **1**
Flipper Lodge **5**
Nautical Inn **7**
Royal Cliff Beach Resort **14**
Royal Cliff Grand **12**
Royal Garden
   Resort Benihana **9**
Royal Jomtien Resort **18**
Royal Wing **13**
Siam Bayshore Resort **11**
Siam Bayview Resort **6**
Sugar Palm Beach Hotel **17**
Surf House International **19**

Dining:
Dolf Riks **2**
Hafen Stubl **4**
Nang Nual (Beach Road) **10**
PIC Kitchen **3**
Thai Market/Seafood Market **15**
Vientiane **8**

Legend
Major Railway
Post Office
Scuba Diving
Tourist Police

Wong Amat
Beach

Phothisan Rd.

To Bangkok

North Pattaya Rd.

Soi 1
Soi 2
Soi 3
Soi 4
Soi 5
Soi
Soi 6

Yodsak

Pattaya Second Rd.

Pattaya Third Rd.

Town
Beach

Soi Sairong

Pattaya

Bay

Railway
Station

Beach Rd.

Central Pattaya Rd.
TAT
Soi 7
Soi 8
Soi 9
Soi 10
Soi 13

Pattaya Second Rd.

Pattaya Third Rd.

Sukhumvit Rd.

Pier

P

Soi Post Office

Pattayaland

South Pattaya Rd.
Soi 14
Soi 15

Soi 17

Tha Lam Nak Rd.

Cliff Rd.

Thappaya Rd.

Pattaya Third Rd.

**Dong Tharn
Beach**

*Gulf
of
Thailand
(Gulf of Siam)*

Pattaya
Park

Pedestrians Walkway

Thep Prasit Rd.

To Sattahip

Jomtien Beach

Jomtien Beach Rd.

143

and are the best and cheapest form of transport. Fares within Pattaya should range from 10B to 30B (25¢ to 80¢); to far-flung beaches such as Jomtien, they're 40B to 90B ($1.05 to $2.35). Rates are fixed by the local governments, but most drivers will try to overcharge you, and you must negotiate firmly. Some hotels operate their own minibuses, but they charge much more for the same bumpy ride.

By Car   There are plenty of car-rental agencies, and you can negotiate the price with most, especially outside the high season. **Avis,** with two branches (Dusit Resort Hotel, ☎ **038/361-627,** and the Royal Garden Resort Hotel, ☎ **038/412-120**), has self-drive rates from about 1,400B ($36.85) per day for a Suzuki Caribian to 2,400B ($63.15) for a Toyota Corona or Honda Accord. All along Pattaya Beach Road, local car-rental agencies offer Caribians and huge souped-up Jeeps for between 700B and 1,500B ($18.40 and $39.45) per day. Car quality and rental agreements can vary, so I recommend shopping around and checking out the vehicles each agency has available. Try **VIA Rent-a-Car** (215/15–18 Pattaya 2nd Rd. opposite Royal Garden Plaza (☎ **038/702-995**). They have a good local reputation (with TAT as well).

By Motorcycle   For those who dare brave the often drunk and reckless foreign drivers in downtown Pattaya, 150cc motorcycles rent for about 200B ($5.25) a day without insurance. (Ask for a helmet!) Big choppers and Japanese speed bikes (500cc) will go for about 500B to 800B ($13.15 to $21.05) per day. Like the independent car-rental agencies, motorcycle rentals also differ in bike quality and insurance agreements.

FAST FACTS   There are many independent money-changing booths; many **bank** exchanges (with better rates) stay open 24 hours. They're all easily located on any of the Pattaya maps available. The **post office** is located on Soi Post Office (how convenient!) about 3 blocks north of South Pattaya Road. There are all kinds of **Internet** access available, at guest houses, cafes, travel agencies—you can't walk a block without finding a giant e-mail sign, so you shouldn't have any troubles there. The most recommended **hospitals** are Pattaya Memorial Hospital 328/1 Central, Pattaya Rd. (☎ **038/429-422**), and Pattaya International Hospital, Soi 4 Beach Rd. (☎ **038/ 428-374**). The **Tourist Police** here are helpful and friendly, on guard 24 hours. Call ☎ **038/429-371** or local fast dial ☎ **1699.**

WHAT TO SEE & DO
HITTING THE BEACH & OTHER OUTDOOR ACTIVITIES

This 4-kilometer-long strip may seem harmless to the naked eye, but be warned, the rumors you've heard are true. It's very, very polluted. Rapid growth of the tourism sector was not accompanied by growth of pubic facilities works, and for years waste has been disposed of improperly, ironically destroying the one thing that drew travelers here in the first place. As if raw sewage isn't enough, it attracts many varieties of poisonous sea snakes. For the record, the local government has launched works to clean the mess up, and has made progress, but it'll be some time before it's all straightened out.

Water sports still reign in the area, but for swimming you should either stick to the very north of Pattaya Beach near the Dusit Resort, or head a little south to Jomtien Beach. Another option is to take a day trip to one of the islands in the Gulf of Thailand.

On Pattaya Beach there's **windsurfing** (150B/$3.95 per hour), **parasailing** (1,000B/$26.30 per hour), canoeing (100B/$2.65 per hour), and **catamaran sailing** (400B/$10.55 per hour). You can either wander along the beach to hire one of these activities, or contact **Bamrung Sport Club & Resort** at 9/6 Moo 8, Sukhumvit Road (☎ **01/354-4986**).

On Jomtien you can find even more activities than on Pattaya Beach. To get to Jomtien Beach, grab a songtao on Beach Road or Pattaya 2nd Road for around 50B ($1.30). Swimming is centered around the northern section of Jomtien Beach, while the southern parts are for other water sports such as catamarans, parasailing, water-skiing, and windsurfing. You'll find a lot of places on the beach to rent equipment and even provide lessons, for prices that are always rising and falling, depending on tourist traffic. Expect to pay around 250B ($6.60) per hour for windsurfing equipment, and up to 1,000B ($26.30) per hour for a jet ski. Parasailing is around 400B ($10.55) per flight. Talk to the guys on the beach for rentals, or contact **Jomtien Water Sport Club,** 59/1 Soi Najomtien 4 (☎ **038/232-2110**). If you are serious about finding a really great beach, move on to nearby Ko Samet; but for convenience, Jomtien is the best in the area.

Game fishing is another very popular activity, with boats going out regularly. You'll get the best rate if you join up with a group, rather than chartering a boat on your own. Contact **Deutsches Haus** (☎ **038/428-725**) or **Pattaya Game Fishing Club** (☎ **038/432-303**) to find out about trips. Packaged excursions usually cost 5,000B ($131.60) per day per boat, including fishing gear.

Snorkeling and **scuba diving** are popular because of Pattaya Bay's clear waters (20m to 25m average visibility), colorful coral reefs (including mushroom, lettuce, brain, and staghorn corals), and tropical fish (white- and black-tip sharks, stingrays, angelfish, and many others). Nearby Ko Larn, Ko Sak, and Ko Kroh can be reached within 45 minutes by boat. There's also diving off of Ko Klung Badan, Ko Man Wichai, or Ko Rin, which are farther offshore. North of Pattaya is Ko Si Chang, once famous as the summer playground of foreign ambassadors to Siam during the 19th century. Here, and off Sattahip to the south, is even better diving, at depths up to 40 meters.

There are a number of good dive shops with PADI and NAUI certified instructors in the area. I liked the people at **Dolphin Diving Center,** 183/31 Moo 10, Soi Post Office (☎ **038/427-185**), who take small groups out for two daily dives—total cost including equipment, two tanks, transport, a hot meal, and a dive master guide costs 2,800B ($73.70). Overnight dives can also be arranged.

For sports enthusiasts, **golf** is second only to water activities in Pattaya. The area around the resort is known as the "Golf Paradise of the East" with international-class courses within a 40-kilometer radius of the city. If you're willing to travel a little, the finest course is at **Bangphra International Golf Club,** 45 Moo 6, Tambon Bang Phra, Sri Racha (☎ **038/341-149**; fax 02/341-150). This par-72 championship course was designed in 1958 by a Japanese team, and redone in 1987. It's considered the prettiest course in the area (greens fees: weekdays 650B/$17.10, weekends 1,320B/$34.75). The **Laem Chabang International Country Club,** 106/8 Moo 4 Tambon Bung, Sri Ratcha (☎ **038/338-350;** fax 038/338-350) is another fair course. Designed by Jack Nicklaus in 1994, this nine-hole course has dramatic scenery (greens fees: weekdays 1,110B/$29.20, weekends 1,980B/$52.10). Another fine choice is the **Siam Country Club,** 50 Tambol Poeng, Banglamung (☎ **038/249-381;** fax 038/249-387) a short hop from Pattaya is believed to be one of the country's most challenging courses (greens fees: all days 1,100B/$28.95).

A WAT, AN ELEPHANT PARK & OTHER ATTRACTIONS

If you feel a need to rise above the earthly distractions of Pattaya or would like some cardiovascular challenge, **Wat Khao Prayai,** a small temple complex, offers excellent vistas and a 32½-foot gold Buddha serenely surveying the western sea. Take a minibus toward Jomtien from the beach road, get off on top of the hill, and walk up between dragon-headed columns. Another wat, on a neighboring rise, can also be visited. Admission is a suggested contribution of 20B (55¢); open daily 6am to 6pm.

There's a huge and highly entertaining **elephant park** only 18km from the city. Nong Nooch stages performances three times daily—with elephants performing alongside some 100 dancers, musicians, and performers for spectator crowds of up to 1,000. Cultural performances, music, Thai boxing, audience participation, and dozens of funny photo ops make this really touristy activity a load of laughs. Make your booking from Nong Nooch directly (☎ 038/429-321). They arrange shuttles from Pattaya at either 8:30am or 1:15pm with return. Tickets cost 250B ($6.60), shuttle 350B($9.20) round-trip.

For those who don't have time to see all of Thailand's many wonders, **Mini Siam,** 387 Moo 6 Sukhumvit Rd., North Pattaya City (☎ 038/421-628), offers a comprehensive tour of the highlights, all shown as miniature models (an example of scale: Bangkok's huge Grand Palace is waist high). Most of Thailand's famous structures, in meticulous detail, are included. Open daily 9am to 9pm; admission 200B ($5.25) adults, 100B ($2.65) children. It's 14km (8.4 miles) north of Pattaya City and can be reached by taxi (about 900B/$23.70 with wait) or by joining a local group tour.

I'm always surprised to see the number of families vacationing in Pattaya—all the main activities are geared for the amusement of bigger kids. If you find yourself there with restless children, a day at **Pattaya Water Park,** 345 Moo 12 Pratamank Rd., Jomtien Beach Rd., Jomtien (☎ 038/251-201), could save you. It's a worn but fun water park with a small Thai restaurant, network of pools, several water slides, a narrow clean beach, and many kinds of water-sports equipment (windsurfing, catamarans, and so on) for rent. The Pattaya Park Tower has a "jump" (100B/$2.65 adults, and 50B/$1.30 children) where you glide down a cable from the top of the 170-meter-high tower. Yikes! Open daily 7am to 6pm; water park admission 100B ($2.65) adults, 50B ($1.30) children under 120 cm (4 feet). Take the minibus to Jomtien to the Pattaya Park Hotel, 8km (5 miles) south of town.

For something completely unusual, the **Ripley's Believe It or Not** showcase, 3rd Floor, Royal Garden Plaza, 218 Beach Rd. (☎ 038/710-294), open 10am to midnight daily (admission 150B/$3.95), is hilarious, with unusual exhibits and odd facts form around the globe. Just next door is the Ripley's Motion Master simulator ride. Both are highly recommended if you're traveling with your children.

The **Pattaya Elephant Village** (see the Elephant Desk at Tropicana Hotel, Beach Road, ☎ 038/423-031), stages elephant shows daily at 2:30pm. You can also arrange for a little jungle trekking on elephant back. If that's not quite your speed, check out **Pattaya Go-Kart,** Sukhumvit Road next to Mini Siam (☎ 038/422-044), with a 400-meter track that is also suitable for children. Rates run between 100B and 200B ($2.65 and $5.25) per 10 minutes, depending on the power of your cart.

DAY CRUISES TO NEARBY ISLANDS

Ko Larn's main port is a long, sandy beach cove facing the mainland, just a 45-minute boat ride away. Dozens of seafood restaurants and snack bars line the beach. **Bamboo Island** and **Ko Man Wichai,** within an hour of Ko Larn, are largely uninhabited and perfect for seekers of deserted tropical islands. Fishing boat and motor boat operators moored on the main part of Pattaya beach offer Ko Larn day trips for about 400B ($10.55) per person on a full boat, or about 1,500B ($39.45) for a privately chartered boat. If you can schedule it, do yourself a favor and take the local ferry boat from the

South Pattaya Pier at 10am, noon, or 6:30pm and return at either 6:30am, noon, or 2pm (it costs only 20B/55¢ each way). It's 2,500B ($65.80) to Bamboo Island. There's lots of competition, so bargain. If you're too shy to organize this on your own, many of the beachside tour operators will sell you a ticket on their day-trip boats. Contact **Pimpar Tour** on Beach Road at ☎ **038/425-762.**

Once you're out on Ko Larn, there's parasailing (350B/$9.20 per hour), jet skiing (1,200B/$31.60 per hour), waterskiing (200B/$5.25 for 5 minutes), and banana boat (sea kayak) rentals (1,200B/$31.60 per hour). Locate operators on the beach.

WHERE TO STAY

Most of these establishments are on Pattaya Beach Road in the middle of the entertainment scene. However, the city's top resorts are in isolated spots—perfect for a sun-and-fun getaway weekend (see "Nearby Places to Stay," below).

All prices listed below are exclusive of the 7% VAT and the 10% service charge and do not reflect the peak-season supplement (usually 600B to 1,200B/$15.80 to $31.60 per room per night) charged by many hotels from mid-December to mid-January. (If business is bad, these fees are often waived and rates are definitely negotiable.) During the high season, reservations are recommended at least 2 weeks in advance. Peak season falls during December and January holidays, while the low season, July through October, offers special rates. Still, weekends tend to be fully booked so plan ahead. (See chapter 2, "Tips on Accommodations.")

The largest resort complex in Pattaya, The Royal Cliff Beach Resort, sports four separate hotels in one—The Royal Cliff Beach Hotel, The Royal Cliff Terrace, The Royal Cliff Grand, and The Royal Wing—offering one of the largest choices of accommodations and facilities in the area. Each has been reviewed separately within the corresponding price category below.

VERY EXPENSIVE

The Royal Cliff Grand. 353 Phra Tamnuk Rd., Moo 12, Pattaya, Chonburi 20260. ☎ **038/250-421,** 02/280-1737 in Bangkok. Fax 038/250-514, 02/282-0294 in Bangkok. www.royalcliff.co.th. 290 units. A/C MINIBAR TV TEL. 7,052B ($185.60) double; from 11,770B ($309.75) suite. AE, DC, MC, V. On cliff, south end of Pattaya Bay.

If columned public spaces with fountains, staircases, chandeliers, and acres of granite mean grand, then this newer addition to the fine Royal Cliff Beach Club Resort complex lives up to the name. Everything about the place is larger than life.

Spacious rooms in the contemporary, scallop-shaped tower have private VCRs and fax setups, as well as marble bathrooms with separate shower stalls and twin sinks. They are elegantly appointed with classic furniture and coffered ceilings in tribute to the era of King Rama V, who inspired the Victoriana/Siam design. The Royal Club on the sixth floor boasts a private spa and sundeck, as well as seven Jacuzzis for its VIP and business guests.

Dining: The Grand Café offers continental and Thai cuisine indoors in a towering sunroom or outdoors on a patio overlooking the gardens. Both quality and service are first rate and prices reasonable. Guests also have access (a pleasant walk) to the many dining options at the Royal Cliff and Royal Wing hotels (see below).

Amenities: Swimming pool, health club, water sports, mini-golf course, 24-hour room service, concierge, limousine service, baby-sitting, house doctor, laundry, no-smoking sections.

The Royal Wing. 353 Phra Tamnuk Rd., Moo 12, Pattaya City 20260, Chonburi. ☎ **038/ 250-421.** Fax 038/250-486. www.royalcliff.co.th. 86 units. A/C MINIBAR TV TEL. From 11,182B ($294.25) suite. AE, DC, MC, V. On cliff, south of Pattaya Beach.

The dazzling Royal Wing is treated both by guests and its capable Swiss management as a separate entity within the impressive Royal Cliff resort. The level of service here is more personal (butlers on call 24 hours), and the rooms are more regally furnished than anywhere else in town.

As opulent as Bangkok's Shangri-La, the Royal Wing is the pinnacle of Hong Kong–style glitz. The lobby is white marble, with lotus bud–capped columns combining Thai and Chinese influences. Each guest is catered to personally, with butlers unpacking your luggage on arrival and beach chaise lounges reserved with your brass nameplate. The large, bright, quietly tasteful rooms—decorated throughout with teak and fine pastel Thai cottons—are spaced around the cliff. For maximum privacy, each has two balconies, draped in fuchsia or orange bougainvillea, overlooking Pattaya Bay. The free-form swimming pool has small bow bridges and waterfalls that add an extra exotic touch. The beach is small but uncrowded and well maintained.

Dining: There is poolside dining at La Ronde, an elegant lobby bar, and the Palm Terrace for breakfast or lighter fare. The Benjarong Restaurant, serves French and continental fare with a hint of Thai. Guests can try the Thai Market or Seafood Market open-air pavilion (see "Where to Dine," below), as well as the facilities at the nearby Royal Cliff or Royal Cliff Grand.

Amenities: Pool, Cliff Club Spa (with sauna, steam bath, and two pools), water sports, minigolf course, tennis courts, jogging track, 24-hour room and butler service, concierge, limousine, baby-sitting, house doctor, laundry, no-smoking rooms.

EXPENSIVE

Asia Pattaya Beach Hotel. 325 Moo 2, Pratamnak Rd., South Pattaya, Pattaya City 20260, Chonburi. ☎ **038/250-602.** Fax 038/250-496. 314 units. A/C MINIBAR TV TEL. 2,119B ($55.75) double; 8,239B ($216.80) suite. AE, DC, MC, V. On cliff above south end of beach; 3km (1.8 miles) south of town.

The Asia Pattaya offers immaculate grounds, all heavily planted, with a topiary A-S-I-A in the middle of a circular driveway. The rooms are aging but well kept and have numerous amenities. Many are decorated with kitschy 1960s paneling or with leather-look furniture. The Dutch-owned Golden Tulip chain manages the resort in a friendly, homey way; European tour groups abound. The well-priced rooms and two-bedroom family suites are a good value if you're looking for a well-groomed private beach, tranquility, and relative seclusion.

Dining/Diversions: The open-air Cliff Top Restaurant offers great views and good continental or typical Thai fare. The Neptune Disco has a popular DJ nightly, with a pretty good selection of European hits and, often, a live band.

Amenities: Swimming pool, 9-hole golf course, shopping arcade, 24-hour room service, concierge, limousine service, baby-sitting (with notice), laundry service.

Dusit Resort. 240/2 Pattaya Beach Rd., Pattaya City 20150, Chonburi. ☎ **038/425-611.** Fax 038/428-239. www.dusit.com. 474 units. A/C MINIBAR TV TEL. 3,960B–7,920B ($104.20–$208.40) double; from 9,240B ($243.15) suite. AE, DC, MC, V. North end of Pattaya Beach.

This beautifully landscaped resort offers water sports, a good health club, and some nightlife (far from the steamier side of Pattaya). Straddling a bluff on the north end of the main beach, the Dusit has two pools and sundecks, access to two small but well-kept sandy beach coves, several dining outlets, and a small shopping arcade.

Most of the balconied rooms overlook Pattaya Bay, but the best values are the garden view rooms in Wing B, which face manicured lawns, hibiscus beds, and a side view of the sea. Tastefully modern rooms trimmed with stained wood offer all-marble bathrooms, hair dryers, and bathrobes. Landmark deluxe rooms have large bathrooms with separate bath tubs and shower stalls, plus outdoor showers on their large balconies, as well as comfortable and luxurious sitting areas.

Dining/Diversions: The Dusit has several dining options, including the Empress for panoramic views and gourmet Chinese food. There's an okay coffee shop and a delightful lobby lounge that serves evening drinks with live musical accompaniment.

Amenities: Two outdoor swimming pools, water sports, health club with daily aerobic classes, sauna rooms with TV sets, pool tables, tennis courts, squash courts, massage, 24-hour room service, concierge, limousine service, baby-sitting, laundry service, and no-smoking rooms.

✪ **Royal Cliff Beach Hotel.** 353 Phra Tamnuk Rd., Moo 12, Pattaya City 20260, Chonburi. ☎ **038/250-421.** Fax 038/250-511. 550 units. A/C MINIBAR TV TEL. 4,944B ($130.10) double; 5,885B ($154.85) minisuite; from 12,146B ($319.65) suite. AE, DC, MC, V. On cliff, above south end of Pattaya Beach.

This is Pattaya's top family resort, on the same garden property as the more exclusive Royal Wing and Royal Cliff Grand. It was built and upgraded in phases: The Royal Cliff Terrace building houses four terraced stories of suites with patios; the nine-story sea-view hotel tower houses most of the guest rooms, including huge, perfect-for-families two-bedroom suites. Rooms are spacious with bleached wood and pastel decor and large terraces, most with bay views. If you tire of the lushly planted grounds, there's an elevator from the precipice down to the sandy beach, which is relatively clean but disappointingly small. Go for the pools, the grounds, the health club, not for the beach. The hotel has a staff of more than 1,500 waiting to serve. I found it friendly, luxurious, and relaxing.

Dining/Diversions: There is an indoor/outdoor poolside coffee shop (delightful for a grand American or Thai-style buffet breakfast), as well as snack bars by the pool and sea, and even in the gardens. For the evening, there's a piano bar off the lobby (for people watching) and one in the open-air Thai Market pavilion. Restaurants include the stately up-country Grill Room, the Thai Market/Seafood Market (see "Where to Dine," below). Guests are also welcome at the exclusive Royal Wing's formal Benjarong Restaurant and the poolside La Ronde.

Amenities: Outdoor swimming pool, spa (with jogging track, sauna, steam bath, and two pools), water sports, minigolf course, tennis courts, squash courts, jogging track, 24-hour room and butler service, concierge, limousine, baby-sitting, house doctor, laundry, no-smoking rooms.

✪ **Royal Garden Village Hua Hin.** 218 Beach Rd., Pattaya City. ☎ **800/344-1212** in the U.S., or 038/412-120. Fax 038/429-926. 300 units. A/C MINIBAR TV TEL. Rates $95–$140 double; $195–$640 suite. AE, DC, JCB, MC, V.

Smack in the center of Pattaya Beach (you really can't get a better location) Royal Garden surprises guests with its large courtyard garden and landscaped pool area. You'd hardly know Pattaya City was just beyond the walls. With their helpful staff and handsome accommodations, this resort makes for a great retreat. Spacious balconied rooms have views of the gardens or the sea, and many creature comforts not found in other hotels, including an in-house video-on-demand service. The adjoining Royal Garden Plaza makes your dining and entertainment options even more attractive. Their pool is the largest in Pattaya, while their fitness center is modern and well equipped. There's also tennis, and the resort can arrange any water-sports activity you so desire.

Dining/Diversions: My favorite here is the Benihana Japanese-American Steakhouse (which I've reviewed separately in this chapter) for fun and great food. The Garden Café Restaurant, for à la carte and buffets, organizes regular food festivals. At night you can relax in the Elephant Lounge, or enjoy beer and pub food at Delaney's Irish Pub.

Amenities: Outdoor swimming pool, lighted tennis courts, water sports, adjacent shopping center.

MODERATE

Siam Bayshore Resort. 559 Beach Rd., Pattaya City 20260, Chonburi. ☎ **038/428-678.** Fax 038/428-730. 272 units. A/C MINIBAR TV TEL. Low season 1,999B ($52.60) double, 2,999B ($78.90) sea-view double; peak season 2,999B ($78.90) double, 3,999B ($105.25) sea-view double. AE, MC, V. Far south end of beach, across from city park.

For comfort, quiet, seclusion, and value in Pattaya, you'll have a hard time beating this excellent hotel. Rooms are large and attractively furnished with most of the amenities of the more luxurious hotels, including individually controlled air-conditioning, free in-house movies, 24-hour room service, laundry, and baby-sitting. The hotel grounds are attractively landscaped and well maintained, and facilities include two pools, a private beach club, four lighted tennis courts, volleyball and table tennis, nearby water-sports facilities, and an exercise room.

Siam Bayview Hotel. 310/2 Beach Rd., Pattaya City, Chonburi 20260. ☎ **038/423-871.** Fax 038/423-879. www.siamhotels.com. 270 units. A/C MINIBAR TV TEL. Low season 3,060B ($80.55) double; peak season 4,777B ($125.70) double. AE, MC, V. Center of beach, between Sois 9 and 10.

The Siam Bayview Hotel is very similar to its sister hotel, the Siam Bayshore (above), except that it's right in the middle of the action—though remarkably quiet for its location. There are two attractively landscaped pools, two lighted tennis courts, nearby water-sports facilities, an exercise room, three good dining venues, and a pleasant pub, plus a friendly and attentive staff.

INEXPENSIVE

Flipper Lodge Hotel. 520/1 Soi 8, Pattaya Beach Rd., Pattaya City 20260, Chonburi. ☎ **038/426-401.** Fax 038/426-403. 126 units. A/C MINIBAR TV TEL. 800B–950B ($21.05–$25) double; 1,500B ($39.45) suite. AE, MC, V. Midbeach strip, off Soi 8.

A life-size statue of Flipper the dolphin dominates the lobby of this fave budget choice in the middle of the beach strip. The decor is basic, but the older rooms are clean and the new ones are quite attractive; their sea-view rooms (with that great view) can't be beat for the price. The pool is a bit on the short side, but the attractive open-air coffee shop serves some pretty good Thai and continental fare.

Nautical Inn. 10/10 Pattaya Beach Rd., Pattaya City 20150, Chonburi. ☎ **038/ 428-110.** Fax 038/428-116. 82 units. A/C MINIBAR TV TEL. 600B to 800B ($15.80–$21.05) double. Rates include tax and service. AE, MC, V. Near center of beach, between Sois 11 and 12.

This good budget choice on the beach strip is a relatively new, though Spartan, facility set well back from the road. Plain tower rooms are worn, but all have sea views, while the garden-view rooms surround a respectably sized pool. If you're staying 2 days or more, ask for their special reduced rates. The daily published rates are often discounted up to 50% in the low season.

NEARBY PLACES TO STAY

Sugar Palm Beach Hotel. 45/16 Moo 12, Sugar Palm Beach, Jomtien, 20260 Chonburi. ☎ **038/231-386.** Fax 038/231-713. 32 units. A/C TEL. 550B ($14.45) double; 750B ($19.75) double with sea view. AE, MC, V. North end of Jomtien Beach, just northwest of Jomtien Plaza Condos, on boardwalk.

A good lower-priced choice for a purely casual, beachy hotel, this place faces the quiet, clean Sugar Palm Beach and its gently lapping surf—far from the crowds on noisy Jomtien Beach Road. The simple rooms are spotless, though only two have ocean views. The Style Restaurant next door offers open-air dining on the beach, with good food and cheap prices.

Surf House International. 75 Jomtien Beach Rd., Jomtien, 20260 Chonburi. ☎ **038/ 231-025.** Fax 231-029. 36 units. A/C MINIBAR TV TEL. 400B–500B ($10.55–$13.15) double. Rates include tax and service. AE, MC, V. East end of Jomtien Beach.

Like most Jomtien accommodations, the Surf House seems to attract a younger, more beach-loving crowd than that which frequents the Pattaya hotels. Rooms are simple and clean, with private baths, and most have balconies and water views—request a seaside room on the top floor for a good panorama of the windsurfers. Because the Surf House is separated from the beach by the busy road, it's a fine second choice to the Sugar Palm Beach Hotel (see above).

WHERE TO DINE
EXPENSIVE

Thai Market/Seafood Market. Royal Cliff Resort Hotel, Cliff Rd. ☎ **038/250-421.** Seafood sold by weight, average portions 350B–800B ($9.20–$21.05); Thai buffet 700B ($18.40). AE, DC, MC, V. Daily 6–10:30pm. South end of Pattaya Beach. THAI/SEAFOOD.

If you've been tempted by the aromas from those tin-and-wood pushcarts parked near the beachside bars, you'll find a hygienic forum to sample everything right here, in this twin-sided "market." On one side of the open-air pavilion you'll find shrimp balls; *garoupa* steamed in banana leaves; beef, chicken, and pork satay; and many other grilled, fried, and boiled Thai standards.

On the other side of the tropical bamboo bar are lobster, crab, prawn, shellfish, and many locally caught fish, all displayed on ice for your choosing. Fresh salads and fruit round out the menu, a perfect finale for fitness buffs here on retreat.

MODERATE

Benihana. 2nd Level, Royal Garden Plaza. ☎ **038/425-029.** Reservations not necessary. Set menus 150B–500B ($3.95–$13.15). Open daily noon–2pm and 5–10pm. AE, DC, JCB, MC, V. JAPANESE-AMERICAN.

Most American readers are thinking, "Benihana? In Thailand?" Well, for those of you who've sampled tom yam gung and paad thai till it's coming out your ears, you'll be happy to visit this place. It has all the fun of Benihana's original restaurants—fantastic teppanyaki grill displays performed by chefs who have as much humor as skill, and the food is just great. The beef is like butter. Come here for a good time and a lot of laughs. You won't be disappointed.

Dolf Riks. 463/77 Sri Nakorn Center, North Pattaya. ☎ **039/428269.** Reservations recommended during high season. Main courses 250B–550B ($6.60–$14.45). AE, DC, MC, V. Daily 11am–midnight. 1 block north of Soi 1. INDONESIAN/EUROPEAN.

Dolf Riks is an Indonesian-born Dutch restaurateur who's also a bit of a character. His restaurant is Pattaya's oldest and remains something of a legend. Although Dolf's menu changes with his whims, he normally serves a delicious Indonesian Rijstaffel (good, but very different from what I had in Jakarta), as well as continental favorites. His regulars prefer the seafood in a wine-drenched broth, the Spanish garlic soup, and his fragrant ramekin Madras, an oven-baked curry ragout.

Hafen Stubl. Nipa Lodge Hotel, Pattaya Beach Rd. ☎ **038/428195.** Main courses 85B–250B ($2.25–$6.60). MC, V. Daily 11:30am–10pm. Corner of Central Pattaya (Pattaya Klang) Rd. GERMAN.

If you're longing for schnitzel and wurst, try this pocket of Germany on the beach. Thai girls in Heidi costumes serve cold steins of Anarist on tap and platters of stout Teutonic fare. I enjoyed it as a break from Thai food, and for the convivial pubby atmosphere.

✪ PIC Kitchen. Soi 5 Pattaya 2nd Rd. ☎ **038/428-374.** Reservations not necessary. 75B–320B ($1.95–$8.40). Daily 8am–midnight. AE, DC, MC, V. THAI.

Named for the Pattaya International Clinic PIC Hospital next door (don't worry, they're unrelated), PIC Kitchen is highly recommended for its wonderful atmosphere. Small Thai teak pavilions, both air-conditioned and open-air, have seating areas on the floor, Thai style, or at romantic tables. Delicious and affordable Thai cuisine is served à la carte or in lunch and dinner sets. The spring rolls and deep fried crab claws are mouthwatering. Other dishes come panfried, steamed, or charcoal grilled, with spice added to taste. At night, groove to a live jazz band from 7pm to 1am.

INEXPENSIVE

Nang Nual. 123/24-25 Moo 12, So. Jomtien Beach Rd., Jomtien. ☎ **038/231-548.** Main courses 60B–300B ($1.60–$7.90). AE, MC, V. Mon–Fri 8am–11pm, Sat–Sun 6am–11pm. Mid-beach in Jomtien. THAI/SEAFOOD.

Nang Nual is an excellent breakfast, lunch, or dinner choice in Jomtien Beach. This Thai restaurant specializes in seafood, which you can select from the tanks out front. A cheery, fluorescent-lit, blue-and-white interior is the setting for steamed butterfish with Chinese lime sauce or the sumptuous seasonal grilled seafood combination. Our combination had grilled prawn, a whole local lobster, and fresh crab; it varies with the catch.

Vientiane. 485/18 Pattaya Second Rd. ☎ **038/411-298.** Main courses 60B–200B ($1.60–$5.25). AE, DC, MC, V. Daily 11am–midnight. On east side of 2nd Rd., between Soi 14 and Soi Post Office. LAOTIAN/THAI.

The large menu of this busy place includes Laotian, Vietnamese, Chinese, and Isan (northeastern Thai) specialties, plus the chef's suggested "not-too-hot dishes." I found the distinctively flavored roast chicken particularly delicious and the seafood fresh, not overcooked, and in generous portions. Excellent sea crab costs 60B per 100-gram portions. The only drawback is its location on a noisy street, so head for the air-conditioned (smoking section) dining room or as far back as possible.

PATTAYA AFTER DARK

At first sight, Pattaya is an assault on the senses. Electricity bills must be staggering from all the neon displays, light-up signs, and flashing bulbs down every soi. Take a stroll down the South Pattaya pedestrian area ("Pattayaland") where every alley is lined with open-air watering holes with bar girls hanging around hoping for a lucky catch. Go-go bars are everywhere, with sex shows the sort you'd find in Bangkok's Patpong. Pattaya Land 1 and Pattaya Land 2, near South Pattaya are "Boyz Town," with rows of gay go-go clubs. This spectacle is the nightlife most come to Pattaya to experience. (Pattayaland is actually pretty cruel in the light of day, when lonely old guys blink bleary-eyed atop barstool perches listening to "Hotel California" for the umpteenth time.)

Most of Pattaya's "physical" massage parlors are on Pattaya Second Road in northern Pattaya. Typically, dozens of girls with numbered signs wait to be selected by clients, who are then whisked away to private massage rooms.

All-night companionship is easy to come by, though payments to club owners, security guards, and so on, mount up. Beware of "companions" bearing drinks laced with "knockout" drugs and watch your wallet. AIDS continues to spread at an alarming rate in Pattaya and all of Thailand. (See chapter 2, "Sex for Sale.") There's also a very active *katoy* (transvestite) scene.

If it's not your scene, you'll be happy to know there are some swell spots that don't have the sleaze. The biggest disco, **Palladium,** 78/33–35 Pattaya 2nd Rd. (☎ **038/424-922**), is cavernous, complete with enormous dance floor, pulsing music, karaoke, snooker—even traditional Thai Massage. The smaller **Disco Duck,** Little Duck Pattaya Resort Hotel, Central Pattaya Road (☎ **038/428-101**), has a fun atmosphere, catering to middle class folks from Bangkok, with live bands, videos, and light shows.

Delaney's, a fun Irish bar hangout, has a branch at the Royal Garden Resort, with the front entrance on Pattaya 2nd Road (☎ **038/412-120**). My favorite place, though, is **Hopf Brewery,** 219 Beach Rd. (☎ **038/710-650**), which brews its own beer served by the glass, goblet, or ampolla. The Hopf Band is the kick—from old Herb Alpert tunes to newer jazzy sounds. Once the general manager jumps up on the stage you're in for a real treat—he sings in native Italian, plus English, Thai, Russian—even songs from Zimbabwe? Wait for the Queen medley.

Be sure to take in a cabaret show: Pattaya's most beautiful *katoeys* (transsexuals) don sequined gowns and feather boas to strut their stuff for packed houses nightly. At **Alcazar,** 78/14 Pattaya 2nd Rd., opposite Soi 5 (☎ **038-410505**), the shows are at times hilarious. If you've seen a cabaret show elsewhere in Thailand, you may be disappointed to see familiar acts, which are standard in almost every show. Special fun are the acts that poke fun at different Asian cultures.

EN ROUTE TO BAN PHE

Rayong Province stretches east along the Gulf of Siam from Pattaya and its ever-mushrooming satellite resorts to the agricultural villages of Chanthaburi. To foreigners, the once sleepy island of Ko Samet, reached by ferry from the fishing village of Ban Phe, is Rayong's greatest attraction.

Most Thai drivers heading east through Rayong leap at the chance to double back through Pattaya, head up Sukhumvit Road, and hop onto the colorless Highway 36, the quick through route to Rayong city, missing out on the meandering coast road.

The warm waters of the Gulf of Thailand support more fishing villages than any other region in Thailand. Each night, hundreds of brightly painted, low-slung trawlers fish for squid, crab, lobsters, oysters, and other fish. The twinkling of lights offshore is one of the unexpected pleasures of sea-view accommodations anywhere on the east coast. When you arrive at Ban Phe's pier, you can inspect these trawlers, some of which are converted to tourist ferries, for the voyage to Ko Samet, during the day.

3 Ban Phe & Ko Samet

220km (137 miles) E of Bangkok via Highway 3, or 185km (115 miles) via Highway 3, and the Pattaya bypass

Ban Phe is 35km (22 miles) east of Rayong city, along Sukhumvit Highway. As you turn south toward the Gulf of Thailand, you'll pass through a bustling village to the seaside main street, dominated by the large pier and its colorful fishing boats destined for Ko Samet.

Ko Samet (also called Ko Kaeo Phitsadan) first became popular with Thais from the poetry of Sunthon Phu, a venerated 19th-century author and Rayong native who set his best-known epic on this "tropical island paradise." Fortunately, despite its appeal to Thais and foreigners, a shortage of potable water kept rampant commerce and tourism at bay for many years. In 1981, Samet became part of the six-island **Khao**

Laem Ya—Samet National Park, a designation meant to preserve its relatively unde-veloped status. Since then, small-scale construction has boomed, and there are more than 50 licensed bungalow hotels with nearly 2,500 rooms on the 6-km-long (3.6 miles) island. In 1990, a TAT-sponsored effort to close the national park to overnight visitors met with such fierce resistance that 4 days later Samet was reopened for busi-ness as usual. Until inadequate water supplies, waste treatment, and garbage disposal are dealt with, the TAT is encouraging visitors to go to the still lovely Samet for day trips only, but that rarely happens.

The small island's northern half is triangular, with a long tail leading to the south that looks somewhat like a kite. Most of the beaches are on the east coast of the tail; although Ko Samet is only about 1km ($^6/_{10}$ mile) wide, it has a rocky spine and there are few paths that connect the two coasts.

Passengers alight from the ferry at **Na Dan,** the island's main port. It's a 10-minute walk south past the **health center** and school to **Hat Sai Kaeo** (Diamond Beach, on the northeast cape), the island's most developed and crowded beach, which is linked by a dirt path to 10 other small beach developments. Most day-trippers take the reg-ular ferry and then catch one of the songtaos that meet the boats and travel inland as far as Wong Duan. You can also catch a ride with one of the individual resort ferries or hike the shoreline path between beaches.

The more developed beaches are Hat Sai Kaeo, Ao Pai, and Vong Deuan beach. Most of the other beaches offer facilities that are barely the basics for human survival. The three most developed beaches are also the most expensive, mostly because every-thing, including water, must be imported form the mainland. And while these beaches can get pretty busy on weekends during peak season, especially Hat Sai Kaeo, which probably should be avoided either way, they are still quite relaxing. The atmosphere here is very laid back. However, even the high-end accommodations are basic. Expect a quaint bungalow with a small deck in the front and a concrete latrine in the back—cold-water shower only. Your first day at Ko Samet will be a little shocking if you've never roughed it before. Your second day will be filled with relaxation and fun. Your third day you won't want to leave. If you stay for a fourth, you'll be redecorating your bungalow.

Ko Samet's peak season follows Pattaya—with July through October brining fewer travelers, so bungalow prices are discounted accordingly. Weekends get busy, however, so discounts may not apply.

ESSENTIALS

GETTING THERE   By Bus   Buses leave Bangkok every hour between 7am and 9pm for the 3½-hour journey, departing from the **Eastern Bus Terminal** (☎ 02/390-1230) on Sukhumvit Road opposite Soi 63, Ekamai Road. The one-way trip to Ban Phe costs 108B ($2.85). From Pattaya, you have to wait along Sukhumvit Road (there are pavilions located across the street from the North Pat-taya Road and Central Pattaya Road intersections. Wait for the Ban Phe bus and flag it down. Buses from Bangkok are very popular on weekends and holidays, so you may not find a seat. Book your return to either Bangkok or Pattaya at the Ban Phe pier bus stop immediately on arrival to make sure you have a seat for your return home.

By Private Bus   Many Bangkok travel agencies operate their own buses to Ban Phe—it's the easiest way to go. **S. T. Travel** has a daily minibus leaving from its office at 102 Rambutri Rd. (at Khao San Road), Banglamphu, daily at 8am (trip time 3½ hours; 350B/$9.20 round-trip). Call them in Bangkok (☎ 02/281-3662) or in Ban Phe (☎ 038/651-461) for schedule information and reservations.

Water Taxi Tip

One note about water taxis and songtaos. They don't like to make the trip if there's only one or two passengers: premiums will be charged. A water taxi could soak you up to 300B ($7.90), and a songtao could run you into the ground for 400B ($10.55), especially if they know you have no other choice. Now's a good time to remember your Thai etiquette, and refrain from blowing your top; otherwise, you'll end up walking.

Several buses a day leave from Pattaya to Ban Phe (trip time: 1 hour; 300B/$7.90 round-trip). Contact **Malibu Travel Service,** Soi Post Office (☎ **038/423-180**).

By Taxi   Malibu Travel Service in Pattaya will arrange a private car to take you to Ban Phe for 900B ($23.70) one-way. Call them at the number above for details and booking.

By Car   Take Highway 3 east from Bangkok along the longer, more scenic coastal route (about 3½ to 4 hours), or the quicker route: via Highway 3 east to Pattaya, then Highway 36 to Rayong, then the coastal Highway 3 to Ban Phe (about 3 hours).

GETTING TO KO SAMET   By Ferry   During the high season, from November to April, ferries leave Ban Phe pier for the main port, Na Dan, every half hour (trip time: 40 minutes; 40B/$1.05). The first boat departs at 9:30am and the last at 5pm. Several other agents in Ban Phe sell passage on their own boats to Wang Duen beach which depart at least a few times daily. One-way fare is 50B ($1.30). Contact Malibu Travel's Ban Phe office at ☎ **038/651-292.**

From the ferry landing on Samet, you must catch a water taxi to the other beaches (20B to 60B/53¢ to $1.60 per person, depending on your destination.) You can also take a songtao to other beaches for between 10B and 50B (25¢ and $1.30). There is one road on Samet connecting the main town, Samet Village, halfway down the eastern shore of the island to Vong Deuan. Beyond that is footpaths.

ORIENTATION   Ban Phe has three streets: The coast road features the ferry pier at the east end of a C-shaped cove; the second road runs westbound and has the town's open-air market; and the third inland road runs eastbound. Buses from Bangkok and Pattaya stop in front of the pier. Everything is within easy walking distance. Buses from the east (Trat and Chantaburi) stop on Sukhumvit Highway, about 4km out, and you'll have to take a songtao (20B/55¢) to the pier.

FAST FACTS   There are no TAT offices in Ko Samet or Ban Phe, but the TAT offices in Bangkok and Pattaya can provide you with information prior to your departure. Ko Samet is pretty much a cash operation only. While there are no ATMs, there is a money changing service at the post office at the Naga Bar along the main road in Ao Pai. (See how laid-back this place is? The post office is at a *bar*.) This same bar also has an international phone and fax service. In Na Dan, also called Samet Village, as well as Vong Duean, there are some small provision shops by the main ferry landing.

EXPLORING THE AREA

Windsurfing is particularly popular with weekenders from Bangkok. The island's best is said to be north of Hat Sai Kaeo (Diamond Beach), around the cape that bulges out of Samet's east side. The rocky north coast is even more challenging, with strong currents and sometimes erratic winds caused by the deep channel between the island and the mainland. Windsurfers are available at most guest houses for 100B to 175B ($2.65 to $4.60) per hour, without instruction. Hat Sai Kaeo also has jet skis for rent at about 1,200B ($31.60) per hour.

Up north on the west coast, is **Ao Phrao** (Paradise Beach), the most isolated cove on the island. Aficionados prefer snorkeling off the rocky west coast where coral reefs have escaped the damage caused by frequent ferries. The western coastline is mostly uninhabited; the easiest access is by sea, though there are two roads and several rough trails across the central spine of the island.

You can book any of the **speedboats** at the beaches for round island tours (about 300B/$7.90 per person), and for **snorkeling** on the rocky uninhabited western side of the island, which is said to be the best for underwater life. They'll be happy to do a morning drop-off and afternoon pickup for 300B ($7.90). Samet's southern, narrow kite tail has calm waters, good for swimming and snorkeling.

WHERE TO STAY

Vong Deaun Resort offers a wide range of accommodations that can be booked in Bangkok, at 359/9-11 Ekamai Complex, Sukhumvit 63 Prakhanong (☎ 02/392-0879, fax 662/391-9571). If you don't book one of the few bungalow complexes with a telephone before your arrival, never fear. Several travel agents, enterprising fishermen, teenage girls, and others hover at the Ban Phe pier with photo albums showing off their rooms to rent. Accommodations are similarly primitive around the island. Note that rates are higher than at other "undeveloped" island resorts because food and water must be imported from the mainland.

There are also many independent bungalows on Ao Wai, Hat Sai Kaeo (Diamond Beach, the longest sandy strip near the island's main port), and Ao Cho, as well as many under-10-room complexes scattered around the shoreline. Rates go as low as 125B ($3.30) for a thatch A-frame with a sleeping platform and shared Asian toilet but no mosquito netting, and as high as 750B ($19.75) for a fan-cooled, screened-window bungalow with linens and a private toilet. Most bungalows have their own dining areas for inexpensive, fresh seafood (don't miss the locally caught squid and cuttle fish, which are barbecued on skewers) and standard Thai rice and noodle dishes.

Ao Kiu Na Nok Villas. c/o Samed Travel Service, Ban Phe, 121160 Rayong. ☎ 01/321-1371. 2,000B ($52.65) single or double with A/C; 800B ($21.05) single or double with fan. Rates include tax and service. No credit cards.

The broad sandy cove of Ao Kiu Na Nok is near the southern tip of the Ko Samet kite tail, and therefore much less busy than other beaches. The fan-cooled, simple bungalows have private bathrooms but only cold water; pricier bungalows are more substantially built and have hot water. All are well located on the beach. Over the holidays from mid-December to mid-January, Samed Travel says they will charge a 300B ($7.90) per room per night supplement.

Ao Pai Huts. Pai Beach, Samet Island, Ban Phe, 121160. ☎ 01/353-2644 in Rayong. 500B ($13.15) bungalow with A/C; 300B ($7.90) bungalow with fan.

Au Pai is a smaller beach, but less developed, with bungalows set in the jungle, just a hop from the beach. It's quiet and you'll feel more privacy. The best of the bungalows

Travel Tip

Arm yourself with mosquito repellent. A flashlight is also a good idea—for finding your way after dark, and for use in the smaller bungalows, which turn off electricity in the late evening. You might want to bring along a towel. Vong Deuan resort has towels, but few of the smaller places do. A good sarong is the ultimate—beach blanket, towel, wrap, bedsheet, sunshield. Don't leave home without at least two.

here is Ao Pai Huts along the main dirt road about 10 minutes ride from the main jetty. These simple bungalows are tidy and well constructed, with clean bathrooms and space to lay your baggage.

Malibu Garden Resort. 77 Wong Duan Beach, Samet Island, Ban Phe, 121160 Rayong. ☎ **038/651-057** in Ban Phe, or 038/710-676 in Pattaya. 1,400B–2,200B ($36.85–$57.90) bungalow with A/C; 800B–1,700B ($21.05–$44.75) bungalow with fans. Rates include tax and service.

These clean concrete bungalows with tin roofs are clustered right on the beach, surrounding a much more picturesque thatch dining pavilion where light meals are served. This is possibly the cushiest of the resorts on Ko Samet—they have hot water and TVs, but you will sacrifice the Robinson Crusoe appeal of the island.

Vongduern Villas. Wong Duan Beach, Samet Island, 22 Moo 4 Pae, 121160 Rayong. ☎ **01/446-1944** for cell phone, or 02/392-4390 in Bangkok. 1,100B–1,200B ($28.95–$31.60) bungalow with A/C; 800B–900B ($21.05–$23.70) bungalow with fan. Rates include tax and service. V.

Simple, solid wood bungalows with air-conditioning and private hot water showers vary in price according to the view and size of room. There are also elaborate VIP bungalows (perhaps the only ones on the island) with carpeting, TV, VCR with a private video collection, intrabungalow phone, and minibar—quite a change from what the average visitor to Ko Samet is seeking.

WHERE TO DINE

All of the bungalows offer some sort of eating experience, mostly bland local food and beer, with some Western breakfast offerings. In the evenings a few places entice dinner guests with video screenings of recently released movies, which are always popular. In Ao Pai, Naga Bar on the main road is quiet, with a fairly decent menu, a beer selection, and a bakery that has surprisingly wonderful fresh goods in the mornings. In Vong Deuan, places like Nice & Easy, Oasis, Baywatch, and Seahorse serve dinner, and get pretty lively later on. You can expect most dishes in these places to cost you between 60B and 100B ($1.60 and $2.65).

EN ROUTE TO CHANTHABURI: RAYONG PROVINCE

If you have lots of time to kill in Ban Phe, the Sopha Botanical Gardens are about 2km (1.2 miles) east of the ferry pier. Run by the private Sawet-Sobha Foundation, this odd collection of ceramics and a few pieces of furniture are placed inside three traditional Thai teak houses on a landscaped piece of property. Only for old-house buffs (open Friday to Tuesday 8am to 4pm; admission 60B/$1.60)!

The long, tree-shaded coastline east of Rayong has several small public beaches and isolated resort properties, with more under development. Just 7km (4.2 miles) east of Ban Phe is the bustling Suan Sum Park, a pine-and-palm-lined, narrow sand beach filled with Thai day-trippers and Thai Guides (Boy Scouts) camping groups. There are dozens of food stalls, picnic tables with cars pulled up nearby, vendors renting inner tubes, modestly clad kids learning to swim, and lots of general hubbub.

From the headland at Wang Kaeo along the stretch of tranquil beach to Laem Mae Phim are several deluxe condo complexes and luxury hotels. The excellent **Palmeraie Princess** (weekday rates from 1,400B/$36.85, weekends from 1,700B/$44.75), is highly recommended to those traveling by car.

As you get farther from the city, mango, coconut, and durian are under cultivation, though the provincial government has begun encouraging rubber plantations as an alternate industry. The old women in tight, flowery sarongs will squat below sun umbrellas to peddle dried squid or grilled octopus and grilled chicken to Bangkok's "Benz families" (the yuppie set in swank cars).

4 Chanthaburi Province

Travelers heading east to the undeveloped, stunning, wooded isles of Mu Ko Chang National Park (see "Trat & Ko Chang," below) will pass through Chanthaburi province and its capital city, Chanthaburi town (Muang Chan). This region is known for its gem mines (a lucrative export industry) and tropical fruit production. Durian, custard apple, longan, and rambutan are grown in large plantations, but small family farms are much in evidence. Don't be startled by the roadside 26-foot-high durian sculpture, or the many watermelon and fruit stands alongside the highway.

Chanthaburi town (Muang Chan) is a large city built on both sides of the Chanthaburi River. In central Taksin Park, there's a statue of King Taksin on horseback, surrounded by sword-brandishing troops, to commemorate his victory over Burmese invaders in 1767, after the fall of Ayutthaya. The city's main avenue is Tha Chalab Road. The taxi stand and bus station (to Trat or Bangkok) are just west of the Chanthaburi Hotel on this street; both flank the central produce and Night Market.

WHAT TO SEE & DO

Most of the area's attractions appeal to Thai tourists seeking the great outdoors: parks, natural sights, and beaches.

PARKS & PUBLIC BEACHES   The 42,000-acre **Namtok Philu National Park,** very popular because King Rama V and his wife, Queen Sunatha, are said to have visited its pretty waterfall, is served by frequent shared taxis (truck taxis or songtao) from the Chanthaburi town market.

Laem Sadet is the best of the nearby beaches, and it's about 35km (22 miles) southwest of the city. From the rocky cape, which forms a picturesque lagoon at Khung Krabane, the pine-shaded coastline has a long, but narrow, sand beach running south for several kilometers. Resort developers are bound to come soon, since the only commercial activities at present are prawn farms and fish-drying cottage industries. Laem Sadet and closer beach destinations can also be reached by shared taxis or public buses.

GEM SHOPPING   In case you were intrigued by the mention of the local gem industry, remember: The best quality gemstones found here are sent to Bangkok for sale. Unless you are an expert, don't expect to find bargains on Gems Street (in Chanthaburi town near the central market), or in any of the many jewelers' shops. For the curious, blue and black sapphires are mined near Wat Khao Ploy Wan, about 15km (9 miles) east of Chanthaburi town. Rubies are mined farther east in Trat and over the Cambodian border. Northeast of Chanthaburi in Nong Bon, and due east of town at Bo Rai (both in Trat province), are the major ruby markets. Each morning, gem sales take place at Bo Rai's central Hua Tung market, and each afternoon at the Khlong Yo Market. The market at Nong Bon (on Route 3299) takes place all day.

A NEARBY ATTRACTION   **Oasis Sea World,** 48/2 Moo 5 Tambon Paknam, Amphur Ramsing, Chanthaburi (☎ **039/399-015**), is Thailand's largest dolphinarium. Partially open at my visit, there were 65 dolphins (some humpback and some Irrawaddi dolphins) housed in more than 25 acres of developed seashore. Feeding and playtime are fun to watch, but the dolphins are trained to do tricks for an audience. The construction of an aviary, swimming pool, water slides, and waterfall are on the agenda. Oasis Sea World is open daily from 9am to 6pm; admission is 60B ($1.60) for adults, 30B (80¢) for children. To get there, take Highway 3 east to Trat city, turn south at the Laem Sing exit, and follow the signs.

WHERE TO STAY & DINE

There's no reason to spend the night in Chanthaburi town, but if you must:

The Chai Lee Hotel. 106 Kwang Rd., Chanthaburi 22000. ☎ **039/311-075.** 66 units. TEL. 170B–300B ($4.45–$7.90) double. Rates include tax and service. No credit cards. In the central market.

These are very simple accommodations, recommended by a Canadian couple I met who became stranded overnight when trying to take a bus from Ayutthaya to Trat for a holiday on Ko Si Chang. Clean-swept, fan-cooled rooms have a private shower inside; choose a back-facing room to avoid the bustle of the Night Market.

The Eastern Hotel. 899 Tha Cha Laeb Rd., Chanthaburi 22000. ☎ **039/312-218.** Fax 039/311-985. 142 units. A/C TV TEL. 550B ($14.45) double. MC, V. Across from Taksin Park, 4km (2½ miles) southeast of town market.

Reputedly the best hotel in town before K.P. Grand opened, this worn and aging structure is right in the middle of Chanthaburi's depressing red-light district. There is actually a pleasant lobby bakery, a cheerful coffee shop mobbed with locals, a dimly lit bar (also mobbed), a loud and seedy nightclub (also mobbed) filled with besequinned young songbirds, and poorly kept but (sort of) clean rooms. Don't let the front desk hustle you into a windowless room; they're no cheaper than the city-view rooms.

K. P. Grand. 35/200-201 Trirat Rd., Chanthaburi 22000. ☎ **039/323-201.** Fax 039/323-214. A/C MINIBAR TV TEL. 202 units. 1,800B ($47.35) double; 20,000B ($526.30) suite. MC, V.

K. P. Grand is the newest and most modern accommodation facility in town. It's a little pricey, but make sure you negotiate—chances are they're more eager to fill rooms in tough times. But if you need a city hotel with Western amenities and comforts, plus nice-sized rooms, you'll be happy to spend the money.

EN ROUTE TO TRAT

The Sukhumvit Highway (Highway 3) east from Chanthaburi town to Trat is just 70km (42 miles) of two-lane blacktop wending through relatively undeveloped terrain. At the 31km marker, two lion statues indicate the turnoff for **Laem Sing,** a cape jutting into the Gulf of Thailand that's said to resemble a resting lion. On a hill above the cape are the remnants of a fortress built by King Rama III. Below Laem Sing, the pier is lined with seafood restaurants and fishing boats and the new Oasis Sea World is nearby, all hoping to appeal to the many traveling Thais.

Along the road you'll see leafy green vines tightly wound around slender poles—it's those small, fiery chiles the Thais love to cook with. Old women in straw hats and brightly patterned sarongs sell bamboo tubes stuffed with sticky rice steamed in coconut milk; these semisweet, chewy cylinders make great road snacks.

5 Trat & Ko Chang

400km (249 miles) E of Bangkok

Trat's dramatic, wooded landscape crests at the Khao Bantat Range, which separates Thailand's easternmost province from neighboring Cambodia (Kampuchea). This region thrives on agriculture (primarily rubber and chili plantations), fish farming, and fishing.

Foreigners and Thai tourists are advised not to travel south of the capital, Muang Trat, especially after dark because of security problems. Navy battle ships moored off Laem Ngop are a reminder of the region's troubled past (every January 13, the Thai

Navy honors those killed in the 19th-century war with France over Cambodian territory) and of its troubled present (ships patrol the coast to monitor activity along the
Cambodian border).

Trat Province is the gateway to the tranquil, unspoiled aches of Mu Ko Chang
National Park, 52 heavily wooded islands, most accessible by ferry from the cape at
Laem Ngop. If no phone or power lines, no discos or video bars, no beach vendors or
mopeds sound like tropical paradise, this is your kind of place. It's naturally pure,
scenically beautiful, and very, very quiet.

ESSENTIALS

GETTING THERE   By Public Bus   Eight air-conditioned buses a day leave from
Bangkok's Eastern or Ekamai Bus Terminal (trip time: 5 to 6 hours; 175B/$4.60).
From Pattaya, you'll have to wait on the side of Sukhumvit Road to flag down one of
the buses heading out that way from Bangkok. There are pavilions at the intersections
of Pattaya North Road and Pattaya Central Road for just this purpose. Talk to TAT
representatives in Pattaya to figure out when the best time to wait would be. The trip
from there is about 3½ hours.

By Private Bus   A few Bangkok travel agencies operate their own transport to Trat—
it's the easiest way to go because you're delivered direct to the Ko Chang ferries. **S.T.
Travel** has a daily minibus leaving from its office at 102 Rambutri Rd. (at Khaosan
Road), Banglamphu, daily at 8am (trip time: 6 hours; 550B/$14.45 round-trip). Call
them in Bangkok (☎ 02/281-3662) or at the ferry pier (☎ 039/597-198) for information and reservations.

By Car   Take Highway 3 east from Bangkok to Chonburi, then Highway 344 southeast to Klaeng (bypassing Pattaya and Rayong), then the coastal Highway 3 east
through Chanthaburi and south to Trat (about 5 to 6 hours).

GETTING TO LAEM NGOP PIER FROM TRAT   There is a constant stream of
shared truck taxis (called minibuses or songtao) departing from Trat's central market,
next to the bus terminal (trip time: 30 minutes; 40B/$1.05). A private truck taxi costs
about 200B ($5.25). Laem Ngop is a tiny village of shops selling shrimp paste and fish
sauce, with a long pier housing dozens of fishing boats. Son Jan Restaurant just south of
the pier is the best place to wait for a boat, have a Thai snack, or a cool drink. The helpful
S.T. Travel desk in front books a private minivan to Bangkok (see "By Private Bus,"
above in this section) and rooms on the island (see "Where to Stay & Dine," below).

GETTING TO KO CHANG   By Ferry   You have to take a ferry from Laem Ngop
to any of Mu Ko Chang National Park's many islands. Boys from the passenger boats
(none too helpful) solicit tourists to go to their assigned Ko Chang beaches (the
fishermen/captains have divided up service to the main island and the park's smaller
islands). However, ferries to the most popular beaches on Ko Chang leave at noon or
3pm (give or take an hour), according to demand and the captain's frame of mind (trip
time: 2 to 4 hours; 50B to 250B/$1.30 to $6.60) depending on destination). Remain
calm and you'll find the right boat.

TRAT ORIENTATION   Arriving visitors will find themselves in the center of Trat,
at the air-conditioned bus terminal on main street, or Sukhumvit Road. Next door is
the central open-air market. Shared taxis going west to Chanthaburi town or east to
Laem Ngop leave from the market throughout the day. Everything is within easy
walking distance.

VISITOR INFORMATION   Happily, TAT has an office in Trat, that also provides
information about the nearby islands. Located at 100 Moo 1 on the Trat-Laem Ngop
Road, you can call them at ☎ 039/597-255.

Malaria Alert

Malaria is endemic to the heavily forested islands of Mu Ko Chang National Park and the jungle-covered foothills of Trat province. Several strains discovered are resistant to all known medical prophylaxis. The only protection you have is to avoid getting bitten. Make sure to purchase insect repellent, preferably one with a high DEET content, in Trat (available at all pharmacies) before proceeding to the islands. Note: Be sure to consult your physician before you make this trip.

WHAT TO SEE & DO IN KO CHANG

Ko Chang, Thailand's second-largest island after Phuket, is the anchor of the 52-island Mu Ko Chang National Park. Thickly forested hills rise from its many rocky bays, forming a swaying hump reminiscent of a sleeping elephant (*chang* means elephant). Accommodations are primitive; budget tourists come for the beaches and the cleanest Mediterranean-blue waters this side of Greece. Pineapple and coconut palms dominate the landscape, with a few scattered fishing villages (established before the island was declared a national park) containing most of the sparse population. Cambodia (Kampuchea) can easily be seen from the eastern shore, the site of a small naval base and the national park office. The **Park Service** has opened some dormitory and camping space; contact their Bangkok headquarters (☎ **02/579-5269**) for reservations and information. Most of the island's development—including a dirt road that stretches around the northern coast and the few pickups that ply it carrying construction materials—is near Thaan Ma Yom pier.

Only a few pristine sand beaches, with newly built thatch bungalows tucked into the treeline, dot its western and southern shores. The best beaches are on the west coast, a 1½ - to 2½ -hour boat ride from Laem Ngop. **Hat Sai Khao (White Sand Beach)** is the closest of the western beaches, with the majority of Ko Chang's bungalow housing set in a narrow ribbon along its kilometer-long, fine-sand beach. Twenty minutes by boat farther south is **Hat Khlong Phrao,** with a pier at its north end to serve some bungalows, an inland canal and fishing settlement in the middle, and one full-service resort and numerous bungalows to the south. This broad, palm-lined cove is one of Ko Chang's prettiest. Since housing is limited, boat captains help direct travelers to the available bungalows by hailing dugouts to come pick you up.

The best **skin diving** or **snorkeling** is around the small islands off Ko Chang's south coast, such as Ko Khlum, Ko Whai (a particularly beautiful island), Ko Phrao (near some wrecks of Thai naval ships), Ko Ngam, and Ko Lao Ya. All of these islands, except Ko Khlum, have some bungalows, but ferry service is erratic, infrequent, and expensive. Ko Lao Ya is the best organized for travelers, with telephone service and a fine resort (see "Where to Stay & Dine," below). Hat Bang Bao is a small cove on the island's southwest corner (within day-trip distance of these islands), whose mixed sand and coral coast supports a few bungalows.

WHERE TO STAY & DINE
IN TRAT

If you get stranded in Trad, the **Muang Trad Hotel,** at 4 Sukhumvit Rd. (☎ **039/ 511-091**), 1 block south of the bus terminal, has 144 rooms with private toilets and Asian *mandi* (ladle shower), which cost 250B ($6.60) single, 450B ($11.85) double with fan; 370B ($9.75) single, 650B ($17.10) double with air-conditioning. They accept MasterCard and Visa and have a nice Thai coffee shop in town (open 6:30am to 9:30pm).

There are only two "full-service" (even this is an exaggeration) hotels in the Mu Ko Chang National Park. Elsewhere, accommodations consist of simple thatch huts and A-frames, most without telephones to accept reservations. Transportation is the biggest problem. Beaches are serviced only by select ferries—it's almost impossible to move from one beach to another without returning to Laem Ngop. The only boats to Laem Ngop return from Ko Chang in the morning, so there's a chance (especially in the high season between mid-December and mid-January) that you'll end up on a great beach with no available bungalows and sleep outdoors overnight.

You can minimize the aura of adventurous unpredictability by checking with travel agents at the Laem Ngop pier or asking your boat captain what's happening at the various beaches. *A reminder:* Take precautions against mosquitoes, as malaria is endemic to this area. Hungry sand flies are also a big problem!

ON KO CHANG

Ko Chang Resort. 39 Moo 8, Ko Chang, Trat 23120. ☎ **039/538-059,** or 02/277-3891 in Bangkok. Fax 02/692-0094 (in Bangkok). 70 units. A/C MINIBAR TV. 2,500B ($65.80) double. MC, V. Hat Khlong Phrao, 2 hr. by ferry.

With hot water, minibars, and even VCRs with Thai-dubbed American B pictures, this resort stands out as the most comfortable and expensive housing on the islands. You can choose between freestanding bungalows (two sizes) and slightly more modern, attached rooms in a two-story hotel block. The best value is found in four beachfront bungalows (priced the same as our no-view hotel room) with delightful verandas and sea views. All rooms are cool and comfortably furnished with minimal decor and pastel tile floors, but cleaning is wildly sporadic.

The beach is superb, with rows of coconut palms marching down to the clear, shallow warm waters. It's a great spot for sitting (canvas deck chairs and no hawkers) or swimming (very few boats and only mild currents). On the outdoor dining patio, an amiable staff serves up typical, but mediocre, Thai fare and a few continental dishes. I found their strong suit was grilled seafood from local waters.

ON KO LAO YA ISLAND

Lao Ya Island Resort. Ko Lao Ya, Trat 23120. ☎ **01/653-8222** resort cellular, 01/818-8386 pier cellular, or 02/391-4425 in Bangkok. Fax 02/381-1463. A/C MINIBAR. 3,400B ($89.45) double, plus boat transfer and all meals. MC, V. Ko Lao Ya, 4 hr. by ferry.

This is the only lodging on this tiny island, making it a destination for those seeking obscure and far-off places. Bungalows have fully functioning air-conditioning, hot-water private showers, full bathrooms, and comfortable bedrooms. They're finished in burnished coconut wood and furnished with some style in tropical rattan. Your only dining option is at the resort, but you'll be happy to note the food is quite good. They say that meals are compulsory—really, you have no other option anyway!

Lao Ya is comparably good value, and ideal for those seeking a tranquil vacation. The beach is lovely but rocky; however, swimming is safe and easy. The marine park's best snorkeling is found in these waters, a real plus if you're so inclined.

The Southern Peninsula

7

Thailand's slim Malay Peninsula extends 1,250km (777 miles) south from Bangkok to the Malaysia border at Sungai Kolok. Just as the beach resort of Phuket in the Andaman Sea dominates the list of west coast pleasures, so Ko Samui, a more laid-back and traditional Thai resort island in the Gulf of Thailand (also known as the Gulf of Siam), dominates the east.

In contrast to the hills of the north and the rice fields in the central region, the south is pure tropical wonder, from it's multitude of coconut plantations worked by monkeys, to a paradise of lush beach-lined islands and lacy coral reefs off each shore. Many southern destinations stand out of the pack. Phetchaburi, the last outpost of the Khmer Empire, delights with ancient temples, while nearby Hua Hin and Cha-Am presents Thailand's first beach resort—the resort of royals. Further south on Ko Samui, Ko Phangngan, and Ko Tao, you can experience an island adventure as exciting as any on Phuket, but without the enormous development of the tourist industry. Across the peninsula on the west side, Krabi is a newcomer to the beach resort areas, popular with backpackers and travelers seeking outdoor adventure. As you venture further down the peninsula, Nakhon Si Thammarat proves itself to be one of the great religious and cultural centers of the region, while Hat Yai, one of Thailand's most visited tourist spots sees mostly Asian visitors (curiously, few Western travelers ever see this small but lively town). By this point you should notice a change in the cultural scenery, for this region is home to most of Thailand's Muslim population. Mosques and Malaysian elements seep into the Thai culture all the way to Sungai Kolok, the border town—where you can eat Malaysian food and buy batiks and other Malaysian crafts at markets.

1 Hua Hin/Cha-Am

Hua Hin is 240km (140 miles) S of Bangkok; 223km (138 miles) N of Chumphon.

Cha-am is 265km (165 miles) S of Bangkok; 248km (154 miles) N of Chumphon

Hua Hin and Cha-Am, neighboring towns on the Gulf of Thailand, are together the country's oldest resort area. Developed in the 1920s as a relaxing getaway for Bangkok's elite, the beautiful seaside of "Thailand's Riviera" was a mere 3 or 4 hours' journey from the capital by train, thanks to the southern railway's completion in 1916. The royal family was the first to embrace these two small fishing villages as the perfect location for both summer vacations and health retreats. In 1924 King Vajiravudh (Rama VI) built the royal Mareukatayawan Palace amid the tall evergreens that lined seemingly endless stretches of golden sands. At the same time, the Royal Hua Hin Golf Course opened as the first course in Thailand. As Bangkok's upper classes began building summer bungalows along the shore, the State Railways opened the Hua Hin Railway Hotel for tourists, which stands today as the Hotel Sofitel Central.

When Pattaya, on Thailand's eastern coast, hit the scene in the 1960s, it lured vacationers away from Hua Hin and Cha-Am with promises of inexpensive holidays with spicy nightlife. Since then, the two villages have yet to reach Pattaya's peak tourist levels, which, if you ask me, makes them still the perfect place for relaxing getaways and health retreats. The clean sea and beaches support some excellent and unique resorts, plus there's the added benefit of nearby Phetchaburi (covered later in this chapter), a fascinating and easy day trip to experience a bit of Thai history and culture.

Plan your trip for the months between November and May for the most sunshine and least rain, but note that from about mid-December to mid-January, Hua Hin and Cha-Am reach peak levels. Bookings must be made in advance and hotels will slap a 500B to 1,500B ($13.15 to $39.45) peak season surcharge onto your nightly room rate. The area is still pleasant during the other months. During the low season, while it's more likely to rain, it is highly improbable it will rain all the time.

ESSENTIALS
GETTING THERE   By Plane   While there is a domestic airport in Hua Hin, no airlines have serviced it for years.

By Train   Both Hua Hin and Cha-Am are reached via the train station in Hua Hin. Ten trains make the daily trek from Bangkok's Hua Lampong Railway Station (☎ 02/223-7010 or 02/223-7020). Fares range from 142B ($3.75) for second class without air-conditioning on a Rapid Train to 182B ($4.80) for air-conditioned second class on a Special Express. The trip is just over 4 hours.

The **Hua Hin Railway Station** (☎ 032/511-073) is at the tip of Damnoenkasem Road, which slices through the center of town straight to the beach. Pickup truck taxis (*songtao*) and *tuk-tuks* wait outside to take you to your hotel.

By Bus   Most agree that the bus is the better choice for travel from Bangkok to Hua Hin because it takes less time. Buses depart from Bangkok's Southern Bus Terminal (☎ 02/435-1199) every 40 minutes from 5am to 10:20pm (110B/$2.90).

Buses from Bangkok arrive in Hua Hin at the air-conditioned Bus Station (☎ 032/511-654 or 032/512-543) on Srasong Road, 1 block north of Damnoenkasem Road. From here it's easy to find a songtao or tuk-tuk to take you to your destination.

By Car   From Bangkok, take Route 35, the Thonburi-Paktho Highway, southwest and allow 2 to 4 hours, depending on traffic.

ORIENTATION   Despite decades of tourist traffic, Hua Hin remains a small town that is simple to navigate. The main artery, Petchkasem Road, runs parallel to the waterfront about four blocks inland. The wide Damnoenkasem Road cuts through Petchkasem and runs straight to the beach. On the north side of Damnoenkasem toward the waterfront, you'll find a cluster of guest houses, restaurants, shopping, and night spots lining the narrow lanes. Across Petchkasem to the west are the bus terminals, railway station, and night market.

The Southern Peninsula: East Coast

Thung Wua Laem
BURMA (MYANMAR)
Chumphon
↑Hua Hin/Cha Am

0 30 mi
0 30 km

Ranong
Lang Suan
RANONG PROVINCE

Ko Tao

Mu Ko Ang Thong National Park
Ko Phangan

Ko Ta Luang
Ko Samui

Chaiya

Surat Thani **1**
No Dog Island (Ko Taen)

Gulf of Thailand
(Gulf of Siam)

Phanom
Sichon

401
Phrasaeng
Tha Sala

4009
41
Nakhon Si Thammarat **2**

Thung Yai

Klong Thom
Hua Sai

403
Huai Yot
41
4

Phatthalung
TRANG PROVINCE
Ko Lanta Yai
Trang
Sathing Pra

Ko Li Bong

Thung Wa
Songkhla **4**

Hat Yai **3**

Pattani

Route 4

Ko Tarutao

YALA PROVINCE
5
Narathiwat
Yala
7
6
Tak Bai

Andaman Sea

MALAYSIA

Sungai Kolok

Legend
Airport ✈
Beach 🏖
Ferry Route – – –
Scuba Diving 🤿

THAILAND
★ Bangkok
The Southeast Coast

Monkey Training Center **1**
Institute for Southern Thai Studies **4**
Khao Noi Hill **4**
Khao Kong Hill (Phra Buddha Taksin Ming Mongkol) **7**
Laem Samila **4**
Songkhla National Museum **4**

Suan Mokkh (Suan Mokkhabalarama) **1**
Wat Chang Hai **5**
Wat Chu Chang **3**
Wat Khuha Phimuk (Wat Na Tham) **6**
Wat Mahatat (Wat Mahathat) **2**
Wat Matchimawat **4**

Cha-Am is a 25-minute drive north of Hua Hin following Petchkasem Road. Cha-Am village is much smaller than Hua Hin, and has a far different feel. Still primarily a fishing town, Cha-Am begins at the piers, which are packed with small local fishing boats. Most of the life is centered on Ruamchit Road, which is also known as Beach Road. Hugging the beach on one side, and rows of shops, restaurants, hotels and motels on the other, it's the part of town that sees the most action. The beach gets crowded here, especially on weekends, but for excitement sleepy Cha-Am can't really compete with Hua Hin, which is a bit more developed.

Cha-Am's resorts line the 8-kilometer stretch of beach that runs south from the village all the way to Hua Hin. If you're staying in one of these resorts, you'll either spend a lot of time in residence, or pay the hotel taxis to take you to either town.

GETTING AROUND   By Songtao   Pickup truck taxis (songtao), make their way along the main streets of Hua Hin passing the railway station and bus terminals at regular intervals. Flag one down that's going in your direction. Fares range from 10B to 20B (25¢ to 55¢) within town, while stops at outlying resorts will be up to 50B ($1.30). Trips between Hua Hin and Cha-Am cost between 100B to 200B ($2.65 to $5.25).

By Tuk-tuk   Tuk-tuks will take you door to door for between 20B and 50B (55¢ and $1.30) within town.

By Motorcycle Taxi   Within each town, motorcycle taxi fares begin at 20B (55¢). The taxi drivers, identified by their colorful numbered vests, are also practically the only way to get to your resort if you're in Cha-Am after hours. The cost is usually 100B ($2.65).

By Samlor   Trishaws, or samlors, can be found around the center of town and can be hired for short distances as low as 20B (55¢). You can also negotiate an hourly rate if you'd like to tour the town.

By Car or Motorcycle   Avis has a desk at both the Hotel Sofitel Central in Hua Hin (☎ 032/512-021) and the Dusit Resort and Polo Club in Cha-Am (☎ 032/520-008). A Suzuki Caribian goes for 1,600B ($42.10) per day, while a Volvo is around 6,000B ($157.90) per day. Make sure you call ahead to reserve at least 1 day in advance. Cheaper alternatives can be rented from stands near the beach on Damnoenkasem Road. A Suzuki Caribian goes for around 800B ($21.05) per day. These places will also rent 100cc motorcycles for 190B ($5) per day.

On Foot   This is the way I recommend seeing Hua Hin. The narrow back alleys reveal a treasure trove of funky guest houses, bars full of local character, and a wide assortment of casual eating venues. Most everything in town is close enough to walk comfortably.

VISITOR INFORMATION   The Hua Hin Tourist Information Center (☎ 032/511-047 or 032/532-433) is in the center of town tucked behind the city shrine at the corner of Damnoenkasem and Petchkasem roads. Opening hours are from 8:30am to 4:30pm daily. In Cha-Am the TAT office (☎ 032/471-005 or 032/471-006) is inconveniently located on the corner of Phetchkasem Road and Narathip Road (the main Beach Road is about 1km away).

A fabulous source of information, *The Hua Hin Cha-Am Observer* packs a lot of advertisers and local tidbits into a small, regularly updated magazine. Better still, it's free! Look for it at the tourism information offices and at travel agents.

FAST FACTS   In Hua Hin, your major banks are along Petchkasem Road to the north of Damnoenkasem, and money changers are peppered throughout the town.

The **main post office** (☎ **032/511-063**) is on Damnoenkasem Road near the Phetchkasem intersection. The best **Internet** in town is at All Nations Guesthouse (☎ **032/512-747**), with service for 2B per minute. The **Hua Hin Hospital** (☎ **032/520-371**) is located in the north of town along Petchkasem Road. Call the **Tourist Police** for either town at ☎ **032/515-995.**

In Cha-Am, banks are centered along Phetchkasem Road, and the **post office** is on Beach Road just south of the Novotel. The **Thonburi Cha-Am Hospital** (☎ **032/ 433-903**) is off Narathip Road close to the Phetchkasem intersection. The nearest Internet cafe is in Hua Hin.

WHAT TO SEE & DO

It should come as no surprise that the main activities here revolve around the long and wide strip of beach. The water is clean, and resorts do a wonderful job keeping their beaches tidy. Be careful of landmines left by the ponies that tool up and down the beach (rides are 200B/$5.25 per half hour). Also keep in mind that after a rain shower, jellyfish come in close to the shore, so it's best to wait a little while before jumping in.

While most of the larger resorts will plan water sports activities for you upon request, you can still arrange your own from shacks on the beach. Jet skis (which most of the resorts have given up due to accidents and pollution) can still be rented for 500B ($13.15) per hour, in addition to windsurfing gear (300B/$7.90 per hour) and Hobie Cats (600B/$15.80 per hour).

Also by the beaches, **mountain bikes** can be rented for 30B (80¢) per hour. Two- and three-seaters go for up to 60B ($1.60) per hour.

Snorkeling trips to outer islands can be arranged through Western Tours, 11 Damnoenkasem Rd., Hua Hin (☎ **032/512-560;** fax 032/512-560) for 1,500B ($39.45) per person. Western Tours accepts AE, DC, MC, and V cards.

Lucky Sea Tours (☎ **01/824-9419** cellular) will also take you snorkeling, island hopping, or **fishing** on a Thai fishing boat. They'll need a minimum of six people to operate the trip, which heads out for nearby Ko Singtao (Lion Island). The day trip is 750B ($19.75) per person.

Scuba diving trips are coordinated by Coral Divers, 7 Naresdamri Road, Hua Hin (☎ **01/432-8180** cellular), in addition to fishing, snorkeling, and island-hopping trips at Ko Singtao. Scuba trips are only as deep as 5 meters around the small island. They charge certified divers 1,500B ($39.45) per dive, while a noncertified diver will pay around 2,000B ($52.65).

Meanwhile, back on terra firma, the other favorite activity in Hua Hin and Cha-Am is **golf,** and some really fine courses may lure you out despite the heat. The best places to try are the centrally located Royal Hua Hin Golf Course and the Springfield Royal Country Club, which is also home to the Springfield Golf Academy staffed with PGA pros. Reservations are suggested and necessary most weekends. **Royal Hua Hin Golf Course,** Damnoenkasem Road near the Hua Hin Railway Station (☎ **032/ 512-475,** or 02/241-1360 in Bangkok), Thailand's first championship golf course, opened in 1924 and was recently upgraded. It features topiary figures along its fairways and is open daily 6am to 6pm. **Springfield Royal Country Club,** 193 Huay-Sai Nua, Petchkasem Rd, Cha-Am (☎ **032/471-303,** fax 032/471-324), designed by Jack Nicklaus in 1993, this course is clever in design in a beautiful valley setting.

Outside the resort areas, there are a few wonderful natural and cultural attractions. A day trip to nearby **Phetchaburi** is the cultural highlight of the region, with enough fascinating temples and palaces to warrant its own section (see "Phetchaburi" following Hua Hin and Cha-Am).

Between Hua Hin and Cha-Am is the **Mareukatayawan Palace,** also known as the Teakwood Mansion (open 8:30am to 4pm daily, free admission). Built and designed in 1924 by King Rama VI, it served for many years as the royal summer residence, but is now open to the public. The maze of elevated rooms and catwalks, all in precious teak, are set in fresh gardens just beyond the beach. It's a pity the mansion is unfurnished, but it's still a beautiful sight.

For a little nature, **Khao Sam Roi Yot National Park** is a nice day trip. The "Mountain of Three Hundred Peaks" is comparatively small in relation to the nation's other parks, but has nice short hikes to see panoramic views of the sea and surroundings, plus a look at wildlife like the serow antelope, macaques, leopards and more than 300 species of birds. Of the park's two caves, Kaew Cave is the most interesting, housing a sala pavilion that was built in 1890 for King Chulalongkorn. The park is a 90-minute drive south from Hua Hin. To get there you can either plan through a tour agency or on your own. **Western Tours (☎ 032/512-560)** will take you for a day trip for 700B ($18.40) per person, or if you contact the **Tourist Information Center** in Hua Hin (☎ **032/532-433**) they'll set you up with a car and driver for the day for 1,000B ($26.30). The information center at the park entrance can set you up with trail information and a guide if you need it.

A half-day trip to the **Pala-U waterfall** close to the Burmese border (63km west of Hua Hin) is another nature trekking option. Nature trails take you through hills and valleys until you end up at the falls. Western Tours (☎ **032/512-560**) does the trip for 700B ($18.40) per person, or you can arrange your own travel through TAT for 1,000B ($26.30) per car. If you do it yourself, the driver can stop at the **Dole Thailand pineapple factory** for a tour and tasting (☎ **032/571-177;** open daily 9am to 4pm; 200B/$5.25 admission), and the Kaew Cave.

Shopping action is had throughout the small streets in the center of Hua Hin, where you can find tailors and souvenir shops. The day market along Damnoenkasem Road just at the beach displays local crafts made from seashells, batik clothing and many other handicraft finds. At night the 2-block-long night market on Dechanuchit Road west of Phetchkasem Road, packs in hawkers with sweet foods, cheap clothes, and all sorts of fun trinkets.

If you're looking for **nightlife** in the area, your best bet is Hua Hin. While Cha-Am has a few notable spots, the Wild West–saloon style **Jeep Pub** (☎ **032/472-311** and the Tiki-style **Bamboo Bar** (☎ **032/433-292**) both on Soi Cattriya off Ruamchit (Beach) Road, Hua Hin has a greater variety of life. A fifteen-minute stroll through the sois between Damnoenkasem, Poolsuk and Deachanuchit Roads near the beach reveals all sorts of small places to stop for a cool cocktail and some fun. Hua Hin's main disco, **Doodles** (☎ **032/512-888**), is at the Melia Hotel on Naresdamri Road. For a little nighttime Thai culture the small shack of a boxing stadium on Poolsuk Road has occasional bouts. Announcements are tacked up around the village, and a truck will cruise the streets to let you know when one is planned.

WHERE TO STAY IN HUA HIN

Hua Hin's resorts are relatively close to the town, with guest houses clustered in the town itself. Most resorts will charge a surcharge of 500B to 1,500B ($13.15 to $39.45) during the high season from December 20 to January 10 and again in late February. (Some Very Expensive and Expensive hotels only quote prices in U.S. dollars; see chapter 2, "Tips on Accommodations," for more details.)

VERY EXPENSIVE

Chiva-Som International Health Resort. 73/4 Petchkasem Road, Hua Hin, 77110 Thailand. ☎ **032/536-536.** Fax 032/511-615. www.chivasom.net. 57 units. A/C MINIBAR TEL.

All double rates are quoted per person. Ocean-view double $315; Thai Pavilion $399; ocean-view suite $540–$900. Nightly rate includes 3 spa cuisine meals per day, health and beauty consultations, daily massage, and participation in fitness and leisure activities. AE, DC, MC, V. 5 min. drive south of Hua Hin.

Chiva-Som will strip away any wear and tear the modern world can dish out, both mentally and physically. This ultrapeaceful resort is a sublime collection of handsome pavilions, bungalows and central buildings dressed in fine teak and sea-colored tiles nestled in landscaped grounds just beyond a pristine beach. Choose a guest room in the main building for the fabulous morning sunrise over the water, or a bungalow with either ocean or garden view for extra privacy. Each are decorated in cooling natural tones and warm wood with traditional Thai touches throughout.

The centerpiece is the spa. Carefully planned to ensure privacy and relaxation, the menu for treatments is phenomenal: health and beauty consultation, numerous facial and body treatments, medical treatments, diet programs, and fitness activities including personal training, swimming, yoga, tai chi, and Thai boxing. Check in with one of their spa packages. Double room package for 3 nights is $945 up to $3,660 for 14 nights. All packages include a fabulous list of treatments.

Dining: The Emerald Room, fine dining in a cooling intimate setting, serves healthful food recommended by resort dieticians using ingredients from Chiva-Som's own organic gardens. You can also dine by the sea at Waves, serving light snacks.

Amenities: Ozonated indoor swimming pool, outdoor swimming pool, stream and hydrotherapy treatments, a truly incredible gym with excellent personal training, beauty treatment and massage center, flotation, medical consultation, beauty salon, library, and water sports.

EXPENSIVE

✪ **Hotel Sofitel Central.** 1 Damnoenkasem Road, Hua Hin 77110. ☎ **800/221-4542** in the U.S., or 032/512-021. Fax 032/511-014. www.sofitel.com. 214 units. A/C MINIBAR TV TEL. 5,600B–7,200B ($147.35–$189.45) double; 12,800B–35,400B ($336.85–$931.60) suite. DC, JCB, MC, V. In the center of town by the beach.

The Hua Hin Railway Hotel opened in 1922 in response to the demand for luxury accommodations in what was then a newly emerging resort town. Adapted from European styles, the brick and wood design incorporated long shady verandas with whitewashed wood detail under a sloped red tile roof. Sofitel treasures the heritage of this old beauty, creating a hotel museum and preserving the hotel's original 14 bedrooms. Subsequent additions and renovations have expanded the hotel into a large and modern full-facility hotel without sacrificing a bit of its former charm.

While the original rooms have their unique appeal, the newer rooms are larger, brighter, and more comfortable. With furnishings that reflect the hotel's old beach resort feel, they are still modern and cozy. Sofitel's three magnificent outdoor pools are landscaped for sundecks with shady spots. The new Spa Health Club, in its own beachside bungalow, provides full-service health and beauty treatments, and the new fitness center sports fine equipment with recent additions.

Dining/Diversions: Of the resort's seven food and beverage outlets, the Palm Seafood Pavilion is the finest, and is reviewed in the "Dining" section. Other options include Thai cuisine at Salathai Restaurant, continental cuisine at the Railway Restaurant, high tea served in the hotel's original lobby, and cocktails at the nostalgic Elephant Bar.

Amenities: Three pools, tennis courts, daily craft and language lessons, billiards room, beauty and barber shop, shopping arcade, water sports, putting green, miniature golf, 24-hour room service, concierge, limousine service, baby-sitting, laundry.

Royal Garden Resort. 107/1 Petchkasem Beach Rd., Hua Hin 77110. ☎ **800/344-1212** in the U.S., or 032/511-881. Fax 032/512-422. 220 units. A/C MINIBAR TV TEL. 4,943B ($130.10) double; 5,767B ($151.75) sea view; 16,748B ($440.75) suite. Peak season supplemental charges Dec 20–Jan 10 $40 per night. AE, DC, JCB, MC, V.

The extremely well-outfitted and maintained Royal Garden Resort is best suited for those in search of beach and sports activities. Singles and families are here throughout the year, lured principally by the ponds, pools, boats, golf, tennis, and other racket sports, as well as by the pet elephant and the junglelike grounds leading out to the calm sea. Top it off with a children's playground and a fitness center, and you have the perfect equation for a family vacation. The hotel is relatively convenient, with complimentary shuttle service into town and to its sister establishment, the more traditional Thai-style Royal Garden Village (see below). Deluxe rooms are the best choice—large, amenity filled, and facing the sea.

Dining/Diversions: The Nautilus Lounge (very clubby) overlooks the pool and is open from 10pm to 1am. The Garden is a cheery coffee shop with an international and Thai menu. On the beach lawn is the Italian Pavilion Restaurant, open daily 10am to 11pm.

Amenities: Pool, tennis courts, beauty and barber shop, shopping arcade, golf, zoo, fitness center, playground, concierge, baby-sitting, house doctor, laundry service, Avis car rental.

○ **Royal Garden Village.** 43/1 Petchkasem Beach Rd., Hua Hin 77110. ☎ **800/344-1212** in the U.S., or 032/520-250. Fax 032/520-259. 162 units. A/C MINIBAR TV TEL. 5,791B ($152.40) double; 7,203B ($189.55) beach terrace; 16,956B ($446.20) suite. Peak season supplemental charges Dec 20–Jan 10 $40 per night. AE, DC, JCB, MC, V.

A series of elegantly designed Thai-style pavilions make up the structure of the lobby and the public facilities at this "village" away from the town center, off the main road. A lovely Kaliga tapestry hangs prominently in the open-air sala-style lobby, which is tastefully decorated with ornately carved teak wooden lanterns, warm wood floors, and furniture with rose-colored cushions. A series of teak pavilions each houses 12 guest rooms. Consistent with the lobby, rooms are furnished Thai style with teak-and-rattan furniture. Superior rooms have a garden view and deluxe rooms overlook the sand and sea. For a few dollars more, the beach terrace rooms have large patios, perfect for requesting a fun (or romantic) barbecue set up by the staff.

Dining/Diversions: Suan Luang, decorated with an elegant, cool green carpet and rattan furniture, is a Thai restaurant serving lunch and dinner. The outdoor Rim Nam Restaurant serves European and seafood dinners only, and there's a pool bar for snacks and drinks.

Amenities: Swimming pool and childrens' pool, rental motorcycles and bicycles, lighted tennis courts, waterskiing, parasailing, sailing lessons (four types of boats), windsurfing, jogging track, shopping arcade, Jacuzzi, playground, 18-hole golf course nearby, 24-hour room service, concierge, limousine service, baby-sitting, house doctor, laundry, complimentary welcome tea, and a fruit basket and flowers in all rooms.

MODERATE

Fresh Inn Hotel. 132 Naresdamri Rd., Hua Hin 77110. ☎ **032/511-389.** Fax 032/432-166. 29 units. A/C MINIBAR TV TEL. 750B ($19.75) double. AE, MC, V.

Opened in 1990, this clean inn is a good choice for location and affordability. Rooms are furnished in very basic fashion with carpeting, small shower stall bathrooms, and tiny balconies with a view of the street below. The hotel's tiled corridors open out to the soi below—a row of bars, which can be a bit noisy on weekends and holidays. Though it's not a fancy place, the Fresh Inn represents good value for its near-to-beach and fishing-pier location. The hotel's popular restaurant located to the side of the lobby (open daily 5 to 10pm) is elevated above the street-side bustle.

Jed Pee Nong Hotel. 17 Damneonkasem Rd., Hua Hin 77110. ☎ **032/512-381.** Fax 032/532-2036. 25 units. MINIBAR. 700B ($18.40) double with A/C; 500B ($13.15) double with fan. No credit cards. On the main street near the town beach.

This recently built hotel with Chinese flair is located less than 100 meters from the Sofitel Central's elegant driveway. It's so clean and well kept that it's a good choice. A bevy of family or local workers maintain the tiny garden filled with songbirds and fountains, a small pool, and the simple balconied rooms. Many rooms are carpeted and have air-conditioning. The higher-priced rooms have better decor and hug the pool, cabana style. There's also a Thai seafood restaurant off the lobby and laundry service.

INEXPENSIVE

✪ **All Nations Guesthouse.** 10–10/1 Deachanuchit Rd., Hua Hin 77110. ☎ **032/ 512-747.** Fax 032/530-474. 12 units. 600B ($15.80) with A/C; 150B–280B ($3.95–$7.35) with fan. No credit cards.

One of those gems you love to stumble upon by sheer word of mouth, All Nations' reputation is golden in the world of backpackers. Opening its doors to short- and long-term guests, from those who just drop in to those who come back again and again, it's a friendly place to meet fellow travelers and locals with stores of information about traveling in the area. Guest rooms vary in size, view, and location and are priced accordingly. Don't expect a lot from the decor, but if you want a TV, they'll provide one for a little extra. None have attached bathrooms, and the ratio of rooms to shared bathrooms is about two to one. The open lobby doubles as a restaurant and bar, and is home to the best Internet cafe in town. I truly recommend reserving a room in advance, as the place runs at high capacity regularly; however, if they're full, they'll direct you to another nearby guest house.

WHERE TO STAY IN CHA-AM

Cha-Am's resorts are, by and large, dotted along the 8-kilometer beach. While there are many hotels in the town itself, the Methavalai is the best, which is reviewed here.

EXPENSIVE

Dusit Resort and Polo Club. 1349 Petchkasem Rd., Cha-Am 76120. ☎ **032/520-009.** Fax 032/520-296. www.dusit.com. 305 units. A/C MINIBAR TV TEL. 5,000B–5,500B ($131.60–$144.75) double; 11,000 ($289.45) Landmark suite. AE, DC, MC, V.

Intended for the country's wealthy elite and the well-heeled foreign tourist, the Dusit combines the amenities and facilities of the best international deluxe resorts with an English country and polo club theme. The grandly elegant marble lobby features bronze horses, plush carpets, and seating areas, with hunting-and-riding oil paintings hung throughout. Hall doors have polo mallet handles; each public area follows suit with "horsey" artwork and decor.

Guest rooms are spacious, with English country touches and oversized marble bathrooms. Room rates vary with the view, although every room's balcony faces out over the lushly landscaped pool, which could very well be the largest in Thailand. Patios for the ground floor Lanai Rooms are landscaped for privacy, but you can still run straight out to the pool and beach. Landmark suites, with a very elegant living room, full pantry area, and dressing room off a huge bathroom, have the finest decor.

For all its air of formality, the resort is great for those who prefer swimsuits and T-shirts to riding jodhpurs. In fact, there's no polo field around at all, but if you'd like to go riding, the resort does care for it's own stables. The beach is meticulous and calm, and all sorts of water sports with instruction are available.

Dining: Palm Court serves breakfast, lunch, and dinner in a huge glass pavilion over a lotus pond. The elegant Ascot Grill, al fresco Italian San Marco, and fine Thai Bencharong, round out your dining options. For atmosphere and amazing seafood, Rim Talay, which is reviewed in this section, is the place to be.

Amenities: Fantastic outdoor pool and Jacuzzi, the Polo Club with horseback riding, weight rooms, squash courts, Ping-Pong, billiards, sauna, aerobics classes, tennis courts, and all water sports, business center, beauty/barbershop, shopping arcade, golf and minigolf, 24-hour room service, concierge, limousine service, baby-sitting, house doctor, laundry, complimentary welcome fruit basket, and Avis car rental.

MODERATE

Beach Garden Hotel Cha-Am. 949/21 Soi Suan Loi, Petchkasem Rd. km 213, Cha-Am 76120. ☎ **032/471-350.** Fax 032/471-291. 244 units. A/C MINIBAR TV TEL. 3,300B–4,800B ($86.85–$126.30) double; 1,500B–2,200B ($39.45–$57.90) bungalow. AE DC MC V.

Located at the southern periphery of Cha-Am is this moderately priced resort favored by European groups. In truth, the place needs to see a little money dumped into it before it regains the style it had when it first opened—the rooms are showing telltale signs of age, especially the sparsely furnished bungalows. But the guest rooms in the main block have held up much better. The main attraction here is the long, sandy beach—it's clean and wide—that abuts the hotel. Facilities include two outdoor pools, two tennis courts, minigolf, and windsurfing gear. Standard rooms have no TV, while superior rooms have all the amenities and are set on high floors with views. The hotel's Chomtalay Restaurant and coffee shop serves breakfast, lunch, and dinner; however, just along the beach are small open-air huts serving yummy seafood in many styles. One of the best is "Family Shop" just north of the hotel.

The Cha-Am Methavalai Hotel. 220 Ruamchit Rd., Cha-Am 76120. ☎ **032/471-028.** Fax 032/471-590. 118 units. A/C MINIBAR TV TEL. 2,500B–2,950B ($65.80–$77.65) double; 5,150B ($135.55) suite. AE, DC, JCB, MC, V.

Compared to the other choices for accommodations in Cha-Am village, the Methavalai is certainly the better bet. This large hotel is modern and well suited for the demands of international travelers. Located on the main Beach Road in Cha-Am, it's convenient to the restaurants, shopping, and small nightlife scene in town. Large guest rooms in soft palettes are peaceful, and all have balconies with a sundeck. The only downfall is you have to share the beach here with residents of the many motels along the strip. Instead you can always opt for their large outdoor lagoon-shaped pool. The Komain Coffee Shop serves room service round the clock, and the Chevalier Supper Club has live music performances nightly. I've reviewed the Sontalay Terrace beachside restaurant in the dining section of this chapter.

Regent Chalet. 849/21 Petchkasem Road, Cha-Am 76120. ☎ **032/451-240.** Fax 032/451-277. www.regent-chaam.com. 660 units. A/C MINIBAR TV TEL. 4,000B ($105.25) double; 5,000 ($131.60) family suite; 6,000B–12,000B ($157.90–$315.80) bungalow suite. AE, MC, V.

I'm sure Regent Chalet gets a lot of business because of name association, but the resort is not related to the famous Regent chain with hotels in Bangkok, Chiang Mai and other Asian cities. Still Regent Chalet is a popular choice in Cha-Am. The entire resort is a huge complex with 660 rooms and suites, three outdoor pools, Jacuzzi, fitness center, massage, four tennis courts, two squash courts, land and water sports, and a choice of restaurants. Sounds overwhelming? Well, in a quiet little section to the side of the resort grounds is the Regent Chalet, the resort's separate bungalow facility. The best part is you enjoy a more relaxed and rustic experience, but still have access to all the offerings of the larger resort—the best of both worlds. Bungalows are either on or close to the beach, with rattan and bamboo furniture in true beach home style.

WHERE TO DINE IN HUA HIN

Itsara. 7 Napkehard St., Hua Hin. ☎ **032/530-574.** Reservations recommended Sat dinner. Main courses 60B–290B ($1.60–$7.65). MC, V. Mon–Fri 10am–midnight; Sat–Sun 2pm–midnight. Seaside, a 40B–70B ($1.05–$1.85) samlor ride north from the town center. THAI.

Formerly called Ban Tuppee Kaow, Itsara is a two-story greenhouse built in the 1920s and not especially well maintained, though it is atmospheric. By the sea, the terrace seating is the best in the house, with views of the beach. During weekend lunches it's quiet and peaceful. Specialties include a sizzling hotplate of glass noodles with prawn, squid, pork, and vegetables. A large variety of fresh seafood and meats are prepared steamed or deep-fried, and can be served with either salt, chile, or red curry paste. Beer, Mekhong whiskey, and soft drinks are available.

Mamma Mia! 19 Damnoeankasem Rd., Hua Hin. ☎ **032/512-250.** Reservations not necessary. Main courses 90B–300B ($2.35–$7.90). DC, MC, V. Daily noon–11:30pm daily. ITALIAN.

Mama Mia! joins Capos, a ribs joint, and Al Fresco, an ice cream parlor, under one roof for one of the most popular dining centers in town. Mama Mia! serves up full Italian courses, including salads, soups, antipasti, pasta, meat, fish, and pizza. Pasta is made fresh in-house, with light sauces, and many dishes feature local seafood catches. The colorful cafe atmosphere has a fun feeling with art posters hung on bright walls. The best tables look out onto Damnoenkasem Road.

Meekaruna Seafood. 26/1 Naratdamri Rd., Hua Hin. ☎ **032/511-932.** Reservations not necessary. Main courses 120B–500B ($3.15–$13.15). AE, DC, MC, V. Daily 10am–10pm. Near the fishing pier. SEAFOOD.

This small family run restaurant serves fresh fish prepared in many Thai and Chinese styles on a wooden terrace overlooking the main fishing pier in Hua Hin. The menu is in English (with photographs), and you'll find the lack of hype—compared to the other fish places with their flashy entrances and hustling touts—refreshing. Among the many good dishes are steamed pomfret with plum sauce, charcoal-grilled shrimp, and the fried vegetable combination with seafood. Wear bug repellent!

Palm Seafood Pavilion. In the Hotel Sofitel Central, 1 Damneonkasem Rd. ☎ **032/ 512-021.** Reservations recommended. Main courses 540B–800B ($14.20–$21.05); seafood buffet 650B ($17.10) per person. AE, DC, MC, V. Daily noon–2:30pm and 6–10:30pm. On the waterfront end of Main St. CONTINENTAL.

Hotel Sofitel Central's crystal pavilion close to the beach offers a very romantic dining experience. Attentive but discreet service, beautiful table settings and linen, soothing mood music, and excellent, elegantly prepared food all contribute in pleasing harmony. The menu changes quite often, but always highlights fresh seafood, which is prepared in continental style with Asian touches. For something different I tried the simmered pomfret with Chinese plums, bacon, and mushrooms smothered in sautéed vegetables, which was light, healthful, and full of flavor. They also do a mean salmon poached with white wine in lobster sauce with sliced lobster and mushrooms. With a fine selection of wines and an eyeful of sweet desserts, this is the best choice for fine dining in Hua Hin. Be sure to call ahead, as they frequently book private barbecues and parties.

WHERE TO DINE IN CHA-AM

Rim Talay. In the Dusit Resort and Polo Club. 1349 Petchkasem Rd., Cha-Am 76120. ☎ **032/520-009.** 170B–350B ($4.45–$9.20). AE, DC, JCB, MC, V. THAI SEAFOOD.

Dusit's version of seaside dining is a casual and fun experience combined with one of the best sea views around. The menu is not as extensive as at other places but the offerings are wonderful. Go for the huge *goong pao*, charcoal grilled prawns filled with succulent and flavorful eggs, *poo ma pad pong karee*, horse crab smothered in thick yellow curry, and *hoi lai pad nam prik pao*, baby clams in a sweet dark chile paste. Expect to get your hands messy and leave with a smile on your face.

Sontalay Terrace. The Cha-Am Methavalai Hotel, 220 Ruamchit Road (Beach Road), Cha-Am. ☎ **032/433-250.** Entrees 80B–250B ($2.10–$6.60). AE, DC, JCB, MC, V. THAI/ WESTERN SEAFOOD.

Operated by the Methavalai Hotel, but located across the street on a beach terrace under the trees, this seafood joint is perhaps the classiest offering in town. In the afternoons, lunch and snacks are served from their menu, which includes sandwiches and burgers, while at dinner, tables are romantically lit by candles and overhead torches hung from the trees. Try the savory baked rice with seafood flavored with ginger and soy and the fried herb chicken wrapped in pandan leaves (with tangy sweet chile sauce on the side).

SIDE TRIPS FROM HUA HIN & CHAN AM
PHETCHABURI

Phetchaburi, one of the country's oldest towns, possibly dates from the same period as Ayutthaya and Kanchanaburi, though it's believed to have been first settled during the Dvaravati period. After the rise of the Thai nation, it served as an important royal military city and was home to several princes who were groomed for ascendance to the throne. Phetchaburi's palace and historically significant temples highlight a fabulous day trip.

There are many tour operators who coordinate day trips to Phetchaburi from Hua Hin, it's a mere 50-minute drive away. **Western Tours,** 11 Damnoenkasem Rd. (☎ **032/512-560**), has day excursions for 700B ($18.40) per person. While the Phra Nakorn Khiri and Khao Luang Cave are the two main stops on every tour itinerary, the city has a few other gems that are never included in the standard package. To see these I recommend arranging your own ride from Hua Hin. A car can be hired through the **Hua Hin Tourist Information Center** (☎ **032/511-047** or 032/ 532-433) for the day for 1,200B ($31.60). All the drivers know how to get to the palace and the cave, but few have ever been to any of the smaller temples in the city. Don't fret, everyone in the town knows where these places are, and the driver need only to stop and ask for directions.

The main attraction is **Phra Nakhorn Khiri** (☎ **032/428-539**), a summer palace atop the hills overlooking the city. Built in 1858 by King Mongkut (Rama IV), it was intended as not only a summer retreat for the royal family, but for foreign dignitaries as well. Combining Thai, European, and Chinese architectural styles, the palace buildings include guest houses and a royal Khmer-style chedi, or temple. The Phra Thinang Phetphum Phairot Hall is open for viewing and contains period art and antiques from the household. Once accessible only via a 4-kilometer hike uphill, you'll be happy to hear there's a funicular railway (called a "cable car," but not really) to bring you to the top. The ride costs 30B (80¢) for adults and 10B (25¢) for children and is open Monday through Friday 8:15am to 5pm and Saturday and Sunday from 8:15am to 5:50pm. The museum is 40B ($1.05) admission, and opens daily from 9am to 4pm.

Another fascinating sight at Phetchaburi, the **Khao Luang Cave,** houses more than 170 Buddha images underground. Outside the cave, hundreds of noisy monkeys descend upon the parking lot and food stalls looking for handouts. Sometimes you'll find a guide outside who'll escort you through the caves for 40B ($1.05). If you're not with a group, it's a good idea—their English isn't too hot, but they do point out many cave features that might otherwise be missed. A 20B (55¢) donation is optional once inside.

A small wonder is **Wat Yai Suwannaram,** a royal temple built during the Ayutthaya period. The teak ordination hall was moved from Ayutthaya after the second Burmese invasion on the city. The proof is in the axe chop battle scar on the building's carved wood doors. Inside, murals represent religious scenes filled with Brahmans, hermits, giants, and deities. The temple complex is usually locked, but if you wander to the back of the complex and talk to some of the young monk apprentices, they'll seek out a key and take you inside.

The other wat with impressive paintings is **Wat Ko Keo Suttharam,** also built in the 17th century, but with murals from the 1730s. These are far more representational and, of some interest to Westerners; there are several panels depicting the arrival in the Ayutthaya court of European courtesans and diplomats (including a Jesuit dressed in Buddhist garb). This one is more likely to be open, but if it's not, there'll be someone around to let you in if you ask.

Another fabulous wat, particularly for fans of Khmer architecture, is **Wat Kamphaeng Laeng,** originally constructed during the reign of Khmer ruler King Jayavaraman VII (1157–1207) as a Hindu shrine. Made of laterite, it was once covered in decorative stucco, some of which still remains. Each of the five prangs, or towers, was devoted to a deity—the center prang to Shiva. During the Ayutthaya period, it was converted to a Buddhist temple. The temple is amazing when you consider how far the Khmer empire extended through Thailand.

If you still have time, the **Phra Ram Raja Nivesana,** or Ban Puen Palace (☎ **032/428-506;** open 8am to 4pm daily, admission free), is a nice stop. A royal palace built by Rama V, the German-designed grand summer home comes alive with colorful tile work, neoclassical marble columns and floor motifs. Today it sits on military grounds and is a popular venue for ceremonies and large occasions.

As for spending the night in Phetchaburi, I don't really recommend it, as there are no comfortable accommodations around. For a lunch break, **Num Tien,** 539 Moo 1, Phetchakasaemkao Rod (☎ **032/425-121**), still reigns as the best lunch eatery in town. An open-air cafe cooled under a columned veranda, this well-established restaurant serves a combination of Thai and Chinese specialties at cheap prices. The menu is in English, and for extra help, Khun Natta, the oh-so-kind proprietor, will make good recommendations.

2 Chumphon

463km (287 miles) S of Bangkok; 193km (120 miles) N of Surat Thani

Chumphon was nearly devastated by Typhoon Gay when it hit the coast of Thailand in 1989. The northern end of town and many outer lying villages were flattened, yet the surrounding hills, denuded of their once fertile fruit trees, have been making a comeback. The plains on the western side of the province are still extremely fertile, with coconuts, mangosteens, durians, rambutans, bananas, and pineapple plantations. Perhaps because of the typhoon's deforestation, Chumphon today is a dusty, buggy town (bring moist towelettes for cooling off and mosquito repellent) with little of interest to the average traveler except a few facilities for backpackers. It is, however, the most convenient departure point for Ko Tao, which offers some of the best scuba diving in Thailand, and there's a growing resort and diving area—best during February to October—on the beach Thung Wua Laem, 12km (7.4 miles) northeast of town.

ESSENTIALS

GETTING THERE   By Plane   The almost unknown **PB Air** flies from Bangkok to Chumphon and back again every Tuesday, Thursday, and Saturday. You can find them in Bangkok at 591 17th floor, UBC II Building, Sukhumvit 33 (☎ 02/261-0220, ext. 106), or call their office at the Chumphon Airport (☎ 077/591-267, ext. 108). For transfers from the airport notify PB Air in advance. For an extra 80B ($2.10), they'll arrange transport to town.

By Train   Ten daily trains stop in Chumphon from Bangkok. Book tickets through the Hua Lamphong Railway Station in Bangkok at ☎ 02/223-7010 or 02/223-7020. The Chumphon Railway Station is on Kromluang Road (☎ 077/511-103), a wide thoroughfare lined with restaurants, hawkers, and guest houses. A songtao or motorcycle taxi can bring you where you need to go for 10B–30B (25¢–80¢).

By Bus   Two air-conditioned buses depart from Bangkok's Southern Bus Terminal (☎ 02/435-1199). The trip time is 6½ hours and costs 245B ($6.45). The bus terminal on Thatapao Road (☎ 077/570-294) is near many travel agencies that specialize in trips to Ko Tao, and the Thatapao Hotel, reviewed in this section.

By Ferry   Songserm Travel Center runs the daily FerryLine service connecting Chumphon with Ko Tao, Ko Phangan, Ko Samui, and Surat Thani. On Ko Tao, their office is at Mae Had Beach (☎ 01/229-5630 cellular); on Ko Phangan at 44/43 Moo 1, Thong Sala Pier (☎ 077/377-046); on Ko Samui at 64/1-2 Na Thon Pier (☎ 077/421-316); and in Surat Thani at 30/2 Moo 3, Bangkung (☎ 077/285-124).

VISITOR INFORMATION   The **Tourist Information Center** is on Paraminmankha Road in the city's Provincial Hall (☎ 077/599-436), but the staff has limited information and English language skills. Better information is found at any of the tour operators by the bus terminal and train station. There's a small D. K. Books shop across from the Jansom Chumphon Hotel that carries a helpful *Map of the Chumphon and Ranong* for about 80B ($2.10).

GETTING AROUND   By Minitruck (Songtao)   They cruise the main roads, and charge about 20B to 40B (55¢ to $1.05) for rides.

By Motorcycle Taxi   Look for the men in colored vests, and they'll take you where you need to go for as little as 10B (25¢) a trip.

ORIENTATION   Chumphon is small enough to walk around easily, but there's not much to see or do in terms of cultural attractions and adventure. The main spots for travelers are Kromluang Road, running from the railway station, with dining options and cheap accommodations, and Thatapao Road, where the bus terminal is located, as well as many tour operators.

FAST FACTS   Bangkok Bank, Thai Farmers Bank, and Bank of Ayudhya are all on Saladaeng Road, running parallel to Thatapao. The main **post office** is on

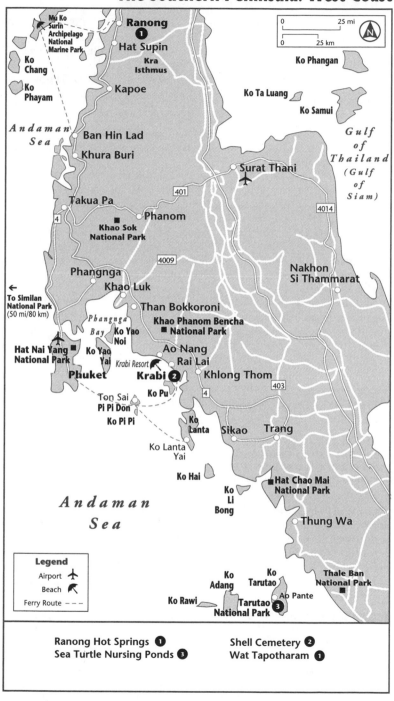

The Southern Peninsula: West Coast

Ranong ❶
Hat Supin
Kra Isthmus
Kapoe

Mu Ko Surin Archipelago National Marine Park
Ko Chang
Ko Phayam

Andaman Sea

Ban Hin Lad
Khura Buri

Ko Phangan
Ko Ta Luang
Ko Samui

Gulf of Thailand (Gulf of Siam)

Surat Thani

401

Takua Pa
Phanom
Khao Sok National Park

4014

4009

Phangnga
Khao Luk

Nakhon Si Thammarat

← To Similan National Park (50 mi/80 km)

Than Bokkoroni
Khao Phanom Bencha National Park

Phangnga Bay
Ko Yao Noi
Ko Yao Yai

Ao Nang
Rai Lai

Hat Nai Yang National Park

Krabi Resort
Phuket
Krabi ❷

Khlong Thom

403

Ton Sai
Pi Pi Don
Ko Pi Pi

Ko Pu

4

Ko Lanta
Sikao
Trang

Ko Lanta Yai

Ko Hai

Hat Chao Mai National Park

Ko Li Bong

Thung Wa

Andaman Sea

Legend
Airport ✈
Beach
Ferry Route - - -

Ko Adang
Ko Tarutao
Ko Rawi
Tarutao National Park
Ao Pante ❸

Thale Ban National Park

0 — 25 mi
0 — 25 km

N

Ranong Hot Springs ❶
Sea Turtle Nursing Ponds ❸

Shell Cemetery ❷
Wat Tapotharam ❶

Paraminmankha Road just down from the city Provincial Hall (☎ 077/272-013). For **Internet** service, I found one terminal in a small shop called Microchip on Saladaeng Road next to the Ocean Shopping Complex (2B per minute). The **Chumphon Hospital** on Kromluang Chumphon Soi 5 can be reached at ☎ 077/ 503-672 for medical emergencies. For **police** assistance call ☎ 077/511-505.

WHAT TO SEE & DO
Most people who come through Chumphon are on their way to Ko Tao, an island near Ko Samui in the Gulf of Thailand—a favorite destination for scuba lovers. Ko Tao is covered in a section later in this chapter, along with information on getting there from Chumphon.

If you're looking for something to do for a day in Chumphon, you can contact **Ekawin Tours,** Kromluang Road (☎ 077/501-821), for a rafting trip to nearby Patho district. After riding rolling waters in a rubber raft, guides will feed you lunch and take you trekking to Heow Loam Waterfall for an afternoon swim. The grand finale is a trip to a local southern fruit farmer's village. You'll need at least four people for them to set out, and the price is 980B ($25.80) per person. Ekawin also coordinates day trips outside the city to visit local waterfalls, caves, beaches and forests, none of which are sensational sights, but make a pleasant way to spend your time if you need to spend a day in the area (500B/$13.15 per person).

Some head out for the beaches near Chumphon, the nicest one being Thung Wua Laen Beach. Ekawin Tours has a minivan service to the beach for 300B ($7.90) each way. If you plan to spend the night, the **Chumphon Cabana Resort and Diving Center,** 69 Moo 8, Saplee, Pathui, Chumphon 86230 (☎ 077/560-245; fax 077/560-247), will accommodate you with 100 hotel rooms (each with minibar, TV, and telephone) and 40 cottages (with rudimentary cold water–only bathrooms). With recreational facilities that include a swimming pool, windsurfing, sailing, mountain biking, and a diving center, plus a pub and restaurant, Chumphon Cabana is a nifty resort find that is more secluded than other options along this coast.

WHERE TO STAY
Chumphon Cabana Resort and Diving Center. 69 Moo 8, Saplee, Pathui, Chumphon 86230. ☎ **077/560-245.** Fax 077/560-247. 100 units. MINIBAR TV TEL. 1,400B ($36.85) double; 1,800B ($47.35) cottage. AE, MC, V.

Located on Thung Wua Laen Beach only 30 minutes from Chumphon town, Chumphon Cabana Resort is a basic bungalow resort, but happens to be the better accommodation in the area. Their bungalow and hotel room options are both outfitted with basic furnishings that are neat but sparse. Hotel rooms are in a low block and each has a small balcony. The hotel will organize windsurfing, sailing and mountain biking, you can take trips to nearby coral reefs with their dive master, or you can just laze by the small outdoor pool. Meals are provided by their Sea View Restaurant and South Sea Pub.

Jansom Chumphon. 118/138 Saladaeng Rd., Tambol Thatapao, Amphur Muang, Chumphon 86000. ☎ **077/502-502.** Fax 077/502-503. 140 units. A/C MINIBAR TV TEL. 638B ($16.80) double. AE, MC, V.

The best accommodation in town, Jansom Chumphon isn't the Oriental, but it's comfortable and reputable. Small rooms can stand some redecorating, but are still the more up-to-date choice in town. The coffee shop serves Thai breakfasts only, so you'll be better off at **Intanil** (☎ 077/503-101), the small coffee shop around the corner from the Ocean department store. American breakfast is only 100B ($2.65), but they don't open till 10am.

Thatapao Hotel. 66/1 Thatapao Rd., Chumphon 86000. ☎ **077/511-479.** Fax 077/ 502-479. 85 units. A/C. 400B–500B ($10.55–$13.15) double. MC, V. Located across the street from the bus terminal.

Once the finest hotel in town, Thatapao can't compete since the Jansom opened, but should not be overlooked if you need a decent place to stay that's convenient and affordable. A peculiar place, on the outside it looks like a government building, while the cavernous lobby—with its tiled floor and wide linoleum-covered stairway—will make you feel as if you are back in grade school. Guest rooms are definitely simple and not too large, but you can expect cleanliness. And if you're in transit from a scuba trip and need to shower up before your bus, they'll offer you a hot shower for 30B (80¢).

WHERE TO DINE

PaPa. Kromluang Rd. ☎ **077/511-972.** 40B–300B ($1.05–$7.90); seafood at market value. Daily 4pm–2am. No credit cards. THAI/SEAFOOD.

Open to the bustling night market outside, PaPa is the largest and most visited restaurant in town. A little on the touristy side (but then again, it's not like Chunphon does a booming tourist trade), the small tables under colorful lamps fill up faster than you'd think. You'll always find a good selection of fresh creatures of the sea prepared in countless ways—Chinese Thai and some Western selections. The Thai dishes are all quite good, especially the grilled crab and the prawns baked in a clay pot.

Suan Rim. 118 Kromluang Rd. ☎ **077/511-531.** 40B–250B ($1.05–$6.60). Daily 10am– 10pm. AE, MC, V. THAI.

While not the most ambient place (and a little tricky to find), Suan Rim makes it into all the guidebooks for being one of the better restaurants to serve authentic Thai cuisine in Chumphon. Walk down Kromluang about 5 minutes through the market, on the right the brightly lit Suan Rim is set back in a car park without a sign. It's good to check it out for *pla ka phon khao,* southern-Thai style extra-crispy fried fish. Ask for Khun Surin, the owner for decades, who speaks English and will be glad to offer suggestions not on the menu.

3 Ranong

568km (352 miles) S of Bangkok; 117km (73 miles) S of Chumphon; 219km (136 miles) NW of Surat Thani; 412km (255 miles) N of Phuket

Situated on the Kra Isthmus, Ranong faces the Andaman Sea and borders the southern tip of Burma (Myanmar) at Victoria Point, a village once famous for its ivory trade and now an important nexus for Thai-Burmese commerce (legitimate and otherwise). This border area was previously closed to western visitors, but today you can cross for day trips into the small town. As the expatriate community in Thailand learn of the border opening, the sleepy Ranong may find more visitors who come to cross the border to update their visa status. Today, most visitors to Ranong are Thai vacationers who come to visit its famous hot springs, located about a half mile east of the town center, just up the road from the Jansom Thara Hotel.

If you plan to visit Ranong, keep in mind that it receives more rain than any other province in Thailand. The least amount of precipitation falls from November to April, while the same holds true from December through March on Ko Surin.

ESSENTIALS

GETTING THERE   By Plane   Bangkok Airways has daily direct flights between Bangkok and Ranong—talk to them about rates and airport transfers. In Bangkok call

☎ **02/229-3456.** In Ranong their office is at 50/18 Moo 1, Petchkasem Road Highway (☎ **077/835-096**).

By Train From Bangkok take the train to Chumphon and from there a minivan to Ranong (trip time from Chumphon: 2 hours; 80B/$2.10). The minivan trip can be arranged without a reservation from the office on Thatapao Road near the Bus Terminal.

By Bus There are two air-conditioned buses daily from Bangkok's Southern Bus Terminal (☎ **02/435-1199**) (trip time: 7 hours; 302B/$7.95). From Phuket there are two daily air-conditioned buses (trip time: 5 hours; 170B/$4.45) from the Phuket Bus Terminal off Phang-Nga Road (☎ **077/211-977**).

By Minivan Private minivan companies connect Ranong to almost all major towns in the southern peninsula. Contact your hotel's front desk for the easiest bookings, they'll have the numbers for vans to Ranong and can communicate with drivers much easier. Minivans will pick you up at your hotel and drop you where you need to go in Ranong.

By Car Travel south from Bangkok by Route 35; then at Pak take Route 4 via Phetchaburi, Pracaub, and Chumphon. From Phuket or Phangnga, take Route 4 north.

GETTING AROUND There is a local *songtao* (minitruck) system in the town, and trips go for about 5B to 10B (15¢–25¢ each). You can also grab a songtao headed for the hot springs for about 20B (55¢). **Motorcycle taxis** (drivers wear colored vests) can be flagged down from almost anywhere in town for quick 10B or 20B (15¢ or 25¢) trips, but the town itself is small and getting around on foot is a snap.

ORIENTATION The town is easily walkable, but unless you like long strolls, you'll probably want to take a songtao to the hot springs. The main street is Ruangrad Road, where you'll find a market, as well as the usual tourist facilities—a bank, a post office, newsstands, drugstores, etc. The bus stop is located on Phetchkasem Road near the Jansom Thara.

FAST FACTS There are many major **banks** along Ruangrad Road, with money-changing services and ATMs. The post office is also on Ruangrad in the center of the town (☎ **077/811-971**). **Internet** service here seems to be targeted toward younger people—the biggest provider is on Ruangrad next to the movie theater across from the post office (no phone). Service is painfully slow and the kids playing video games are noisy. For hospital emergencies contact the **Ranong Hospital** (☎ **077/811-574**) on Kamlansap Road, just west of Highway 4. **Police** (☎ **077/811-173**) are on Ruangrad Road, near the north end of town.

WHAT TO SEE & DO

The **natural hot spring** that attracts so many visitors is located within the Wat Tapotharam compound, about 2km (1.2 miles) east of Ranong town center. The site is set in a lovely forested area, complete with pools (in which locals boil eggs!), trails, and thermal runoffs. The temperature of the water reaches 149°F (65°C) and is best appreciated in the pools at the Jansom Thara Hotel, where it's cooled to a more tolerable temperature; they charge 100B ($2.65) for nonguests to use the pools. At the market on Ruangrad Road, try the cashews grown on a nearby island, dried red dates and prunes, Burmese sweets, and a distinctive green vegetable called a *lieng* that finds its way into most shrimp-based soups.

Half-day trips across the border to **Kowthuong,** or **Victoria Point,** in Myanmar (Burma) are favorites for Thais, and now that the border is open to Westerners, you can join in too. **Jansom Travel,** 5/28–29 Petchkasem Rd. (☎ **077/835-317**), is the only operator with a contract with Myanmar to coordinate the trips. A 15-minute boat ride with accompanying guide opens up Burma, with a trip to Kowthuong's huge reclining Buddha, and other temples displaying Burmese architectural heritage. A final stop at the local market is better for browsing than for picking up souvenirs and gifts. The 3-hour package is 750B ($19.75) per person.

Mu Ko Surin Archipelago National Marine Park is for those who wish to lose the crowds on such popular beaches as Phuket, Krabi, or Ko Samui and find the pristine sand and sea of a protected national park. Similar to Ko Similan, off the Phuket coast, Ko Surin is best appreciated for its fine sand beaches, clean waters, and exquisite coral reefs. There is little development on the main island and literally no development on the surrounding three islets. Jansom Travel (☎ 077/835-317) offers a 3-day/2-night snorkel package for 3,500B ($92.10) per person, but only during December through April. Other times of the year, the seas are too choppy for boats to get out to the islands, and the weather is far too rainy to appreciate the park.

WHERE TO STAY

Jansom Thara. 2/10 Phetchkasem Rd., Ranong 85000. ☎ **077/822-516.** Fax 077/ 821-821. 200 units. A/C MINIBAR TV TEL. 942B–1,648B ($24.80–$43.35) double; from 2,119B ($55.75) suite. AE, MC, V.

The Jansom Thara is *the* hotel in Ranong because of its proximity and connection with the hot springs as well as the fact that it's a fully equipped resort. The main attractions are the gender segregated thermal pools, outdoor swimming pool, health/fitness club, and an in-house doctor who consults with those who've come to "take the waters." The rooms are nicely decorated and of decent size. Unfortunately, the lowest-price rooms are nearly always booked, so you'll likely end up in a superior room or junior suite. Even so, we think these rooms plus all of the facilities add up to a pretty good value.

Dining/Diversions: You can choose between the more formal Palm Court or the Namtarm, the latter sports an evening show featuring a live band and local Thai girl singers. The Hills Cocktail Lounge is about as discreet as you can get; it's so dark that you can barely see your hand in front of you!

Amenities: Outdoor pool, Jacuzzi with mineral-spring water, beauty/barber shop, gift/drugstore, and massage (4pm to midnight), room service 6am to 2am, concierge, limousine service, house doctor, laundry service, complimentary welcome drink.

The Spa-Inn Ranong. Phetchkasem Rd., Ranong 85000. ☎ **077/811-715.** 70 units. A/C TV TEL. 380B ($10) double. MC, V.

This recently expanded inn is conveniently located down the street from the Jansom Thara and, given its location close to the town and the springs, basic facilities (only slightly shabby), and ultralow price, stands as the best value in Ranong. The coffee shop isn't the best, but you're close enough to Jansom to take advantage of their offerings. Plus, for 100B ($2.65), Jansom Thara will let you use their spa pool.

WHERE TO DINE

Khun Nunt. 35/3 Lu Wang Rd. ☎ **077/821-966.** Main courses 50B–200B ($1.30–$5.25). Daily 9am–midnight. No credit cards. At the intersection of Chanra-U Rd. THAI.

This thatched, open-air pavilion with simple metal tables and chairs is a favorite lunch spot for government and hospital workers. Great dishes to try are deep-fried soft-shell crabs in bread crumbs or with garlic and pepper or the fried fish balls in sweet tangy dipping sauce. Venison is a specialty during the hunting season (September to December); it can be prepared barbecued-style or fried with garlic and pepper.

Somboon Restaurant. 2/63 Petchkasem Rd. ☎ **077/822-722.** Main courses 70B–350B ($1.85–$9.20). V. Daily 11am–11pm. Across from Jansom Thara. THAI/CHINESE/SEAFOOD.

Somboon was originally downtown on Ruangrad Road, but still enjoys great popularity here on Phetchkasem. The atmosphere is casual, with terrace dining in the back of the shop facade, and the food is excellent. Among the best dishes are steamed bass with Chinese sauce, fried prawn with vegetables, and squid fried with garlic, peppers, and onions. Go for the fried crab with curry and barbecued crab.

4 Surat Thani

644 km (400 miles) S of Bangkok

Surat Thani is believed to have been an important center of the Sumatra-based Srivijaya Empire in the 9th and 10th centuries. Today, it's known to foreigners as the gateway to beautiful Ko Samui and to Thais as a rich agricultural province.

The favorite food product is **oysters,** farmed in Ka Dae and the Tha Thanong Estuary (30km/18 miles south of Amphur Muang, the capital town), where more than 16,000 acres are devoted to aquaculture. Fallow rice paddies now support young *hoi takram,* or tilam oysters, which cling to bamboo poles submerged in brackish water. After 2 years they can be harvested; the summer months yield the best crop. Surat Thani's other famed product is the Rong Rian rambutan (*ngor* in Thai). The industry has blossomed since 1926, when a breed of the spine-covered fruit grown in Penang was transplanted here; now more than 125,000 acres of the Nasan district (40km/24 miles south of town) are devoted to plantations. Each August (the harvest is August through October) a Rambutan Fair is held, with a parade of fruit-covered floats and performances by trained monkeys.

ESSENTIALS

GETTING THERE   By Plane   Thai Airways (in Bangkok (☎ **02/232-8000**) has two daily flights from Bangkok to Surat Thani (trip time: 70 minutes). Thai Airways has a minibus (70B/$1.85) between the airport and its office at 3/27–28 Karoonrat Rd. (☎ **077/272-610**), just south of town. For Surat Thani Airport information call ☎ **077/253-500.**

By Train   Ten trains leave daily from Bangkok's Hua Lampong station to Surat Thani (trip time: 13 hours; second-class sleeper 468B/$12.30, second-class seat 288B/$7.60). The Surat Thani train station is very inconvenient, but minitrucks meet trains to transport you to town for 20B (55¢) shared ride.

By Bus   Five air-conditioned buses leave daily from Bangkok's Southern Bus Terminal (☎ **02/435-1199**) (trip time: 11 hours; 346B/$9.10 air-conditioned bus; 535B/$14.10 for VIP). Six air-conditioned buses leave daily from Phuket's Bus Terminal off Phang-nga Road opposite the Royal Phuket City Hotel (☎ **076/211-977**) (trip time: 5 hours; 150B/$3.95). Also from Phuket, six minivans travel to Surat Thani daily (trip time: 4 hours; 160B/$4.20). Find them across from the Montri Hotel on Suthat Road. The Surat Thani Bus Terminal is on Kaset II Road a block east of the main road (☎ **077/200-032**).

By Minivan   The best way to travel between southern cities is by privately operated air-conditioned minivans. Frequently used by locals, they're cheap and run on very regular schedules from around 6am to 7pm daily. They'll connect you to Surat Thani from Chumphon, Ranong, Nakhon Si Thammarat, Hat Yai and beyond. Since many different companies cover each individual route, I've found the best way to arrange

Surat Thani

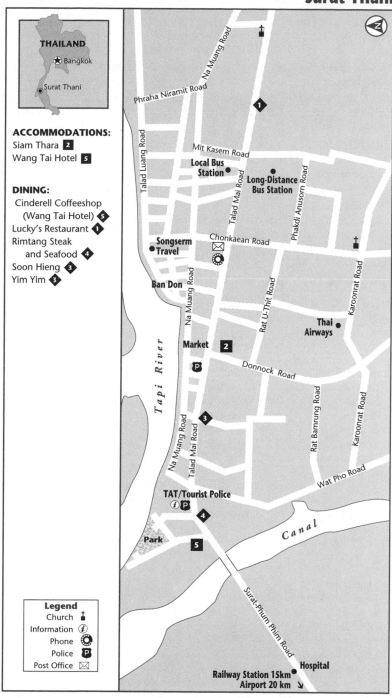

THAILAND
★ Bangkok
● Surat Thani

ACCOMMODATIONS:
Siam Thara **2**
Wang Tai Hotel **5**

DINING:
Cinderell Coffeeshop
  (Wang Tai Hotel) **5**
Lucky's Restaurant **1**
Rimtang Steak
  and Seafood **4**
Soon Hieng **3**
Yim Yim **3**

Legend
Church ✝
Information *i*
Phone ☎
Police **P**
Post Office ✉

Na Muang Road
Phraha Niramit Road
Talad Luang Road
Talad Mai Road
Mit Kasem Road
Local Bus Station
Long-Distance Bus Station
Phakdi Anusorn Road
Chonkaean Road
Songserm Travel
Ban Don
Na Muang Road
Rat U-Thit Road
Karoonrat Road
Thai Airways
Market 2
Donnock Road
Rat Bamrung Road
Karoonrat Road
Na Muang Road
Talad Mai Road
3
Tapi River
Wat Pho Road
TAT/Tourist Police
4
Park 5
Canal
Surat-Phum Phim Road
Hospital
Railway Station 15km
Airport 20 km ↘

these trips is to consult your hotel's front desk. They almost always have reservation numbers, and can book your trip and arrange hotel pickup with great efficiency. I've yet to pay more than 100B ($2.65) for any minivan trip in the south.

By Car Take Highway 4 south from Bangkok to Chumphon, then Highway 41 south direct to Surat Thani.

VISITOR INFORMATION For information about Surat Thani, Ko Samui, and Ko Phangan, contact the **TAT office,** 5 Talad Mai Rd., Surat Thani (☎ 077/ 288-818), up the street from the Wang Tai Hotel.

ORIENTATION Surat Thani is built up along the south shore of the Tapi River. Talad Mai Road, 2 blocks south of the river, is the city's main street, with the TAT office at its west end, and the bus station and central market at its east end. Frequent songtao ply Talad Mai; prices are based on distance but rarely exceed 25B (65¢).

FAST FACTS Major banks along Talad Mai Road have ATMs and will perform currency exchanges. The **Post Office** and **Overseas Call Office** (☎ 077/272-013) are together on Na Muang and Chonkasean roads near the center of town. The **Taksin Hospital** (☎ 077/273-239) is at the north end of Talad Mai Road. The **Tourist Police** (☎ 077/281-300) are with the TAT on Talad Mai Road.

WHAT TO SEE & DO

This pleasant but rather confusing town is little more than a transportation hub to Ko Samui and its less-developed satellite island, Ko Phangan. Most people will want to press on. Those with an extra day or two (especially those with children) may want to organize a visit to a local Monkey Training Center, where monkeys are taught how to harvest ripe coconuts, or to Suan Mokkh Monastery, a renowned Buddhist retreat with meditation study programs in English.

Monkeys have been trained to harvest fruit from south Thailand's particularly tall breed of coconut palm since the 1950s. In that time, dozens of private schools have opened, each accepting up to about 50 monkeys per year. The Macaca nemestrina, or pig-tailed macaque (*ling kang* in Thai), is the only suitable breed; a farmer pays about 3,000B ($78.95) for a 1- to 3-year-old male, then another 3,000B for training the animal to eventually pick 800 coconuts a day. At the **Monkey Training College,** 24 Moo 4, Tambon Thungkong (☎ 077/227-351), Khun Somphon Saekhow teaches monkeys to distinguish ripe from unripe or rotten fruit, how to spin coconuts around their stems to break them off the tree, and how to pitch them into receptacles below. A charming man, he'll be glad to "perform" with his monkeys to show you their learned skills and amazing abilities. You can find the place by following Talad Mai Road east of town for about a half hour; daily shows begin at 9am (the best time to come) until 6pm and cost about 300B ($7.90) per person. The TAT (see "Visitor Information" above) can assist in making travel arrangements.

Suan Mokkhabalarama (the Grove of the Power of Liberation, better known as Suan Mokkh) was founded in 1932 and moved to this forest in Chaiya about 10 years later. Its abbot, Ajahn Buddhadasa, spent years traveling around Thailand teaching the elemental principles of the Buddha. His fame as a teacher spread, and his fluent English lured foreigners to Suan Mokkh to study under him. Today, many foreign monks and nuns continue the aging Ajahn's teachings in the simplest of settings, with no elaborate temple to contain their meditation and no Buddha images to pray to.

The 1st through 10th days of every month are dedicated to a 10-day **Buddhist Meditation Course.** The daily program typically includes a 4am wake-up and meditation session, breakfast, chores around the compound, lunch, private study, afternoon tea, an evening lecture, and evening meditation. The retreat has limited accommodations for visitors who are asked to "stay here as individuals committed to self-exploration." There are several rules of conduct. Applicants are accepted on a first-come basis; the 10-day course, dorm lodging, and meals cost 1,200B ($31.60) total. Suan Mokkh accepts students at other times of the month free of charge, although beginners will find it awkward to fit into the self-motivated meditation routine. Write to Suan Mokkh, Tambon Lamet, Amphur Chaiya, Surat Thani 84110. Or contact the **Dhamma Study and Practice Group,** 309/49 Moo 2, Vibhavadi Rangsit Road, Tung Song Heng, Bangkhen, Bangkok 10210, or call them direct at ☎ **077/431-552.** The monastery is at Amphur Chaiya, 50km (31 miles) north of Surat Thani on Highway 41; long-distance buses and minitrucks pass by the entrance throughout the day.

KHAO SOK NATIONAL PARK

One of the largest jungle parks in the south, Khao Sok is regularly frequented for its stunning scenery and exotic wildlife as much as it is for the convenience of the trip. If you're traveling overland from Surat Thani to Phuket, you'll pass the park headquarters. Take buses from either town, and ask to be dropped off at the park entrance. To get back, just pick up the next bus heading in your direction.

Within the park's 646 square kilometers, you'll swoon over the beauty of the limestone craggy cliffs—imagine the jutting formations of Phangnga Bay, only on land. Rising some 1,000 meters, and laced with shaggy patches of forest, these are the main focal point for landscape photographers and ogglers alike. Living within the dense jungle habitat, with vines dripping form the tall canopy above, tigers, leopard species, golden cats, and elephant herds still wander freely, but you may be hard-pressed to actually spot any. More commonly visitors see guar, Malaysian sun bear, gibbons, mangur, macaques, civets, flying lemur, and squirrels. Keep your eye peeled for the over 200 species of birds like hornbills, woodpeckers and kingfishers. As for the flora, the Raffelesia, the largest flower in the world, finds vines to suck its parasitic subsistence from. The largest are up to a meter wide.

Well-marked trails lead you through the park to the main attraction, the **Rajprabha Dam** and reservoir. Here you can go boating, rafting, and fishing among the **limestone cliffs** that act as islands in the swelling waters. There's also a park office here. Neither office provides camping equipment, but at either office you can arrange accommodation in simple bungalows or bamboo shacks, with only basic meals. Hanging around each office, guides will offer their services through the main paths and help plan your itinerary.

For more details contact the **National Park Division,** Natural Resources Conservation office, Royal Forestry Department, 61 Pahonyothin Rd., Chatuchak, Bangkok 10900 (☎ **02/579-7223**), or the TAT office in either Phuket Town or Surat Thani.

WHERE TO STAY

Siam Thara. 1/144 Donnock Rd., Surat Thani 84000. ☎ **077/273-740.** 172 units. A/C TV TEL. 395B ($10.40) double. MC, V. Middle of town near bus station; corner of Talad Mai Rd.

Worn but well-kept rooms, with dull beige and brown upholstery, are a good value because of Siam Thara's central location, but not too attractive. Still, it's close to the center of town. The lobby coffee shop has some pretty good food, and becomes an evening nightclub from 8pm to 2am; high-floor rooms are quieter.

Wang Tai Hotel. 1 Talad Mai Rd., Surat Thani 84000. ☎ **077/283-020.** Fax 077/281-007. 238 units. A/C TEL. 850B–1,000B ($22.35–$26.30) double; from 2,000B ($52.65) suite. AE, MC, V. South side of town near TAT.

The best quality choice is a bit inconvenient, but only 25B (65¢) by tuk-tuk from the bus terminal or ferry company offices. This newer hotel tower features a coffee shop, where acceptable Thai food and good salads are served at tables overlooking the Tapi River and a pleasant pool and sun deck. There's also a lobby cafe with coffee and pastries, for a quick bite while you're running to catch your morning ferry to Samui. Spacious rooms are clean and comfortable, a great value for the money (rates vary according to view).

WHERE TO DINE

Locally farmed, succulent oysters are served at most restaurants in town for as little as 10B (25¢) each. To sample this gustatory highlight, try **Soon Hieng** (near the Jula Department Store off Bandon Road)—also try their crab salad, and **Yim Yim,** Talad Lang Road, about 3 blocks northeast of the ferry terminal, both specializing in Thai and Chinese cuisine.

In the north end of town, **Lucky's Restaurant,** at 452/84-85 Talad Mai Rd. (☎ **077/273-267**), has an open-air dining room and an air-conditioned hall, both filled with locals enjoying the inexpensive, well-cooked food. Pork curry with coconut milk, ginger, and peppers is a spicy but tolerable brew, and deliciously tender. The *tom yam klung,* a shrimp soup with straw mushrooms, makes a good starter before their superb fried oyster omelette. Main dishes range from 45B to 180B ($1.20 to $4.75).

5 Ko Samui

644km (400 miles) S of Bangkok to Surat Thani; 84km (52 miles) E from Surat Thani to Ko Samui

The island of Ko Samui lies 84km (52 miles) off Thailand's east coast in the Gulf of Thailand, near the mainland commercial town of Surat Thani. Since the 1850s, Ko Samui has been visited by Chinese merchants sailing from Hainan Island in the South China Sea to trade coconuts and cotton, the island's two most profitable products.

Ko Samui's coconuts are among Southeast Asia's most coveted, principally for their flavor. More than two million coconuts a month are shipped to Bangkok. Much of the fruit is made into coconut oil, a process that involves scraping the meat out of the shell, drying it, and pressing it to produce a sweet oil. To assist farmers with Ko Samui's indigenous breed of tall palm trees, monkeys are trained to climb them, shake off the ripe coconuts, and gather them for their master. (See "Surat Thani," above, for information about visiting a monkey training school.)

You'll hear Ko Samui compared to Phuket all the time. While Phuket enjoys international fame (or notoriety, depending on your point of view) as a gorgeous beach resort heaven, Ko Samui attracts those who want to avoid the hype and settle down for more down-to-earth relaxation. Once upon a time Ko Samui's fine beaches were less crowded, and simple bungalow accommodations and eateries made for a more authentic Southeast Asian island experience. As Ko Samui's reputation as the "alternative Thai island" grew, so did the number of visitors landing on its shores. Increasing demand inspired the opening of an international airport in 1988, which now has more than 20 packed daily flights. In recent years big resorts are getting in on the action, opening up huge accommodations a la Phuket. While they provide more comforts and facilities, they lack the carefree Ko Samui charm that drew travelers here in the first place.

Ko Samui is still in some places an idyllic tropical retreat with little traffic, clean warm water, fine sand beaches, and simple bungalows—but hotels, some of them quite luxurious, have sprung up like mushrooms, and some beaches see heavy tourist

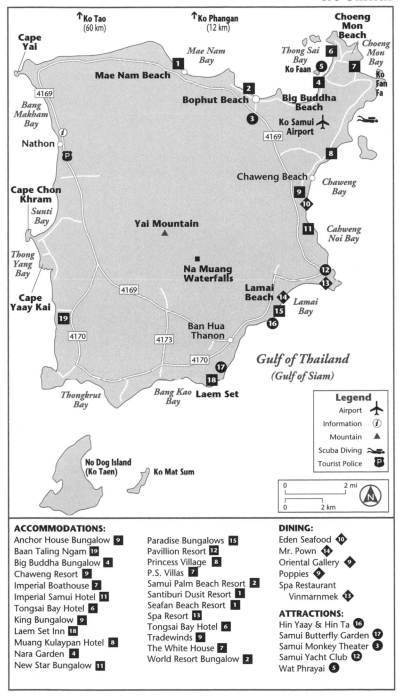

Ko Samui

↑Ko Tao (60 km) ↑Ko Phangan (12 km)

Cape Yai

Mae Nam Bay

Mae Nam Beach 1

Choeng Mon Beach

Thong Sai Bay
Ko Faan

Choeng Mon Bay

6
5
7

Ko Fan Fa

4

4169

Bang Makham Bay

2

Bophut Beach

Big Buddha Beach

Nathon

ⓘ

P

3

Ko Samui Airport ✈

4169

8

Cape Chon Khram

Sunti Bay

Chaweng Beach

Chaweng Bay

9
10

Thong Yang Bay

Yai Mountain ▲

11

Cahweng Noi Bay

Cape Yaay Kai

Na Muang Waterfalls ■

12
13

4169

Lamai Beach 14

15

Lamai Bay

19

Ban Hua Thanon

16

4170

4173

4170

17

18

Laem Set

Gulf of Thailand *(Gulf of Siam)*

Thongkrut Bay

Bang Kao Bay

No Dog Island (Ko Taen)

Ko Mat Sum

Legend

Airport ✈
Information ⓘ
Mountain ▲
Scuba Diving
Tourist Police P

0 ———— 2 mi
0 ———— 2 km
N

ACCOMMODATIONS:

Anchor House Bungalow 9
Baan Taling Ngam 19
Big Buddha Bungalow 4
Chaweng Resort 9
Imperial Boathouse 7
Imperial Samui Hotel 11
Tongsai Bay Hotel 6
King Bungalow 9
Laem Set Inn 18
Muang Kulaypan Hotel 8
Nara Garden 4
New Star Bungalow 11

Paradise Bungalows 15
Pavillion Resort 12
Princess Village 8
P.S. Villas 7
Samui Palm Beach Resort 2
Santiburi Dusit Resort 1
Seafan Beach Resort 1
Spa Resort 13
Tongsai Bay Hotel 6
Tradewinds 9
The White House 7
World Resort Bungalow 2

DINING:

Eden Seafood 10
Mr. Pown 14
Oriental Gallery 9
Poppies 9
Spa Restaurant Vinmarnmek 13

ATTRACTIONS:

Hin Yaay & Hin Ta 16
Samui Butterfly Garden 17
Samui Monkey Theater 3
Samui Yacht Club 12
Wat Phrayai 5

traffic. If you're looking for a true isolated tropical paradise, you'll have to look a little harder. Below, in "Orientation," we'll help you out with a beach by beach account of what you can expect from each location on the island.

The high season on Ko Samui is from mid-December to mid-January. January to April has the best weather, before its gets hot. October through mid-December are the wettest months, with November bringing extreme rains and fierce winds that make the east side of the island rough for swimming. Some years, the island's west side is buffeted by summer monsoons from the mainland.

ESSENTIALS

GETTING THERE   Getting to Ko Samui is more simple than it at first appears. Direct flights from Bangkok, Phuket, Pattaya, and even Singapore make visiting the island a snap. In addition there are several bus and train options to Surat Thani (the nearest mainland town); a ferry from a canal in south Surat Thani and express ferries from Thathon, another port 5km (3 miles) south of Surat Thani.

By Plane to Ko Samui   Seventeen flights depart daily from Bangkok on **Bangkok Airways** (☎ 02/229-3456 in Bangkok), pretty much one every 40 minutes between 6:20am and 7:40pm. A daily flight from Phuket (Bangkok Airways Phuket office, ☎ 076/225-033), and another daily from the U-Tapao airport near Pattaya (Bangkok Airways Pattaya office, ☎ 038/411-965) connect these major beach destinations, with additional Bangkok airways flights connecting the northern cities through Bangkok. From Singapore, Bangkok Airways flies direct each day (Singapore office, ☎ 65/546-8982). Their offices in Samui are at 54/4 Moo 3 in Bophut (☎ 077/422-512) and at the airport (☎ 077/425-012).

Ko Samui Airport is a little slice of heaven—open-air pavilions with thatch roofs surrounded by gardens and palms. For airport information call ☎ 077/425-012. If you're staying at a larger resort, airport minivan shuttles can be arranged when you book your room. If not, just out at the main road you'll find songtaos (pickup truck taxis) that can take you to the beach you're staying at. If there are many of you, trips can be as low as 30B (80¢), depending on how far you're going. For one or two people going a longer distance, they may try to up the price to over 100B ($2.65). If you depart Ko Samui via the airport, there's an additional 150B ($3.95) airport tax that's usually added to your ticket charge.

Another flight option, while more cumbersome, is also available. Thai Airways operates two daily flights to Surat Thani (Bangkok reservations, ☎ 02/232-8000; Surat Thani office, ☎ 077/272-610). While Thai Airways runs a shuttle to Surat Thani town, if you're moving on to Ko Samui, your best bet is to prearrange a combined airport shuttle and ferry trip through Songserm Travel. Detailed contact information is listed below in "By Bus/Ferry Packages."

GETTING TO KO SAMUI VIA SURAT THANI   By Air Ferry Package   Thai Airways (☎ 02/232-8000 in Bangkok, or 077/272-610 in Surat Thani) has two daily flights from Bangkok to Surat Thani (trip time: 70 minutes). While Thai Airlines offers a shuttle to Surat Thani town, if you're heading direct to Ko Samui, you'll want to prearrange a combination shuttle bus and ferry trip through Songserm Travel. Songserm's main office is in Bangkok, 33/11–12 Changwattana Rd., Pakkret (☎ 02/984-5600, fax 02/984-5641), with branches in Surat Thani, 30/2 Moo 3 (☎ 077/285-124, fax 077/285-127, and on Ko Samui, 64/1–2 Nathon Pier (☎ 077/421-316, fax 077/420-167).

By Train/Ferry Package   Ten trains leave daily from Bangkok's Hua Lampong station to Surat Thani (trip time: 13 hours; second-class sleeper 468B/$12.30, second-class seat 288B/$7.60). Minitrucks meet trains to transport passengers to Surat Thani, but Songserm Travel can arrange a train station pick up to take you direct to the ferry to Ko Samui. Songserm's main office is in Bangkok at 33/11–12 Changwattana Rd., Pakkret (☎ 02/984-5600, fax 02/984-5641), with branches in Surat Thani, 30/2 Moo 3 (☎ 077/285-124, fax 077/285-127), and on Ko Samui, 64/1-2 Nathon Pier (☎ 077/421-316, fax 077/420-167).

By Bus/Ferry Packages   Songserm has daily bus and ferry packages from Bangkok, and other cities in the peninsula. Buses depart from **Bangkok's** Khao San Road, 172 Khao San Rd., Banglamphu (☎ 02/281-1463), and their main office, 33/11–12 Changwattana Rd., Pakkret (☎ 02/984-5600, fax 02/ 984-5641); **Chumphon,** 66/1 Thatapao Rd. (☎ 077/502-023); **Phuket,** 51–53 Satun Rd. (☎ 076/222-570); **Krabi,** 92/94 Kongka Rd. (☎ 075/630-470); and **Ko Phi Phi,** Phi Phi Natural Resort, Leam Tong Beach (☎ 075/396-3769). Prices vary; from Bangkok an air-conditioned bus/ferry package is 230B ($6.05), while if you want VIP travel (with larger reclining seats) you'll pay 500B ($13.15) for the combination ticket. From Phuket, the air-conditioned package trip costs 350B ($9.20).

Songserm has offices in Surat Thani, 30/2 Moo 3 (☎ 077/285-124, fax 077/ 285-127), and on Ko Samui, 64/1–2 Nathon Pier (☎ 077/421-316, fax 077/ 420-167).

By Express Boat from Surat Thani & Chumphon   Early morning boats connecting Ko Samui to the mainland run a circuit from Surat Thani to Ko Samui, Ko Phangan, Ko Tao, and on to Chumphon and back again. The total trip is about 4 hours, while the Surat-Samui leg is 2½ hours. Rates are as follows: Surat-Samui 150B ($3.95); Samui-Phangan 95B ($2.50); Phangan-Tao 250B ($6.60); Tao-Chumphon 400B ($10.55). Contact Songserm in Surat Thani, 30/2 Moo 3 (☎ 077/285-124, fax 077/285-127); Ko Samui, 64/1-2 Nathon Pier (☎ 077/421-316, fax 077 /420-167); Ko Phangan, 44/43 Moo 1, Thong Sala Pier (☎ 077/377-046); Ko Tao, Mae Had Beach (☎ 01/229-5630 cellular); and Chumphon, 66/1 Thatapao Rd. (☎ 077/502-023). In most cases, they can arrange your transportation to the ferry pier.

If you miss the morning boat from Surat Thani, **Phantip** (☎ 077/421-221) has an afternoon bus and ferry package for comparable prices.

You probably won't have to worry about transportation once you reach Nathon, Ko Samui's ferry pier. Touts on the ferry offer very cheap rides, some as low as 20B (55¢) if they can get a packed truckload from the boat (and be warned, they'll tie people to the roof if they can get an additional 20B/55¢ for it). If you have no accommodations booking, many will even make a few stops along the way so you can check a few places out before deciding. If you wait until you reach the pier, there are many more songtao waiting to take people to their destinations.

ORIENTATION   Though Ko Samui is the country's third-largest island, with a total area of 90 square miles, its entire coastline can be toured by car or motorcycle in about 2½ hours. The island is hilly, densely forested, and rimmed with coconut palm plantations. The Ko Samui airport is in the northeast corner of the island. The hydrofoils, car ferry, and express boats arrive on the west coast, in or near (depending on the boat) Nathon. The island's main road (Highway 4169) circles the island.

Most of Samui's fine beaches are on the north and east coasts. The long east coast stretch between Chaweng and Lamai beaches is the most popular destination for visitors and, consequently, where you'll find the greatest concentration of hotels and bungalows. The south coast is home to the island's small fishing fleet, dating back to the era of the China trade. The west coast has a few sandy strips, but the busy boat traffic lessens its surfside appeal.

Nathon, on the west coast of the island, is the main transportation hub for ferry arrivals and departures. A tiny town, the presence of banks, money exchange booths, the TAT office, main post office, and local transportation makes it convenient, but there are no resorts near here—most folks head straight for the beaches. The main road, Thaweerat Phakdee Road (aka Nathon Road aka Highway 4167), runs parallel to the waterside road by the ferry pier (Chonwithee Road).

Clockwise from Nathon, **Mae Nam Bay** is 12km (7½ miles) from the ferry pier, at the midpoint of Samui's north shore, facing nearby Ko Phangan. The beach is on a par with Lamai but narrower; it's long, with coarse sand and shaded by trees. The water is deep enough for a great swim (on other beaches the water is shallow unless you walk out very far). This bay is often spared the fierce winds that whip during the stormy months, making it popular during the winter. Mae Nam is relatively isolated, and there are a number of simple, charming beach bungalows on unpaved roads off Highway 4169, which offer some of the most secluded accommodations on the island. Ban Mae Nam, the commercial center, is just east of the Dusit Santiburi Resort, one of the best resorts on the island, and has several restaurants, laundries, shops, a medical clinic, and a gas station.

Bophut Beach, on the north coast just east of Mae Nam, is one of the island's fastest developing areas. Unfortunately, Highway 4169 (the main circle road) runs very close to the shore all along the sandy stretch. The presence of many small Thai restaurants, businesses, shops, and taxis creates a busier pace than is evident at other, more removed beaches. Bophut's very long (usually crowded in the high season) sand beach narrows considerably in the monsoon season, but the water remains fairly calm year-round. At present, some of the myriad cheap bungalows and hippie compounds are being replaced by upscale accommodations.

Big Buddha Beach is a more recently developed cove (east of Bophut, on the north coast) that's becoming popular with young, low-budget families. There's a fairly clean, coarse sand beach (narrow in the monsoon months) and a calm, shallow swimming bay. Some small hotels and many simple bungalows look out over Ko Faan (also written Ko Farn), the island home of Ko Samui's huge seated Buddha, which is also a good place to purchase seashells. Fishing boats and long-tail water taxis servicing Ko Phanghan create some traffic (especially around the full moon when they work double-time to carry passengers out for the Full-Moon Party (see "Ko Phangan"), but it's very picturesque.

Ko Samui juts out at the northeastern tip in a rough, irregular coastline. Bold rock formations create private coves and protected swimming areas, though from mid-October to mid-December the monsoon whips up the wind and waves, creating a steep drop-off from the coarse sand beach and strong undertow. **Thong Sai Bay** is a beautiful cove dominated by one resort (Thong Sai Bay Cottages); its privacy is a plus and a minus. While exclusively tranquil, it's difficult to reach by cheap public transport.

At the southeast end of Thong Sai Beach, you'll come to a fairly formidable set of rocks (they can be climbed safely if you wear decent footwear). Just over these craggy cliffs is the fine sand beach of **Choeng Mon,** a gracefully shaped crescent about a half mile long. Palm trees shading sunbathers reach right to the water's edge; swimming is excellent, with few rocks near the central shore. Across the way is Ko Fan Fa, a deserted island with an excellent beach. You can swim or, if the tides are right, walk there, but be careful of the rocks at low tide. Although Choeng Mon is as isolated as Thong Sai Bay, there are many small hotels and bungalows hidden in the hills and public mini-truck service.

The two Chaweng beaches (the main "**Chaweng**" and south "**Chaweng Noi**") are undoubtedly the most popular destinations on Ko Samui—for better or worse. The benefits of Chaweng are the many conveniences provided by consumer demand—you have more money changing, Internet, laundry, travel and rental agencies, medical facilities, shopping, restaurants, and nightlife, not to mention more choices for accommodations. Chaweng can be a blast if you don't mind a little hustle and bustle. If you bore easily from hours on the beach or get waterlogged from the surf, there are plenty of activity options just near the beach.

The drawback of Chaweng is the crowds. Travelers draw businesses, which in turn draw more travelers. It seems the latest sport is Chaweng bashing—putting the place down for being grotesquely touristy and overdeveloped, preferring the quieter comforts of the more isolated bays. In defense of Chaweng, most of the people I heard putting the place down ended up spending time here for one reason or another! Some resort owners, who have been here for over 20 or so years, lament the peaceful secluded days of yesterday (but secretly adore the increase of their prime beach real estate). Chaweng, the north or main bay, was the first to be developed and is crowded at its north end with simple, budget bungalows whose cafes turn into an active nightlife scene; Chaweng Noi is more peaceful day or night.

The main island circle road (Highway 4169) is $^3/_{10}$ to 1.8 miles inland from the beach, but there's a one-lane road (which has been dug up for repaving for the past year) closer to the water. The beach here is the longest on the island, and despite the crowds remains surprisingly clean, with soft white sand edged with coconut palms. The water is very shallow, however, making swimming activities a little difficult unless you go far from the shore. Head for the southern parts for great snorkeling views.

The long sand beach on **Lamai Bay** is comparable to Chaweng's, but the clientele is decidedly rowdier and more colorful, if not always younger. Though there are many bungalows, few are above the most primitive standard—they tend to attract backpackers. However, there's lots of new construction, most of it in the budget category, and a range of cafes, bars, discos, tourist services, and bungalows make Lamai the cheapest resort on the island.

Laem Set Bay is a small rocky cape on Samui's southeast coast, with dramatic scenery that has prompted the construction of a few hotels. The Highway 4169 is nearly 2km (1.2 miles) inland, but motorcycle taxis will give you a ride for 25B/65¢, waiting at the public minitruck junction to transport you out to the point.

On the west coast, from Laem Phang Ka, one of Samui's better beaches on the island's southwest tip, the Highway cuts inland, heading north past **Ban Taling Ngam** and the cutoff running west to the car-ferry jetty. These beaches are the most isolated on the island, with few facilities to support resorts and waters filled with rocks, making the beaches barely swimmable. Many Thai families stop for picnics at Hin Lat Falls, a rather uninteresting, littered site 2km (1.2 miles) south of Nathon, which supplies the town with its drinking water.

VISITOR INFORMATION   The TAT Information Center operates a small kiosk on Chonwithee Road (☎ 077/420-504), the north end of the main waterfront street in town. A good place to stop, they distribute, in addition to TAT pamphlets, the thin *Accommodations Samui* guidebook, a free booklet packed with information on hotel, dining and activity options. Bangkok Airways produces the free *Samui Guide*, a color magazine with advertisements and practical information about the island. I like Bangkok Airways' free *Samui Guidemap*, an accurate map indicating locations for most major businesses and landmarks. All are distributed at TAT, the airport and many hotels and restaurants. At magazine stands, look for the *Greater Samui Guide* (80B/$2.10) a brand-new glossy magazine with travel articles, photos and advertisements for up-market establishments.

GETTING AROUND   By Songtao   Pickups outfitted with bench seats, called *songtao* in Thai, are the easiest and most efficient way to get around the island. They advertise their destinations—to such beaches as Lamai, Chaweng, and Mai Nam—with colorfully painted signs. There are two primary routes, with songtao plying the circular Highway 4169 making stops between Nathon on the west coast over the north side of the island to Chaweng on the east coast, and another route between Chaweng and Nathon along the southern coast. For some trips, you have to change trucks between north and south routes. Some branch off to hit Choeng Mon in the northeastern tip of the island. You can hail one anywhere along the highway and along beach roads. To visit a site off the beaten track (or one other than that painted on a truck's sign), ask the driver to make a detour. Check when the songtao stop running, usually around sundown, after which some will hang around outside the discos in Chaweng to take night owls home to other beaches. The cost is 20B to 40B (55¢ to $1.05) one way, with steep fares (up to 300B/$7.90) after hours.

By Rental Car   Ko Samui's roads are narrow, winding, poorly maintained, and dark at night. In the island's first decade of tourism, more than 350 foreigners died in vehicle accidents. Still, renting a car is safer than a motorcycle. Your defensive driving skills will be required to navigate around slow motorcycles at the side of the road and the occasional wandering dog.

From **Avis'** office at Santiburi Dusit Resort (☎ 077/425-031), you can have your vehicle delivered to your hotel, to the ferry pier or the airport. Avis provides excellent insurance, but costs far more than local rental firms. Their brand new fleet of Suzuki Caribians go for 1,600B ($42.10) a day each, while a Volvo sedan can run up to 6,000B ($157.90) per day.

Local rental companies and travel agents have great deals for car rentals, and while vehicles are sometimes a little beat up, they're generally mechanically sound. Look for bargains as low as 700B ($18.40) per day, but don't expect solid insurance policy coverage. Read all fine print, and make sure, if you don't have an international driver license, that your local license is acceptable under the terms of the insurance agreement. In the event of an accident, you don't want to lose insurance eligibility for not being properly licensed according to the contract. A standard contract allows for liability coverage with a 5,000B ($131.60) deductible.

By Motorcycle   Upon first arrival, it's easy to see that motorcycles are the top choice for locals as well as visitors. Driving on the left, most motorcyclists stick to the side of the road, but where shoulders are narrow, they drift into car lanes. Keep to the side as much as you can to make way for passing cars and trucks, and be mindful of other bikes. Helmet laws exist, but aren't always enforced. Travel agencies and small operators rent motorcycles in popular beach areas. A 100cc Honda scooter goes for 150B ($3.95) per day, while a 250cc chopper is as expensive as 700B to 900B ($18.40 to $23.70) a day. Insist they provide a helmet.

FAST FACTS   All the major **banks** are in Nathon, along Taweerat Phakdee Road, running parallel to the waterfront road where the pier is. While there's only one bank (Siam City Bank in the north of the beach road) in Chaweng, there are a multitude of money changers in Chaweng, Lamai, and some at other beach locations. Hotels and guest houses also accept traveler's checks—your safest bet here—but use conversion rates to their favor. The **main post office** (☎ 077/421-013) is opposite the TAT kiosk on Chonwithee Road in Nathon, but you'll probably not hike all the way back to the main pier for posting. Any hotel or guest house will handle it for you, and stamps can be purchased in small provision shops in beach areas.

For **Internet** service on Chaweng head for the **Go Internet Café** opposite the Central Samui Beach Resort (☎ **077/230-535**). The best Internet (and business services) can be found at **Sawadee Internet Service,** 131 Moo 4, T. Maret Lamai, Lamai Beach (☎ **077/231-176**).

A good **hospital** with excellent emergency care, Bandon International Hospital has English-speaking physicians and good facilities. Located in the north of Chaweng off Highway 4169, doctors can also make house calls. Call ☎ **077/425-382.** For tourist police emergencies dial ☎ **077/421-281.**

WHAT TO SEE & DO

Local aquanauts agree that the best **scuba diving** is off Ko Tao, a small island north of Ko Phangan and Ko Samui. Since conditions vary with the seasons, the cluster of tiny islands south of Samui, Mu Ko Angthong National Park, are often more reliable destinations. Follow the advice of a local dive shop on where to go. **Easy Divers,** in operation for 10 years, has locations in Chaweng, on the beach road next to Silver Sand Resort (☎ **077/230-548**), and Lamai, main road between Sand Sea Resort and Lamai Resort (☎ **077/231-190**). They offer all sorts of PADI courses, daily dive tours to 13 different sites, international safety standard boats, good equipment and complete insurance packages. Daily dives (two dives per day) range from 2,750B to 3,150B ($73 to $83) per person including land transportation, breakfast, equipment, lunch, and drinks. For speedboat scuba trips pay around 3,600B ($94.75) per person.

Some of the finest **snorkeling** off Ko Samui is found along the rocky coast between Chaweng Noi and Lamai Bays. Several shops along Chaweng Beach rent snorkeling gear for about 100B ($2.65) per day.

Blue Stars Sea Kayaking, at the Gallery Lafayette next to the Green Mango in Chaweng (☎ **077/230-497**), takes people kayaking and snorkeling to the Marine National Park. The rubber canoes are perfect for exploring the caverns underneath limestone cliffs. If you can't get to Phang Nga, for the most fantastic sea cave scenery, this trip is a fun alternative. The 4-hour trip costs 1,990B ($52.35) per person.

For **catamaran sailing,** check out **Tradewinds Resort** in Chaweng (☎ **077/230-602**). Run by John Stall, one of the pioneer bungalow operators here, he is familiar with local sailing conditions and great routes. He'll also provide instruction for 2,500B ($65.80) (3-hour course), while straight rentals are 800B ($21.05) per hour (with a guide if you'd like).

Fishermen should talk to **Camel Fishing Game,** in Lamai across from Bauhaus Pub (☎ **077/424-523**), about daily trips with all equipment and lunch provided. Prices range from 230B to 270B ($6.05 to 7.10) for a day trip.

EXPLORING THE ISLAND

Ko Samui's famed **Wonderful Rocks**—the most important of which are the sex-organ-shaped **Hin Yaay & Hin Ta** (Grandmother and Grandfather Stones)—are located at the far southern end of Lamai Beach. To get to them, walk about an hour south of Chaweng Beach, or take any minitruck to Lamai Beach and get off at Paradise Bungalows.

The gold-tiled **Wat Phrayai** (Big Buddha), more than 80 feet tall, sits atop Ko Faan (Barking Deer Island), a small islet connected to the shore by a dirt causeway almost 1,000 feet long. Though of little historic value, it's an imposing presence on the northeast coast and is one of Samui's primary landmarks. It's open all day; 20B (55¢)

contribution recommended. It's easy to reach, just hop on any songtao going to Big Buddha Beach. You can't miss it.

The main island road forks at Ban Hua Thanon in the southeast corner. Past the village of Ban Thurian, the road climbs north past **Na Muang Falls,** a pleasant waterfall once visited by many kings of the Chakri dynasty. After the rainy season ends in December, it reaches a height of almost 100 feet and a width of about 66 feet. Na Muang is a steamy 5km (3 mile) walk from the coast road and makes for a nice bathing and picnic stop. Feel free to trek to the falls on the back of an **elephant. Na Muang Trekking** (☎ 01/397-5430 cellular) will take you for a half-hour trip (600B/$15.80), or longer.

For something a little more tranquil visit the **Butterfly Garden** (☎ 077/424-020), off the 4170 Road near Laem Din on the southeast corner (open daily 9am to 5pm; adults 120B/$3.15, children 60B/$1.60). Near the Butterfly Garden, at the Samui Orchid Resort, is the **Samui Aquarium** (☎ 077/424-017) with sealife in huge aquariums lining a 120 meter passageway (open daily 9am to 5pm; admission 250B/$6.60 adult, 150B/$3.95 child.)

OTHER THINGS TO SEE & DO IN KO SAMUI

Along Samui's main roads, you'll find little hand-painted signs along the lines of "Monkey Work Coconut." These home-grown tourist spots show off monkey skills involved in the local coconut industry—they're trained to climb the trees, spin the coconuts to break them off their stems, and collect them from the bottom when they're finished. Trainers really use the beasts' natural smarts and talents—these monkeys might otherwise end up picking through resort garbage cans to eke out an existence. The proper **Samui Monkey Theater** (☎ 077/245-140) is just south of Bophut village on 4169 Road. Shows are a little more vaudeville than the "working" demonstrations—with costumes and goofy tricks—and are a lot more fun for kids than for adults, who'll just feel sorry for the animals. Show times at 10:30am, 2pm, and 4pm daily cost 150B ($3.95) for adults, 50B ($1.30) for children.

I defy you to find a Thai tourist spot without the requisite **snake farm,** complete with young men who taunt audiences with scary serpents, catching them with their bare hands (and sometimes their teeth). If you're really scared of snakes, keep away—this stuff is fodder for months of nightmares. On the other hand, it's a lot of laughs to see the audience squirming all over each other in semiamused horror. Samui's snake farm is at the far southwest corner of the island on 4170 Road (☎ 077/423-247), with daily shows at 11am and 2pm; tickets cost 250B ($6.60).

Although there's a cleared corral in every village around the island, **buffalo fights** now take place only on holidays. This equitable sport, popular in south Thailand, pits male water buffaloes in a contest of locked horns. Endurance, chutzpah, and brute strength determine the winner; the loser usually lies down or runs away. (Buffalo rarely hurt one another, though fans have been trampled!) Authorities have tried to curb gambling, but the event is still festive; shamans are called in to rile up the bulls, ribbons are hung around their necks, and buffalo horns are decorated with gold leaf. Contact the TAT office about when and where specific bouts will be held.

The spa scene on Ko Samui has really skyrocketed in recent years. Resorts like **The Spa Resort,** between Chaweng and Lamai Beaches (☎ 077/230-855), **Health Oasis Resort,** Bang Po Beach near Mae Nam (☎ 077/420-124), and **Axolotl Village,** Bang Po Beaach near Mae Nam (☎ 077/420-017), offer full service health and beauty treatments, including yoga, meditation, chi kung, international styles of massage, herbal steam treatments, facials, and body wraps, plus lectures on health. All feature health cuisine in their restaurants and long and short-term health programs for guests.

I also recommend these places for people who just want to pop in for a day of relaxation. If it happens to be bad weather—can you think of a better way to get out of the rain and still enjoy Samui? I've recommended The Spa Resort in the "Where to Stay" section above, mainly because its location is both secluded, but near the conveniences of Chaweng and Lamai Beaches. Understand, however, the health resorts on Ko Samui are not Chiva Som or Banyan Tree—they're more New Age than Guerlain (no doubt the effect of Ko Samui's development as an alternative vacation island). Health Oasis Resort, famous for its Healing Child Center, is pretty hard core, offering fasting and colonic programs, a holistic education program (for parents as well), and vortex destiny astrology (vortex destiny astrology?). Axolotl Village does all of that, plus tarot readings and lessons, past life analysis, aura readings, and more.

Also recommended: The brand-new **Bodycare Spa** at Poppies in Chaweng Beach (☎ 077/422-419) features natural Thai skin-care products (we highly recommend) from The Hideaway Spa in Phuket, and **Tamarind Springs** in Lamai (☎ 077/424-436) has a lovely hillside location, providing comforting surroundings for massage, even acupuncture.

Samui is not exactly a hotbed of **shopping.** There's very little in terms of local crafts production on the island—most everything is imported from the mainland. Do yourself a favor by saving your money for Bangkok or Chiang Mai, where you'll find a better selection of the same items for a better price.

One thing we can suggest is to take a peek at local **pearls** from oysters that thrive in this area. For those seriously interested in learning about pearl cultivation and jewelry crafting, I recommend a trip offshore to the Naga Pearl Shop. The day trip includes a 20-minute boat ride to and from the island shop, the grand tour of the operation, lunch, and shopping at their showroom. All for only 1,300B ($34.20) per person—one of the few places in the world that actually charges *you* to shop in their store! Call ☎ 077/423-272 to make a booking.

WHERE TO STAY ON KO SAMUI

Development has changed the face of resorts on Ko Samui. Twenty years ago, some resourceful souls opened makeshift beachside bungalow compounds along the long beaches. Today, all sorts of accommodations, in every price range, snuggle up to the bay to take advantage of prime real estate. Everything from motel cellblocks to gracious Thai style pavilions to chic modern facilities to homey guest houses share the same strips of beaches. Even if you're budget is tight, you can still enjoy the same sand as those is the more exclusive joints. Of course, like anywhere else in Thailand, all beaches are public, so feel free to hang out on any beach you wish.

Above, in island "Orientation," I've given you a breakdown of the island bay by bay so you can weigh the advantages of each. Below I've listed the better choices of accommodations in a variety of price categories in each bay area so you can pick the best one for your ideal vacation.

MAE NAM BAY

Mae Nam is relatively isolated, and there are a number of simple, charming beach bungalows on unpaved roads off the highway, which offer some of the best-secluded accommodations on the island. All are very simple with small snack bars, screened windows, common toilets, and no phones—a few have a pool—prices range from 200B to 500B ($5.25 to $13.15). A couple of the more attractive places are **Coco Palm** (☎ 077/425-321), with a nice pool and restaurant; and **Palm Point Village** (☎ 077/247-372). Close by you may also be interested in two spa resorts, the New Age **Health Oasis Resort** (☎ 077/420-124, www.healingchild.com), with its popular Healing Child Center, or the even more new age **Axolotl Village** (☎ 077/ 420-017, www.axolotlvillage.com), great for vegetarians and those interested in yoga and meditation.

⭗ **Santiburi Dusit Resort.** 12/12 Moo 1, Tambol Mae Nam, Ko Samui, Surat Thani 84330. ☎ **077/425-031.** Fax 077/425-040. www.dusit.com. 73 units. A/C MINIBAR TV TEL. $340–$520 Equatorial rooms and suites; $380–$460 Deluxe villa; $900 two-bedroom beach suite. AE, DC, JCB, MC, V.

For the best relaxation on the island, our money is on Santiburi. Fifteen minutes from the crazy life of Chaweng Beach, this resort is designed with a wink at the famous royal palace at Phetchaburi, with spacious and airy interiors—a simplicity accented with luxurious Jim Thompson Thai silks and tidy floral arrangements. The gardens and beachfront are picturesque and quiet and the staff is motivated to please, making this not only the finest resort on the island, but a solid competitor for Phuket's luxury travel market.

The higher priced villas front the beach, while the rest snuggle up to fabulous landscaping beyond. Each is a suite, with living and sleeping areas divided by glass and flowers. The bathroom is masterful, in masculine wood and black tiles, the centerpiece is the large round sunken tub. Standard features such as a video player and stereo system make each villa as convenient as your own home. The 12 Equatorial rooms, located in a building overlooking the large outdoor pool area, offer similar comfort at a slightly more affordable price.

You won't have to worry about noisy jet skis at this quiet beach, but you're welcome to take advantage of windsurfing and sailing on the house. They also have their own gorgeous Chinese junk anchored in the bay for dinner cruises or for hiring out to tour surrounding islands. Santiburi's two tennis courts, squash court, modern gymnasium and driving range will appeal to the sports set. A self-contained unit, the resort also has a salon, video library, tour counter, scuba counter, and a car rental desk.

Dining: The Sala Thai, serves rich royal Thai cuisine, and Vimarnmek, which combines Eastern and Western tastes for its delicious menu. Santiburi is more than happy to accommodate your desires, from a private barbecue at your villa, to a romantic supper on the beach. In addition they also serve light meals at Rim Talay by the beach, the pool bar, and Taksin Lobby Lounge.

Amenities: Swimming pool, children's pool, tennis and squash courts, fitness center, golf driving range, sailing, windsurfing, 24-hour room service, concierge, babysitting, and laundry.

Seafan Beach Resort. Mae Nam Beach, Ko Samui 84140, Surat Thani. ☎ **077/425-204.** Fax 077/425-350. www.kosamui.net/seafan. 37 suites. A/C MINIBAR. 2,950B ($77.65) includes breakfast; peak season (Dec–Jan) $120, beachfront $132, second row $128. AE, DC, JCB, MC, V. West end of beach.

With Thai ambience and low-key elegance, these deluxe beach-style bungalows are tucked into eight acres of landscaped grounds fronting the bay. Each "primitive" rattan and coconut-wood house has two queen-size beds, an extra rattan daybed, a bamboo makeup table, hair dryer, bathrobe and slippers, pastel-cotton seating area, and a large, all-tiled bathroom. Each has a terrace and is spaced far enough from its neighbors to ensure privacy, but the front beach-view bungalows (the same rate) really stand out. A small pool with kiddy pool and a snack bar overlook the beach. The nearby restaurant features Thai, continental, and several seafood specialties. Rates include use of windsurfing boards, snorkeling gear, and other water-sports activities. Service is attentive.

BOPHUT BEACH

Bophut beach is fast growing, but there are still some nice charming places to try. **The Lodge** (☎ 077/425-337), a cozy guest house, comes highly recommended but only has 10 rooms, so book early.

Samui Palm Beach Resort. 175/3 Thaveerat-Pakdee Rd., Bophut Beach, Ko Samui 84140, Surat Thani. ☎ **077/425-494.** Fax 077/425-358. 50 units. A/C MINIBAR TEL. 5,000B ($131.60) double. AE, V. Center of beach strip.

These attractively built, modern minihouses are spaced apart from one another along a boardwalk facing the sea. Each has a large porch with comfortable furniture, polished hardwood floors, a seating area, and tiled bathrooms with hot-water showers. Big picture windows and louvered ventilation windows with screens and curtains add a bit of luxury. A small pool, beachside restaurant, and 20 smaller bungalows with the same amenities but limited sea views, have been added. All are attractive, but we prefer the relative privacy of the older, freestanding bungalows.

World Resort Bungalow. Bophut Beach, Ko Samui 84320, Surat Thani. ☎ **077/425-355.** Fax 077/425-355. 32 units. A/C. 1,350B–1,550B ($35.55–$40.80) double. MC, V. Center of beach strip.

This is a large compound of simple, wood-paneled bungalows facing each other around a well-kept garden. The communal lawn area and beachfront are well maintained by a friendly staff. Kudos to the much-respected Mr. Pinyo Sritongkul, World's friendly owner, who organized the planting of 1,200 trees along Samui's north coast road in a conservation drive to celebrate Mother's Day! Rates are based on the proximity to the beach. There's a pleasant, seaside cafe and good pool. A special discount is offered to return visitors.

BIG BUDDHA BEACH

Big Buddha Beach is pretty laid-back. If you find the following places full, you can have your songtao driver drop you at the center of the beach to walk around the dozen or so guest houses to find one you like.

Big Buddha Bungalow. B34/1 Moo 4, Big Buddha Beach, Ko Samui 84140, Surat Thani. ☎ **077/425-282.** 14 bungalows. 500B ($13.15) double with fan, 1,300B ($34.20) double with A/C. Rates include tax and service. No credit cards. East side of beach near Nara Lodge.

These coconut wood, split-log cabins are the best deal on this beach, and one of the best on the island. They're large, with big porches, comfy furniture, screened windows, fans, and private showers. Rates vary according to size, and some rooms are air-conditioned, but all near the well-swept beach, meticulously clean, and face a large lawn. During our most recent visit, we found new owners busily sprucing up the place and building a few more bungalows. Let us know how you find it.

Nara Garden Resort. 88 Moo 4, Big Buddha Beach, Ko Samui 84140, Surat Thani. ☎ **077/425-364.** Fax 077/425-292. 43 units. A/C MINIBAR TV TEL. 1,500B–1,800B ($39.45–$47.35) double. MC, V. East end of beach.

The recently remodeled Nara is one of the island's older inns, with attached rooms as close to an American motel as you'll come in Ko Samui. A well-kept lawn leads to an acceptable beach with gentle swimming. The Nara has a slightly suburban ambience that makes it especially comfortable for families.

THONG SAI BAY

Tongsai Bay Resort is one of only a few accommodations here. If you can't get a reservation, you're better off trying at another beach area.

Tongsai Bay Resort. Ban Plailaem, Bophut, Ko Samui 84140, Surat Thani. ☎ **077/ 425-015.** Fax 077/425-462. All reservations through Bangkok office ☎ **02/254-0056,** fax 02/254-0054. 72 units. A/C MINIBAR TV TEL. 10,000B ($263.15) beachfront or cottage suites; 20,000B ($526.30) grand Tongsai villa (great discounts are available throughout the year). AE, DC, MC, V. Northeast tip of island; call for hotel pickup or charter private minitruck (about 250B/$6.60 from pier).

Built amphitheatrically down a hillside, the white stucco, red-tile roofed bungalows and buildings remind one of the Mediterranean, though the palm and bougainvillea are pure Thai. Between the half-moon cove's rocky bookends, the coarse sand beach invites you to idle away the days. The free-form saltwater pool, landscaping (tended by 36 gardeners), tucked-away tennis courts, and myriad flowers delight the eye. Most guests admire the grounds and sunset from the spacious balconies of the three-story hotel wing or from the large, tiled patios of freestanding two-room bungalows. Suites are stocked with toiletries, hair dryer, bathrobes, slippers, fresh roses, a fruit basket, houseplants, lacy mosquito netting, and plush rattan furniture.

Water sports are taught by enthusiastic young pool boys: Windsurfing, snorkeling, sailing dinghies, canoes, and a catamaran or speedboat (the last two at additional charge) await you. Service, from the comfort-conscious front desk to the amiable restaurant staff, is good. Advance reservations (up to 3 months) are a must from mid-December to February and in August. Our only caveat: The many steps between the hilltop reception area, the bungalows, and the beach challenge the elderly and may thwart travelers with disabilities.

There's a pleasant poolside cafe for breakfast and lunch, and a more formal dining terrace that has a commanding view from the hill.

CHOENG MON

Choeng Mon also has few accommodations to choose from, and the White House, as the centerpoint of the beach, overshadows all of its competition.

Imperial Boathouse. 83 Moo 4, Choeng Mon Beach, Tambon Bophut, Ko Samui 84320, Surat Thani. ☎ **077/425-041.** Fax 077/425-460. 216 units. A/C MINIBAR TV TEL. 5,445B–9,075B ($143.30–$238.80) double. AE, DC, MC, V. Southern part of beach.

You've a pretty unique concept here—34 authentic teak rice barges have been dry-docked and converted into small "suites." These suites are full of everything you'll ever need, including private bathrooms, in-house videos, and coffee-/tea-making facilities in each room. Go for the "Boat Suite," your own minihouseboat—very, very charming. Naturally, the less-expensive rooms in the three-story buildings aren't as atmospheric. If you still long for boats, you can swim in their boat-shaped swimming pool, or go windsurfing and canoeing. For relaxation try the pleasant lounge or the game room.

P.S. Villa. Choeng Mon Beach, Ko Samui 84320, Surat Thani. ☎ **077/425-160.** 18 units. 600B–1,200B ($15.80–$31.60) double with A/C; 400B ($10.55) double with fan. MC, V. North end of beach.

These spick-and-span bungalows with plenty of space between them for extra quiet are an excellent value. The friendly staff maintains a large lawn, lots of flowering plants, and a seaview bamboo bar and dining pavilion. Large, attractively patterned thatch and rattan bungalows with bamboo porch furniture have three comfortable beds, fans, and tiled cold-water showers. Smaller, equally nice thatch bungalows with only two beds cost less. Good for families.

The White House. 59/3 Moo 5, Choeng Mon Beach, Ko Samui 84320, Surat Thani. ☎ **077/245-315.** Fax 077/245-318. 40 units. A/C MINIBAR TV TEL. Low season (May–July,

Sept–Nov) 3,000B–3,600B ($78.95–$94.75) double; from 4,200B ($110.55) suite. Peak season (Aug, Dec–Apr) 3,900B–4,500B ($102.65–$118.40) double; from 5,100B ($134.20) suite, plus peak-season supplement 2,500B ($65.80) per night. AE, MC, V. On Choeng Mon Beach.

This resort in the graceful Ayutthaya style, built around a central garden with a lotus pond and swimming pool, is by far the top choice in Choeng Mon. The lobby—almost a museum—is impeccably decorated with original Thai artwork and images. Spacious and elegant rooms with tea and coffee service flank a central walkway that's lined with orchids. Houses accommodate four rooms each, which are large with separate sitting areas and big showers. By the beach there's a pool with a bar and an especially graceful teak *sala*. The resort's quality Swiss management team, with proven success on Ko Samui, assures a pleasant stay. There are Jeep and motorbike rentals, Jacuzzi and Thai massage, and even a business conference facility.

CHAWENG & CHAWENG NOI BAYS

By far the largest assortment of accommodations is at Chaweng. Every inch of the beachfront is divvied up between all sorts of hotels and resorts—some are unique and lovely, some I wouldn't let my dog stay in. The following are my favorites.

Very Expensive

Imperial Samui Hotel. 86 Moo 3, Ban Chaweng Noi, Ko Samui 84320, Surat Thani. ☎ **077/422-020.** Fax 077/422-396. www.imperialhotels.com. 155 units. A/C MINIBAR TV TEL. 5,000B ($131.60) double; from 7,000B ($184.20) suite. AE, DC, MC, V. Middle of Chaweng Noi Beach.

This is one of the few luxury resorts on this long coastline; like its sister, the Boat House at Choeng Mon, it's a member of the Thai-owned Imperial Hotel chain. The hotel's two original wings are built up on a hill in a grove of coconut palms, overlooking Chaweng Noi; two newer wings, a second pool (with fewer people), and another indoor/outdoor restaurant have been added higher up the hillside.

Spacious rooms have sea views, lots of floral prints and rattan, large bathrooms with potted plants, and easy access (via steps) to the beach. Amenities include large balconies, tiled floors that seem impervious to sand, and an odd-shaped saltwater swimming pool that looks ready to spill into the bay. The staff was helpful, many with great senses of humor. Check to see if a local travel agent can get you a good rate here; it's a very pleasant resort.

Dining: Jarmjuree serves Thai food, while Le Tara features international cuisine and seafood. The poolside Le Sandy beach bar has drinks, snacks, and good sandwiches.

Amenities: The freshwater pool is relatively peaceful compared to the lively seawater pool by the beach. A diving club, Jacuzzi, water sports activities, tennis court, snooker and badminton, plus in-house videos.

Expensive

Chaweng Resort. Chaweng Beach, Ko Samui 84140, Surat Thani. ☎ **077/422-230,** or 02/651-0016 in Bangkok. Fax 077/422-378. 70 units. A/C MINIBAR TV TEL. 1,800B ($47.35) double. AE, DC, MC, V. Middle of Chaweng Beach.

Like a quaint Florida resort development, the Chaweng Resort consists of two columns of freestanding bungalows, all alike, facing each other down to the sea. Cottages are comfortable and spacious, with one queen-sized bed, one single bed, a spotless bathroom, and personal safe in each. Grounds are nicely landscaped, with a medium-sized pool and Thai/continental restaurant overlooking the fine beach. A good family choice.

✪ **Muang Kulaypan Hotel.** 100 Moo 2, Chaweng Beach Rd., Ko Samui 84320, Surat Thani. ☎ **077/230-850,** or 02/713-0668 in Bangkok. Fax 077/230-031, or 02/713-0667 in Bangkok. Kulaypan@sawadee.com. 40 units. A/C MINIBAR TV TEL. Low season 3,000B–4,500B ($78.95–$118.40) double; 5,500B ($144.75) honeymoon suite. Peak season 5,000B–7,500B ($131.60–$197.35) double; 8,500B ($223.70) honeymoon suite. AE, MC, V. Northern tip of Chaweng Beach.

I've never seen a resort like this in Thailand. Within this 3-year old two-story building, some imaginative soul has combined warm natural woods and rich local textiles with clean contemporary lines and stylistic minimalism. While rooms are sparse, it's all part of the design concept—think of it as a sort of Shaker approach to resort decor. Grace in simplicity, with some tasteful Thai touches. The four-poster platform bed is the centerpiece, and all rooms have either balconies or private gardens. Budsaba Restaurant serves all kinds of cuisine—including many vegetarian selections. The pool is just lovely.

Dining: Budsaba, their open-air restaurant and bar, serves excellent Thai cuisine.

Amenities: Beachside swimming pool with lovely landscaping, open-air fitness center, gift shop, and massage.

✪ **The Princess Village.** 101/1 Moo 3, Chaweng Beach, Ko Samui 84320, Surat Thani. ☎ **077/422-216.** Fax 077/422-382. 12 units. A/C MINIBAR. Low season (May–July, Sept–Nov) 2,400B–3,800B ($63.15–$100) double; from 4,000B ($105.25) suite. Peak season (Aug, Dec–Apr) 3,000B–4,400B ($78.95–$115.80) double; from 4,600B ($121.05) suite, plus peak-season supplement 2,500B ($65.80) per night. AE, MC, V. Middle of Chaweng Beach.

If you've wondered what sleeping in Jim Thompson's House or the Suan Pakkard Palace—both in Bangkok—might be like, try the regal Princess Village. Traditional teak houses from Ayutthaya have been restored and placed around a lushly planted garden. Several have sea views and each is on stilts above its own lotus pond; use-worn stairs lead up to a large veranda with roll-down bamboo screens.

Inside, you'll find a grand teak bed covered in embroidered silk or cotton and antique furniture and artwork worthy of the Ramas. Small, carved dressing tables and spacious bathrooms contain painted ceramics, silverware, a porcelain dish, a large khlong jar for water storage, or other Thai details amid the modern conveniences. Traditional shuttered windows on all sides have no screens, but lacy mosquito netting and a ceiling fan, combined with sea breezes, create Thai-style ventilation. There is air-conditioning for skeptics.

Dining: A lovely beachside restaurant serves breakfast and lunch, with an evening Thai and seafood barbecue dinner.

Amenities: Car and motorcycle rentals, tour counter, massage.

Moderate

New Star Bungalow. Chaweng Noi Beach, Ko Samui 84320, Surat Thani. ☎ **077/422-407.** Fax 077/422-325. 50 units. A/C. 1,800B ($47.35) double. MC, V. North of Imperial Samui Hotel on Chaweng Noi.

This newer establishment offers a wide range of facilities clustered on Chaweng Noi. All are freestanding buildings with porches. Eight deluxe bungalows sit slightly up the hill with full sea views, large rooms, air-conditioning, and charming stonework in the private bathrooms. Smaller, slightly cheaper, superior rooms with air-conditioning sit on the beach, but five rows deep, so that only the first row is really desirable (the best value). However, prices include one full-size bed and an alcove single bed, ideal for small families. Most of the rooms are air-conditioned, but some are back from the beach and small, with fans and twin beds.

Tradewinds. 17/14 Moo 3, Chaweng Beach, Ko Samui 84320, Surat Thani. ☎ **077/230-602.** Fax 077/231-247. 20 units. A/C MINIBAR. Dec 20–Jan 10 2,500B–3,000B

($65.80–$78.95); Jan 10–June and Aug 2,000B–2,500B ($52.65–$65.80); other months 1,500B–2,000B ($39.45–$52.65). AE, DC, MC, V.

In the center of Chaweng, Tradewinds has one of the best locations. Step out of the front entrance and you're in the center of it all: restaurants, clubs, shopping. However, the other side of the resort opens out to Chaweng's long lovely beach. From the higher priced bungalows you can step right off your front porch into the sand. The other bungalows are placed in shady secluded gardens, not far from the beach. The bungalows here are modern and fully furnished with large beds and rattan furnishings. Spotless and bright, they're perfect for travelers who want the intimate feeling of a bungalow village, but don't want to sacrifice modern conveniences. If you don't want to go out for a meal, their superb Thai restaurant (with Western selections as well) is situated on the beach. Tradewinds is also home of Samui's catamaran sailing center.

Inexpensive
Anchor House Bungalow. 167-1 Moo 2, Chaweng Beach, Ko Samui 84320, Surat Thani. ☎ and fax **077/230-586.** 20 units. 1,200B ($31.60) double with A/C; 200B ($5.25) double with fan. AE, MC, V. In the center of Chaweng Beach.

Recommended by the Thai Hotels Association, Anchor House is very well patronized. Swiss owned, you'll find a lot of Europeans here, attracted by friendly multilingual staff and its great location (as well as the outstanding value for money). Bungalow accommodations are simple, newly renovated, and clean.

King Bungalow. 12 Moo 2, Chaweng Beach, Ko Samui 84320, Surat Thani. ☎ **077/422-304.** Fax 077/424-029. 40 units. 1,500B ($39.45) double with A/C; 500B ($13.15) double with fan. Rates include tax and service. No credit cards. Middle of Chaweng Beach.

These simple bungalows are fairly new, spacious, and comfortable, with fans and cold-water showers. The older, smaller cottages are closer to the beach and cheaper, but lack window screens. A larger, higher-priced cottage has air-conditioning and is a better value, only about 100 feet back from the beach.

LAMAI BAY
Despite the popularity of this beach, it's slim pickins in terms of decent accommodations. Most places are bargain hunters' dreams, at the expense of comfort. And sometimes this beach can be rowdier at night than its more infamous neighbor Chaweng.

Expensive
The Pavillion Resort. Lamai Beach, Ko Samui 84140, Surat Thani. ☎ **077/424-030.** Fax 077/424-420. 50 units. A/C MINIBAR. 2,200B ($57.90) double in hotel wing; 3,000B ($78.95) double bungalow. Extra person 500B ($13.15). Rates include tax and service. AE, DC, MC, V. North end of Lamai Beach.

One of Lamai's newer facilities, this resort has attached rooms in a hotel block and Polynesian-style octagonal bungalows, all scattered throughout the beachfront grounds (limited sea views). Hotel rooms are nicely appointed, each with its own safe, and have good-sized patios for sunbathing. The larger bungalows have a campy primitive feel, as well as the comfort of a private bath and hot water. The pool and dining pavilion are right on the surf—combined with ground-floor hotel rooms, it makes a comfortable, easy access resort for travelers with disabilities. The proximity to Lamai's nightlife is a plus for most guests.

Moderate
Samui Yacht Club. Ao Tongtakian, between Chaweng and Lamai Beaches, Koh Samui 84320, Surat Thani. ☎ **077/422-225.** Fax 077/422-400. 43 units. A/C MINIBAR TV. Low season 1,200B–1,700B ($31.60–$44.75) garden bungalow; 2,100B ($55.25) sea-view bungalow. Peak season 2,000B–2,500B ($52.65–$65.80) garden bungalow; 3,000B ($78.95) sea-view bungalow. MC, V.

This tidy bungalow resort has an almost exclusive location in a small cove just north of Lamai Beach. Very quiet, and close to one of the best snorkeling areas off the island. Each bungalow has a little porch, glass wrap-around windows (with drapes), canopy beds with romantic mosquito netting, clean tiled floors, and rattan furnishings. I like the ample closet space. Best are the beachfront bungalows (which also have stereos), where you can just step off the porch into the sand. The restaurant is fine for breakfast, but I'd go out for dinner. This place is best for people who want to be left alone.

Inexpensive

Paradise Bungalows. Lamai Noi, Ko Samui 84140, Surat Thani. ☎ **077/424-290.** 37 units. 300B ($7.90) double with fan. Rates include tax and service. No credit cards. South end of Lamai Beach.

The oldest, simple, wood-and-thatch cabins on stilts have a wood platform bed, overhead light bulb, and access to toilets and cold-water showers out back. They're a bargain for their beachside location. The newer brick-and-concrete bungalows have their own cold-water plumbing. The grounds are plain but well swept, the cafe is still cheap and good, with steady reggae music, and the friendly staff maintains a safe for valuables (use it!).

The Spa Resort. 171-2 Moo 4, Lamai Beach, Ko Samui 84320, Surat Thani. ☎ **077/ 230-855.** Fax 077/424-126. 18 units. 200B–550B ($5.25–$14.45). MC, V. North of Lamai Beach.

For long-term stays or just a daytime spa visit, The Spa Resort Health Center has one of the best reputations on the island. From Chi Kung, Yoga, Thai massage, fasting, herbal cleansing, plus health and beauty face and body treatments—they'll plan everything, and at an affordable price. Their latest promotion was for Thai massage, herbal steam, cleansing facial and body wrap for only 700B ($18.40)! Accommodations are the simplest of the simple—no air-conditioning, TV, or telephones, just fans and private bathrooms. Higher priced bungalows are those situated closer to the beach. Their vegetarian restaurant serves dishes with particular care to cleansing bodies.

LAEM SET BAY

Laem Set is a small rocky cape on Samui's southeast coast, with dramatic scenery that has prompted the construction of a few hotels. The main island circle road is nearly 2km (1.2 miles) inland, but mototaxis (kids who will give you a ride on the back of their motorcycle for 25B/65¢ wait at the public minitruck junction to transport you out to the point.

✪ **Laem Set Inn.** 110 Moo 2, Hua Thanon, Laem Set, Ko Samui 84310, Surat Thani. ☎ **077/424-393.** Fax 077/424-394. www.laemset.com. 15 units. Low season $100 bungalow with A/C; $50–$60 bungalow with fan; $200–$370 suite. Peak season $120 bungalow with A/C; $60–$75 bungalow with fan; $200–$400 suite. AE, MC, V. Call for pickup or refer to paragraph above for location and information on mototaxi rides.

Lauded in fashion magazines, newspaper travel sections, and guidebooks as one of the most delightful small resorts blending a cozy hideaway into the handsome hillside. Kayaks, mountain bikes, and snorkel gear are available to explore this location's stunning scenery. The elevated pool seamlessly blends with the gulf, reflecting sea and sky. The pavilion restaurant serves gourmet fare and delicious Thai seafood.

The most exclusive accommodation is the private two-bedroom house, transplanted from a nearby island and converted to a suite, decorated with hand-hewn furniture and native grace. The Ma-rat suites are two connected bedrooms and an open, eight-bed sleeping loft draped with mosquito netting that's perfect for a bevy of children. Large porches bookend the bedrooms and provide a perch for drinking in views beyond the pounding surf of No Dog Island. The basic screened-window, fan-cooled rooms are comfortable, but less charming than the thatched bungalows, which have beds canopied with mosquito netting and a large loft above. This boutique inn (it was built as a private club) has a handcrafted feel, far from the crowds, rustic and intimate. It's unique—an ideal getaway.

WEST COAST

Le Royal Meridien Baan Taling Ngam. 295 Moo 3, Taling Ngam Beach, Ko Samui, Surat Thani 84140. ☎ **800/225-5843** in the U.S., or 077/423-019. www.lemeridien-hotels.com. 82 units. A/C MINIBAR TV TEL. $300–$330 double; $550 suite; $400–$3,000 villa. Peak season (Dec 20–Jan 10) $600–$660 double; $1,100 suite; $800–$6,000 villa. AE, DC, JCB, MC, V.

One of two five-star resorts on Ko Samui, Le Royal Meridien is peaceful and isolated on the western side of the island, about forty minutes' drive from the Samui Airport. Built up the side of a hill, the resort's accommodations include deluxe rooms and suites, as well as one- to three-bedroom beach and cliff villas. The hilltop lobby and restaurant, as well as the guest rooms, have fantastic views overlooking the sea and resort gardens, and the main pool appears to spill over its edges into the coconut palm grove below.

Guest rooms combine Thai furniture with great textiles and louvered wood paneling, including the sliding doors to the huge tanning terrace. The bathroom's highlight, an oversized tiled tub, is accented by sleek and sophisticated black slate and wood paneling. The villas are comfortable enough to be your own home and handsome enough to fill a few pages of a home design magazine. The two-bedroom villas afford the most value and convenience for families.

To be honest, there are a couple of drawbacks to Le Royal Meridien. Like all the beaches on the west side of Samui, Taling Ngam beach is small and the water is filled with coral, restricting most beach activities including swimming. And while some may seek out the privacy this resort promises, the cost is isolation from the "action" on the other parts of the island—at least a 30-minute drive away. However, the resort has kayaks, catamarans, snorkeling gear, and Windsurfers, as well as tennis courts, mountain bikes, a massage spa, PADI dive school and no fewer than seven outdoor swimming pools, in case you're worried about boredom. Dining at the hilltop Lom Talay is as gorgeous as the Thai and Asian cuisine served, while The Promenade serves locally caught fresh seafood by the beach.

WHERE TO DINE
CHAWENG BEACH

Eden Seafood. 49/1 Moo 3, Chaweng Beach. ☎ **077/422-375.** Reservations not necessary. Main courses 100B–250B ($2.65–$6.60). AE, MC, V. Daily 4pm–midnight. South end of Beach Rd.; call Eden for free pickup from hotel. SEAFOOD.

From this pleasant group of thatch pavilions—some overlooking a winding creek from several different levels—diners can choose from the freshest pomfret, red or white snapper, lobster, tiger prawns, mussels, or the catch of the day (priced per kilogram), or select from the à la carte menu. Fish is steamed, fried with sweet-and-sour sauce, grilled, or poached with garlic and peppers. Don't forget the oysters, fresh from the famed farms of Surat Thani. The guy with the Casio accompanying Thai women warbling ballads sounded like tryouts for the Twin Peaks soundtrack—a surreal but admittedly enjoyable touch. The gracious staff proudly presents an extensive drink list, which includes very sweet, Thai-produced red and Australian house wines.

○ **The Oriental Gallery.** 39/1 Moo 3, Chaweng Beach. ☎ **077/422-200.** Reservations recommended during peak season. Main courses 60B–200B ($1.60–$5.25). AE, MC, V. Daily 2–11:30pm. THAI.

Opened in 1991, the Oriental Gallery combines a fine arts and antiques gallery with a swanky little cafe. Gorgeous treasures fill the dining area, both under cover and in the small outdoor patio garden. You'll almost be too busy admiring the pieces to look at the menu. Thai dishes are prepared and presented with similar good taste, and are not too spicy for tender foreign tongues. The friendly and knowledgeable gallery owners are around to chat about Thai antiques and art, and to explain any pieces that catch your eye.

Poppies. South Chaweng Beach. ☎ **077/422-419.** Reservations recommended during peak season. Daily 7am–10pm. Entrees 80B–240B ($2.10–$6.30). AE, MC, V. THAI/ INTERNATIONAL.

Famous for its Bali-style feel, Poppies is equally famous for fresh seafood by the beach. The romantic atmosphere under the large thatch pavilion is enhanced by soft lighting and live international jazz music. Guest chefs from around the world mean the menu is ever changing, but you can be sure their seafood selections are some of the best catches around. A good place, especially if you're romancing someone special.

LAMAI BEACH

Mr. Pown Restaurant. 124/137 Moo 3, Lamai Beach. ☎ **01/970-7758.** Reservations not necessary. Seafood at market prices. 10am–10pm. MC, V. SEAFOOD.

Of all the seafood places along the main drag in Lamai, Mr. Pown is the nicest. Fresh seafood is carefully laid on ice in front of the entrance, so you can choose your own toothy fish or local lobster. A patio of a restaurant, tables near the front railing are great fun for people watching. The menu is an extensive list of seafood of all kinds prepared in many Chinese, Thai and western styles. There's also an assortment of accompanying Chinese and Thai soups, vegetable and meat dishes. Be warned, the lobster is delicious, but expensive.

The Spa Restaurant. Route 4169 between Chaweng and Lamai Beaches. ☎ **077/ 230-855**. Reservations recommended in peak season. 30B–150B (80¢–$3.95). Daily 7am–10pm. MC, V. VEGETARIAN.

I don't just recommend Spa Restaurant to vegetarians (they serve a few seafood and chicken dishes as well), but to anyone who'd like to relax with their feet in the sand, eating a healthful, tasty dish. Go for the delicious curries, or try the excellent local dishes. But leave plenty of time for an herbal steam and massage at their Health Center. I think for a vacation activity, this is tops for relaxation—an afternoon of pure indulgence, and it's good for you!

AROUND THE ISLAND

○ **Vinmarnmek.** Santiburi Dusit Resort. 12/12 Moo 1, Tambol Mae Nam, Ko Samui, Surat Thani 84330. ☎ **077/425-031.** Reservations recommended for peak season. 170B–350B ($4.45–$9.20). 10am–10pm. AE, DC, JCB, MC, V. ASIAN FUSION/SEAFOOD.

You'll think you'd died and gone to heaven. Chef Khun Tangkuay, the genius behind the menu, knows his local cuisine like the back of his hand and has studied in prestigious kitchens abroad. He combines his knowledge of many cultural tastes to invent dishes with the best elements of the East and West, crafted from the freshest local ingredients. Presentation is perfect, service is true Dusit charm, and the atmosphere is royal elegance.

KO SAMUI AFTER DARK

Some of the nights that you're on Samui, your dinner will be interrupted by a roaming pickup truck with a crackling PA system blaring out incomprehensible Thai. They're advertising local Thai boxing bouts. Grab one of their flyers for times and locations, which vary. It's iffy whether or not the TAT office can tell you about upcoming bouts, but you can try.

Some resort restaurants stage **dinner theater** with Thai performances, but the schedules change regularly. Check with the **Santiburi Dusit Resort** (☎ 077/ 425-031). They do wonderful poolside theme nights, and the food is always excellent. Ask about their Floating Market parties, where people float various Thai foods around on wooden canoes in the pool, right up to your table! Another venue known for throwing fine dinner performances is the **Imperial Samui Hotel** (☎ 077/422-020). With back-to-back shows featuring dances, Thai boxing, sword fighting, fruit and vegetable carving, and palm reading—they really put on a show.

Talk about shows—of course Ko Samui has a **drag queen review. Christy's Cabaret** (☎ 01/676-2181 cellular) on the north end of Chaweng puts on a hilarious show that's free of charge. Come well before the show starts at 11pm to get a better seat, and be prepared to make up for that free admission with cocktail prices.

For **bars and discos,** Chaweng has the action. The main fun seems to always be happening at **The Reggae Pub** (indicated on just about every island map—back from the main road around the central beach area). A huge thatch mansion, the stage thumps with some funky international acts, the dance floor jumps (even during low season they do a booming business) and the upstairs pool tables are good for sporting around. Just outside is a collection of open air bars, also found along Chaweng's beach road. Spots like **Doors Pub** and **Blues Brothers** compete for business with the dozen or so other places that look all the same. Over at Lamai Beach, the open-air bars get a little sleazier, with even less originality but more bar girls. The big nightclub in Lamai is supposed to be **Bauhaus** (located in the center of the beach road), but when I was there it was empty save a few in to watch the satellite football match.

We suggest that you have an alfresco picnic: Purchase a bottle of wine and some snacks from a grocer or your hotel, walk to the beach, spread out a sarong and gaze at the stars. But, if it happens to be Sunday afternoon, truck on over to **The Secret Garden Pub** on Big Buddha Beach (☎ 077/245-253) for live music and a barbecue on the beach. Many a famous performer has jumped up on the stage here, including a *certain* guitarist for a *certain* Grateful Dead. Call ahead of time and they can book you on one of their free shuttles (one at 3pm and another at 4pm). There have been times where the pub has hosted thousands. Not exactly "secret," but highly recommended.

SIDE TRIPS FROM KO SAMUI

Just as Ko Samui developed as a more secluded alternative to busy Phuket, Ko Phangan developed as an alternative to the alternative. After an afternoon on Ko Samui's Chaweng Beach, it's not hard to figure out why. Like the kids in Alex Garland's *The Beach,* many come to Thailand to find that island paradise that has been unspoiled by the tacky trappings of mass tourism. The message of that novel is a perfect example of what eventually happens—paradise seekers inevitably bring their own standards of comfort and values, ironically turning their utopia into what they have strived to escape. Ko Phangan, while still somewhat alternative, suffers from shoddy, unplanned development. It's sister island, Ko Tao, serves the scuba community well. Most resorts on this quiet island specialize in under-the-sea activities. For beach life, snorkeling and diving, Ko Tao remains one of the better developed choices in the Gulf of Thailand. Finally, the Mu Ko Ang Thong National Marine Park, accessed easily from Ko Samui for day trips, opens gorgeous scenery to kayakers, beach bums, snorkelers, and some adventurous campers. A far better choice for isolation and simple life.

KO PHANGAN

Ko Phangan, easily visible from Ko Samui and about two-thirds its size, with similar terrain and flora, does have beautiful beaches and inexpensive, primitive bungalows, but it's definitely not what you probably have in mind. Rather than paradise, it resembles an environmental nightmare of the nineties.

Ko Phangan is extremely popular with budget tourists; the misinformed, clean-cut kids, backpackers, and aging hippies come to find cheap beer, easy drugs, New Age massages, good street food, and $5 bungalows just a Frisbee throw away from a white sand beach. Magic mushrooms are advertised alongside nightly showings of the latest pirated VDO CDs and Zen meditation workshops.

Most tourists head for the southwestern peninsula called **Haad Rin,** which has developed into a T-shirt and vegetarian restaurant village, replete with mopeds and VDO (big-screen video) bars. On the east side of Haad Rin, there's one of the most beautiful white powder beaches, arched in a gentle cove enclosed by rocky cliffs, that you'll ever see. It's covered with garbage: plastic bags, discarded thongs, water bottles, dead coconut shells, food packaging, cigarette butts and boxes, plant matter, and myriad other fly-encrusted items are washed up from the litter-filled sea or tossed wholesale from the hillside bungalows down to the shore. No one pays enough rent to justify organized trash collection, and for generations (before the age of plastic) the Gulf of Thailand was counted on to absorb all the islanders' waste. Consider yourselves warned.

Haad Rin's claim to fame is the infamous Full Moon Party. What started about a decade ago as a secret word-of-mouth affair with only a few hundred participants has erupted into a highly publicized event—written up in every local magazine, and reported in every (ahem) travel guide. Not like I'm ruining the secret—the latest parties have hosted up to and over 7,000. A giant rave on a small beach, party people spend an entire night hopping from beachfront bars, thrashing or grooving to tracks spinned by imported DJs, smoking pot, downing mushrooms, popping Ecstacy, and whatever else is available. If you're interested in attending, boats leave from piers at either Big Buddha Beach or Bophut—leaving at regular intervals all day and night (stopping at around 1am). However, if you plan to have a place to crash, you'll have to get there well in advance (in peak season up to five or so days) to secure a bungalow. They go fast. If you don't have a place to stay, you can always join the rest who eventually collapse somewhere on the beach waiting for the morning ferries back to Samui. *A word of warning:* Busts are made regularly, by both uniformed and plainclothes police officers. Penalties include jail time, exorbitant fines, and possible persona non grata status (Thailand will revoke your travel privileges in the kingdom for the rest of your life—believe me, it happens). Also beware of theft—do yourself a favor and lock all your valuables in a hotel safe back in Ko Samui. Thieving hands are common.

GETTING THERE   By Boat   Early morning boats link Surat Thani, Ko Samui, Ko Phangan, Ko Tao, and Chumphon and back again. From Samui's Nathon Pier the trip to Ko Phangan takes just over an hour and costs 95B ($2.50). Contact Songserm in Ko Samui, 64/1–2 Nathon Pier (☎ **077/421-316,** fax 077/420-167), or Ko Phangan, 44/43 Moo 1, Thong Sala Pier (☎ **077/377-046**). If you're near Big

Buddha Beach or Bophut Beach, walk down to the pier to arrange passage on one of three daily ferries (80B/$2.10).

WHERE TO STAY & DINE   Most of Ko Phangan's development (primitive bungalows with their own electric generators and simple snack bars) is along the south coast facing Ko Samui. No one stays in the port of Thong Sala, on the southwest tip. Instead, moving east to parallel the south coast access road, you first get to **Ban Tai Beach,** a quiet, though not extraordinary, sand beach about 5km (3 miles) from Thong Sala, reachable by minitruck. The **Charm Beach Resort** offers decent sea-view bungalows for 60B to 350B ($1.60 to $9.20); the cheaper ones are quite Spartan, and the more expensive ones have toilets, cold showers, and a fan. **Green Peace** is another good inn, with acceptable accommodations for less than 100B ($2.65). Between Ban Tai and Haad Rin on the south coast there are many small, very isolated bungalows that can be reached by local long-tail boats from Thong Sala or Ban Tai. These beaches are narrow, but very quiet and clean. The **Blue Hill Bungalows,** a collection of old Thai-style A-frames rising up the gentle hill above a pretty beach (120B to 250B/$3.15 to $6.60).

Haad Rin is a narrow peninsula on the island's southeast tip, with a large number of bungalows on both the west and east sides and a footpath leading between them. The most attractive bungalows on the busier west side are **Coral Bungalows** (85B to 120B/$2.24 to $3.15), about 550 yards north of the footpath, and the **Sunset Bay Resort** (80B/$2.10 to 350B/$9.20), about 275 yards farther north. Both are more substantial and better maintained than their neighbors. The **Lighthouse Bungalows,** on the very tip of the peninsula (reached by a boardwalk built out over the sea from the west beach), are scenic-view huts for 80B ($2.10) to 350B ($9.20), but don't expect much in the way of service—anywhere on the island, for that matter.

On the east side of Haad Rin, **Serenity Bungalows** sit high above the north end of the beach. These Spartan bungalows with dramatic sea views cost 80B ($2.10) double with shared toilet, twice that with cold-water facilities. The 29 bungalow **Palita Lodge** (☎ 01/213-5445) with some private showers and toilets (150B to 500B/$3.95 to $13.15) may be the best on the littered beach, and the food is said to be quite good.

As Haad Rin gets unbearable, travelers are spreading out to other parts of the island. The **Bovy Resort** on Laem Son Beach, booked by the Bovy Market in Thong Sala, offers beachfront bungalows (85B/$2.24) with a freshwater lake for swimming nearby. **Haad Khuad Bay** and **Haad Naay Paan,** both on the remote northeast corner of the island and accessible by private minitruck from Ban Tai (about 75B/$1.95), are becoming the new hot spots.

KO TAO

Tiny **Ko Tao** has been developed so recently that it skipped the slow-growth years of thatch shacks and candlelit meals and went straight to corrugated tin roofs and VDO bars. There are a few primitive bungalows on the west and south coasts, with most activity provided by the **scuba tours** that come from Ko Samui for the best coral diving in the area. Avoid Ko Tao in the stormy fall season, when the monsoon whips up and winds cloud the normally transparent seas. For a reliable ride, call Songserm, who can get you to Ko Tao from Surat Thani, Ko Samui, Ko Phangan, or Chumphon. From Chumphon the fare is a steep 400B ($10.55), from Ko Samui 300B ($7.90) and from Ko Phangan 250B ($6.60). Songserm's contacts are as follows: Ko Samui, 64/1–2 Nathon Pier (☎ **077/421-316,** fax 077/420-167); Ko Phangan, 44/43 Moo 1, Thong Sala Pier (☎ **077/377-046**); Ko Tao, Mae Had Beach (☎ **01/229-5630;** and Chumphon, 66/1 Thatapao Rd. (☎ **077/502-023**).

Many arrive on Ko Tao via group booking with a scuba operation, who will plan accommodation, meals, diving trips, and provide apparatus. Ban's Diving has a simple resort and restaurant with nightly video entertainment. During the day, you'll be busy with either certification classes, open water practice dives, or morning and afternoon dive trips aboard their dive boat. The basic Discover Scuba course (no certification) is 1,400B ($36.85), while the open-water PADI course will run you 7,800B ($205.25), and a dive master course is 20,000B ($562.30). You can also water-ski and snorkel if you like. Call Ban's at Ko Tao (☎ 01/229-3181, fax 01/229-4465) or Ko Phangan (☎ and fax 077/337-057). Also try Buddha View, a high quality PADI outfit with instruction and dives for all levels of experience. Their bungalow accommodations seem slightly nicer, and prices are comparable (☎ 01/229-3948 cellular, fax 077/229-4693, www.buddhaview-diving.com).

MU KO ANG THONG NATIONAL MARINE PARK

Forty islands northwest of Ko Samui have recently been designated a national park. **Mu Ko Ang Thong National Marine Park** is known for its scenic beauty and rare coral reefs. Many of these islands are limestone rock towers (similar to Phangnga Bay off Phuket), once used by pirates marauding in the South China Sea.

Ko Wua Ta Lap (Sleeping Cow Island), the largest of the 40, is home to the **National Park Headquarters,** where there are several dormitory bungalows sleeping 10 to 20 people, and some two-person tents. These facilities can only be booked at the park's Bangkok office (☎ 02/579-0529), although visitors with their own camping gear can stay for free. The island has freshwater springs and a park service restaurant as well.

Mae Ko (Mother Island) is known both for its beach and Thale Noi, an inland salt-water lake that is mysteriously replenished through an undiscovered outlet to the sea. Known to the Thais as **Ang Thong,** or **Golden Bowl,** this yellowish-green lagoon gave its name to the entire archipelago.

The marine park can be reached by day-excursion boats from Nathon pier run by Samui Holiday Tours. The 450B ($11.85) tariff includes round-trip cruise and lunch; overnighters can arrange to return on another day.

6 Krabi

814km (505 miles) S of Bangkok; 165km (109 miles) E of Phuket; 42km (26 miles) E of Ko Pi Pi; 276km (171 miles) N of Satun; 211km (131 miles) SW of Surat Thani

Lately Krabi has become quite the alternative to the overdevelopment of Phuket and Ko Phi Phi, or at least has gained popularity as a nice stop along the way. But for whatever reason, people are coming. The town of Krabi isn't much to see, but as the main hub, everyone ends up here at least for a few minutes. Ferries and minivans from other destinations connect via songtao and boats to nearby Ao Nang, the center of holiday activities, and to the farther flung beaches at Rai Ley and Phra Nang, referred to collectively as Krabi Resort. Of course, they too are well developed and rather crowded in the high season, but the environment is more pristine and life is a bit more relaxed. Lesser-known islands, such as Ko Lanta, Ko Pu, and Ko Hai are certainly in the process of becoming the latest and greatest, but most party people will find the Krabi beaches just fine. If you need quiet and tranquility, you may want to head farther south to Ko Tarutao and even farther out to Ko Adang and Ko Rawi. For those planning trips to Ko Phi Phi, many resorts and businesses on the island have head offices in Krabi.

The best time to visit the Krabi area is November through April, with January and February the ideal months. The rainy season runs May through October; it's wet nearly every day, the beaches are strewn with sea debris, and many accommodations and businesses are closed.

ESSENTIALS

GETTING THERE   People arrive in Krabi one of two ways—either via Phuket and Ko Phi Phi in the Andaman, or via Surat Thani or Nakhon Si Thammarat on the eastern coast of the peninsula. Many take the latter route and stop in Krabi on the way to Phuket.

By Plane   You'll have to fly into either Phuket or Surat Thani airports then connect from there. Refer to each town's "Getting There" section for flight details.

By Boat   Twice daily trips leave from Ko Pi Pi to Krabi (trip time 2 hours; 150B/$3.95). There are two daily boats from Ko Lanta to Krabi in the high season (trip time: 1 hour; 150B/$3.95).

By Bus   Seven air-conditioned buses leave daily from Bangkok's Southern Bus Terminal (☎ **02/435-1199**) (trip time: 13 hours; 290B/$7.65 air-conditioned; 425B/$11.18 VIP) to Krabi town. For Krabi bus information call ☎ **075/611-804.** Frequently scheduled air-conditioned minibuses leave daily from Surat Thani to Krabi (trip time: 2¾ hours; ☎ **077/286-131;** 150B/$3.95). Three air-conditioned minibuses leave daily from Phuket town to Krabi (trip time: 2½ hours; 200B/$5.25).

GETTING TO KRABI RESORT   There is frequent songtao service between Krabi town and Ao Nang and Rai Lai Beach (Take the white songtao. trip time: 30 minutes; 20B/55¢). You can charter a long-tail boat near the main ferry pier in Krabi town for a more interesting trip (1 hour; 50B/$1.30), but don't forget protection from the sun.

VISITOR INFORMATION   There's a small branch of the TAT on the north end of the esplanade along the river in Krabi town (☎ **075/612-740**). Check in the small shops around town for the *Guide Map of Krabi,* by V. Hongsombud, with excellent information about the town, resort and region (60B/$1.60).

FAST FACTS   There are several **banks** on U-Trakit Road, paralleling the waterfront (to the right as you alight the ferry). The **post office** (☎ **075/611-050**) and **police station** (☎ **075/637-208**) are located on U-Trakit Road, to the left as you leave the pier. There are two **banks** in Ao Nang, near the Phranang Inn, but make sure you have cash before you head out, just to be safe.

WHAT TO SEE & DO

Krabi has a number of sites that are touted as required viewing, but while a pleasant way to spend your time, none of these are must sees. Stay on the beach and relax, take a boat trip to snorkeling sights, or join the rock climbers on the cliffs at Rai Ley.

Just outside the Felix Phra-Nang Resort, across from the songtao stop, long-tail boats wait to take you out to nearby islands, with scenery similar to the limestone outcroppings at Phangnga, 85km (53 miles) to the north. Although Phangnga is of equal appeal, the water and area around Ao Nang is considerably cleaner, and less crowded.

Be Like the Monkey

A priceless grammatical error in TAT literature about the town of Krabi declares, "In recorded times it was called 'Ban Thai Samor,' and was one of 12 towns that used, before people were widely literate, the monkey for their standard." What could they possibly have been trying to say? It probably refers to the monkey as the town's historic mascot—the name Krabi contains a reference to the beast.

Look for the sign that says "Ao Nang Long Tail Boat Club." Scenic day-trips for swimming, snorkeling, and sunbathing at nearby islands cost 800B ($21.05) for a half-day, 1,500B ($39.45) for a full day, or between 200B and 250B ($5.25 and $6.60) for an island drop-off and pickup. Rent snorkel gear from any of the tour operators along Ao Nang for 50B ($1.30) per day.

There are some dive operators, but it's a better idea to save your money and time for Ko Phi Phi or Phuket—from Krabi you'll have to travel farther to reach the better sites.

If the **limestone cliffs** above Rai Ley take your breath away, imagine how incredible it would be to climb them. One of the top climbs in the world—even the pros look forward to this one—these cliffs have views of the sea and surrounds that are so unbelievable, you'll lose your grip. Better still, you don't have to be an expert to participate. King Climbers, P.O. Box 34, Krabi 81000 (☎ 02151 pager; fax 075/612-914), 50 meters behind Ya Ya Restaurant on Ao Nang, do a half-day intro course for 700B ($18.40), a full-day course for 1,400B ($36.85), and a 3-day course for 4,000B ($105.25), all equipment included.

Okay, here's one for compulsive sightseers, or Ripley's Believe it or Not: The **Shell Cemetery,** otherwise known as Su San Hoi, is 17km (11 miles) from town in Ban Laem Pho. Is this a rare, 75-million-year-old petrified rock cliff composed of ancient seashells, or is it a slab of parking lot that broke off from the shopping area above? The best part of the visit here is that it's on the way to Ao Nang Beach.

WHERE TO STAY ON AO NANG, AO PHRA NANG & RAI LAI BEACH
VERY EXPENSIVE

✪ **Rayavadee Premier Resort.** 67 Moo 5, Susan Hoy Rd., Tambol Sai Thai, Amphur Muang, Krabi 81000. ☎ and fax **075/620740.** 100 units. A/C MINIBAR TV TEL. Low season 10,578B ($278.35) double; peak season 21,400B ($563.15) double. AE, DC, MC, V. 30 min. northwest of Krabi town by long-tail boat or 70 min. from Phuket on the resort's own launch.

Anyone who knows this resort will tell you it's one of the finest in Thailand. Handsome two-story pavilions are large and luxurious, offering every modern convenience and utmost privacy—but what's most impressive is the impeccable way each is integrated into its beautiful environment, sparing every tree and natural feature possible. Situated between the two gorgeous beaches at Rai Ley and Phra Nang, where fantastic limestone cliffs tower above, this Dusit resort takes your breath away. The staff is thoroughly professional yet relaxed, and the ambience is one of a peaceful village with paths meandering among lotus ponds and lovely landscaping. The sunsets at the big, beautiful round pool hovering over the ocean or on Rai Lai Beach itself are sensational.

Dining: The Raya Dining Room serves a sumptuous breakfast and select international cuisine until midnight. The Krua Phranang serves traditional Thai cuisine and fresh seafood for lunch and dinner overlooking Phranang Beach in a setting made for romance.

Amenities: Swimming pool, whirlpool, children's pool, two lighted tennis courts (in a beautiful setting), air-conditioned squash court, fitness center (with good views), library, video library, massage and sauna, water sports center with facilities for sailing, scuba, snorkeling, and windsurfing, personal host, room service, car rental, laundry service.

MODERATE
The Felix Phra-Nang Inn. 119 Ao Nang Beach, P.O. Box 25, Krabi 81000. ☎ **075/637-130.** Fax 075/637-134. 83 units. A/C MINIBAR TV. Low season 1,4000B ($36.85) double; peak season 2,800B ($73.70) double. DC, MC, V. Overlooking beach at Ao Nang-Rai Lai boat dock.

Felix Phra-Nang wins first runner-up in the Weirdest Hotel in Thailand Competition (First Hotel in Mae Sot took the roses down the catwalk). The outside looks like a rustic woodland lodge, built with pine and palms, with papasans (those round comfy sink-in chairs) arranged overlooking the garden. Inside, the rooms are a mix of sight sensations—Chinese tiled floors, concrete furnishings built into the walls (which are covered in stucco and seashells), and a twisted wood canopy bed hung with strands of shells. Even the bathroom is odd, with concrete and slate built-in shower and vanity. The rooms form a U around a tiny pool, while the Phra Nang's restaurant (with a varied Thai/continental menu) overlooks Ao Nang Beach.

Krabi Resort. 53-57 Patthana Rd., Ao Nang Beach, Krabi 81000. ☎ **075/637-030.** Fax 075/637-051. 75 units. A/C MINIBAR TV TEL. 1,657B ($43.60) double; 1,146B–3,850B ($30.15–$101.30) bungalow; 4,455B ($117.25) suite. Peak season (Nov–Apr) 3,584B ($94.30) double; 2,386B–6,271B ($62.80–$165.05) bungalow; 8,524B ($224.30) suite. MC, V. Overlooking beach at Ao Nang.

Unlike other accommodations in the area, the Krabi Resort is a compound with two hotel buildings in addition to a full array of bungalows. Nicely maintained grounds with a swimming pool, an aviary, playground, tennis courts, and health club mark this as a fully equipped facility. Choose the thatched-roof bungalows for privacy, especially with a sea view—these are the more expensive in the category. In addition to the property in Ao Nang, the Krabi Resort also books 18 A-frame bungalows on Poda Island; cold shower only and limited electrical service.

INEXPENSIVE

Ao Nang Villa. 125-127 U-Trakit Rd., Ao Nang Beach, Krabi 81000. ☎ and fax **075/637-270.** 75 units. 1,380B ($36.30) low season double; 2,500B ($65.80) peak season double. MC, V. On the beach, beyond the Felix.

The lesser-priced accommodations here are traditional thatched bungalows, while the more expensive units are small prefab houses. Suites have air-conditioning. The pretty, open-air restaurant's got a nice atmosphere.

7 Nakhon Si Thammarat

Nakhon Si Thammarat, one of the oldest cities in south Thailand, has long been its religious capital. Formerly known as Tamphonling, it was the center of Buddhism for the Malay peninsula during the Srivijaya Empire, about 1,200 years ago. At that time, records show that a relic of the Lord Buddha was transported from Sri Lanka to Hat Sai Kaeo, the Beach of Crystal Sand. Today, the ancient beachfront chedi built to house this relic is at Wat Mahatat, a site now 32km (20 miles) from the seaside. Tamphonling was an active port and a busy trading partner with other Asian nations. Many Indian merchants settled around the region and built Buddhist and Brahman Hindu temples.

By the late 13th century, Nakhon Si Thammarat (or Muang Nakhon), the dominant power in south Thailand, adopted the Sri Lankan school of Hinayana Buddhism. Because of Nakhon's spiritual influence, it was eventually adopted by the rulers at Sukhothai and became the country's official religion. Nakhon Si Thammarat came to be known as Muang Phra or Town of Monks.

Today, tourist facilities aren't so hot, and many people here do not speak English. While the city gets a ton of travelers every year, only about 15,000 of them are non-Malaysian.

Thai Airways flies once daily from Bangkok (☎ 02/232-8000); trip time: 1½ hours. Arrange transportation to town through the airline when you purchase your ticket. From Bangkok two daily trains stop in Nakhon Si Thammarat (trip time: 15

hours, 1,172B/$30.85 first-class cabin, 578B/$15.20 second-class berth). Contact Bangkok's Hua Lampong station at ☎ 02/223-7010. Muang Nakhon's Railway Station is in the middle of town at the end of Pak Nakhon Road (☎ 075/356-364). Private minibuses from neighboring towns travel regularly throughout the day. Contact your hotel's front desk for the minibus to Nakhon Si Thammarat—they have the most current information, and can reserve your spot in Thai. In the town, songtao and motorcycles are cheap (about 5B/15¢ per trip).

The best place to start your day is at the **TAT** office, Sanam Ma Muang, Ratchadamnoen Road (☎ 075/346-515). I found the staff knowledgeable and incredibly chatty about the region. They also have a good map with very handy information. The post office is on Siprat Road (☎ 075/356-135), as well as the Nakhorn Christian Hospital (☎ 075-356-214). If you need Internet, you can try Plug & Play on Paknakhon Road across from the market, but good luck getting a fast connection. In an emergency call the police at ☎ 075/356-026.

EXPLORING THE CITY

One of south Thailand's most revered shrines, the huge chedi at **Wat Mahatat** is said to contain relics of the Buddha brought from Sri Lanka more than a millennium ago. The chedi is 250 feet tall with a point decorated in sculpture and gold leaf. The wat's museum is composed of several small pavilions lined with dusty cupboards and old, carved woodwork. There are thousands of votive offerings, large and small Buddhas, porcelain, lacquerware, jewelry, and other presents left at the shrine (open daily 8:30am to 4:30pm). Study the site plan at the main gate, opposite the TAT office, before you begin your tour. Outside the compound walls are several small food stalls and an open-air market selling local handicrafts and souvenirs. Donations (about 20B/55¢) are gratefully accepted toward the restoration of the chedi.

Still a region noted for its **craftspeople,** Muang Nakhon offers a large variety of *niello* (silver oxidized a shiny blue black, much like polished hematite), repoussé, silver, brass work, and woven straw products made from the superfine, locally cultivated liphao vine. Bronze and metalware designs are old-fashioned, but the workmanship is very high quality and prices are reasonable. Rice serving bowls, betel-nut boxes, serving pieces, and some traditional jewelry are available at several shops on Tha Chang Road, just behind the TAT. These stores also carry a small selection of woven pillboxes, handbags, evening purses, and decorative items, as well as some newly made shadow puppets (another cottage industry). The best shops have been designated by the TAT with their logo; most take credit cards and are open daily 9am to 6pm.

A real treat in this city is a rare performance of Thai nang, or **shadow-play.** While the puppets, delicate stencils carved out of hide and held behind a skrim on sticks, are available in markets and souvenir shops everywhere, actual performances are rare. Mr. Suchart Subsin, an award-winning puppet master, keeps the faith alive at his home in this city. Suchart House, his home, is open for visitors to appreciate his collection of puppets from around the world (some as old as 200 years), and the venue for talks and performances. Call Ban Nang Thalung Suchart Subsin, 110/18 Si Thammasok Soi 3, near Wat Mahathat (☎ 075/346-394), for a demonstration (about 50B/$1.30). In late August join in the Shadow Puppet Festival.

Religious holidays are celebrated with fervor. The Hae Pha Khun, or **Homage Paying Ceremony,** is one local event celebrated for 3 days in the third lunar month (usually February or March) to honor the relics of Buddha. The Prapheni Duan Sip or **Tenth Lunar Month Festival** (usually October) runs for 10 days from the waning of the moon. Locals make elaborate preparations to receive their pret (ancestors who were condemned to hell), who take a 15-day leave to visit the living.

WHERE TO STAY & DINE

You'll find the best hotels and restaurants near the train station, in a central but seedy part of town. Around Thailand you'll hear warnings that the town can be a little rough, and to be honest, I was heckled on the street by some outgoing young guys—sort of unusual behavior. But I never felt like I was in any real danger. Still, be careful walking around after dark. Besides the hotel listed below, try the **Grand Park Hotel,** 2 blocks down from the Thai Hotel, 1204/79 Phaknakorn Road (☎ **075/317-666;** fax 075/317-674), a brand-new hotel with squeaky clean rooms—fabulous value for money (700B/$18.40 double).

Thai Hotel. 1375 Ratchadamnoen Rd., Amphur Muang, Nakhon Si Thammarat 80000. ☎ **075/341-509.** Fax 075/344-858. 251 units. A/C TV TEL. 700B ($18.40) double. AE, MC, V. Two blocks from train station.

This was one of the first decent establishments in town, but these days it seems a bit run down—catering mainly to regional businessmen all of whom seem to be loitering in the lobby at all hours of the day and night. The front desk staff speaks little English, but tries hard to please. Tidy carpeted rooms (with writing desks and private baths) aren't extraordinary, but reasonably comfortable. If you choose this place it'll be for the very convenient location alone. Their coffee shop off the lobby is busy, with inexpensive Thai, Chinese, and a few continental dishes served under a blaring TV set. The "Stop Child Prostitution" sign under the king's portrait at the elevators is a bit freakish.

If you'd like a meal outside your hotel, head for Bovorn Bazaar on Siprat Road just down from the Thai Hotel. Krour Nakorn (no telephone) an open air pavilion under the trees, is as much a folk museum as a cafeteria. Food is spicy, and the decor is cute—coconut huskers and old fishing baskets line the walls. For a jug of beer, just next door is Rock 99 Bar & Grill, across from a coffee shop and ice-cream parlor.

EN ROUTE TO SONGKHLA

If you take Route 401 southwest from Nakhon Si Thammarat, at Hua Sai it joins the coast, becoming a two-lane blacktop wedged between the South China Sea and Songkhla Lake. Soon, dense groves of papaya, coconut palm, and cashew nut trees give way to flooded paddies. This was the rice bowl of the Malay Peninsula until skyrocketing land costs and diminishing yields forced rice farmers to sell their land to tiger prawn growers. The air is abuzz with small generators driving fans to aerate the water as the fish mature. In the evening, exposed fluorescent tubes illuminate the prawn pools so villagers can watch over their investment.

East of Phattalung town, in this region and neighboring Trang Province, are the remnants of the Sakai people, an aboriginal tribe whose hilltop habitats have slowly eroded with modern development. The few dozen Sakai who've been discovered in the jungle continue to hunt with blowpipes, chasing after gibbons, their sons in tow to learn these vital skills. Motivated by the difficulty of surviving on dwindling natural resources, Sakai youth have begun going to the nearby cities to find manual work. Soon their villages will give way to condominiums, and the traditional Sakai will become the object of tribal treks for tourists.

8 Hat Yai & Songkhla

1,013km (629 miles) S of Bangkok; 350km (217 miles) S of Surat Thani

Although it's one of the most popular destinations for foreign visitors to Thailand, most Western tourists never reach Hat Yai. But millions of Malaysian and Singaporean visitors do frequent this rowdy, slightly sleazy, inexpensive, consumer-oriented playground, turning it into Thailand's most homogenous, pan-Asian city. Hat Yai's draw is a bit rough around the edges—with a nightlife full of illicit goings-on, and daytime jaunts in markets for pirate goods and knock-offs.

A major transportation hub, travelers exploring south Thailand or Malaysia will not surprisingly find themselves spending the night. If you do, don't miss the vibrant Night Market, the city's neon-lit venue for clothes and souvenir merchants, produce farmers, and food vendors. The nearby Songkhla's natural beauties—an inland lake, a long broad beach, a smattering of wooded islands, and forested rolling hills—endear it to the Thais; and it makes a relaxing, pleasant day trip.

ESSENTIALS

GETTING THERE   By Plane   Hat Yai International Airport welcomes flights from Malaysia and Singapore frequently throughout the week. Silk Air (☎ 074/ 238-901) and Malaysia Airlines (☎ 074/243-729). Thai Airways has five flights daily to Hat Yai from Bangkok direct or via Phuket (trip times: 85 minutes/45 minutes respectively). Call Thai Airways (☎ 02/232-8000 in Bangkok, 076/212-400 in Phuket, or 074/233-433 in Hat Yai). The Thai Airways minibus from the airport costs 80B ($2.10) to Hat Yai and 200B ($5.25) to Songkhla. There are regular taxis (180B/$4.75) and songtao to Hat Yai for 60B ($1.60) per person.

By Train   Five trains depart daily from Bangkok's Hua Lampong station to Hat Yai (trip time: 16½ hours; second-class sleeper 615B/$16.18, second-class seat 405B/$10.66). For information, contact Bangkok's Hua Lamphong Railway Station (☎ 02/223-7010) or the Hat Yai Station on Thammanoonvithi Road (☎ 074/ 243-705). Songtao wait outside the station which is in the middle of town, and can take you anywhere locally for about 20B (55¢).

By Bus   Six air-conditioned buses leave daily from Bangkok's Southern Bus Terminal (trip time: 14 hours; price 319B/$8.40 air-conditioned; 400B/$10.55 VIP). Call the Bangkok Southern Bus Terminal (☎ 02/435-1199), or the Hat Yai Bus Terminal (☎ 074/232-404). There is regular air-conditioned bus connection with Phuket (☎ 076/211-977) for 243B ($6.40) (trip time: 7 hours).

By Minivan   There are frequent minivans linking the cities in the south. They're very popular, and so depart regularly from about 7am to 7pm daily. The best way to make arrangements for Hat Yai is to book your seat through your hotel's front desk. Private companies service different towns, and operators rarely speak English—your hotel's staff can arrange it far more efficiently, with door-to-door service. From anywhere in the south, the trip shouldn't be any more than 100B ($2.65), a little higher from Surat Thani.

By Car   Take Highway 4 south from Bangkok to Chumphon, then Highway 41 south to Phattalung, then again Highway 4 south to Hat Yai.

VISITOR INFORMATION   The **TAT** office is at 1/1 Soi 2 Niphat Uthit 3 Rd., a few kilometers southeast of the train station (☎ 074/231-055 or 074/238-518). There are a few colorful maps available for free in hotels, most notably the Amazing Thailand Welcome to Hatyai map, with lots of nightlife adverts.

ORIENTATION   Hat Yai is a big city, but most of the tourist services can be found a few blocks on either side of the main east-west street, Thammanoonvithi, which runs from the train station east to the highway to Songkhla. There isn't much to see or do beyond the winding Klongtoey River further east, north of Suphasanrangsan Road, or south of Siphunawat Road. Niphat Uthit Road, two blocks east of the train tracks, is one of the main streets; Niphat Uthit 2 Road and Niphat Uthit 3 Road—both parallel to it to the east—are the other major thoroughfares and home of the lively Night Market.

GETTING AROUND   Walking is the easiest means to reach most tourist services in the city of Hat Yai or the sites within the town of Songkhla. To travel between them, take a minivan from the Hat Yai bus terminal on Ranchanawanit Road (☎ **074/ 232-404;** every half hour 5am to 7:30pm; 15B/40¢). It arrives in Songkhla near the central clock tower. Hat Yai's main thoroughfares are served by frequent minitruck taxis (here called tuk-tuks, even though they are bench-seat pickups); just hail one heading in your general direction and bargain; the fare should be no more than 10B for most destinations. From the taxi stand outside the Regency Hotel (☎ **074/ 350-039**) you can hire a private car to take you to Songkhla for 400B ($10.55) one way, or 500B ($13.15) round-trip. You can also negotiate trips to other cities in the region for under 500B ($13.15).

FAST FACTS   There are several bank exchanges in the city center either on or just off Niphat Uthit 2 and 3 Roads. The **post office** (☎ **074/244-480**) is on Nasatanee Road, not far from the Railway Station. For the **Hat Yai Hospital** (Rattakarn Road) phone ☎ **074/230-800. Songkhla Hospital** is on Ramwhithi Road, 4 blocks south of the clock tower (☎ **074/321-072**). For theft or loss of property, contact the **Tourist Police** (☎ **074/246-733**) at the TAT office on Soi 2, Niphat Uthit 3 Rd. For other problems, call the **Hat Yai Police** (☎ **074/243-021**) or the **Songkhla Police** (☎ **191**). There have been minor robberies (in the Night Market and from the bottom-rung hotels) and some unfortunate tourist/local drug-trade violence. The Overseas Call Office is next to the main Post Office on Niphat Songkrao Road, on the north side of town (open daily 7am to midnight).

WHAT TO SEE & DO
HAT YAI

Hat Yai's **Night Market** is the city's most interesting attraction for Western tourists. It features the variety and vitality of a Singapore Hawkers Center or an Indonesian Pasar Malam more than the bargain-hunting frenzy of Chiang Mai's Night Bazaar. Most of the activity is centered on the north stretch of Niphat Uthit 3 Road, at the intersection of Pratchathipat Road, down to Niphat Uthit 2 Road, and up around the Regent Hotel and the small sois encircling it. There are a number of barbers and beauty parlors (open till 8:30pm); sidewalk vendors selling imitation "Lacoste," "Dior," "Gucci," and other T-shirts; Chinese bakeries catering to the large, local Hokkien population; a Hawkers Center (market described above) with 30 different food stalls; the multistory, bargain-priced Ocean and Diana department stores (open 10am to 9:30pm); and myriad stalls of audio- and videotape dealers, dried shrimp and fish vendors, and housewives selling their dried sour plums, fresh durian (in June and July), and luscious, moist raisins. Thai fruits are highly prized in Malaysia and Singapore, and these stalls are usually the most crowded.

In front of the food stalls at the Hawkers Center, you'll find a Chinese Buddhist temple, **Wat Chu Chang,** where services are held in Mandarin. On the three nights of the full moon of the eighth lunar month, the **Moon Festival** is celebrated (October/November). Illuminated with lanterns, the city comes alive, and tables are set with beautifully displayed offerings for heroic ancestors. A parade and dragon dance, as well as fireworks, are always part of the holiday.

Hat Yai's sleazy side makes Malaysian and Singaporean tourists' mouths water. Their restricted societies back home make Hat Yai a tantalizing opportunity to get down and dirty—and they do. The main discos—the nucleus of activity—are **Discovery,** 408 Thammanoonvithi Rd. (☎ 074/356-710), and **Hollywood,** 94 Thammanoonvithi Rd. (☎ 074/350-775), with the best sound systems, light shows, nightly sexy performances, and the smell of marijuana permeating the air. Numerous massage parlors offer massages with the promise of much more, and deliver. The **Pink Lady Club** at the Pink Hotel complex near Hollywood (☎ 074/240-960), is popular for "special" massages and other physical recreation. The **Diana Club** (☎ 074/234-420), in the Lee Gardens Hotel on Lee Pattana Road, and the **Aladdin Club** (☎ 074/244-711), in the Kosit Hotel at 199 Niphat Uthit 2 Rd., are popular choices for a drink or dinner accompanied by pretty Thai songbirds. Charges for alcohol and "escorts" can mount up quickly.

SONGKHLA

A day trip to Songkhla should include a visit to the Songkhla National Museum, the beach, and a fresh seafood lunch. The **Songkhla National Museum** is housed in the well-restored home of Songkhla's former deputy governor on Platha Road. It was built in the Chinese style in 1878; red-tiled pagoda roofs crown a two-story, teak-beamed house centered around a large courtyard. While it was used as the State Hall for Nakhon Sim Thammarat province, it hosted royalty and the bed that King Rama V slept in is on display. On the ground floor are two framed flags from Siam—regal white elephants on a red field. The other dusty displays of local archaeological finds are not of much interest, with the exception of some finds from the Srivijaya period. The museum is two blocks east of the clock tower and taxi stand. Open Wednesday to Sunday 9am to noon and 1 to 4pm; admission is 30B (80¢). Across the street, you'll find a section of Songkhla's original fortified wall, built in 1839 under King Rama III.

There are many impressive wats in this town, once a distinguished merchant and maritime center. **Wat Matchimawat** on the Saiburi Road, built in the 16th century, includes a classic temple (to the left as you enter) in the style of Bangkok's royal Wat Phra Kaeo. The frescoes within are rumored to be painted by the same royal artists. There is another, newer pavilion housing a collection of votive offerings and relics from regional archaeological sites. If the door isn't open (Wednesday through Sunday 9am to 4:30pm), ask the abbot for the key. The wat is about a 15-minute walk south, down Ramvithi Road, from the clock tower.

Laem Samila, 3km (1.8 miles) north of the Municipal Market on Ratchadamnoen Road, is the quintessential Asian beach. Thai, Malay, Singaporean, and Chinese tourists descend from minibuses with their cameras and children. They step off the beachside walkway to inspect the clean gold sand, climb on the bronze mermaid statue for photos, or look more closely at Cat and Rat (the nearer, humpbacked ones) islands. If the weather's clear and seas are calm (usually from April to October), they may spread tatami mats on the sand for a picnic or allow their children to swim. Otherwise, it's straight to one of the seafood restaurants where fish, crab, and prawns can be selected for cooking.

Up above Samila is **Khao Noi Hill,** a forested slope whose foot is decorated with topiary animals and has swings; its peak (a hardy 45-minute walk) provides great views over land and sea.

Some visitors come solely to study at the ✪ **Institute for Southern Thai Studies,** part of Srinakharinwirot University (☎ 074/331-184). This well-documented collection and research facility is housed in 24 modern Thai-style pavilions on wooded Ko Yo Island, across the lake from the main town of Songkhla. At the roadside information building, pick up a site plan and brochure, then head up the steep hill to the first room of pottery and proceed through the collections of beads, cloth weaving, metalwork, religious displays, model boats, instruments, folk crafts, weapons, and household objects. If you're interested in the very old, traditional Thai-Malay culture, you'll want to spend a few hours here. There's a cafeteria on the premises and nice gardens.

The museum is open daily 8:30am to 5pm; admission is 50B ($1.30). It's 28km (17 miles; a 30-minute drive) from either Hat Yai or Songkhla; public buses to Ko Yo cost 10B (25¢) and group minitruck taxis cost 25B (65¢); a more convenient private taxi will cost about 500B ($13.15) for a half day.

WHERE TO STAY

Hat Yai has dozens of hotels, many not well suited to Western tastes. Here are a few convenient recommendations, plus two choices in Songkhla for those who want a peaceful retreat.

BP Samila Beach Hotel. 8 Ratchadumnurn Rd., Amphur Muang, Songkhla 90000. ☎ **074/440-222.** Fax 074/440-442. 200 units. A/C MINIBAR TV TEL. 1,150B ($30.25) mountain-view double; 1,250B ($32.90) seaview double. AE, DC, JCB, MC, V. Along Samila Beach, northeast of town.

By the time I arrived in Songkhla, all anyone could talk about was Samila, the newest resort opening along the beach strip. Having checked in before the soft opening, I didn't get the chance to see the place in full force—I was one of few guests as facilities were still being completed. Still, the place is full of promise. A landmark on the beach, the large hotel has rooms with balconies, sisal carpeting, and sea tone schemes, plus bathrooms have separate tubs. To be truthful, the beach here isn't the finest in the land, but it is more peaceful than other tourist spots along the gulf. By the time this hits the bookshelves, Samila's two swimming pools, restaurants, and water-sports center should be fully functional.

Cathay Guest House. 93/1 Niphat Uthit 2 Rd., Hat Yai 90110. ☎ **074/243-815.** 28 units. 80B ($2.10) dorm bed; 220B ($5.80) double. Rates include tax and service. No credit cards. Two blocks east of train station, 15 meters south of Thammanoonvithi Rd.

The extensive bulletin board tells you that this is one crossroad for budget Asia travelers. The Cathay offers travel services, such as bus and train tickets and hotel bookings (for a small commission), and provides clean rooms with fan and private cold shower and toilet, at very cheap prices. Get there at breakfast if you want a room; it's pretty much first come, first served.

The Florida Hotel. 8 Sripoovanart Rd., Hat Yai 90110. ☎ **074/234-555.** Fax 074/234-553. 119 units. A/C MINIBAR TV TEL. 1,000B ($26.30) double. AE, MC, V. South end of town between Niphat Uthit 2 and 3 rds.

If you're surprised to find a hotel named Florida, you'll be equally surprised at how nice it is. It's a first-class place with all the expected services, and large, comfortable, modern, and well-priced rooms. The staff is friendly and professional. The Florida has a popular outdoor restaurant and is fairly well located, making it more quiet and peaceful than many other accommodations in the city—and only a 15-minute walk south of the train station.

Narai Hotel. 14 Chai Khao Rd., Songkhla 90000. ☎ **074/311-078.** 13 units. 200B ($5.25) double. No credit cards. South of town, 5-min. walk from beach.

This old house, like a country cottage set away from the town but near the beach and seafood restaurants, will please those in search of quiet and simplicity. *Tip:* The friendly proprietor is a good source of information about local sights and events.

The Regency Hotel. 23 Prachathipat Rd., Hat Yai 90100. ☎ **074/234-400.** Fax 074/234-102. 436 units. A/C MINIBAR TV TEL. 1,300B ($34.20) old wing double; 3,000B ($78.95) new wing double. AE, DC, MC, V. North end of Sangchan Rd.

The best address in Hat Yai, near the night market and shopping, plus the option of two types of rooms depending on your budget. Regency's new wing sports some of the finest rooms in the city—with plenty of space and modern touches like marble bathrooms and fully stocked minibars. The older wing is definitely older—rooms are smaller, more worn-in, yet are still quite acceptable. Ask about rates as low as 750B ($19.75) per night for one of these rooms. The old wing does get a bit rowdy, however.

Sook Som Boom 2 Hotel. 18 Siburee Rd., Songkhla 90000. ☎ **074/311-149.** Fax 074/321-406. 53 units. A/C 500B ($13.15) double. No credit cards. Near the center of town, 1 block west of the clock tower.

One of the better, more pleasant alternatives in town—not to be confused with the Sook Som Boon #1, a shabbier, older place. Choose this place for the location, close to transportation and sights within town.

WHERE TO DINE

The **Hawkers Center (market),** a clean, hygienic street-food extravaganza, opens about 6pm but comes to life after about 8:30pm. Head for the northern part of Niphat Uthit 3 Road, at the intersection of Pratchathipat Road, down to Niphat Uthit 2 Road, and up around the Regent Hotel and the small sois encircling it. Chefs prepare their specialties in chrome steam carts. Roam from cart to cart, assembling a full meal, then settle in at anyone's table. Go for the crab-and-egg noodle soup, fried spring rolls, crisp-fried black-eyed pea cakes, steamed vegetable dumplings, taro root and rice noodle cakes, and vegetable egg foo yung. Many vendors sell sweets and condiments, particularly brightly colored jellies, stewed sweet corn and stewed fruits, and Chinese-style sugar donuts. Sample everything.

If you'd like to try some of the region's Malay specialties, head for **Salma Makanan Muslim Seafood Bakar** (☎ 074/350-216) on Pratchathipat Road 1 block east of the Regency Hotel. A spotless coffee shop, you can rest for an afternoon tea and try a light roti canai—a fried flat bread with dipping curry, or go for the more substantial murtaba, a roti wrapped around savory meats. **Ta-Lae Thai Seafood,** about a 5-minute taxi ride from the town's center, Ratch Uthat Road near Hansa Café (☎ 074/359-682), is probably the most famous place for southern Thai style seafood in the city. Al fresco dining, the atmosphere is like a carnival on busy nights, and food is fresh and well prepared, and prices aren't too bad (if only slightly more expensive).

Seafood in Songkhla is incredible. Laem Son Onn, the area just to the northwest of Samila Beach has about a dozen food vendors under the pine trees near the water. Local seafood here is fresh and delicious, prepared in simple styles. Among the best choices are *pla klapong,* a fleshy white fish cooked in a red chile sauce with bits of pork; steamed crabs served plain but very tender; and fiery *tom yam* with shrimp in soothing coconut milk. Prices average 80B to 160B ($2.10 to $4.20) for seafood.

In Songkhla town, there are a few bar and restaurant combos, supported by the demands of a large expatriate community working the oil industry here. While their numbers have grown smaller in the face of economic troubles, many of these establishments are still open and not half bad. Places like **The Skillet,** 2/8 Saket Rd. (☎ 074/314-784), **Parlang Bar & Restaurant,** 5/14 Sai-Ngam Road (☎ 074/440-801), and **Karl's Place,** 9 Srisuda Rd. (☎ 074/326-217), are good places to drink and eat Western or Thai food, and meet expatriates.

9 South to Malaysia: Pattani, Narathiwat & Sungai Kolok

From Bangkok: 1,055km (656 miles) S to Pattani; 1,149km (714 miles) S to Narathiwat; 1,215km (755 miles) S to Sungai Kolok

In Isan you can't help but notice influences spilled over from neighboring Laos and Cambodia, just the same as there are Burmese elements all over the northern parts of Thailand. Southern Thailand is no different. With deep historical ties to Malaysia, southern Thai provinces are undoubtedly linked to their southern neighbor through religious affiliation, cultural flair, and cuisine. In fact, before a 1909 agreement with the British colonial government in Malaya, Malaysia's northern states of Kelantan, Kedah, and Terengganu were controlled by Siam. In the agreement, the border was drawn at the Kolok River (Sungai Kolok), dividing this common people between two countries.

To understand this part of Thailand's south, it's helpful to understand a little of what is going on on the other side of the border. Kelantan is a unique state in Malaysia. Cut off from the colonial developments and booming trade of the peninsula's west coast, Kelantan developed its own character—very conservative, very Muslim. The government in this state is today the only Malaysian local government led by the Islamic party, and the law of Islam is stronger than in any other part of the country. In Kelantan there are no bars or discos, and women are forbidden from dancing or performing in public. It is widely understood, however, that many Malaysian men from this area cross the border to take advantage of Thailand's open attitude toward wine and women. Border towns such as Sungai Kolok, have become mini Tijuanas. (Hat Yai, just to the north, is the epitome of this phenomenon).

If you venture beyond the sleazy bars and massage parlors, there's a heritage here unique to Thailand—a Muslim heritage. The Thai Muslim population is large in this area, yet struggles to have a voice in Thai political policy. A minority for sure, despite deep Buddhist traditions in the rest of the country, their rights are protected by the state. The king, as protector of faith, holds it as his responsibility to ensure Muslim religious freedoms just the same as Buddhist.

While ports elsewhere in Southeast Asia were fast becoming cosmopolitan trading centers, this region was primarily bypassed, save for a few Arab, Indian, and Chinese traders. As some settled here, you find an interesting, yet subtle blend of international character. Chinese temples, Malay mosques (masjids), and Thai wats are common in each town. You won't find handicrafts like in other parts of the country, instead Malay styles of silverworks, basket weaving and traditional batik cloth prints reign. Shopping for sarongs is especially recommended here. And while Thai food still dominates most menus, almost every restaurant serves Chinese dishes, and you'll find small eateries serving up halal Muslim food from Malaysia. Look for yummy murtabak—a fried flat bread wrapped around chicken or mutton served with delicious curry gravy, or nasi kebu, a rice dish with curry chicken that you smother in a sweet chile sauce (usually served in coffee shops and markets—a real local specialty).

You'll find the people in the south are more conservative. I recommend wearing less revealing clothing here, especially for women. And ladies, if you plan to visit any of the mosques, you must wear a long skirt or slacks, long sleeved shirt and a scarf covering your head, as required by Islamic law. Women are also not permitted to enter a mosque during menses, and are forbidden from entering the main prayer hall.

ESSENTIALS

GETTING THERE **By Plane** Thai Airways connects Bangkok to Narathiwat via Trang once daily (trip time: about 3 hours). In Bangkok, **Thai Airways** on Lan Luang Road can be phoned at (☎ 02/232-8000), and in Narathiwat at 322-4 Phupha Phakdi Rd. (☎ 073/511-161). Although there's no airport in Sungai Kolok, you can book tickets through an authorized agent located behind the Genting Hotel at 53 Charoenkhet Rd., Soi 1 (☎ 073/611-417). For the airport in Narathiwat call ☎ 073/514-570.

Thai Airways provides shuttles to and from the airport. Most times the shuttle is waiting for the flight to disembark and will charge up to 80B ($2.10) for trips to town. To get to the airport from town, call the appropriate Thai Airways office and request pick up at your hotel.

By Train Two trains a day depart from Bangkok to Sungai Kolok (trip time: 20 hours; 457B/$12.05 second-class seat, 617B/$16.25 second-class sleeper). In Bangkok call **Hua Lamphong Railway Station** at (☎ 02/223-7010 or 02/223-7020). The **Sungai Kolok Railway Station** (☎ 073/614-060) is on Asia 18 Road, across from the Genting Hotel.

By Minivan While public buses run between towns, you won't find air-conditioned coaches. Group taxis also make runs, but sometimes you'll be stuffed inside with up to five other passengers. The most common, and best, way to get around via air-conditioned minivans. Most services begin at around 6am and stop at 7pm. Fares range from 60B to 100B ($1.60 to $2.65) for jumps in between destinations. What I really like about minivan services is they'll pick you up at your hotel and drop you off wherever you want to go in your destination town without a problem. Reservation information is given for each town in the appropriate section, but I suggest you let your hotel reception call to make the booking for you, to prevent language barrier problems.

By Car Take Highway 4 south from Bangkok to Chumphon, then Highway 4/41 south to Hat Yai/Songkhla, then Route 42 south to Pattani, Narathiwat, and Sungai Kolok.

DEPARTING/ENTERING THAILAND The Thai/Malay land border is open daily 5am to 9pm Thailand time or 6am to 10pm Malaysia time. The **immigration office** in Sungai Kolok can be reached at ☎ 073/611-231.

If you want to hop over the border to Malaysia you must have a valid passport. Citizens of the United States do not need visas for tourist and business visits. Citizens of Canada, Australia, New Zealand, and the United Kingdom do not require a visa for tourist or business visits not exceeding 1 month.

If you are entering Thailand from this point either by train or bus (see "Getting There" in chapter 2), visa applications are not required if you are staying up to 30 days and are a national of 41 designated countries, including Australia, Canada, Ireland, New Zealand, the United Kingdom, and the United States (New Zealanders may stay up to 3 months.)

VISITOR INFORMATION There's a Tourism Authority of Thailand office in Narathiwat, but it's not very conveniently located. On Takbai Road just over the Bangnara River, you can call them at ☎ 073/516-144 or head out there on a motorcycle taxi. In Sungai Kolok, the TAT office is just near the border crossing on Asia 18 Road (☎ 073/612-126).

GETTING AROUND By and large, these places are small, and can be walked pretty easily, but the best way around is by motorcycle taxi—the guys in the colored vests—who'll charge between 5B and 20B (15¢ and 55¢) for most trips around town. I did have a hard time finding drivers in Pattani, so you may want to stick to songtao here, the minitrucks that cruise the streets looking for fares. Like motorcycles, trips on the minitrucks are around 5B to 20B (15¢ to 55¢), depending on how far you go.

PATTANI

Due south of Songkhla, past miles of coconut palm plantations and pine trees along the winding coastal Route 408, is Pattani province. Once famous for having a woman ruler, today Pattani is primarily agricultural oriented, with palm oil and rubber plantations as well as fruit orchards dominating the economy. Within the town, the small, orange-tiled, green-roofed, onion-dome **Central Mosque** on Pipit Road provides the cultural and religious center for the city's Muslim community. Its arched stained-glass windows and two slender minarets distinguish it from an otherwise typical Thai townscape.

Along the Pattani River, which dissects the city, some older wooden houses on stilts are moored next to long-tailed, striped *korlae* (fishing boats).

On Arnoru Road, the Leng Chu Kieng Shrine is a peek into the Chinese heritage behind this small town. Also called the Lim Korn Niew Chinese temple, for the local Chinese goddess Korniew, a local legendary figure who's image is immortalized within (see below).

The Kruese Mosque, on the Pattani-Narathiwat Road (Route 42) about 7km outside of town, a simple and slightly dilapidated mosque constructed of brick and mortar in Arabic style, was designed by Lim To Kiem, the goddess Korn New's older brother. According to local legend, Korn Niew tried to persuade her brother to return to China. Her failure made her so disturbed that she killed herself under a cashew tree, but not before cursing the temple to never be completed. To be sure, the temple's dome remains unfinished to this day. Korn New's body is buried beside the building.

Thirty kilometers (18 miles) south of town, near the Hat Yai-Sungai Kolok Railroad line, is the 300-year-old **Wat Chang Hai,** built to commemorate a very famous Thai monk who's said to have crossed the sea by foot, distilling salt from the water with every step. Everywhere you'll see fish farms, with large nets draped over raised platforms to control the amount of heat and sun the growing fish will receive.

To get to Pattani from any southern city or town is easy. Private minivans shuttle passengers at regular intervals from about 6am to 7pm. There are many private companies for each route—I recommend you make your booking through your hotel's front desk. They always have the latest contacts for where you want to go, and will simplify the arrangement for you, as the minivan operators rarely speak English. Vans will pick you up at your hotel and drop you at your hotel in Pattani, no problem.

In case there's an emergency while you're in town, the **Pattani Hospital** is on Nongchik Road (☎ **073/331-860**).

WHERE TO STAY & DINE

My Gardens Hotel. 8/28 Charoenprathet Rd., Amphur Muang 94000, Pattani. ☎ **073/331-055.** Fax 073/336-217. 135 units. A/C TV TEL. 600B ($15.80) double with A/C; 550B ($14.45) double with fan. Rates include tax and service. MC, V. North side of town at clock tower.

My Gardens is a contemporary high-rise in the town center, with rooms that are curiously Chinese in style. Or maybe it's just the bright red wall to wall carpeting that gives it a Sino-style feel. Bathrooms are like new, with fresh yellow tiles and longbaths.

Few of the staff speak English, but manage to help you out, or to grab someone who knows how to communicate a little.

The Pailin hotel restaurant is your best bet in town. Fashioned like a diner, with booths along the windows overlooking Charoenprathet, it's not much for the eye, but the menu's got plenty of Thai dishes, and an equal amount of Chinese specialties.

NARATHIWAT

Narathiwat, meaning "Home of Good People," was named by Rama VI. Like it's neighboring province, Pattani, the main industry here is agriculture—palm oil, coconuts, rubber and fruits, as well as fishing. While there's not much to do in Narathiwat town, there are some great cultural treats just outside town. From the central area, a 2-kilometer walk north on the main street, Pichitbamrung, leads to **Narathat Beach,** a broad, fine sand stretch shaded by coconut trees, which define a public park. In the rainy season (July to December), the seas will likely be rough, but it's the Muslim sense of modesty that deters most visitors from having a swim.

For boating enthusiasts, also north of town, about 16km north near the Narathiwat Airport, Banthorn, a fishing village, is known for boat building. The korlae boats, long fishing boats in elaborate colors and decorations, are made here, both real-sized and boat models for purchase as souvenirs.

The Yahkang fishing village (also known as Bangnara village), about 4km to the south of town, seen from the Bangnara River bridge is worth a short trip out of the town proper. The naked young boys playing in the water, wiry elders polishing their korlae (boats), and women with covered heads mending fishing nets, are rare glimpses of an almost bygone rural life. To the right just as you cross the bridge, a batik factory for which Narathiwat is famous rolls out huge quantities of unique batiks in traditional patterns and colors.

Narathiwat's other unexpected treat is at **Khao Kong Hill,** about 8km (5 miles) south of town (along the same road as Yahkang), where the Phra Buddha Taksin Ming Mongkol, a 24-meter-tall rotund Buddha, gazes serenely over the rice paddy.

To see the sights outside of town, it's easy to charter a taxi and provide the driver with a list of the places you wish to see. It'll cost around 200B ($5.25) including waiting time. The taxi stand is on Pichitbamrung Road (☎ 073/513-470).

To get around between Narathiwat, Pattani, Sungai Kolok, Songkhla, Hat Yai, or any other southern town, I recommend the same situation for travel for each place. Wherever you happen to be, chat up the front desk of your hotel to arrange an air-conditioned minivan to your destination. Every time I've called these numbers myself, my Thai is so bad the minivan operator must think I'm ordering a ham sandwich served in a shoe.

Your major **banks** are on Phupapakdee Road, down from the Narathiwat Hotel. The **post office** is on Pichitbamrung Road (☎ 073/511-093), across from City Hall. **Narathiwat Hospital** (☎ 073/513-480) is just south of town on Rangaemanka Road. For **police** emergencies call ☎ 073/511-236.

SRINDHORN PEAT SWAMP FOREST

While evergreen peat swamp forest reserves exist in other provinces, Srindhorn is the largest protected forest of this type—home to many varieties of wildlife. The forest, named after Her Royal Highness Princess Maha Chakri Srindhorn, was on the brink of destruction before the royal family stepped in to found the Srindhorn Peat Swamp Forest Nature Study and Research Center to study the life here. With far more diversity than other geological zones, some of the plants and creatures of the swamp are unique to this small area, such as the sealing wax palm and a great number of orchid species. Small wildlife is abundant, such as the macaque, otter, flying squirrel, civet, and crocodile. Larger animals like the Malaysia sun bear and black panther manage to survive in the damp forest. With a total 50 types of mammals, 195 types of birds, 30 types of reptiles, and 14 types of amphibians, the 125,000 rai preserve throbs with life.

Nature treks begin at the Research Center, where visitors can learn about the paths, peat swamps, and the wildlife they're likely to see. The nature study trail is a board-walk snaking through the forest with stops to educate hikers about the origins of peat swamp forests, unique soil and root networks, aquatic life, vegetation, and land animals. A suspension bridge and bird-watching tower provide great views and photo ops.

It's best to visit the preserve between February and April for ideal weather. Admission is free. For more information, contact the **Srindhorn Peat Swamp Forest Nature Study and Research Center** at P.O. Box 37 Sungai Kolok, Narathiwat 96120 (☎ **01/715-0159** cellular). It is reachable via both Narathiwat or Sungai Kolok—arrange trips with the help of the TAT office in either city.

WHERE TO STAY & DINE

Tanyong Hotel. 16/1 Sopapisai Rd., Amphur Muang 96000, Narathiwat. ☎ **073/511-477.** Fax 073/511-834. 84 units. A/C MINIBAR TV TEL. 600B ($15.80) double. MC, V. Located in the town center, 2 blocks from the clock tower.

This is a surprisingly fine hotel for such a small city. Large rooms are bright and comfortable; the staff speaks little English but tries hard to please. Beware, the shower heads are placed low, so you'll need to be a contortionist to rinse the top of your head. There is a pool hall (open daily 9am to 2am), the Ladybird Ancient Massage Parlor, a barbershop, and an espresso bar off the lobby.

The Tanyong Restaurant serves a few continental and Chinese dishes to round out its terrific Thai menu. Locally raised duck (served grilled or cooked in a brown sauce) and fresh seafood are popular, but oh so spicy! Previous editions of this book reported a nightly parade of lovely young girls in the wildest prom outfits belting out Thai love songs to the accompaniment of an electric synthesizer. You'll be thrilled to know they're still going strong.

SUNGAI KOLOK

The Thai town with the Malay name, Sungai Kolok, named for the Kolok River that separates Thailand from Malaysia, is a typical border town. Sign boards start to display Thai and Malay messages, both languages are spoken, and either currency is accepted as legal tender. At the time of this writing one Malaysian ringgit was worth about 10 Thai baht. Many shops and taxi drivers quote prices in Malaysian "dollars," but will accept Thai equivalency.

A much smaller and not as glitzy version of Hat Yai, the purpose of tourism here is basically the same. Malaysian tour groups come for day trips to shop and see the sights of Narathiwat, and Malaysian men venture over the border to spend a little time in liberated Thailand. You'll see all sorts of bars, lounges, and massage parlors that cater to these tourists.

There's a little shopping around. Behind the Genting Hotel begins a sprawl of fruit and vegetable vendors. Look for the man who sells the beautiful songbirds in delicate cages. A day market nearby displays Chinese-made cheap chic clothing for a song. In the town streets beyond wander past clothing shops with ready-made batik clothing, and some really nice selections of sarongs, both in batiks for ladies and madras plaids for gents.

To get to Sungai Kolok, arrange minivan service through your hotel's front desk for door to door service. The cost is usually under 100B ($2.65) (more if you're coming all the way from Hat Yai). Train service between Sungai Kolok and Hat Yai is frequent, but make sure you catch the daily air-conditioned express train at 2pm, otherwise you'll be riding for hours on an open air train with wooden benches and people squirming all over the place to make room for piles of produce and shopping finds.

Within Sungai Kolok, banks are clustered mainly at Charoenket Road in the center of town. The **post office** (☎ 073/611-141) is on Thespathom Road near the Plaza Hotel. The **Sungai Kolok Hospital** (☎ 073/611-109) is on Saithong 6 Road, across the railroad tracks from the customs office. If you should need the **Tourist Police**, dial ☎ 073/612-008.

WHERE TO STAY & DINE

Genting Hotel. 141 Asia Rd. 18, Sungai Kolok 96120, Narathiwat. ☎ **073/613231.** 190 units. A/C MINIBAR TV TEL. 450B ($11.85) double. MC, V. 2 blocks from the border crossing.

Most of this border town's hotels do a brisk business by the hour. The modern, clean, and comfortable Genting has a pool, pool hall, massage parlor, and lively Chatvarin Restaurant, with a mixed Thai/continental/Chinese menu, plus live bands. It's located a short distance from the TAT office, and just behind, the streets of the town open all sorts of small town possibilities.

The hotel's restaurant is a safe choice, and while the food is not bad, the service is lousy. Fast, but not very willing to listen to a special request.

Out and about, you'll find a number of coffee shops with local cuisine.

10 Tarutao National Park

973km (603 miles) S of Bangkok; 30km (19 miles) W of Ban Pak Bara; 276km (171 miles) S of Krabi; 100km (62 miles) S of Trang

The 51-island chain known as Tarutao National Park is located off of Thailand's far southwestern coast, only a few miles from the Malaysian border in the Strait of Malacca (leading out to the Indian Ocean). This fringe setting goes a long way toward explaining Tarutao's legacy. Originally settled by sea gypsies, it wasn't until 1939 that the main island received its first load of settlers. These pioneers were political detainees, enemies of the incipient Thai democracy, who were given the charge of constructing their own prison. More prisoners arrived and the facilities spread to other parts of the island. After the Japanese invasion of Thailand during World War II, the chain of command to Tarutao was broken, and the prisoners and guards turned the place into a Devil's Island, preying on passing ships for booty. These feared pirates patrolled the Strait of Malacca until British troops, stationed in nearby Malaya, overcame the guerrilla forces to return the island to Thai peasants; they in turn established farms and plantations. The spirit of resistance continued well into the 1980s—and the battle is still being played out—between environmentalists and proponents of the national park, and factions of the local fishing industry. Some illegal trawlers have used destructive means (such as dynamiting coral reefs) to pursue their trade. As recently as 1981, illegal fishermen fired on park service workers in their offshore patrol boats.

Perhaps it's due to the chain's pioneering legacy or, more to the point, its Wild West environment, but it has been spared the scars of mass tourism. Due to the heroic efforts of both Thai and foreign workers, and especially Mr. Booruang Saison (the champion of Thailand's burgeoning national park system), the islands are protected for now, but there are plans to begin development. Currently there's a limit on the number of visitors to Tarutao at any one time (more than 10,000 travelers come to the chain annually), so it's important to check with the authorities to ensure that you'll be allowed to stay overnight.

Once there, you'll find islands the likes of which you thought disappeared decades ago. With only rough accommodations and facilities and few if any vehicles, life on Tarutao's islands is as primitive and pristine as exists in the country. Those in search of serenity, tranquil bays, long hiking trails, nearly deserted beaches, a seemingly endless number of islands, good snorkeling and diving, and cheap travel will think they've died and gone to heaven. Go now or forever hold your peace.

The season for travel to Tarutao and beyond is November through May. Monsoons dump rain during the balance of the year, severely hampering boat travel in the area.

GETTING THERE   The jumping-off point for Tarutao is Ban Pak Bara, a port city roughly 100km (62 miles) south of Trang. The best access to the park is through Hat Yai. Thai Airways has five flights daily to Hat Yai from Bangkok direct or via Phuket (trip times: 85 minutes/45 minutes respectively). Call Thai Airways (☎ **02/232-8000** in Bangkok, 076/212-400 in Phuket, or 074/233-433 in Hat Yai).

From Hat Yai, you can take the public government bus service, but you'll have to transfer buses in the town of Satun to continue the trip. Instead, I recommend a direct minivan from Hat Yai to Pak Bara. They leave every hour from the stand at Prachathipat Road (☎ **074/245-655**) between 6am and 4pm.

The Pak Bara–Tarutao boat service will only carry you to the islands during mid-November through mid-May. Other times of the year, the waters are too choppy, and everything's closed down for the monsoon season. The trip takes 2 hours, but there are only two daily boats—one at 10am and one at 3pm (110B/$2.90). Since the van service takes about 2 hours from Hat Yai, make sure you leave the town around either 7am or noon to make sure you catch these boats.

By Car   From Bangkok, take Route 4 south to Pettalung; then travel west on Route 406 to Satun Province and then northwest on Route 4073 at Chalung for Ban Pak Bara, where you can take a songtao to Ban Pak Bara.

VISITOR INFORMATION   The governing entity of the Tarutao archipelago is the **National Park Division,** Department of Forestry in Bangkok (☎ **02/579-0529**). There's a **Tarutao National Park** office in Ban Pak Bara (☎ **074/781-285**), adjacent to the pier. The national Park Division handles all accommodations on the island, which are extremely basic, fan-cooled huts with cold-water showers. Reservations may be made with either office; however, the local office has the most up-to-date information on the islands.

ISLAND ORIENTATION   Boats to Ko Tarutao arrive at Ao Pante, the island's most important settlement, near the northwest end of the island, where you'll find the park headquarters, visitors center, tourist police, emergency services, sea turtle nursing ponds, food, and basic accommodations. Tarutao is a lush and rocky place, almost 180 square miles in area. The interior is covered half by rain forest and the balance by mangrove swamps, plains, and mountains.

The visitor's center on Ao Pante has a few basic supplies, a small library, and sometimes a useful guide, *The Traveler's Adventure Handbook to Tarutao.* The park rangers are friendly and a few of them speak some English, and there are usually a few "young old hands" hanging about to give you some advice. The island's two most popular beaches, Ao Jak and Ao Sone, are to the south.

The archipelago's next largest island is Ko Adang, about 40km (25 miles) west, and Ko Rawi lies just beyond it; both of these are surrounded by many smaller islands, such as Ko Lipe, Ko Kra, Ko Jabang, and Ko Yang, all considered fine diving and snorkeling destinations due to their intact coral reefs.

GETTING AROUND   Other than hiking, the only other means of transport is via long-tail boats. Most people pool their resources to hire a boat, especially for long-distance trips. Expect to pay about 250B ($6.60) for 10 people to travel south to Ao Sone Beach.

As for getting between islands, there's a mail boat that usually leaves Ao Pante for Ko Adang and smaller Ko Lipe, to its south, three times a week January to April. Be warned that the water can get quite rough, and the boats are small and frequently have problems navigating the seas. In some cases they will simply not run or will turn back after reaching open water. It's a good idea to plan on adding a few days to your itinerary if you intend to visit these areas. Even the two diminutive boats that shuttle people between Ban Pak Bara and Tarutao are on the dodgy side, which is all the more obvious when the weather gets rough. Be prepared to improvise.

WHAT TO SEE & DO IN AO PANTE

There are several exhibits that are worth visiting at the park headquarters. The library and adjacent visitors center have interesting displays about the ecology and history of Ko Tarutao, as well as books on the subject; open daily 8am to dusk. Nearby, to the left as you alight from the pier, are the **Sea Turtle Nursing Ponds.** Green, hawksbill, and Pacific Ridley turtles in various stages of growth (from 2 to 7 years old) swim in shallow pools; try to visit during feeding time. This is part of the park's greater program to repopulate the ever-dwindling number of these species.

EXPLORING THE KO TARUTAO

At low tide it's possible to walk a long way down the west coast of Ko Tarutao. There are excellent and wide sandy beaches with an amazing variety of marine life (sea horses, sand dollars, starfish, and hermit crabs galore) on or near the shoreline. A small trail snakes through the interior of the island to Ao Sane, and there are mangrove swamps, rain forests, and a variety of wildlife on this three- to four-hour hike. The more fit and intrepid might want to make the 6-hour (12km) trek along an overgrown trail across to the east side of the island at Ao Talo Wao, where there's a small ranger station. Those with the energy might want to push south to Ao Talo Udang to see the remnants of the prison camp. There are small settlements on Ao Sane, Ao Talo Wao, and Ao Talo Udang, as well as good places to set up camp.

For those who want a scenic overview, take the 15-minute hike up to **To Boo Cliff** that starts behind the library. It's especially nice at sunset. More adventurous travelers will enjoy a trip to **Crocodile Cave;** take a flashlight and expect to get wet wading through the mangrove swamps.

EXPLORING THE WESTERN ISLANDS OF THE ARCHIPELAGO

A few hardy souls make their way west to the many smaller islands in the archipelago. The most popular destination is **Ko Adang,** and there's ferry service three times a week (January to April) from Ao Pante (3 hours; 400B/$10.55 round-trip), with possible connection to surrounding islands. Many travelers push on to **Ao Rawi,** with a stop at **Ko Lipe,** a relatively flat island that has been settled by people known as *Chao Le* (or *Chao Nam,* "Water People"), a dark-skinned people probably originally from Indonesia who speak their own language and are famous for their diving ability; here their principle occupation is coconut farming. In addition to Ko Lipe, the islands of **Ko Kra, Ko Jabang,** and **Ko Yang** are also excellent places for snorkeling or diving because of their fine coral reefs. If you want to stay on Ko Adang, the boat docks at Laem Sone, where there is a park headquarters office, as well as two bamboo long-houses, each sleeping four people; expect to pay 400B ($10.55). There is also a simple restaurant nearby.

Phuket | 8

No other Thai destination has changed as rapidly as Phuket—not all for the worse—and it remains Thailand's finest resort destination. At its best, this island in the Andaman Sea is almost idyllic: It has long sandy beaches (some with dunes), warm water, excellent snorkeling and scuba diving off Ko Similan, ideal windsurfing conditions, mountains, and the best seafood in all of Thailand.

During the past decade the Thai government has granted economic incentives to encourage developers to shape the island into an international first-class resort. Hotels—some of them enormous—are taking over every beach where once only a smattering of modest bungalows stood. As groups pour in from Singapore, Hong Kong, Germany, and Italy, backpackers head off to nearby Ko Pi Pi, or Ko Samui on the Gulf.

But some of the resorts are disarmingly attractive and elegant. The "Miami Beach" strip of concrete and steel is rarely seen on Phuket. In its place are serene bays framed by tastefully designed retreats that are modeled after hillside villas or luxury bungalows. It's nearly impossible to find a totally secluded beach, but there are a number of very attractive and comfortable facilities with a high level of service—not a bad trade-off for those in search of all the luxuries. If you're traveling with a family, want to be pampered, or are looking for action, Phuket might be the place for you.

The season on Phuket extends from September to March, with the 4 months between November and March being prime time. The monsoon strikes from April to August; during the period from late June through August, the so-called promotional season, many hotels and other establishments and services offer discounts up to 50%. During the monsoon season few people come to Phuket due to the perception that it rains all day and night, every day. It doesn't, so for the more flexibly minded, it's an ideal time to make a visit.

The name "Phuket" is derived from the Malay "Bukit," meaning hill, and hills dominate much of the island, spilling their craggy rocks on the gentle beach coves below. From most high points you can see a number of nearby islands and islets, among them hourglass-shaped Ko Pi Pi, off the southern shore. In parts of the interior, rubber plantations still operate, and open-pit mining for tin and other metals has scarred the land.

1 Orientation

ARRIVING

BY PLANE   Thai Airways (☎ 02/280-0070 in Bangkok) flies more than 10 times daily from Bangkok from 8am to 9pm (trip time: 1 hour and 20 minutes); and a daily morning flight from Hat Yai (trip time: 45 minutes). In Hat Yai, its office is at 190/6 Niphat Uthit Rd. (☎ 074/233-433). Thai Airways' office in Phuket is at 78 Ranong Rd. (☎ 076/211-195). Also keep in mind Thai Airways connects Phuket with international flights to and from Singapore and Kuala Lumpur in Malaysia.

Bangkok Airways (☎ 02/229-3434 in Bangkok; 077/425-011 in Ko Samui) connects Phuket with Ko Samui once daily. The Bangkok Airways office in Phuket is at 158/2–3 Yaowarat Rd., Phuket town (☎ **076/225-033,** or 076/327-114 at Phuket Airport).

The attractive, modern Phuket International Airport is located in the north of the island, about 40 minutes drive from town or from Patong Beach. There are banks, money-changing facilities, car-rental agents (see "Getting Around" later in this chapter), and a post office. The Phuket Tourist Business Association booth can help you make hotel arrangements if you haven't booked a room.

Many resorts will pick you at the airport upon request for a fee, usually steep. The airport limousine counter, operated by **Tour Royale** (☎ 076/341-214), offers many options for getting to your hotel from the airport. The cheapest way is the minibus, which operates every hour on the hour from 9am to 11pm daily. Stopping between Patong, Kata, Karon, and Phuket town, prices run from 80B to 180B ($2.10 to $4.75), depending on how far you're going. Taxi service from the airport, also arranged at the limousine counter, will cost from between 360B ($9.45) to Phuket town and 540B ($14.20) to Kata beach. The VIP Volvo transfer will set you back between 480B and 750B ($12.65 and $19.75).

BY BUS   Three air-conditioned VIP buses leave daily from Bangkok's Southern Bus Terminal (☎ 02/435-1199), on Charan Sanitwong Road (trip time 14 hours; 690B/$18.15), as well as an additional government air-conditioned bus (446B/$11.75).

The **intercity** bus terminal is at the city Park Complex on Phangnga Road (☎ 076/211-480), east of Phuket town just opposite the Royal Phuket City Hotel. For information on how to get from here to the beaches, see "Getting Around" below.

BY MINIVAN   Minivans from Surat Thani leave on a regular schedule throughout the day. Call ☎ 077/286-131 for booking and hotel pickup (160B/$4.20). From Krabi near the TAT office there are three daily minivans that will take you for 200B ($5.25).

VISITOR INFORMATION

The **Tourism Authority of Thailand** is on the ball in Phuket. Unfortunately you have to travel all the way into Phuket town to see them at 73–75 Phuket Rd. (☎ 076/211-036). It is well worth the trip, as they have all sorts of information, and the people behind the counter know everything there is to know about travel in the area.

Some great local publications to pick up include the free *Phuket Food-Shopping-Entertainment,* packed with hotel and restaurant write-ups, and ads for many of the island's activities. Another free publication, *What's on South Thai,* is not as comprehensive, but has some information on Ko Phi Phi and Krabi. The bimonthly ultra-glossy *Greater Phuket Magazine* provides in-depth articles and photo essays about the island and its people. Pick it up at bookstores in Phuket and Bangkok for 80B ($2.10).

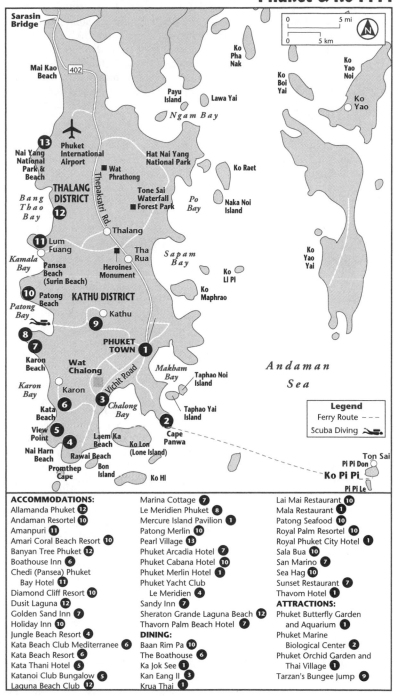

Phuket & Ko Pi Pi

Sarasin Bridge

Mai Kao Beach

402

Ko Pha Nak

Ko Yao Noi

Ko Boi Yai

Ko Yao

Payu Island

Lawa Yai

Ngam Bay

13 Nai Yang National Park & Beach

Phuket International Airport

Hat Nai Yang National Park

Ko Raet

Wat Phrathong

THALANG DISTRICT

Tone Sai Waterfall ■ Forest Park

Po Bay

Naka Noi Island

Bang Thao Bay

12

Thalang

Sapam Bay

Ko Li Pi

Ko Yao Yai

11 Lum Fuang

Tha Rua

Kamala Bay

Pansea Beach (Surin Beach)

Heroines Monument

Ko Maphrao

10 Patong Beach

KATHU DISTRICT

Patong Bay

9 Kathu

8

PHUKET TOWN

1

Andaman Sea

7

Karon Beach

Wat Chalong

Makham Bay

Taphao Noi Island

Karon Bay

6 Karon

3 *Chalong Bay*

Taphao Yai Island

Kata Beach

Legend

Ferry Route ---

Scuba Diving

5 View Point

4

Laem Ka Beach

Ko Lon (Lone Island)

2 Cape Panwa

Nai Harn Beach

Rawai Beach

Promthep Cape

Bon Island

Ko Hi

Ton Sai

Pi Pi Don

Ko Pi Pi

Pi Pi Le

ACCOMMODATIONS:
Allamanda Phuket **12**
Andaman Resortel **10**
Amanpuri **11**
Amari Coral Beach Resort **10**
Banyan Tree Phuket **12**
Boathouse Inn **6**
Chedi (Pansea) Phuket Bay Hotel **11**
Diamond Cliff Resort **10**
Dusit Laguna **12**
Golden Sand Inn **7**
Holiday Inn **10**
Jungle Beach Resort **4**
Kata Beach Club Mediterranee **6**
Kata Beach Resort **6**
Kata Thani Hotel **5**
Katanoi Club Bungalow **5**
Laguna Beach Club **12**

Marina Cottage **7**
Le Meridien Phuket **8**
Mercure Island Pavilion **1**
Patong Merlin **10**
Pearl Village **13**
Phuket Arcadia Hotel **7**
Phuket Cabana Hotel **10**
Phuket Merlin Hotel **1**
Phuket Yacht Club Le Meridien **4**
Sandy Inn **7**
Sheraton Grande Laguna Beach **12**
Thavorn Palm Beach Hotel **7**
DINING:
Baan Rim Pa **10**
The Boathouse **6**
Ka Jok See **1**
Kan Eang II **3**
Krua Thai **1**

Lai Mai Restaurant **10**
Mala Restaurant **1**
Patong Seafood **10**
Royal Palm Resortel **10**
Royal Phuket City Hotel **1**
Sala Bua **10**
San Marino **7**
Sea Hag **10**
Sunset Restaurant **7**
Thavorn Hotel **1**
ATTRACTIONS:
Phuket Butterfly Garden and Aquarium **1**
Phuket Marine Biological Center **2**
Phuket Orchid Garden and Thai Village **1**
Tarzan's Bungee Jump **9**

229

Maps are abundant and most of them are free. For getting around Phuket town I like the detail, accuracy, and clarity of the free map given out by the TAT, but for driving around the island the Periplus Editions *Map of Phuket* (at bookstores) is easier to use. The Periplus map also features good layouts of the major beaches. Also check out the booklet of coupons found at the airport, which offers discounts on activities and meals all over the island. *Visitors' Privilege Vouchers* are also at the TAT office in town.

CITY LAYOUT

If you arrive by car or coach, you cross over to Phuket from the mainland at the northern tip of the island via the Sarasin Bridge. A few miles east of the inland road is the Khao Phra Thaeo Wildlife Park, notable for Ton Sai falls, a lovely spot for a cool break on a blistering day. The park is home to a variety of birds and other fauna, as well as diverse flora, including a variety of palm that is unique to the island. The road continues south to the middle of the island and the largest town, Phuket.

In the southeastern quarter, Phuket is the island's commercial and transportation nexus. Most, if not all, local buses go to Phuket town (usually called simply "Phuket"). Because inland Phuket is often very hot and noisy with buzzing motorcycles and cars, most tourists usually head for the shore, where the blazing sun, fine white sand, and the refreshing sea encourages a longer stay than planned.

Phuket's most attractive beaches are on the west coast, extending from Nai Harn, on the southern tip, to Bang Tao, about 30km (19 miles) north. Most bungalows and new resorts are in between, along the Kata, Kata Noi, Karon, Karon Noi, Patong, and Surin corridor. A coastal road linking most of these beaches has been completed. For now, travel between some of the beaches north of Patong requires a detour to the interior, although some stretches are navigable with four-wheel-drive vehicles.

THE BEACHES

Each beach has its own distinct character, so selecting the appropriate one for your perfect vacation can make all the difference in the world. **Nai Harn,** the southernmost bay on the west coast, is home to only one major resort, plus a few scattered bungalows in the forested hills that rise from the shore. Although the beach here is not as long as others, there are fewer people and it's more laid back and quiet. The sand is fine and the water deep. There's also some great coral and marine life just to the north side of the beach. As a public beach, with restaurant facilities, both local and resort class, it makes for a great day trip if you're staying at a more populated beach and want to run away for the day.

North of Nai Harn, **Kata, Kata Noi, Karon, and Karon Noi Beaches** are more developed, but not to the point of distraction. Here you'll find both large resorts and smaller, less expensive facilities. The beaches here are long and picturesque, and the water is deep with some nice wave breaks. This beach area has more restaurants than the remote bays, and some shopping, nightlife, and travel agent options as well. But you won't find rowdy crowds here. Despite resort development, there are still lots of open land, and the area manages to maintain a relaxed and laid back character.

A short drive north takes you to **Relax Bay,** a small cove with nice swimming and some coral for snorkeling. Relax Bay has the dual advantage of a small secluded spot that is still close to the two most developed beaches on Phuket.

North of the Kata and Karon bays, you'll find **Patong Beach,** the most famous (or infamous, depending on your point of view) strip on the island. Patong's draw is its accommodations—from five-star resorts to budget motels, the largest and most diverse selection of dining facilities on the island, a high concentration of tour and dive operators, water sports activities, tons of shopping, and the most extensive nightlife "scene" on the island. The drawbacks—it is a not-so-ideal parade of tourists and touts, prices for souvenirs and handicrafts are highly inflated, and the nightlife can be risque at best or sleazy and pathetic at worst. If you love to be in the center of it all, stay in Patong. If you want to chill out in peace, stay away.

Still north of Patong, **Kamala Bay, Surin Beach and Pan Sea Beach** have more secluded resorts on lovely beaches. For those who still want the convenience of nearby Patong, but cherish the serenity of a private resort, these beaches are highly recommended.

About two-thirds of the way to the northern tip of the island, **Bang Tao Beach** is home to the Laguna Resort Complex, a partnership of five world-class resorts sharing excellent facilities and a fabulous beach. While this area is rather far from both Patong beach and Phuket town, the endless dining and activity options will keep you very happy here.

Finally, the northernmost recreation beach is at the **Had Nai Yang National Park.** This remote area with limited facilities may not appeal to most, but for real beach lovers it's a dream come true. Best yet, the coral reef just 1,400 meters to sea is the best off the island. If you're looking to get back to nature, Had Nai Yang is your best bet.

2 Getting Around

Public transportation is a problem on Phuket that never seems to get solved. It's also very confusing for a few reasons. First of all, if you've spent any time in other parts of the country, you'll know that the covered pickup trucks that cruise the streets picking up and dropping off passengers are called *songtao,* while the noisy motorized three-wheel demon vehicles are known as *tuk-tuks.* Not so on Phuket! Here, the people call the minitrucks *tuk-tuks,* while *songtao* are the giant colorful buses that ply the main roads (a few people also call them "baht buses").

Here's the problem: Tuk-tuk drivers, in an attempt to generate more business, have lobbied successfully for exclusive rights to transport people *between* beaches. This means the songtao buses are only permitted to travel from each beach to Phuket town. You can't hop from beach to beach on them. For these trips you have to negotiate with the tuk-tuk drivers. Below, I've provided some bargaining tips.

BY SONGTAO   The local bus terminal is in front of the Central Market on Ranong Road in Phuket town. Fares to the most popular beaches range from 15B to 25B (40¢ to 65¢). Buses are typically scheduled to operate every 30 minutes from 7am to 5pm, but usually run whenever there is a full load of passengers or produce. As mentioned above, you can only take these buses from town to beach or back again. They do not operate routes between beaches.

BY TUK-TUK   Within Phuket town, tuk-tuks cost about 10B to 20B (25¢ to 55¢) for local trips, more or less, depending on your destination. They also wander up and down the beach areas for short trips along the strip.

Tuk-tuks are the only way to travel between beaches, and these guys will try to eke every baht out of you. Here's your rule of thumb: 300B ($7.90) from town to the airport, 150B ($3.95) from town to Patong Beach, 150B ($3.95) from Patong Beach to Karon Beach.

BY MOTORCYCLE TAXI   Drivers in colored vests will try to talk you into a ride as you pass by, both in Phuket town and Patong Beaches. As in other towns, drivers here are identified by their colored vests. For a quick jot within town or Patong beach, they're recommended, but don't let them talk you into a trip between beaches. I really doubt it's safe enough.

BY CAR   When you self-drive on Phuket, you have to be especially careful. Coastal and inland roads have serious hills and curves that appear out of nowhere. Motorcycles swarm like bees, and Thai drivers will pass anything on a blind curve without so much as a care. Your defensive driving skills will come in handy.

Avis has quite a few counters on Phuket. At Phuket Airport, they can be reached at ☎ **076/351-243.** They also have counters at Le Meridien Phuket (☎ **076/340-480**) and the Sheraton Grande Laguna Beach (☎ **076/324-101**). Budget around 1,800B ($47.35) for a Suzuki Caribian, or higher if you'd prefer a sedan.

Inexpensive Suzuki Caribians, four-wheel drive sport vehicles, can be rented from almost all travel agents and from hotels at the beach areas. Prices range from 700B to 900B ($18.40 to $23.70) per day. **World Rent-a-Car** (opposite the airport (☎ **076/205-359**) goes as low as 700B ($18.40) per day, and can greet you at the airport with a car or deliver one to your resort. They accept American Express, MasterCard, and Visa.

Lining the beach at Patong, there are oodles of Caribian cars for rent from independent agents who hang around under umbrellas. They'll charge 700B ($18.40) a day for Caribians, and 800B ($21.05) and over for open-top Jeeps and souped up four-wheel drive off-road vehicles. While many resorts will rent you a car, I've found that the independent dealers have the same product for less money.

BY MOTORCYCLE   Also along the Patong strip, the same car-rental people will provide you with a bike for cheap. A 100cc Honda scooter goes for 200B ($5.25) per day, while a 400cc Honda CBR or a 600cc Honda Shadow chopper will set you back 500B ($13.15) per day. If you plan to rent for longer, make sure to negotiate for a discount rate. Wear your helmet, keep to the left and let cars pass. For God's sake, watch it out there—they're animals. I shudder to think of all the horror stories I've heard about vacation motorcycle accidents.

Fast Facts: Phuket

American Express   The American Express agent in Phuket is Sea Tours (☎ **076/218-417**), 95/4 Phuket Rd., Phuket town, 1 block south of the TAT.

Banks   Banks are located in Phuket town, with many larger branches on Ranong and Rasada roads. There are bank offices at the airport, as well as branches of major Thai banks at Kata, Karon, and Patong beaches. See each section for more complete information. **Money changers** are also around, at banks and in major shopping areas on each beach.

Bookstores   Near the TAT office in Phuket town, look for **The Books** on Therkrasatri Road (☎ **076/224-362**).

Post Office   The General Post Office in Phuket town (☎ **076/211-020**) is at the corner of Thalang Road and Montri Road. For post offices in the beach areas, see each corresponding section.

Hospitals   The Bangkok Phuket Hospital at 2/1 Hongyok-Uthit Rd. (off Yaowarat Road in Phuket town) (☎ **076/254-421**) has English-speaking staff and high quality facilities.

Internet   Internet service is fairly easy to find on the island. In Phuket town, head for Internet KSC at the ECC Building, 73/1–2 Rasada Rd., across from Thavorn Hotel (☎ **076/214-496**); rates are 3B (10¢) per minute.

Police   The emergency number for the **Tourist Police** is ☎ **1699.** For **Marine Police** call ☎ **076/342-518.**

3 Where to Stay & Dine

I've divided the hotels, resorts, and restaurants on the island into beach areas to make it easier to select a great hotel, and to find restaurants nearby. However, if you have your own transportation, can make transfer arrangements with your resort or are open to tuk-tuk rides, most every restaurant is an option, no matter what area you're staying in. For more tips on accommodations and dining see "Tips on Accommodations" in chapter 2 and "Tips on Dining" in chapter 4.

PHUKET TOWN

Phuket town is not the first choice for vacationers who come to Phuket for beaches and sunshine. The island's capital city, the small town does have some good high-class facilities, and more moderately priced ones as well. However, most will only stay in town if they're overnighting before the early boat to surrounding islands.

WHERE TO STAY

Expensive

Royal Phuket City Hotel. 154 Phang-Nga Rd., Amphur Muang, Phuket 83000. ☎ **076/233-333.** Fax 076/233-335. www.royalphuketcity.nu. 251 units. AC MINIBAR TV TEL. 3,400B–4,100B ($89.45–$107.90) double; from 5,800B ($152.65) suite. AE, DC, JCB, MC, V. Located to the east of Phuket town, across from the intercity bus terminal.

For a small town like Phuket, this hotel is surprisingly cosmopolitan. A true city hotel, Royal Phuket's facilities include possibly the largest and most modern fitness center facility on the island, an excellent spa and massage center, outdoor swimming pool, and an executive business center good enough for even Bangkok itself. Above the cavernous marble lobby, guestrooms are smart—in contemporary hues and style, with amenities that simplify your stay. Don't expect too much from the views.

Pickles Restaurant serves international cuisine, with monthly regional features. At the time of writing, they highlighted the mouthwatering foods of Malaysia. At the Chinatown Restaurant you can dine in one of the poshest establishments in town.

Moderate

The Tavorn Hotel. 74 Rasada Rd., Amphur Muang, Phuket 83000. ☎ **076/211-333.** Fax 076/215-559. 200 units. A/C TV TEL. 550B ($14.45) double. V, MC. Rasada Rd. is in the center of Phuket town.

Talk about character! The lobby of this unique and informal hotel doubles as a museum exhibit dedicated to the history of the island. Old photos and antiques create a fascinating period tone to the dark wood paneled entry hall and surrounding chambers. Too bad the ambience doesn't spill over into the rooms. Still, they're quite cheap, and in not too bad condition, although some renovations here and there would help. Besides, for in-town accommodations, you can't find a better location—close to the TAT office, banks, shopping, and dining.

WHERE TO DINE

✪ **Ka Jok See.** 26 Takuapa Rd., Phuket town. ☎ **076/217-903.** Reservations recommended for weekends. 150B–380B ($3.95–$10). 6pm–midnight (kitchen closes around 11pm). Closed Mon. No credit cards. A short walk from Rasada Rd. THAI.

This is one of my favorite restaurants in Thailand. I love the ambience—a small shop in town with tiled floor and wood-beamed ceiling, antiques lit by candlelight, and classic jazz wafting throughout. Ka Jok See is smart and chic, cozy and intimate. They prepare fabulous dishes like the house specialty, goong-saroong—vermicelli-wrapped shrimp fried quick and light and served with a velvety mustard dipping sauce. I also sampled smoky grilled eggplant and shrimp salad and the stir-fried beef curry, which were both heavenly. This place is well worth a venture from the beach for an evening. Look for the shop hidden behind all the plants—they have no sign.

Mala. 5/73 Mae Luan Rd., ☎ **076/214-201.** Reservations not necessary. 30B–150B (80¢–$3.95). Daily 7am–9pm. No credit cards. Located between Satun and Yaowarat rds. THAI/INTERNATIONAL.

Mala serves inexpensive breakfast, lunch, and dinner in a small open-air coffee shop setting. Spacious and cooled by overhead fans, the charming wood and tile tables look out at the street scene past a potted terrace garden. With a full selection of Thai curries, Thai and Chinese dishes, plus some Western selections, you can't go wrong. Like many restaurants in town, Mala serves prawn wrapped with vermicelli and deep fried, only theirs is served with a more traditional sweet chile sauce. I also recommend the mee-sua, a noodle soup with pork that is a local specialty.

CHALONG BAY

Chalong Bay was Phuket's original resort area—oh so many years ago. Today, with the development of the far superior beaches on the western side of the island, and the establishment of Phuket's public marina, Chalong isn't the most ideal place to stay. However, you'll still find fantastic restaurants here, especially if you crave some of Phuket's famous seafood.

WHERE TO DINE

Kan Eang 2. 9/3 Chaofa Rd., Chalong Bay. ☎ **076/381-323.** Reservations recommended if you'd like a seaside table. 30B–120B (80¢–$3.15); seafood sold per gram. AE, DC, JCB, MC, V. THAI SEAFOOD.

Seafood lovers rejoice! Of course I just had to have the Phuket lobster, which almost escaped from his tub by the kitchen. With nine preparation styles to choose from— baked with butter, sashimi, baked with chile paste, you'll never go wrong. I had mine baked with garlic. Yum. I also adored the delicately fried crab meat Kan Eang style—dipped in a sweet chile sauce. They also prepare king prawns, various fish, squid, and shellfish in a million different ways. Set under trees on the beach looking out at distant boats twinkling in the bay, the tables next to the sand are the best in the house.

NAI HARN BEACH
WHERE TO STAY & DINE

Jungle Beach Resort. 11/3 Viset Rd., Ao Sane Beach, Phuket 83130. ☎ and fax **076/ 228-264.** 44 units. A/C MINIBAR TV TEL. 600B–1,800B ($15.80–$47.35) double; 2,100B–2,640B ($55.25–$69.45) bungalow. AE, MC, V. Beyond the Phuket Yacht Club.

Half a mile beyond the Phuket Yacht Club along a dirt road is this bungalow compound, recently upgraded and now sporting a new swimming pool. The bungalows are in a natural cove above Ao Sane Beach, but there's no access other than from Nai Harn. The setting is equatorial: Monkeys swoop down at night from the hills and climb the resort's trees; during the long rainy season, water cascades over the rocks. The bungalows are equipped in several configurations, some with fans or air-conditioning, hot and cold water, and a large deck. It's pretty buggy at night, so bring repellent, but otherwise this is pretty comfortable. Be prepared for rustic. Phone ahead to arrange a transfer from the airport or town.

✪ **Le Royal Meridien Phuket Yacht Club.** 23/3 Viset Rd., Nai Harn Beach, Phuket 83130. ☎ **800/225-5843** in the U.S., or 076/381-156. Fax 076/381-164. 110 units. A/C MINIBAR TV TEL. $250 double; from $450 suite. Peak season (Nov–Apr) $380 double; from $550 suite. AE, DC, JCB, MC, V. Above Nai Harn Beach, 18km (11 miles) south of Phuket.

Le Meridien recently took over the Phuket Yacht Club, one of the earliest luxury accommodations in Phuket, and have taken the resort to new heights in quality. Perched above the northern edge of Nai Harn, looking down at the public beach and yachts beyond, the Yacht Club rivals nearly anything on the island for setting—from its pagoda-style entryway to the terraced gardens overflowing with pink and white bougainvillea. All rooms view the beach, the Andaman Sea, and Promthep Cape from their landscaped, red-tiled balconies. Newly redecorated guestrooms are spacious and decorated with cheerful fabrics and wicker furniture; most bathrooms have sunken tubs and are fully stocked with high-quality amenities. The Phuket Yacht Club has a pool, a newly renovated fitness center, and three dining venues—beachside Mediterranean fare, Italian in the elegant dining room, or Asian and International cuisine on the patio.

KATA & KARON

In Karon there's a small post office on the north end of Karon Beach Road between My Friendship Hotel and South Sea Resort. At Karon, try the **Karon Beach Internet Center** at 36/31 Patak Rd. (☎ **076/286-086**).

WHERE TO STAY IN KATA BEACH

Expensive

The Boathouse Phuket. 2/2 Patak Rd., Kata Beach, Phuket 83100. ☎ **076/330-557.** Fax 076/330-561. 36 units. A/C MINIBAR TV TEL. Low season 4,500B ($118.40) double; from 10,000B ($263.15) suite; peak season 8,700B ($228.95) double; from 11,053B ($290.85) suite. AE, DC, MC, V.

With its own beach at the quieter south end of Kata Beach, this small inn is a favorite. All the comfortable, attractive rooms face the sea, each with a terrace overlooking the huge Jacuzzi pool in the courtyard. The beach-side pool is small, with nearby massage and therapy facilities. Nothing about the hotel calls attention to itself; it's the well-trained, friendly, attentive staff that makes it special. The Boathouse high-style Thai and continental restaurant serves some of the best food on the island and boasts one of the best wine "cellars" in Thailand. They also offer discount theme packages: Health Holidays, inclusive of massage and herbal steam treatments, and a Thai Cooking Class weekend getaway.

Kata Beach Club Mediterranee. 7/3 Patak Rd., Kata Beach, Phuket 83000. ☎ **02/ 253-0108,** or 076/330-455 in Bangkok. Fax 02/253-9778, or 076/330-441 in Bangkok. (The resort does not accept direct reservations.) 300 units. A/C. Low season 4,300B ($113.15) per night per adult; 2,460B ($64.75) per child. Midseason (Feb–Apr) 3,500B ($92.10) per night per adult; 2,100B ($55.25) per child. Peak season 8,000B ($210.55) per night per adult; 4,800B ($126.30) per child. Includes 3 meals a day and all activities (no water sports from May–Oct). Walk-in rate, without reservation 5,700B ($150) per night. AE, DC, MC, V. North end of Kata Beach.

Though there has been some recent renovation, the Club Med still lacks luxury. Quarters contain two tiny bedrooms, divided by a rattan wall, with a shared bathroom and foyer; in other words, unless you pay a 20% premium, you'll share a room.

Set in its own sealed compound, Club Med commands an enormous and enviable piece of beachfront real estate. In typical Club Med fashion, the Kata Beach facility is so completely equipped that contact with the outside world is hardly required. A full range of water sports is available, and if you do feel compelled to wander off, various excursions around the island are offered. Special kudos for the food, including much locally caught Phuket seafood.

Among the many positive aspects of staying at this Club Med is its provision for children. There is the Mini-Club (open daily 9am to 9:30pm), which involves play groups, special classes for craft making, supervised activities, and baby-sitting (for kids under 4), all performed by people who are well versed in child care. Many vacationing parents leave their kids in the Mini-Club in the morning, eat lunch with them in the afternoon, and pick them up at the end of the day, leaving them to enjoy their vacation relatively unburdened by family demands. For teenagers there's an equivalent service called the Cadets Club—and the kids certainly seemed to be enjoying themselves during our last visit. Shuttle service, baby-sitting, laundry service, excursion boat are provided. Facilities include swimming pool, health club, tennis courts, beauty salon and barbershop, shopping arcade, game room, water sports, bowling, gymnasium, archery, volleyball court, soccer field.

Kata Beach Resort. 5/2 Patak Rd., Kata Beach, Phuket 83100. ☎ **076/330-530,** or 02/939-4062 in Bangkok. Fax 076/330-128. 200 units. A/C MINIBAR TV TEL. 5,400B ($142.10) double. Peak-season supplement 1,000B ($26.30). AE, DC, MC, V. In the Kata Beach strip.

As soon as you pull up to the soaring granite and marble lobby, you'll realize that you've arrived at the most formal facility on the Kata coast. I prefer the beach-view rooms in the central building—the higher-priced choice, of course, but they really are lovely. All rooms are well equipped and attractively decorated. This deluxe establishment is the glitziest accommodation in the area.

Dining: The Terrace has nightly seafood barbecues. Thai and continental food are served at the Orangerie Coffee Shop, while the Silk Road offers a range of Asian cuisine.

Amenities: Swimming pools, health club and sauna, beauty salon and barbershop, shopping arcade, water sports, business center, nursery and Children's Club, in-house video, 24-hour room service, concierge, limousine service, laundry service, tailor and dressmaker.

Kata Thani Hotel. 3/24 Patak Rd., Kata Noi Beach, Phuket 83100. ☎ **076/330-124.** Fax 076/330-426. 433 units. A/C MINIBAR TV TEL. 2,772B ($72.95) double; sea view 3,102B ($81.65); from 3,432B ($90.30) suite. Peak season (Dec–Jan) 5,808B double ($152.85); 6,413B ($168.75) sea view; from 7,018B ($184.70) suite. AE, DC, MC, V. North end of Kata Noi Beach. Peak season surcharge (20 Dec–Jan 31) 1,000B ($26.30).

The Kata Thani is the dominant structure on lovely Kata Noi Beach and is a haven of quiet luxury. The top-end deluxe rooms are especially attractive, but even the standard ones are a good value, especially those with a sea view. A wide, well-groomed lawn surrounds two sizable pools and leads to the graceful curve of the pristine cove. There is a nightly poolside buffet. Breakfast and snacks are available at the coffee shop, while more elegant dining takes place in the Grill. The Rendezvous Cocktail Bar has music well into the night. Twenty-four-hour room service, concierge, limousine service, and laundry service are provided. Facilities include swimming pools, health club and sauna, tennis courts, beauty salon and barbershop, shopping arcade, and water sports.

Moderate/Inexpensive

Katanoi Club Bungalow. 3/25 Patak Rd., Kata Noi, Phuket 83100. ☎ **076/330-194.** 16 units. 500B ($13.15) double. Rates include tax and service. No credit cards. South end of Kata Noi Beach.

These Thai-style bungalows on a large lawn are more substantial than the old thatch ones that once lined Phuket's beach coves, and the location is excellent—just 50 feet from the quiet south tip of a sandy beach cove. The guest quarters are very roomy, with ceiling fans and screened, shuttered windows. Each contains a small writing desk, armoire, and a tiled bathroom with a cold-water shower. In front of the small snack bar and reception area is a windsurfing rental shop. Several concrete bunkers, with shared Asian toilet facilities, are offered for only 350B ($14) for two, but they're rather grim. Call early to reserve one of these good-value bungalows.

Marina Cottage. 120 Patak Rd., Kata Karon Beach, Phuket 83000. ☎ **076/330-625.** Fax 076/330-999. 104 units. A/C MINIBAR TV TEL. Low season 2,394B ($63) garden double; 3,192B ($84) pool-view double; 3,724B ($98) ocean view. Peak season 3,800B ($100) garden double; 5,320B ($140) pool-view double; 5,700B ($150) ocean view. MC, V. On bluff at south end of Karon Beach Rd.

These simple cottages, tucked in the woods above the cusp of Kata and Karon beaches, are slightly more comfortable than the older thatch bungalows nearby. All are a hike down to the rocky shore; rates vary according to the view. Some rooms have air-conditioning. The staff could be a bit more amiable. The Marina Cottage is home to **Marina Divers** (☎ **076/381625**), a PADI International Diving School, which conducts classes, rents equipment, and leads expeditions around the island reefs. The pleasant restaurant cottage serves good, inexpensive Thai food.

WHERE TO STAY IN KARON BEACH
Expensive
Phuket Arcadia Hotel. 78/2 Patak Rd., Karon Beach, Phuket 83100. ☎ **076/396-433.** Fax 076/396-136. www.phuketarcadia.com. 475 units. A/C MINIBAR TV TEL. 4,500B–4,800B ($118.40–$126.30) double; from 8,500B ($223.70) suite. AE, DC, MC, V. Middle of Karon Beach Rd.

This modern, full-facility resort is a massive presence on Karon Beach, and quite pleasant if a bit expensive for a not-so-great beach area. Rooms are attractive but rather bland, with standard bathroom facilities, all overlooking the beach and ocean. The landscaping is a little stark, but the elevated pool and sundeck offer wonderful views of the bay.

    Dining: The hotel offers up the Garden Coffee Shop for Thai, Chinese, and Western cuisine, San Marino for great Italian, and Tai Kong for local seafood and grilled meats.

    Amenities: Health club with sauna, large outdoor pool, tennis courts, putting greens, windsurfing, game room, 24-hour room service, concierge, taxi service, baby-sitting, house doctor, bathrobes, and hair dryers in room.

Thavorn Palm Beach Hotel. 128/10 Moo 3, Karon Beach, Phuket 83110. ☎ **076/ 396-091.** Fax 076/396-555. 210 units. A/C MINIBAR TV TEL. 6,400B ($168.40) double. Peak-season supplement 750B ($19.75) per room per night. AE, DC, MC, V. In mid–Karon Beach area.

Most rooms have fine views overlooking the Karon dunes. The decor is minimal but pleasant, and there are four good pools and a kiddie pool, along with a fitness center, tennis courts, and four restaurants. The beach is lovely, but it's across the busy beach road, and the roar of the road can sometimes drown out the sound of the surf.

    Dining: The Thavorn has nine dining possibilities. A favorite is the outdoor terrace venue called Sansai, which specializes in seafood; but there's certain to be a dining facility to your liking.

    Amenities: Health club, four outdoor pools, tennis courts, windsurfing, snooker room, 24-hour room service, concierge, taxi service, baby-sitting, house doctor, bathrobes, hair dryers.

Inexpensive
Golden Sand Inn. Karon Beach, Phuket 83100. ☎ **076/396-493.** Fax 076/396-117. 125 units. 1,500B ($39.45) double room; 3,500B ($92.10) double bungalow. AE, DC, MC, V. Across highway from north end of beach above traffic circle.

Budget accommodations are disappearing on this part of the island. After looking hard and finding little, this is one of a couple of places that's fine to recommend. It's clean, reasonably quiet, and well maintained, and the management is friendly. Rooms are large and motel-like, but you can't see much of the nearby beach. There's a pleasant cafe-style coffee shop, swimming pool, safety boxes in the rooms, and VDO. Rooms are 50% less in the low season.

Sandy Inn. 102/12 Patak Rd., Karon Beach, Phuket 83100. ☎ **076/340-275.** Fax 076/341-519. 12 units (with showers, no hot water). A/C MINIBAR. 800B ($21.05) double. No credit cards. Near south end of beach, inland on small road south of Thavorn Hotel.

Those who don't require hot water or a view will find this a good-value choice. It's a 5-minute walk from the beach, near some inexpensive restaurants and a laundry. Rooms are simple, clean, and cool.

WHERE TO DINE

✪ **The Boathouse.** The Boathouse Inn, 114 Patak Rd. ☎ **076/330-557.** Reservations accepted. 200B and up ($5.25); seafood sold at market price. Daily 7:30am–11pm. AE, DC, MC, V. THAI/INTERNATIONAL.

So legendary is the Thai and Western cuisine at the Boathouse, that the inn where it resides offers popular holiday packages for visitors who wish to come and take cooking lessons from its chef. Inside the restaurant, a large bar and separate dining area sport nautical touches, while outside huge picture windows, the sun sets on a deep blue sea. Cuisine is nouvelle, combining the best of East and West and the finest ingredients in satisfying portions. If you're in the mood for the works, the Phuket lobster is one of the most expensive dishes on the menu, but is worth every baht. The Boathouse also has an excellent selection of international wines. *Bon appétit.*

Sunset Restaurant. 102/6 Patak Rd., Karon Beach. ☎ **076/396-465.** Reservations not necessary. Entrees 80B–180B ($2.10–$4.75); seafood at market price. Daily 8am–11pm. AE, DC, MC, V. SEAFOOD.

While Patak Road, running perpendicular to the main beach road, doesn't really have a view of the sunset, this restaurant is notable for its fine seafood, prepared in both local and Western styles. Their lobster thermidor and western-style steamed fish are fresh and scrumptious, as are their mixed seafood platters. Thai dishes are either spicy or tempered upon request, depending on your preference. Simple tables have neat batik cloths, which is as stylish as the restaurant's decor gets. Nevertheless, it's a favorite spot for foreigners living in Phuket, and one of the best places in this part of the island.

San Marino. Phuket Arcadia Hotel, Karon Beach Rd. ☎ **076/396-038.** Main courses 120B–380B ($3.15–$10). Daily 6–10pm. AE, DC, JCB, MC, V. ITALIAN.

White linens and candlelight soften the huge Roman coliseum setting—complete with columns—in this pretty Italian restaurant, one of the finest on the island. Pastas are fresh, as is the seafood, although the menu selection is a bit limited. Still, my lobster ravioli was excellent—a generous portion drenched in a rich Alfredo sauce. Try the tiramisu.

RELAX BAY
WHERE TO STAY & DINE

Le Meridien Phuket. 8/5 Tambol, Karon Noi, P.O. Box 277, Relax Bay, Phuket 83000. ☎ **800/225-5843** in the U.S., or 076/340-480. Fax 076/340-479. 470 units. A/C MINIBAR TV TEL. May–Oct $180–$220 double; from $470 suite. Nov–Apr $200–$240; from $490 suite. AE, DC, EURO, MC, V. Relax Bay airport shuttle bus.

Le Meridien Phuket is tucked away on secluded Relax Bay, with a lovely 600-yard beach and 40 acres of tropical greenery. This is one of the largest (verging on huge) resorts on the island, and during the high season it's almost always packed with European vacationers. The advantages of a larger resort are its numerous facilities—two swimming pools huge enough to windsurf in, beach water sports, four tennis courts, putting green and practice range, and one of the best fitness centers I've ever seen. My favorite amenity, though, is the brilliant Penguin Club, a professionally staffed and highly creative day-care center that kids just seem to love. The large building complex combines Western and traditional Thai architecture, and one of the advantages to its U-shape layout is that it ensures that 80% of the rooms face the ocean. The modern furnishings in each cheerful room are of rattan and teak, with a hi-fi and balcony with wooden sundeck chairs. No fewer than 10 restaurants give you all kinds of choice: Asian, beachside barbecue, Italian, Japanese, seafood, royal Thai, plus pubs with games and live shows.

PATONG

In Patong the post office is on Thaveewongse Road (the main beach road) in the center of the strip near the Banthai Hotel. My favorite place to frequent is **Pizzadelic,** a combination pizzeria, bar, and Internet cafe at 93/3 Taveewongse Rd. in Patong (☎ **076/341-545**). They have fairly reliable service, plus you can have a beer while you check your e-mail.

WHERE TO STAY

Expensive

Amari Coral Beach Resort. 104 Moo 4, Patong Beach, Phuket 83150. ☎ **076/340-106.** Fax 076/340-115. 200 units. A/C MINIBAR TV TEL. Low season $107–$121 double; from $200 suite. Peak season $145–$165; from $243 suite. AE, DC, MC, V. Far south end of Patong Beach.

The Coral Beach stands on the rocks high above Patong, at the southern tip well away from the din of Patong's congested strip, but close enough to enjoy the mayhem. While the beachfront is lacking—the rocks prevent swimming and water sports other than snorkeling—the two swimming pools overlook the huge bay, as does the terrace lobby, resort restaurants, and guest rooms. The rooms have seafoam tones, balconies, and full amenities, so you'll not miss any of the comforts of home.

Dining: The nicest restaurant here is La Gritta Italian, which has bay-side views from atop the bluff at the far south of the bay. The Kinaree Thai and coffee shop offer other cuisine options.

Amenities: Outdoor swimming pools, car rental, shuttle to Kata Beach, tour desk, baby-sitting, massage, beauty parlor, laundry, tennis court, dive center, and game room.

Diamond Cliff Resort. 284 Prabaramee Rd., Patong, Phuket 83150. ☎ **076/340-501.** Fax 076/340-507. www.Diamondcliff.com. 222 units. A/C MINIBAR TV TEL. 6,800B ($178.95) double; from 8,800B ($231.60) suite. Peak season (Dec–Feb) supplement 1,500B ($39.45). AE, DC, MC, V. Far south end, on the road to Kamala Beach.

Located a 10-minute walk from the center of Patong Beach, the Diamond Cliff is a gleaming, well maintained, full-facility resort, with rooms done in soothing sea greens and blues and light wood trim. All guest quarters command an ocean view and the grounds are attractively landscaped (they even have a boardwalk to Patong that winds through the rocky coastline). Our one caveat (other than the high price) is that the Diamond Cliff is for those who enjoy a view but don't require a beach on the premises; they do operate a shuttle to a small private bit of sand across the bay, but for the money, you might want your own bit of sand. However, for facilities they sport quite a selection—with three outdoor pools, a spa, games room, tennis, and beach club activities.

Dining: There are eight restaurants including Japanese, Western grill, Korean barbecue, Italian, Thai, and seafood.

Amenities: Health club, minigolf, swimming pool, scuba diving lessons, tennis courts, private beach, barber and beauty shop, shopping arcade, children's game room, sauna, 24-hour room service, concierge, taxi service, baby-sitting, house doctor.

Holiday Inn Resort Phuket. 52 Thaweewong Rd., Patong Beach, Phuket 83150. ☎ **800/HOLIDAY** in the U.S., or 076/340-608. Fax 076/340-435. 272 units. A/C MINIBAR TV TEL. 5,200B ($136.85) double; from 6,800B ($178.95) suite. Peak season surcharge 1,200B ($31.60) Dec 25–Jan 31. AE, DC, EURO, MC, V. Patong Beach strip.

The buildings at this Holiday Inn are modern, concrete blocks; guest rooms are furnished with rattan furniture and have balconies. The resort fronts the beach and offers water sports, including diving. This property has become especially popular with European groups, as is reflected in its restaurant offerings. Although there is little to distinguish it, the Holiday Inn is one of Patong's better accommodations.

Dining: The Seabreeze Café, Sam's Steakhouse, Suan Nok Thai Restaurant, and The Pizzeria Restaurant give you quite a few dining options.

Amenities: No-smoking floors, outdoor swimming pool, tennis courts, fitness club, water sports, self-service laundry, game room, Kids Club, sauna, massage, 24-hour room service, concierge, shuttle service, baby-sitting, house doctor, laundry service.

Patong Merlin. 99/2 Moo 4, Patong Beach, Phuket 83150. ☎ **076/340-037.** Fax 076/340-394. 386 units. A/C MINIBAR TV TEL. Low season 4,591B ($120.80) double; from 13,536B ($356.20) suite. Peak season 4,944B ($130.10) double; from 14,124B ($371.70) suite. Christmas and New Year's surcharges 3,000B ($78.95) per person. AE, DC, MC, V. On Patong strip near south end of town.

The Merlin is well maintained and has a particularly attractive center courtyard. All rooms have balconies, some of which overlook the three swimming pools (each with a pool bar) and a nicely manicured garden. The lobby is spacious and airy with comfortable, clubby rattan furniture. Facilities also include a fitness club, water sports, a game room, gym, sauna, and snooker.

Phuket Cabana Resort. 41 Thaweewongse Rd., Patong Beach, Phuket 83150. ☎ **076/340-138.** Fax 076/340-178. 81 units. A/C MINIBAR TV TEL. 4,500B–5,600B ($118.40–$147.35) double; from 9,000B ($236.85) suite. AE, DC, MC, V. Middle of beach road.

These Thai island cabins are closely packed but are quiet and have some character: exposed wood beams, dark lacquered bamboo, rattan wall coverings, and stone floors. Though crowded, the closeness of the beach, the seaside Aquatique Restaurant, the resident PADI-dive instructor, and the hotel's enticing pool make this one of Patong's better-value lodgings. Ask about their May to October discounts!

Moderate

To be honest, the lower-priced accommodations near the beach are noisier and tawdrier than ever. If you're looking for bargains in Patong, go up Soi Bangla away from the water to Soi Saen Sabai, where you'll find several small, newer hotels, including the following:

Andaman Resortel. 65/21–25 Soi Sansabai, Patong Beach, Phuket 83150. ☎ **076/ 341-516.** Fax 076/341-712. 45 units. A/C TV TEL. 1,200B ($31.60) double. MC, V. Off Soi Bangla.

The most attractive of the newer alternatives, the Andaman offers both warmth and modern Thai style. The rooms are light with simple and comfortable furnishings.

Royal Palm Resortel. 66/2 Taweewong Rd., Patong Beach, Phuket 83150. ☎ **076/ 292-510.** Fax 076/292-512. 43 units. A/C TV TEL. 1,800 ($47.35) double. MC, V. In the middle of the Patong Beach strip.

If you want to be in the center of it all, Royal Palm is pretty great—in the middle of the crazy main thoroughfare, just across the street from the beach. Rooms are not bad—with king-size beds, closet space, and a bathroom that has a long bathtub. I was surprised to find such an inexpensive place at this location (during off-peak season you can get a room for under 1,000B/$26.30). But I wasn't surprised to hear so much noise outside the window.

WHERE TO DINE

Baan Rim Pa. Kalim Beach Rd., north end of Patong Beach. ☎ **076/340-789.** Reservations necessary. Entrees 250B–1,200B ($6.60–$31.60). Daily noon–2:30pm and 6–10pm. AE, DC, MC, V. THAI.

In a beautiful Thai-style teak house, Baan Rim Pa has dining in the romantic indoor setting or with a gorgeous view of the bay from outdoor terraces. This restaurant is one of the most popular restaurants on the island, for locals who wish to entertain as well as for visitors, so be sure to reserve your table early. Thai cuisine features seafood, with a variety of other meat and vegetable dishes, including a rich duck curry and a sweet honey chicken dish. The seafood basket is a fantastic assortment of prawns, mussels, squid, and crab.

Patong Seafood Restaurant. Patong Beach Rd., Patong Beach. ☎ **076/340-247.** Reservations not accepted. 80B–250B ($2.10–$6.60); seafood at market price. Daily 7am–11pm. AE, DC, MC, V. SEAFOOD.

Take an evening stroll on the lively Patong Beach strip and you'll find quite a few open-air seafood restaurants displaying their catches of the day on chipped ice at their entrances. The best choice of them all is the casual Patong Seafood, for the freshest and the best selection of seafood, including several types of local fish, lobster, squid (very tender), prawn, and crab. The menu has a fantastic assortment of preparation styles—with photos of popular Thai noodles and Chinese stir-fry dishes. Service is quick and efficient. The place fills up quickly, so it's best to arrive here early.

Sala Bua. In the Phuket Cabana Hotel, 94 Thaweewong Rd., Patong Beach. ☎ **076/ 342-100.** Reservations recommended for weekends. Entrees 120B–260B ($3.15–$6.85). AE, DC, MC, V. At the north end of the beach at Phuket Cabana Hotel.

Dining is breezy at Sala Bua, one of the few restaurants in Patong that enjoys beach-side views. The lunch menu features light Thai dishes, and Western sandwiches and burgers are inexpensive and well prepared. Dinners are wonderful, especially the southern-Thai style seafood favorites—local Phuket lobster, huge juicy tiger prawns, and fresh fish steaks in a variety of local preparation styles. Sala Bua is a far more intimate option from the crowded seafood joints across the street. Under the pavilion, candlelight and local decor make for a nice touch, but to see the beach you must sit on the patio.

✪ **Sea Hag Restaurant.** 78/5 Soi Permong III, Patong Beach. ☎ **076/341-111.** Reservations recommended for weekend dinner. 80B–200B ($2.10–$5.25). Daily 11am–2pm, 5pm–midnight. No credit cards. THAI.

The name is far from appealing, but everything else about the place is, making it one of Patong's favorite joints for local residents and travelers. The food is superb (I loved my baked seafood in curry), and the casual dining atmosphere captures a local style of grace with an easy charm.

THE NORTHWEST COAST
PANSEA BEACH (SURIN BEACH)
Also known as Surin Beach, the Pansea area has coconut plantations, steep slopes leading down to the beach, and small, private coves dominated by two of the best hotels on the island.

Where to Stay & Dine
✪ **Amanpuri.** Pansea Beach, Phuket 83110. ☎ **076/324-333.** Fax 076/324100. 43 units. A/C MINIBAR TEL. $390 garden-view pavilion; $900 ocean view pavilion. Peak season (Oct–May) $490 garden-view pavilion; $1,120 ocean-view pavilion. AE, DC, MC, V. North end of cove.

The discreet and sublime Amanpuri is the Phuket address for visiting celebrities, from Hollywood and elsewhere. Small wonder, it is the most elegant and secluded resort in Thailand and quite possibly Southeast Asia, for that matter. The lobby is an open-air pavilion with a standing Buddha near a lovely swimming pool, and stairs leading to the beach. Superior Pavilions are freestanding houses creeping up the dense coconut palm grounds from the main building. Each is masterfully designed in a traditional Thai style, with teak and tile floors, sliding teak doors, exquisite built-ins, and well-chosen accents, including antiques. Private *salas* (covered patios), are perfect for romantic dining or secluded sunbathing. For special mood setting, check under the bathroom sinks for heavenly incense and burners. Less expensive suites are available inland from the resort, across the road.

Dining: Two restaurants, the Restaurant Amanpuri and the Terrace, serve Western cuisine, including imported rarities that are hard to find in Thailand, and great Thai dishes.

Amenities: They have their own yacht fleet, water-sports equipment and instruction, swimming pool, tennis and squash courts, fitness center, sauna, and private beach. For quiet times, there's a library with books, videos, and CDs (stereo systems are standard in each room), room service (6am to midnight), concierge, complimentary airport taxi service, house doctor.

The Chedi Phuket. 118 Moo 3, Choeng Talay, Pansea Beach, Phuket 83110. ☎ **076/ 324-017.** Fax 076/324-252. www.ghmhotels.com. 110 units. A/C MINIBAR TV TEL. $150 hill cottage; $170 superior cottage; $200 deluxe cottage; $250 beach cottage. Peak season (Nov–Apr) $320 hill cottage; $340 superior cottage; $380 deluxe cottage; $430 beach cottage. AE, DC, JCB, MC, V. Next to the Amanpuri.

These bungalows have been constructed in a manner that owes something to its august neighbor, the Amanpuri (see above in this section). It, too, is located well above the beach, and it commands an excellent view as well as having its own private stretch of sand. It is one of the most enticing accommodations on the island—from the sophisticated lobby (with columns and lily pond) to sleek and handsome private bungalows. From beachside or hillside location, one or two bedroom, each is a mini-isuite with a lovely private sundeck. The swimming pool is gorgeous, with views of the beach, and they'll also arrange any water sports, sightseeing tour or activity you could ever want. While it may not be as outwardly impressive as its extraordinary neighbor, The Chedi is more affordable and it's quiet, comfortably informal, and very relaxing. The dining options are wonderful, too: Lomtalay for Thai, Beach Restaurant for seafood and daytime snacks, and the Poolside Café, open to fabulous sunsets over the bay.

BANG THAO BAY (THE LAGUNA RESORT COMPLEX)

This area, 22km (14 miles) west of Phuket town, 20 minutes south of the airport, has been transformed into an "integrated resort." With five major resorts all sharing top-rated facilities like a world-class health spa and the island's best golf course, plus countless excellent restaurants, it's an enclave carefully segregated from any down-scale development. Besides the two hotels recommended here, there are luxury accommodations at the **Laguna Beach Club** (☎ 076/324-352), the **Sheraton Grande Laguna Beach** (☎ 076/324-101), and the **Allamanda Phuket** (☎ 076/324-360). The grounds are impressively landscaped, and several lagoons give the complex a lush and more humid environment than found elsewhere on the island (as well as more mosquitoes).

Where to Stay

✪ **Banyan Tree Phuket.** 33 Moo 4, Srisoonthorn Rd., Cherngtalay District, Amphur Talang, Phuket 83110. ☎ 800/525-4800 in the U.S., or 076/324-374. Fax 076/324-375. 86 units. A/C MINIBAR TV TEL. $170–$350 bungalow; $600 2-bedroom bungalow. AE, DC, MC, V. North end of beach.

Far from the crowds of rowdy Patong and Karon Beaches, Banyan Tree is a famous hideaway for honeymooners and people who just want to relax. Private villas with walled courtyards (many with private pool or Jacuzzi) are spacious and grand, lushly styled in teakwood with an outdoor bath, and a platform bed under large Thai murals depicting the Ramakien, the story of the Ramayana. The resort can arrange private barbecues at your villa, and massage under each villa's *sala*, (outdoor Thaian-style pavilion). The reception area is a large open *sala* with lovely lotus pools. The Banyan Tree Spa wins awards every year. A small village in itself, the spa provides a wide range of beauty and health treatments in relaxing rooms, plus Jacuzzi, sauna, steam, hair styling, fitness pavilion (with daily meditation lessons), separate spa pool and cafe serving delicious, light and healthy dishes. The main pool is truly impressive—a free-form lagoon, landscaped with greenery and rock formations—with a water canal (currents that gently pull you through the passage).

Dining: Within the main building the resort's five main restaurants serve a choice of Thai, Mediterranean, Southeast Asian, and other international cuisine.

Amenities: Spa; fitness pavilion; beauty garden; two pools; water sports; three tennis courts; squash court, snooker room; adjacent golf course, 24-hour room service, concierge, shuttle service, baby-sitting, laundry service. For added options, Banyan Tree guests have signing privileges at the sister resorts of the Laguna consortium.

Dusit Laguna Resort. 390 Srisoontorn Rd., Cherngtalay District, Phuket 83110. ☎ 076/324-320. Fax 076/324-174. 226 units. A/C MINIBAR TV TEL. Low season $196 double; from $312 suite. Peak-season $270 double; from $430 suite. AE, DC, JCB, MC, V. South end of beach.

Dusit is undoubtedly the finest hotel group in Thailand, and this particular Dusit has linked itself with five other fine resorts in this northern area of the island. Although sharing restaurants and facilities with the others, this resort has three fine restaurants of its own. The rooms are tastefully, if a bit fussily, decorated; mosquito nets that are part of the decor may charm some, but they reminded us of the pests humming outside. Bathrooms are large but a bit cluttered and certainly not airy. I suggest requesting a sea-view room. The well-landscaped gardens have an especially delightful waterfall and an excellent pool, and the grounds open onto a long, wide, white sand beach flanked by two lagoons. The facilities for kids are pretty good: a Kids Corner, open daily 10am to 8pm, for children 2 years old and up; baby-sitting; a playground; and computer games.

Dining: The JunkCeylon fine dining room specializes in fresh seafood and meats; La Trattoria is a lunch-and-dinner venue for pizza, pasta, and other Italian dishes; the Ruenthai Restaurant, overlooking the South Lagoon, offers regional dishes from all over the country; Laguna Café has a view of the pool, waterfall, and gardens; there's also an al fresco barbecue terrace lounge that overlooks the water.

Nai Yang Beach

Nai Yang National Park is an expanse of haphazardly (and illegally) developed shoreline, framed by a dense forest of palms, casuarina, and other indigenous flora. It's good for those who want to leave the densest crowds behind, but be warned that it has become exceedingly popular with Thai campers, as well as foreign backpackers. There are a few bungalows, but most people bring a tent.

Nai Yang has been known for its part in National Fish Species Multiplication Day, when the Phuket's Marine Biological Center released its crop of sea turtles back into the Andaman Sea. In more recent years, however, most turtles have been brought to safer waters. The turtles weigh from 100 to 1,500 pounds and swim the waters around Phuket, unprotected from fishermen. If not for the efforts of the Marine Biological Center, these creatures would probably be locally extinct. April 13, during the Songkran holiday, continues to be the day of release, and activities are organized on this day.

Where to Stay

Pearl Village. Nai Yang Beach and National Park, Amphur Talang, Phuket 83104. ☎ **076/327-006.** Fax 076/327-338. www.phuket.com/pearlvillage. 226 units. A/C MINIBAR TV TEL. 2,460B ($64.75) double; 2,640B ($69.45) cottage; 3,000B ($78.95) family cottage; 3,000B ($78.95) suite. Peak season 5,000B ($131.60) double; 5,300B ($139.45) cottage; 5,900B ($155.25) family cottage; 5,900B ($155.25) suite. AE, DC, V. Five min. south of the airport.

Not as glitzy as some of Phuket's newest resorts, the Pearl Village nevertheless holds its own due to its location, facilities, and friendly atmosphere. On the periphery of the national park, the Pearl Village is relatively isolated from the ravages of overdevelopment and, in comparison to other shorelines, has a cleaner stretch of beach. The facilities are excellent, particularly for families, such as an excellent swimming pool with a powerful waterfall. The friendly personal service is as homey as the scale of the place. Special kudos go to the landscape architect and the gardening staff who maintain one of Phuket's loveliest grounds.

Only caveat: The hotel is on the far north of the island (about 45 minutes from Phuket town) and isn't for those who need to be near the action. Michael Jackson, Prince Phillip, and King Gustav of Sweden have stayed here.

Dining/Diversions: Among the several dining outlets are the Village Café, the Palm Court (for steak and seafood), and Thai and Japanese cuisine at Pae Thip, located in the center of a small lake. There are evening shows for kids, including magic, movies, and Thai dancing.

Amenities: Windsurfing, scuba center, fishing, two pools (one for children), kindergarten, game room, barber and beauty shop, golf green, tennis courts, weight room, jogging track, horse and elephant riding, snooker, table tennis, 24-hour room service, concierge, shuttle service, baby-sitting, laundry service.

Mai Khao Beach

Like Nai Yang, Mai Khao is a marvelous beach on the northeastern shore that's even closer to the airport. It's Phuket's longest beach and is the site where a few sea turtles try to lay their eggs during December and January. Unfortunately their eggs are coveted by Thai and Chinese people, who eat them for the supposed life-sustaining power.

4 Exploring Phuket

As you can see from the length of the section that follows, you can spend a lot of time on Phuket and still not do everything. Thanks to years of resort growth, there are well-developed activities here, and literally something for everyone. Upon arrival you can't help but notice the hundreds of tour operators, each vying for your business. For each activity I've provided the most reputable firms, those with the best quality of activities, and even some of the more unusual, to help steer you clear of any shoddy operators.

WATER ADVENTURES

Most of your water sports activities are almost exclusively on Patong Beach—centralized for convenience, but restricted to one beach, so swimmers can enjoy other beaches without the buzz of a jet ski or power boat. There are no specific offices to organize such activities, just walk to the beach and chat up the guys under the umbrellas who'll set up activities from impromptu operations. **Jet skis** can be rented out for 30 minutes at 700B ($18.40), and a 10-minute **parasailing** ride is 600B ($15.80). You'll also find **Hobie Cats** for around 600B ($15.80) per hour, as well as **windsurf** boards for 200B ($5.25) per hour.

For yachting, Phuket can't be rivaled in Southeast Asia. Facilities from recreational boating are better than anywhere else, while Phuket is a **sailing** dream come true, with the crystal blue waters of the Andaman Sea, and gorgeous island scenery. A great guide, *Sail Thailand,* accurately documents all of them. It's distributed in the United States, the United Kingdom, and Australia, or you can contact **Artasia Press** at ☎ 02/861-3360; fax 02/861-3363.

Every December Phuket hosts the increasingly popular **King's Cup Regatta,** in which almost 100 international racing yachts competed. For more information check out www.kingscup.com.

If you don't have your own yacht, but still want a taste of the sea, you can charter a bareboat or crewed boat from **Thai Marine Leisure** (c/o Phuket Boat Lagoon, 22/1 Thepkasatri Rd., Tambon Koh Kaew Amphur Muang, Phuket 83200; ☎ 076/239-111; fax 076/238-974; www.thaimarine.com). **Sunsail,** Phuket Boat Lagoon, Unit 20/5 (☎ 076/239-057; fax 076/238-940), one of the best charter companies in the world, also handles charters from Phuket. Contact them to discuss prices and availability.

Sport fishers will appreciate **game fishing** for marlin, sailfish, and wahoo organized through **Phuket Sport Fishing Center,** P.O. Box 214, Phuket (☎ 076/214-713, fax 076/236-182, e-mail: wahoo@phuket.loxinfo.co.th). Also contact **Thai Marine Leisure** (c/o Phuket Boat Lagoon, 22/1 Thepkasatri Rd., Tambon Koh Kaew Amphur Muang, Phuket 83200; ☎ 076/339-111; fax 076/238-974). For game fishing talk to **Blue Water Anglers,** deep-sea fishing experts with well-equipped boats. They'll take you out for marlin, sailfish, swordfish, and tuna, and also have special night-fishing programs. Stop by at 35/7 Sakadidet Rd., Phuket town or call ☎ 076/391-287, fax 076/391-342. Or you can e-mail them at info@bluewater-anglers.com.

For a very unique water adventure, try a **sea kayak** trip to Phang-nga Bay National Park, 1½-hour drive north of Phuket (3 hours by boat) off Thailand's mainland. Between 5 and 10 million years ago, limestone thrust above the water's surface, creating more than 120 small islands. These craggy rock formations (the famous scenery for the James Bond classic, *The Man with the Golden Gun*) look like they were taken straight from a Chinese scroll painting. Sea kayaks are perfect for inching your way into the many breathtaking caves and chambers that hide beneath the jagged cliffs. Most companies will drive you to Phang-Nga province where you'll pick up the kayaks for the water adventure, then bring you back to Phuket. The company to pioneer the cave trips, **Sea Canoe,** in Phuket town, 367/4 Yaowarat Rd. (☎ **076/212-252**), is a very ecofriendly group, and the most professional around. The full day trip is 2,970B ($78.15) per person.

For a different view of the gorgeous Phang-Nga Bay, book a trip aboard the *June Bahtra,* a restored Chinese sailing junk, to **cruise** the islands. Full day trips include lunch and hotel transfers. Adults are 2,200B ($57.90) per person (alcoholic beverages are separate), while children are 1,500 ($39.45) each. Contact East West Siam, 119 Rat-U-Thit 2000 Year Road, Patong (☎076/340-912).

You can also book a **speedboat** for private trips to nearby Similan Islands, Ko Phi Phi, Phang-Nga Bay, and other small beach paradises. Day and half-day excursions are incredibly expensive so consider getting a group together to chip in for the 25,000B ($657.90) per day for a speedboat with two engines. Call **Phuket Water Taxi,** Canal Village, Laguna Phuket (☎ 076/324-453; fax 076/270-563).

In the smaller bays around the island, such as Nai Harn Beach or Relax Bay, you'll come across some lovely **snorkeling** just close to the shore. For the best **coral** just off the shoreline, trek up to Had Nai Yang National Park for the long reef in clear shallow waters. Most skin divers prefer day trips to outer islands such as the Similan Islands, Ko Phi Phi, or the newest favorite Raya Island (pronounced by the Thais as "Laya" Island). The best times to snorkel are from November to April before the monsoon comes and makes the water too choppy. Almost every tour operator arranges group day boating trips with hotel transfers, lunch, and gear—they all book people for groups on the same boats, so services are all the same, and the prices are under 2,000B ($52.65) a day per person.

The island's more than 45 **scuba** operators are testimony to the beautiful attractions that lie deep within the Andaman Sea. Sites at nearby coral walls, caves, and wrecks can be explored in full day, overnight, or long-term excursions. All operators advertise full PADI courses, Divemaster courses, and 1-day introductory lessons. Let me rave for a moment about **Dive Master's** EcoDive 2000, which is timely and innovative. A program of special dives planned under the supervision of marine biologists and environmentalists, this unique program takes small groups beyond the standard dive routes to pristine areas, educating divers about sea creatures and ecodiving. Contact Dive Master in Phuket at 75/20 Moo 10, Patak Road, Chalong (☎ 076/280-330); or plan your trip in advance through their Bangkok office (☎ 02/259-3195; fax 259-3196). For a 5-day live-aboard trip, you will pay around 31,000B ($815.80).

Fantasea Divers is the oldest and most reputable firm on Phuket. Their main office is at Patong Beach at 219 Ratchautit Rd. (☎ 076/340-088; fax 076/340-309), but they have other branches along Thaveewongse Road (the main beach road) in Patong. Dive packages include a 6-day and 7-night trip for $1,650, or a 9-day and 10-night trip that includes diving off the Burmese coast for $2,475 plus $130 for Myanmar entry fee. They also have a 4-day PADI certification course for 11,000B ($289.45).

If you can only spare a day for diving, great day trips to nearby reefs and wrecks are put together by **Sea Bees Diving,** a highly respected firm on the island. Day trips go for 2,400B ($63.15). Visit them at 1/3 Moo 9, Viset Road, Chalong Bay, or phone/fax ☎ 076/381-765. Find them on the Web at www.sea-bees.com.

TREKKING & OTHER ACTIVITIES

To experience the wild side of Phuket's interior, try a **rainforest trekking** journey through the Khao Phra Thaew National Park. Jungle Tours operates an ecofriendly small group trek through 3.5km of jungle paths past waterfalls and swimming holes. The half-day excursion costs only 650B ($17.10) per person including hotel transfers, English-speaking jungle guides, and drinks. Booking is made by calling ☎ 076/285-223.

Then there's **elephant trekking,** a perennial favorite for children, and a great time for adults too. While it makes sense to think elephant tourism is harmful to these creatures, environmentalists claim the industry is a win/win situation. Elephants can no longer support themselves in the wild in Thailand, and many working elephants have found themselves out of jobs. Victims of starvation and ivory poachers, or on city streets parading for tourists, these beasts are far better off under the expert care of quality tourism firms. Siam Safari Nature Tours, winner of numerous tourism awards, coordinates daily treks on elephants, Land Rovers and river rafts. Their three-in-one Half-Day Eco-Adventure includes 4 hours of elephant treks through jungles to rubber estates, Jeep tours to see local wildlife, and a light river rafting journey to Chalong Bay. The cost is 1,350B ($35.55) for adults and 800B ($21.05) for children. A full day tour is the three in one plus a trek on foot through Khao Pra Taew National Park and a Thai lunch. Cost is 1,950B ($51.30) adults; 1,200 ($31.60) children. Siam Safari's office is at 70/1 Chaofa Rd. in Chalong (☎ 076/280-116; www.siamsafari.com).

Island Safari Adventure Company, 77 Moo 6 Chalong (☎ 076/280-858), also does the elephant trekking thing, but it's geared more for those who can't invest a whole 3 hours for the experience. A half-hour elephant trek is only 600B ($15.80) for adults and 400B ($10.55) for kids; an hour costs 1,000B ($26.30) adults and 700B ($18.40) kids. Check out their free elephant shows daily at 8:45am, 9:45am, 10:45am, 2:45pm, 3:45pm, and 4:45pm. The babies are heartbreakingly cute.

Meanwhile, back on terra firma, it wouldn't be an Asian resort without **golf.** The best course on Phuket is the **Banyan Tree** Club & Laguna, 34 Moo 4, Srisoonthorn Road, at the **Laguna Resort Complex** on Bang Tao Bay (☎ 076/324-350, fax 076/324-251), a par-71 championship course with many water features (greens fees: weekdays and weekends 2,335B/$61.45; guests of Laguna resorts pay 1,635B/$43.05). The **Blue Canyon Country Club,** 165 Moo 1, Thepkasattri Road, near the airport (☎ 076/327-440, fax 076/327-449), is a par-72 championship course with natural hazards, trees, and guarded greens (greens fees: weekdays and weekends 3,400B/$89.45). An older course, the **Phuket Country Club,** 80/1 Vichitsongkram Rd., west of Phuket town (☎ 076/321-038, fax 076/321-721), has beautiful greens and fairways, plus a giant lake (greens fees: weekdays and weekends 2,540B/$66.85).

CULTURAL PURSUITS

When you're ready to take in a little culture, the first place to stop is the **Thalang National Museum,** toward the eastern side of the island on Sri Soonthorn in Thalang District off Highway 402 just past the Heroine's Monument (☎ 076/311-426; open daily from 9am to 4pm; admission 30B/80¢). They have extensive displays on Phuket's indigenous cultures, the history of the Thais on Phuket, and crafts from the southern Thai regions. There's also a fascinating image of the Hindu god Vishnu that was uncovered from forest overgrowth in Phang-Nga in the early 1900s. The image dates from the 9th century A.D.—evidence of the presence of Indian merchants long ago, and their influence on the Thai people.

Phuket may not be the center of traditional Thai culture like its northern cousins, Bangkok or Chiang Mai, but there are a few **Buddhist temples** on the island that are quite notable. I highly recommend this little window on Thai culture, especially if Phuket is your only stop in Thailand. The most unique temple is **Wat Pra Tong,** located along Highway 402 in Thalang just south of the airport. Years ago, a boy fell ill and dropped dead after tying his buffalo to a post sticking out of the ground. It was later discovered that the post was actually the top of a huge Buddha image that was buried under the earth. Numerous attempts to dig out the post failed—during one attempt in 1785, workers were chased off by hornets. Everyone took all this failure to mean that the Buddha image wanted to just stay put, so they covered the "post" with a plaster image of The Buddha's head and shoulders and built a temple around it.

Near Wat Pra Tong, **Wat Pra Nahng Sahng** (also on Highway 402, at the traffic light in Thalang) houses three very interesting Buddha images. Made from tin, a local natural resource once considered semiprecious, each image has a smaller Buddha in its belly.

The most famous temple among the Thais is **Wat Chalong.** Chalong was the first resort on Phuket, back when the Thais first started coming to the island for vacations. Nowadays, the discovery of better beaches on the west side of the island has driven most tourists away from this area, but the temple still remains the center of Buddhist worship. While the temple compound itself is pretty standard in terms of modern temples, the place comes to life during Buddhist holy days. See the section on "When to Go" in chapter 2 for dates and descriptions of religious holidays. The temple is on the Bypass Road, about 8km south of Phuket town.

Sea Gypsies, considered the indigenous people of Phuket, are fast disappearing from the island and surrounds. Commercial fishing interests and shoreline development continue to threaten their existence, which is primarily subsistence fishing. These people are related to both the Orang Laut, sea people of Malaysia, and the Sakai tribes on Thailand's southern peninsula. While many live primarily at sea, there remains two small settlements on Phuket island, one on Ko Sirey east of Phuket town, and another at Rawai Beach just south of Chalong Bay. The small **fishing villages** are nothing more than simple shacks and long-tail boats. It's an enlightening trip to see these people and their disappearing culture. Be prepared for panhandling children.

When just eating Thai cuisine isn't enough, you can learn how to make it yourself at The Boathouse. Weekend **cooking classes** (from 10am to 2pm) with Chef Tummanoon introduce students not only to preparation styles and ingredients, but to Thai culture as well. Two half-day sessions are 2,000B ($52.65) per person. Call **The Boathouse** at ☎ 076/330-015, or fax 076/330-561.

A touristy cultural attraction, the **Phuket Orchid Garden & Thai Village** does have regularly scheduled **music and dance performances** typical to southern Thailand, which seem harder and harder to find these days. After each show stick around to see the trained elephants. They're open from 11am to midnight daily, but shows are only at 11am and 5:30pm. You'll also find crafts and local industry demonstrations. On Thepkasatri Road call ☎ 076/214-860 for more information. Admission is 230B ($8.40) for adults; 120B ($3.15) for children.

NATURAL TREASURES

Had Nai Yang National Park, 90 square km of protected land in the northwest corner of the island, offers a peaceful retreat from the rest of the island's tourism madness. There are two fantastic reasons to make the journey out to the park. The first is for Phuket's largest coral reef in shallow water, only 1,400 meters from the shore. The second is for the giant leatherback turtles that come to nest every year between

November and February. Park headquarters is a very short hop from Phuket Airport off Highway 402.

Playful **monkeys** add a fun dimension to bars, restaurants, and guest houses around Thailand, where the adorable creatures are kept as pets. Many times, however, these gibbons are mistreated. Raised in captivity on unhealthful food in restricted living conditions, and subjected to human companionship exclusively, many develop psychological problems. Depression and despondency becomes common for maladjusted monkeys, with violent outbursts occurring sometimes. Bar monkeys end up drinking alcohol, and are force-fed uppers to keep them awake and lively—to the delight of tourists who aren't aware of the inevitable destruction it causes. The **Gibbon Rehabilitation Project,** off Highway 4027 at the Bang Pae waterfall in the northeastern corner of the island (☎ 076/260-492), cares for wayward gibbons, offering them a safe haven and teaching them how to relate with other gibbons in natural surroundings. Volunteer staff guide visitors to see gibbons that are still "humanized," some of which are hard-luck cases. The rest are strictly secluded to ensure their rehabilitation. Open daily from 10am to 4:30pm, admission is free, but a donation is desperately needed. 1,000B ($26.30) takes care of one gibbon for a year.

The **Phuket Aquarium** at the Phuket Marine Biological Center seeks to educate the public about local marine life and nature preservation. Unfortunately most of the signs throughout are in Thai (very disappointing). I'd have to say my favorite part was the drive to and from the aquarium through little suburban neighborhoods that were alive with flowering trees and shrubs. Open 8:30am to 4pm daily, admission is 20B (55¢) for adults and 5B (15¢) for children. Call ☎ 076/391-126 for more information.

The **Butterfly Garden & Aquarium,** Soi Phaniang, Samkong, Phuket town (☎ 076/215-616), captures and breeds hundreds of gorgeous butterflies in a large enclosed garden. Photo ops are great, so bring film. The aquarium may not be as large as the Marine Biology Center's, but here the tanks are filled with great "show fish," fascinating for their beautiful or unusual appearances rather than for marine education. Open daily from 9am to 5pm, adult admission 150B ($3.95), children below 10 years of age 60B ($1.60).

You'd never think seashells were so fascinating until you visit the **Phuket Shell Museum.** The largest shell museum in the world, this rare collection is simply beautiful. I especially love the gift shop full of high quality shell products. Huge gorgeous whole shells make very well received gifts for friends back home. Open daily from 8am to 7pm, the museum is at 12/2 Moo 2, Viset Road, Rawai Beach (just south of Chalong Bay) (☎ 076/381-266). Admission 100B ($2.65) for adults; children free.

OTHER ACTIVITIES

A romantic and charming way to see Phuket's jungles and beaches is on **horseback.** Phuket Riding Club, 95 Viset Rd., Chaweng Bay (☎ 076/288-213), and Phuket Laguna Riding Club, 394 Moo 1, Bangthao Beach (☎ 076/324-099), welcome riders of all ages and experience levels and can provide instruction for beginners and children. Prices are about 500B ($13.15) per hour.

Jungle Bungy Jump has to be the wackiest thing I've seen on Phuket. If you have the nerve to jump out 50 meters over the water, call their "Bungy Hotline" at ☎ 076/321-351. They're in Kathu near Patong. They charge 1,400B ($36.85) per jump.

PHUKET'S SPAS

If you've come to Phuket to decompress from daily life, slow down and cool out, I can't think of a better way to accomplish this than a visit to one of Phukets' **spas.** The most famous and exclusive facility here is **The Spa** at the Banyan Tree Phuket (see its listing above). Operated by the Banyan Tree Resort, this spa has won Condé Nast reader's choice awards for best spa in the world. In pavilions secluded by garden settings, choose from many types of massage, plus body and facial treatments for health and beauty. To make reservations call ☎ **076/324-374.** Expect to pay for the luxury—figure an average of 1,500B ($39.45) per treatment.

If the expense of a spa visit makes you even more stressed out, then **The Hideaway Herbal Aromatic Spa,** 47/4 Soi Nanai, Patong (☎ **076/340-591**) and a new location at 116/9 Moo 6, Patak Road, Kata (☎ **076/330-914**), is the place for you. A tiny compound of open-air thatch salas are tucked into a hillside, where the relaxed and informal staff prepare baths, and perform traditional Thai massage and aromatic herbal face, foot, and hair treatments using age-old Thai beauty treatments. Their signature skin-care products will make your body feel like silk. For those used to the usual generic spa routine, this homegrown place is a welcome retreat, and surprisingly affordable, too. At around 400B ($10.55) for a single treatment, you can have the works for what it costs for a single treatment at a resort spa.

Hideaway has also recently opened the **Kata Institute of Thai Massage,** 116/9 Patak Rd., Kata Beach (☎ **076/333-194**), for lessons in traditional Thai or Swedish massage.

5 Shopping

Patong Beach is the center of handicraft and souvenir shopping in Phuket. By day and night a journey through the main streets and small sois is an assault on anyone's shopping senses. Tailors, leather shops, jewelers, and ready-to-wear clothing boutiques occupy storefronts, while vendors line the sidewalks selling everything from batik clothing, T-shirts, pirate CDs, local arts and handicrafts, northern hill tribe handicrafts, silver, and souvenir trinkets. You'll also find people standing on corners holding out sarongs, fabrics, even luggage, in the hopes someone will stop and buy. The shops and vendors stay open until around 10 or 11pm nightly, so it's a fun stroll after dinner. But be warned. Heavy tourist traffic has inflated prices in Patong to unbelievable levels (a batik sarong that costs 100B ($2.65) in Bangkok was quoted as 380B ($10) in Patong!), so be prepared to bargain. It helps to know how much these items go for in other parts of the country. But my advice: If you are going to other parts of Thailand, do your shopping there. You can find any of these items in Bangkok. As for handicrafts, if something catches your eye, ask where it was made. Many northern hill tribe crafts are sold here, and if you're headed up to Chiang Mai later in your trip you'll find the selection there much wider, the quality of handicrafts better and the prices far more realistic.

For other shopping around the island it's best to have your own wheels. There are some cute shops in Phuket town and others on Highway 402 (Thepkrasattri Road),

The Best Sunset

There's a small point at the southern tip of the island that everybody will tell you has the best view of the sunset. And they're right. From the cliffs atop Promthep Cape, the view of the sky as it changes colors from deep reds to almost neon yellows can't compete with the best fireworks. The sun usually sets between 6:15 and 6:45pm. Get there early on weekends. The place isn't exactly a secret.

the airport access highway. In town you can find antiques at **Ban Boran Antiques,** 24 Takuapa Rd. (☎ 076/212-473), and **The Loft,** 36 Thalang Rd. (☎ 076/258-160). Along Highway 402, Chan's Antiques, 26/3 Thepkrasattri Rd. (☎ 076/215-229), is also a treat, as well as **Thai Style Antique and Décor,** 25/7 Thepkrasattri Rd. (☎ 076/215-980). They are easily spotted as you drive on the highway.

I like to do my gift shopping at the Phuket Shell Museum. Their huge gift shop has high quality shell products for the home, novelty items and fun shell souvenirs. They also have all varieties of gorgeous perfect seashells for sale, some of them massive. You could only pray to find one of these on the beach. Friends and family love them.

6 Phuket After Dark

From the huge billboards and glossy brochures, **Phuket FantaSea,** the newest theme attraction, seems like it could be touristy and tacky. But, to be perfectly honest with you, I had a fabulous time. A giant theme park, Phuket FantaSea is as slick as Universal Studios. The festival village entrance, lined with more shopping than you can imagine plus games, entertainment and snacks, keeps you busy until dinner. The buffet is served in the palatial Golden Kinaree Restaurant, with decor fashioned after the *kinaree* mythical half-woman half-bird creatures. After, proceed to the Sukhothai-styled Palace of the Elephants for the show. Frankly, the shopping is expensive and the dinner is nothing to rave about, but the show is incredibly entertaining, very professional, and oftentimes amazing. Don't fear the hype. Phuket FantaSea is at Kamala Beach, north of Patong, on the coastal road. Call ☎ 076/271-222 for reservations. The park opens at 5:30pm; the buffet begins at 6:30pm and the show at 9pm. Tickets for the show are 1,000B ($26.30) for adults and 700B ($18.40) for children, while dinner is 500B ($13.15) adults and 300B ($7.90) children. Hotel transfers are extra.

Phuket also has a resident cabaret troupe at **Simon Cabaret,** 100/6-8 Moo 4, Patong Karon Road (☎ 076/342-011). There are shows at 7:30pm and 9pm nightly, costing 750B ($19.75) between Patong and Karon beaches. It's a featured spot on every planned tour agenda, so be prepared for busloads. However, I still think the cabaret is a fun and interesting thing to see—many of the tourists who attend are Asians, and the show mainly caters to them, with lip-sync performances that in turn make all the Koreans laugh, the Japanese laugh, and the Chinese laugh. It can be a lot of fun. In between the comedy are dance numbers with pretty impressive sets, costumes, and naturally, transsexuals.

Every night you can catch **Thai boxing** at Vegas Thai Boxing in Patong at the Patong Simon Shopping Arcade on Soi Bangla. Bouts start every night from 7pm and last until 3am. Best of all, admission is free.

Patong nightlife is a wild time. Lit up like Las Vegas, the beach town hops like Saturday every night of the week. Shops and restaurants stay open late, and there's a never-ending choice of bars (both straight and gay), nightclubs, karaoke lounges, snooker halls, massage parlors, go-go bars, and sex shows à Patpong). Needless to say, Patong has a draw for those interested in sex tourism—most of the bars have hostesses who are not shy.

Patong has a couple of worthwhile discos. The centrally located **Banana Club,** 94 Thaweewong Rd. (☎ 076/340-301), has a fun mix of foreigners and locals, a good DJ spinning dance music and chart hits, and is almost always packed to the gills. My other favorite choice is **Safari,** 28 Sririrat Rd., Patong Hill (☎ 076/340-310), just south of Patong Beach. This giant Polynesian tiki-hut throbs with dance music, provided either by resident DJs or, in peak season, live international bands.

Muay Thai—Are You Ready to Rumble?

Want to taste some real Thai spice? The action in a Thai boxing ring is as much a sporting match as a spectacular cultural event, and it's as hot as ever. With hundreds of years of tradition, a deep spiritual core, and dangerous feats of physical violence, *muay thai,* or Thai boxing, is some of the best pure Thai entertainment for your money. While Thailand becomes increasingly adept at packaging its cultural gems for the tourism industry, muay thai retains a true cultural authenticity. In short, this is not a parade of costumes for tour buses. It's the real thing.

Although Thai boxers weigh in anywhere between 115 to 135 pounds (very small by western boxing standards), their forceful offensive moves include not only power punches, but elbow jabs, knee thrusts and charges, and fast kicks connecting hard shin to head, ribs or any other body part that gets in the way. Each bout lasts five rounds with 2-minute breaks in between. Except for the occasional KO or penalty dismissal, fighters usually go the distance, with the winner determined by a tally of effective blows: kicks gain the most points, while punches earn the fewest.

In the world of Thai sports, the best boxers enjoy quite a bit of fame. Training for years under a master teacher, each boxer is affiliated with a camp—a muay thai training center where he lives and trains. Once he is accepted to a camp, he attends a ceremony where he is blessed by a monk and presented with a *kruang rang,* a sacred amulet believed to ward off injury.

To many, the motions a boxer goes through at the start of a fight is as important as the fight itself. Before entering the ring, a *monkhon* is placed upon his head. This stiff, colorful headband is the mark of his camp. A sacred crown blessed by monks, the monkhon serves as a reminder that he not only fights for himself, but for his family, his camp and his teacher. Once inside the ring, he circles the perimeter counterclockwise to dispel bad vibes that could cause him defeat. He then kneels in the center of the ring, facing his camp. With boxing gloves laced, he *wais* a traditional Thai bow three times; one for the Buddha, one for the *sangha* (the order of monks), and one for the *Dhamma* (the Doctrine). At the same time he honors his teacher and his camp. The boxer is focused in meditation, centering his inner calm in preparation for the violence soon to come.

The dance that follows is full of grace and flowing movements. During the *ram muay* dance the boxer turns to each of the four primary directions, seeking

7 Side Trips from Phuket

PHANG-NGA

The landscape of Phang-Nga is quintessentially Asian, similar to Chinese scroll paintings of the Li River Valley (near Guilin), with plant-covered stone outcroppings rising majestically from tranquil water. On each formation there are craggy pinnacles with an occasional pine. Solitary fishermen navigate around these huge rocks and through mangrove swamps.

These unique geologic forms are thought to have been created between 2 million and 10 million years ago when tectonic plates pushed up layers of limestone and gave birth to the dramatic-looking outcroppings with their caves and stalactites. Many people have seen this area on film, in particular the 1973 Bond classic, *The Man with* protection and balance from the four noble truths of the Buddhist doctrine; compassion, temperance, prudence, and justice. As he kneels, he circles his gloves over his head to ask for courage. The monkhon is removed, and with his kruang rang tied firmly to his bicep, he enters the fight.

It is a curious act of spirituality for outside observers, but to the Thai fighter these opening elements are critical to his powers of strength, endurance, balance, and concentration. It is also watched with a keen eye by the audience, which feels it can gauge the power of a fighter based upon the integrity of his ritual. Needless to say, muay thai draws out the gambling crowds in hordes, who can be seen shaking hand signals in the air through every round of each fight.

To see Thai boxers in action, the best stadiums are in the capital city; however, numerous other cities and towns have local stadiums with weekly or biweekly fights. The action usually starts anywhere between 6:30pm and 7:30pm, depending on the stadium, and a string of up to 15 fights will keep you busy all night. Don't rush through dinner, though. The better fighters are saved until the end, so if you show up at around 9:30 you'll be right on time. In Bangkok, the **Ratchadamnoen Stadium** on Ratchadamnoen Nok Avenue (☎ 02/281-4205) hosts bouts every Monday, Wednesday, Thursday, and Sunday, while the **Lumphini Staduim** on Rama IV Road (☎ 02/251-4303) has bouts on Tuesdays, Fridays, and Saturdays. Tickets are 1,000B ($26.30) for ringside seats, 440B ($11.55) standing room only, and 220B ($5.80) if you don't mind crowding in the cage at the back. For other cities, stadium locations are given in each corresponding section.

For some it's not enough to be a simple spectator. If the sport inspires you to jump in the ring, you'll be happy to know about the Muay Thai Institute, which accepts foreign pupils for muay thai training in English. The 10-day Fundamental Muay Thai course costs $160, plus $8 per day room and board. After the introductory course, students can decide if they wish to continue with intermediate, advanced or professional level instruction, and special programs for trainers and referees. For more information contact the **Muay Thai Institute** at 336/932 Prachatipat Thanyaburi, Pathumthani, Rangsit 12130, Thailand (☎ 02/992-0099; fax 02/992/0100). Their Web site is at http://ite.nectec.or.th/; e-mail: muaythai@a-net.net.th.

the Golden Gun, which gave rise to the name James Bond Island (Ko Tapu and Ko Pingan). Lesser known are the rock paintings on Ko Kian, dating from more than 3,000 years ago.

There seems to be an endless stream of excursion boats, stinky and noisy, filled with day-trippers from Phuket slashing their way across this very much discovered waterway (it sometimes feels like taking the Jungle Cruise at Disneyland). In fact, Phang-Nga Bay has been the subject of recent controversy. While the area is protected by the government, some businessmen have acquired licenses to gather swallows' nests—the valuable main ingredient of the Chinese delicacy bird's nest soup—from the island caves. Public buses travel the 87km (54 miles) distance from Phuket town to Phangnga throughout the day (trip time: 2½ hours; 31B (80¢).

SIMILAN NATIONAL PARK

The nine islands that form the Similan archipelago are so pristine that they have been cited by diving authorities as among the best in the world for undersea exploration. I think you'd be hard put to find cleaner, clearer water than that around these utterly fantastic islands. The beaches that encircle all nine are fine, white sand bordered by lush forests that lead to rocky interiors. The only development is on **Ko Muang** (also known as Ko 4), which has a park's office and a few very basic bungalows (☎ **076/411-913; 400B/$10.55** per night). Many people head to Ko 9 for its superb diving as well as interesting caves; you'll see an amazing variety of brightly colored fish off Ko 9's coral reefs!

The Similan archipelago is 80km (50 miles) northwest of Phuket. Excursion boats take both day-trippers (it's a long way but worth it) and campers to Similan daily for about 1,700B ($44.75) including food and snorkel equipment, or 850B ($22.35) for a one-way transfer. **Seatran Travel** (☎ **076/211-809**) has a boat that departs every morning at 8am, and can provide hotel transfers. Note that this trip is very much affected by weather conditions (both for travel and for diving), so plan to visit from November to May (February and March are the best months) when the western monsoons are at their quietest. Under no circumstances should you fail to bring sunscreen with the highest possible rating; it's likely that the sun will be as hot and bright as you've ever encountered, and you can seriously burn within 10 minutes on the beach!

8 Ko Phi Phi

40km (25 miles) SW of Phuket; 42km (26 miles) W of Krabi

Ko Phi Phi, actually a pair of islands—Phi Phi Don and Phi Phi Le—were once the darlings of the backpacker set. Phi Phi Don, the larger of the two, was loved for its fabulous beaches, great snorkeling and remote location. As dozens of bungalow complexes sprouted along the beaches, development went unchecked, pollution got out of hand, and corals started to fall to pieces. You'll be happy to know that Ko Phi Phi has started cleaning up its act as Thailand has become more aware of its environmental problems. The winter of 1998–99 saw this small pair of islands making national headlines when Hollywood came to town to shoot *The Beach* based upon the Thailand-based novel by Alex Garland. The film's star, Leonardo DiCaprio, drew all kinds of rubberneckers to these parts, as well as environmental protection groups that, after years of turning a deaf ear, ironically howled loudly about the negative effects the production might have on the environment here.

ESSENTIALS

GETTING THERE   Quite a few companies provide daily trips to Phi Phi and back to Phuket. Boats to Phi Phi generally leave at 8:30am and take 1½ hours to complete the journey. Companies will arrange for your transfer to the jetty for an extra cost (from 50B to 200B/$1.30 to $5.25, depending on your hotel's location). During the high season—from November to April, these companies will sometimes run an afternoon boat at 2:30pm if there's demand. **Songserm** (☎ **076/222-570**) has both ferries (250B to 350B/$6.60 to $9.20 per person) and a speedboat (350B/$9.20). Round-trip, with returns in the afternoon, cost between 450B and 650B ($11.85 and $17.10). While the boats depart for Phi Phi year-round, you may want to be careful from May through October, when monsoon winds cause them to rock heavy—I've seen more than a few people lose their lunch over the side of the boat. Not a pretty sight.

Boats from Krabi on the mainland depart daily at 9:30am for the 2-hour trip (150B/$3.95). Head for the Chao Fah Pier in Krabi Town.

ORIENTATION & GETTING AROUND   Pi Pi Don, which most people refer to simply as Pi Pi, is an hourglass-shaped islet with a narrow middle only a few hundred yards wide. There are long beaches on both sides (Ton Sai Bay and Lo Dalham Bay), but the deeper water is on the south and east coasts. The town that has grown up around Ton Sai is actually turning into a fairly pleasant place now that islanders have learned something about the disposal of sewage and trash. The main jetty here serves as the central docking point for all boats, incoming and outgoing, plus island shuttles. Ton Sai is especially nice after all the day-trippers have departed back to Phuket, and you'll find most of the island's services and better eateries there. It's about a 15-minute walk north to Long Beach, for the best nearby swimming and fair accommodations.

The northern part of the island and the long east coast are far less built up, particularly around Laemthong Beach. One of the best parts about staying on Pi Pi is that cars are not seen on the island. All travel is by foot (be careful on the steep trails) or boat. Unfortunately, the water taxis (long-tail boats) make a lot of noise and add to the island's pollution problem.

By Boat   Long-tail boats may be hired all along the Ton Sai Bay waterfront; however, there's a main dock where they tend to congregate. There's a fairly standard rate that fluctuates according to season and demand. Expect to pay about 25B (65¢ to go to Long Beach, about 500B to 600B ($13.15 to $15.80) for a 5-hour tour of the island (good for a whole boatload of people), and in excess of 1,200B ($31.60) to go to the northern end of the island. It's a good idea to ask long-staying travelers what the current rates are to avoid overpaying.

FAST FACTS   Bring Thai baht and traveler's checks with you—Phi Phi has no banks with regular hours, but hotels can change money for you. There's a small **post office** off the main street (and I use the term *street* lightly). You can access the **Internet** there for 5B (15¢) per minute. They believe their telephone number is ☎ **01/ 464-2888,** but nobody ever calls it, so they're not sure. Get the picture? Phi Phi is a real small homegrown kind of place—don't expect big-time development. And if you run into any trouble, talk to your hotel staff, who will hook you up with a doctor from the local clinic (that has no phone) or local authorities.

WHAT TO SEE & DO

The best place to begin your exploration of the island is along the **Mountain View Trail,** which starts at the back of Ton Sai town; turn right (east) from the docks and follow the signs. The hike takes about 45 minutes to the top, but the vista is unforgettable. When the trail passes the water tanks, veer to the right for an easier path, or to the left for rock scrambling. I suggest doing this at the beginning or end of the day as it gets very hot; wear sturdy shoes and bring sunblock, a hat, and water. There's a thatched-hut snack bar atop the mountain.

Pi Pi Le proves the most popular day trip from Pi Pi Don, and it's a fun excursion. Boats depart from Ton Sai town and take you on a tour that includes stops at the Viking Cave, known for its swallows' nests (which fetch up to $2,000 per kilo and are the key ingredient of bird's nest soup), cave paintings with vessels that look like Viking ships (thus the name of the cavern), inland bays with dramatic rock formations, and small beaches for swimming and snorkeling. **Songserm** (☎ **01/229-2480**), along the main street in town will take you on a day trip there, plus lunch and snorkel gear, for 350B ($9.20) per person. *Note:* Some of the Phuket-based day trips include stops at Pi Pi Le.

There are a few companies that charter boats for game fishing around the area. Andaman Sea Adventure Fishing, along the main street, have a full day trip for 1,400B ($36.85) for a Thai fishing boat or 4,000B ($105.25) for a fully equipped speed boat.

The best scuba operator, **Mosquito Diving,** off the main street (☎ and fax **01/229-2802**), comes highly recommended by locals on the island. Trips to nearby island bays aboard their custom dive boat give divers access to the best reefs the area has to offer. A 1-day trip with two dives is 1,800B ($47.35). Special trips for wreck diving (2,200B/$57.90) or to see Shark Point with its black-tip reef sharks (2,600B/$68.40) can also be arranged. In addition, Mosquito provides all levels of instruction, from beginner to instructor development courses.

For fun around the island's bays, look for **Sea Fun Water sports** (☎ 1/396-2253 cellular) on the beach between P. P. Princess Resort and Charlie Bar. They rent sea sports equipment for the day or by the hour. A fiberglass kayak is 300B ($7.90) per hour or 1,000B ($26.30) per day; windsurfing gear is 300B ($7.90) per hour; a motorized dinghy (to take yourself around snorkeling) is 1,500B ($39.45) per hour with additional hours 1,000B ($26.30) each; Hobie Cats are 1,000B ($26.30) per hour with additional hours 500B ($13.15) each. Talk to them about yacht charters for beach barbecues on neighboring beaches, fishing, or sunset cruises. These you'll have to set up in advance. For advance chapters only, you can e-mail Mike at sea_fun@ hotmail.com to hash out the details.

WHERE TO STAY

✪ P. P. Princess Resort. 103 Moo 7, Tambon Ao Nang, Amphur Muang, Krabi 81000. ☎ **075/612-188.** Fax 075/620-615. Office on Phuket 2/39 Montri Rd., Phuket town (076/210-928, fax 076/217-106). 79 units. A/C MINIBAR TV TEL. Low season 1,490B–1,990B ($39.20–$52.35) garden bungalow; 2,190B ($57.65) beachfront bungalow; 3,290B ($86.60) suite bungalow. High season 2,190B–2,890B ($57.65–$76.05) garden bungalow; 3,290 ($86.60) beachfront bungalow; 4,590B ($120.80) suite bungalow. AE, MV, V. Center of Loh Dalum Beach.

Back-to-basics was never so wonderful. These beach bungalows are different from any others I've seen, especially within this moderate price category. Incorporating natural materials in contemporary design, P. P. Princess creates a close-to-nature feel enhanced by style and comfort. While the bungalows and private decks are not huge, smooth stained woods and huge glass windows bring the outside indoors. The garden and beachside bungalows are identical, only the location changes with the price. Beachside bungalows are just that—walk off your deck and hit the shady tree-lined sands. P. P. Princess also runs my favorite restaurant on the island, The Waterfall Restaurant, which is reviewed below. Just next door is Sea Fun, where you can arrange all your water activities.

Phi Phi Hotel. 129 Moo 7, Ao Nang, Ko Pi Pi, Krabi 81000. ☎ and fax **01/230-3138.** In Krabi, 15 Phattana Rd. (☎ 075/611-658; fax 075/611-658). In Phuket, 95/2 Phuket Villa 1, Yaowarat Rd, Soi 1, Phuket town (☎ 076/219-298; fax 076/254-668). 64 units. Low season 1,500B–1,700B ($39.45–$44.75) double. High season 1,800B–2,000B ($47.35–$52.65) double. AE, MC, V. Look for the tallest building, a short walk inland from the ferry pier.

This attractive new first-class hotel has clean, comfortable rooms that are surprisingly quiet for its central location. It offers the widest range of services on the island, including a coffee shop and restaurant, a bakery, gift and drug store, tour and travel agency, diving center, laundry service, and 24-hour room service.

Phi Phi Island Cabana Hotel. Ao Nang, Ko Pi Pi, Krabi 81000. ☎ **075/620-634,** or 075/611-496 in Krabi. Fax 075/612-132. 38 units. 1,00B ($26.30) bungalow with fan; 2,000B ($52.65) double with A/C. Peak season 1,800B ($47.35) bungalow with fan; 3,400B ($89.45) double with A/C. AE, MC, V. West (left) from dock, near beach.

This is easily the most attractive hotel on Ton Sai Bay, built in the style its name implies, with a particularly beautiful free-form pool surrounded by several coconut palms. The rooms are spacious, tastefully furnished, and very comfortable, with lots of light.

Phi Phi Palm Beach Resort. Laemthong Beach, Ko Pi Pi, Krabi 81000. ☎ **01/476-3787** on Phi Phi, or 076/214-654 in Phuket. Fax 076/215-090. 70 units (all with shower). A/C MINIBAR. Low season 5,049B ($132.85) double bungalow; 9,451B ($248.70) family cottage. High season 7,750B ($203.95) double bungalow; 14,853B ($390.85) family cottage. AE, MC, V. North side of the island.

Fairly isolated on the far northern end of Pi Pi, this is the best of the high-end resorts on the island. The coconut palm–fringed beach is excellent, and on calm days you can visit Bamboo Island, one of the best beaches in the region. The facilities, including a freshwater swimming pool, are comparable to the midlevel resorts on Phuket, including tennis, windsurfing, scuba diving, sauna, Jacuzzi, kiddie pool, game room, and two restaurants. Cottages include king-size beds, writing tables, and refrigerators. Larger family-style layouts with suitelike space are available. The Palm Beach Resort has a booking office in Phuket at 196/1–3 Phuket Rd., Phuket town 83000; contact them for reservations and transfer from Ton Sai harbor.

Phi Phi Pavilion Resort. Ko Phi Phi, Krabi 81000. ☎ and fax **075/620-633.** Office in Krabi 201/5 Uttrakit Rd., Muang, Krabi 81000, (☎ 075/611-295; fax 075/611-578). 50 units. A/C. Low season 1,200B ($31.60) bungalow with A/C; 700B ($18.40) bungalow with fan. High season 1,800B ($47.35) bungalow with A/C; 1,200B ($31.60) bungalow with fan. MC, V. Loh Dalum Beach.

On a grassy plain shaded by tall coconut palms, the bungalows at Phi Phi Pavilion are charmingly rustic. Close to the beach, the bamboo walls and thatch-roofed bungalows are scrupulously maintained. Plenty of windows allow for abundant sunlight, and the light interiors add to a clean open feeling. Simple bathrooms are spotless, with standing hot water showers. A capacious Italian restaurant and bar on a wooden beachside terrace gets lively at night.

WHERE TO DINE

Small Ko Phi Phi doesn't have the variety of Phuket, but you'll still find a decent meal. My favorite place for food and atmosphere is **The Waterfall Restaurant** at P. P. Princess Resort (☎ **075/612-188**). Dine on the beach with the sand in between your toes, at tables with linens and candles looking out at the twinkling lights on the bay. The menu features local seafood such as Phuket lobster and king prawn prepared in continental and Thai styles. I enjoyed their very reasonably priced set dinner, which included a seafood salad, lobster bisque, king prawn thermidor, fried ice cream, coffee, and white wine for only 360B ($9.45).

Also on the bay, the Italian Ciao Bella is on the beach atop a wood terrace, while a little further on, Charlie Bar has beachside drinks and snacks, while Charlie Restaurant shows the latest video CD movie releases during dinnertime.

Through the winding streets of the town you'll come across **Garlic Restaurant** (☎ **01/476-4830**), one of the better local joints not affiliated with a resort. Their Thai and sandwich menu is fairly decent and prices are fair.

9

The Central Plains

The vast Central Plains are known as the Great Rice Bowl of the country. This region, the source of Thailand's major crop, is also the source of the country's cultural wealth. Washed by rivers, including the Chao Phraya, the land sweeps on with rice field after rice field, many hosting incredible archaeological sites, including the nation's greatest wonder, Sukhothai. It's where the Thai kingdom was founded and where you'll still find much traditional Thai culture. Although Phitsanulok is the region's major commercial hub, with a variety of tourist facilities, travelers with limited time and an archaeological bent should definitely stay in the hotels near the Sukhothai Historical Park.

1 Phitsanulok

377km (234 miles) N of Bangkok; 93km (58 miles) SE of Sukhothai

Phitsanulok is a bustling agricultural center, with a population of 80,000, on the banks of the Nan River in the heart of the country's fertile rice bowl. If you're planning an all-encompassing tour of northern Thailand, Phitsanulok is roughly equidistant between Chiang Mai and Bangkok and is a good base for visiting Sukhothai and Si Satchanalai. Because of its strategic location, the city enjoys prosperity and some historic importance, but it's not especially attractive and can get rather hectic and noisy.

The terrain is flat, and the rice paddies seem endless, their vivid green especially delightful in the late spring. In winter, white-flowering tobacco and pink-flowering soybeans are planted in rotation. Rice barges, houseboats, and long-tail boats ply the Nan and Song Kwai rivers, which eventually connect to the Chao Phraya and feed into the Gulf of Thailand (Gulf of Siam).

Phitsanulok is the birthplace of King Naresuan (the Great) and his less famous brother, Prince Ekatosarot. The Ayutthaya king is legendary in Thai history for his gallant defense against the forces of the invading Burmese army during the 16th century. There are many paintings of Naresuan in hand-to-hand combat, on elephant back, with a Burmese crown prince. Other Ayutthaya kings used Phitsanulok as a staging and training ground for battles with the Burmese, and for 25 years it served as the capital of the Ayutthaya kingdom.

When most of the city burned in 1959, one of the only original buildings to survive was Wat Yai, one of the most holy temples in the country, and the city's most important site. For the Thais a trip to

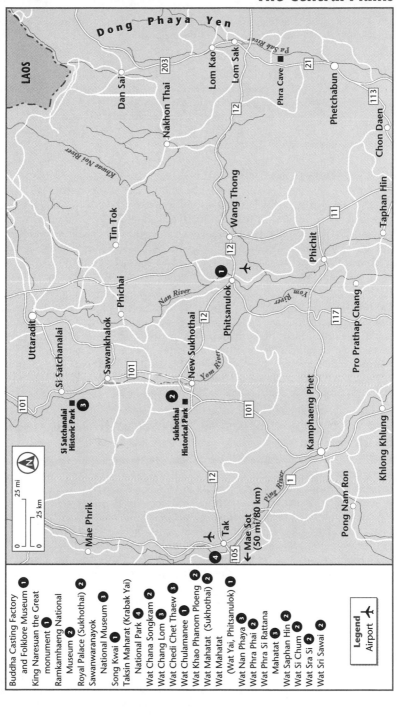

The Central Plains

Dong Phaya Yen

LAOS

Pa Sak River

Khwae Not River

Nan River

Yom River

Yom River

Ping River

- Dan Sai
- Nakhon Thai
- 203
- Lom Kao
- Lom Sak
- Phra Cave
- Phetchabun
- 21
- 113
- Chon Daen
- 12
- Wang Thong
- Taphan Hin
- 11
- Tin Tok
- 12
- Phichai
- Phichit
- Uttaradit
- Si Satchanalai
- Sawankhalok
- 101
- New Sukhothai
- Phitsanulok ✈ **1**
- 12
- 117
- Pro Prathap Chang
- Si Satchanalai Historic Park ■ **3**
- 101
- Sukhothai Historical Park ■ **2**
- 101
- Kamphaeng Phet
- Khlong Khlung
- 12
- Mae Phrik
- Tak ✈
- Mae Sot (50 mi/80 km)
- 105 **4**
- 1
- Pong Nam Ron

0 25 mi
0 25 km

Buddha Casting Factory and Folklore Museum **1**
King Naresuan the Great monument **1**
Ramkamhaeng National Museum **2**
Royal Palace (Sukhothai) ■ **2**
Sawanwaranayok National Museum **3**
Song Kwai **1**
Taksin Maharat (Krabak Yai) National Park **4**
Wat Chana Songkram **2**
Wat Chang Lom **3**
Wat Chedi Chet Thaew **3**
Wat Chulamanee **1**
Wat Khao Phanom Ploeng **2**
Wat Mahatat (Sukhothai) **2**
Wat Mahatat (Wat Yai, Phitsanulok) **1**
Wat Nan Phaya **3**
Wat Phra Phai **2**
Wat Phra Si Rattana Mahatat **3**
Wat Saphan Hin **2**
Wat Si Chum **2**
Wat Sra Si **2**
Wat Sri Sawai **2**

Legend
✈ Airport

Phitsanulok is a chance to pay respect to the famous Buddha image inside. For travelers, it's a great way to start your tour of the region—at the TAT office.

ESSENTIALS

GETTING THERE   By Plane   Thai Airways has either four or five flights a day to Phitsanulok from Bangkok (flying time: 45 minutes); and either one or two flights daily from Chiang Mai via either Nan or Mae Sot (flying time: 2 hours). Taxis cost 50B ($1.30) into town from the airport. The **Thai Airways** office is at 209/26–28 Boromtrailokanart Rd., Phitsanulok (☎ **055/258-020**), near the TAT. To call Phitsanulok airport direct, dial ☎ **055/258-029.**

By Train   Ten trains per day travel to Phitsanulok from Bangkok (trip time: 6 hours; 199B to 239B/$5.25 to $6.30 for an air-conditioned second-class seat). There's also rapid train connection between Phitsanulok and Chiang Mai (7 hours; 310B/$8.15 for a second-class seat). For information and reservations, call Bangkok's **Hua Lamphong Railway Station** (☎ **02/223-7010** or 02/223-7020), Chiang Mai Railway Station (☎ **053/242-094,** for advance booking), or the Phitsanulok Railway Station (☎ **055/258-005**). You won't have any trouble finding transportation to your hotel. Throngs of samlors, songtao, and motorcycle taxis are waiting for you. The station is right in town, so expect to pay only 20B (55¢) or 40B ($1.05) to get where you need to go.

By Bus   Air-conditioned buses leave daily every hour for the trip to Phitsanulok from Bangkok, starting at 7am to 11pm (trip time: 6 hours; 194B/$5.10). Six buses a day depart from Chiang Mai (trip time: 6 hours; 146B/$3.85). The intercity bus terminal in Phitsanulok is 2km east of town on Highway 12; local bus no. 1 will take you to the center of town. Contact **Bangkok's Northern Bus Terminal** (☎ **02/272-5761**) or the **Arcade Bus Station** in Chiang Mai (☎ **053/247-462**). Call the **Phitsanulok Bus Terminal** at (☎ **055/242-664**).

By Car   Take Highway 11 north from Bangkok.

VISITOR INFORMATION   The helpful **TAT** office (☎ **055/252-742**) is on Boromtrailokanart Road, two blocks south of the Clock Tower.

ORIENTATION   The town is fairly compact, with the majority of services and sights for tourists concentrated along or near the east bank of the Nan River. A bridge connects the two banks along the central east-west street, Naresuan Road, which leads from the railway station on the city's main north-south road, A-Kathotsarot Road. The day market for housewares, Buddhist amulets, and knickknacks is along the eastern bank south of the bridge, Buddhabucha Road. In the evening it becomes a lively Night Market with food stalls and a large assortment of inexpensive merchandise.

Phyalithai Road, 2 blocks south of central Naresuan, leads from the Market perpendicular to the river directly to the Clock Tower, one of the town's principal landmarks. Just east of the Clock Tower, Boromtrailokanart Road is the central north-south commercial artery. Boromtrailokanart runs parallel to the river through most of the city, but on its northern end it turns back toward the river near a second bridge that carries the traffic of busy Highway 12, Singhawat Road. Wat Yai and its museum are just beyond this bridge on the right (east).

GETTING AROUND   By Tuk-Tuk & Song Tao   Tuk-tuks (called taxis here) are common near the bus and train stations. Fares have to be negotiated but should range from 20B to 40B (53¢ to $1.05) in town. Songtao (pickup trucks with covered beds and benches) are group taxis, which leave from the bus or train station for nearby villages.

By Bus   There's a well-organized city bus system with a main terminal south of the train station on A-Kathotsarot Road. There are five main routes: no. 1 goes to the intercity bus terminal and Wat Yai; no. 2 serves the southeast sector of the city; no. 3 goes west across the river; no. 4 goes to the airport; and no. 5 goes north to the Topland Plaza, across Highway 12. Trips are between 5B and 10B (15¢ and 25¢).

There is frequent (every half hour 6am to 6pm), inexpensive, bus service from the intercity bus terminal east of town to New Sukhothai (trip time: 1 hour; 27B (70¢).

By Hired Minivan   **Able Tour and Travel** (☎ 055/055-242-206), just next to the TAT office, offers vans with a driver for 1,200B ($31.60) per day to take you around Phitsanulok's sights, and beyond to Old Sukhothai, even Si Satchanalai.

By Rental Car   If you'd like to rent a car to drive around the central plains areas, Avis has a small operation in Tak, but make sure you call ahead for booking, as they only have a few cars available. Call ☎ 055/242-060 for reservations and information.

SPECIAL EVENTS   The Buddha Chinarat Festival is held annually on the sixth day of the waxing moon in the third lunar month (usually late January or early February). Then, Phitsanulok's Wat Yai is packed with well-wishers, dancers, monks and abbots, children, and tourists, all converging on the temple grounds for a 6-day celebration.

FAST FACTS   There are several **banks** located along Boromtrailoknart Road. The **General Post Office** (☎ 055/258-013) is on Bhuddabucha Road, along the river 2 blocks north of Naresuan Road. The **Overseas Call Office** is on the second floor of the post office. For **Internet** access, cross the bridge at Naresuan Road. To the left is Phitsanulok Plaza, where you'll find **Speedy Net** (☎ 055/283-030) with service for 20B (55¢) per hour. The main **police** station (☎ 055/245-856) is near the intersection of Naresuan and Boromtrilokanart roads. Dial ☎ 1699 for the Tourist Police. **Ruamphaet Hospital** (☎ 055/242-574) on Boromtrailokanart Road, near the market, is the closest private facility.

WHAT TO SEE & DO

Other than leaving the city to visit the historical parks at Sukhothai or Si Satchanlai, there is only one major must-see in Phitsanulok: ✪ **Wat Yai** (its full name is **Wat Phra Sri Ratana Mahatat**), one of the holiest and most beautiful Buddhist temples in the country. It's one block north of the Highway 12 bridge, on the right. Its brilliant and powerful late Sukhothai–period Phra Buddha Chinarat is a bronze image cast in 1357 under the Sukhothai king Mahatmmaracha; its most distinctive feature is its flamelike halo (*mandorla*), which symbolizes spiritual radiance. This image serves as a model for ideal representations of the Buddha in contemporary statue factories, and only Emerald Buddha is more highly revered by the Thai people.

The wihaan that houses this illustrious Buddha is a prize example of traditional Thai architecture, with three eaves, overlapping one another to emphasize the nave, and graceful black and gold columns. Be sure to examine the excellent late Ayutthaya period, mother-of-pearl inlaid doors leading into the chapel; similar to those in Bangkok's Royal Chapel, they were added in 1576 as a gift from King Borommakot of Ayutthaya. Inside, besides the beautiful image, note the Italian marble floor, the two painted *thammas* (pulpits) to the side, and the murals illustrating the life of Buddha.

Other than the main bot, the wat's most distinctive architectural aspect is the Khmer-style prang, rebuilt by King Boromtrilokanart, that houses the relic from which the wat takes its name; Mahathat means "Great Relic." The gilding on the top half is probably recent, but it complements the Khmer temple decor. There's a small museum that houses a good collection of Sukhothai- and Ayutthaya-era Buddhas.

The wat is always packed with worshippers paying their respects, making offerings, and praying for a healthy mind and body. During the winter Buddha Chinarat Festival, it's transformed into a cultural circus! (See "Special Events," earlier in this section.)

Admission is a suggested contribution of 20B (55¢), a strict dress code is imposed—wear long pants or skirts (dresses) and shirts with sleeves that reach at least to your elbow. It's open daily 6am to 6pm (during the Buddha Chinarat Festival 6am to midnight); the museum is open Wednesday to Sunday 9am to 4pm.

From Wat Mahatat, you might want to stroll south along Buddhabucha Road, inspecting **Song Kwai,** the "Two River" city of semipermanently moored houseboats on the banks of the Nan River. You can cross the bridge near Wat Yai to see the King Naresuan the Great Monument. It was built on the site of the Chandra Palace, where he was born in 1555. Nearby are the city and provincial government buildings. Farther south on the east bank is the day market with a panoply of everyday items, Buddha images, and a smattering of hill-tribe crafts for sale at relatively low prices.

The **Sgt. Maj. Thavee Folk Museum,** 26/43 Wisutkasat Rd. (☎ **055/258-715**), is a private collection of antique items from Thai rural life. Farming and trapping equipment, household items, and old photographs of the city are lovingly displayed by the good sergeant major in two beautiful Thai houses on quiet landscaped grounds. The museum is open every day from 8:30am to 4:30pm, except Mondays, with free admission (a small donation is requested, say, 20B/55¢ per person). Across the street is the **Buranathai Buddha Image Factory,** where you can witness artisans crafting Buddha images of bronze in the style of Wat Yai's Buddha Chinarat. A small display walks you through the bronze casting process. Outside the factory are caged bangkaew dogs—a famous breed from Phitsanulok. They bark a lot. The factory is open from 8am to 5pm daily, and admission is free. From the train station, it's a 20-minute walk through the city, or you can catch bus no. 3.

Wat Chulamanee, south of Nakorn Sawan Highway, is the oldest temple in this Phitsanulok area and the site of the original city. Like the prang at Wat Yai, this Khmer-built spire was rebuilt by King Boromtrailokanart after his instruction in the architecture of nearby Sukhothai. The wat, still an active monastery, was restored in the 1950s and is studied particularly for its fine laterite cactus-shaped prang and the elaborate stucco designs decorating the structure. The compound is open to the public daily from 6am to 7pm; 20B (55¢) is the suggested contribution. It's on Boromtrailokanart Road, and can be reached by bus no. 4 from the city bus stand, south from the train station.

WHERE TO STAY

Amarin Lagoon Hotel. 52/299 Moo 6, Praongkhao Rd., Amphur Muang, Phitsanulok 65000. ☎ **055/220-999.** Fax 055/220-944. A/C MINIBAR TV TEL. 301 units. 1,000B ($26.30) double. AE, MC, V. On Hwy. 12 east of town.

The best and most attractive resort hotel in the area, Amarin is particularly recommended for those who are driving. (The hotel offers free transfer from the airport and a shuttle bus into town.) The rooms are spacious, attractive, and quiet—a big plus in noisy Phitsanulok. The hotel has a big handsome pool, a 24-hour cafe, the excellent Aranyika Restaurant (with Thai, Chinese, and Vietnamese cuisine), and a fitness center. Services include baby-sitting, laundry, valet, car rental, and safety deposit boxes.

Amarin Nakorn Hotel. 3/1 Chaophrya Rd., Phitsanulok 65000. ☎ **055/219-069.** Fax 055/219-500. 132 units. A/C TV TEL. 480B ($12.65) double. AE, MC, V. One block west of train station on left.

This tall white hotel, within sight of the train and bus stations, was built back in 1972. It's well maintained and still an acceptable choice for convenient lodging. It offers clean rooms, a 24-hour coffee shop, a Chinese restaurant, and a barber shop and beauty parlor. Their minivan will pick you up at the airport.

Pailyn Phitsanulok Hotel. 38 Boromtrailokanart Rd., Phutsanulok 65000. ☎ 055/252-411. Fax 055/258-185. 212 units. A/C MINIBAR TV TEL. 700B ($18.40) double. Rates include breakfast. AE, MC, V. Two long blocks north of Naresuan Rd.

The Pailyn, one block from the river, is Phitsanulok's best in-town lodging, with a bright marble lobby that gives it panache. The rooms have textured wallpaper and rattan decor; they're clean and fairly quiet and priced according to size (though there are no double beds and the mattresses are very firm). Unfortunately, the staff can get overworked by the many tour groups that come overnight. There's a very good coffee shop, a popular disco, sauna, and massage parlor.

Phitsanulok Youth Hostel. 38 Sanambin Rd., Phitsanulok 65000. ☎ 055/242-060. 5 rooms, 40 beds. 120B ($3.15) dorm bed; 400B ($10.55) double with A/C; 300B ($7.90) double with fan. No credit cards. 4km (2.4 miles) southeast of clock tower, about 1km from airport; take bus no. 1 to technical school, then bus no. 4.

This hostel, known to locals as "No. 38," is distinguished by its owner, Mr. Sapachai, considered by his wards to be the most helpful, caring host in the country. It gets a great crowd of enthusiastic young travelers who overlook the Spartan lodgings for the enjoyment of making new friends. The quaint five rooms in an old teak house, outfitted with wood furnishings, hold two to eight persons each. It offers a densely planted garden, cold-water shower, clean toilet, bikes, and breakfast.

Rajapruk Guesthouse. 99/10 Pra-Ongdam Rd., Phitsanulok 65000. ☎ 055/259-203. Fax 055/251-395. 40 units. TEL. 360B ($9.45) double with A/C; 280B ($7.35) double with fan. No credit cards. Behind Rajapruk Hotel.

This appears to be a converted apartment building, and the rooms have simple linoleum floors, twin beds, a hot shower, and a fan. Though worn, they're clean. One of the town's best deals.

Rajapruk Hotel. 99/9 Pha-Ong Dum Rd., Phitsanulok 65000. ☎ 055/258-477. Fax 055/251-395, or 02/229-4496 in Bangkok. 101 units. A/C TV TEL. 500B ($13.15) double. MC, V. 1km (6/10 mile) northeast of Clock Tower, near bus terminal.

The Rajapruk is a bit worn, but it has a small swimming pool, and its simple guest rooms are clean. The open-air Garden Bar is pleasant, and there's a coffee shop, Thai massage parlor, and a boisterous disco.

WHERE TO DINE

Basically, the food in Phitsanulok isn't the best, but be sure to try the local specialty, *khaew tak,* delicious sun-dried banana baked with honey; a small package costs 30B (80¢) and is widely sold. There's an okay bakery across the street north of the Clock Tower. I don't recommend the food in the Night Market unless you're interested in increasing the variety of your intestinal flora, as there seems to be less attention paid to hygiene than usual. Some people will be amused by the "flying vegetables"—morning-glory greens sautéed, tossed high in the air, and caught by a waiter. Check it out at the night market by the river.

Mangkla Restaurant. In the Pailyn Hotel, 38 Boromtrailokanart Rd. ☎ 055/252-411. Main courses 60B–240B ($1.60–$ 6.30). AE, MC, V. Daily 6am–10:30pm. Two long blocks north of Naresuan Rd. THAI/CHINESE/INTERNATIONAL.

This is about the best you can do in town. They serve an excellent breakfast buffet for 80B ($2.10), about the best going in these parts. The menu is fairly large, and everything was excellent, but your best bet is to stay with the Thai dishes. The service is friendly, and there are Thai songbirds at night.

Songkheaw Houseboat Restaurant. 21 Phuttabucha Rd. ☎ **055/242-167.** Main courses 50B–120B ($1.30–$3.15). No credit cards. Daily 11am–midnight. On Nan River. THAI/CHINESE.

This is one of a few houseboats that serves Thai and Chinese cuisine; locals claim it has the best food, though it's actually just mediocre—but an interesting dining experience. Try the tasty *tom mon pla* (fried fish cake), grilled chicken, or "light noodle" salad of glass noodles and seafood. (Don't make the mistake of crossing over to the old, worn boats moored alongside; they pull out about 8:15pm and cruise the river.)

2 Sukhothai & Si Satchanalai Historical Parks

Sukhothai: 427km (265 miles) N of Bangkok; 58km (36 miles) E of Phitsanulok. Si Satchanalai: 56km (35 miles) N of Sukhothai

The emergence of Sukhothai ("Dawn of Happiness" in Pali) in 1238 as an independent political state signified not only the birth of a unified kingdom, but also of Thailand itself. It was here that Phor Khun Bangk Klang Hao became the first Thai monarch, as King Sri Indrathit, in what would become the country's most influential religious and cultural center. Today Sukhothai is a world-renowned historical site; it is to Thailand what Borobudur is to Indonesia, or Angkor Wat is to Cambodia.

While the Sukhothai Historical Park is the main attraction, New Sukhothai is also called simply Sukhothai, and has a better range of facilities for travelers.

Si Satchanalai is another richly endowed legacy of the Sukhothai Kingdom, a city thought to have been built around the same time. The ancient city isn't in a fine state of repair; nevertheless, it's absolutely worth a detour.

If you're traveling from Phitsanulok, the drive takes you across wide plains where there are rice paddies, cotton fields, and mango-and-lemon groves. Though some peasants have purchased tractors (which locals call the "iron buffalo"), most still use traditional methods, water buffalo and manual plow.

In addition to the two main attractions in the area, the Sukhothai Historical Park and the Si Satchanalai Historical Park, there are numerous chedis and wats in the area, particularly in the hills around ancient Sukhothai; however, many guides will not take you to them because of their unpaved, sometimes treacherous, off-road locations.

ESSENTIALS

GETTING THERE   By Plane   Bangkok Airways has a private airport between New Sukhothai and Si Satchanalai. They have a daily flight connecting Bangkok, Sukhothai and Chiang Mai. Contact them in Bangkok at ☎ 02/229-3456 or Chiang Mai at 053/281-519. Their office in New Sukhothai is at 10 moo 1, Jarodvithithong Road (055/613-310, ext. 8891), or at the airport (055/612-803). They also have an office at Pailyn Sukhothai Hotel. They'll provide minivan transfer to and from the airport to their town office for 80B ($2.10) at the time of ticket purchase, or 100B ($2.65) upon arrival.

By Train   Phitsanulok has the nearest railroad station (see section 1, earlier in this chapter).

By Bus   Daily air-conditioned buses leave every hour from Bangkok (trip time: 6 to 7 hours; price 230B/$6.05), departing from the **Northern Bus Terminal** (☎ 02/ 272-5761). There's also air-conditioned bus service from Chiang Mai six times daily (trip time: 5 to 6 hours, price 196B ($5.15) from the **Arcade Bus Station** (☎ 053/242-664).

Sukhothai

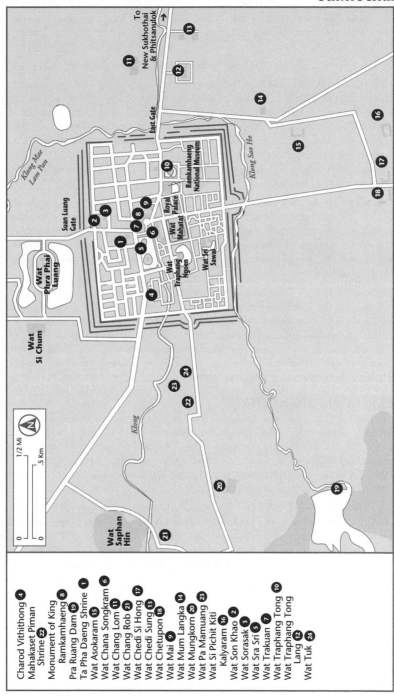

Charod Vithithong **4**
Mahakaset Piman Shrine **22**
Monument of King Ramkamhaeng **8**
Pra Ruang Dam **19**
Ta Pha Daeng Shrine **1**
Wat Asokaram **15**
Wat Chana Songkram **6**
Wat Chang Lom **11**
Wat Chang Rob **21**
Wat Chedi Si Hong **17**
Wat Chedi Sung **13**
Wat Chetupon **18**
Wat Mai **9**
Wat Mum Langka **14**
Wat Mungkorn **20**
Wat Pa Mamuang **23**
Wat Si Pichit Kiti Kalyaram **16**
Wat Son Khao **2**
Wat Sorasak **3**
Wat Sra Sri **5**
Wat Trakuan **7**
Wat Traphang Tong **10**
Wat Traphang Tong Lang **12**
Wat Tuk **24**

By Local Bus from Phitsanulok   From Phitsanulok, local bus no. 1 runs to the intercity terminal on Highway 12, where buses leave hourly for New Sukhothai (trip time: 1 hour; 27B (71¢).

By Car   Take Singhawat Road east from Phitsanulok, then Highway 12.

VISITOR INFORMATION   Sukhothai has no TAT office; the closest one is in Phitsanulok ☎ **055/252-742**. New Sukhothai is a friendly town, not large enough to get lost in for long, and you can negotiate your own tour with a tuk-tuk driver. **Sky Tours** (☎ **055/612-237**), 28–30 Prasertpong Rd., around the corner from the bus station, offers tours and information. Most hotels and guesthouses can also help you arrange a tour. You can pick up an information booklet for 50B ($1.30) at the museum, which has a slightly more detailed map than ours (but personally I thought ours was easier to follow).

ORIENTATION   **Sukhothai Historical Park** (or Muang Kao, Old City) is located 12km (7.5 miles) east of New Sukhothai. The modern town offers a few good hotels and useful services; it's built along the banks of the **Yom River** and is best traversed by tuk-tuk or songtao. **Si Satchanalai Historic Park** is on the Yom River 56km (35 miles) north of new Sukhothai, and 17km (10.5 miles) south of Sawankhalok, the closest modern town.

SPECIAL EVENTS   **Loi Krathong** is a visually delightful, 3-day festival held on the full moon of the 12th lunar month (usually October/November) in honor of the water spirits. Around the country, crowds gather at ponds, klongs, rivers, and temple fountains to float small banana-leaf boats bearing candles, incense, a flower, and a coin. This is done as an offering and to wash away the previous year's sins. Since this festival dates from the Sukhothai era, celebrations (including a parade, fireworks, and beauty pageant) are widespread throughout the province.

EXPLORING SUKHOTHAI

In 1978, UNESCO named Sukhothai a target for preservation of world culture and heritage, along with Venice, Borobudur, Mohenjo-Daro, Carthage, and Nubia. In 1988, the Thai government, international and regional archaeologists, and art historians under the direction of the Fine Arts Department, with financial assistance from UNESCO, completed the preservation of these magnificent monuments and an excellent museum in one large park.

GETTING TO THE SIGHT   You can reach the historic park of Sukhothai by public bus, samlor, or private car. On Jarodvhithithong Road, west of the traffic circle, you can catch an open-air public bus to the park entrance for 10B (25¢). The samlors (motorcycles carting flatbeds with bench seats) that cruise around New Sukhothai can be hired to trek you out to the park and around it for 3 or so hours. They'll do it for 300B ($7.90).

TOURING THE SITE   Early morning and evening bring fewer buses and groups, and the site is cooler and more serene.

The historical park is open daily 6am to 6pm; admission is 40B ($1.05). You can purchase a combination ticket with admission to the National Museum, Historic Park, Si Satchanali National Park and Sawanvorangayok National Museum for 150B ($3.95). It's something of a deal because they list extra charges (30B/80¢ each) for touring areas outside the city (East, West, and North).

On Foot   If you're walking, the sites outside the park will be somewhat of a hike. Count on spending 3 to 6 hours visiting sites in and outside of the park. Start by exploring the museum, then buy a guidebook and map (the temples are well labeled). It's pleasant walking, with several soda and snack stalls en route.

By Bicycle My favorite method of exploration here. The area is flat, and cycling is easy. Bikes give you the freedom to go where you want, but are quiet and slow enough to let you take it all in. Rent them from one of the many stalls right outside the park gate (across from the Museum) for 20B (55¢) per day.

By Samlor These motorcycles with two bench flatbeds are noisy but fun, and can seat six people fairly comfortably. You can hire one in New Sukhothai to take you to the site and even around it. If you don't hire your samlor in New Sukhothai town, you can negotiate with one of the guys hanging around the park entrance, and even get him to take you to your hotel when you're done.

By Tram Several beige trams wait in front of the museum to take visitors around. They circle the major sites (20B/55¢) in about half an hour, returning you to the museum entrance.

SEEING THE HIGHLIGHTS

A network of walls and moats defines the perfect rectangle that is the central city. (It is thought that the original moat connected Sukhothai with Si Satchanalai.) The Phitsanulok-Sukhothai highway runs right through the east or Kam Phang Hak Gate to the museum, a good beginning.

RAMKAMHAENG NATIONAL MUSEUM The museum houses a detailed model of the area, and an admirable display of Sukhothai and Si Satchanalai archaeological finds largely culled from the private collection of the abbot of Wat Ratchathani. It's located in the center of the old city, opposite the historic park's pedestrian gate. Before exploring the site, stop here for maps and guidebooks. It's open Wednesday through Sunday 9am to 4pm (closed Mondays, Tuesdays, and public holidays); admission is 30B (80¢).

WAT MAHATAT Begin your exploration of the ancient city at the central area (5 minutes' walk west of the museum). Wat Mahatat, part of the royal compound, is the most extraordinary monument in the park, a multichedi edifice that's dominated by a 14th-century lotus-bud tower and encircled by a moat. Surrounding its unique Sukhothai-style chedi are several smaller towers of Sri Lankan and Khmer influence and a grouping of Buddhist disciples in the adoration pose. An imposing cast-bronze seated Buddha used to be placed in front of the reliquary (this image, Phra Si Sakaya Muni, was removed in the 18th century to Bangkok's Wat Suthat). The viharn that housed this figure was built in 1362 by King Lithai. The small viharn to the south contains a fine Ayutthaya-era Buddha. Be sure to examine the large chedi: the lowest platform (south side of Wat Mahatat) and its excellent stucco sculpture, the crypt murals, and two elegant Sri Lankan-style stupas (equivalent to Thai chedi) at the southeast corner of the site. Some of the best architectural ornamentation to Sukhothai is found on the upper, eastern-facing levels of the niche pediments in the main reliquary tower. Dancing figures, Queen Maya giving birth to Prince Siddhartha, and scenes from the life of Buddha are among the best-preserved details.

THE ROYAL PALACE Between the museum and Wat Mahatat are the remains of the Royal Palace. Although this once-grand complex contained the throne and stone inscription of King Ramkamhaeng (there's a copy in the Ramkamhaeng Museum; the original is in the National Museum in Bangkok), today it's a shambles.

WAT SRI SAWAI Southwest of the palace you'll come to the 12th-century Wat Sri Sawai, a Hindu shrine later converted to a Buddhist temple. The architecture is distinctly Khmer, with three Lopburi-style prangs commanding center stage. The viharns around the central prangs (cactus-shaped towers) are of more traditional Sukhothai design.

OTHER MONUMENTS IN THE PARK   Circling north, just west of Wat Mahatat, is **Wat Traphang Ngoen,** set in its own pond. Though little remains other than an attractive chedi, the vistas of the surrounding monuments are among the most superb in the park. North past Wat Mahatat, is **Wat Chana Songkram,** where there's a Sri Lankan–style stupa of note. Nearby is **Wat Sra Si,** with a Sri Lankan chedi and viharn set on a small island in Traphang Takuan pond. Take a moment to examine the stucco Buddha in the fore viharn.

TAKE A BREAK AT DONGTARN   This open-air cafe is located by the cool, tree-shaded entrance to the historical park. Thai and Chinese cuisine are served, as well as some continental dishes. It's a very convenient choice, just across from the Ramkamhaeng Museum. Main courses are 50B to 120B ($1.30 to $3.15). It's open daily from 10am to 6pm.

Sights Outside the Historical Park

The remainder of monuments worth seeing are outside the historic central park, most to the north. You'll need to purchase another 30B (80¢) ticket; the sites are open 8am to 4:30pm.

If you leave the park at the northern San Luang Gate and continue about 500 feet, you'll arrive at **Wat Phra Phai Luang,** similar to Wat Sri Sawai because of its three prangs. However, only the north tower still shows off its exquisite stucco decoration. This monument, originally a Hindu shrine, once housed a lingam, a phallic sculpture representing Shiva. Conversion to a Buddhist sanctuary is evidenced by the mondop, a square building containing a Buddha image illustrating the four postures: sitting, standing, reclining, and walking.

One of the more astonishing and beautiful monuments in Sukhothai is found at **Wat Si Chum,** where there's a majestic 50-foot-tall seated Buddha, in the mudra (pose) of Subduing Mara (evil). When the narrow passageway to the top was open you could admire the 700-year-old slate reliefs within. Don't let fatigue deter you from seeing this celebrated image, still actively worshipped, but keep a hand on your bag. There have been past reports of purse snatchings in these areas.

About 550 yards away from Si Chum are the womblike brick remains of the Thuriang Kiln, where Sawankhalok ware was once produced. A few kilometers west, atop a 660-foot hill and visible from afar, is **Wat Saphan Hin.** It's well worth the steep, 5-minute climb to study the towering Phra Attaros Buddha, a 41-foot-tall figure, his right hand raised in the Dispelling Fear mudra, which towers above the wat's laterite remains.

EXPLORING SI SATCHANALAI

Ancient Si Satchanalai developed between the Yom River and the Khao Phra Si Valley, on more than 800 acres of land. The 228 acres contained within the old laterite ramparts and moats of the city wall are the focus of sightseeing in the historical park.

A LOOK AT THE PAST   Although a stone inscription found at Sukhothai refers to Si Satchanalai as a protectorate of King Ramkhamhaeng (possibly its founder), most historians believe that Rama I expanded a city that was built by Khmer settlers, and which was well established by the 13th century, or even earlier. During the Ayutthaya period the town was named Sawankhalok (now the nearest modern town) because of the area's highly prized product, its famous ceramics, which were exported throughout Asia. Si Satchanalai's riverside site was crucial to the development of the ceramics industry; there were literally more than 1,000 kilns operating along the river. These kilns have been excavated by a Thai-Australian team, led by archaeologists from the University of Adelaide. Their findings contradict the prevailing view that Chinese traders brought the method of producing celadon to Sukhothai in the 13th century. Instead they hypothesize that ceramic manufacture began more than 1,000 years ago at Ban Ko Noi (there's a small site museum 6km/3.7 miles north of Satchanalai), strong evidence that it's an indigenous Thai art form. Don't miss the Sawanwaranoyok Museum's collection.

TOURING THE SITE   Taking Route 101 north from Sukhothai through sugar-cane and tobacco fields, one must cross the Yom River to enter the historical park's central city. The remains of the 22 monuments inside the old city rank well below those of Sukhothai in importance, yet the crumbling grandeur of the buildings and the relative isolation of the site add to its allure.

A taxi, private car, or guided tour are the best ways to see the spread-out sites of Si Satchanalai (see "Touring the Site" in Sukhothai, for more information). However, public buses to **Si Satchanalai** and **Sawankhalok** (18B/45¢) depart every half hour from a bus stop on Jarodvithitong Road just east of the traffic circle. It drops you about 2km from the site, but you can rent a bicycle for 20B (55¢) per day. At the front gate of the park you can also rent bicycles for the same price (and these are of much better quality). Enterprising locals have organized an **elephant ride** around the park (three passengers fit in the howdah, one rides the neck, and the mahout sits on the head). It costs 50B ($1.30) to 100B ($2.65) per person, depending on whether you choose a half-hour or hour-long trip.

Admission to the park is 40B ($1.05), and you can purchase a nice 5B (15¢) map and pamphlet when you pay at the gate. It is open daily except national holidays 8am to 5pm.

SEEING THE HIGHLIGHTS

The first two monuments that you'll encounter are the largest and most impressive in the city.

WAT CHANG LOM   This compound, to the right of the entrance, is distinctly Sri Lankan, with a characteristic stupa and 39 laterite elephant buttresses. (It's unusual to find so many elephant sculptures still intact.) If you ascend the stairs, you can walk around the base of the stupas and admire the 19 Buddhas that are installed in niches above the terrace. The discovery of the Buddha's relics at the site during the reign of King Ramkhamhaeng prompted the construction of this temple, an event described in stone inscriptions found at Sukhothai.

WAT CHEDI CHET THAEW   Opposite Wat Chang Lom to the south, within sandstone walls, is Wat Chedi Chet Thaew. Like Wat Mahatat at Sukhothai, this wat is distinguished by a series of lotus-bud towers and rows of chedis thought to contain the remains of the royal family. The chedis are adorned with 33 Buddha images and other stucco decorative images, and some have traces of color.

OTHER MONUMENTS IN THE PARK   The balance of monuments within the ancient city walls can be inspected within an hour. **Wat Nan Phaya,** southeast of Chedi Chet Thaew, is known for the stucco bas-reliefs on the remains of a seven-room viharn. It's easily spotted by their tin-roof shelter. Nothing compares to **Wat Phra Si**

Rattana Mahatat, located 1km ($^6/_{10}$ mile) southeast of the bridge. The most prominent feature of this 13th-century temple is the Khmer-style prang, thought to date from the renovation of the original Sukhothai design made under the rule of the Ayutthaya King Borommakot in the 18th century. The exterior carving and sculpture are superb, in particular a walking Buddha done in relief. Some of the more delicate fragments of the wat, including very rare wooden doors, have been removed to the Ramkamhaeng National Museum in Sukhothai.

SIGHTS OUTSIDE THE HISTORICAL PARK

Private transport will enable you to wander at will around the hundreds of archaeological sites and kilns that dot the landscape. **Wat Khao Phanom Ploeng,** a nearby hill topped by two wat compounds, offers an excellent vantage of the historic city from the top of its steep 112-step staircase.

Sangkhalok Museum, Tambon Muang, Sawankhalok, 12km from the historical park, houses the superb collection of Sawankhalok ceramics, the ancient pottery of the Sukhothai kingdom. Utensils, bowls, decorative items, and toys from the kingdom are on display, plus many other ceramic treasures from the Lanna Kingdom to the north. It's open Monday to Friday 10am to 6pm; Saturday and Sunday 10am to 8pm; admission is 250B ($6.60) for adults (you'll get a free souvenir guide), children under 17 are 50B ($1.30).

SHOPPING IN THE AREA

In Sukhothai, the **Boonchew Antique Shop** in the Sukhothai Cultural Center, 2km (1.2 miles) east of the historical park at 214 Jarodvithithong Rd. (☎ 055/612-275), offers a collection of Sawankhalok ceramics and religious figures, some reputed to date from the 14th to 17th centuries. (Feel free to be skeptical.) Prices are somewhat better than in Bangkok, but the large selection is generally of lesser quality. Mr. Boonchew issues certificates of authenticity, but, of course, buyer beware.

Those who would like to buy modern reproductions of Sawankhalok ceramics should stop at **Kingdom of Fathers Ceramics** (☎ and fax 055/612180), 1/29 Moo 3, Tambon Muang-Kao, on the left just before you enter the Sukhothai Historical Park. Somdet Phuangphaen has an interesting museum gallery and sells his very convincing work at reasonable prices. (Knock a piece around a little, scuff it up, soak it in strong tea, bury it for several months, and voilà! you too can make an antique.)

WHERE TO STAY

Ban Thai Guesthouse. 38 Pravet Nakhon Rd., Sukhothati 64000. ☎ **055/610-163.** 15 units. 120B ($3.15) double; 200B ($5.25) bungalow. No credit cards. On the west side of Yom River, 1km ($^6/_{10}$ miles) northwest of bus station, 300m south of bridge.

This is a good budget choice in Sukhothai proper, because it's got hot water (in shared showers) and the staff is friendly and informative. It's conveniently located, scrupulously clean, and has a small, lushly planted garden with a Thai-style open pavilion where travelers of all ages sit around and swap stories. The A-frame teak bungalows with private toilets and bathrooms with only cold water are the best deal. But the rooms in the one-story modern house are nicely papered with coconut matting and have a few touches of Thai style.

Northern Palace Hotel. 43 Singhawat Rd., Sukhothai 64000. ☎ **055/611-193.** Fax 055/612-038. 67 units. A/C TV. 450B ($11.85) double. MC, V. On Main St., 2 blocks southeast of traffic circle.

This is a very good, recently renovated choice. Most of the street frontage is taken up by the coffee shop, which is sparse and not too great (head for the Dream Café across the street). The granite and chrome lobby is perky and small; rooms are plain, and just a little drab, and have small showers. Still, it's a good deal for the great location.

Pailyn Sukhothai Hotel. 10/2 Moo 1, Jarodvithithong Rd., Sukhothai 64210. ☎ **055/613-310.** Fax 055/613-317. 238 units. A/C MINIBAR TV TEL. 650B ($17.10) double; from 1,200B ($31.60) suite. MC, V. 4km (2.4 miles) east of historical park, 8km (4.8 miles) from the town center.

This recently completed roadside resort is bright, modern, and the most luxurious Sukhothai has to offer. Beyond the rattan and granite lobby, an elevator leads to comfortable, carpeted rooms built in two four-story sextagonal wings, one of which encircles a small pool and sundeck. Rates vary according to room size and amenities; higher rates bring minibars and TVs. The suites are enormous but their bathrooms are surprisingly small. The food in the Thai/Chinese and continental restaurant is very good, attracting locals as well as hotel guests.

Rajthanee Hotel. 229 Charodwithithong, Sukhothai 64000. ☎ **055/611-031.** Fax 055/612-878. 62 units. A/C TV TEL. 300B–600B double ($7.90–$15.80). MC, V. On west side of Yom River, 1km ($^6/_{10}$ mile) northwest of bus station.

This acceptable new city lodging has guestrooms that are relatively clean; more expensive rooms have carpeting, a balcony, and TV, but even the cheapest rooms are adequate. There's a Thai coffee shop and a fancier, second-floor Krua Thai restaurant.

Thai Village Hotels. 214 Jarodwithithong Rd., Muang Khao, Sukhothai 64000. ☎ **055/611-049.** Fax 055/612-583. 120 units. A/C MINIBAR TEL. 500B ($13.15) single; 600B ($15.80) double; 700B ($18.40) triple. MC, V. 2km (1.2 miles) east of Sukhothai Historical Park.

You'll love the old-style Thai Village Houses, set in gardens at the Sukhothai Cultural Center (a kind of minimall with souvenirs, handicrafts, and an "antiques" shop). The quarters are semiattached teak bungalows, attractive from the outside, clean and simple inside. Larger "suites" have a minibar and quaint charm. The Nam Khang garden restaurant is locally known for serving *hommok pao,* a curried fish soufflé made according to the traditional Sukhothai recipe. If you've come only for old Sukhothai and don't care to explore the new town, this is an excellent budget choice.

WHERE TO DINE IN THE AREA

Dream Cafe. 86/1 Singhawat Rd., Sukhothai. ☎ **055/612-081.** Main courses 40B–130B ($1.05–$3.40). No credit cards. Daily 10am–midnight. Center of new city. INTERNATIONAL.

Dream Cafe, the creation of Ms. Chaba Suwantmaykin, has a cozy teak and stucco decor, including an eclectic collection of ceramics, copperware, memorabilia, glass, textiles, and old jewelry. Besides the Thai dishes, including many of the Chaba family recipes, Dream also serves excellent European and Chinese dishes, good burgers, beer, and ice-cream sundaes. A small annex has opened across from Win Tours, right near the Night Market.

Kang Sak Restaurant. Si Satchanalai Rd. No phone. Main courses 40B–120B ($1.05–$3.15). No credit cards. Daily 9am–6pm. 1.2km (¾ mile) before entrance to Si Satchanalai Historical Park. THAI/CHINESE/CONTINENTAL.

This huge restaurant, on quaint terraces and covered patios in tree-shaded gardens, overlooks the Yom River. Make sure you walk all the way back to the riverside tables, which are the best in the house. It's obviously designed to feed busloads, but the food is quite tasty, and if you come at around 2:30 in the afternoon, just after the last bus has left, it's nice and peaceful.

3　Tak & Mae Sot: The Burma (Myanmar) Border

Tak: 426km (265 miles) NW of Bangkok; 138km (86 miles) W of Phitsanulok. Mae Sot: 80km (50 miles) W of Tak

Most travelers will never reach Tak Province, unless they're passing through on a Bangkok–Chiang Mai overland trip, or an east-west journey on the Asia Highway between Thailand's Northeast and Mae Sot at the Burmese border. Tak province is known to Thais for two attributes: the Bhumipol Dam, the country's largest, and for having the hottest weather in Thailand. In contrast, Mae Sot, in the nearby forested hills, is popular with vacationing Thais for its cool weather. The capital Tak (or Amphur Muang) is worth a stopover if you're traveling during the Taksin Festival (see "Special Events," following), when the King Taksin Shrine in the city center is showered with more than the usual incense, candles, and flower offerings.

ESSENTIALS

GETTING THERE　By Plane　There's an airport in Tak, but these days routes to and from the city are canceled. **Thai Airways** has one flight each on Tuesday, Thursday, Saturday, and Sunday to Mae Sot from Phitsanulok. Call them in Bangkok at ☎ **02/280-0070**, or in Phitsanulok at 055/258-020. Thai Airways Mae Sot contacts are 05/251-671 office, or 055/258-029 airport.

By Bus　Fourteen buses to Tak leave daily from Bangkok (trip time 7 hours; 183B/ $4.80, and three buses to Mae Sot (trip time 8 hours; 272B/$7.15) from the Northern Bus Terminal (☎ **02/272-5761**). Government buses leave daily from Phitsanulok's bus terminal (☎ **055/242-430**) to Tak (departures every hour; trip time 3 hours; 44B/$1.15) and to Mae Sot (eight buses; trip time 5 hours; 74B/$1.95). Privately operated minivans connect Tak and Mae Sot, leaving when they get a full van (about every half hour). Trip time is 1½ hours; 33B (85¢). To contact the bus terminal in Tak dial ☎ **055/511-057**. In Mae Sot call ☎ **055/532-949**. From each terminal it's not hard to find either a motorcycle taxi, samlor, or songtao to take you to your hotel for about 10B to 20B (25¢ to 55¢).

By Car　Take Highway 1 north from Bangkok to Tak. From Phitsanulok, take Route 12 west to Tak, then Route 105 west to Mae Sot.

VISITOR INFORMATION　Tak has a brand new TAT office near the bus terminal, 193 Taksin Rd. (☎ **055/514-341**) in an attempt to boost tourism to the area. Most of the information is geared toward Thai nationals. In Mae Sot, stop by Maesot Conservation Tours on Tangkimchiang Road, 1 block past the main intersection, for their free map of the town.

SPECIAL EVENTS　Every January, around the New Year, a provincial festival is held in Tak to honor King Taksin the Great. The streets around his shrine (on Taksin Road at the north side of town) fill with clothes, produce, and food vendors and stalls piled high with Thai sweets and cakes. Dancers, musicians, and monks come out to celebrate. The shrine is showered with floral wreaths and decked out in gold fabric to impress the Thais who come from afar to pay their respects.

EXPLORING THE AREA

Other than the vigorous trading that goes on with Burma (Myanmar) at the tiny border town of Mae Sot, there's not much to see in the Tak province. One nice spot on the Asia Highway, 25km (15 miles) east of Tak, is the **Taksin Maharat (Krabak Yai) National Park,** known for having Thailand's largest tree. Once you've entered the park, the partially paved road goes uphill through forested terrain for a few kilometers, till it dead-ends in a large stand of bamboo. From here, it's a fun and rigorous 20-minute descent to a stream overshadowed by a huge Krabak tree. It would probably take about 16 long-armed people to encircle it.

Mae Sot's border at Rim Moei is no closer to Burma (Myanmar) than the northern towns of Mae Hong Son or Mae Sai, and the lively trade here is always interesting. There's something really unusual about the Mercedes-Benz and two-story brick homes lining this village's main street. The wealth derives mostly from the trade (legal and otherwise) in Burmese jade, bought mostly by Hong Kong and Taiwanese dealers. Despite the volume of illicit trade, most visitors will only see bags of Thai-produced dried shrimp, cuttlefish, black fungus, soybean, and chickpea snacks traded for Burmese woven cotton blankets, lacquer-ware items, ruby jewelry (gems from Burma with Thai workmanship), newly made bronze Buddhas, cotton sarongs, and wicker ware. Goods can be paid for in Burmese kyat and Thai baht.

The border between Rim Moei (Mae Sot) and Myawaddy, Burma, is open daily 8am to 5:30pm, and you can cross the bridge over to Burma on foot or in a car with an on-the-spot day visa for $10.

Most Western tourists come for the rather spectacular scenery and shopping—**jade, lacquerware, and gems** (I only recommend gem shopping here if you know what you're doing, synthetics are getting harder and harder to detect). **Trekking** in the remote and still unspoiled area is becoming somewhat popular, but Mae Sot is far behind its northern neighbors when it comes to organized trips. The one agency that has their act together is **Mae Sot Conservation Tours,** 415/11–12 Tangkimchiang Road (☎ and fax **055/532-818**). They have wonderful 1-day trips for trekking, bamboo rafting, and elephant trekking (4,000B/$105.25) per person for two people, with discounts for larger groups. Longer term trips into Umphang to the north has rubber rafting in some nice rapids with bamboo rafting in tranquil spots on the Mae Krung River. You'll spend your overnights either camping in the jungle or in a Karen village—3-day/2-night stays cost 4,500B ($118.40) per person or 5,500B ($144.75) for 4 days/3 nights. They recommend the full 4-day trip—the jungle mountain and river scenery is absolutely breathtaking, and the trip is magnificently relaxing. Another interesting option is their trips to Burma. They'll take you in to the border town Mawlamyine, to the Pha-an Golden Rock and on to Bago and Yangon on a 4-day, 3-night overland trip. It costs $830 per person, not including return transportation. Other Burma trips up to 9 days can be arranged, which include Mandalay and Inle Lake on the itinerary. E-mail Khun Boon at a1travel@hotmail.com for more information.

WHERE TO STAY & DINE
TAK

I recommend you push on to Mae Sot if you've come this far, but in case you get caught in Tak, I'll recommend one place there, too (really, the only choice these days).

Viang Tak Hotel 2. 236 Jompol Rd., Tak 63000. ☎ **055/511-910.** Fax 055/512-687. 100 units. A/C TV TEL. 550B–1,000B ($14.45–$26.30) double. AE, DC, MC, V. On the Mae Ping River, about 5 min. ride from bus terminal.

This is a surprisingly plush hotel for these prices, with an extremely helpful, polite staff. Large rooms are comfortable and spotless; higher-priced rooms in the new wing are nicer and boast a minibar. The restaurant serves some great Thai and Chinese selections, and there's a small pool. Viang Tak's big brother, the Viang Tak 1 hotel, is presently closed for renovations, with no specific estimated date for reopening. If it's up and running while you're in town, it's also an excellent choice.

MAE SOT

There are a number of inexpensive guest houses in Mae Sot, but I found most of them to be really shabby and lacking in charm. If you're still interested, try the **Number 4 Guesthouse** (☎ 055/544-976) on Intharakiri Road, 5 minutes' walk west of the main intersection in town.

✪ **First Hotel.** 444 Intharakiri Rd., Mae Sot, Tak 63110. ☎ **055/531-233.** Fax 055/ 531-340. 45 units. 450B ($11.85) double with A/C; 270B ($7.10) double with fan. No credit cards. Just north of the main intersection in town, across from the Thai Commercial Bank.

From the street the building is old and weathered, its parking lot like a dirty alley. Look closer and you'll find Mercedes Benzes and Volvos parked here, because the drivers know that inside, First Hotel is really, really cool. Corridors are floored in marble, with intricate three-dimensional woodwork carvings of crazy flora and demonic fish creeping up every wall and dripping from paneled ceilings. Rooms carry the same theme throughout, with carved wood furniture and marble bathrooms—most unusual for this price category. I crown First Hotel The Weirdest Hotel in Thailand.

Mae Sot Hills Hotel. 100 Asia Hwy., Mae Sot, Tak 63110. ☎ **055/532-601.** Fax 055/ 532-600. 114 units. A/C MINIBAR TV TEL. 900B ($23.70) double; from 1,500B ($39.45) suite. MC, V. 17km (10 miles) west of border.

This contemporary four-story hotel is built in two long wings fanning out from a glitzy atrium lobby. All comfortable rooms have modern amenities (suites also have work desks and a bar alcove) and nice views over the mist-shrouded, wooded hills. There's a popular coffee shop and supper club/disco. The Mae Sot Hills also lures group tours, which favor its pool and tennis courts. Songtao on the highway can take you to town or to the border.

In small and cozy Mae Sot, there are a few good choices for dining. My favorite is **Pim Hut** (☎ 055/532-818)on Tangkimchiang Road, 1 block east of the town's main intersection. The casual and comfortable atmosphere works well for family dining or sitting around relaxing with a beer. The moderately priced menu includes excellently prepared Thai dishes, which are the most recommended. The **Kura Internet Restaurant** (☎ 055/534-658), in Intharakiri Road across from the Police Station, serves an all-day breakfast plus fresh local dishes, and has fast Internet service upstairs for 1B per minute.

Exploring Isan: Thailand's Frontier
10

The northeast of Thailand, called Isan (*Ee*-saan) in Thai, accounts for roughly one-third of the country's land mass; yet until recently, only a few intrepid visitors, many of whom were aid workers in refugee and displaced-persons camps, made their way into the area. Bordered by Laos to the north and east (along the famed Mae Khong) and by Cambodia to the south, the region has long suffered political, military, and ethnic upheavals, stemming largely from the Vietnam War, and more recently from the civil war in Cambodia.

A trip to the Northeast is particularly recommended for those who have visited Thailand's better-known destinations, such as Chiang Mai, Mae Hong Son, or Chiang Rai, and who are looking for an adventure. The hotels are less luxurious and English is less widely spoken, but you'll discover exciting archaeological sites (mostly dating from the Khmer period), lovely river towns, finely made crafts, and fiery hot food—all this and few foreign visitors, inexpensive accommodations, surprisingly good roads, and friendly people.

Much of Isan, particularly in the south, is a wide, infertile plain that's reminiscent of parts of Oklahoma and Texas. To the far east, as you approach the confluence of the Mae Khong and Moon rivers, the semifertile grasslands give way to arid, charred sandstone plateaus. The land has a primeval quality, as if an ocean had receded millions of years ago, leaving water-scarred ruts and ripples in the rock. (It's not surprising that paleontologists have found fossils and other evidence of prehistoric life.)

The northern and western sections of Isan are more fertile and mountainous (particularly around Loei), resembling northern Thailand more than the Isan plains. Farms are organized on a much larger scale and the local economy is considerably richer.

Although there are many new small-scale industrial enterprises cropping up in Isan, the economy of the area is still primarily dependent on subsistence farming. After the crops are planted or harvested, many villagers produce handmade crafts, especially silk and cotton, woven in the traditional mutmee or ikat pattern. High-quality silver work, ceramics, and basketry are also produced in Isan.

Trade with Laos is expanding rapidly now that the international bridge has been completed across the Mae Khong at Nong Khai. There are plans to build additional bridges across the mighty river at Nakhon Phanom or Mukdahan and eventually at Loei and Ubon. Meanwhile, Laos is not only opening itself up to tourism but actually promoting it. You can obtain a visa through travel agents or the Laos embassies in Bangkok and Khon Kaen for 1,200B ($31.55) good for 15 days in country, and you can cross at Nong Khai (still the major entry point), Mukdahan, and Nakhon Phanom, as well as at Chong Mek further north.

The weather in Isan is much like the rest of Thailand. The cool season runs from November through February and is similar to summer in Southern California, with very warm days and cool nights. March to May is the dry season, which in Isan is considerably drier than in other sections of the country. The rains begin in earnest in June and there's nary a letup until October.

1 Nakhon Ratchasima (Khorat)

259km (160 miles) NE of Bangkok; 417km (259 miles) W of Buriram; 305km (189 miles) S of Udon Thani

Nakhon Ratchasima, popularly known as Khorat, isn't a wildly interesting city but makes a good base for excursions to such highly recommended sites as Khao Yai National Park, Phimai, Phanom Rung, and other nearby Khmer ruins. It's called the "Gateway to Isan" and is generally considered its major city because of its rapid industrialization and spread-out city plan, though its population is actually less than that of Khon Kaen—or at least we read that recently.

Nearly all of the region's infrastructure emanates from Khorat; train lines, bus routes, roads, communications, and shipping (via the deepwater port to the south) all pass through. It has the largest number of new hotels in the area, and even the TAT office seems to have information beyond that of other regional outposts. All of this makes Khorat a good place to begin your exploration of Isan—though, to be honest, it's not the place for travelers of modest means.

ESSENTIALS

GETTING THERE By Plane Two flights per day leave from Bangkok (flying time: 45 minutes) on Thai Airways. For Bangkok booking call (☎ 02/232-8000). Thai Airways office in Nakhon Ratchasima is Prayoolkit Building, 40–44 Suranaree Rd. (044/252-114). The airport is about 40km east of the city (044/254-834), in Chalerm Prakiet. Thai Airways will arrange ground transportation from the airport at the time of booking.

By Train Nakhon Ratchasima is well connected by rail to Bangkok and major destinations north to the Laos border. Seven trains a day depart from Bangkok (trip time: 6 hours) on ordinary train, 4 hours by express train, which is faster than flying, when you consider trips to and from airports, and less expensive; second-class ordinary costs 115B ($3.05), express is 175B ($4.60). Six trains leave daily from Ubon Ratchathani, with stops in Si Saket, Surin, and Buriram (trip time: 6 hours; 106B/$2.80).

The Khorat (Nakhon Ratchasima) Railway Station is on Mukkhamontri Road, not far from the center of town (☎ 044/242-044). From there, a number of songtao can take you to your hotel for about 10B to 20B (25¢ to 55¢). For Bangkok booking, call the Hua Lampong Railway Station (☎ 02/223-7010). For information about departures from other cities, railway station contacts are provided in each section.

By Bus There are air-conditioned buses departing from the **Northern Bus Terminal** (☎ 02/272-5761) in Bangkok on Paholyothin Road approximately every 20 minutes (trip time: 3 hours; 115B/$3.05). Four buses leave daily from **Chiang Mai Arcade Bus Station** (☎ 053/242-664) (trip time: 11 hours; 325B/$8.55), and hourly buses to and from **Udon Thani Bus Terminal** (☎ 042/222-916) (trip time: 3 hours;

Isan

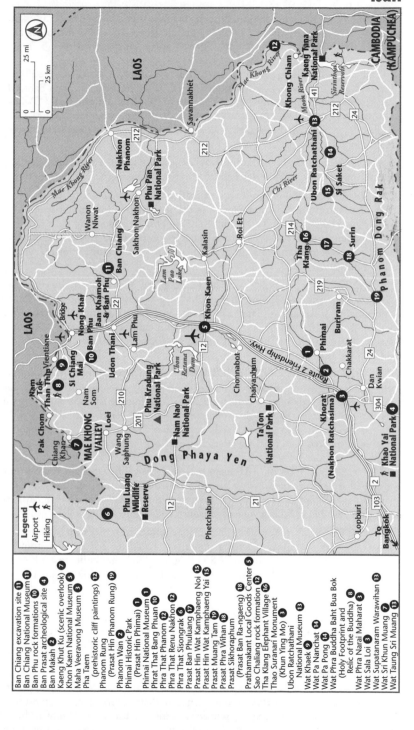

Legend
- ✈ Airport
- 🚶 Hiking

Ban Chiang excavation site 11
Ban Chiang National Museum 10
Ban Prasat archeological site 4
Ban Makah 2
Kaeng Khut Ku (scenic overlook) 7
Khon Kaen National Museum 5
Maha Veeravong Museum 3
Pha Taem
  (prehistoric cliff paintings) 12
Phanom Rung
  (Prasat Hin Phanom Rung) 19
Phanom Wan 2
Phimai Historic Park
  (Prasat Hin Phimai) 1
Phimai National Museum 10
Phrat That Bang Phuan 12
Phra That Phanom 12
Phra That Renu Nakhon 12
Phra That Sisongrak 6
Prasat Ban Phuluang 17
Prasat Hin Wat Kamphaeng Noi 15
Prasat Hin Wat Kamphaeng Yai 15
Prasat Muang Tam 19
Prasat Phra Wihan 18
Prasat Sikhoraphum
  (Prasat Ban Ra-ngaeng) 18
Prathamakant Local Goods Center 5
Sao Chaliang rock formation 12
Tha Klang Elephant Village 16
Thao Suranari Monument
  (Khun Ying Mo) 3
Ubon Ratchathani
  National Museum 13
Wat Khaek 9
Wat Pa Nanchat 14
Wat Pa Pong 14
Wat Phra Buddha Baht Bua Bok
  (Holy Footprint and
  Relic of the Buddha) 8
Wat Phra Narai Maharat 3
Wat Sala Loi 3
Wat Supataniram Warawihan 13
Wat Sri Khun Muang 7
Wat Taung Sri Muang 13

135B/$3.55). Three air-conditioned buses daily run between Nong Khai and Nakhon Ratchasima (trip time: 4 hours; 157B/$4.15), and three air-conditioned buses daily connect Nakhon Ratchasima and Ubon Ratchathani (trip time: 5 hours; 125B/$3.30).

There are two bus terminals in the city. **Bus Terminal I** (☎ **044/242-889**), on Nakhon Ratchasima Road next to the First Hotel, serves buses to and from Bangkok, plus buses making short trips around the province. **Bus Terminal II** (☎ **044/ 256-006**), on Off Highway 2 near St. Mary's Hospital (across from the Tourist Police), handles all long-distance bus routes around Isan. Songtao pass by these stations regularly for local transportation.

By Car   The most direct road from Bangkok is along Route 1 to Saraburi, turning east on Route 2 into Nakhon Ratchasima (trip time: 4 hours).

VISITOR INFORMATION   The **TAT office** (☎ **044/262-505**) is located at 997/5 Mittraphap Rd. (Highway 2), next to the Sima Thani Hotel on the west side of town. Plan to take a songtao to the office. They publish a good map of the city, as well as maintaining up-to-date information about transportation, jungle trekking programs, and hotel and restaurant listings. There's also a small tourist information desk at the train station.

SPECIAL EVENTS   A special fair is held during New Years. Khorat also commemorates the city's heroine, Thao Suranari, in a 10-day fair during the end of March and the beginning of April (see "Things to See & Do," below). During this celebration there are bazaars, parades, historic exhibitions, and cultural performances. A special longboat regatta is held on the second weekend in October to celebrate the end of the Buddhist Rains Retreat.

ORIENTATION & GETTING AROUND   Nakhon Ratcahsima spreads outward from an historical core, an east-west elongated rectangle surrounded by a moat and reconstructed city gates dating back to the city's founding by King Narai during the Ayutthaya period. Just outside the western end of the old city is a zone bordered by Chomsurangyart Road to the south and Suranari Road to the north. Nearly all hotels, restaurants, markets, and tourist services are contained within this area, although the TAT office and the newest hotels are situated on the periphery. The distances between 3 or 4 blocks (as seen on the TAT map) may seem walkable, especially those within the central area, but in most cases a songtao is a better idea. You should pay no more than 20B to 50B (50¢ to $1.30) to get anywhere within the city, though you may have to bargain hard or get help in your negotiations.

FAST FACTS   Nakhon Ratchasima is a major commercial center with banks located all over the city. A money changing booth, on Phoklang Road across from the Chumphon City Gate, is open until 8pm nightly. Find the **main post office** on Assadang Road between Manat and Prajak roads (☎ **044/247-537**) in the old city center. You'll find the overseas telephone office here, too. There's another post office branch on Chomsurangyard Road, next to the Klang Plaza shopping center. The **Maharat Hospital** (☎ **044/254-990**) is on Changphuak Road, north of Mittraphap Road (Highway 2). For police emergencies, call the **Tourist Police** at ☎ **044/ 341-777,** or stop by their office across from Bus Terminal II on Highway 2.

WHAT TO SEE & DO

There are a couple of minisites in Nakhon Ratchasima (Khorat) that will appeal to those who have a proclivity toward completeness in their travels; otherwise, most head out of town for the more engaging excursions. A trip to **Phimai** (see "Phimai," below in this chapter), 60km (37 miles) north of town, is a terrific trip if you have any interest in archaeology. **Phanom Rung,** to the east, is only slightly less interesting (see "Side Trips from Surin," later in this chapter). Nature buffs will certainly enjoy a day trip, or longer, to **Khao Yai National Park** (see "Side Trips from Khorat," below in this section), while shoppers will decide for themselves about the quality of silk at famed **Pak Thong Chai** as well as the equally lauded pottery made in **Dan Kwian village** (see "Side Trips from Khorat," below in this section).

Khorat is 600 years old (postdating the classical Khmer period), dating from the unification of two villages into a larger provincial town. Little remains from this period other than pieces of city walls and gates as well as sections of a moat. The most highly regarded in-town site is the **Monument of Thao Suranari (Khun Ying Mo),** located on Chumphon Road in front of the sandblasted Chumphon Gate and overlooking the town square. The statue is of little aesthetic interest, but the story behind it merits retelling. During the reign of Rama III (19th century), Prince Anuwong of Vientiane led an invasion of Khorat, scoring an initial success with his rout of local forces. His intention was to establish a colony and enslave the local population. Khun Ying Mo, the wife of Khorat's deputy governor, enticed the Laotian officers to celebrate and got them all drunk. Then she and a band of women killed the officers, and in the confusion Prince Anuwong's army fled in defeat. It took about 100 years, but in 1934 a monument was built in her honor, and today it serves as a reminder that freedom must be defended.

The most interesting in-town Buddhist wat houses an image of Narayana, a sacred Hindu deity, at **Wat Phra Narai Maharat;** this testament to religious diversity can be found along Prajak Road, where you'll also find the **City Pillar.** Also in town is the **Maha Veeravong Museum,** on Ratchadamnoen Road just south of the intersection with Mahatthai Road, which has a small historical collection, open Wednesday to Sunday 9am to noon and 1 to 4pm; 30B (80¢) admission.

Wat Sala Loi is notable for its modern main chapel, designed in the shape of a Chinese junk. The distinctive design has won it several architectural awards and is worth a look for those who relish the unusual. It's on the far northwestern end of town along the Lam Tha Khong River.

WHERE TO STAY

The better hotels are located on the outer parts of the city, but at these places you can get a top quality hotel room for about 1,000B! In town, you'll find even cheaper places, but they won't be as plush.

Chomsurang Hotel. 547 Mahatthai Rd., Khorat. ☎ **044/257-088.** 119 units. A/C TV TEL. 850B–1,270B double ($22.37–$33.42). AE, MC, V. Near the Night Market on Manat Rd.

A fully featured hotel with a swimming pool, restaurant, and the typical niceties found in the city's better places. I found it a bit worn, with some fresh paint here and there indicating an effort at keeping up.

Khorat Doctor's Guest House. 78 Sueb Siri Rd., Khorat. ☎ **044/255-846.** 6 units. 300B ($7.90) double with A/C, 150B ($3.95) double with fan. No credit cards.

A lucky few will find absolutely rock-bottom accommodations at this popular guest house (sometimes it's closed, though). Services and facilities include hot-water showers, breakfast and dinner, laundry service, as well as full guide services. The staff is friendly and speaks English. For the money you can't beat it.

King Hotel. 1756 Mittraphap Rd., Khorat. ☎ **044/253-360.** Fax 044/262-048. 64 units. TV TEL. 500B ($13.15) double with A/C. MC, V. Far northwest edge of town, near the river.

A good value, but the location isn't convenient, and very little English is spoken. Some of the rooms have air-conditioning.

Royal Princess Khorat. 1137 Suranarai Rd., Naimuang District, Khorat 30000. ☎ **044/256-629.** Fax 044/256-601. 186 units. A/C MINIBAR TV TEL. 900B ($23.70) single or double. AE, DC, MC, V. Northeast of town, near the stadium.

The best hotel in Khorat, with a friendly and helpful staff, a little removed from the hubbub of this very busy city and yet convenient to transportation—the Princess offers all the usual amenities plus the best pool in town, a tennis court, a business center, meeting rooms, boutiques, laundry and room service, a nightclub, and two restaurants. Its Empress Chinese Restaurant is probably the finest in Khorat.

Sima Thani Hotel. Mittraphap Rd., Khorat 30000. ☎ **044/213-100.** Fax 044/213-121. 265 units. A/C MINIBAR TV TEL. 750B ($19.75) double. AE, DC, MC, V. Next to the TAT office, west of town.

Second only to the Royal Princess, Sima Thani is a first-rate city hotel. Its new wing adds more than 100 brand new rooms, and while the hotel is situated just along the main highway, it's surprisingly quiet. The spacious five-story atrium lounge is especially handsome and inviting. The rooms are large and modern; the gray granite bathrooms are particularly attractive. There's a good pool, a fitness center with excellent saunas, two restaurants, a pub, and a bar. (By the way, Sima Thani wins the prize for in-house videos, VDO-CDs that are so current they can't be legal.)

WHERE TO DINE

There are several acceptable eateries in the center of town, near the intersection of Phoklang and Chumpon roads, notably **Ploey,** which serves some Western food, including pizza. The Klang Plaza 2 shopping center, at Ratchadamnoen and Jomsurangyat roads, has a **KFC, Dunkin Donuts,** and other American-style eateries, as well as a big supermarket.

Lisa Steakhouse. Jomsurangyat Rd. ☎ **044/242-279.** Sandwiches 35B–60B (90¢–$1.55); steaks 90B–200B ($2.35–$5.25). MC, V. Daily 11am–midnight. Across road from Wat Chaeng Nai, next to VIP Karaoki. WESTERN/THAI/CHINESE.

If you can read Thai, you may be able to make out the name; otherwise, find the vine-covered arbor and look through it for the waterfall cascading down an impressive rock facade to spot the most pleasant outdoor restaurant around. There's a large Thai and Chinese menu, in Thai, but the friendly staff speaks some English.

Thaweephan. Sueb Siri Rd. ☎ **044/257-775.** Main courses 35B–200B (90¢–$5.25). No credit cards. Daily noon–11pm. South of the rail lines and 1 big block east of Mittraphap Rd.; near the TAT office. THAI/CHINESE.

This is a typical Thai restaurant conveniently located near the TAT office. Thaweephan has a large menu that includes mild but tasty Chinese dishes. The staff is friendly but speaks little English.

NAKHON RATCHASIMA AFTER DARK

You can have an interesting evening at the Khorat **Night Market,** on Manat Road south of Chumphon Road, where there are more than 100 stands selling everything from cooking utensils, jeans, and nylon bags to a wide variety of snack food—you can hop from one stand to another for an inexpensive meal. It opens daily at dusk, about 6 to 10pm, depending on the time of year. Around the New Year it gets especially festive.

You can take a stroll along Chomsurangyat Road west from the center of town and check out the bars and clubs—there's something for everyone. The **Plaza Cinema,** behind the Klang Plaza 2 shopping center, at Ratchadamnoen and Jomsurangyat roads, frequently has English-language movies.

SIDE TRIPS FROM NAKHON RATCHASIMA

You'll notice all of Nakhon Ratchasima's interesting attractions are actually located outside the city. I've provided local transportation directions to each sight, but if you're not into the added time you can call **Nanta Travel Service,** 168 Mahatthai Rd. (☎ 044/257-359). They organize very convenient 1-day excursions to each of the following places for between 980B and 1,150B ($25.80 and $30.25) per person (with discounts for three or more people), inclusive of all transfers, lunch, and admission fees.

PRASAT HIN PHANOM WAN & BAN MAKAH   These two stops combine a Khmer historical stone castle with a small village, Ban Makah, that specializes in the manufacture of handmade knives. Phanom Wan, smaller and less restored than Phimai, is of architectural significance and still in use by monks. The main structure at Phanom Wan is crumbling, and the long-term plan is to dismantle and reconstruct it on a new foundation—though this apparently isn't imminent. The trip to Phanom Wan is best done by car, though those with plenty of time can do it by bus. Phanom Wan and Ban Makah are only 20km (12 miles) from Khorat on the way to Phimai. Air-conditioned minivan service departs from Bus Terminal II. The 15-minute trip costs only 7B (20¢), but doesn't take you all the way to the site. From the drop-off on the main highway, you'll have to negotiate with one of the motorcycle taxis waiting under the shady trees for the final 7km of the trip (and have a ride back). You can also grab a songtao from Assadang Road, across from Thai Prokkhaphan Hotel to take you direct (about 20B/53¢ one-way). If you do this, have someone at your hotel write Prasat Hin Phanom Wan for you in Thai to show the driver. To get there by car, travel north on Route 2 for 11km (6½ miles) and take the turnoff for Phanom Wan; en route you'll pass through Ban Makah. Open daily 8:30am to 6pm; admission 30B (80¢).

PAK THONG CHAI   This village, located approximately 30km (18 miles) south of Khorat along Route 304, is known for its handwoven silk. In addition to the small factories and home shops where residents still engage in the craft of silk weaving, there are a handful of shops that carry a wide range of silk products. Fabrics and patterns are attractive though somewhat pricey. Professional silk buyers warn that much of the silk produced in Pak Thong Chai (as with other silk villages) incorporates varying blends of polyester—usually in the warp, which isn't visible. So exercise caution if you want 100% silk; burn a thread, if it's silk, it will smell like singed hair or feathers.

To get there from Khorat, take a bus from Bus Terminal I. It will cost about 11B (30¢) for the fan bus, which leaves every 30 minutes throughout the day.

Among the more reputable shops are **Srithai Silk,** with a new showroom at 333 Sueb Siri Rd. (☎ 044/441-588), open daily 7am to 6pm; and **Praneet Thai Silk,** 96–97 Sriphonrat Rd. (☎ 044/441-173).

DAN KWIAN VILLAGE   The only reason to visit Dan Kwian is for the distinctive pottery that's produced by the descendants of the Mon tribespeople who settled here in the early 18th century. Their ceramics may not suit your taste, but we recommend a visit for anyone who wants to see how this unusual pottery is manufactured. This will be especially interesting for those who intend to visit Ban Chiang (see "Udon Thani & Ban Chiang," in this chapter), where ceramic pots are made in a similar technique used nearly 5,000 years ago.

There are still about 20 families engaged in the traditional manufacture of ceramic pots. Clay is gathered from the banks of the nearby Moon River during low water (between January and April). Prepared clay is built up to form the basic shape, then the potter places it on a wheel and refines the vessel while an assistant turns the wheel. The pottery is then left to dry outdoors before being fired in a wood-fueled kiln.

From Khorat, buses run every 20 minutes from Khorat's Bus Terminal I. (Trip time: 30 minutes; fare 10B/25¢).

KHAO YAI NATIONAL PARK   Of all Thailand's national parks, Khao Yai is the most notable for many reasons. Not only is it the oldest national park in Thailand (established in 1962), the third largest (2,172 square kilometers), and the second-most visited park (well over half a million per year), but it's also one of the few places where you're likely to see this country's wildlife in its natural environment. Khao Yai has wild elephant herds, two kinds of gibbon, macaques, tigers, leopards, Malaysian sun bears, Asian black bears, and a multitude of other mammals. Bird species are counted at more than 320, but the stars are the hornbills; there are four species that call the park home. Snuggled well in the tropical evergreen forest, you're not guaranteed to see all of these animals, but chances are good you'll see something creeping around. If you have time to stick around for a night view, it'll increase your chances. Other attractions include the **Heo Suwat Waterfall** (the waterfalls are at their peak from September to November) and the bat-populated **limestone cave** at **Khao Rub Chang** (located at the periphery of the park).

Of the 12 trails that are open to the public, the Krong Thaew Nature Trail is the most traveled. A short 1-km-long hike, it begins behind the park's visitors' center, and has been designed as a sort of short introduction to the park habitat. The other trails are up to 8km long, for those who want to venture further.

It used to be easier to experience this beautiful place, before the National Parks Division closed the resorts to overnight stays to prevent tourist encroachment. Recently, however, they've been permitting overnight visitors at their own overnight facilities—simple bungalows. You have to contact them directly (☎ 037/319-002) at their office in Bangkok to obtain permission. In Pak Chong at the Tourist Service Center, call Khao Yai National Park (☎ 037/319-002).

There are two entrances to Khao Yai, one south in Nakhon Nayak province closer to Bangkok, and another in the north in Nakhon Ratcahsima province. While the southern entrance is geographically closer to Bangkok, public transportation is almost nonexistent—you'd have to have your own car, or hire a car and driver. But the one nearest to Khorat (Nakhon Ratcahsima) has better access by far from both Bangkok and Khorat. Take one of the buses that ply between Bangkok's Northern Bus Terminal and Khorat's Bus Terminal I, and ask the driver to drop you at Pak Chong. From the market there, you'll have to arrange a songtao to take you to the park entrance. You may have to flag down an additional ride to the Headquarters—it's about 12km back from the main road. Once you reach the Khao Yai Headquarters and visitors' center, you can pick up maps and detailed information about the park, and rangers can arrange tours and guides for reasonable fees.

Unless you rough it in government accommodations in the park, you'll be staying with other overnighters in Pak Chong. Try the **Khao Yai Garden Lodge,** Km. 7 Tanarat Road (☎ 044/365-167; fax 044/365-179); it will cost between 100B and 1,200B ($2.65 and $31.60) for a double or the **Juladis Khao Yai Resort,** 45 Moo 4, Tanarat Road (☎ 044/297-297, or 02/255-1712 in Bangkok); double rooms begin at 2,300B ($60.55). Khao Yai Garden Lodge (see above) arranges tours, driving you more remote sites and arranging night views, plus stops at waterfalls for swimming (950B/$25 per person).

From Khorat you can enjoy a day trip organized by **Nanta Travel Service,** 168 Mahatthai Rd. (☎ 044/257-359) for about 1,150B ($30.25) per person, including transportation and lunch.

If you plan on visiting Khao Yai National Park during the cool season (December and January), remember to bring a sweater; temperatures drop below 50°F in the evening. Year-round, you're advised to bring plenty of mosquito repellent, as well as leech repellent.

2 Phimai

319km (197 miles) NE of Bangkok; 60km (37 miles) N of Khorat; 245km (152 miles) S of Udon Thani

Along with Prasat Hin Phanom Rung (see "Side Trips from Surin," in this chapter), the completely restored ruins at Phimai are a highlight of any tour of Isan. In fact, because the site is in such a good state of repair, it's the best place to begin your tour of the Khmer ruins in Isan, so that you'll have a better idea of the original condition and design of lesser reconstructed/excavated archaeological destinations.

ESSENTIALS
GETTING THERE

By Bus There aren't any direct bus routes from Bangkok, so you'll have to stop in Khorat first. From the **Bus Terminal II** (☎ **044/256-006**) off Mittraphap Road, buses run every 30 minutes between 5:30am and 10pm. (trip time: 90 minutes; 16B/40¢). The bus lets you off at the end of Chomsudasadet Road.

By Car The most direct route is north from Khorat on Route 2; take the eastbound Phimai turnoff.

ORIENTATION Basically, the main roads for getting your bearings are Anantjinda Road and Chomsudasadet Road. If you arrive by bus, you'll let out at the dead end of Chomsudasadet—look down to the other end of the street to see the tall prang of the Prasat Hin Phimai at the historical park. Along Chomsudasadet there are some convenient restaurants and accommodations. Walk toward the temple, and Chomsudasadet intercepts Anantjinda. Look to the left and you'll find the Tourist Police office. Look to the right and you'll see the national park entrance. If you turn right and travel down Anantjinda for one block, you'll hit the intersection with Buchayan Road. The museum is north of this intersection, just off Buchayan.

Because Phimai is so small, you can basically walk from the main attractions to the major points in town. Bicycles can be rented on the cheap from a few shops along Chomsudasadet Road by the bus stop. You'll also find lots of guys who still make their living peddling trishaws, a good option if you're traveling out to the museum and you're just too hot to deal with the 15-minute walk.

FAST FACTS The best traveler information I found was at the **Tourist Police office** (☎ **044/341-777**). They've got a good map of the town, and are happy to answer all your questions. The **Bai Teiy Restaurant** (☎ **044/471-725**), on Chomsudasadet Road about midway between the bus stop and the historical park, has a map and info—you can't miss their big sign. You'll find a couple of **banks** with ATMs on Anantajinda Road near the main entrance of the historical park—one just across from the Tourist Police office and one in the opposite direction at the intersection of Anantajinda and Buchayan roads (this one also has currency exchange).

SPECIAL EVENTS A celebration of dance, lights, and music honoring Phimai is held annually in late October or early November (contact the TAT for this year's date) as part of the **Phimai Festival.** Lopburi-period stage performances and a play depicting scenes from the *Ramayana* are presented at the Sanctuary. Other aspects of the festival include the Northeastern Boat Racing Championship, historical and cultural exhibitions, and a costume parade.

WHAT TO SEE & DO

Phimai Historic Park (Prasat Hin Phimai). Anantjinda Rd. ☎ **044/471-518.** Admission 40B ($1.05). Daily 7:30am–6pm.

Prasat Hin Phimai, Thailand's best-known and best-restored Khmer site, is a stone sanctuary built in the style, if not the scale, of Angkor Wat in Cambodia. It is thought to have been constructed during the reign of King Suriya Woraman I, who ruled the Khmer Empire from A.D. 1002 to 1050.

The Khmer people worshiped Hindu deities, in particular Brahma and Shiva, and consistent with Shiva worship, many of the *prasats* (cactus-shaped towers atop multi-storied bases) contained *lingams* (phallic-shaped columns that represent the generative power of Shiva) in their central chambers. The most distinctive evidence of the Hindu origin of Phimai are the intricately carved sandstone lintels (several on display in the museum) above the main doorways in the central prasats and *gopuras* (gate towers); images of a dancing Shiva and Vishnu are among the most prominent. After the decline of the Khmer Empire in Thailand, Phimai was rebuilt by Thai artisans and decorated with Mahayana Buddhist imagery. Lingams were replaced by Buddhas, and lintels depicting Hindu deities were incorporated with figures from the story of Buddhism, usually with the Buddhist figure positioned above the original Hindu deity. New buildings were added; in general, the lower, less-decorated structures were constructed after the 12th century by Thai architects.

The renovation of Phimai has turned what once was a moat-surrounded site into a groomed lawn park with neatly trimmed trees; a rebuilt stone wall, overflowing with pink and white bougainvillea, encircles the site. A single *naga* bridge, with Anglo-style cobras, leads up to the main sanctuary. Massive sandstone columns form the entrance to the gallery. One very distinctive Khmer architectural motif is the balustrade window; archaeologists believe that many of these windows contained other decorative elements that haven't survived. The well-proportioned doorways are particularly sublime.

✪ **Phimai National Museum.** Buchayan Rd. ☎ **044/471-167.** Admission 30B (80¢). Wed–Sun 9am–4pm.

The handsome new building finished by the Thai Fine Arts Department in 1993 is a significant addition to this major site—and a must-see. You'll pass it on your way to the ruin, but it's better to save it until after you see the historical site, both to take a break from the sun and to better appreciate the experience. Downstairs are the superb archaeological remains of Phimai—stone carvings, jewelry, and other artifacts that give a very good picture of the ancient city, its art, architecture, and culture. Artifacts of more recent origin are exhibited upstairs, along with displays that provide views of the social, economic, political, artistic, and cultural development of Isan. Guided tours and books are available.

Outside, but within the museum compound, you'll also find an open-air wing with a small collection of some of the finest carved lintels in Isan—some from other sites in Si Saket, Buriram, and Khorat. It's open daily 8:30am to 4:30pm and there's no admission charge

WHERE TO STAY & DINE

If you find yourself spending the night in Phimai, there are two small and inexpensive inns just in town: The **Old Phimai Guest House** (☎ **044/471-918**), a teak mansion with dormitory beds and small fan-cooled rooms for 120B to 260B ($3.15 to $6.85); and the slightly more upscale **Phimai Hotel** (☎ **044/471-306;** fax 044/471-940), with air-conditioned rooms that run 400B to 600B ($10.55 to $15.80) and cheaper fan-cooled rooms. Both are on Chomsudasadet Road, just around the corner from the historical park.

There are a few dining options in and around Phimai. Near the site is the **Bai-Teiy Restaurant** (☎ 044/471-725), with a convenient location and facilities that draw all sorts of independent travelers. The **Rim Moon Restaurant** (☎ 044/471-692) and **Toiting** (no phone) are on the northern end of town beyond the museum, overlooking the Moon River. All are open daily for lunch and dinner. There is a **Night Market,** located near the southeast corner of the site, for extremely inexpensive food and casual dining; open nightly 6pm to midnight.

EN ROUTE TO THE NORTH

For a place that's largely escaped the stamp of group tourism, **Chaiyaphum,** located approximately midway between busy Khorat and Khon Kaen (take Route 202) is far enough off national Route 2 to be largely overlooked.

One event that may eventually put little Chaiyaphum on the map is the increasingly popular **Chaiyaphum Elephant Roundup** that takes place each year in February (contact the TAT for this year's date).

There's a Dvaravati era (A.D. 6th–11th c.), Khmer-style sandstone sanctuary (with a carved bodhisattva) at Prang Ku (2km/1.2 miles from the center) and a bathing ritual that takes place here on the first day of the full moon in April. Otherwise, the main attraction here is Chaiyaphum's most famous product, silk. The material woven in the Chaiyaphum area is made of 100% silk and is favored by the royal family. If you wish to see the finest examples of weaving, visit people's houses instead of the shops and stands. You'll have to spend several hours searching out such people, but you'll have a memorable time—and probably find some exquisite silk at bargain prices.

If you end up spending the night, there is the **Lert Nimitra Hotel,** at 447 Nivetrat Rd. (☎ 044/811-522), where rooms run 150B to 1,100B ($3.95 to $28.95). Another alternative is **Yin's Guest House** (no phone), near the bus station, which will arrange inexpensive excursions to view the natural scenery around Chaiyaphum as well as visits to silk-weaving establishments. Expect to pay 60B to 110B ($1.60 to $2.90) for a dormitory room.

There are hourly air-conditioned buses daily that navigate the 119km (74 miles) distance to Chaiyaphum from Khorat for 59B ($1.55).

Those interested in archaeological digs may want to check out **Ban Prasat,** 45km (2.8 miles) north of Khorat on the way to Phimai, 2km (1.2 miles) left, off the main road. There are presently three pits, one about 3,000 years old, with human skeletons, stone weapons, and ornaments of animal bones and shells. A second (about 1,600 to 1,800 years old) also contains red-and-black pottery with incised decorations and gold wrist and ankle bracelets. The third (about 600 years old) includes a kiln and pottery in both Khmer and contemporary styles, as well as weapons. If you go by bus, ask the conductor to let you off at the roadside pavilion, where you can catch a later bus to continue on to Phimai or return to Khorat.

3 Khon Kaen

449km (278 miles) NE of Bangkok; 190km (118 miles) N of Khorat; 115km (71 miles) S of Udon Thani

Khon Kaen is best known by travelers as a stopping-off point en route to northern Isan. With a large commercial airport, a stop along the northern railway line, and a site along Highway 2 (between Nakhon Ratchasima and Nong Khai), most who come here are on their way to other destinations. Khon Kaen is a relatively new city, having been established in 1783, so there's not much history here. Nationally it's known for Khon Kaen University, the largest in Isan, and as the home of Channel 5 (one of the region's largest television stations), as well as for its gigantic branch of the Bank of Thailand. It's a pleasant, thriving city with a vibrant nightlife; however, there's not much to see and do here. Better to move on, especially if you're on a tight program, than to try to fashion a tour. However, those interested in silk may want to make time to visit the silk village of Chonnabot.

ESSENTIALS

GETTING THERE **By Plane** **Thai Airways** flies four times daily to Khon Kaen from Bangkok (flying time: 55 minutes). For Bangkok booking contact them at (☎ **02/232-8000**), and in Khon Kaen contact them at 183/6 Maliwan Rd. (043/334-112). There are several tour operators in Khon Kaen that provide airport transfers. Arrange the 15-minute trip through **Kaen Khun Travel** (☎ **043/239-458**) for 50B ($1.30).

By Train Khon Kaen is connected by rail to Bangkok via Nakhon Ratchasima (the same train that heads north to Udon Thani and Nong Khai). Three trains a day leave from Bangkok (trip time: 8 hours on rapid train, 7 hours by express train; second-class ordinary 179B/$4.70, express 239B/$6.30). Make sure you're on the right train, as the northern line branches off—one branch for Nong Khai (which stops in Khon Kaen— the one you want) and the other to Ubon Ratchathani. Bangkok's Hua Lampong Station can be reached at ☎ **02/223-7010.**

The **Khon Kaen Railway Station** (☎ **043/221-112**) is at the end of Ruenrom Road, which leads you to Nangmuang Road and Klangmuang Road, the main arteries of the town. Frequent songtao, minitruck taxis, can take you to your hotel from the station for between 20B and 40B (55¢ and $1.05).

By Bus Sixteen air-conditioned buses and one VIP bus leave daily from Bangkok's Northern Bus Terminal (☎ **02/272-5761**) (trip time: 6 hours; 193B/$5.08 for the standard buses; 295B/$7.76 for the VIP bus). Hourly air-conditioned buses leave daily from Nakhon Ratchasima's (Khorat) Bus Terminal II (044/256-006) (trip time: 2½ hours; 86B/$2.25). Many buses depart daily from Udon Thani Bus Terminal (042/222-916), about one every 15 minutes from 8:30am to 11pm (trip time: 2 hours; 68B/$1.80). In Khon Kaen call (043/239-910) for schedules for air-conditioned buses from the city. The bus terminal is located in the heart of the town, on Soi Ruajit between Srichan and Ammart roads. Songtao can take you to your hotel from here for about 10B (25¢).

By Car The most direct route from either Bangkok or Udon Thani is on Route 2.

ORIENTATION The city is laid out in a simple grid system. The railway station is on the southwestern edge of town on Rueorom Road. The two main north-south boulevards are Na-Muang Road on the west and Klang Muang Road on the east, while Phimpasut Road forms a northern perimeter in the central section.

FAST FACTS The **TAT office** (☎ **043/244-498**) is on Prachasamosorn Road between Klangmuang and Langmuang roads. The **Tourist Police** share the TAT building and can be reached 24 hours a day at ☎ **043/236-937.** The **Thai Airways** office (☎ **043/334-112**) is located at 183/6 Maliwan Rd. The **Khon Kaen Hospital** (☎ **043/236-005**) is on Sichan Road.; for **emergencies** dial ☎ **191.**

SPECIAL EVENTS In December of each year is the **Khon Kaen Silk and Friendship Fair.** Silk weavers, large and small, from the surrounding area display their wares along with other locally manufactured handicrafts. In addition to the market, there are other cultural performances and demonstrations.

WHAT TO SEE & DO

The **Khon Kaen National Museum** houses one of the better small collections in this area of Isan. Archaeological finds from nearby sites are on display spanning the major periods of historic development. The most significant holdings are an excellent collection of Ban Chiang clay pots and a fine exhibit of carved stone markers from the Dvaravati period. The museum is located in the Provincial Civil Service Center, to the north of Khon Kaen's central district. Open Tuesday to Saturday 8:30am to 4:30pm; admission 30B (80¢).

For shoppers the **Prathamakant Local Goods Center,** 79/2–3 Ruenrom Rd. (☎ 043/224-080), is the number one handicrafts emporium in Khon Kaen, if not in this section of Isan. They stock an incredible selection of silk woven in Khorat, Chonnabot, Chaiyaphum, and other smaller villages at retail prices. They also have cotton weaves of various styles, especially mutmee or ikat. Their selection of hill-tribe appliqué work, beadwork from Chiang Mai, and basketry is also extensive. You can purchase silver jewelry produced in Surin and Laos (more expensive than in those locations but still cheaper by 25% to 50% than it is in Bangkok). Their beautiful shirts and blouses made with panels of antique silk are irresistible. The helpful staff speaks English. Open daily 8am to 8:30pm; Visa and MasterCard are accepted.

WHERE TO STAY & DINE

Although there are coffee shop–style restaurants in the major hotels, I recommend dining al fresco at the **Khon Kaen Market,** off Klang Muang Road near the department store. The area has a well-deserved reputation for the piquancy of its food, so easy does it at first.

Charoen Thani Princess. 260 Srichan Rd., Khon Kaen 40000. ☎ **043/220-400.** Fax 043/220-438. 320 units. A/C MINIBAR TV TEL. 2,160B ($56.85) double. AE, DC, MC, V. Midway between train and bus stations, off Srichan and Na-Muang rds.

This handsome 20-story hotel is a good choice for location and convenience. Facilities include a swimming pool, fitness center, business center, 24-hour room service, laundry service, bakery, drugstore, shops, meeting rooms, lobby lounge, Chinese restaurant, and coffee shop with international cuisine. Attractive, comfortable rooms have quality amenities plus a room safe, international direct dial telephone, and color TV.

Hotel Sofitel Raja Orchid Khon Kaen. 9/9 Prachasumran Rd., Khon Kaen, 40000. ☎ **043/322-155.** Fax 043/322-150. 297 units. A/C MINIBAR TV TEL. 1,754B ($46.15) double; from 2,900B ($76.30) suite. AE, DC, MC, V. Behind Charoen Thani Princess Hotel.

You can't miss this, the tallest building in town, and the newest modern structure to grace Khon Kaen's skyline. Hotel Sofitel provides excellent service and the finest facilities available. Rooms are large, modern, and elegant—a great facility for an upcountry provincial capital. Facilities include top-notch health and fitness center, beauty salon, outdoor swimming pool, and spa. Sofitel's dining and entertainment options are second to none—with Western, Chinese, and Vietnamese restaurants, plus bakery and sushi bar. Come here in the evenings for a great time at Kronen Brauhaus, Studio 1 Karaoke, the lobby lounge, a modern disco, and live music. Definitely the best choice for entertainment in the city.

Kaen Inn Hotel. 56 Klang Muang Rd., Khon Kaen, 40000. ☎ **043/245-420.** Fax 043/239-457. 162 units. A/C MINIBAR TV TEL. 800B ($21.05) double. AE, MC, V. At the intersection with Ammart Rd. near the National Bank of Thailand.

The Kaen Inn is a good quality, provincial hotel with fair service, in a busy central location. Decor is standard as are the many facilities including a coffee shop, bar, and restaurant. The guest rooms are basically clean and well maintained.

Khon Kaen Hotel. 43/3 Phimpasut Rd., Khon Kaen, 40000. ☎ **043/237-711.** Fax 043/237-744. 130 units. A/C TEL. 700B ($18.40) double. AE, MC, V. Near the intersection with Na-Muang Rd.

The Khon Kaen Hotel is very popular with Thai businesspeople. Rooms are clean, worn, Spartanly furnished, and acceptable. The plus is a quieter location in an inner courtyard near a school.

SIDE TRIPS FROM KHON KAEN

About the only place that I'd recommend touring is the silk-weaving village of **Chonnabot,** located southwest of the city. Take Route 2 south and turn at the 399km marker for an additional 12km (7 miles). The quality of the silk and the prices compare favorably with that in Pak Thong Chai. (The Thai silk experts feel that it was of good quality, but not up to the standards of material from Chaiyaphum.) Among the larger shops, with a wide selection of locally made silk and mutmee cotton, is **Ratree Thai Silk** (☎ **043/286-054**), 246–248 Sriboonreung Rd., where a 6-foot length of finely made silk runs 800B to 1,500B ($21.05 to $39.45).

4 Udon Thani & Ban Chiang

564km (350 miles) NE of Bangkok; 305km (189 miles) N of Khorat; 115km (71 miles) N of Khon Kaen; 51km (32 miles) S of Nong Khai; 152km (94 miles) E of Loei

Udon Thani, known simply as Udon, is a provincial center that once was the base for a large contingent of U.S. armed forces and their families, particularly during the Vietnam War. Today there are only a handful of American military advisors and a slightly larger number of retirees, who've either stayed or returned, from the more active days of the 1960s and 1970s. The most obvious reminder of American military presence in Udon is the enormous air base that now serves both military and civilian sectors of the Thai air infrastructure. The only public access to this installation is when flying on a commercial airliner, so if you arrive by car, bus, or train you'll miss this unusual tourist site. Until early 1999, there was a branch of the U.S. consulate here, but it has since closed.

About the only reason to stop in Udon is easy access to Thailand's premier Bronze Age excavation at Ban Chiang. This world-renowned archaeological site has attracted interest from both scholars and travelers since its excavation dating back to the 1970s, and was the subject of a traveling exhibition organized by the Smithsonian Institution in the 1980s. If you plan to visit Ban Chiang, remember it's closed on Mondays, Tuesdays, and national holidays.

ESSENTIALS

GETTING THERE   By Plane   Thai Airways (in Bangkok (☎ **02/232-8000)** has three flights daily from Bangkok (flying time: 55 minutes). The **Thai Airways** office (☎ **042/243-222**) is at 60 Makkang Rd. **Angel Air** also offers service between Chiang Mai and Udon Thani four times a week. Call them in Bangkok at ☎ **02/953-2260** weekdays or 02/535-6287 weekends. Airport transfers can be arranged at the airport for 50B ($1.30) to town.

By Train   Udon Thani is connected by rail to Bangkok via Nakhon Ratchasima (Khorat) as well as to Nong Khai to the north. Five trains a day leave from Bangkok

Hua Lamphong Railway Station (☎ 02/223-7010) (trip time: 10 to 11 hours on rapid train, 8½ hours by express train; second-class ordinary 219B/$5.75, express 279B/$7.35). Four trains leave daily from Khorat (trip time: 4½ hours; 104B/$2.75).

The **Railway Station** in Udon (☎ 042/222-061) is on the very east side of town. From there, you can catch a songtao to your hotel starting from 30B (80¢).

By Bus   Nineteen air-conditioned buses a day leave from Bangkok Northern Bus Terminal (☎ 02/272-5761) (trip time: 9 hours; 241B/$6.34). Hourly air-conditioned buses leave from Nakhon Ratchasima (Khorat) (trip time: 4 hours; 135B/$3.55). Many buses leave daily from Nong Khai (trip time: 45 minutes; 70B/$1.85).

There are several bus stations in Udon Thani. Buses to and from Bangkok and Nakhon Ratchasima (Khorat) stop on Wattana Road, on the southeast side of town, to the right and north of the train station. Buses to and from Ban Chiang and Sakhon Nakhon stop on Phosi Road, south of town, to the left and south of the train station (☎ 042/222-916). Buses to and from Nong Khai stop at the corner of Rop Muang Road and Udon Dutsadee Road in the north of town (☎ 042/222-916). Buses to and from Loei, Phitsanulok, and Chiang Mai stop on the Phosi Road and north of town (☎ 042/247-788).

By Car   The most direct route from either Bangkok or Nong Khai is on Route 2 (Friendship Highway).

CITY LAYOUT   The airport, train station, and bus depot are all located on the southeast end of town as are many tourist services. The main north-south artery is Phosi Road (often spelled Phosri), which is the largest commercial strip in Udon. The hospital is located on the northeast side of town along Nong Phra Jak, an inland water park. The city is compact enough and not yet so developed that you can still get around by *samlor* (pedicabs), that are humorously called "skylabs."

FAST FACTS   A small **TAT** office, 16/5 Kukkhamontri Rd. (☎ 042/325-406), can be found in the government complex across from the lake, about 100m off Phosi Road. The **Udon Thani Hospital** (☎ 042/248-586) is on Pho Niyom Road; the emergency number for the **police** is ☎ 042/222-285. Most national **banks** have branch offices on Phosi Road. The post office is on Wattana Road, near the lake. There's **Internet** service on Prachak Road just across from the shopping mall, and two other Internet cafes on Srisuk Road across from the high school on the way toward Loei.

WHAT TO SEE & DO

The city of Udon offers little to see for most travelers, as the main attractions, such as **Ban Chiang** or **Wat Phra Buddha Baht Bua Bok,** are located more than 50km (32 miles) out of town (for details on both, see "Side Trips from Udon Thani," below in this section). Mak Khaeng Road has the highest concentration of gift shops for local crafts, modern pottery in the style of Ban Chiang (see below), and silk made in nearby villages. Try **Porntip,** 331 Mak Khaeng (☎ 042/223-407), **Mae Oun,** 11/12 Sang Luang Rd. (☎ 042/246-305), and **Pra Thammakhan,** 183 Mak Khaeng (☎ 042/221-154).

WHERE TO STAY & DINE

If you crave a good American meal, and the company of expatriates, try **T-J's,** run by an American who stayed on after the war, which turns out hamburgers and fries, among other specialties; it's located near the lake, on Nongsamrong Road, near the old U.S. Consulate.

More interesting options are across Prachak Road from the Charoensri Grand Royal Hotel—local places with al fresco dining and good local food. The signboards are in Thai, but the places are hard to miss with party lights and plenty of diners. Also along this strip are a couple of beer gardens with live music—a nice entertainment option.

Charoen Hotel. 549 Phosi Rd., Udon Thani, 41000. ☎ **042/248-155.** Fax 042/241-093. 250 units. A/C TEL. 500B–800B ($13.15–$21.05) double. AE, DC, MC, V. Near the train station.

This was the best hotel in town before Charoensri was built a few years ago. The rooms, quiet, clean, and large, are equipped to varying degrees. Standard rooms have no TV or minibar, while deluxe accommodations have TVs but no minibar; junior suites have both. There's a pool in the front yard, immediately adjacent to the new 100-room addition that's completely equipped and very modern. There's also the adequate Poovieng Restaurant for inexpensive buffet meals.

✪ **Charoensri Grand Royal Hotel.** 277/1 Prachak Rd., Udon Thani, 41000. ☎ **042/343-555.** Fax 042/343-550. 255 units. A/C MINIBAR TV TEL. 1,900B ($50) double; from 2,900B ($76.30) suite. AE, DC, MC, V. West of the railway station, you can't miss the mall just next door.

I am constantly impressed with the quality of hotels that have been opening in Isan these past few years. This one was especially impressive. Quiet and quite plush rooms are outfitted in handsome colors and deep wood furnishings—a first-class city hotel. Elegant marble bathrooms and nice amenities are also a swell touch. With discounts as low as 900B ($23.70) including American breakfast, you'd be nuts to pass it up. They have a small pool and health club, but the best facility is the Krau Tung Srimuang restaurant. Fantastic service and excellent Thai, Chinese, and European food, in a white linen and candlelight setting make it the top restaurant in town.

Udon Hotel. 81-89 Makkang Rd., Udon Thani. ☎ **042/248-160.** Fax 042/242-782. 190 units. A/C MINIBAR TV TEL. 500B–1,000B ($13.15–$26.30) double. MC, V. Near the intersection with Prajak Rd., in the central area.

The Udon is not as modern as the Charoen (see above), but it's friendly and the facilities are similar. It has a new wing. Aside from the slightly worn rooms, the more downtown location makes it a noisier establishment. If you take one of the older rooms, avoid those facing the street.

EXPLORING THE AREA

BAN CHIANG NATIONAL MUSEUM The tiny hamlet of Ban Chiang, a prehistoric village that's more than 5,000 years old, is located approximately 50km (31 miles) east of Udon, on the Sakon Nakhon highway. It's based upon the findings here that Thailand, and all of Southeast Asia, stakes its claim to historic and technological parity with its larger and more influential neighbors, China and India.

In the years 1974–75 the governmental Fine Arts Department, in conjunction with the University of Pennsylvania, led a major excavation of sites within the village. This in turn led to the discovery of ceramic vessels, metal implements and tools, woven fabric, and human skeletons that date from 3,600 B.C. More recent dating of the metal objects has revised their date of manufacture forward to about 2,000 B.C., but this still places a technologically advanced civilization in northeast Thailand earlier than in any other area of eastern Asia.

Although little is known about the people who inhabited the village, it's thought that they descended from the so-called Hoabinhians, Stone Age people who lived in Southeast Asia from 12,000 to 5,000 B.C. Excavation indicates three separate periods of development. The Early Period lasted for approximately 2,600 years, while the so-called Middle Period began in 1,000 B.C. and continued to 300 B.C. The Late Period extended through A.D. 200, after which Ban Chiang is thought to have been deserted.

Objects from these periods of development are on display at two separate museums in the town—they are across from one another on a common ground. The smaller, older museum (on your right as you enter) was founded in 1976 as a housing for the excavations conducted during the previous 2 years. The far more impressive collection is displayed in the new wing (to your left as you enter) opened in 1986 and built by the Kennedy Foundation.

The museum is open Wednesday to Sunday 8:30am to 5pm, closed all national holidays; admission is 30B (80¢). To get there, take a Ban Chiang—bound minivan (10B to 15B/25¢ to 40¢) from Muang Tong Market in Udon along Route 22, which will let you off on the main road, some 6km (4 miles) south of the site. From there you can take a motorcycle taxi or samlor to the museum for about 20B (55¢). *Note:* Both the bus and the minivan will often stop in the town, but ask before assuming, otherwise you may overshoot the town. If you plan on continuing your tour to Sakon Nakhon or Nakhon Phanom, remember to bring your luggage, as there's no need to return to Udon; you can flag down the eastbound bus on the main road.

BAN CHIANG EXCAVATION SITE   One of the archaeological pits in Ban Chiang is open to the public—and you should go if you've come this far—although, there's nothing truly special to see. It's within the grounds of Wat Pho Si Nai, only a 5-minute walk from the museum. It is open every day from dawn to dusk, and admission is free with museum ticket.

BAN KHAMOH & BAN PHU   If you admire the earthenware in the Ban Chiang Museum, you'll likely appreciate the ceramics produced by Mr. Suewai Janjaroon, his wife, Rien, and their fellow villagers in Ban Khamoh, located along the main road near Ban Chiang. Seven families reproduce Ban Chiang–era pottery for the Thai and tourist market. These pots have been known to be sold as "antiquities," yet the villagers consider their work a revival of an ancient craft instead of fashioning fakes. These pots do make fine souvenirs. (There has been a major problem with looting in the area, as residents were offered enormous amounts of money by dealers to "excavate" their fields and beyond for antiques that found their way to Japan, Europe, and America.)

Although the villagers in Ban Khamoh produce pottery, the vessels are painted in Ban Phu, where local craftspeople decorate the pots in swirling geometric forms. These are then taken directly to the souvenir stands opposite the Ban Chiang Museum or sold to distributors in other parts of Thailand.

The larger, 3-foot-high decorated ceramics cost about 800B ($21.05), while the smaller souvenir-size pieces start at 75B ($1.95). Mr. Suewai can arrange shipping through a freight company in Chiang Mai, but we caution you that these are extremely fragile and may not make it to you in one piece. (But then, they might look even more authentic broken.)

Ban Phu is the village that you pass through traveling from the main road to Ban Chiang, while Ban Khamoh is but 3km (2 miles) west of Ban Phu. There are no shops in these villages; you'll have to ask for Khun Suewai. He's usually found along the road, working on his pots.

WAT PHRA BUDDHA BAHT BUA BOK   Fifty km (31 miles) northwest of Udon is a 1,200-acre park containing a shrine dedicated to the Holy Footprint and Relic of the Buddha that's under development as a historical park by the Thai Fine Arts Department. These are contained within a 12-foot-high pagoda that's the subject of a festival in March when worshippers pay homage to Buddha. Prehistoric wall paintings—particularly those on Tham Wua and Tham Khon rocks—have also been found within the confines of the park. It's interesting that this area, as indicated by the later Buddhist presence, was also revered during the Dvaravati and Lopburi periods, and the painted geometric forms seen on the rocks may also contain some religious references.

The wat is built at the base of Khao Phu Phan, near Ban Phu, and can be reached either from Udon, Si Chiang Mai, or Nong Khai by bus.

5 Loei & the Mae Khong Valley

520km (322 miles) NE of Bangkok; 344km (213 miles) N of Khorat; 206km (128 miles) NW of Khon Kaen; 202km (125 miles) W of Nong Khai; 269km (167 miles) NE of Phitsanulok

As you enter Loei, you're likely to come across a billboard that reads, "WELCOME TO LOEI, THE COLDEST PLACE IN ALL SIAM." This is a town with a sense of humor, which is a good thing since little happens here, except for the annual Cotton Blossom Festival the first week in February, when it gets really crowded.

Not only is the place nice for its small scale and friendly folks—don't expect anyone to speak more than a few words of English—but it's a wonderful jumping-off point for two national parks, **Phu Kradung** and **Phu Luang,** as well as a gateway to the Mae Khong district, beginning at Chiang Khan and leading to Nong Khai. By the way, that coldest place in all Siam business is no joke; take a sweater or jacket—at least in the cool season.

ESSENTIALS

GETTING THERE   By Bus   Six air-conditioned buses a day leave for Loei from Bangkok's Northern Bus Terminal (trip time: 9 hours, 279B ($7.35) air-conditioned; 340B/$8.95 VIP). Buses leave every hour from Chiang Khang (18B/45¢).

By Car   The most direct route from Khon Kaen is west on Route 12 and north on Route 201. From Udon, travel west on Route 210 and north on Route 201. From Nong Khai, travel west along the Mae Khong on Route 212.

FAST FACTS   There's no TAT presence in Loei, but in a pinch you can try the **Tourist Information Center** at City Hall, located across the highway from the main part of town along Hiasoke Road. Not much English is spoken here, but they're happy to dig up a City Hall worker who can speak with you to answer any questions you may have. They also have a fabulous three-dimensional display of the national parks territories around Loei—a good thing to see before you head out. The **Loei Hospital** (☎ 042/811-806) is on Loei-Chiang Khan Road; the emergency number for the **police** is ☎ 042/811-254. Most national **banks** have branch offices in town with normal operating hours; if you intend to travel north to Chiang Khan, change money in Loei as there are no other banks in the area.

WHAT TO SEE & DO

Only a few streets hold anything for travelers. The most important is Charoenrat Road, where you'll find, among other things, a bank, the Night Market, hotels and restaurants, and shops open at night. Perpendicular to it is Haisoke Road, another commercially significant thoroughfare. Most of the official Loei is located across the Loei-Chiang Khan highway, where you'll find the Tourist Information Center.

WHERE TO STAY & DINE

As usual, the **Night Market,** just off Charoenrat Road, is the cheapest dining in town; the food stalls are set up at about 6pm and close around 11pm—a stroll through the market is a delicious feast of savory smells.

King's Hotel. 1241 Haisoke Rd., Loei 42000. ☎ **042/811-701.** 46 units. TEL. 450B ($11.85) double with A/C; 400B ($10.55) double with fan. MC, V. Southeast side of town, across the street from the Green Laserdisc Club.

The King's is the best hotel in Loei, but not by much. Accommodations are very basic with Spartanly furnished rooms and reasonably clean bathrooms; 30 rooms have air-conditioning. There's a small lobby with an attached coffee shop, but there's little else in the way of services and facilities. The staff is friendly, though very little English is spoken.

Phu Luang Hotel. 55 Charoenrat Rd., Loei 42000. ☎ **042/811-532.** Fax 042/811-532. 86 units. TEL. 400B ($10.55) double with A/C. No credit cards. East side of town near the river.

A close second to the King's (see above), but just a tad less well run and less clean; nevertheless, it's an acceptable alternative. Forty guest rooms have air-conditioning.

Savita Bakery. 137 Charoenrat Rd. ☎ **042/811-526.** Main courses 60B–240B ($1.60–$6.30). Daily 6am–10:30pm. In the central area. WESTERN/THAI.

This is the only place for late-night snacks or early breakfast. At night, the cheery staff doles out Foremost ice cream by the bucket, and you can get a complete breakfast with eggs, sausage, toast, and jam for 40B ($1.05). They also have a complete and varied lunch and dinner menu, mostly Thai dishes.

SIDE TRIPS FROM LOEI

PHU KRADUNG NATIONAL PARK   Phu Kradung may be Thailand's most dramatic, mountainous national park. To say mountainous is both descriptive and misleading. The whole park consists of a giant mountain (in girth not height; the summit is just under 4,000 feet) with a wide, heart-shaped plateau at the "peak." On the high table summit, some 9km (5½ miles) from the Sithan trailhead and information station, there are 50km (31 miles) of hiking trails to explore, a tent village with basic facilities, waterfalls, breathtaking sheer cliffs, and numerous panoramic spots from which to gaze out over the nearby Phetchabun Mountains—you'll understand why Loei is referred to as the Province of a Sea of Mountains.

The name Phu Kradung means Bell Mountain, which connects with the Buddhist legend that the mountain once rang like a bell on a Sabbath day. Of course, the fact that it's bell-shaped might have played some part. The park is popular with both Thai and foreign travelers, especially from October to January, and even more so on weekends. Park rangers suggest visiting during weekdays and, if possible, in May and June—just at the beginning of the rainy season, when it's not too wet.

The park has a wide variety of animals—though I won't promise that you'll see anything exotic—and some glorious wildflower fields (best seen from February through May). Phu Kradung is one place in Thailand that actually has a fall season, though it arrives in December. Whole stands of deciduous trees, including maple, oak, and beech, turn golden. The park closes during the rainy season, July through October.

The main place to stay is up top, at Phu Kradung House, at the park headquarters. Down below, at Sithon, you can arrange for a porter to carry your bags. You'll also find restaurants, an information office, and a few bungalows. Up top accommodations are in tents, and there's a simple Thai restaurant serving hot food, which is especially nice when the temperature drops. Questions should be directed to the Bangkok office of the **National Park Division,** Forestry Department, 61 Paholyothin Rd. ☎ 02/ 579-5734). If you arrive in Loei and need additional assistance, contact the people at the tourist information center at City Hall.

Phu Kradang National Park is located 82km (51 miles) south of Loei. To reach it, take Route 201 south and travel 8km (5 miles) west along Route 2019. Buses heading for Khon Kaen depart approximately every 30 minutes from Loei for 25B (65¢); some minivans or buses go directly to the park while others stop along the main road, where you'll have to flag a ride into the park.

PHU LUANG WILDLIFE RESERVE   Access to Phu Luang Wildlife Reserve is controlled by the Forestry Department to protect the many species of wildlife that live atop this wide plateau. The summit of Phu Luang is only about 500 feet higher than Phu Kradung, yet the ecology is more varied. In the reserve tropical flora gives way to deciduous and coniferous zones, which in turn host a wider array of fauna. Elephants and tigers are reputed to be within the bounds of the reserve, but it's unlikely that you'll see them as they shy away from humans.

Questions should be directed to the Bangkok office of the **National Park Division,** Forestry Department, 61 Paholyothin Road (☎ 02/579-5734). If you arrive in Loei and need additional assistance, contact the people at the Tourist Information Center at City Hall.

EN ROUTE TO NONG KHAI
ALONG THE MAE KHONG FROM CHIANG KAN THROUGH SI CHIANG MAI

This has to be one of the most scenic areas in Thailand. Almost totally unexploited and delightfully secluded, the northern perimeter of Isan runs along the famed Mae Khong River, which forms the border with Laos. This is probably the best cycling route in Thailand. The terrain is relatively flat, the road is lightly trafficked and in a good state of repair, and there are a number of villages where you can stop. A few guest houses in the area rent bicycles, though they are of the three-speed variety, and in general, are haphazardly maintained.

If you take the bus or songtao north from Loei (trip time: 45 minutes; 18B/45¢) you'll reach the riverside town of **Chiang Kan,** opposite Sarakham, Laos. If you decide to travel here directly from Bangkok, there's twice daily overnight air-conditioned bus service to Chiang Kan (trip time: 10 hours; 261B/$6.85 air-conditioned; 405B/10.65 VIP). Here you'll find a guest house or two, a wat worth visiting, a couple of fun excursions, and many expatriates who've discovered that life is fine in a simple Thai border town. The most highly recommended activity is cruising west (upriver) on the Mae Khong. The trip, motoring in long-tail boats, traverses some of the most sublime scenery in all of Isan. **Boat trips** can be booked by the owner of your guest house with a typical price of 400B ($10.55) for 1 hour or 500B ($13.15) for two. There is regular boat service between Chiang Kan and Pak Chom, another riverside town (1,200B/$31.60 per person); I heartily recommend the ride, as it follows some of the most interesting scenery in Isan.

Wat Sri Khun Muang, next to the town market, is constructed in the northern style and features walls of glassy materials. Notice the guardian demons and lions in the main chapel area and the primitively painted murals of the life of the Buddha.

In-town accommodations at the **Friendship Hotel,** 300 ChaiKong Rd. (☎ and fax **042/821-547; 200B/$5.25** double) are homey with personalized service from Swedish owner Jan and his wife, Luck. They can rent bicycles (50B/$1.30), motorbikes (200B/$5.25), or a car (800B to 1,000B/$21.05 to

Swimmer's Alert

If on your Mae Khong trip or at any point during your travels you take a swim in the river, be aware that each year many Thai residents drown due to the treacherous currents. Stay close to the shore and make sure that you swim with someone else, or request that somebody keeps an eye out.

$26.30), arrange all river trips, and provide maps and directions for all the interesting sights in and around the town. They also have the only Internet service in the town.

Five kilometers (3 miles) east of Chiang Khan is **Kaeng Khut Khu,** a particularly scenic Mae Khong overlook reminiscent of a Mississippi River stop—lazy, wide, and muddy. There are a few dozen food stalls lining the shore, which offer a fine vista and a good lunch; try the *som tam* or *pla yang.* There's songtao service for 10B (25¢) and tuk-tuk service for 50B ($1.30), but I suggest taking a 25-minute bike ride. For the height of luxury you can cruise downriver to Kaeng Khut Khu for about 150B ($3.95) per person. If you want to spend the night near the rapids, there's the **Seeview Hut** (no phone) which has four bungalows that rent for 300B ($7.90). (Remember to change money in Loei or Si Chiang Mai as there are no banks in Chiang Kan.)

Highway 2186 continues along the Mae Khong passing through Pak Chom and Si Chiang Mai before arriving in Nong Khai. Lush banana plantations, terraced fruit farms, manganese mines, and cotton and tomato fields reach deeply into the verdant flood plains of the Mae Khong basin. Farther inland are lovely waterfalls such as **Nam Tok Than Thip** (between Pak Chom and Si Chiang Mai), which are fun for hiking and ideal for picnics.

Si Chiang Mai is opposite Vientiane, the capital of the Lao People's Democratic Republic, and is but 58km (36 miles) due west of Nong Khai. The town is one of those perfect Thai backwaters that offers lots of nice day trips on bicycle to see and do, yet is nearly idyllic. A trip to the bakery, watching Lao and Thai long-tail boats silently ply the Mae Khong, or taking a walk to a spring-roll factory are among the major in-town excitements. Or you can rent bicycles (30B/80¢ per day) or motorcycles (150B to 200B/$3.95 to $5.25 per day) to see the scenery, nearby wats and waterfalls, plus the lovely rock formations at Ban Phu (see below). Boat trips around the river area run for 500B ($13.15) per boat (less if you have more than three people). There's even booking for service connecting Si Chiang Mai to Nong Khai (at the Thai-Lao crossing) for 800B ($21.05) per boat. You can have lunch overlooking the river and Vientiane, which is possibly the most surrealistically serene capital city you'll ever see. Try the candied tomatoes sold outside of the restaurants; they're scrumptious. During the dry season you can sunbathe on the beach or on one of the nearby islands—but remember my warning about the currents.

If a stay in Si Chiang Mai sounds appealing, try **Tim Guest House** (☎ and fax **042/451-072;** www.nk.ksc.co.th/timgh/; e-mail: timgh@ksc.th.com), on the quay about 200 yards from the bus stop on the main road, where singles and doubles run 70B to 110B ($1.85 to $2.90). Manager/owners Daniel and Noy pioneered this guest house in this town, and know all about the attractions of the surrounding areas plus local transportation between towns. The restaurants about 200 yards east of Tim's are okay and inexpensive.

Outside of Si Chiang Mai is another Isan town called **Ban Phu** (not to be confused with the Ban Phu near Ban Chiang), where there are stone pinnacles similar to those in the Stone Forest in China's Yunnan Province. This is a worthwhile excursion, but accomplished more easily by car than bus (a mototrbike from Si Chiang Mai is a good option). If you do bus it, take the coach directly to Ban Phu town via Thabo followed by the Nam Som–bound bus, getting off at Ban Tiew. After that you'll have to take a 4-km (2½-mile) tuk-tuk ride to the park. Nearby is the restored 17th-century temple complex known as **Phrat That Bang Phuan,** thought to have been originally constructed around the same time as Phra That Phanom, between A.D. 500 and 1000. As with many shrines in Thailand, it's said to entomb relics of the Buddha, specifically his pelvis (according to Urangkhathat legend). The lotus-bud-shaped central building is Lanna (northern Thai) architecture; the other buildings are influenced by Laotian styles.

Public transportation from Chiang Kan to Nong Khai via Si Chiang Mai is somewhat involved. Take a green bus (trip time: 45 minutes; 50B/$1.30) from Chiang Kan to Pak Chom and change to another green bus to So Chiang Mai and on to Nong Khai (trip time: 3 hours and 1.5 hours; 40B/$1.05 and 18B/45¢ respectively). Some of the guest houses in the area have tried bike-swapping ventures with guest houses in other towns, so you could hire a bike in one town and drop it at another to move on from there, but as of yet nobody had forged a truly reliable agreement. Still, ask around at guest houses if you're interested—maybe something's set up already.

Torsak and Katie Murray Tiparos, a Thai-American family in Chiang Khan, operate one of the most unique bike tour companies I've seen in Thailand. Experts in bike touring as well as the local culture in this region, they plan fantastic **bike trips** that include homestays with local families, opportunities to participate in daily activities such as rice farming and weaving, plus in-depth glimpses of Thai festivals and Buddhist traditions. Torsak and Katie like small groups (between 4 to 10 people) and welcome riders of all ages and abilities (actual cycling is only 30 miles per day). Their 10-day and 9-night "Mae Khong Journey" costs $1,615 per person, plus $178 for (top quality) mountian bike and $150 room supplement. The 5-day and 4-night "Extension to the North" follows the river to more northern parts of the kingdom and costs $925 per person, plus $89 for bike rental and $75 for room supplement. They're glad to take smaller groups and plan personalized itineraries. Contact them at **One World Bike Expeditions,** 356 Chaikong Road, Chiang Khan, Loei 42110 ☎/fax **042/821-825,** or e-mail them at info@bike thailand.com; Web site www.bikeland.com.

6 Nong Khai

615km (381 miles) NE of Bangkok; 51km (32 miles) N of Udon Thani; 356km (221 miles) N of Khorat; 202km (125 miles) E of Loei; 303km (188 miles) W of Nakhon Phanom

With the completion of the Friendship Bridge spanning the Mae Khong to Tha Dua, Laos, increased international commerce and travel is bringing many changes to Nong Khai. There are new first-class hotels and several others in the planning. Travel restrictions to Laos have eased considerably now that country's government has finally accepted the economic advantages of tourism.

Nong Khai remains well worth a visit, retaining much of its small town charm—though I can't promise how much longer that will continue to be the case—with the added excitement of a booming border town. It occupies a strip not much more than 3 blocks deep, running about 4km along the banks of the river. You can still easily walk anywhere in its downtown area centered on its main pier, Tha Sadet, though it's a 25B (66¢) tuk-tuk ride to the railway station and another 20B (55¢) to the bridge. Even if you're not crossing to Laos, you can get a good view of it, get in some shopping, and make connections to the scenic Mae Khong basin and even the archaeological site at Ban Chiang.

ESSENTIALS

GETTING THERE   By Plane   The nearest airport is in Udon Thani, but from there you can hire a transfer from the airport to Nong Khai for 100B ($2.65). For information on flights to Udon Thani, see "Getting There" in that section.

By Train   Nong Khai is connected by rail to Bangkok via Khorat. Three trains a day depart from Bangkok (trip time: 11 hours on rapid train; second-class air-conditioned 278B/$7.30).

By Bus   Six daily air-conditioned buses leave from Bangkok's Northern Bus Terminal to Nong Khai (trip time: 11 hours; 263B/$6.90 air-conditioned; 405B/$10.65 VIP). Seven air-conditioned buses leave daily from Nakhon Ratchasima (Khorat) Bus Terminal II to Nong Khai (trip time: 5 hours; 157B/$4.15)—most leave late at night, so check the schedule beforehand. Many buses travel to Nong Khai daily from Udon Thani (trip time: 45 minutes; 17B/45¢). From Loei to Pak Chom, switch to a Nong Khai bound green bus (total trip time: 6 hours; about 60B/$1.60)

By Car   The most direct route from either Bangkok or Udon Thani Khai is on Route 2 (Friendship Highway). Take Route 211 west to travel along the Mae Khong to Loei, via Si Chiang Mai, Pak Chom, and Chiang Khan.

VISITOR INFORMATION   Although there is no TAT office or municipal information booth, the bulletin boards and maps at both the **Mut-mee Guest House,** 1111/4 Kaeworawut Rd., and **Sawasdee Guest House,** 402 Meechai Rd., offer all of the help you might need.

The only map of the town is available at the restaurant/bar **Meeting Place,** 1117 Soi Chuenchitt (☎ **042/421-223,** fax 042/460-975); sometimes known locally as Soi Si Chomchuen. It's managed by Australian Alan Patterson, who also offers guest rooms and motorcycles for rent, the latest information, and visa service. At the time of writing, the Meeting Place claimed to process visa requests to Lao in under an hour. The visa itself costs 1,200B ($31.60), but Mr. Patterson charges only an additional 300B ($7.90) for the service. The visa is valid for 15 days travel, with exit from any official port in Laos. He also has current information on travel in the country. See his Web site at www.mekongriviera.com or e-mail him at flxs@udin.ksc.co.th

ORIENTATION   Nearly all tourist facilities and sites are located on three parallel streets running along the Mae Khong. The closest to the river is **Rimkhong Road,** and it's where you'll find the Immigration Office, where those who need to can get an extension on their Thai tourist visa. **Meechai Road** is a commercial thoroughfare along which is the post office, the hospital, and Bangkok Bank, at 374 Si Saket Rd., open Monday to Friday 8am to 8pm. The farthest of the three main roads is **Prajak Road,** on which you'll find Thai Airways, the air-conditioned and VIP bus terminals, and Pochai Market, near the regular bus station on the east side. The train station is on the western edge of town.

No distance—with the exception of the train station—within town is beyond a long walk, or if you have luggage, a 10B (25¢) *samlor* (bicycle trishaw) or tuk-tuk ride.

SPECIAL EVENTS   A **Rocket Festival,** on a lesser scale than that held in Yasothon in May, begins on the full moon in June. Its purpose is to appeal to the heavens as a reminder to bring plentiful rain in the upcoming season. The event takes place at Wat Pho Chai, the home of Nong Khai's most revered Buddha.

WHAT TO SEE & DO

There's an interesting hybrid architectural style in Nong Khai. On the east side of town, along Meechai Road, are several mansions built in the early 20th century in what might best be described as French-Chinese colonial style.

A couple of in-town wats are worth exploring, but the most unusual structure is located about 4 to 5km (3 miles) east of town at **Wat Khaek** on Route 212 (the Nakhon Phanom Rd.). Here you'll find recently cast concrete Buddhas, Hindu deities, and other fantastic figures of enormous proportions in an attractive garden setting. This imaginative theme park was constructed under the direction of a colorful Thai religious leader, Luang Phu Boonlua Surirat, who studied with an Indian guru in Vietnam and taught in Laos until the communists kicked him out. (More recently Luang Phu was imprisoned for insulting King Bhumibol—a charge some say was trumped up by jealous neighbors.)

WHERE TO STAY

Mekong Royal Nong Khai. 222 Jommanee Beach, Nong Khai 43000. ☎ **042/420-024.** Fax 042/421-280. 208 units. A/C TV TEL. 1,000B ($26.30) double; from 1,500B ($39.45) suite. AE, DC, MC, V. West of bridge, about a mile west of town.

This handsome new high-rise, with a swimming pool and half a dozen restaurants, is all you'd expect from the Holiday Inn chain and more. However, we recommend it only for those touring by private car.

Mut-Mee Guest House. 1111/4 Kaeworawut Rd., Nong Khai. No phone. 14 units. 150B ($3.95) double with fan. No credit cards. Half a block from the waterfront next to Wat Haisok.

Near the waterfront, this guest house is favored by some travelers for its garden that overlooks the Mae Khong and beyond (to Laos), as well as for its proximity to Nong Khai's vibrant market. The rooms are more basic and higher priced than those at the Sawasdee (see below), but the staff is well-informed and helpful. The Mut-Mee rents bicycles; expect to pay 40B ($1.05) per day.

Nong Khai Grand Thani Hotel. 589 Moo 5, Nong Khai-Poanpisai Rd., Nong Khai 43000. ☎ **042/420-033.** Fax 042/412-026. 126 units. A/C MINIBAR TV TEL. 900B ($23.70) double; from 1,500B ($39.45) suite. AE, DC, MC, V. Just south of town on highway.

A good choice for convenient location plus quality facilities, I was immensely pleased with this lovely new hotel, far enough off the main highway to be quiet, yet close enough to town for an easy walk. Facilities include a swimming pool, lobby lounge/music room, restaurant, cafe, rooftop grill, business center, meeting rooms, discotheque, massage parlor, snooker club, and jogging track.

Sawasdee Guest House. 402 Meechai Rd., Nong Khai, 43000. ☎ **042/412-502.** Fax 042/420-259. 16 units. 200B–280B ($5.25–$7.35) with A/C; 120B ($3.15) with fan. No credit cards. 1 block from the waterfront on the east side.

The oversized doors to this unassuming guest house lead to a spacious lobby with an eclectic selection of furniture. Wagon-wheel Western and traditional Thai decor, with a curio cabinet, make for an odd and satisfying mix. Off the lobby is an open courtyard where guests congregate after a long day of touring. The rooms (six have air-conditioning) are clean and of guest house standard. This the best value for accommodations in Nong Khai. There are bicycles for rent at nominal prices.

WHERE TO DINE

If you're hungry late at night, **Khun Dang Thai Food** at 406 Rimkhong Rd. (☎ **042/411-709**) is open 24 hours. It's just a small cafe overlooking the river with simple Thai dishes (between 30B and 150B/80¢ and $3.95), it's a favorite for backpackers. During the day the covered terrace is shaded by bamboo trees.

Bird's Eye Restaurant. In the Nong Khai Grand Hotel 589 Moo 5, Nong Khai-Poanpisai Rd. ☎ **042/420-033.** Entrees 60B–250B ($1.60–$6.60). AE, DC, MC, V. Just south of town on highway. THAI/INTERNATIONAL.

A fine selection of local river fish prepared in a range of styles draws diners to this restaurant. Not to mention the place has the best view. Arrive before sunset to see across the river for a panoramic view of Laos. Try their local specialties, including papaya salad. Later in the evening a live band plays Western music and soft pop.

Udomros Restaurant. 423 Rimkhong Rd. ☎ **042/421-084.** Main courses 40B–200B ($1.05–$5.25). No credit cards. Daily 11am–10pm. Next to the Immigration Office, overlooking the Mae Khong. THAI.

This riverside eatery is popular with both locals and travelers alike and serves very simple but tasty Thai cuisine. The delicious chicken with basil dish and a bubbling hot pot with meat and vegetables are specialties.

SHOPPING

This is a major activity in Nong Khai and shouldn't be ignored, although prices have been getting a little higher with increasing tourist traffic. The nexus of activity is the waterfront market on Rimkhong Road, just east of the Immigration Office. Many crafts are on display, including Laotian silver work, but if you're heading out to Nakhon Phanom and Ubon you'll find better goods at better prices. If not, Nong Khai is still fine.

Village Weaver Handicrafts (☎ **042/411-236**), at 786/1 Prajak Rd. (factory and showroom) and 1151 Soi Jittapunya Rd. (showroom only), began as a self-help project in 1982 and has flourished as a cooperative enterprise. The goal of the project is to provide a means by which local weavers can practice their art and remain in their home village while making a living. Weaving masters oversee the work to maintain quality and to introduce advanced techniques. The two shops—the Prajak Road location doubles as a factory and demonstration center—offer a wide selection of fabric, ready-to-wear clothing, and a variety of pillow covers, eyeglass cases, and other household items. Prices are fair. Many products from this shop are featured in the Oxfam gift catalog.

Similar goods, though perhaps not quite as well tailored, are produced at the shop known as **House of E-San,** located south of Nong Khai in Ban Nong Song Hong on the Udon highway. The shop is only a part of a complex that includes a series of small buildings where fabric is spun, dyed, woven, and cut, all on display for the interested shopper. They have a small but nice collection of older weavings, but you'll find a large assortment of material and clothing for sale here at prices that are similar to those at Village Weaver Handicrafts. **Nisa Chon,** the gregarious proprietor of the establishment, has a modest **guest house** on the premises (☎ **042/410-137**). To get there, take a public bus to the checkpoint, approximately 12km (7½ miles) south of Nong Khai. The shop is located about 100 yards south of the guard station.

SIDE TRIPS FROM NONG KHAI

Aside from visiting Laos, the two most frequently requested excursions are to **Ban Phu** (with a side trip to Phra That Bang Phuan) and Ban Chiang. The former is a visit to a park with unique rock structures (see "En Route to Nong Khai," above in this chapter). The significant archaeological finds at **Ban Chiang** (see "Exploring the Area," above in this chapter) can be explored from Nong Khai instead of the usual base in Udon Thani. Most travel agents in Nong Khai book a 1-day excursion including transport, food, guide, and admission fees for 500B ($13.15) per person. Contact your hotel or an agency to make reservations.

Many people who come to Nong Khai contemplate a visit to **Laos.** It's tantalizingly close, but you'll have to plan in advance to get there. You'll need a tourist visa, which you'll need to acquire either in your home country, or in Lao consulates in Bangkok or Khon Kaen. In Bangkok the **Lao Embassy** is at 193 South Sathorn Rd. (☎ 02/ 539-667) and in Khon Kaen at 19/123 Nonthan village, Phoathisan Road (043/ 223-698). The price for a 15-day tourist visa is 1,200B ($31.60), and the visa will only allow you to exit Laos from the port at which you entered, although you will be allowed to travel freely within the country itself. These days, thanks to relaxed regulations, you can also apply for a visa on the spot at the border crossing over the bridge. A few people have reported minor hassles with the bureaucracy here—more bother than real trouble—so if you want to play it safe, it's better to arrange beforehand. The price of the visa is still the same either way.

Another option if you haven't acquired your visa beforehand is to visit Alan Patterson at the Meeting Place (see "Visitor Information," above). He can help you process your paperwork and grease the wheels for you before you head for the checkpoint. He says his arrangement will allow you to exit Lao from any port.

To get to the border checkpoint from Thailand, the best way is to hire a tuk-tuk in Nong Khai to take you to the bridge. From there, you'll have to take a special minivan ride over the bridge to the checkpoint (10B/25¢). After you've cleared immigration, a 150B ($3.95) taxi ride should get you where you need to go in Vientiane. While there are public buses available for cheaper, they're not very dependable and can be quite frustrating.

Once in Vientiane, you can get travel information for the capital and the country from the **Tourist Information Center** (☎ 856-21/212-248).

7 Nakhon Phanom

740km (459 miles) NE of Bangkok; 252km (156 miles) E of Udon Thani; 481km (298 miles) NE of Khorat; 271km (168 miles) N of Ubon Ratchathani; 303km (188 miles) E of Nong Khai; 93km (58 miles) E of Sakon Nakhon

It's a rare traveler who makes it out to these parts of the kingdom—if you find yourself dispirited by the tourist industry in other parts of Thailand, this place could be the cure for you. In Thai, Nakhon means "religious," and it's this spiritual connection that attracts many travelers to Nakhon Phanom: They come to visit **Phra That Phanom,** the Northeast's most sacred Buddhist site, located about 76km (47 miles) south of the town on Route 212. The town is set along the Mae Khong, bordering Laos; across the way is the smaller Laotian town of Ta Kaek. Although there's a fair amount of traffic between the two towns, Nakhon Phanom is not a primary crossover point for foreign tourists, but you can make the trip with a visa from the Bangkok or Khon Kaen Lao embassies, in Bangkok at 193 South Sathorn Rd. (☎ 02/539-667) and in Khon Kaen at 19/123 Nonthan village, Phoathisan Road (☎ 043/ 223-698)—or talk to the people at North by North-East Travel if you haven't gotten your visa in advance. Their contact information is listed under "Things to See & Do" later in this section.

It's a little-known fact that during the Vietnam War, while American GIs headed to Pattaya for R&R, the Viet Cong came to Nakhon Phanom for downtime. The town was, for about 6 years, home to Ho Chi Minh, who donated the clock tower in the town's center. His old home is about 5km outside of the town proper. To this day, the population is about 30% Vietnamese, although today these people have adopted Thai lifestyles typical to the region.

ESSENTIALS

GETTING THERE   By Plane   Thai Airways has one flight daily from Bangkok to Nakhon Phanom (flying time: 65 minutes). The airport is located 15km from town (☎ 042/513-264). You'll have to arrange ground transportation form **Bowon Travel**

at 13 Ruamjit Thawaey Rd. (☎ 042/512-940) for about 40B ($1.05) per person. Bowon Travel is the official Thai Airways representative in Nakhon Phanom, so you can contact them for ticket booking and confirmations. In Bangkok call **Thai Airways** at ☎ **02/232-8000.**

By Bus Six VIP air-conditioned buses a day leave from Bangkok's Northern Bus Terminal to Nakon Phanom (trip time: 13 hours; 421B to 585B/$11.10 to $15.40), passing through Nakhon Ratchasima and sometimes Ubon Ratchathani. Numerous buses leave daily from Udon Thani to Nakon Phanom (trip time: 5 hours; 76B to 100B/$2 to $2.65). You can also ask these buses to drop you at Ban Chiang World Heritage along the way—and pick one up on the highway when you're ready to continue your journey. Many buses travel from Ubon Ratchathani to Nakhom Phanom daily (trip time: 4½ hours; 81B to 146B/$2.15 to $3.85), stopping at Phra Phanom Phamom upon request.

The bus terminal in Nakhon Phanom is at the corner of Highway 22 and Klang Muang Road (☎ **042/511-403**). From here, a short "skylab" (samlor) ride can take you where you need to go for under 30B (80¢).

By Car The most direct route from either Bangkok or Khorat is on Route 2 (Friendship Highway) either north to Udon Thani and east on Route 22 or east on Route 24, north on Route 219 to Buriram, northeast on Route 213, and east on Route 22. The former includes a visit to Phimai and Ban Chiang, while the latter passes through Prasat Hin Phanom Rung and the less-explored central Isan region.

FAST FACTS There's a new **TAT** information office 18 4/1 Sunthon Wichit Rd. (the road that follows the banks of the river) ☎ 042/513-490. The **post office** (☎ 042/512-945) is on Sunthon Whichit Road south of the TAT office. The **Nakhon Phanom Provincial Hospital** (☎ 042/511-422) is on Aphibanbuncha Road, beyond the Overseas Telephone Office (at the corner of Aphibanbuncha and Salaklang rds.). Call the emergency number for the **police,** on Sunthon Wichit Road just next to the post office, at ☎ **042/511-266.** There's also a great **Internet cafe** in the center of town, just opposite the clock tower on Sunthon Wichit Road.

SPECIAL EVENTS Nakhon Phanom hosts two river spectacles to celebrate the end of the Rains Retreat. The first is the renowned **Mae Khong longboat race,** while the second is an illuminated **boat procession,** called "Lai Rua Fai" or the Fire Boat Festival, where barges float downstream, twinkling with small candles in the night. The festival is accompanied by cultural programs, Buddhist rituals, and a craft and food fair. Both celebrations normally take place in October, specifically on the 13th day of the waxing moon during the 11th lunar month. The **Phra That Phanom Festival** takes place in February (see "Side Trips from Nakhon Phanom," below).

WHAT TO SEE & DO

From the main ferry pier across from the Indochina market, take a boat tour of the Mae Khong River for about 500B to 1,000B ($13.15 to $26.30). The trip across to Laos costs 500B ($13.15). The scenery here is different from other parts of the river, so even if you've taken trips up north or further south, you'll see something different every time.

There are also some scenic riverside bike routes, including a nice daylong trip north along the river toward the town of Tha-uthen.

Nakhon Phanom is a good place to buy **silver**—in several shops near the pier—some of it fashioned by the skillful local craftsmen, some by Laotians in nearby refugee settlements, even some machine-made in Bangkok (though in Nakon Phanom, it's considerably cheaper). The town is pleasant enough, though few people speak English. If you're traveling south to Ubon you might consider staying at the Phra That Phanom site, where there are some rudimentary accommodations, and continuing your journey after a morning visit.

For something truly unique, contact **North by North-East Tours,** at the Mekong Grandview Hotel, 527 Sunthon Wichit Rd. (☎ 042/513-572; fax 042/513-573; e-mail: nxne@esan.inet.co.th). They coordinate a fabulous tour of Isan (Nakhon Phanom, Phra That Phanom; see "Side Trips" and "Simply Isan," below), through Ubon Ratchasima and major sights to Khorat, with return to Bangkok. The 6-day trip will run you about 4940B ($130) per day for a private tour (you can basically tailor your trip to suit your schedule and desires) or about 3800B ($100) if you join a pre-planned outing (which happens every 2nd and 4th Monday of each month). The best part of the trip is the visit to Ban Nong Hoi Yai, a small village full of some of the nicest people you've ever met. They'll show you how they process and weave cotton and make baskets, and you'll be entertained with live Isan country music and local dancing. The highlight of your visit will be the official welcoming ceremony, in which all village members participate—it will be one of your favorite memories from your trip here. Talk to North by North-East Tours about specialized itineraries, too, including excellent **trips to Laos and Vietnam.**

WHERE TO STAY

There are several adequate hotels, including the **River Inn** (the oldest guest house in town, and one of the best known) with rates from about 100B to 400B ($2.65 to $10.50).

Nakhon Phanom Hotel. 403 Aphibanbuncha Rd., Nakhon Phanom 48000. ☎ **042/511-455.** Fax 042/511-074. 58 units. A/C TV TEL. 450B ($11.85) double. MC, V. South center of town, near bus station.

The NPH is centrally located, clean, comfortable enough, and air-conditioned, and the friendly manager speaks English. There's a good restaurant, pool, and snooker parlor. Insist on a rear-facing room, as the plaza out front is a popular late-night gathering place for local young people.

Nakhon Phanom River View Hotel. 9 Nakhon Phanom-Thad Phanom Road, Nakhon Phanom 48000. ☎ **042/522-333.** Fax 042/522-780. 122 units. A/C MINIBAR TV TEL. 1,500B–1,800B ($39.47–$47.37) double; from 4,500B ($118.42) suite. MC V. Along Mae Khong River, in the south of town.

The River View is the newest and best accommodation in the town. A modern hotel, with marble lobby, rooms to Western standards of convenience, attentive service, and a great restaurant and lobby cocktail lounge, I recommend this place highly. Nothing beats coming home to comfort after a long day of sightseeing. It's worth the extra money. Make sure you request river views when booking your room.

A SIDE TRIP TO PHRA THAT PHANOM

The origins of this most sacred shrine are somewhat undetermined, though archaeologists have concluded that the first building was put up about 1,500 years ago (the spire is said to date from the 9th century). The legend associated with the temple is that the monk Maha Kasapa brought a breastbone of the Buddha to this location, whereupon five local princes built a stupa to house the relic—just eight years after the Buddha's death. After that, successive rulers built smaller shrines, and most importantly, rebuilt the original structure; it's been restored seven times. The most recent restoration took place in 1977 after the tower had collapsed in 1975. A museum at the

Simply Isan

Traveling in Isan always promises unusual experiences, but I was unprepared for the day I was welcomed in a small farming village. Ban Nong Hoi Yai, about an hour south of Nakhon Phanom, is a lovely village filled with some of the most friendly people I've ever met. I was greeted with smiles by ladies spinning cotton, and got a full demonstration of all the processes to turn the crop into thread. Under another *sala* (pavilion), huge wooden looms clacked as more ladies wove the threads into the fabulous cotton patterns you see in all the local markets (it was a thrill to buy the fabrics from the people who'd actually made them). Further beyond, a group of men wove baskets very carefully, accompanied by other men tweedling and plucking and pounding out local Isan country songs. Some of the cotton spinners came to dance, and we had a little country disco out under the trees. Later, inside one of the houses, some of the local girls had rehearsed a few traditional dances, and everyone in the town gathered to watch and heckle. The girls smiled and joked with all of the onlookers—everyone was just having a ball.

My friend Kaew is from this village, and she and her husband, Nick, have an agency in Nakhon Phanom that will bring travelers out to the village to meet her people and witness their lives. So few people get to these parts that the event is far from being touristy. And the village folks have just as much fun as their visitors do. For them it's a time to meet new people, and to celebrate their lives and traditions.

For the grand finale, the village headman performs a traditional welcoming ceremony. I sat quietly while every villager chanted, calling out to my spirits to return to my body for blessing. Apparently everywhere I've been in my life, I've left a piece of my spirit behind. I figured it would take about 4 months to call all my bits back to me, but they did it in about 5 minutes. They placed an egg and a lump of sticky rice in each hand. As each villager approached me, they tied a piece of string around my wrist and said a special wish for me. Safe travels, good luck, a handsome husband. It was just a wonderful day. If you've wanted to see how the country folk live, this is about the most wonderful way you can experience it. See North by North-East Tours in this section above for more information about setting this day up for yourself.

---

back of the complex displays the multitude of artifacts, pottery, Buddha images, and the like that were found inside the tower after it collapsed.

The shrine is venerated throughout the year by both Thai and Laotian people; however, for 7 days beginning on the full moon during the third lunar month, Phra That Phanom hosts a fair for worshippers. The fair, in honor of the Buddhist Rains Retreat, features food and craft stalls and a variety of cultural programs.

On the way to the shrine, at **Renu Nakhon,** is a crafts center where locals produce a wide range of embroidered material. There's also a diminutive version of the shrine with the appropriate name, Phra That Renu Nakhon.

Public buses travel between Nakom Phanom and the site for 20B (55¢). There are a few guest houses located near the site of Phra That Phanom that, while being merely functional, may be just the thing for those who are heading south to Ubon. Although none are very clean, the **Saeng Thong,** 34 Mu 1, Phanom-Phanarak Road (no phone), where fan-cooled doubles run 140B ($3.70) is an okay choice. Another, possibly cleaner alternative, is the **Lim Charoen,** 167/67 Mu 13, Chayangkun Road (☎ 042/541-019); fan-cooled rooms range from 110B to 175B ($2.90 to $4.60) for singles and doubles, respectively.

8 Ubon Ratchathani

629km (390 miles) NE of Bangkok; 271km (168 miles) S of Nakhon Phanom; 370km (229 miles) E of Khorat; 227km (141 miles) E of Surin

A visit to Ubon Ratchathani is most compelling for its proximity to the prehistoric cave paintings at Pha Taem, Rivers. The city, one of Isan's most developed, is being positioned as Thailand's international gateway to nearby Laos (it's near one of two official crossover points for foreigners), Cambodia, and beyond, to Vietnam. The proximity of these countries to Ubon Province accounts for the overwhelming military presence of the Thai army; wherever you wander from the town you're likely to encounter a well-established base.

Although there's little to see and do within Ubon, it's a fine place to start or end a tour of the region's southern cities, as it's connected by plane to Bangkok and close to Si Saket. Lastly, if you can manage to visit during the **Candle Festival** (usually in late July) you'll be rewarded with a genuine Thai spectacle (see "Special Events," below).

ESSENTIALS

GETTING THERE   By Plane   Two Thai Airways flights a day leave from Bangkok (flying time: 65 minutes). The **international airport** (☎ 045/263-916) is located near Ubon's city center, and is easily reached by tuk-tuk or taxi. Visit **Thai Airways** in Ubon at 364 Chayangoon Rd. (☎ 045/313-430) or call for reservations in Bangkok 02/232-8000.

By Train   Ubon Ratchathani is connected by rail to Bangkok via the Nakhon Ratchasima, Buriram, and Surin line. One express (second-class sleeper 421B/$11.10), three rapid (second-class sleeper 441B/$11.60), and two ordinary (second-class 221B/$5.80) trains leave daily from Bangkok's **Hua Lamphong Railway Station** (☎ 02/223-7010). The Railway Station (☎ 045/321-004) is across the Moon River from the city. Take the no. 2 bus to the center of town for a nominal charge.

By Bus   There are eight air-conditioned VIP buses departing daily from the Northern Bus Terminal in Bangkok on Paholythin Road (trip time: 9½ hours; 393B/$10.35). These buses stop in Nakhon Ratchasima (Khorat) and other towns along the way. The bus terminal in Ubon is near the Railway Station, south of the city across the Moon River. You'll have to take bus no. 2 into the town center.

By Car   The most direct road from Bangkok is Route 1 to Saraburi, turning east on Route 2 into Khorat (trip time: 4 hours); travel south on Route 304 and continue east on Route 24 (taking side trips to Buriram, Surin, and Si Saket); proceed north on Route 212 into Ubon (trip time: 5 hours).

VISITOR INFORMATION   The **TAT** (☎ 045/243-770) operates a helpful branch office at 264/1 Khuan Thani Rd. They publish a good map of the town and other very useful information—as well as answering specific questions about the city and region.

ORIENTATION   The town is built along the banks of the Moon River. The most important area for travelers is within a 4-square-block area proceeding north from the river. Running parallel to the river are **Prommathep Road;** followed by **Prommaraj** (with many banks); **Khuan Thani Road** (where you'll find the TAT); and **Srinarong**

Road, with the General Post Office, the telephone office, and the National Museum. The main north-south intersecting artery is **Auparat Road,** which is an extension of the bridge that spans the **Moon River** (the lesser suburb of Warinchamrab is located on the other side of the Moon). As Auparat extends northward, it becomes **Chayangkul Road** where the public bus terminal and Thai Airways office are located. The air-conditioned bus terminal is located on Phalorangrit Road, 1½ blocks north of the TAT office.

FAST FACTS   Banks are centered along Auparch Road down to and along Promtap Road and Promrach Road, just north of the Moon River and south of the TAT office. The **Rom Gao Hospital** (☎ 045/254-053) is on Auparch Road, on the south side of town; **Tourist Police** on Suriyat Road near the airport can be reached at ☎ 045/245-505. The **post office** is on Srinarong Road; the **telephone office** (☎ 045/254-001), also on Srinarong Road, is open daily 24 hours. The airport has a **currency exchange** bureau open every day; hours are determined by Thai Airways flights. **Chow Watana** (☎ 045/242-202) operates the best **car-rental** agency in town; expect to pay about 1,000B ($26.30) a day without gas. They can also arrange vans with drivers.

SPECIAL EVENTS   Normally beginning in July (the full moon during the eighth lunar month), Ubon Ratchathani hosts its **Candle Festival** to honor the start of the 3-month-long Buddhist Rains Retreat. The highlight of this period is the Candle Parade in which giant decorated beeswax-cast figures and floats are trekked through the town. During this celebration there are also bazaars, a beauty parade, Buddhist rituals and merit making, and dance performances.

WHAT TO SEE & DO

The National Museum provides a good overview of the historical development of lower Isan. It's particularly interesting for its diverse collection of Indian, Khmer, and Thai art and objects that demonstrate interaction of these competing cultures. There's also an ethnographic section that highlights Thai and Laotian costumes and customs. The structure that houses the collection was built in the mid–19th century and served as the provincial governor's office. Admission is 30B (80¢). It's open Wednesday to Saturday 8:30am to 4:30pm (the museum is often closed during lunch).

The **Wat Supatanaram Warawihan** complex demonstrates how Ubon Ratchathani is a significant crossroad in Southeast Asia. Originally built in 1853 by Vietnamese craftspeople in a Vietnamese/European style, it was financed by the Thai king Rama IV to house 7th-century Khmer lintels, an ancient figure of the Indian Hindu deity Ganesha, Dvaravati stone boundary markers—all placed in front of the viharn as memorials—and a Buddha of Chinese influence, Pra Sapphayu Chao. This aesthetically eclectic shrine is revered by both Thai and Laotian people, adding to the cultural mélange of historic and regional modes. Within the complex is a sonorous wooden bell that's reputed to be the largest of its kind in Thailand. The wat is located along the Moon River, a good place to take in the sunset.

Wat Tung Sri Muang, a temple complex situated smack in the center of town and around the corner from delightful Ubon restaurants, is worth a visit. Actually this wat is renowned for its mural paintings as well as the gracefully designed compound, including a pond and an all-teak library with a collection of antique books.

WHERE TO STAY

Laithong Hotel. 50 Pitchit Rangsan Rd., Ubon Ratchathani, 34000. ☎ **045/264-271.** Fax 045/264-270. 124 units. A/C MINIBAR TV TEL. 1,900B ($50) double; 2,500B ($65.80) suite. AE, DC, MC, V. Near the airport.

The best address in town, Laithong has all you'd want from a top-class city hotel, and room rate discounts are as low as 900B ($23.70) per night. Tha Laithong has a polite staff, big rooms, great bathrooms with nice long bathtubs, a host of amenities, plus a swimming pool and dining facilities. I recommend it if you demand a better place to lay your head. Plus, great restaurants are a short tuk-tuk ride away.

Pathumrat Hotel. 337 Chayangkul Rd., Ubon Ratchathani. ☎ **045/241-501.** 138 units. MINIBAR TV TEL. 450B–550B ($11.85–$14.45) double with A/C. MC, V. To the northwest of the river.

This older seven-story high-rise offers plain accommodations—a bit of a seventies revival, so maybe it's time for a little work. The lobby is often crowded with Thai tourists who congregate in the coffee shop area around the large television or who are reading the newspaper while waiting for their tour bus. There is a tiny swimming pool just off of the lobby. The management is a bit friendlier than in most Isan accommodations and the level of service is adequate.

WHERE TO DINE

Indochin Restaurant. 168-170 Subpasit Rd. ☎ **045/254-126.** Entrees 60B–120B ($1.60–$3.15). MV, V in air-conditioned room only. 2 blks. east of Auparch Rd. VIETNAMESE.

The sign may be in Thai, but you can't miss the giant teak Thai-style building that houses Indochin. At sidewalk level there's an open-air coffee shop–style eatery (good for casual lunches), behind is an air-conditioned restaurant. It gets quite crowded at lunch and dinner—this place is easily one of the best restaurants in town. Vietnamese cuisine is at its finest—excellently prepared sweet and spicy dishes with fresh ingredients. Expect the overworked service staff to ignore you.

Khun Tei Restaurant. 10/18 Nakhon Ban Rd. ☎ **045/242278.** Main courses 10B–50B (25¢–$1.30). No credit cards. Mon–Sat 10am–10pm. Around the corner from Wat Tung Sri Muang. THAI.

There won't be a word of English spoken here and the menu won't help you out either, but the food at the Khun Tei could be about the best I've sampled in town. The specialties are Isan-style Thai food, which basically means hotter than hot. The *som tam* (papaya salad with a cornucopia of accompanying ingredients) was incendiary but utterly fresh and delicious. Similarly tasty but considerably toned down was a plate of chicken *larb*. Our *gai yang* (fried chicken) was crisp and inexpensive. Speaking of price, a complete meal for two should run no more than about 150B ($3.95).

SHOPPING

The best single place to buy silk, *khit* patterned cloth, ready-made garments, silver, and other local wares is **Phanchat Esan Folk Arts and Handicrafts,** 158/1–2 Ratchabut Rd., between TAT and the Ratchathani Hotel (☎ **042/243-433**). It's open 9am to 8pm daily except Wednesday; MasterCard and VISA are accepted. The friendly English-speaking owner is knowledgeable and informative.

Watanasilp, 104 Ratchabut Rd. (☎ **042/255-661**), has a large selection of silver, ranging from cultural handicrafts to sophisticated machine-made items from Bangkok (less expensive here than in the capital), as well as exquisite pieces in gold and hematite.

SIDE TRIPS FROM UBON RATCHATHANI

PHA TAEM CLIFF PAINTINGS & SAO CHALIANG Well-preserved cliff paintings, dating from 4,000 to 2,000 years ago, are the principal attraction of Pha Taem, located 95km (59 miles) northeast of Ubon Ratchathani. The site is located along the base of sandstone cliffs that overlook the broad Mae Khong basin; I like this particular stop as much for its panorama as for the paintings. After arriving at the site, you'll have to walk down, a shade less than a mile, to the cliffs.

The prehistoric abstract forms are thought to have been painted by a migrating tribe that had a developed agricultural society. Figures of humans, domestic animals, and fish seem to connect with similar images found at such Neolithic sites as Ban Chiang (see "Side Trips from Udon Thani," above in this chapter). There are two basic stretches of cliff paintings, which are thought to be the longest in Southeast Asia. For the best view, climb up the low observation towers. The more intrepid hiker can either continue along the trail or scramble down to the village below. In any case, be sure to wear a hat and good shoes and plan on buying a bottle of water (there are stalls at the top, adjacent to the parking lot) to take with you.

Along the road to Pha Taem is a wonderful rock formation, **Sao Chaliang,** that's especially popular with kids who enjoy climbing. Although it's small, it might remind them of a real-life Bedrock—minus the Flintstones.

The best way to get to Pha Taem is by hired car (contact Chow Watana ☎ 045/242/202. Address 39/8 Surivat Road, opposite Nikko Massage, for car and driver), especially as there is no direct public transportation to Pha Taem. It's possible to take a bus from the bus terminal to Khong Chiam (only three every day) for 40B ($1.05). In Khong Chiam you'll have to hire a tuk-tuk or motorcycle taxi to the site, which is about 20km away. However, you should contact the TAT for the current bus schedule to ensure that this is still a viable option. The site is open from dawn to dusk. Admission is free.

KAENG TANA NATIONAL PARK   There are several scenic overlooks and parks along the Mae Khong and its confluence with the Mae Moon. The Kaeng Tana National Park includes both the confluence as well as inland forested areas that have hiking trails, bungalows, and rock formations similar to Sao Chaliang's (see above). During low water, roughly February through May, there are islets to explore, while waterfalls are best seen during and after the rains, from June through November. There's a short ferry that traverses the Moon River from **Khong Chiam** (50B/$1.30) per vehicle. In the town of Khong Chiam, there are a few restaurants, a market, and an emerging cluster of primitively equipped guest houses; nice for a stay for those who are really trying to escape the tourist hordes.

Traveling west, back toward Ubon Ratchathani, is the well-developed overlook at **Sapue Rapids.** Here you'll find a wide stretch of water with fishermen casting nets into the rushing water. There are food and drink stalls immediately adjacent, so it's possible to join the many Thai families picnicking on the rocks while taking in the lovely river scenery.

Just a few kilometers west is the newly built, ceramic tile covered temple at **Wat Phokhaokaew.** It's gaudy, but if you're in the neighborhood it might be worth a stop.

CHONGMEK   For those who have arranged their Laotian visa in advance (at the Bangkok embassy or in Khon Kaen), Chomgmek is an official crossing point. The ferry trip is about 200B to 300B ($5.25 to $7.90). Crossing to Laos is really the only reason to come out here: A dreary fenced-in hamlet visited by a few lucky Laotians buying Thai and foreign goods is what they call a border market. Other than that, there is no compelling reason to visit.

EN ROUTE TO SURIN

There are two wats—**Wat Pa Pong** and **Wat Pa Nanachat**—located midway between Ubon Ratchathani and Si Saket that are home to forest-dwelling Buddhist monks, many of whom hail from the United States, Canada, and Europe. The spiritual leader at Wat Pa Pong, 12km (7 miles) from Warinchamrab (south of the Ubon-Si Saket

Highway), is Acharn Cha, who leads a contingent of devoted acolytes in the study of Vipassana (insight-oriented) meditation. Visitors are welcome at Wat Pa Pong, but they are requested to arrive in the morning, as the afternoon is devoted to silent meditation. The related complex, Wat Pa Nanchat (temple of the International Forest), is located north of the main highway and is home exclusively to foreign monks; visitors are similarly welcomed and advised.

The best way to get there, other than by private car, is to take a bus to Warinchamrab and hire a tuk-tuk or take a songtao.

SI SAKET

Pronounced "*see*-Sket," this province is among the most ancient in Isan and, correspondingly, has several excellent Khmer sites worth visiting.

PRASAT HIN WAT KAMPHAENG NOI   Located about 8km (5 miles) off Route 226 on the road to Surin, this Khmer sanctuary is thought to have served as a so-called healing house. Intact are the foundation and central prang, but the structure of the site can be imagined based on the crumbling laterite remains and the familiar style developed during the 13th-century reign of King Jayavarman VII. Among the highlights of this ruin are the decorative lintels that depict Hindu scenes, such as Baruna carried by three swans. It's open daily 8:30am to 4:30pm. Admission is 25B (65¢).

PRASAT HIN WAT KAMPHAENG YAI   The largest of the Khmer sanctuaries in this part of Isan, Kamphaeng Yai is thought to have been finished in 1042 and was dedicated to the Hindu deity Shiva. Although Angkor architectural design is evident, there's a strong Indian influence throughout, particularly on the northern (Vishnu in Slumber) and southern (Shiva with Uma riding on Nandi the bull) lintels adorning the central prang. Like Phimai (see section 2 of this chapter), the temple was converted from a Brahmanic Khmer-based shrine into a Mahayana Thai-Buddhist complex after the 13th century.

Much of the Prasat has been reconstructed using modern bricks, but the Thai Fine Arts Department has made an attempt to integrate as many of the original decorated columns and lintels as possible. Kamphaeng Yai is located on Route 2080, about 15 minutes farther west from Kamphaeng Noi. It's open daily 8:30am to 4:30pm. Admission is 25B (65¢).

PRASAT PHRA WIHARN   For the truly dauntless traveler, there's a visit to Khao Phra Wiharn, which is actually in Cambodia. "Hm, Cambodia, you say?" The Thai government has negotiated a special right for foreign visitors who wish to visit this impressive Khmer temple set in the hills overlooking that war-weary country. Like the vista at Phanom Rung (see "Side Trips from Surin," below in this chapter), the view from Khao Phra Wiharn is remarkable and, in its day (the 12th century), it was on par with Phimai and Phanom Rung as one of the major Khmer satellite stops from Angkor Wat. It's a big-time site and it takes a major effort to get there. The complication and time involved is actually not worth the frustration—most travelers, both budget and well heeled alike agree that the best way to see it is with your own vehicle or through a tour. The best is from Surin—talk to Khun Pirom at Pirom Guest House. More information is provided in the next section.

9 Surin

457km (283 miles) NE of Bangkok; 227km (141 miles) W of Ubon Ratchathani; 111km (69 miles) E of Buriram; 198km (123 miles) E of Khorat

Surin is elephant country. Its festivals, excursions, and identity are intricately tied to ethnic Suay history and one of the great legends in Thai history. It seems that a tribal people, who were of either Laotian or Thai ancestry, migrated from the Mae Khong valley into what was later to become Ayutthaya-ruled Thailand. The villages that became Surin weren't under the direct rule of the kingdom, yet when a royal white elephant escaped from Ayutthaya, the Suay were brought in to capture King Suriyamarin's prized animal. As a reward, the king conferred the honorific "Luang" on six men, one of whom was Luang Surintarapakdee Srinarongchangwang. He later moved his village to the site of present day Surin, which officially become a Thai-ruled city under the Chakri dynasty in 1756.

Surin is home to some of the best silver work in Thailand, with finely made silver bracelets, baubles, and beads selling in high-end Bangkok shops (such as Gifted Hands), which would suggest that would-be buyers should attend Surin's markets to sample the locally made wares.

ESSENTIALS

GETTING THERE By Train Surin is connected by rail to Bangkok via the Nakhon Ratchasima (Khorat), Buriram, Ubon line. Seven trains a day leave from Bangkok (trip time: 10 hours on ordinary train, 8½ hours by express train; second-class ordinary 169B/$4.45, express 229B/$6.05).

By Bus There are five air-conditioned buses departing daily from the Northern Bus Terminal in Bangkok on Paholyothin Road (trip time: 6 hours; 195B/$5.15). Four buses depart daily from Nakhon Ratchasima Bus Terminal II (trip time: 3 hours; 100B/$2.65). Many daily buses connect Surin and Ubon Ratchanthani every half hour (trip time: 3½ hours; 250B/$6.60 VIP or 180B/$4.75).

By Car The most direct road from Bangkok is along Route 1 to Saraburi, turning east on Route 2 into Khorat (trip time: 4 hours); travel south on Route 304 and continue east on Route 24.

VISITOR INFORMATION There is no official information office in Surin; however, Khun Pirom and his wife, Khun Aree, at the **Pirom Guest House** (☎ 044/ 515140) are very friendly and helpful.

ORIENTATION Surin is a compact, though growing, city with a central market and a main street, **Thanasarn Road.** Behind Thanasarn is the train station (on the northern end of Surin), and along it are nearly all of the foreign exchange banks. Near Thanasarn are Tesabarn I, II, and III roads, where you'll find a large number of tourist services and establishments such as car-rental agencies, department stores, and restaurants. The two most central landmarks in town are the market and the post office, just about in the exact center of Surin. In the same central area is Chitbumrung Road, the location of the Petchkasem Hotel, which hosts the Bangkok Airways office. The bus station is located in the northeast quadrant of town, a very short tuk-tuk or samlor ride to most hotels.

FAST FACTS The **Provincial Hospital** (☎ 044/511-006) is on Tambon Nai Muang Rd; the emergency number for the **police** is ☎ 044/191 or 044/511-007; the **border police** number is ☎ 044/511-386. **Mengthai Hongyen** (☎ 044/511-715) and **Gopchai** (☎ 044/511-775) both **rent cars** and are located on Tesabarn III and Tesabarn I, respectively; expect to pay 1,000B ($26.30) a day without gas.

SPECIAL EVENTS Many people associate Surin solely with its famed **Elephant Roundup,** and though there are other compelling reasons to come here, this event is certainly a regional highlight. Each year, on the third Saturday and Sunday in November, the main events of the roundup take place in the town stadium. Accompanying the roundup is a weeklong **Elephant Fair,** a greatly expanded version of a typical Thai market, with food and crafts stalls, performances (including Surin folktales), a rocket show, and rides. The fair begins about a week in advance of the roundup. Aside from the actual roundup, there are elephant tugs-of-war, an elephant talent contest, elephant soccer games, an elephant procession over their trainers, and a re-creation of a war formation involving elephants and soldiers. Since Surin is jammed with tourists from around the world during this event, you are well advised to make hotel and travel reservations as soon as possible.

ELEPHANTS, TEMPLES & SILK

For most of the attractions in and around Surin, I recommend booking a guided trip with Khun Priom at the **Pirom Guest House (☎ 044/515-140)**. He's been here for 12 years, and in the business for 10—but he only has weekend trips because he hasn't yet retired from his day job as a social worker. Popular tours are to the Khmer temples in the region, plus a Khmer village (full-day tour 690B/$18.15 per person); a handicrafts tour to silk villages, silverware villages, and to the elephant village (690B/$18.15 full-day), and a tour of the weekend market at the Cambodian border (590B/$15.55 per person).

In case you're wondering where the elephants that participate in the annual roundup live during the rest of the year, many of them reside in **Tha Klang Elephant Village** in the village of Tha Klang, located 58km (37 miles) north of Surin. The villagers are reputed to be descendants of the Suay who have long worked as elephant capturers and trainers, largely in and around the Cambodian border area. Today they train elephants for labor as well as to perform in the region's two roundups, in Surin during November and Chaiyaphum in January. Visitors are welcome in the village; however, few elephants are in Tha Klang during the day. They only return in the evening hours after putting in their work near the river. Some tours, such as that organized by Mr. Pirom (see The Pirom Guest House, under "Where to Stay," below, for details), include a trip here combined with other attractions.

Once again the Thai Fine Arts Department is restoring a Khmer temple, and as with most in this part of Thailand, it was built during the 11th century in Angkor style. Like many of its kind, **Prasat Sikhoraphum (Prasat Ban Ra-ngaeng)** was converted during the 17th century from a Hindu to a Buddhist shrine. Of particular note are the carvings, excellent examples of Khmer limestone work, adorning the doorway columns as well as the Shiva carved lintel above the main doorway of the central prang. It's open daily 8:30am to 4:30pm. Admission is 25B (65¢).

Located about 30km (19 miles) north of Surin, the recently restored **Prasat Ban Phuluang** is admired as much for its surroundings as for its elegantly carved sandstone and laterite Khmer architecture. As with most Khmer sites in Isan, Phuluang is thought to have been built in the 11th or 12th century during the reign of King Suriyaworamun I. The highlight here is the east-facing lintel above the main entrance with a delightful scene of Indra riding an elephant.

In the modern village of Ban Pluang, there are opportunities to watch and purchase silk weaving. It's open daily 8:30am to 5:30pm. Admission is 25B (65¢).

Located 12km (7 miles) east of Surin, off Route 226, is **Butom,** a rural **basket-weaving village.** If you wander into the village, you're bound to see a group of women weaving sturdy and attractive baskets under their stilt houses, usually accompanied by a Thai soap opera on a generator-run television. It's an odd sight but the work is incredible; people come from Bangkok to make their purchases. There are several roadside stands that sell baskets, but you can also buy directly from the craftspeople.

Two **silk-weaving villages,** both within about 20km (13 miles) of Surin, welcome visitors who wish to see demonstrations of traditional methods of manufacturing silk. **Khawao Sinrin** and **Chanrom** (the former on Route 214 north of Surin, the latter on

Route 2077 to the east of town) are centers of handmade silk products, from thread to finished lengths of material, which are sold locally and in shops in Surin.

WHERE TO STAY

Some hotels will add a surcharge during the Elephant Roundup, so if you plan on visiting during the festival, expect to pay as much as a 50% premium. The prices quoted are the normal prices.

Memorial Hotel. 186 Lak Muang Rd., Surin 32000. ☎ 044/511-288. 56 units. TEL. 400B ($10.55) double with A/C; 275B ($7.25) double with fan. No credit cards. In the center.

This is a small hotel, that, nevertheless, offers decent value for the money, especially for the fan-cooled rooms; some rooms have air-conditioning. I like its central location, clean rooms, and proximity to restaurants and services.

Petchkasem Hotel. 104 Chitbumrung Rd., Surin 32000. ☎ 044/511-274. Fax 044/514-470. 162 units. A/C TV TEL. 500B ($13.15) double. MC, V. In the center.

Until recently, this six-story high-rise offered the best that Surin had to offer (it's since been surpassed by the Tharin, see below), but don't expect much in the way of luxury or service: It's rather Spartanly furnished, poorly maintained, and a tad worn. Nevertheless, the Petchkasem has a restaurant, coffee shop, disco, pool, and other services that make it a center, not only for its guests, but for locals as well.

Pirom Guest House. 242 Krungsrinai Rd., Surin, 32000. ☎ 044/515-140. 6 units and dormitory. 150B ($3.95) double with fan; 70B ($1.85) dormitory room. No credit cards. West of the center, 2 blocks west of the market.

The Pirom is a small guest house with style and personal service. In a dark-wood, older Thai house, it avoids the banality of the modern-style hotels so ubiquitous in Isan. There are no amenities to speak of (bathing facilities are outside the rooms), and the rooms themselves are very basic and small, but Mr. Pirom (who speaks excellent English) and his wife, Aree, are lovely hosts and both are extremely well informed about the area. Pirom leads daily excursions (see "Things to See & Do," above) to the more remote destinations around Surin, especially to Tha Klang Elephant Village. He also guides cultural tours through Isan.

Tharin Hotel. Sirirat Rd., Surin 32000. ☎ 044/514-281. 240 units. A/C TV TEL. 1,250B ($32.90) double. MC, V. In the center.

Since the tourist explosion hit Thailand, there have been few hotels built in Surin; however, the town finally has a good standard in the Tharin Hotel, which has a fine restaurant, a nightclub, and a very nice pool. All rooms are equipped in a clean and modern fashion, and the service and maintenance is a notch better than in other Isan hotels of this caliber. If you plan on visiting during the roundup, try to reserve a room as early as possible.

WHERE TO DINE

There are several attractive restaurants on the small street between the bus station and the Tharin Hotel, including **Low Jar,** across from the temple (one of the best restaurants in the town). **Somboonpochana** near the Bor Kor Sot bus station serves a combination of Isan and Thai specialties at low to moderate prices.

SIDE TRIPS FROM SURIN

BURIRAM Buriram, about halfway between Surin and Khorat (and easily reached by either bus, train, or car), is the capital of the province of the same name. The main reason for a stop there would be a visit to **Phanom Rung,** one of the best Khmer ruins in the world—but as facilities for foreign tourists have not developed as anticipated, we currently recommend you visit the site from Khorat or Surin.

If you have the time, there are a number of interesting lesser sites in the province, and the TAT in Khorat publishes a good guide pamphlet (see "Visitor Information," in section 1 of this chapter). **Phanom Rung Tours** (formed by two assistant professors at Buriram Teachers College), 131 Buriram-Prakhnochai Rd., Buriram (☎ **044/ 612-046,** fax 612-691), can arrange tours, accommodations, and meals, with packages starting at about 1,500B ($39.45).

Should you wish to overnight in Buriram, the **Thep Nakron Hotel,** 139 Isan Rd. (☎ **044/613-400**), on the main highway, where air-conditioned singles go for about 600B ($15.80) and doubles for 800B ($21.05) is a good choice. Visa and MasterCard are accepted. An acceptable downtown alternative is the **Thai Hotel,** 38/1 Romburi Rd. (☎ **044/611-112**), with rooms ranging from 300B ($7.90) for a single with fan to 500B ($13.15) for an air-conditioned double. Visa and MasterCard are also accepted. There's an inexpensive Chinese restaurant adjacent to it and an unnamed shop about 100 yards south that sells groceries and baked goods.

In the first week of November the annual **Longboat Races** are held at Amphoe Satuk; an elephant procession and elephant swimming contest are part of the festivities. **Songkran** (full moon of the fifth lunar month) is celebrated by a special pilgrimage to Phanom Rung. Early December brings a colorful **Kite Festival.** Contact the TAT in Khorat for more information.

PHANOM RUNG Perhaps due to its isolated hilltop location, **Prasat Hin Phanom Rung** (Great Mountain), one of the major stops on the road to Angkor Wat, was deserted from its fall in the late 13th century until its "rediscovery" in 1935. Full-scale restoration began in 1972, and in early 1988, it opened to the public, instantly becoming one of the region's most popular Khmer sites. The shrine was the subject of an international dispute when one of its exceptionally well-carved sandstone lintels, depicting a reclining Vishnu, showed up in the Art Institute of Chicago. It was returned to Thailand and reinstalled just after the site's opening.

The temple, built on the summit of an inactive volcano, sits majestically above the wide plains, facing southeast toward Angkor in Cambodia. The approach is via a stairway, interrupted by pavilionlike bridges, lined on both sides with a multiheaded cobra, or *naga* (mythical serpent), in Angkor style. The base of the central structure was built in the 10th century and almost certainly housed Shiva imagery, such as a phallic lingam (the pipe that allowed water to cascade over the lingam is still in place) in a small temple enclosure. This building was expanded by the 12th century and is the main prang of the site. Above the finely carved Lopburi-period doors are lintels, each portraying an important Hindu character or incident, the most famous of which is that of the reclining Vishnu. Look carefully at the columns and supporting stones on the central buildings, as many are festooned with ornately carved Shivas, galloping elephants, and shapely Khmer dancers. At the periphery of the central buildings are several 13th-century structures, which are thought to have functioned as libraries.

To reach Phanom Rung by public transport from Khorat, take a Surin-bound bus to Ban Tak Ko (trip time: 2 hours; 50B/$1.30) and take a tuk-tuk or songtao to the site. It's open daily 8am to 5pm. Admission is 25B (65¢).

Down the hill and about 8km (5 miles) from Phanom Rung in Ban Chorake (Village of Crocodiles) is **Prasat Muang Tam,** a largely unreconstructed Khmer site that features a series of ponds, framed by *nagas* (similar to the stairway at Phanom Rung), surrounding a gallery of prangs or stupas. Again, lintel carvings indicate a Brahmanic tradition, with the most significant frieze illustrating Shiva riding on the back of

Nandi the Bull. It highlights the difference between a "found" site and one that has been reconstructed.

There is no public transportation to Muang Tam; however, taxis or tuk-tuks will take you there from Ban Tak Ko (and sometimes from Phanom Rung). The site is open daily 7:30am to 6pm. Admission is 25B (65¢).

Prasat Ta Muen Toj and **Ta Muen Tom,** two halts on the Angkor road, are part of a larger cluster of Khmer buildings, constructed in the 11th century, that are located exactly on the current Thai-Cambodian border. At Muen Toj, the main stupa is, like Ban Pluang, of square design. Muen Tom is a larger complex that incorporates a remarkable sandstone wall and base with a triple stupa on the central porch.

Don't be surprised if you see soldiers armed with automatic weapons. They will carefully guide you through the sites, aware that mines have not been completely cleared in the adjoining area. The buildings, which may have had religious or possibly healing functions attached to them, are a jumble of sandstone and laterite bricks and columns. Thick trunk banyans have grown up in the midst of this cacophony of stones; brush fires, lit by the armed soldiers to keep the jungle from overwhelming the site, complete the scene. It's no wonder that I felt a strong kinship with Indiana Jones at the Muen Toj and Tom.

You'll likely be the only ones at this particular stop, so make the most of it. This is the kind of place where, once you overcome the feeling that a band of Khmer Rouge soldiers might open fire at any moment, you'll relax and attend to the sounds, sites, and smells of a little-visited, wild location.

You'll have to hire a car in order to visit, or talk to Khum Pirom in Surin about a tour. Plan on being stopped by no less than six military checkpoints.

11

Exploring Northern Thailand

Exotic Northern Thailand is home to the majority of Thailand's half-million-plus tribal peoples, many of whom emigrated from Laos, southwestern China, Burma, and Tibet. Because of the ethnic, cultural, and language ties to these neighbors, the hill tribes have retained their traditional costumes, religion, art, and way of life. These distinctive ethnic cultures continue to make the rural north one of the country's most popular tourist destinations.

Most of the hill tribes have traditionally subsisted on shifting agriculture: burning forests to clear land, planting poppies as a cash crop, then setting up new bamboo and thatch villages whenever their farmland's soil became depleted. This nomadic existence has meant that travelers interested in hill-tribe culture have had to go out and look for it. Contact with the cultural traditions and simple rural life of these hospitable peoples is only one of the attractions of trekking, a popular way to explore this region. The crafts of the hill tribe peoples and local cottage industries also make shopping in this part some of the most exciting in the country.

Other parts of the north are affiliated with the historic Lanna (often written Lan Na) Kingdom. Thailand's second city after Bangkok, Chiang Mai was the Lanna Thai capital from the 13th to 18th centuries, when it was a powerful ally of the central Sukhothai Kingdom. Using this exciting city as a base for travel by bus, car, or motorcycle, you can visit the ruins of fortifications, ornately decorated wats, and museums preserving the Lanna culture.

1 The Land & Its People

THE REGION IN BRIEF

Northern Thailand is comprised of 15 provinces, many of them sharing borders with Burma (Myanmar) to the north and west and Laos to the northeast. (Thailand's eastern areas bordering Laos and Cambodia are covered in chapter 10, "Exploring Isan: Thailand's Frontier.") This verdant, mountainous terrain, including Thailand's largest mountain, Doi Inthanon, at 2,563 meters (8,408 ft.) supports nomadic farming and teak logging at high altitudes and systematic agriculture in the valleys. The hill tribes' traditional poppy crops have largely been replaced with rice, tobacco, soybeans, corn, and sugarcane.

North and east of Chiang Mai, lowland farmers also cultivate seasonal fruits such as strawberries, longan, mandarin oranges, mango, and melon; the lush, tended fields and winding rivers make sightseeing, particularly in the spring, a visual treat.

In addition to agriculture, lumber (especially teak), textiles, some mining, and handicrafts and tourism-related cottage industries contribute to making northern Thailand one of the country's fastest-growing economies.

A LOOK AT THE REGION'S PAST

In the late 13th century, King Mengrai united several Tai tribes that had migrated from southern China and built the first capital of the Lanna Kingdom in Chiang Rai. Mengrai, whose brilliant rule was aided by useful alliances, saw a threat in the Mongol emperor Kublai Khan's incursions into Burma (Myanmar) and quickly forged ties with the powerful Kingdom of Sukhothai in the south. The Lanna Thai king moved swiftly to consolidate his position when he vanquished the vestiges of the Mon Empire in Lamphun (Nakorn Hariphunchai), and in 1296 moved his new capital south to what is now Chiang Mai. There is a monument to King Mengrai, across from Chiang Mai's Wat Phan Tao, where he is said to have been struck by lightning and killed in 1317.

For the next century, Chiang Mai prospered and the Lanna Kingdom grew, absorbing most of the present-day northern provinces. In alliance Chiang Mai and Sukhothai were able to repulse any significant attacks from Khmer and Mon neighbors. After the ascendant Siam Kingdom at Ayutthaya absorbed Sukhothai, Ayutthaya forces tried repeatedly to take Chiang Mai, but the kingdom did not yield. Instead, Chiang Mai strengthened itself, and from the late 14th century until its eventual fall to the Burmese in 1556, it enjoyed tremendous affluence and influence.

After 2 centuries of relentless warfare, the Burmese captured Chiang Mai in 1556, and for the next 2 centuries the Lanna Kingdom was a Burmese vassal—the Burmese cultural influence is still evident today. After Siam's King Taksin recaptured Chiang Mai from the Burmese in 1775, the city was so weakened that Taksin moved its surviving citizens to nearby Lampang. For 2 decades Chiang Mai was literally a ghost town. Though the city was still nominally under the control of local princes, their power continued to decline, and in 1939, Chiang Mai was formally incorporated into the modern Thai nation.

A PORTRAIT OF THE HILL-TRIBE PEOPLE

The ethnic hill-tribe people of the north help make this area an important destination for visitors to Thailand. Most tribes migrated from China or Tibet to Burma, Laos, and Vietnam and ultimately settled in Thailand's northern provinces such as Chiang Rai, Chiang Mai, Mae Hong Son, Phayao, and Nan. The six main tribes are the Karen, Akha (also known as the Kaw), Lahu (Mussur), Lisu (Lisaw), Hmong (Meo), and Mien (Yao), each with subgroups that are linked by history, lineage, language, costume, social organization, and religion.

Hill tribes are divided into two linguistic categories, the Sino-Tibetan and Austro-Asiatic, though only descendants of the Mon-Khmer speak a dialect of the latter category. In addition, tribes are divided geographically into lowland, or valley, dwellers who grow cyclical crops, such as rice or corn, and high-altitude dwellers who grow opium poppies. The so-called indigenous tribes, who have occupied the same areas for hundreds of years, are those that tend to inhabit the lower valleys in organized villages of split-log huts. The nomadic groups generally live above 1,000 meters (3,250 ft.) in easy-to-assemble bamboo and thatch housing, ready to resettle when nearby fields grow less fertile or when political strife overspills the borders of Burma (Myanmar) and Laos.

Nearly all tribal villages have a headman who performs most of the political and social functions, including welcoming guests. The nomadic, high-altitude villages are led by village elders or a shaman who consults spirits. If the community is threatened by agricultural losses, disease, or by the bandits in the area, the whole village may disband and move to a more advantageous location. Villages also break up over internal disputes, and families will separate and take up new residences. Most often, the social unit is characterized as the extended family; this is especially true among the Hmong (Meo) and Mien (Yao), who practice polygamy.

Highland minorities believe in spirits, and it's the role of the shaman, or head religious figure, to read into every situation the workings of spiritual forces. Most villages practice rites that are meant to appease the spirits, with the shaman or headman chosen to determine the problem, prescribe the solution, and perform the ritual. Remarkably enough, neither the shamans nor headmen have higher status than the other villagers; they merely render a service. If a shaman or headman becomes too grandiose in his political aspirations, the villagers will often decide collectively to disband.

Karen A quarter million Karen make up the largest tribal group in Thailand, accounting for more than half of all tribal people in the country. In nearby Burma (Myanmar), it's estimated that there are more than four million people of Karen descent (and of Buddhist belief), many of whom have settled along the Thai-Burmese border. For years the military government has been battling Karen rebels seeking an autonomous homeland—and there are many Burmese Karen who have sought refuge in Thailand. In Thailand, the Karen are geographically dispersed, living as far north as Chiang Rai and as far south as Kanchanaburi.

The Karen are among the most assimilated among the hill tribes of Thailand, making it difficult to identify them by any outward appearance; however, the most traditional tribespeople wear silver armbands and don a beaded sash and headband, and the single women wear all white.

Hmong (Meo) The Hmong are a nomadic tribe scattered throughout Southeast Asia and China. About 65,000 Hmong live in Thailand, with the greatest number residing in Chiang Mai, Chiang Rai, Nan, Phetchabun, and Phrae provinces; there are approximately four million Hmong living in China. Within Thailand there are several subgroups; the Hmong Daew (White Hmong) and the Hmong Njua (Blue Hmong) are the main divisions, and the Hmong Gua Mba (Armband Hmong) is a subdivision of the Hmong Daew.

In Thailand, the Hmong generally dwell in the highlands, where they cultivate opium poppies more extensively than any other tribal group; corn, rice, and soybeans are also grown as subsistence crops. The Hmong are also excellent animal breeders, and their ponies are especially prized.

As with other nomadic tribes, the Hmong maintain much of their wealth in silver jewelry. Neck rings are given to Hmong babies as a sign of their acceptance into the material world. During the December New Year festival, families wear their silver jewelry and ornaments in an impressive display of craftsmanship. The women are particularly distinctive with knotted, long dark hair woven with horse- or human-hair switches to create an enormous bun on the top of their heads. Though most men take only one wife, a wealthier one will take two.

Also like most of the other tribes, the Hmong are pantheistic and rely on shamans to perform spiritual rites, though their elite is staunchly Catholic. In a perceived

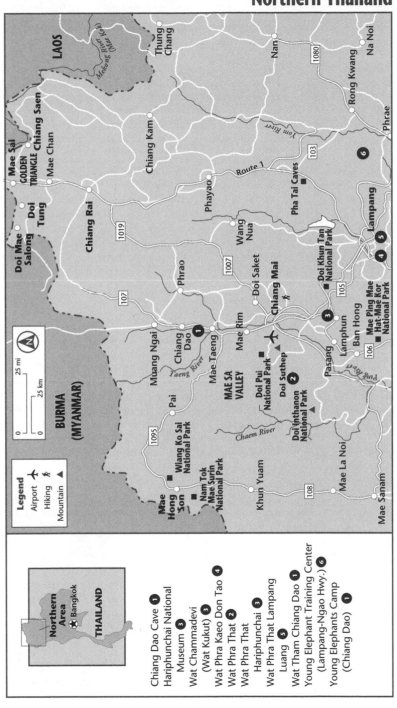

LAOS

BURMA
(MYANMAR)

THAILAND

Mehong River (Mae Kok)

Thung
Chang

Nan

Na Noi

Rong Kwang

1080

Mae Sai

GOLDEN
TRIANGLE Chiang Saen

Mae Chan

Chiang Kam

Yom River

Route 1

103

Phrae

6

Doi Mae
Salong

Doi
Tung

Mae Chan

Chiang Rai

1019

Phayao

Wang
Nua

Pha Tai Caves

Lampang

5

4

Doi Khun Tan
National Park

105

Phrao

1007

Doi Saket

Chiang Mai

Mae Ping Mae
Hat-Mae Kor
National Park

3

107

Muang Ngai

Chiang
Dao

1

Mae Taeng

Mae Rim

Mae Rim

Ban Hong

Taeng River

Lamphun

Pasang

106

Wang River

Pai

MAE SA
VALLEY

Doi Pui
National Park

Doi Suthep

2

1095

Wiang Ko Sai
National Park

Nam Tok
Mae Surin
National Park

Doi Inthanon
National Park

Chaem River

Mae La Noi

Mae
Hong
Son

Khun Yuam

108

Mae Sanam

Legend
✈ Airport
🚶 Hiking
▲ Mountain

25 mi

25 km

0

0

Northern
Area

★ Bangkok

THAILAND

Chiang Dao Cave ❶
Hariphunchai National
Museum ❸
Wat Chammadevi
(Wat Kukut) ❸
Wat Phra Kaeo Don Tao ❹
Wat Phra That ❷
Wat Phra That
Hariphunchai ❸
Wat Phra That Lampang
Luang ❺
Wat Tham Chiang Dao ❶
Young Elephant Training Center
(Lampang-Ngao Hwy.) ❻
Young Elephants Camp
(Chiang Dao) ❶

spiritual crisis, shamans practice animal sacrifice and perform rituals, contacting the spirit world in a trancelike state. They place particular emphasis on the spirit of doors: doors for entering and exiting the human world, doors to houses, doors to let in good fortune and to block bad spirits, and doors to the afterlife. The Hmong also worship their ancestors, another echo from their Chinese past.

Like the Chinese, with whom they resided for so many centuries, Hmong are skilled entrepreneurs, and many are beginning to move down from the hills to pursue a less rigorous and more profitable life in other occupations. But as long as the trade in opium remains lucrative, most Hmong will remain in the highlands, cultivating poppies.

Lahu (Mussur)   The Lahu people, of which about 40,000 abide in Thailand, are a fractured group with a great many subdivisions. The differences can even be seen from their clothing. The two main bands are the Lahu Na (Black Lahu) and the Lahu Shi (Yellow Lahu), with a much smaller number of Lahu Hpu (White Lahu), La Ba, and Abele. Most Lahu villages are situated above 1,000 meters (3,250 ft.) in the mountains around Chiang Mai, Chiang Rai, Mae Hong Son, Tak, and Kamphaeng Phet, where poppies, dry rice, corn, and other cash crops are grown.

Lahu Na, similar to Tibetan, is so well accepted that other tribal people and Yunnanese Chinese have adopted it as their common tongue. The Lahu are skilled musicians, and their bamboo and gourd flutes are the most common instruments. Flutes are often used by young men to woo the woman of their choice. (You can buy their instruments in the Night Market in Chiang Mai.)

If any tribe reflects the difficulties of maintaining a singular cultural identity in the tumult of migration, it's the Lahu. Consider Lahu religion: Originally animist, they adopted the worship of a deity called G'ui sha (possibly Tibetan in origin), borrowed the practice of merit making from Buddhism (Indian or Chinese), and ultimately incorporated Christian (British/Burmese) theology into their belief system. G'ui sha is the supreme being who created the universe and rules over all spirits. Spirits inhabit animate and inanimate objects, making them capable of benevolence or evil, with the soul functioning as the spiritual force within people. In addition, they practice a kind of Lahu voodoo as well as following a messianic tradition. They welcome strangers more than any other tribe in Thailand.

Mien (Yao)   There are now estimated to be 33,000 Mien living in Thailand, concentrated in Chiang Rai, Phayao, Lampang, and Nan provinces. The Mien are still numerous in China as well as in Vietnam, Burma (Myanmar), and Laos. Like the Hmong, tens of thousands of Mien fled to northern Thailand from Vietnam and Laos after the end of the Vietnam War.

Even more than the Hmong, the Mien (the name is thought to come from the Chinese word for "barbarian") are closely connected to their origins in southern China. They incorporated the Han spoken and written language into their own, and many Mien legends, history books, and religious tracts are recorded in Chinese. The Mien people also assimilated ancestor worship and a form of Taoism into their theology, in addition to celebrating their New Year on the same date (relying on the same calendar system) as the Chinese.

Mien farmers practice slash-and-burn agriculture but do not rely on opium poppies; instead they cultivate dry rice and corn. The women produce rather elaborate and elegant embroidery, which often adorns their clothing. Their silver work is intricate and highly prized even by other tribes, particularly the Hmong. Much of Mien religious art appears to be strongly influenced by Chinese design, particularly Taoist motifs, clearly distinguishing it from other tribes' work.

Lisu (Lisaw)   The Lisu are one of the smaller ethnic minorities in northern Thailand, representing less than 5% of all hill-tribe people. They arrived in Chiang Rai Province in the 1920s, migrating from nearby Burma. The Lisu occupy high ground and grow opium poppies as well as other subsistence crops. Lisu people, like their Chinese cousins (many have intermarried), are reputed to be extremely competitive and hardworking. They also frequently intermarry with the Lahu. Even their clothing is brash, with brightly colored tunics embellished with hundreds of silver beads and trinkets.

The Lisu are achievers who live well-structured lives. Their rituals rely on complicated procedures that demand much from the participants. Everything from birth to courtship to marriage to death is ruled by an orthodox tradition, much borrowed from the Chinese. Possibly because of their structured, goal-oriented society, the Lisu have the highest suicide rate among Thailand's tribal people.

Akha (Kaw)   Of all the tradition-bound tribes, the Akha, accounting for only 3% of all minorities living in Thailand, have probably maintained the most profound connection with their past. At great events in one's life, the full name (often more than 50 generations of titles) of an Akha is proclaimed, with each name symbolic of a lineage dating back more than 1,000 years. All aspects of life are governed by the Akha Way, an all-encompassing system of myth, ritual, plant cultivation, courtship and marriage, birth, death, dress, and healing.

The strength of the Akha Way may be the key to maintaining their identity, for the Akha are widely spread throughout southern China, Laos, Vietnam, and Burma (Myanmar). The first Akha migrated from Burma to Thailand in the beginning of the 20th century, originally settling in the highlands above the Mae Kok River in Chiang Rai Province. Now they are moving down to lower heights in search of more arable land. They are "shifting" cultivators, depending on subsistence crops, planted in rotation, and raising domestic animals for their livelihood.

The clothing of the Akha is among the most attractive of all the hill tribes. Simple black jackets with skillful embroidery are the everyday attire for both men and women. The Akha shoulder bags are adorned with silver coins, baubles, and found beads and are woven with exceptional skill.

2 When to Go

THE CLIMATE   Northern Thailand has three distinct seasons. The hot season (March through May) is dry with temperatures up to 86°F (30°C). Still cooler than the southern parts of the country, many Thais vacation in this region to get away from scorching temperatures elsewhere. The rainy season (June through October) is cooler, with the heaviest daily rainfall in September. While trekking and outdoor activities are still carried out, mud and rain conditions should be taken into consideration when packing for your trip. The cool season (November through February) is brisk, with daytime temperatures as low as 59°F (21°C) in Chiang Mai town, and 41°F (5°C) in the hills. Bring a sweater and some snuggly socks. November to May is the best time for trekking, with February, March, and April (when southern Thailand gets extremely hot) usually being the most crowded months. In October and November, after the rainfalls, the forests are lush, rivers swell, and waterfalls are more splendid than usual.

FESTIVALS   Northern Thailand celebrates many unique festivals, as well as many nationwide festivals in an unusual way. Check the calendar below so that you can plan your trip to coincide with one of them. Many Thais also travel to participate in these festivals (particularly the Winter Fair, Flower Festival, Songkran, and Loi Krathong), and advance hotel reservations are a must.

Songkran

April 13th marks the first day of *Songkran,* the Thai New Year. In traditional times, the Thais would celebrate by visiting local temples to wash the Buddha images. Afterward they would sprinkle water on the hands of their elders as a show of filal piety. These days Songkran has escalated into something completely different. You see, more than anything in the world, the Thais love *sanuk,* fun, and the celebration has turned into a nationwide water fight. In most places the battle lasts for 3 days, but in the north it goes on for up to 10.

Moms and dads fire up the pickup truck, load the back with garbage cans filled with water, toss in all the neighborhood kids (teenagers, playful grown-ups, and wacky grannies included) and drive around town throwing water at everybody in sight. Others wait on street corners, to nail the menacing truckloads, as well as assorted passersby. No one is spared.

Well, it didn't take me too long to be out there with all the kids on the side of the road. I had to suffer my initiation soaking, the kids squealing to have a *farang,* a foreigner, in their midst. Farangs are the preferred targets of the Thai, so I might as well have worn a bull's-eye on my back. I spent half the afternoon teasing one tiny girl, who was fascinated with pouring water over me when I wasn't looking. Needless to say, she met the business end of my water bazooka—giggling the whole time.

By five, I was an ever-lovin' mess, only to find the party had just begun. I headed off to Khao San Road, the nucleus of Songkran festivities in Bangkok. Khao San Road is a small street in Bangkok where you find all the backpacker hostels and cheap guest houses. On any normal day the cafes and bars are pretty lively, and the sides of the street are lined with hawkers making spicy noodles and vendors selling handicrafts and souvenirs. Not today. The street was a mob scene, packed side to side with wet dancing people, smeared from head to toe with talc paste. I could barely move through the swelling crowd. Every beautiful smile said "Happy New Year!" before the hands came and gently wiped the goo down my face. Then there would be a splash of water, washing it all away, only to have someone new come and reapply the powder to my clean face. And it went this way over and over. Thais, farangs, everybody was a fright, throbbing to the loud music and wriggling through the slippery bodies. From time to time someone in an upstairs window would chuck a bucketful—splash! and the crowd would roar. It took me 3 hours to get as many blocks. By the end I was joyously exhausted, wet to the bone, caked with chunks of powder, and aching from laughter.

This is only one of the many festivals celebrated in the kingdom. For a listing of events happening during your stay, see "When to Go" in chapter 2.

Northern Thailand Calendar of Events

Many of these annual events are based on the lunar calendar. Contact the TAT (☎ 02/282-9773) in Bangkok for the exact dates.

January

- **Winter Fair,** Chiang Mai. Special theatrical events, a Beauty Queen pageant, and art exhibits are held at the Municipal Stadium.

- **Umbrella Festival,** Bo Sang. Held in a village of umbrella craftspeople and painters about 15km (9miles) east of Chiang Mai, the Umbrella Festival features handicraft competitions, an elephant show, and a local parade.

February

- **Flower Festival,** Chiang Mai. Celebrates the city's undisputed position as the "Flower of the North," with concerts, flower displays and competitions, a food fair, and a beauty contest. The pace of the long parade of the first weekend—the focal point of the festival—is decidedly Asian, not nearly as rushed as something like Macy's Thanksgiving Day Parade, but the streets are just as jammed.

  The Buak Hat park is the location for most of the other events in the festival, including an exquisite orchid competition/display, flower-arranging demonstrations, and a pageant to elect a Miss Chiang Mai Flower Festival.
- **King Mengrai Festival,** Chiang Rai. Known for its special hill-tribe cultural displays and a fine handicrafts market (early February).
- **Sakura Blooms Flower Fair,** Doi Mae Salong. Celebrates the sakura of Japanese cherry trees, imported to this northwestern hill village by former members of China's nationalist Kuomintang party (early February).

March

- **Poy Sang Long.** A traditional Shan ceremony honoring Buddhist novices, widely celebrated in the northwestern village of Mae Hong Son (late March or early April).

April

- **Songkran (Water) Festival.** Celebrated over the Lanna Thai New Year, most of the ceremonies take place at the wats. Presents and merit-making acts are offered, and water is sprinkled over Buddhas, monks, elders, and tourists—those who don't want a good soaking should avoid the streets—to celebrate the beginning of the harvest and to ensure good fortune. The festival is celebrated in all northern provinces, and throughout the country, but Chiang Mai's celebration is notorious for being the longest (up to 10 days) and the rowdiest. The first day is April 13.

May

- **Visakha Bucha.** Honors the birth, enlightenment, and death of the Lord Buddha on the full moon of this month. Celebrated nationwide, it's a particularly dramatic event in Chiang Mai, where residents walk up Doi Suthep in homage.
- **Harvest Festival,** Kho Loi Park, Chiang Rai. This festival honors the harvest of litchis. There is a parade, litchi competition and display, a beauty contest to find Miss Chiang Rai Litchi Nut, and lots of food (mid-May).
- **Mango Fair,** Chiang Mai. A fair honoring mangoes, the local's favorite crop (second weekend).

August

- **Lamyai or Longan Fair,** Lamphun. Celebrates the town's favorite fruit and one of Thailand's largest foreign-exchange earners. Yes, there is a Miss Longan competition, too (first or second weekend).

October

- **Nan Province** sponsors 2 days of boat racing, with wildly decorated, long, low-slung craft zipping down the Nan River. The Lanna Boat Races are run 7 days after the Rains' Retreat, marking the beginning of the dry season.

November

- **Loi Krathong.** Occurs around the country over 2 nights of the full moon in the 12th lunar month. Crowds float small banana-leaf boats bearing candles, incense, a flower, and a coin as an offering and to carry away the previous year's sins and bad luck. In Chiang Mai, brightly colored lanterns are strung everywhere; enormous, flaming hot-air balloons are released in the night sky; and there's a parade of women in traditional costumes, as well as a Miss Noppamas Beauty Pageant. The offering boats or krathongs are floated on the Ping River. In Sukhothai, there's a spectacular sound-and-light show.

December

- **Day of Roses,** Chiang Mai. Exhibitions and cultural performances are held in Buak Hat Park (first weekend).

3 Getting There & Getting Around

GETTING THERE

Before the 1920s, when the railway's Northern Line to Chiang Mai was completed, one traveled either by longboat or elephant; the trip took more than 2 weeks and was considered fairly arduous. Today, commerce and tourism together have generated several much faster and more comfortable transportation options. See chapter 12, "Chiang Mai," and chapter 13 "Touring the Northern Hills," for more specific schedule and price information.

BY PLANE   Thai Airways (☎ 02/232-8000 in Bangkok) flies from Bangkok to Chiang Mai, Lampang, Chiang Rai, Mae Hong Son, Nan, and Phrae. There are also flights between many of these destinations and between them and Phitsanulok in central Thailand. **Bangkok Airways** (☎ 02/229-3456 in Bangkok) connects Bangkok and Chiang Mai with a stop in Sukhothai in the central plains.

BY TRAIN   Express and rapid trains leave Bangkok for Chiang Mai several times a day. Sleeper cars are available on certain trains, and should be reserved as early as possible.

BY PRIVATE BUS   There are dozens of daily and nightly private, air-conditioned buses to Chiang Mai and other northern cities, as well as cheaper, less comfortable, public buses from Bangkok's Northern Bus Terminal.

GETTING AROUND

BY PUBLIC BUS   Chiang Mai has a fairly efficient if somewhat confusing and often crowded public bus system. There's frequent, inexpensive bus service between Chiang Mai and other northern cities. You'll also find *songtao,* pickup trucks fitted with long bench seats (also known locally as *seelor* or four wheels), that ply the streets of Chiang Mai as well as all the major roads throughout the north, with no fixed schedule or stopping points.

BY CAR   Renting your own car not only allows you freedom, but gives you the chance to see the beautiful countryside as well. Roads are well paved and safe, with frequent petrol stations and restaurants in towns. Avis has branches in Chiang Mai, Chiang Rai, and Mae Hong Son (which is great if you'd like to rent the car in one city and drop it off at another). While larger rental companies have better insurance policies, they're expensive. Local companies in Chiang Mai, Chiang Rai, and Mae Hong Son will save you money, and in many instances their insurance coverage isn't half bad. Most will meet you at the airport with your car for no extra charge. If you'll be

A Serious Warning to Explorers

Motorcyclists and trekkers face a real danger in northern Thailand that mustn't be downplayed or overlooked. Thailand's national border with neighboring Burma (Myanmar) isn't marked with signs along the frontier. Even the most innocent wanderings across the border can land you in custody of Shan State rebels, who don't care if you have a visa, and don't accept American Express. Travelers have been held in custody for weeks, interrogated, and harassed. Sure, your travel journal will look really cool, but your vacation will be miserable.

When touring these areas, don't rely too heavily on your map, which is probably not completely accurate, or your navigational skills, which will be off-kilter in a foreign environment. Stay with an experienced guide, or, if by yourself, keep a very wide safety distance from border territories to allow for miscalculations.

Still, if you're nervous, you can register with your home country's consulate in Chiang Mai or Bangkok, notify them of your travel plans, and provide them with your return date. If you disappear, they'll have a clue. If you plan to cross the Burmese border, and are permitted at the official border crossing at Mae Sai (it opens and closes on whim), do plenty of research before making the trip. There are some nongovernmental organizations (NGOs) that are familiar with the ins and outs of the area. Talk to United Nations agencies, foreign embassies, the Myanmar embassy, or use the Internet to identify other related nongovernmental organizations, and chat them up for current, practical advice.

driving out to mountain destinations, work with them to pick the most sound cars on the lot. Older cars are reserved for in-town drivers. Refer to the "Getting Around" section in chapters 12 and 13 for office locations and rates.

BY MOTORCYCLE   Seven- to ten-day motorcycle circuits of northern Thailand have become popular, particularly with those who like to explore with freedom, and experience the great outdoors up close. Motorcycles get you from place to place with exhilarating liberty, bringing you closer to the landscape, people, and life around you. Gas stations, small noodle shops, and lodgings along main highways provide peace of mind, while adventures down back roads, and even along jungle trails (for off-road riders), open up worlds unseen to travelers who restrict themselves to buses, or enclose themselves inside a rented motor vehicle. Several tour operators offer guided motorcycle tours from Chiang Mai. See chapter 12 for details.

Many opt to take the plunge themselves, renting bikes in Chiang Mai and taking off for the hills. While there are a few guidebooks on the shelves in Chiang Mai's bookshops that specialize in motorcycle touring in the region, of the ones I've found, most haven't been updated regularly. The most threatening danger comes when bikers are unaware of international border crossings. Steer clear of gray areas on maps where you feel you might be approaching the Myanmar border a little too close (see the warning above). Road conditions change frequently, and maps of off-road paths are especially dicey. Common sense says if you're heading out solo, take the time to talk with folks around town—in guest houses and coffee shops—to find someone who's been there and done it. It will help if you are familiar with motorcycle maintenance and basic repair, so you can inspect your motorcycle before your trip and make quick fixes on the road.

Most riders rent motorcycles in Chiang Mai, and average 100 kilometers to 150 kilometers (62 to 93 miles) a day. Cheaper motorcycles give you the same flexibility as a car; off-road dirt bikes provide access to remote hill-tribe villages. Off-road bikes, such as the 250cc Honda, are commonly available and a good choice because of their added power and large fuel tanks; they rent for about 550B ($14.45) a day or 425B ($11.20) per day on a weekly basis. Small 150cc motorbikes are sometimes the only things available in the smaller villages outside of Chiang Mai. Small fuel tanks make them impractical for longer trips, and they usually aren't sturdy enough for off-road adventure, but they have enough power for most day trips. They rent for about 200B ($5.25) a day or 150B ($3.95) per day on a weekly basis.

Many rental motorcycles are very old and patched together from several different models. Before you make a deal with a rental shop, read the contract. Make sure it includes insurance (only liability coverage for the other party is sold, not for damage to your bike), and make sure that if the motorcycle breaks down due to wear, it's the rental company's responsibility to transport it back home.

Once you've located an acceptable bike and bargained for it, test it on the local streets before departing on a longer trip. Helmets are required by local ordinance in Chiang Mai, and the law was being enforced during our last visit. Be alert and on the defensive with Thai drivers, who often drive recklessly; the British left-hand drive system prevails, but on uncrowded roads they will often take their half of the middle. Watch out for pedestrians, stray dogs, chickens, and water buffalo, which can be especially unpredictable. Always move to the shoulder of the road if a bus or truck tries to overtake you.

4 Tours & Trekking

Tourism in the north developed slowly during the 1970s, but really took off in the early '80s, when backpackers and other assorted intrepids made their way north to see this unique region. The colorful tribal peoples of the hills were an explorer's dream. Isolated from the rest of the country, and the globe, their cultures and lifestyles hadn't yet been influenced by the modern world. For early adventurers, a stay in a tribal village was like living an entry in an anthropologist's journal.

Recent developments have changed the nature of jungle trekking in these parts. Of course, with growing tourism the tribal peoples have been exposed to the outside world. However, modernization within Thailand itself has changed the way these people live. The government has made efforts to incorporate them into the national political culture, environmentalists have worked to spare forests that are destroyed by their slash-and-burn agricultural techniques, and the royal family has taken huge strides to introduce crops to replace their staple opium production. Within these influences the tribal peoples have struggled to maintain their cultural identities, livelihoods, and centuries-old ways of life.

Still, many travelers are drawn to the hill-tribe villages in search of the "authentic" travel experience—to touch a "primitive" culture, unspoiled by modern man, to witness life for these people as it has been for past centuries. Every tour and trekking operator in the region knows about this dream, and is quick to exploit it. All advertise their offerings as "nontourist," "authentic," "alternative," or "remote" to set their tours and treks apart from tacky tourist operations or staged cultural experiences. I'll be honest with you. I can almost guarantee that there are no villages here that are untouched by foreign curiosity. There are no villages that have not experienced the modern world in any way. But don't be discouraged from joining a trek or tour, just be smart about it. If you seek a truly authentic experience, come not to see primitive people, as the tour promoters suggest. Rather, come to learn how these cultures on the margin of society grapple with complex pressures from the national and international scene while maintaining their unique identities. Within this frame of reference you will find your authentic experience.

There are two kinds of hill-tribe operators in northern Thailand: those that offer **tribal village tours** and others that coordinate jungle treks. The former puts together large and small groups to visit villages that are close to major cities and towns. If you join one of these groups, you'll travel by van or coach to up to three villages, each inhabited by a different tribe, and you'll spend about an hour in each one. These villages have had decades of exposure to foreigners, and because they are connected by roads, have some modern conveniences. Some overnight trips will put you up in small hotels or hostels that have been built especially for foreigners. You'll find all sorts of crafts for sale from roadside vendors, elephant trekking, and staged cultural performances that include costume parades with music and dance. These short trips are great for those who would like a closer view of these cultures, but have neither the time nor the physical endurance for a 3-day trek through the jungle.

The second kind of trip is the **jungle trek,** which is longer, with smaller groups (about 4 to 10 people) and closer contact with tribal people. These will last anywhere from 3 days and 2 nights to 2 weeks if enough people are interested to make the longer trip worthwhile. Your journey will combine trekking both by Jeep and on foot, accompanied by a local guide, with some bamboo rafting and elephant trekking thrown in for variety. Most guides come from the low-lying areas in the south of Chiang Mai or from Isan. Few are native to these jungles, although some have quite a few years of experience. All guides are required to attend a special 1-month course at Chiang Mai University and must be licensed by the Tourism Authority.

Don't be intimidated by the trekking aspect, the guides keep a controlled pace, and even if you're not perfectly fit, you shouldn't have a problem keeping up. Most guides have some knowledge of a few tribal languages and will serve as your go-between. They are familiar with the villages they'll take you to, will rehearse you in etiquette and protocol, and will negotiate the terms of your "invitation" with the local village leaders. Your guides will also feed you "jungle food," which is usually simple meals of rice and fish. Don't be surprised if the village slaughters a pig for your coming. If you're a vegetarian, it's a good idea to discuss this with your guide well in advance. Many times in the evenings, villagers will entertain guests with music and dance. All guests are invited to sleep in a separate area of the headman's house, which is usually the largest in the compound. You'll be on mats on the floor, and believe me it ain't Shangri-la.

Some truly adventurous travelers may want to buy a trail map and head out for a village experience sans guide. One word of warning: In addition to knowledge about trails and terrain, guides also understand tribal customs and beliefs, some of which are delicate and not obvious to a newcomer who's just walked in out of the trees. Consider this: Not only would you be running the risk of making a cultural faux pas, you'd be an unexpected guest and could be a terrible inconvenience. There's another reason why you shouldn't go trekking by yourself in these areas. There is a very real danger that you might accidentally cross the border into Myanmar or run into unsavory situations that you will be unprepared to get yourself out of.

There have been incidents of banditry on the trails between villages. Although the authorities have tried their best to cut back on robbery occurrences, it's impossible to police the jungle. Do yourself a favor and don't bring any valuables with you on your trek. You can make arrangements with your hotel or guest house in town to stow these things in the hotel safe while you're away.

One notorious aspect of trekking in the north is the availability of drugs, especially opium. You will more than likely be offered opium directly from a villager, but while this area is rich with secret poppy fields and opium factories, the stuff doled out to trekkers is rarely of high quality. Often diluted with tree sap and tamarind, it's a poor mixture that usually is accepted well by those who have no prior experience with the drug to know the difference.

Be warned that narcotics usage is still illegal, and if you do chance to get caught, you face strict fines, jail time, or perhaps even loss of your right to travel in Thailand. Although the Thai government is serious about tackling the problem, they feel that busting short-term visitors (who are usually only trying it once out of curiosity) doesn't get to the heart of the problem. In May 1999, the authorities began a new campaign of financial incentives for villages that clean up their acts and have started to test guides for usage. Guides that are found to be addicted (as many of them are) have their licenses revoked. There's a fund available to rehabilitate them and find placement in other industries. Tour operators also run the risk of being shut down if found to promote drug usage, or if too many of their guides fail urine tests.

TREKKING COMPANIES

The TAT publishes a list of trekking companies that operate out of Chiang Mai and Chiang Rai, but elsewhere, you're on your own. Be warned that the TAT, as a government agency, is very hesitant to recommend specific operations to travelers, for fear of being criticized for favoritism. However, the problem isn't finding a trek—there are several leaving every day from Chiang Mai, and a growing number from Chiang Rai, Mae Hong Son, and Pai—it's finding one that combines experienced and knowledgeable guides, an intelligent itinerary, a compatible group, and appropriate timing, all at an acceptable price. I've talked with trekking companies and interviewed trekkers and residents (both local and foreign) to glean information about operations with the best reputations, the most unique tours, and the most reliable guides, and have listed my picks in the "What to See & Do" section for each northern destination. My recommendations are sound, yet you might want to check around on your own before you select one. Some elements you should weigh in choosing a trek are explained below.

The Guide   If there's one single element of a trek that will make or break the experience, it's the guide. Although most claim to speak a number of hill-tribe languages, it's impossible to be fluent in so many different dialects with no written alphabet; besides, their command of English is the most important thing. Hill-tribe guides usually know key phrases in other tongues, are familiar with the best trails, are well informed about the area and people, and are usually pretty interesting characters themselves. Try to meet your prospective guide and ask lots of questions.

Also ask if there are two guides for your trek. A backup is always a good thing if you should run into trouble somewhere.

The Itinerary   Several well-known Chiang Mai agencies offer prepackaged routes that leave on a regularly scheduled basis. If you intend to head for more remote spots, you might either have to arrange a custom tour (more expensive) or call around to see if anyone happens to offer such a trip.

For those who intend to visit the Golden Triangle or Mae Salong or Pai in the northwest, most trekking companies offer a 2- or 3-day trek. Those who want to travel east to Phayao or Nan will have to dig a little to find an appropriate outfit. If you're not up to trekking—usually 3 to 6 hours of unhurried walking—but want to visit some of the hill-tribe villages, inquire about Jeep trips. Nearly all trekking itineraries list the various hill-tribe villages visited; try to read as much as you can and decide for yourself which you'd most like to see.

Most treks start with a Jeep or minibus drive, or a raft or boat trip, to the head of the trail, which can take up to a full day. Plan on spending 2 or 3 days for a nearby trek and between 5 days and 2 weeks for the more remote spots.

The Group   Treks can made more enjoyable or annoying by the composition of the group. If you're planning a long, arduous trip, try to meet your fellow travelers before committing; you might find that their stamina, assumptions, interests, and/or personalities are not compatible with yours. Look for an agency that limits the number of people to about 10 per trek. Having at least 4 in the group minimizes personality clashes and adds conviviality.

The Season   Seasonality plays some part in trekking; see "When to Go," above, for more information.

What to Bring   Most trekkers come to Thailand on vacation, totally unprepared for a serious trek. That's fine because most treks are on well-traveled paths, up and down rolling, cultivated hillsides, and require no special equipment. Good sneakers or walking shoes are usually adequate, though rainy season trekkers will fare better in waterproof, nonskid hiking boots. A wool sweater for evenings and some outerwear to sleep in will come in handy. (Many trekking companies only provide blankets.) We suggest long pants rather than shorts because of the sometimes dense underbrush and the nightly mosquito raids. A flashlight, supply of tissues or toilet paper, mosquito repellent, and a basic first-aid kit with blister remedies is also recommended.

Some people like to bring gifts for the villagers they encounter. The best and most convenient gifts to bring are coloring books, crayons, pencils, and paper for the children. You can also ask your guide for other recommendations before the trip. He may know the specific needs of the villagers in the places you'll be visiting.

Price   The last criterion is price, though you shouldn't get too stingy here because even the most expensive treks cost less than 1 night at a hotel and three restaurant meals. Some negotiation may be in order, especially if you are traveling with a larger group of people. However, these days, most of the treks are fixed price. At the time of writing, treks ranged from about 500B to 2,000B ($13.15 to $52.65) per person per night, with prices changing inversely with the number of participants and length of a longer trek. Typically, food is included in the fee. Some budget operators charge separately for transportation to and from the trailhead. Some companies provide sleeping bags, backpacks, and water bottles free of charge, while others rent them.

12 Chiang Mai

Chiang Mai ("New City") was founded in 1296 by King Mengrai as the capital of the first independent Tai state, Lanna Thao (Kingdom of One Million Rice Fields). It became the cultural and religious center of the northern Tai, those who had migrated from southern China to dwell in Thailand, and remained so throughout the turbulent period of recurring Burmese attacks. The Burmese finally captured Chiang Mai in 1556 and occupied it until King Taksin recaptured the city in 1775 and drove the Burmese forces back to the approximately present border. Burmese influence on religion, architecture, language, cuisine, and culture, however, remains strong.

Local princes, *chao,* remained in nominal control of the city, though they deferred to the king of Siam in Bangkok. In 1874, King Chulalongkorn (Rama V), concerned with encroachment by the British (who had teak-logging interests as occupiers of Burma) and fearful of a conflict with them, sent a commission to Chiang Mai, which eventually limited the power of the local princes and brought the Lanna kingdom further under the control of the central government in Bangkok. In 1939, the city was formally and fully integrated into the kingdom of Thailand, becoming the administrative center of northern Thailand. In 1996, the city celebrated its 700th anniversary.

In the last half century, the population of the city has grown rapidly, so that it's now Thailand's second city, with a population of more than 200,000. With this growth have come the attendant problems of air pollution, rush-hour traffic, and water shortages, though not quite nearly as bad as Bangkok, as well as the displacement of tribal people in the nearby hills and valleys to make way for the development of retirement and vacation-home communities.

It would be difficult to find a city that reflects more of the country's diverse cultural heritage and modern aspirations than Chiang Mai. Tour buses crowd Burmese-style wats ablaze with the color of saffron and humming with the chanting of monks. Traditional open-air markets sell handicrafts, produce, plastic utensils, and motorcycle parts. Narrow streets lined with ornately carved teak houses lie in the shadow of contemporary skyscrapers. Chiang Mai's heart is its Old City, an area surrounded by vestiges of walls and moats originally constructed for defense. Yet Chiang Mai as a whole is a modern city, with the usual advantages and disadvantages. No visitor to Thailand should miss it.

Because of its temperate climate (similar to the hill stations in nearby Myanmar), many Thais choose Chiang Mai as a summer retreat during March, April, and May, when the rest of the country is wilting under the heat. Its central location makes Chiang Mai an excellent base for exploring the north of Thailand.

1 Orientation

ARRIVING

BY PLANE   In planning your trip, keep in mind that Chiang Mai connects with many other cities outside of Thailand. **Lao Aviation** (☎ 053/418-258) links Chiang Mai to Vientiane and Luang Prabang twice weekly, while Air Mandalay also has twice-weekly flights to Yangon, traveling on to Mandalay, in Myanmar. **Malaysia Airlines** (☎ 053/276-523), and **Silk Air** (☎ 053/276-459) each fly to and from Kuala Lumpur and Singapore, respectively. Both make the trip two times a week. Within Thailand, **Thai Airways,** 240 Propokklao Rd. (☎ 053/210-210) flies from Bangkok to Chiang Mai 10 times daily (trip time: 1 hour, 10 minutes). There's a daily flight from Phitsanulok with a stop in Mae Hong Son (trip time: 1 hour, 45 minutes); and one daily from Chiang Rai (trip time: 40 minutes). Call Thai Airways in Bangkok at 02/232-8000, in Phitsanulok at 055/258-020, and in Chiang Rai at 053/740-309.

 Bangkok Airways, Chiang Mai International Airport, Level 2 (☎ 053/281-519; in Bangkok 02/229-3456), has a daily flight from Bangkok with a stop in Sukhothai. **Angel Air,** 2/1–2 Prachasumpun Rd. (☎ 053/279-172) has four flights weekly from Udon Thani in Isan.

 The **Chiang Mai International Airport** (☎ 053/270-222) houses several banks, a post and overseas call office, and an information booth.

 Thai Airways can provide minivan service for the airport with advance notice. Taxis from the airport are expensive, once you realize how close the airport is to the center of town. Still, if you've never been here before, it's the most convenient way to get to your hotel. Find taxis just outside the arrival hall. They'll charge up to 120B ($3.15) for the service.

BY TRAIN   Of the seven daily trains from Bangkok to Chiang Mai, the 8:10am Express Diesel Railcar (11 hours; 681B ($16.25) second-class sleeper berth) is the quickest. The other trains take between 13 and 15 hours for the trip, but second-class sleeper berths are comparable in price (but some trains don't have sleeper cars at all). Private sleeper cabins (1193B/$31.40), available on certain express and rapid trains, should be reserved as early as possible. Purchase tickets at Bangkok's **Hua Lampong Railway Station** (☎ 02/223-7010) up to 90 days in advance. For local train information in Chiang Mai call ☎ 053/245-363, for advance booking call 053/242-094.

BY BUS   There are several buses to choose from, depending on your budget and the level of comfort you desire—either one you choose, the trip is still 11 hours. From Bangkok's **Northern Bus Terminal** (☎ 02/272-5761) on Phahonyothin Road near the Chatuchak Weekend Market, five daily VIP buses provide the most comfort, with larger seats that recline (470B/$12.35), government air-conditioned buses cost 237B ($6.25). There's also frequent service between Chiang Mai and Mae Hong Son, Phitsanulok, and Chiang Rai.

 Most buses arrive at the **Arcade Bus Station** (☎ 053/242-664) on Kaeo Nawarat Road, 3km northeast of the Tha Pae Gate; a few arrive at the **Chang Puak station** (☎ 053/211-586), north of the Chang Puak Gate on Chotana Road. Some of the private bus companies drop their passengers off on the Superhighway, where guest house touts await them. Unless you're exhausted, don't accept their offers and make the extra effort to get to your place of choice on your own. You should be able to find a tuk-tuk or songtao.

VISITOR INFORMATION

The **TAT** office is at 105/1 Chiang Mai-Lamphun Rd., 400 meters south of the Nawarat Bridge on the east side of the Ping River (☎ **053/248-604**). There are a couple of free magazines available at hotels and businesses—*Guidelines Chiang Mai* and *Welcome to Chiang Mai and Chiangrai*—which contain detailed maps, as well as useful and interesting information. I personally think the latter is better for maps and useful information.

CITY LAYOUT

The heart of Chiang Mai is the **Old City,** completely surrounded by a well-tended moat (restored in the 19th century) and a few remains of the massive wall, laid out in a square aligned on the cardinal directions. Several of the original gates have been restored and serve as handy reference points. Within the Old City are three of the area's more important wats: Wat Chedu Luang, Wat Phra Singh, and Wat Chiang Man.

Most of the major streets radiate from the Old City and fan out in all directions. The main business and shopping area is the half-mile stretch between the east side of the Old City and the Ping River. Here you will find the Night Market, many shops, better hotels, guest houses and restaurants, a slew of trekking companies (especially along Tha Pae Road), and some of the most picturesque back streets in the area. The main post office and train station are farther east on Tha Pae Road, known as Charoen Muang after it crosses the river on Nawarat Bridge.

As you exit the Old City on the west side from the Suan Dok Gate, Suthep Road leads out to Wat Suan Dok, with its whitewashed chedis. The road leading out from the northwest corner of the Old City is Huai Kaeo, with a strip of modern hotels, the zoo, university, and ultimately Doi Suthep mountain. Atop this peak is the most regal of all Chiang Mai Buddhist compounds, Wat Phra That Doi Suthep.

The Superhighway circles the outskirts of the city from west of town north from Suthep Road around to the airport on the southwest.

2 Getting Around

BY BUS Local minibuses cost 5B to 40B (15¢ to $1.05) for most in-town destinations, but they are often packed and follow rather confusing routes that are more for out-of-town destinations. The minibus to Wat Pra That on Doi Suthep mountain costs 35B (90¢)and 25B (65¢)to return.

From Chang Puak Bus Station, there is frequent, inexpensive bus service to the nearby villages of Sankamphaeng (red-white buses cost 4B/10¢, Lamphun bus no. 181 or 35 costs 8B/20¢, Bo Sang bus no. 2259 costs 4B/10¢, and the Hang Dong minibus costs 55B/$1.45). These buses can also be flagged down on the highways that lead out of town to these destinations.

BY SONGTAO These red pickup trucks fitted with two long bench seats are also known locally as *seelor* (four wheels). They ply all the major roads throughout the city, day and night, with no fixed stopping points. Hail one going in your general direction and tell the driver your destination. (*Tip:* Have your hotel or guest house concierge write your destination in Thai before you head out). If it fits in with the destinations of other passengers, you'll get a ride to your door for only 5B to 20B (15¢ to 55¢). If you can deal with a bit of uncertainty along the confusing twist of roads, it's a great way to explore the city—cheap, fast, and the drivers are honest.

BY TUK-TUK   The ubiquitous tuk-tuk (motorized three-wheeler) is the next best option. The fare within Chiang Mai is always negotiable—and you will have to bargain hard to get a good rate—but expect to pay about 30B to 100B (80¢ to $2.65) for an in-town ride.

Many tuk-tuk drivers will hustle you with a shopping tour of their "favorite" shops and factories, then pocket hefty commissions on your purchases. And be careful of the drivers who lurk around major hotels, hounding guests as they exit. Their prices are always inflated. Still, many drivers have emigrated from Bangkok, speak good English, and are fun to ride with. Just make sure you go where *you* want to go: A favorite ploy is pretending they have never heard of your destination.

BY CAR   **Avis** has an office at 14/14 Huai Kaeo Rd. (☎ and fax **053/221-316**), opposite the Chiang Mai Orchid Hotel. Self-drive rental rates for cars and Jeeps start at 1,800B ($47.35) a day or 9,000B ($236.85) a week for unlimited kilometers. Expect to pay 6,300B ($165.80) per day for a Volvo with a driver.

There are dozens of local car-rental companies that rent self-drive sedans for 1,000 to 1,400B ($26.30 to $36.85) per day, and Suzuki Caribians for as low as 750B ($19.75) per day (if you bargain well). Most travel agents will arrange a car and driver for about 1,600B ($42.10) per day. I've used **North Wheels,** 127/2 Moonmuang Rd. (☎ **053/216-189**), with great success. They'll greet you at the airport, and drop you there when you leave, or make deliveries to your hotel, no problem. They even took me back to the lot to let me inspect and select the car I wanted myself.

BY BICYCLE   Biking in the city isn't exactly the best way to get around for safety reasons, but if you'd like to try your hand, stop in one of the many guest houses in or around the old city for a rental. Pay about 30B (80¢) per day. Pay attention to one-way streets, as well as tuk-tuks, motorcycles, samlors, and other smaller vehicles that are known to weave through slower traffic, and try to avoid rush-hour jams.

BY MOTORCYCLE   Many guest houses along the Ping River and shops around Chaiyapoom Road (north of Tha Pae Road in the Old City) rent 100cc motorcycles for about 200B (5.25¢) per day. The 250cc Hondas are commonly available and a good choice because of their added power and large fuel tanks; they rent for about 550B ($14.45). Make sure you have the necessary insurance, wear a helmet, and expect to leave your passport as security (don't leave any credit cards). Traffic congestion makes driving within the city dangerous, so employ all your defensive driving techniques.

Fast Facts: Chiang Mai

Airport   See "Arriving," above in this chapter.

American Express   Sea Tours Co. Ltd., 2/3 Prachasampan Rd., off Chang Klan Road (☎ **053/271-441**), is the American Express representative.

Area Code   The area code is 053 for the Chiang Mai region.

ATMs   For ATMs and money changers, go to Chang Klan Road and Charoen Prathet Road, around the Night Market, for the most convenient major bank branches.

Bookstores   There are a few with a good selection of English-language novels and travel books. The best is **Suriwong Book Centre,** 54/1–5 Sri Dornchai (☎ **053/281-052**). **D. K. Books,** 234 Tha Pae Rd. (☎ **053/251-555**), has a good selection as well, but beware—they have a "store policy" 3% credit-card surcharge.

Car Rentals   See "Getting Around: By Car," above in this chapter.

Climate   See "When to Go" in chapter 11.

Consulates   There are many representative offices in Chiang Mai. Contacts are as follows: **American Consulate General** (☎ 053/252-629), **Canadian Honorary Consul** (☎ 053/850-147), **Australian Honorary Consul** (☎ 053/221-083), **British Consul** (☎ 053/203-405).

Dentist/Doctor   The American Consulate (see Consulates above) will supply you with a list of English-speaking dentists and doctors. There are also several medical clinics; check with your hotel about the best and nearest facility.

Emergencies   Dial ☎ **199** or 191 in case of emergency.

Holidays   See "When to Go" in chapter 2 and the "Northern Thailand Calendar of Events" in chapter 11, "Exploring Northern Thailand."

Hospitals   In Chiang Mai hospitals offer excellent emergency and general care, with English-speaking nurses and physicians. The best private hospital is **McCormick** on Kaeo Nawarat Road (☎ **053/241-107**) out toward the Arcade Bus Terminal.

Internet   If you're looking for a good Internet cafe, there are a few around, especially in or around guest houses in the Old City. **Assign Internet** has two branches, the most convenient across from MacDonald's in Chiang Mai Pavilion at the Night Market on 145/23 Chang Klan Rd. (☎ **053/818-911**), with another branch outside the northwest corner of the Old City at 12 Huay Kaew Shopping Center, Huay Kaew Road across from Central Department Store (☎ **053/404-550**).

Pharmacies   There are dozens of pharmacies throughout the city; most are open daily 7am to midnight.

Police   For police assistance, call the **Tourist Police** at ☎ **053/248-130,** or see them at the TAT office.

Post Office   The most convenient branch is at 186/1 on Chang Klan Road (☎ **053/222-483**), with another branch at the airport 053/277-382). The General Post Office is on Charoen Muang (053/241-070), near the train station. The Overseas Call Office, open 24 hours, is upstairs from the GPO and offers phone, fax, and telex services.

Rest Rooms   Large hotels and most restaurants have public rest rooms. Outside the city, small restaurants may charge 2B (10¢) for the use of an Asian toilet. Bring your own toilet paper.

3 Accommodations

NEAR THE PING RIVER
VERY EXPENSIVE

Chiang Inn Hotel. 100 Chang Klan Rd., Chiang Mai 50100. ☎ **053/270-070.** Fax 053/274-299. 190 units. A/C MINIBAR TV TEL. 1,815B ($47.75) double; from 7,000B ($184.20) suite. AE, DC, MC, V. 2 blocks south of Tha Pae Rd., 2 blocks west of river, just north of Night Market.

The renovated Chiang Inn is right across the street from the Chiang Inn Plaza, an arcade of Western chain eateries like MacDonald's and Dunkin Donuts, but it's set back from the lively street and quieter at night than you'd expect. The compact, teak-paneled lobby has a homey yet elegant feel and is almost always crowded with

Europeans. Spacious rooms are clean but are decorated in a bland fashion that's not much in keeping with the price of the facility. Still, for location, the Chiang Inn is tops. After touring the city and its sights, you'll appreciate relaxing around the large pool and sundeck, or playing tennis on the outdoor courts. Be warned, though, the Chiang Inn is a favorite hangout for tuk-tuk drivers who try to charge visitors an arm and a leg and take them to places they don't wish to visit.

Dining/Diversions: The coffee shop is popular and good, but the real star is their French restaurant, La Grillade. There is also a lobby cocktail bar and the city's favorite disco, "The Wall."

Amenities: Large pool with a sundeck, tennis courts, business center, shopping arcade, excellent traditional Thai massage on the basement level, room service, concierge, laundry service, and complimentary airport transfer.

Chiang Mai Plaza Hotel. 92 Sri Dornchai Rd., Chiang Mai 50100. ☎ **053/270-036.** Fax 053/279-457. 444 units. A/C MINIBAR TV TEL. 2,400B–2,800B ($63.15–$73.70) double; from 10,000B ($263.15) suite. AE, DC, MC, V. Between Chang Klan and Charoen Prathet rds., midway between Old City and river.

These two 12-story towers, completed in 1986, form a typically bland, modern Western hotel, but guest rooms are large, plush, and offer city and mountain views. The lobby is so spacious that the especially attentive staff and decorative furniture seem almost lost in acres of brilliantly polished granite. The Plaza is also well located— in town, but just far enough away, toward the Ping River, to be out of the congestion. The swimming pool area is surrounded by Lanna-style pavilions, a view that is shared with the fitness center.

Dining/Diversions: The huge Fai Kum restaurant serves Thai and continental cuisine. There is a lobby bar, where a classical Thai quartet performs traditional music nightly. For more action try the Twinkle Lounge hostess club or the popular Plaza Disco.

Amenities: Swimming pool, fitness center, and shopping arcade, 24-hour room service, concierge, limousine service, baby-sitting (with notice), laundry service.

The Empress Hotel. 199/42 Chang Klan Rd., Chiang Mai 50100. ☎ **053/270-240.** Fax 053/272-467. 375 units. A/C MINIBAR TV TEL. 3,000B–4,000B ($78.95–$105.25) double; from 8,400B ($221.05) suite. AE, DC, MC, V. A 15-min. walk south of Night Market, 2 blocks from river.

This 17-story tower, opened in 1990, is a little bit south of the main business and tourist area, which makes it especially quiet. The impressive public spaces are filled with glass, granite, and chrome and well-integrated touches of Thai style. The large rooms with picture windows are done in a tasteful, modern interpretation of Asian decor, using primarily rose-and-peach tones. Bathrooms are small but include many toiletries.

Dining/Diversions: Panda Palace, a Peking-style Chinese restaurant, is located on the mezzanine level. La Brasserie is a formal continental grill with an attached wine cellar. There's a coffee shop, an Asian cocktail lounge with live entertainment, and several bars and lounges, plus the very popular Crystal Cave Disco.

Amenities: Fitness center, 24-hour room service, midsized outdoor pool, concierge, limousine service, laundry service.

✪ **Royal Princess Hotel.** 112 Chang Klan Rd., Chiang Mai 50100. ☎ **053/281-033.** Fax 053/281-044. www.royalprincess.com. 198 units. A/C MINIBAR TV TEL. 3,000B–3,300B ($78.95–$86.85) double; from 9,500B ($250) suite. Peak season (Dec–Jan 10) 500B ($13.15). AE, DC, MC, V. Located just at the Night Market, across from Chiang Mai Pavilion (shopping center).

The northern cousin of Bangkok's deluxe Dusit Thani is a first-rate city hotel. Furnishings are tasteful, with elements of Thai art and discreet luxury. The extremely busy staff is always helpful and courteous. Surprisingly quiet rooms overlook the glittering lights of the city. They're a good size, clean, and—though not new—impressively well maintained. Cotton bathrobes and slippers, a hair dryer, and personal safe are standard amenities. The sometimes frenetic lobby has a comfortable bar. The pleasant coffee shop serves an elaborate breakfast buffet with delicious pastries and the Jasmine restaurant serves excellent dim sum at lunch. While the small swimming pool isn't the most atmospheric, their traditional Thai massage service in the basement is excellent (300B/$7.90 per hour).

Suriwongse Zenith Hotel. 110 Chang Klan Rd., Chiang Mai 50100. ☎ **053/270-051.** Fax 053/270-063. 168 units. A/C MINIBAR TV TEL. 2,200–2,600 ($57.90–$68.40) double; from 4,700 ($123.70) suite. AE, DC, JCB, MC, V. Corner of Loi Kroa Rd., just southwest of Night Market, halfway between Old City and River.

The unique hardwood paneling that covers every inch of the lobby of this comfortable hotel gives it an appealing warmth—this much wood is hard to find in newer places these days. The spacious, teak-trimmed twin bedrooms are among Chiang Mai's better values. Unlike the woody decorative scheme downstairs, the colors in the upstairs guest areas are cheerier off-white and pastel. Higher-priced rooms offer a balcony and better views, but all are equipped with first-class amenities.

Dining/Diversions: The Bistro and its sidewalk cafe serve pricey French and Italian fare but are popular at teatime, when serious shoppers stoke up for a Night Market assault, and make for a great centralized meeting point. The northern-style Thai restaurant, Fueng Fah, has an excellent reputation for local food in an up-market setting. It's also popular with local officials and dignitaries.

Amenities: Room service, concierge, laundry service, fitness center, small shopping arcade.

✪ **The Westin Chiang Mai.** 318/1 Chiangmai-Lamphun Rd., Chiang Mai 50007. ☎ **053/275-300.** Fax 053/275-299. 528 units. A/C MINIBAR TV TEL. 5,200B–8,200B ($136.85–$215.80) double; from 12,500B ($328.95) suite. AE, DC, JCB, MC, V. South of city center, across Mengrai Bridge on east bank of river.

Chiang Mai's newest and best high-rise hotel is isolated across the river just south of town. The attractive lobby is both spacious and welcoming, and the staff is friendly and well trained (making this place particularly suited for business travelers). The rooms are large and plush with subdued colors and attractive teak furnishings, each with a view.

Dining/Diversions: The River Terrace Restaurant serves the best buffet lunch in Chiang Mai, and the Castana, which serves Mediterranean cuisine, the China Palace (with chefs from Hong Kong), and a cafe beside a picturesque outside pool provide an array of dining options. The lobby Vienna Lounge offers a touch of old-world elegance with live music, and the Stars nightclub features a Hollywood theme.

Amenities: Swimming pool, fitness center, beauty salon, 24-hour room service, tour desk, complimentary shuttle to and from airport, voice mail.

EXPENSIVE

The Imperial Mae Ping Hotel. 153 Sri Dornchai Rd., Chiang Mai 50100. ☎ **053/270-160.** Fax 053/270-181. 371 units. A/C MINIBAR TV TEL. 1,648B ($43.35) double; from 4,700B ($123.70) suite. AE, DC, MC, V. Corner of Kampaengdin Rd., 2 blocks southwest of Night Market.

This newer tower hotel is one of the city's best values because of its attractive style and excellent location—a stroll away from the Night Market, yet far enough to get a good

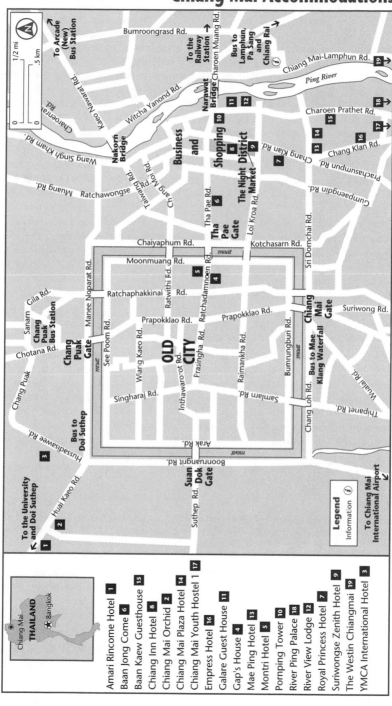

Chiang Mai Accommodations

Amari Rincome Hotel **1**
Baan Jong Come **6**
Baan Kaew Guesthouse **15**
Chiang Inn Hotel **8**
Chiang Mai Orchid **2**
Chiang Mai Plaza Hotel **14**
Chiang Mai Youth Hostel 1 **17**
Empress Hotel **16**
Galare Guest House **11**
Gap's House **4**
Mae Ping Hotel **13**
Montri Hotel **5**
Pornping Tower **10**
River Ping Palace **18**
River View Lodge **12**
Royal Princess Hotel **7**
Suriwongse Zenith Hotel **9**
The Westin Chiangmai **19**
YMCA International Hotel **3**

night's sleep without springing for the 14th- and 15th-floor Executive Club rooms. The unusual double height lobby interprets Thai architectural elements in bold white-and-gold decor, with shops, a tour desk, and other services discreetly included. Large, bright guest rooms have contemporary blond teak furnishings upholstered in peach, jade, or blue, modern conveniences, and mountain views. Sculpted lamp bases and reproductions of temple murals add a classic touch.

Dining/Diversions: There's a coffee shop with a bounteous international lunch buffet, the elegant Ming Ming Chinese Restaurant, the Mae Ping Khantoke with local traditional cuisine and dance performances, plus a lively beer garden.

Amenities: Small swimming pool, shopping arcade, room service, concierge, limousine service, baby-sitting (with notice), laundry service.

Pornping Tower. 46–48 Charoen Prathet Rd., Chiang Mai 50100. ☎ **053/270-099.** Fax 053/270-119. 318 units. A/C MINIBAR TV TEL. 2,399 ($63.15) double. AE, DC, MC, V. Corner of Loi Kroa Rd., 1 block from river.

This 20-story hotel bustles with evening activity at the Bubbles Discotheque, the lower-level cocktail lounge, the lobby bar, and even in the coffee shop. The Hong Kong–style public spaces are of polished marble, glass, and mirrors. Rooms are elegantly furnished in cool colors and contemporary styles. There's an excellent pool with an inviting sundeck, a friendly staff, a popular Chinese restaurant, a rooftop international grill room, and other services that make it one of the best buys in the city.

✪ **River View Lodge.** 25 Charoen Prathet Rd., Soi 2, Chiang Mai 50100. ☎ **053/271-109.** Fax 053/279-019. 36 units. A/C TEL. 1,450B–1,800B ($38.15–$47.35) double. MC, V. On river 2 blocks south of Thae Pae Rd.

Veteran shopper and mapmaker Nancy Chandler stays here when in Chiang Mai, and for good reason. First of all, River View's location makes for a peaceful retreat, and yet it's only a short hop to the city's main business and shopping district. Second, the atmosphere is fabulous, from the antiques (all for sale) scattered throughout the hotel's public spaces to the quaint, shady garden that separates the small swimming pool from the open-sided cafe restaurant. Large guest rooms have fresh terra-cotta tile floors with simple but well-maintained wood furnishings and no fuss decor. Bathrooms have shower stalls only, and some of the rooms have wall-to-wall carpeting, which doesn't feel as cooling as the tiled rooms. Rates vary depending on the view, and many rooms have balconies.

MODERATE

Baan Kaew Guesthouse. 142 Charoen Prathet Rd., Chiang Mai 50100. ☎ **053/271-606.** Fax 053/273-436. 20 units. TEL. 450B ($11.85) double with A/C; 350B ($9.20) double with fan. Rates include tax and service. No credit cards. South of Loi Kroa Rd. opposite Wat Chaimongkol; enter gate, turn left, and find guest house well back from street.

This motel-style guest house, in an enclosed compound in a peaceful neighborhood, has a well-tended garden and a manicured lawn large enough for kids to play. Rooms are simple and spotless, with tiled bathrooms with hot-water showers. Fan-cooled rooms have screened windows overlooking the grounds. Breakfast is served in a shaded pavilion, and snacks can be had all day at picnic tables on the lawn.

Galare Guest House. 7 Charoen Prathet Rd., Soi 2, Chiang Mai 50100. ☎ **053/818-887.** Fax 053/279-088. 35 units. A/C TEL. 680B ($17.90) double. MC, V. On river south of Tha Pae Rd.

If the River View Lodge (see "Expensive," above) is booked or you want to save the baht, try the smaller Galare, almost next door. It's a modern, Thai-style, three-story, brick and wood motel, with broad covered verandas overlooking a pleasant garden and courtyard. Rooms are small but have air-conditioning and king-size beds. They're comfortable and tastefully furnished. The very affordable restaurant serves breakfast, lunch, and dinner on a covered deck overlooking the river. Sam's Trekking, based at the Galare, organizes treks to hill-tribe villages as well as local tours of Chiang Mai.

✪ **River Ping Palace.** 385/2 Charoen Prathet Rd., Chiang Mai 50100. ☎ **053/274-932.** Fax 053/273-675. 11 units. A/C MINIBAR. 600B–900B ($15.80–$23.70) double; 1,400B ($36.85) suite. AE, MC, V. On the river, a 20-min. walk south of the Night Market, between Monfort College and the Mengrai Bridge.

If you really want a taste of old Thailand, check into the River Ping Palace for a night. This old lovingly restored compound of teak houses that were once a private residence has been converted into a guest house, dressed in four-poster beds with romantic mosquito netting, antique cabinets, rattan armchairs, Victorian brass wall sconces, framed historical photos, and unique accessories. The upstairs lanai overlooking the river is especially wonderful for enjoying lazy afternoon cocktails. The only complaint is that the facility is not exactly modern—it's difficult fitting so many functioning bathrooms into the old dame, so you must sacrifice a little convenience, especially during rainstorms when the roof gets leaky in spots. The management fights a never-ending battle to keep up with maintenance. At the time of writing, the suite room, located in its own teak house, was under renovation. Still in all, it's ambience and authenticity in one wild package. Its restaurant, Once Upon a Time, serves excellent northern cuisine, and is reviewed later in this chapter.

INEXPENSIVE

Chiang Mai Youth Hostel. 21/8 Chang Klan Rd., Mooban Oon-Ruen, Chiang Mai 50000. ☎ **053/276-737.** Fax 053/204-025. E-mail Chiangmai@tyha.org. 16 units. 180B ($4.75) double. Rates include tax and service. MC, V. 1.5km (1 mile) south of Night Market.

Though the location isn't convenient, this is by far the best youth hostel in town; it's especially quiet, and a good spirit prevails. Spotless, twin-bedded rooms have private hot-water showers and either a fan or air-conditioning; bunks in the spick-and-span dorm are fan-cooled. There's laundry service and a highly recommended trekking company. Breakfast is served in a proper dining room. A free nightly shuttle takes you to the Night Market.

IN THE OLD CITY
MODERATE

Baan Jong Come. 47 Soi 4, Tha Pae Rd., Chiang Mai 50100. ☎ **053/274-823.** 28 units. 450B ($11.85) double with A/C; 350B ($9.20) double with fan. Rates include tax and service. No credit cards. 3 blocks east of Tha Pae Gate, 2 blocks south, on left.

This attractive, three-story lodge is one of the best guest houses in this part of town. It's conveniently located, yet fairly quiet. Bright, airy rooms, as well as the fully tiled bathrooms with showers, are very clean. All have a comfortable seating area, screened windows, and fans; higher-priced rooms also have air-conditioning, though you probably won't need it—unless you need some extra quiet. The open-sided ground floor has a TV lounge, a good inexpensive restaurant (try their *kuai tiao* rice noodles), and a reputable trekking office.

Gap's House. 3 Soi 4, Ratchadamnoen Rd., Chiang Mai 50000. ☎ and fax **053/278-140.** 18 units. 450B ($11.85) double; 600B ($15.80) suite. Rates include American breakfast, tax, and service. MC, V. 1 block west of Tha Pae Gate on left.

Gap's House is centrally located yet quiet, comfortable yet traditional, recently built yet with plenty of Lanna Thai style. Excellent values, but book ahead for the less expensive rooms. Most of the rooms are tucked into free-standing teak houses, with polished floors and walls, woven rattan beds, kitschy upholstered chairs, and clean, tiled bathrooms. There's a block of four attached rooms that are smaller and usually rented to singles, as well as a double suite with a TV and minibar. Bargain rates include breakfast, served in the teak dining pavilion in the middle of their flower-filled garden. The manager, Mr. Preecha, is friendly and informative.

Montri Hotel. 2–6 Ratchadamnoen Rd., Chiang Mai 50100. ☎ **053/211-069.** Fax 053/217-416. 80 units. TV TEL. 560B ($14.75) double with A/C. Rates include tax and service. MC, V. Just northwest across from Tha Pae Gate.

This is a good, inexpensive choice in a very convenient and busy location. Ask for a back room—don't accept a fan-cooled room because of the street noise, but the renovated rooms with air-conditioning are attractive, comfortable, and a very good value. The Montri also boasts JJ's Coffee shop and Bakery, a great place to eat Western food.

INEXPENSIVE

✪ **Top North Guest House.** 15 Moon Muang Rd., Soi 2, Chiang Mai 50100. ☎ **053/298-900.** Fax 053/278-485. 90 units. 500B ($13.15) double with A/C; 300B ($7.90) double with fan. MC, V.

This is not your average guest house. Tucked away on one of the Old City's narrow lanes, the quiet Top North is like a minihotel. It's quiet and comfortable, and guests are invited to relax by the pool, which is large for the price, or sit for a spell in the laid-back Thai/Western coffee shop. Rooms are big, with clean tiled floors, large bathrooms (with bathtubs!), and the most unique blue-and-white stencil painting on the walls. Top North also has a good tour operation that organizes treks and an Internet cafe on premises.

WESTSIDE/HUAI KAEO ROAD
VERY EXPENSIVE

The Amari Rincome Hotel. 1 Nimmanhaeminda Rd., off Huay Kaeo Road, Chiang Mai 50200. ☎ **053/221-130.** Fax 053/221-915. www.amari.com. 158 units. A/C MINIBAR TV TEL. $170–$241 double; from $188 suite. AE, DC, MC, V. Near Superhighway northwest of Old City.

This tranquil hotel complex is a favorite because of its elegant, yet traditional, Thai atmosphere. The public spaces are decorated with local handicrafts, and the professional staff wears intricately embroidered costumes. The large, balconied guest rooms are elaborately adorned with Burmese tapestries and carved wood accents in local style, and the bathrooms are plush. At press time they were undergoing a massive renovation project of many of the public spaces, and the final results expect to be quite lovely.

Dining/Diversions: The Gritta Italian Restaurant is excellent and well known in the city. Coffee shop and lobby lounge, the Thing Kwow is a hearty handsome teak restaurant serving a hearty lunch buffet and international cuisine by candlelight.

Amenities: Two swimming pools (one Olympic-size), tennis courts, jogging track, shopping arcade, 24-hour room service, concierge, limousine service, baby-sitting (with notice), laundry service.

Chiang Mai Orchid. 100-102 Huai Kaeo Rd., Chiang Mai 50200. ☎ **053/222-099.** Fax 053/221-625. Bangkok reservations call 02/252-5265, fax 02/251-0936. 262 units. A/C MINIBAR TV TEL. 1,848B–1,980B ($48.65–$52.10) double; 5,940B ($156.30) suite. AE, DC, JCB, MC, V. Northwest of Old City, next door to Gad San Kaew/Central Shopping Complex.

The Orchid has a well-deserved reputation for sophisticated facilities and friendly service. The lobby and other public spaces are furnished with clusters of chic, low-slung rattan couches and chairs and decorated with flowers. Spacious, quiet rooms are pleasantly decorated with local wood carvings. There's a children's play center and a knowledgeable tour desk.

Dining: There's an excellent continental restaurant, Le Pavillon; an open-air Thai restaurant/coffee shop for northern specialties; a new Chinese restaurant; and a poolside snack bar. The lobby's coffee bar serves European pastries, tea, and 11 brewed coffees, 2 to 9pm.

Amenities: Large swimming pool, health club with aerobics classes, traditional Thai massage parlor, shopping arcade, 24-hour room service, concierge, limousine service, baby-sitting (with notice), laundry service.

Holiday Inn Green Hills. 24 Chiang Mai-Lamphang Superhighway, Chiang Mai 50200. ☎ **053/220-100,** or 02/245-1383 in Bangkok. Fax 053/221-602, or 02/248-2264 in Bangkok. 200 units. A/C MINIBAR TV TEL. 2,825B–3,296B ($74.35–$86.75) double; from 5,297B ($139.40) suite. AE, DC, MC, V. On Superhighway north of Huai Kaeo Rd., 6km (3.7 miles) north of airport.

This recently completed deluxe facility offers the bland Western comfort and glossy style of the chain. It's right around the corner from the Nimhaeminda Arcade, which houses some of Chiang Mai's nicest stores. The lobby has a striking peaked orange ceiling with dark green inset circles and some touches of Thai style in carved furniture and wall hangings, but the large rooms are strictly Western, with flowered spreads, blond wood, and plush armchairs around small tables. The staff is warm, efficient, and speaks especially good English.

Dining/Diversions: The ornate Cherry Blossoms restaurant specializes in Chinese banquets with exotic dishes like shark-fin soup. The Salathong Thai restaurant serves up traditional local dishes. For a lower-key, lower-priced Italian meal, try Pinocchio's (the wooden puppet on its door is especially inviting to children). The Mariko Karaoke bar and a poolside cafe serve lighter fare.

Amenities: Large swimming pool, health club with aerobics classes, traditional Thai massage parlor, shopping arcade, 24-hour room service, concierge, limousine service, baby-sitting (with notice), laundry service.

EXPENSIVE

Holiday Garden Hotel. 16/16 Huai Kaeo Rd., Chiang Mai 50200. ☎ **053/210-901.** Fax 053/210-905. 200 units. A/C MINIBAR TV TEL. 900B ($23.70) double garden wing; 1,600B–1,900B ($42.10–$50) tower double. AE, DC, MC, V. 4km (2.5 miles) northwest of Old City, past Superhighway on right.

Most of the hotel, opened in 1987, is in well-kept buildings set in a U-shape around a small pool and garden. In 1990, a sparkling 12-story tower was built, adding an ultramodern glass-walled elevator, a large gray granite lobby, a pool-view coffee shop, and more than 100 compact, well-designed, tasteful guest rooms. Rates vary according to location and view. The older, high-ceilinged garden wing rooms seem more colonial and are a bit worn, but they're very comfortable and an excellent value. The hotel retains its Thai homeyness, and the management is very friendly. Besides the coffee shop, there is a casual Thai restaurant and outdoor bar by the pool.

INEXPENSIVE

YMCA International Hotel. 11 Sermsuk Rd., Mengrairasmi, Chiang Mai 50200. ☎ **053/221-819.** Fax 053/215-523. 31 units. TEL. 600B ($15.80) double with A/C. AE, MC, V. West off Hatsadhisawee Rd., north of the Thai Public Library.

The YMCA is convenient, but difficult to find. (From the northwest corner of the Old City, continue north past the Public Library, take the first left and find it on the right.) The hotel has a studious, clean-cut aura, and the modern, carpeted rooms are quiet, and cheap. There are many choices, ranging from a suite with minibar and TV; to private rooms with fans, air-conditioning, and private shower; to dorm-style with common bathroom. Access to the YMCA's laundry, recreation, and business center facilities is included in the price. There's also a good cafeteria, tour desk, and crafts shop.

OUTSIDE CHIANG MAI
VERY EXPENSIVE

✪ **The Regent Chiang Mai.** Mae Rim–Samoeng Old Rd., Mae Rim, Chiang Mai 50180. ☎ **800/545-4000** in the U.S., or 053/298-181. Fax 053/298-190. 67 suites. A/C MINIBAR TV TEL. $320–$410 pavilion suite; $900–$2,00 residence suite. AE, DC, MC, V. 20 min. north of city off Chiangmai-Maerim Rd.

Northern Thailand's finest resort is well isolated from the bustle of the city on 20 acres of landscaped grounds in the Mae Rim Valley. The beautiful central garden includes two small lakes, lily ponds, and terraced rice paddies (which are maintained by the resort), and two story Lanna-style pavilions are clustered informally around it. Spacious suites are understatedly elegant with polished teak floors and vaulted ceilings, decorated with traditional Thai fabrics and art, each with an adjoining private *sala* (open-air pavilion). Bathrooms are particularly large and luxurious, with two vanities, a big sunken tub, and separate shower, overlooking a secluded garden.

The pool is a spectacle. As you stand at the head, the false edge at the opposite end seems to drop off into the paddy fields below and rise into the mountains beyond. At night, torches are lit in the fields, lending a mysterious aura to the views from the resort's restaurants. On a whimsical note, Regent is the only resort in the world to boast its own resident family of water buffalo. For sure, they are the most pampered and prissy beasts you've ever seen. If you're worried about being far from Chiang Mai, the resort provides regular shuttles to and from the main business and shopping district.

Dining/Diversions: The Sala Mae Rim features fine Thai cuisine, including Northern specialties. The Pool Terrace and Bar serves continental breakfast, lunch (including salads, sandwiches, and pizza), and barbecue dinners. The Elephant Bar is a more elegant, open pavilion with a view across the valley, especially sensational at sunset, offering afternoon tea, cocktails, and after dinner drinks.

Amenities: Modern fitness studio, luxurious spa with massage and sauna, two lighted tennis courts with full-time pro, and mountain bikes with maps of the surrounding countryside, 24-hour room service, twice-daily maid service, laundry and pressing service, limousine, personalized sightseeing and excursions.

EXPENSIVE

Chiang Mai Sports Club and Clubhouse Inn. 284 Moo 3, Tambon Donkaew, Amphoe Maerim, Chiang Mai 50180. ☎ **053/298-326.** Fax 053/297-897. 48 units. 2,400B–2,800B ($63.16–$73.68) double; 6,500B ($171,05) suite. A/C MINIBAR TV TEL. AE, DC, MC, V. 7km (4.3 miles) north of center off Chiangmai-Maerim Rd.

This exceptional facility occupies a large park among litchi and longan trees with the sports facilities its name implies. The Inn has a handsome open-air lobby with an excellent restaurant (with Swiss chef) and coffee shop. Very comfortable and attractive guest rooms are isolated beyond the sports facilities, for extra quiet. The staff is friendly and professional, and there's free shuttle service into town twice a day. They even organize local handicraft lessons in pottery, cane seating and basket weaving. This resort is a very unique choice for vacationers.

Amenities: Sports facilities are what distinguishes this place from others. Olympic-size pool, horseback riding lessons, pony trekking, and trail riding.

MODERATE

Chiang Mai Holiday Resort. 39/3 Soi 6, Rat Uthit Rd., Chiang Mai 50000. ☎ **053/277-104.** Fax 053/279-913. 40 units. A/C. 1,000B ($26.30) double room or bungalow. AE, MC, V. East side of river beyond Chiangmai Gymkhana Club; take first right after club.

This small resort isn't exactly out of town, but it will make you feel it is. Lanna-style villas have been integrated into a pretty litchi and longan orchard and landscaped to give a village feel. There's a lot of variation in the rooms, but all are charming and will take you back to earlier times. The staff doesn't speak much English, but they're friendly and cooperative, and if you're patient you'll find a room to your liking.

4 Dining

Northern-style or Lanna Thai cooking has been influenced by the Burmese and other ethnic minorities who live in the area. Among the most distinctive northern Thai dishes are *khao miao* (glutinous or sticky rice) often served in a knotted banana leaf), *sai-ua* (Chiang Mai sausage); *khao soi* (a spicy, curried broth with vegetables and glass noodles), and many other slightly sweet meat and fish curries. You may be relieved to know that chile peppers are used less than in other Thai cuisines.

The formal northern meal is call *khan toke,* referring to the custom of sharing a variety of main courses (eaten with the hands) with guests seated around *khan toke* (low, lacquered teak tables). Most of the restaurants that serve in the khan toke–style combine a dance performance with the meal. These are covered in the nightlife section later in this chapter.

Chiang Mai is also blessed with good street food and markets. The best food markets for tasting local favorites are the Anusarn Market, on the corner of Sri Dornchai and Chang Klan roads near the Night Market, and Somphet Market, on the northwest interior perimeter road in the Old City. You can also try the food stalls on Moon Muang Road at the southwest corner of the Old City, or the outdoor restaurants and stalls on the east side of the Old City at the gate near Loi Kroa Road.

NEAR THE PING RIVER
EXPENSIVE

Jasmine. Royal Princess Hotel, 112 Chang Klan Rd. ☎ **053/281-033.** Reservations recommended. Main courses 250B–1,400B ($6.60–$36.85). AE, DC, MC, V. Daily 11am–2:30pm and 6:30–10pm. CHINESE.

Jasmine is an intimate, quiet, tastefully decorated, and expensive Cantonese restaurant that specializes in dim sum (about 75B/$1.97 for each three- to five-piece serving) at lunch. The variety changes often, but there are normally 12 different mildly spiced, freshly steamed treats from which to choose. Dinner and lunch main courses are deliciously prepared by a Chinese chef. Specialties include bird's-nest and shark's-fin soups, barbecued pig, crystal prawns, and minced squab with lettuce.

La Grillade. In the Chiang Inn Hotel, 100 Chang Klan Rd. ☎ **045/270-070.** Reservations recommended. Main courses 275B–600B ($7.25–$15.80). AE, MC, V. Daily 11:30am–2pm and 6:30–10pm. FRENCH.

The Chiang Inn Hotel's formal Thai-style dining room serves some of the best continental fare in the city, with an emphasis on French cuisine. Comfortable armchairs, crisp linens, gleaming crystal, and attentive service distinguish this from your average casual Thai dining experience. For starters, enjoy fresh asparagus with hollandaise, vegetable salads, and several potages. The red snapper, panfried with capers, is flown in daily from the south, and imported Australian tenderloin is marinated in red wine and cooked with artichoke hearts. French wines are served by the bottle or glass.

✪ **Le Coq d'Or.** 68/1 Koh Klang Rd. ☎ **053/282-024.** Reservations recommended for weekend dinner. 320B–850B ($8.40–$22.35). Daily 11am–2:30pm and 7–11pm. AE, DC, MC, V. 5-min. drive south of the Westin, following the river. FRENCH.

In a romantic English country house setting, Le Coq d'Or is second to none in Chiang Mai for excellent atmosphere, food, presentation, and service. Well-trained waiters serve a small, but mouthwatering assortment of imported beef, lamb, and fish in French and continental styles on white linen and china. My chateaubriand came perfectly rare, with a delicate gravy and béarnaise on the side. For starters, the salmon tartar wrapped in smoked salmon is served with toast, a sour cream and horseradish sauce, and capers. They have a nice wine list to complement your meal. Don't wait for a special occasion.

Piccola Roma. 3/2–3 Charoen Prathet Rd. ☎ **053/271-256.** Reservations recommended. Main dishes 160B–400B ($4.20–$10.55). AE. Daily 11am–2pm and 5–11pm. Near river, south of Nawarat Bridge. ITALIAN.

Locals praise this *taverna* as the best of the city's many Italian restaurants. The northern Italian setting and cuisine is as memorable as your host, executive chef Angelo Faro. Make sure to ask him about his daily recommendations, which depend upon his latest fresh finds at the markets. If you're lucky enough to select a dish that is prepared at your table, there's no extra charge for the entertainment. A good regularly featured menu item is the black linguine in inky squid sauce. A small selection of wines is available to accompany your meal.

White Orchid. Diamond Riverside Hotel, 33/10 Charoen Prathet Rd. ☎ **053/270-080.** Reservations recommended at dinner. Main courses 80B–600B ($2.10–$15.80). MC, V. Daily 11am–2pm and 5–10:30pm. Near river, north of Loi Kroa Rd. and New (Iron) Bridge. CHINESE.

Go past the hotel's tolerable coffee shop and teak Lanna khan-toke house to find this riverside restaurant at the back of the courtyard. You can sit under the covered pavilion or outside in the garden cafe overlooking the river and enjoy such specialties as Peking duck, sliced noodles with shrimp, chicken with cashews, and stir-fried mixed vegetables.

MODERATE

Once Upon a Time. 385/2 Charoen Prathet Rd. ☎ **053/274-932.** Reservations recommended. Main courses 80B–200B ($2.10–$5.25). AE, MC, V. Daily 4:30pm–midnight. Lunch is served during festivals or by request. West side of the river, just north on Mengrai Bridge. THAI.

If you want the best Thai food, in the most beautiful compound of restored teak houses, there's no better choice. The two-story teak dining pavilion shares a tranquil garden with the charming River Ping Palace guest house. Downstairs serves specialties such as *hohmok,* an array of seafood soufflés made with prawn, mussels, or fish and coconut milk; mildly spiced grilled duck in a coconut-milk curry; *pla chon* (fresh river fish served with dipping sauces) and delicious and distinctive *gai yang* (barbecue chicken). Upstairs, under the peaked roof, diners can sit on cushions in the khan toke style and sample the same specials or an array of northern Thai dishes, including pork curry and piquant chile pastes.

The Riverside. 9–11 Charoenrat Rd. ☎ **053/243-239.** Reservations recommended for weekend dinner. Main courses 65B–200B ($1.70–$5.25). Daily 10am–1am. AE, MC, V. East side of river, north of Narawatt Bridge. THAI/INTERNATIONAL.

Casual and cool is what Riverside is all about. It's a tavern with riverside terrace views—make sure you get there before the dinner rush so you get your pick of tables.

Chiang Mai Dining

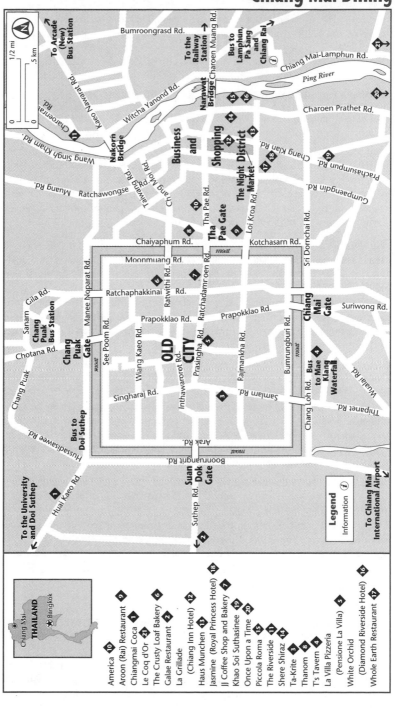

America **10**
Aroon (Rai) Restaurant **1**
Chiangmai Coca **21**
Le Coq d'Or **6**
The Crusty Loaf Bakery **2**
Galae Restaurant **12**
La Grillade
(Chiang Inn Hotel) **13**
Haus Munchen **18**
Jasmine (Royal Princess Hotel) **7**
JJ Coffee Shop and Bakery **19**
Khao Soi Suthasinee **20**
Once Upon a Time **15**
Piccola Roma **11**
The Riverside **14**
Shere Shiraz **3**
Ta-Krite **8**
Thanom **4**
T's Tavern **5**
La Villa Pizzeria
(Pensione La Villa) **16**
White Orchid
(Diamond Riverside Hotel) **17**
Whole Earth Restaurant

There's live music, from blues to soft rock, great Thai and Western food (including burgers), and a full bar. Even if you just stop by for a beer, it's a convivial place that always has a jolly crowd. Full of conversation and laughter, small wonder it's such a favorite with travelers, locals, and expatriates. Riverside also operates a night cruise at 8pm for 50B ($1.30) per person.

☻ **Whole Earth Restaurant.** 88 Sri Dornchai Rd. ☎ 053/282-463. Reservations recommended. Main courses 60B–250B ($1.60–$6.60). No credit cards. Daily 11am–10pm. 2 blocks west of river, off Chang Klan Rd. VEGETARIAN/ASIAN.

If you're looking for Asian food in the typically California/health food/Western vein, head for this New Age place in a traditional Lanna Thai pavilion. The extensive menu is prepared by a gifted Pakistani chef and is part vegetarian, Thai, and Indian. The old pavilion has an indoor air-conditioned no-smoking section, and a long open-air veranda set for dining with a view of the gardens (they'll bring a fan to your table upon request). In a good location, near to the main shopping and business areas, Whole Earth gets busy at lunch and dinner, so try to call ahead if you can.

INEXPENSIVE

Haus München. 115/3 Loi Kroa Rd. ☎ 053/274-027. Main courses 90B–140B ($2.35–$3.70). No credit cards. Daily 9am–11pm. At the corner of Chang Klan Rd. around corner from Night Market. GERMAN/CONTINENTAL.

This popular place is usually filled with shoppers in the evening. You can eat wurst, delicious Kasseler (smoked pork), fish-and-chips, spaghetti, or many German favorites, including homemade brown bread. You can also drink draft Amarit beer and check in with the international expatriate community.

Khao Soi Suthasinee. 164/10 Chang Klan Rd. No phone. Main courses 20B–140B (55¢–$3.70). No credit cards. Daily 9am–8:30pm. South of Sri Donchai Rd., just south of junction with Prachasamphan Rd., across from Saengtawan Cinema. THAI.

This small Formica and fluorescent shop house isn't easy to find, but it's a sure bet for authentic *khao soi*—an aromatic concoction of coconut curry soup with noodles, *gai* (chicken), or *moo* (pork), including greens and seasonal vegetables, such as tangy green eggplant. It's an unusual taste sensation, and a large bowl costs only 20B (80¢). The restaurant isn't touristy, so you may have to ask for help finding it.

Shere Shiraz. 23–35 Charoen Prathet Soi 6. ☎ 053/276-132. Main courses 50B–130B ($1.30–$3.40). AE, MC, V. Daily 9:30am–11pm. 3 blocks south of Tha Pae Rd., left across from Galare Bazaar. INDIAN/PAKISTANI/ARABIAN/THAI.

One step in the door and the aroma of coriander, cardamom, and anise will convince you the tastes are going to be authentic. It's also especially good for vegetarians—the *aloo paratha* (potato-stuffed bread) and the *bindi masala* (okra in tomato) melt in your mouth.

AROUND THE OLD CITY
MODERATE

La Villa Pizzeria. Pensione La Villa, 145 Ratchadamnoen Rd. ☎ 053/277-403. Main courses 50B–150B ($1.30–$3.95). MC, V. Daily 11am–10pm. West of Prapokklao Rd., on left. ITALIAN.

La Villa is part of a friendly, Italian-run guest house, where an occasional "Ciao, bambina!" is heard. Main courses include *fegato alla veneziana* (beef liver fried with onions and butter) and several pastas in a variety of sauces. Thin-crust pizzas with authentic tomato sauce and various vegetable and meat toppings are some of the best pizza I've had in Thailand, and they start at 80B ($2.10).

INEXPENSIVE

America. 402/1–2 Tha Pae Rd. ☎ **053/252-190.** Main courses 40B–220B ($1.05–$5.80). No credit cards. Daily 11am–10pm. 2 blocks east of Tha Pae Gate, on left. MEXICAN/ITALIAN/THAI.

Tony Moon, a friendly restaurateur from Salt Lake City, operates this small restaurant, a hangout of an interesting expatriate crowd in Chiang Mai. The place is by no means fancy, but it's pleasant and the food is quite good. Especially recommended are authentic-tasting Mexican specialties, a rarity in Thailand. The salads are also fresh and tasty, and the ice cream is good, particularly the chocolate chip.

✪ **Aroon (Rai) Restaurant.** 45 Kotchasarn Rd. ☎ **053/276-947.** Main courses 20B–60B (55¢–$1.60). No credit cards. Daily 9am–2:30pm and 5:30–1pm. 2 blocks south of Tha Pae Gate outside Old City. NORTHERN THAI.

For authentic northern food, adventurous eaters should try this nondescript garden restaurant. Their *khao soi*, filled with egg noodles and crisp-fried chicken bits and sprinkled with dried, fried noodles, is spicy and coconut-sweet at the same time. Chiang Mai sausages are served sliced over steamed rice; puffed-up fried pork rinds are the traditional (if not cholesterol-free) accompaniment. Dishes are all made to order in an open kitchen, so you can point to things that interest you, including the myriad fried insects, beetles, and frogs for which this place is famous. They've added a new attraction—prepackaged spices and recipes for make-it-yourself back at home.

The Crusty Loaf Bakery. 24–24/1 Ratwithi Rd. ☎ **053/214-554.** Main courses 30B–40B (80¢–$1.05). No credit cards. Daily 8am–9pm. 1 long block north of Tha Pae Gate in Old City, turn left; on right near end of block. WESTERN.

Even if you don't notice the handsome display of different breads in the front windows, the smell of fresh-baked loaves will draw you into this cheerful, unpretentious little joint run by a nice Irish-Thai couple. The long tables covered with green-checked oilcloth, wooden benches, clutter of plants, and lighthearted Irish pictures on the wall make this a very pleasant place to start a day of exploring wats in the Old City.

JJ Coffee Shop and Bakery. Corner of Moonmuang and Ratchadamnoen rds. ☎ **053/211-070.** Main courses 40B–220B ($1.05–$5.80). V. Daily 7am–10pm. In Old City across from Tha Pae Gate. INTERNATIONAL.

Probably the closest thing I've seen to a diner in Thailand, JJ's has spotless booths and tables lining the long window front, rock-and-roll music, and a wait staff with personality. The extensive menu includes excellent sandwiches and burgers, with good fries. They also have Thai dishes, but the Western food is particularly recommended. Breakfasts are tops, and reasonably priced. Excellent bakery goods are sold next door, in the lobby of the Montri Hotel. There's a second branch at the Chiang Inn Plaza, 100/1 Chang Klan Rd., with the same hours.

T's Tavern. 1 Chang Loh Rd. ☎ **053/271-950.** Main courses 50–230B ($1.30–$6.05). Daily 11am–11pm. Outside Old City, west of Chiang Mai Gate. THAI/EUROPEAN.

Outside this looks like a traditional Thai establishment, but inside it's more Western, and it draws a sophisticated expatriate crowd. Among the European dishes are fish-and-chips, lamb chops, smoked salmon, and a number of Swedish specialties. The wine list is the most impressive we've found in Chiang Mai, including French, Italian, South African, Hungarian, and Australian—the house wine—as well as Guinness.

✪ **Ta-Krite.** 7 Samlarn Rd., Soi 1. ☎ **053/278-298.** Reservations not necessary. 50B–120B ($1.30–$3.15). Open daily 10am–11pm. No credit cards. Walk south from Wat Phra Sing and turn right on Soi 1. THAI.

This small restaurant packs a lot of charm, with lots of green plants, lovely locally made blue-and-white pottery, and old finds here and there. Serving Thai cuisine more common to the central parts of the country, the house specialty is the duck curry in a coconut gravy hot with chilies and sweetened with fruits. It's also nice to know that their produce comes from the Royal Project. A great place to stop for a sightseeing lunch break, their Quick Lunch specials are numerous and only cost between 25B and 30B (65¢ and 80¢)!

Thanom. 8 Chaiyaphum Rd. No phone. Main dishes 25B–90B (65¢–$2.35). No credit cards. Daily noon–2pm and 6–8pm. North from the Tha Pae Gate outside the Old City, on right. NORTHERN THAI.

It's easy to walk by the gates of this drab open-air restaurant and miss an outstanding northern Thai meal. In addition to the usual tourists, you'll see plenty of Thai couples drawn by the excellent *khao soi* (spicy curried noodles with crispy noodles on top) and *khanom jin nam giaw* (chicken with curried noodles, Chinese style). *But be advised:* no alcohol, no sleeveless shirts, and the kitchen closes by 8pm.

WESTSIDE/HUAI KAEO ROAD

Chiangmai Coca. 9912 Huai Kaeo Rd. ☎ 053/220-569. Main courses 30B–85B (80¢–$2.25). No credit cards. Daily 10am–10:30pm. 1 block east of and across street from Chiang Mai Orchid Hotel. THAI.

Look for the Coke sign with a steaming sukiyaki cooker above it. This lively restaurant has seating outdoors in a huge gravel lot or under a huge, fan-cooled hangar, and it's always packed with Thai families enjoying the cook-it-yourself, inexpensive fare. The roast duck is tender and served with a bittersweet plum sauce. Delicious "fresh" spring rolls are steamed with rice-flour wrappers filled with mushrooms, bean curd, fish, and chopped vegetables. There's a large choice of entrees for the sukiyaki cooker—shrimp dumplings, meatballs, sliced chicken—all fresh and served with a tray of condiments (MSG is used).

Galae Restaurant. 65 Suthep Rd. ☎ 053/278-655. Main courses 70B–145B ($1.85–$3.80). No credit cards. Mon–Fri 10am–9pm, Sat–Sun 10am–10pm. 5km (3 miles) west of the Old City up the hill toward Doi Suthep. THAI.

Dining is casual, with tables on several grass plateaus under cool shade trees in a wooded compound overlooking a lake. The menu includes typical Thai rice and noodle dishes, including Chiang Mai sausage, but the specialty is beef cooked on a nearby spit—with its tempting aroma of roasting garlic, lemon juice, and chile. Their unusual pomelo and fried catfish salad is a deliciously pungent combination of flavors.

5 Exploring Chiang Mai

THE WATS

Except for Bangkok, Chiang Mai, with more than 700, has the greatest concentration of exquisitely crafted **wats,** or temples, in the country. If you start in the early morning, you can see all of the principal sights in one day, particularly if you travel by tuk-tuk.

Wat Chedi Luang. Prapokklao Rd. south of Ratchadamnoen Rd. Suggested contribution 20B (55¢). Daily 6am–5pm.

Because Wat Chedi Luang is near the Tha Pae Gate, most visitors begin their sightseeing here, where there are two wats of interest. This complex, which briefly housed the Emerald Buddha now at Bangkok's Wat Phra Kaeo, dates from 1411 when the original chedi was built by King Saen Muang Ma. The already-massive edifice was expanded to 280 feet in height in the mid-1400s, only to be ruined by a severe earthquake in 1545, just 11 years before Chiang Mai fell to the Burmese. (It was never rebuilt.) A Buddha still graces its exterior, and it's not unusual to spot a saffron-robed monk bowing to it as he circles the chedi.

Wat Phan Tao, also on the grounds, has a wooden wihaan and bot, reclining Buddha, and fine carving on the eaves and door. After leaving the temple, walk around to the monks' quarters on the side, taking in the traditional teak northern architecture and delightful landscaping.

Wat Phra Singh. Samlarn and Ratchadamnoen rds. Suggested contribution 20B (55¢). Daily 6am–5pm.

This compound was built during the zenith of Chiang Mai's power, and is one of the more venerated shrines in the city. It's still the site of many important religious ceremonies, particularly during the Songkran Festival. More than 700 monks study here, and you will probably find them especially friendly and curious.

King Phayu, of Mengrai lineage, built the chedi in 1345, principally to house the cremated remains of King Kamfu, his father. As you enter the grounds, head to the right toward the 14th-century library. Notice the graceful carving and the characteristic roof line with four separate elevations. The sculptural *devata* (Buddhist spirits) figures, in both dancing and meditative poses, are thought to have been made during King Muang Kaeo's reign in the early 16th century. They decorate a stone base designed to keep the fragile *sa* (mulberry bark) manuscripts elevated from flooding and vermin.

On the other side of the temple complex is the 200-year-old **Lai Kham ("Gilded Hall") wihaan,** housing the venerated image of the Phra Singh or **Sighing Buddha,** brought to the site by King Muang Ma in 1400. The original Buddha's head was stolen in 1922, but the reproduction in its place doesn't diminish the homage paid to this figure during Songkran. Inside are frescoes illustrating the stories of Sang Thong (the Golden Prince of the Conchshell) and Suwannahong. These images convey a great deal about the religious, civil, and military life of 19th-century Chiang Mai during King Mahotraprathet's reign.

Wat Suan Dok. Suthep Rd. Suggested contribution 20B (55¢). Open daily 6am–5pm From the Old City, take the Suan Dok Gate and continue 1 mile west.

This complex is special less for its architecture (the buildings, though monumental, are undistinguished) than for its contemplative spirit and pleasant surroundings.

The temple was built amid the pleasure gardens of the 14th-century Lanna Thai monarch, King Ku Na. Unlike most of Chiang Mai's other wats (more tourist sights than working temples and schools), Wat Suan Dok houses quite a few monks who seem to have isolated themselves from the distractions of the outside world.

Among the main attractions in the complex are the bot, with a very impressive **Chiang Saen Buddha** (one of the largest bronzes in the north) dating from 1504 and some garish murals; the chedi, built to hold a relic of the Buddha; and a royal cemetery with some splendid shrines.

Wat Chet Yot. Superhighway near the Chiang Mai National Museum. Suggested contribution 20B (55¢). Open daily 6am–5pm. North of the intersection of Nimanhemin and Huai Kaeo rds., about half a mile, on the left.

Wat Chet Yot (also called Wat Maha Photharam) is one of the central city's most elegant sites. The chedi was built during the reign of King Tilokkarat in the late 15th century (his remains are in one of the smaller chedis), and in 1477, the World Sangkayana convened here to revise the doctrines of the Buddha.

The unusual design of the main rectangular chedi with seven peaks was copied from the Maha Bodhi Temple in Bodh Gaya, India, where the Buddha first achieved enlightenment. The temple also has architectural elements of Burmese, Chinese Yuan, and Ming influence. The extraordinary proportions, the angelic, levitating devata figures carved into the base of the chedi, and the juxtaposition of the other buildings make Wat Chet Yot (Seven Spires) a masterpiece.

The Lanna-style Buddha hidden in the center was sculpted in the mid–15th century; a door inside the niche containing the Buddha leads to the roof on which rests the **Phra Kaen Chan (Sandalwood Buddha).** There is a nice vista from up top, but only men are allowed to ascend the stairs.

Wat Chiang Man. Wiang Kaeo and Ratchaphakkinai rds. Suggested contribution 20B (55¢). Open daily 6am–5pm. In the Old City near the northern Chang Puak Gate.

Thought to be Chiang Mai's oldest wat, it was built during the 14th century by King Mengrai, the founder of Chiang Mai, on the spot where he first camped. Like many of the wats in Chiang Mai, this complex reflects many architectural styles. Some of the structures are pure Lanna. Others show influences from as far away as Sri Lanka; notice the typical row of elephant supports. Wat Chiang Man is most famous for its two Buddhas: Phra Sritang Khamani (a miniature crystal image also known as the **White Emerald Buddha**) and the **marble Phra Sri-la Buddha.** Unfortunately, the wihaan that safeguards these religious sculptures is almost always closed.

TOURS & TREKS

There are so many tour groups in Chiang Mai that specialize in trekking, that it can seem impossible to choose. I've narrowed down the different types of hill-tribe tour offerings below, and provided information on what I have found to be the better, more reputable operators for each type of trip. Most of the smaller operators have offices along Tha Pae Road, in guest houses, and all along the major tourist routes in the city. You might like to talk to some of them for yourself to see if they have anything you might be interested in. Many adventure tours mix mountain biking or motorcycling with tribal village tours, so be sure to refer to the "Outdoor Adventures" section if you're interested in combining such activities. See "Tours & Trekking," in chapter 11 for more information on the hill tribes themselves, descriptions of what to expect on tours, how to select a good operator, and how to prepare for your trip.

Day-trip village tours are carried out professionally by **Gem Travel,** 29 Charoen Prathet Rd. (☎ **053/272-855;** fax 053/271-255). They'll provide transportation, a guide, and lunch for a day trip to 6 different hill-tribe villages. For two, the cost is 1,500B ($39.45) per person, but this figure decreases if you can join a group.

For **short-term jungle trekking,** The Wild Planet is a highly reputable outfit. Combining treks and village stays with elephant treks, visits to caves, and relaxing bamboo raft river trips, they have quality guides and can even provide English-speaking guides upon request. Treks from Chiang Mai stop at Lisu, Lahu, and Karen villages. A 2-day/1-night trip is 3,200B ($84.20) per person if you join their regular tour; the 3-day/2-night tour is 4,200B ($110.55). Private group trips can also be arranged, and Wild Planet will be happy to help tailor yours for special requests. Their head office in Bangkok is at no. 9 Thonglor Soi 25, Sukhumvit 55, Prakanong (☎ **02/233-0997;** fax 02/712-8748; www.wild-planet.co.th). In Chiang Mai, their office is on Charoen Prathet Road between Diamond Hotel and SK Money Changer (☎ **053/277-178**).

Long-term jungle trekking up to 20 days in small groups can be arranged through **The Trekking Collective,** a reputable operation started 12 years ago by a

Chiang Mai Attractions

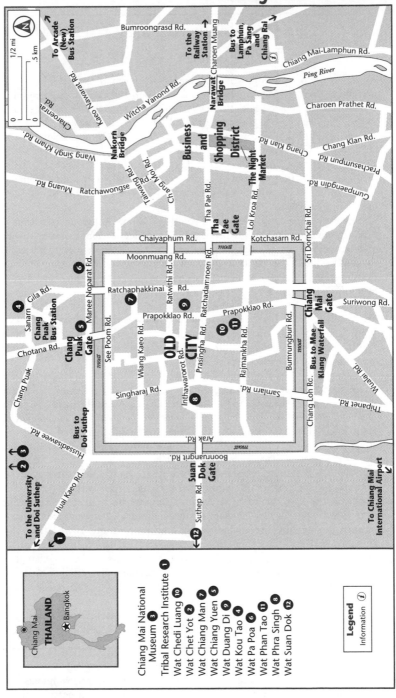

Chiang Mai National Museum ❶
Tribal Research Institute ❸
Wat Chedi Luang ❿
Wat Chet Yot ❷
Wat Chiang Man ❼
Wat Chiang Yuen ❺
Wat Duang Di ❾
Wat Kou Tao ❹
Wat Pa Poa ❻
Wat Phan Tao ⓫
Wat Phra Singh ❽
Wat Suan Dok ⓬

Legend
ⓘ Information

Temple Murals: Understanding Thailand Through Religious Paintings

In the days before universal schooling, the temple served as a school for religious and moral teaching. Monks relied on oral narration and visual interpretation to advance the learning to a population who was largely illiterate. These stories contained examples of moral conduct and Buddhist virtues that are central to divine knowledge and happiness. A heritage of temple mural painting developed—one of Thailand's finest contributions to the world's body of religious art. Unfortunately, the artists (usually uncredited monks and dedicated laypeople) used a technique of dry fresco painting that deteriorated rapidly in the humid climate. As a result the oldest murals date back only as far as the early 1700s, and these are disappearing fast.

One fascinating element of mural paintings are the background elements— little vignettes of everyday life painted with sometimes hilarious characters—men and women flirting, groups gossiping, conducting chores or playing games. A window on life in the old days, costumes are realistic and facial expressions are detailed enough to reveal familiar expressions. These elements are most whimsical in northern temples, especially those of Chiang Mai.

Outer temple arcades will oftentimes illustrate the stories of the Ramakien in bright colors, lively characters, and vivid action sequences. This story, inherited from the Indian Ramayana of Hindu origin, is explained more fully in Appendix A. Once you know the basic story, these murals are fun to interpret, but the events are rarely in chronological sequence.

Inside the *bot* (main ordination hall), where you find the principal Buddha image, murals depict stories from previous incarnations of the Buddha, known as the Jatakas. While there are 547 in total, the Thais concern themselves with the Tosachat, the ten lives that lead directly to the Buddha's last incarnation as Siddhartha. These lives depict the **10 virtues** the Buddha perfected in order to attain enlightenment. You'll see different episodes from each story, but each has a principal identifying scene, described below.

The future Buddha learns **renunciation** as Prince Temiya, who turns down his place on the throne to prevent himself from hurting others with his power. The main mural scene is the prince raising a chariot over his head at the end of the story to reveal himself as a *Bodhisattva* (a future Buddha). **Perseverance** is learned through the story of Prince Mahajanaka, a prince separated at birth from his kingdom who endures a shipwreck in dangerous seas to eventually claim his throne; look for the prince swimming among sea monsters. In the story that illustrates **loving kindness,** Sama cares dutifully for his blind parents, until he is shot by a greedy king in the forest; look for Sama surrounded by deer beside a lake, falling from the blow of the king's arrow.

In another incarnation, the future Buddha practices **resolution** as Nemi, who had to choose between a holy life or a life giving alms. In his quest, he visited

Thai/Western couple. They combine the thrills of adventure touring with longer-term stays in villages (for a deeper cultural experience) where you will be encouraged to become involved in daily activities such as farming, or may even accompany men on the hunt. Treks will include visits to Hmong, Karen, Akha, Lisu, Lahu, Yao, Mlabri, heaven and hell, the latter of which is the leading picture of the story in graphic detail (usually found on the wall behind the principal Buddha image). The story of Mahosodh tells a story of **wisdom.** The wise sage was the subject of jealousy from other wise men in the kingdom and was put to a series of tests by them. In the main scene he cleverly thwarts an invasion from a neighboring kingdom—the warriors often include foreigners in the jumble of activity. Not so unthinkable, as many Portuguese and Dutch fought alongside the Thais during the battle-scarred Ayutthaya period. We see the Bodhisattva learn **moral practice** in his incarnation as Bhuridatta, son of the Naga (serpent) king of the underworld. He is captured by greedy travelers and forced to perform in markets—this being the identifying scene of the story.

For a lesson in **forbearance,** the Boddhisattva is incarnated as Prince Chandrakumard, who falls victim to a jealous official in his father's kingdom. The official convinces the king to sacrifice his son, and in the main and final scene, the god Indra flies over Chandrakumard, saving him. The boddhisattva practices **equanimity** as Narada, an ascetic who teaches the doctrine to a wayward king. Look for the image of a monk in an antelope hide with a golden bowl raised above him on a stick. **Truth** is the lesson through the incarnation of Witoon. A wise minister, he is summoned by the queen of the Nagas (serpents) to instruct her of his wisdom. Her servant misunderstands her orders and instead tries to kill Witoon. The main scene shows Witoon holding onto the tail of a flying horse, and being flung over a cliff.

The final incarnation before he is born as Siddhartha is perhaps the most often told story. Consisting of 1,000 verses in 13 cantos, its recitation at the close of the Buddhist Lent is the centerpiece of temple activities. Many times you'll find an individual scene for each canto of the story, which teaches the virtue of **charity.** You'll see Prince Wetsandon giving away his sacred white elephant, being led into exile with his wife and children, giving away his chariot, and carrying his tired children. Another character, Chuckok (an old Brahmin), is seen with his young wife, who persuades him to find slaves for her. In the forest he encounters Wetsandon, who gives his children to Chuchok as slaves while the Princess is held back by tigers. The prince eventually gives her away, too. At the end of the story, all are returned to the kingdom in a grand royal procession.

While these murals surround bot walls, the rear wall facing the Buddha image is usually reserved for a painting depicting the story of the Buddha subduing Mara. Mara tempts the Buddha, sending his beautiful daughters to seduce the Great Sage. The Buddha is victorious, as he calls the earth to witness his great knowledge and wisdom. The finest examples of Tosachat murals are in Wat Saket and Wat Po in Bangkok, Wat Phra Singh in Chiang Mai, and Wat Machimawas in Songkhla.

Palong, or Lawa tribes—and with longer trips, you'll obviously have the opportunity to visit the more remote areas in this region. Expect the cost to start from 2,000B ($52.65) per day per person. Contact them at 25/1 Ratchawithi Rd. (☎ **053/419-079;** fax 053/419-080); e-mail: trek-collective@cm.ksc.co.th.

Towns that develop on river banks become increasingly dependent on the water that flows through them for providing food, a place to wash, and water to drink. Where in the past you would have seen folks doing daily chores down by the river, in metropolitan Chiang Mai you're hardly likely to see such sights today. Still, a **long-tail boat trip** provides a different angle of the city, with views of old teak riverside mansions behind which arise the tall skyline of the modern city, while on the outskirts of town, villages offer scenes of more suburban and rural lives beyond the city limits. Boat operators begin at 9am and continue until 5pm, leaving whenever someone comes by to hire their boats. Head for the boat landing at Wat Chaimongkol on Charoen Prathet Road opposite Alliance Francais. The tour lasts about 2 hours and costs 300B ($7.90); fruit and drinks are included.

Chiang Mai Nature Tour has a great full-day trip to Doi Inthanon for **birdwatching.** Accompanied by a local bird expert, you'll spend the day in the national park where you may see local species, including eagles and hawks, and up to 3,000 others (if you have time!). In a few areas of the park, the birds are unafraid of humans and can allow some pretty close encounters. The best bird watching is from February to May when birds are breeding. The months following are when they raise their young. Trips start early in the morning—from 6am and finish up after dark. Somebody should teach those birds to sleep in! The cost is 3,900B ($102.65) per person. Chiang Mai Nature Tour is located at 9 Soi 4, Viengbua Rd. (opposite Rayabhat Institute) (☎ and fax **053/210-917**).

Here's something you won't see on other tour operator agendas. The Trekking Collective has small-group camping trips to an isolated **animal sanctuary** on the Burmese border to watch indigenous creatures in the wild. Sometimes rugged, they recommend at least 4 days for a better chance to see more wildlife. Trips will depend on the season (mating season) so plan with them in advance. You quite possibly will see a herd of wild elephants, plus several species of deer, monkey and the Malaysian sun bear. Contact them at 25/1 Ratchawithi Rd. (☎ **053/419-079,** fax 053/419-080, e-mail: trek-collective@cm.ksc.co.th).

CULTURAL PURSUITS

While its collection of historical treasures is not nearly as extensive as that of Bangkok's National Museum, the **Chiang Mai National Museum** does provide something of an historical overview of the region, the city, and historical highlights. The Lanna Kingdom, Tai people, and hill tribes are highlighted in simple displays with English explanations. It's small, but interesting. Located on the Superhighway northwest of the Old City, it's near Wat Chet Yot. The museum is open Tuesday through Sunday from 8:30am to 4pm (☎ **053/221-308**); admission 80B ($2.10).

The **Tribal Museum,** formerly at Chiang Mai University's Tribal Research Institute moved location to the peaceful Ratchamangkla Park just north of the city, not far from the Chiang Mai National Museum. It's a small but well-executed exhibit showing the cultures and daily lives of the hill tribes people of Thailand's north. It is especially recommended as an intro course for those who plan to visit the villages. The museum is in Ratchamangkla Park on Chotana Road (☎ **053/210-872**). It's open daily from 9am to 4pm; admission is free.

If you love the food, why not learn how to make it yourself? At **Sompet Thai Cookery School** you can learn how to make green curry, tom yam, phad thai, and all those other dishes you've grown to love during your trip. There are day and evening courses where you'll prepare at least seven dishes yourself. You'll also get a tour of their herb garden and receive a recipe book for all that you've learned. Prices range from 800B to 1,500B ($21.05 to $39.45) per person. **Sompet's** booking office is on the ground floor at Chiang Inn Plaza on Chang Klan Road (☎ 053/281-354; e-mail: sompet67@hotmail.com).

If you adore the handicrafts you see here in the north, **The Trekking Collective,** run by a Thai/Western couple, offers **courses in weaving, ceramics, basketry, and wood carving.** You'll be taught by local handicraft artisans with the assistance of guide interpreters. These courses are hit or miss, as the main handicrafts activities happen only during low farming seasons, but if you contact them in advance you just may be in season. While they can arrange short 3-day weekend courses, they recommend at least a week for more complete learning. Groups are very small, and cost about $100 per person per day. They are located at 25/1 Ratchawithi Rd. (☎ 053/419-079; fax 053/419-080; e-mail: trek-collective@cm.ksc.co.th).

For a fabulous **traditional Thai massage,** while there are many places around town to choose from, I recommend **Yogi** at the Royal Princess Chiang Mai Hotel in the basement at 112 Chang Klan Rd. (☎ 053/281-033). Quiet and peaceful, with walls and floors covered in matting, the atmosphere is perfect for a Thai experience—far more creativity at play than in many other joints. The excellent massage goes for 300B ($7.90) per hour, and I recommend at least 2 hours to take advantage of the true benefits of the massage.

The **Thai massage schools** in Bangkok and Phuket teach the southern style of Thai massage, which places pressure on muscles to make them tender and relaxed. Northern-style Thai massage is something closer to yoga, where your muscles are stretched and elongated to enhance flexibility and relaxation. **International Training Massage,** or ITM, has small but popular courses in English to learn these techniques at introduction, intermediate, and advanced levels. Each 5-day course is 1,800B ($47.35). Contact them at 17/7 Morakot Rd., Hah Yaek Santitham (☎ 053/218-632; fax 053/224-197).

If you've come to Thailand because you *really* want to give yourself relief from the pressures of life back home, then a course in **meditation** techniques is highly recommended. The **Northern Insight Meditation Center** at Wat Rampoeng (Kan Klongchonprathan Road) is a well-respected center for learning vipassana meditation techniques. While other techniques focus on developing concentration, **vipassana** works to empty the brain completely—perfect for those who can't seem to relax, or whose brains are always working double-time. While the center does have short 10-day intro courses, they really emphasize their full 26-day in-depth training program. During this period you will live in the monastery with other students, you'll practice the lifestyle of monks and nuns (yes, they welcome women), and will undergo training supervised by resident monks and nuns. There is no charge for the course, but you will be asked to make a contribution to the temple of whatever amount you see fit. My advice is to contribute an amount equal to what you'd pay outside the center—if you normally stay in guest houses, donate 26 (nights) × 300B (hotel) + 26 (days) × 200B (meals) = 13,000B ($342.10); if you normally stay in resorts, then 26 × 5,000B + 26 × 1,000B = 156,000B ($4,105.25). If it seems steep, keep in mind you are not paying for a service; you're making merit. Pay what you can afford. They don't accept reservations, but call a day ahead to see if they have space at ☎ 053/278-620; fax 053/810-197.

OUTDOOR ADVENTURES

Mountain biking is perhaps the best way to see this part of the country. Out in the fresh air there's a more up close and personal view of nature, sights, and people. The **Wild Planet** coordinates 2-, 3-, and 4-day trips from Chiang Mai, taking you to elephant camps, hill-tribe villages (with an overnight stay in the headman's house), temples, and some cave exploration. Some trips even end up in Chiang Rai—much more interesting than taking a Thai Airways flight, no? Two days cycling is 4,000B ($105.25); 3 days, 6,000B ($157.90); 4 days, 9,000B ($236.85). Call them in Bangkok at ☎ **02/233-0997** or in Chiang Mai, Charoen Prathet Road between Diamond Hotel and SK Money Changer at 053/277-178.

Chiang Mai Green Tour, 29–31 Chiangmai-Lamphun Road (☎ and fax **053/247-374**), organizes half-day or full-day mountain bike trips to Chiang Mai's city attractions, Lamphun, the Elephant Conservation Center, or to nearby farming villages. The full day trip runs 1,400B ($36.85) per person.

A homegrown operation, the **Chiang Mai Sunday Bicycle Club** (☎ 053/ **418-403**) gathers up to 200 people every Sunday morning for either sightseeing trips around the city (light cycling), trips to handicraft villages (15km), or through the northern countryside (20km). Meet up with them at 7am at the Old City's Tha Pae Gate. The trip is free.

Want to take your **motorcycle adventure off-road**? Talk to **The Wild Planet,** which coordinates 250cc dirt bike trips on dirt paths, with some rough single tracks that can be steep or rutted (make sure you're confident of your abilities here). From Chiang Mai a 3-day adventure (8,000B/$210.55 per person) takes you to tribal villages, natural wonders, and cultural sights. The 2-day weekend trip (5,000B/$131.60 per person) has stops in many tribal villages between Chiang Mai and Pai with an overnight in one of the villages. Their guides are also experienced with motorcycle mechanics. Call Wild Planet in Bangkok at ☎ **02/233-0997;** in Chiang Mai, Charoen Prathet Road between Diamond Hotel and SK Money Changer (☎ **053/277-178**).

From atop Doi Inthanon, Thailand's highest peak, flows the Mae Chaem River. Winding through ravines, past tall cliffs, and small settlements, the river makes for a gorgeous and fun **river-rafting** trip. Maesot Conservation Tour puts together a 2-day/1-night trip that includes a drive to the summit of the mountain followed by rafting (a rubber inflatable raft) with stops at villages and archaeological sites along the way. All equipment is provided. Contact them at 175/18 Ratchadamnern Rd. (☎ and fax **053/814-505**). The cost is 3,500B ($92.10) per person, everything included.

HITTING THE LINKS

The best golf course open to the public is the **Chiang Mai Green Valley Country Club** (☎ **053/298-249;** fax 053/279-386), 183/2 Chotana Rd. (Route 107), in Mae Rim, in excellent condition, the flat greens and fairways slope toward the Ping River (greens fees: weekdays 750B/$19.75); weekends 1,5000B/$39.45). At the nearby **Lanna Golf Club** (☎ **053/221-911;** fax 053/221-743), on Chotana Rd. 2km north of the Old City, this tree-lined 18-hole course has views of nearby Doi Suthep; (greens fees: weekdays 500B/$13.15; weekends 700B/$18.40). Both are open daily 6am to dusk; clubs are available for rent.

The **Chiang Mai–Lamphun Country Club** (☎ **053/248-3397;** fax 053/ 248-937), Baan Thi Road, 10km east of Sankamphaeng, is another good 18-hole course set in a valley (greens fees: weekdays and weekends 1,200B/$31.60). The **Gymkhana Club Golf Course** (☎ **053/241-035;** fax 053/247-352), on Ratutit Road, off the Chiang Mai-Lamphun Road (Route 106), has a wooded nine-hole course with small greens (greens fees: weekdays 130B/$3.40; weekends 200B/$5.25).

6 Shopping

The joys of shopping in Chiang Mai are endless. There's just so much to buy here that shopping has become a sport. Better still, so much of the merchandise is of great quality at incredible prices. If you plan to shop in Thailand, save your money for Chiang Mai—you won't be disappointed.

Thailand has a rich tradition of handicrafts, developing over centuries as people used the many natural resources around them—mixing their own diverse creativities with ideas introduced from distant China and India. Hardwoods, precious metals and stones, raw materials for fabrics and dyes, bamboo, and clay were fashioned into practical items for everyday use and intricately ornamented ceremonial objects. While these days, there's little demand for many of these traditional items (can you picture yourself at the grocery store back home in full hill-tribe garb?), most craftspeople have adopted traditional styles for the realities and tastes of the modern, international world, opening up new markets. But while the majority of craft items are modernized, the materials remain top quality, and fortunately, craft skills are still very refined.

So what can you buy here? Well, for starters, the tribal crafts you see all over Thailand—those brightly embroidered bags, household textiles, and clothing—are made in the north, so not only are the prices better here, but the selection is far superior. Traditional **tribal embroidery crafts** have been modified over the years, so you can find their delicate styles on shoulder bags, carry-ons, and backpacks. The markets even sell tribal clothing—jackets with embroidered lapels or long skirts with colorful detail.

The hill tribes' **handwoven textiles** are rich in texture and natural tones, colored with plants from local sources. The cotton fabric can be bought in bulk in the markets, and you can find ready-made clothing everywhere for a song. Most styles carry Asian and hill-tribe signature styles with straight lines and handsome simplicity.

Some tribes are also known for their fine **silver jewelry**—necklaces, bangles, and earrings—in unusual traditional ethnic designs or more ordinary Western styles. For all hill-tribe handicrafts, the best place to shop is at the Night Markets.

Fine silver works are synonymous with Chiang Mai. Early smiths are believed to have immigrated from Burma with the coming of Kublai Khan, and skills have been passed from generation to generation. While silver is not a local resource, early raw materials were acquired from coins brought by traders. These days, all of it is imported from foreign sources, most of it about 80% pure. Traditional bowls feature intricate raised floral designs—the deeper the imprint, the higher quality the silver. Jewelry items are crafted in delicate filigree designs in styles copied by many Western manufacturers. Many families set up shop along Wulai Road, south of the Old City, while outlets on Sankamphaeng Road carry large selections.

Gemstones can be good buys here, where the larger stores are honest and reasonably priced (but to be perfectly honest, you'll probably find more competitive prices in Bangkok). I'll recommend you stick to the better-known establishments. While you may find bargain deals elsewhere in comparison—you run the risk of purchasing manufactured stones. With Myanmar and China so close by, you'll find jade and other precious stones in very unique designs. There are some good shops in town, with others out on Sankamphaeng Road.

Chiang Mai is also one of the major centers for fine **Thai silk** production. While shops in town have fine selections, the larger outlets on Sankamphaeng Road have a larger quantity to chose from. As for tailoring services, in the "Shopping in the City Center" section that follows, I've provided contact information for my favorite dressmaker in Thailand. Buy your silks, then pop in for a visit.

The early royals commissioned carvers to produce wood furnishings for use in palaces, thrones, temple doors and adornments, carriages, pavilions, howdahs for riding elephant back, and royal barges. The excellent quality of hardwoods in Thailand's forests allowed these items to be adorned with grand and intricate **wood carvings.** The skills survive in gifted artisans throughout the country, especially in Chiang

Mai, where craftspeople produce furniture, boxes, and all varieties of gift items imaginable. Wood carving is perhaps more influenced by foreign preferences than other crafts. Products are molded to fit modern uses and conveniences. And while too many decorative items today look similar to wood crafts from Bali, there are still elements of Thai design in many.

Lacquer skills are believed to have been carried from China with early migrants. Sap applied in layers to wooden, clay, or bamboo items can be carved, colored, and sometimes inlaid with mother-of-pearl for a very elegant finished product. Today it is acknowledged as a traditional Chiang Mai craft, having been perfected over centuries by the Khoen people who live in communities outside the city. **Laquerware** vases, boxes, bangles, and traditional items are lightweight gifts, practical for carrying home. Larger tiered boxes and furnishings can be shipped.

Celadon pottery, designed with clean lines and understated simplicity in tones of the palest gray-greens, looks both classic and contemporary. For these reasons this style of pottery has won the affections of decorators and collectors around the world. The distinctive color of the glaze comes from a mixture of local clay and wood ash. Chiang Mai has some of the largest and best celadon factories in the country, the trade passing down through local families. The best places to purchase celadon are out on Sankamphaeng Road, in the large factory outlets.

Antiques in Thailand are not as old as those of Europe—most old objects have disintegrated, disappeared, or were burned or stolen in any one of many Burmese invasions. And while most authentic antiques are snatched up almost immediately by museums or expert collectors, there are still some finds around. Most of the shop owners can produce certificates of authenticity to prove the antiquity of your purchases; however, only specialists in the Fine Arts Department have enough knowledge about these things to truly know which pieces are true antiques or not. Buyer beware. As my dear old dad always says, "When you buy art and antiques, buy what you love. If it turns out to be worthless, you've still bought something you can enjoy." Please refer to the section on "Export of Antiquities or Art from Thailand" in chapter 2 regarding removal of these objects from the country.

MARKETS

Some consider the Night Market (also called the Night Bazaar) the city's premier attraction, though it's becoming increasingly homogenized.

The Night Market on Chang Klan Road between Tha Pae and Loi Kroa roads is open daily from 6 to 11pm. The actual Night Bazaar is a modern, antiseptic, three-story building, but the indoor and outdoor market extends south to Sri Dornchai Road and far beyond. Many shops and stalls remain open throughout the day and evening, especially along Chang Klan Road. The Anusarn section closes at 10pm, so if you want a chance to browse through some of the best deals, come early.

The stalls have grandiose names, like Harrods (with the familiar logo), and most carry Bangkok-produced counterfeits of international name-brand clothing, watches, and luggage. There are thousands of pirated audiotapes and videodiscs, acres of burnished brown "bone" objects, masks, wood carvings, opium pipes, opium weights, you name it.

Inside the Night Bazaar building itself are primarily modern, mass-manufactured goods, with an occasional stand selling wonderful tribal tchotchkes. They range from pretty good, low-cost Thai fashions to typical souvenirs. The top floor has booths selling locally produced handicrafts, some "antiques," and some decorative arts.

The Anusarn Night Market, down Charoen Prathet Road, south of Suriwongse Road, closes about an hour earlier than the main Night Market, but carries more

---

Shopper's Tip

Pack a "goodie bag"—an extra bag to stuff with purchases so you can carry them back with you. You'll fill it in an hour. If you're buying something that is too large or cumbersome to carry back, almost every shop has a shipping service that they work with to deliver goods to your home back home. Shops will advise you, and you can trust the shippers, who are known to pack things well and are honest about shipments.

I recommend renting a car or hiring one with a driver for your shopping excursions—many places are far apart, and your own transportation will be far more convenient. If you'd like, you can join a tour group—every travel agent in hotels and elsewhere has half-day and full-day "tours" of the main shopping areas.

---

hill-tribe goods in authentic traditional styles. The prices are also considerably better here.

The Warowot Market on Changmoi and Wichayanon roads opens every morning at 7am and stays open until 4pm. This central indoor market is the city's largest. Produce, colorful fruits, spices, and food products jam the ground floor. On the second floor, things are calmer, with dozens of vendors selling cheap cotton sportswear, Thai-made shoes, and some hill-tribe handicrafts and garments. Fun and inexpensive.

SHOPPING IN THE CITY CENTER

The many hotels in this area make it attractive for retailers to open shops here. But while you'll find a good concentration of shopping options, shops tend to be smaller, which means they'll have less selection inside. Still, there are many places with great reputations, unique items, lovely displays, and reasonable prices.

Exotic Thai silks and luxurious gemstones light up shop windows all over town. **City Silk** at 336 Tha Pae Rd., 1 block east of the gate (☎ **053/234-388**), has a fine selection, but compare prices a bit. As for tailoring, there are a number of places that vie for your business, but I'll tell you about **Chick & Charm,** 204 Rajchiengsaen Rd., just south of the southeast corner of the Old City (☎ **053/271-208**). Even though I live in Bangkok, I send my business to these two brilliant ladies, who produce excellent work, will direct you to the best fabric bargains around, and are unbelievably affordable.

Your main concern about buying gemstones and jewelry will be the honesty of the dealer. For reputation, you can try **Shiraz Jewelry,** 170 Tha Pae Rd. at the corner of Kampeangdin Road (☎ **053/252-382**), for gemstones, loose or set. **Princess Jewelry,** 147/8 Chang Klan Rd. opposite Royal Princess Hotel (☎ **053/273-648**), also comes with local recommendations. If you seek some of Chiang Mai's famous silver visit **Dynasty's Silver,** 6 Chaiyapoom Rd. just near the Tha Pae gate (☎ **053/ 874-095**).

Asia Eco-Touch, in the basement of Chiang Inn Plaza (☎ **053/332-008**), sells very unique garments made from natural materials, mostly cottons, that are tie-dyed, batik, or embroidered. If you fancy some of the hemp products from the area, shop at the **Cotton & Hemp Shop,** 185 Tha Pae Rd. near Thapae Place Hotel (☎ **053/ 208-505**). Chiang Mai also has some of the finest featherweight cottons, which you'll find made into beautiful shirts and blouses, sundresses, nightgowns, and undergarments—all in the coolest of white shades. I like the selection at **Pik Lik,** Chiang Mai Pavilion across from Suriwongse Zenith Hotel on Chang Klan Road (☎ **053/818-539**), the best.

Sleek Asian designs steal the show at **Living Space,** 276–278 Tha Pae Road (☎ 053/874-299), where celadon and laquerware decorative items are both contemporary and timeless. And if you're looking for really unique designs on T-shirts, **Chiang Mai by Pairoj Studio,** 118 Chang Klan Rd. near Royal Princess Hotel (☎ 053/204-224), has the most handsome Thai designs I've ever seen. Very interesting handmade silver jewelry, too.

OLD CITY

Mengrai Kilns 9/2 Araks Rd., Soi Samlarn 6 near the southwest corner of the Old City (☎ 053/272-063), is one of the biggest names in town, specializing in celadonware, and in handsome decorative and household items. **Thai Tribal Crafts,** 208 Bamrungrad Rd. near the southeast corner of the Old City (☎ 053/241-043), has a better selection of tribal crafts than just about anyplace else in the Old City. Teak woodcarving designs at **Vichitslip Furniture,** 54/5–7 Singharaj Rd. toward the northwest corner of the Old City (☎ 053/221-024), are exceptional, and with countless pieces in oodles of designs, it's fun to see even if you're not buying. **Ban Phor Liang Meun's Terra Cotta,** 36 Prapakklao Rd., Soi 2 near the Chiang Mai (South) Gate (☎ 053/278-187), is the king of this ancient art in Chiang Mai. Huge statues and murals in traditional Khmer, Indian, Chinese, Burmese, and Thai designs are as stunning as in any temple.

WEST SIDE OF THE OLD CITY

At 95 Nimanhemin Rd. across from Amari Rincome Hotel, **Nantawan Arcade** has many notable antiques, crafts, and curios shops that make for fun browsing. Here you'll find places like **Sipsong Panna** (☎ 053/216-096) for the finest collection of hill-tribe silverware and folk jewelry—the handiwork of Tai, Burmese, Chinese, and Laotian artisans. **Nandakwang** (☎ 053/222-261), a branch of the popular Bangkok store, sells first-rate goods of homespun Thai cotton. A treat for anyone interested in weaving. **P. N. Precious Stones** (☎ 053/222-396), the only precious gems dealer that was recommend to *Frommer's* without hesitation, is known for the quality of stones, workmanship of the settings, and reasonable prices.

Part of Natawan Arcade, **Duangjitt House** (☎ 053/215-167), a three-story, contemporary teak house is the elegant gallery of Duangjitt Thaveesri, a distinguished woman who has spent her life collecting Thai and tribal clothing and Southeast Asian handwoven materials. **Michi Gallery** on the 3rd floor (☎ 053/217-767) specializes in the craft of papermaking. Different grades of local *sa* paper (mulberry bark), are handcrafted to copy Buddhist scriptures.

While you're in the neighborhood, feel free to trek up near Wat Suan Dok to drop some cash at the **Hilltribe Products Promotion Center,** 21/17 Suthep Rd. (☎ 053/277-743).

This large shop is under the patronage of His Majesty the King, and was established to sell Akha, Karen, Yao, Hmong, Lisu, and Lahu crafts to provide an alternative income to poppy cultivation. **The Y Shop** at the YMCA, 11 Sermsuk Rd. off the northwest side of the Old City (☎ 053/221-819), returns profits to the community through rural development projects, handicraft training, and marketing and export assistance.

WULAI ROAD

Here's the home of Chiang Mai's cottage silver crafts industry. Families operate shops and factories along this road, just south of the Chiang Mai Gate. Walk along the street and stop in the small shops. **Siam Silverware,** 5 Wua Lai Rd., Soi 3

(☎ 053/279-013), sports a huge selection of new tableware and serving pieces (some in beautiful, traditional Thai designs) and a few decorative objects, plus a variety of well-priced jewelry.

SANKAMPHAENG ROAD

Dedicated shoppers will have to devote at least half a day to shopping along the Chiang Mai-Sankamphaeng Road (Route 1006). It runs due east out of Chiang Mai, and after several kilometers becomes lined with delicious shops, showrooms, and factories extending another 9km (5.4 miles). You can drive yourself along the route, or take one of the white songtao that ply the road, stopping from shop to shop (which is definitely a pain if you're lugging parcels). Most opt for one of the many shopping tours to the area, which are a great bargain, at about 200B ($5.25) per person for a half-day outing. Call **Gem Travel,** 29 Charoen Prathet Rd. (☎ 053/272-855, fax 053/271-255). There are oodles of outlets along the strip, so the following list is definitely not inclusive. However it will give you an idea of what you're in store for.

If you're looking for good gift ideas, check out **Laitong Lacquerware,** 140/1–2 Moo 3, Chiang Mai-Sankamphaeng Road (☎ 053/338-237). Some of the smaller items, like jewelry boxes, can be quite lightweight, so you won't have to lug 10 tons home with you. Saa paper cards (with pressed flowers), stationery, notebooks, and gifts are not only top quality, but they're perfect for light travelers. **Mesa U&P Company's** selection is quite good. Head for 78–78/3 Moo 10, Sankamphaeng Road (☎ 053/331-141).

For larger housewares and objets d'art, **Pa Ker Yaw Basket & Textile,** 136/1 Moo 2, Sankampheang Road (☎ 053/338-512), deals in fabulous baskets of all shapes and sizes, featuring weaving techniques from hill tribes in Thailand, Burma, Laos, and Vietnam. For a large selection of celadonware in traditional Thai designs, **Baan Celadon,** 7 Moo 3, Chiang Mai-Sankamphaeng Road (☎ 053/338-288); and **Siam Celadon,** 38 moo 10, Chiang Mai-Sankamphaeng Road (☎ 053/331-526), have the best selections. Smooth and lustrous vases, jars, bowls, and decorative objects spring to life from local hardwoods, you'd almost think these turned wood products were porcelain. **Aroon Colorware,** 67 Moo 4, Baan Sankaokaepgang (☎ 053/881-605), turns out mod gifts—very unique. **Iyara Art,** 35/4 Moo 3, Sankamphaeng Road (☎ 053/339-450), showcases all sorts of curio items and antiques, plus Buddha and other religious images. At **Chiang Mai Silverware,** 62/10–11 Sankamphaeng Rd. (☎ 053/246-037). you can watch silversmiths hammer and polish their work (most of it serving pieces and utilitarian items). The majority of goods are ornate and expensive.

When you're ready for a little fashion, let **Jolie Femme Thai Silk,** 8/3 Sankamphaeng Rd. (☎ 053/247-222), hit the spot. Weaving traditional silks in rich colors, they fashion much of their stock into modern ready-to-wear creations. There's also **Shinawatra Thai Silk,** 145/1–2 Sankamphaeng Rd. (☎ 053/338-053). An outlet of the high-quality Bangkok chain, rivaled only by Jim Thompson's in Bangkok, Shinawatra sells handwoven and hand-painted silk and cotton by the meter, a wide range of men's and women's conservative silk fashions, cushions, drapery, ties, and dozens of silk accessories. **Asia Eco-Touch,** 78 Sankamphaeng Rd. (☎ 053/332-008), retails casual clothing in local cottons that are colored in natural dyes, and sometimes delicately embroidered.

VILLAGES

Many of the handicrafts you find in town and out at Sangkamphaeng Road are the fine work of local villagers around Chiang Mai. They welcome visitors to their villages to see their traditional craft techniques that have been handed down through generations. Purchase these items directly from the source, sometimes at a savings. While some drive out to these places (which are indicated on most of the maps available), for convenience, I recommend a guided tour. **Gem Travel** (☎ 053/272-855) makes the trip for just over 200B ($5.25) for a half day.

East of Chiang Mai, Moo Baan Sri-pun-krua (near the railway station) specializes in bamboo products and lacquerware. Out off of Sangkamphaeng Road, Moo Baan Tohn Pao (about 8km outside the city) produces sa paper products; Moo Baan Bor Sarng (10km) is a nationally renowned center for painted paper umbrellas and fans; and Moo Baan Tohn (13km) makes fine wood carvings, in addition to umbrellas. Just to the south, Moo Baan Pa-bong (about 6km down Superhighway 11) manufactures furnishings and household items from bamboo.

South of the city, Moo Baan Muang Goong (along Highway 108) is a center for clay pottery; Moo Ban Roi-Jaan (about 8km along the same highway) weaves cottons, dying them in natural colors extracted from natural products; while Moo Baan Tha-wai (14km) has families that craft carved wood antique reproductions.

7 Chiang Mai After Dark

Most folks will spend at least one night at the Night Bazaar for an evening full of shopping adventure, and if you get tired and hungry along the way, stop at **Galare Food & Shopping Center,** 89/2 Chang Klan Rd., on the corner of Soi 6, behind the bazaar (☎ 053/820-320). Free nightly traditional **Thai folk dance** and musical performances grace an informal beer garden where shoppers stop for a drink or pick up inexpensive Chinese, Thai, and Indian food from stalls around. Just behind, local singer-guitarists play more modern selections. For an impromptu bar scene, duck into one of the back alleys behind the Night Bazaar mall that are lined with tiny bars.

For a more studied **cultural performance,** the **Old Chiang Mai Cultural Center,** 185/3 Wulai Rd. (☎ 053/274-093), stages a good show at 7pm every night for 270B ($7.11), which includes dinner and the show. Live music accompanies female dancers in handsome costumes who perform traditional dances. In between sets, men dance with knives and swords. A *khan toke* dinner is served, and despite the crowds, the wait staff remains quite attentive. Yes, it's touristy—busloads find their way here—but I still managed to have a great time. Call ahead, and they'll plan transportation from your hotel.

Most **discos and lounges,** located in major hotels, feature live music, whether it's a quiet piano bar or a rock pub featuring a Filipino band. The lobby bar at the **Empress Hotel,** Chang Klan Road (☎ 053/270-240), features live R&B and pop songs in a relaxed lounge setting, and well as **The Royal Princess Hotel's Casablanca Room,** 112 Chang Klan Rd. (☎ 053/281-033). The casual tavern atmosphere and live pop and rock nightly at **The Riverside Restaurant & Bar,** 9–11 Charoenrat Rd. (☎ 053/243-239), gets my business every time. The **Bubble Disco in Pornping Tower,** 46 Charoen Prathit Rd. (☎ 053/270-099), and **Crystal Cave Disco at Empress Hotel,** Chang Klan Road (☎ 053/270-240), are two of the most popular discos in the city. Pick up a copy of *Welcome to Chiang Mai & Chiang Rai* magazine at your hotel for listings of events that are happening while you're in town.

8 Side Trips from Chiang Mai

If you have time for only one day trip, I recommend taking a minibus up to Wat Phra That and touring Doi Suthep Mountain. If you have more time, you might want to journey to Lamphun or to the elephant training camp in Lampang.

WAT PHRA THAT   The jewel of Chiang Mai, Wat Phra That glistens in the sun on the slopes of Doi Suthep Mountain. One of four royal wats in the north, at 1,000 meters (3,250 ft.), it occupies an extraordinary site with a cool refreshing climate, expansive views over the city, and the mountain's idyllic forests, waterfalls, and flowers.

In the 14th century, during the installation of a relic of the Buddha in Wat Suan Dok (in the Old City), the holy object split in two, with one part equaling the original size. A new wat was needed to honor the miracle. King Ku Na placed the new relic on a sacred white elephant and let it wander freely through the hills. The elephant climbed to the top of Doi Suthep, trumpeted three times, made three counterclockwise circles, and knelt down, choosing the site for Wat Phra That.

The original chedi was built to a height of 26½ feet. Subsequent kings contributed to it, first by doubling the size, then by adding layers of gold and other ornamentation to the exterior. The gilded-copper decorative umbrellas around the central chedi and the murals showing scenes from the Buddha's life are especially attractive.

Other structures were raised to bring greater honor to the Buddha and various patrons. The most remarkable is the steep 290-step naga staircase, added in 1557, leading up to the wat—one of the most dramatic approaches to a temple in all of Thailand. To shorten the 5-hour climb, the winding road was constructed in 1935 by thousands of volunteers under the direction of a local monk.

Visitors with exposed legs are offered a sarong at the entrance. Most Thai visitors come to make an offering—usually flowers, candles, incense, and small squares of gold leaf that are applied to a favored Buddha or to the exterior of a chedi—and to be blessed. Believers kneel down and touch their foreheads to the ground in worship, then often shake prayer sticks to learn their fortune. Reverential Westerners may also participate.

Wat Phra That is open daily 7am to 5pm; come early or late to avoid the crowds; the suggested contribution is 20B (55¢). To get there, take the minibus from Chang Puak (White Elephant) Gate on the north side of the Old City. The fare is 35B (90¢) going up and 25B (65¢) for the descent. The ride can get cool, so bring a sweater or jacket. The bus stops at the base of the naga staircase. If you'd rather not climb the 290 steps—a special part of the experience—there's a motorized gondola to the top for 5B (15¢).

The **Phuping Palace (Doi Bua Ha)** is the summer residence of Thailand's royal family, which is 4km (2½ miles) beyond Doi Suthep, 22km (14 miles) west of the Old City off Route 1004. When the royal family isn't present, visitors are allowed to enter and stroll its beautiful gardens. When it's open (check with the TAT), the hours are usually Friday to Sunday 8:30am to 4:30pm, and admission is free. You really have to dress conservatively for this one. Military guards at the gate are more like the fashion police—tuck in your shirt, unroll your trousers, don't tie your sweater around your waist, and the like. The Doi Suthep minibus continues to the Phuping Palace from Wat Phra That (see above).

LAMPHUN   The oldest continuously inhabited city in Thailand, just 26km (16 miles) south of Chiang Mai, Lamphun was founded in A.D. 663 by the Mon Queen Chammadevi as the capital of Nakorn Hariphunchai. Throughout its long history, the Hariphunchai Kingdom, an offspring of the Mon Empire, was fought over, often conquered, yet it remained one of the powers of the north until King Mengrai established his capital in neighboring Chiang Mai.

The best way to get there is by car, taking the old highway Route 106 south to town. The Superhighway no. 11 runs parallel and east of it, but you'll miss the tall *yang* (rubber) trees, which shade the old highway until Sarapi, and the bushy yellow-flowered *khilik* (cassia) trees. Buses to Lamphun and Pasang leave from the Chang Puak Bus Station (☎ 053/211-586); the 45-minute ride costs 8B (20¢).

The town is legendary for its beautiful women. There are some historical wats, including excellent Dvaravati-style chedis, and a fine museum. Longan (*lumyai*) is a native fruit that resembles clusters of fuzzy brown grapes, which peel easily to yield luscious crisp white flesh. The trees can be recognized by their narrow, crooked trunks and large, droopy oval leaves. On the second weekend in August, Lamphun goes wild with its **Longan Festival,** with a parade of floats decorated only in longans and a beauty contest to select that year's Miss Longan. Lamphun and Pasang (to the south) are also popular with shoppers for their excellent cotton and silk weaving.

The highlight of Lamphun is **Wat Phra That Hariphunchai,** one of the most striking temples in all of Thailand. (Wat Phra Ihat Doi Suthep was modeled after it.) The central chedi, in Chiang Saen style, is said to house a hair of the Buddha and is more than 150 feet high and dates from the 9th century, when it was built over a royal structure. The nine-tiered umbrella at the top contains 6,498.75 grams of gold, and the chedi's exterior is faced with bronze. Also of interest in the temple complex are an immense bronze gong (reputedly the largest in the world), and several wihaan (rebuilt in the 19th and 20th centuries) containing Buddha images. According to legend, the Buddha visited a hill about 16km (10 miles) southeast of town, where he left his footprints; the site is marked by Wat Phra Bat Tak Pha. During the full-moon day in May, there's a ritual bathing for the Phra That.

The new **Hariphunchai National Museum,** Amphur Muang (☎ 053/511-186), is across the street from Wat Phra That Hariphunchai's back entrance. It's worth a visit to see the many bronze and stucco religious works from the wat. The museum also contains a fine collection of Dvaravati- and Lanna-style votive and architectural objects. Open Wednesday to Sunday 9am to noon and 1 to 4pm; admission 10B (40¢).

Wat Chammadevi (Wat Kukut) is a large complex located less than 1km (⁶/₁₀ mile) northwest of the city center. The highlights here are the late Dvaravati-style chedis, and Suwan Chang Kot and Ratana, built in the 8th and 10th centuries respectively, and modeled on those at Bodha Gaya in India. The central one is remarkable for the 60 standing Buddhas that adorn its four corners. The wat itself was built by Khmer artisans for King Mahantayot around A.D. 755. The relics of his mother, Queen Chammadevi, are housed inside, but the gold-covered pagoda was stolen, earning this site its nickname Kukut (topless).

LAMPANG The sprawling town of Lampang (originally called Khelang Nakhon) had been romanticized for its exclusive reliance on the horse and carriage for transportation, a throwback to its 19th-century European legacy. These buggies can still be rented near the center of town, next to the City Hall or in front of the Tipchang Hotel, for about 200B ($5.25) an hour, but they have to share the streets with noisy tuk-tuks and motorcycles, and the modern town offers little in the way of enchantment.

Lampang is graced with some of the finest Burmese temples in Thailand and supports the nearby celebrated Young Elephant Training Camp. Because of the region's fine kilns, there are dozens of ceramics factories producing new and "antique" pottery. For visitor information, contact the **Lampang District Tourist Center,** Chatichai Rd. near the central clock tower (☎ 053/226-810), open daily 8:30am to noon and 1 to 4:30pm.

The easiest way to reach Lampang is by car, taking the old highway Route 106 south to Lamphun, then Superhighway no. 11 southeast for another 64km (40 miles).

Buses to Lampang leave from Chiang Mai's Arcade Bus Terminal (☎ 053/242-664). The 2½-hour trip costs 35B ($1.40).

For a lunch break or an overnight sojourn, the **Tipchang Hotel,** 54/22 Tarkraonoi Rd. (☎ 053/226-501; fax 053/225-362), is the most comfortable in town, with large, air-conditioned doubles for 840B to 1,500B ($22.10 to $39.45).

Lampang's wats are best toured by car or taxi. **Wat Phra Kaeo Don Tao** is on Tambon Wiang Nua, 12km (6.2 miles) southwest of the town center. For 32 years, this highly revered 18th-century Burmese temple housed the Emerald Buddha that's now in Bangkok's Wat Phra Kaeo. Legend has it that one day the prince of Chiang Mai decided to move the Emerald Buddha from Chiang Rai to Chiang Mai. His attendants traveled there with a royal elephant to transport the sacred icon. But when the elephant got to this spot, it refused to go on to Chiang Mai with its burden, and so a wat was built here to house the Buddha. There's an impressive carved wooden chapel and Buddha; a 162-foot-high pagoda houses a strand of the Buddha's hair. Poke around in the small **Laan Thai Museum** to the left of the entrance, it contains some fine woodwork and old *phra wihaan* (spirit houses).

Wat Phra That Lampang Luang is on Tambon Lampang Luang, in Ko Kha, 18km (11 miles) south of the center of Lampang. This impressive complex is considered one of the finest examples of northern Thai architecture. If you mount the main steps toward the older temples, you'll see a site map, a distinguished wihaan (inspired by Wat Phra That Haripunchai in Lamphun), and behind it to the west, a chedi with a fine seated Buddha. Go back to the parking area and cross through the lawn filled with contemporary, painted-plaster Chinese gods. Past the old, old Bodhi tree—whose stems are supported by dozens of bamboo poles and ribbons—you'll see signs for the Emerald Buddha House. The small Phra Kaeo Don Tao image wears a gold necklace and stands on a gold base; it's locked behind two separate sets of gates and is very difficult to see.

The **Young Elephant Training Center,** on Lampang-Ngao Highway ☎ 053/229-042), is 54km (33 miles) east of Lampang. Demonstrations are given daily at 10am and 11am, with an extra show at 1:30pm on weekends and during festivals; the suggested contribution is 50B ($1.30). (Before your visit check with the TAT office in Chiang Mai to confirm the elephants are in training.) This center is run by the Veterinary Section of the Northern Lumber Production Division of the Forest Industry Organization, and is unlike the other elephant camps that are set up for tourists. The 3- to 5-year-old elephants train at this facility to harvest hardwoods, specifically teak, in the government-controlled forests. At any one time, there are about 100 elephants, all supervised by a veterinary staff and *mahouts* (handlers and trainers). Among the tasks that the elephants learn are pushing logs with both trunk and tusks, log hauling and piling, walking in procession, and crouching down to allow mahouts to mount and dismount. Elephants train throughout the year, except the hot season (March to May). You may see them frolicking in the Huai Mae La, too.

DOI INTHANON NATIONAL PARK   Thailand's tallest mountain, Doi Inthanon—2,563 meters (8,408 ft.)—is 47km (29 miles) south of Chiang Mai. It crowns a 360-square-mile national park filled with impressive waterfalls and wild orchids. Doi Inthanon Road climbs 48km (30 miles) to the summit. Along the way is the 100-foot-high Mae Klang Falls, a popular picnic spot with food stands. Nearby **Pakan Na Falls** is less crowded because it requires a bit of climbing along a path to reach. At the top of the mountain, there's a fine view and two more falls, **Wachirathan** and **Siriphum,** both worth exploring.

Admission to Doi Inthanon National Park is 10B (40¢). It's open daily from sunrise to sunset. Camping is allowed in the park, but you must check with the TAT or the national park office to obtain permits, schedule information, and regulations.

The area is a popular day-trip destination for residents of Chiang Mai. Take a blue bus to Chom Thong from the Chiang Mai Gate (1 hour, 20B/55¢). Day trips organized by Chiang Mai companies cost 1,200B ($31.60) including lunch. By car, take Route 108 south through San Pa Tong; continue south following signs to the national park. If you travel by private car, you can take an 8-mile side trip to Lamphun on Route 1015.

THE MAE SA VALLEY   The lovely Mae Sa Valley area, more developed than Doi Inthanon National Park, is about 20km (12 miles) northwest of Chiang Mai. A rash of condo construction and the sprouting of roadside billboards all indicate that Mae Sa Valley is being developed as a rural tourist resort, but it still has an unhurried feel. Current attractions include an elephant show (including rides), a cascade, and a nature park, as well as orchid nurseries. Most of these attractions are packaged by Chiang Mai tour operators as a half-day trip costing 500B ($13.15).

CHIANG DAO   The town of Chiang Dao, 56km (35 miles) north of Chiang Mai, and its environs offer several small resort hotels and a few fun activities, but if you don't have a car, the easiest way to sightsee is by joining a day trip organized by Chiang Mai operators, which costs about 900B ($23.70) per person. The Young Elephants Training Camp in Chiang Dao is rather touristy and not as good as that in Lampang (see above in this section), but it's still a nice treat for kids. The adventure begins as you cross a rope bridge and walk through a forest to the camp. After the elephants bathe in the river (showering themselves and their mahouts) they demonstrate log hauling and log rolling. There's an interesting free pamphlet. The shows are given daily at 9am and 10am; admission is 60B ($1.60) for adults and 25B (65¢) for children. After the show, you can climb into a howdah and take a safari across the Ping River and through the forest to a Lisu village. It's a 2½-hour trip and costs 300B ($7.90) per person. Brief elephant rides on the grounds are only 20B (55¢). To get there from Chiang Mai, take the bus from Chiang Puak Bus Terminal (☎ 053/211-586); the 1½-hour ride costs 21B (55¢). By car, take Route 107 north.

Sixteen kilometers (10 miles) north of the Young Elephants Training Camp is the **Chiang Dao Cave (Wat Tham Chiang Dao),** one of the area's more fascinating sites. Two caverns are illuminated by electric lights, and you can see a number of Buddha statues, including a 13-foot-long reclining one. The row of five seated Buddhas in the first cavern is particularly impressive. The cave and two connected caverns extend over 10km (6 miles) into the mountain, but you'll have to hire a local guide with a lantern to explore the unlighted areas. It's open daily from 8:30am to 4:30pm; admission is 10B (25¢). From Chiang Mai, take Route 107 north for 72km.

Touring the Northern Hills

Once you leave the bustle of urban Chiang Mai and its satellite cities, you begin to discover the heart of the north. The area's mountainous terrain, its proximity to the borders of Burma (Myanmar) and Laos, and the diverse ethnic hill tribes that have colored its history and culture are what distinguish northern Thailand from the rest of the country. There are dense jungles and teak forests logged by elephants. The Mae Khong River flows southeast down from the Golden Triangle, the opium-producing region straddling Burma and Laos.

Connected by highways that wind through forested mountains, descend into picturesque valleys, and pass through quaint farming villages, northern points are best explored overland, in a rented vehicle. If you can plan the time to drive, there are lookout viewpoints along the way, and places to stop and have a bite and relax. Treks, by foot, Jeep, elephant back, or boat, through the forested hill-tribe homelands—either north from Chiang Mai to Chiang Rai, north from Chiang Rai to the Burma/Laos/Thai border at the Golden Triangle, or northwest around Pai and Mae Hong Son, are a popular means to explore this region and get to know its unique people.

1 Mae Hong Son

924km (574 miles) NW of Bangkok; 355km (220 miles) NW of Chiang Mai via Pai; 274km (170 miles) NW of Chiang Mai via Mae Sariang

In Mae Hong Son, a province bordering Burma, you can discover large areas of scenic woodlands, waterways, and hill-tribe villages little affected by change. The verdant hills, mist-shrouded year-round, burst into color each October and November when *tung buatong* (wild sunflowers) come into bloom. The province's crisp air and cool climate guarantee a refreshing, relaxing sojourn.

This forested, mountainous region was little known until recently. Mountains scarred by slash-and-burn agriculture and logged teak forests indicated hill-tribe habitation, but the lack of infrastructure kept Mae Hong Son from public view. Change came in the mid-1980s, when Thailand's rapid industrialization began to incorporate hill-tribe peoples into the modern economy. Roads, airfields, and public works projects opened up the scenic province to all. Poppy fields gave way to terraced rice paddies and garlic crops. Simultaneously, the surge in tourism brought foreigners trekking into villages where automobiles were still unknown.

TAT efforts to promote tourism in this region, combined with the completion of two large hotels in the early 1990s, augured even greater change for the rapidly expanding provincial capital. Although Mae Hong Son will continue to be the focus of development for several years, its picturesque valley setting and lovely Burmese-style wats are worthy of a visit.

The mountains create more extreme **weather** here. The hot season (March to April) has temperatures as high as 104°F (40°C), and the rainy season is longer (May to October), with several brief showers daily.

THE PADUNG

Postcards, T-shirts, and dish towels emblazoned with the head of a young woman wearing a tall gold collar advertise one of Mae Hong Son's most intriguing attractions. She is from the Padung tribe, with a heart-shaped face, framed by short black bangs, that's different from that of most Thai tribal peoples.

The Padung, originally from Burma, are thought to be an aristocratic subgroup of the Karen tribe. Legend has it that many generations ago, when their kingdom was threatened by attacking Burmese troops, the Padung princess uprooted a solid gold tree that grew near the border of their territory and tied it around her neck for safe-keeping. As victory approached, the ruthless Burmese chopped off the princess's head in order to capture the tree. Thus, Padung women came to wear *moodee* or golden collars (now made of shiny brass) in her honor.

At the age of 9, Padung girls get their first half-inch-wide collar; they add one per year until they get married. A foot-long neck is highly prized; you'll see women with brass bands around their forearms and shins as well. The rings are mysteriously added by a local witch doctor; these women become so accustomed to them that by the time they are adults, the Padung women can no longer hold up their heads without the rings' support. The practice is dying out, but young women have been sighted wearing their first rings in other areas.

Unfortunately, seeing the Padung has become a political decision in our complicated world. It's estimated that fewer than 50 currently live in Thailand, mostly in Karen villages, on provincial land donated by the Thai government to Karen rebel groups expelled by Burma's military dictatorship. Because the Karen charge each visitor a 250B ($6.60) fee to see and photograph them (no video cameras are allowed), it's widely assumed that the Padung are kept at these villages to help fund rebel activities. I was told that the women are obligated to weave and sell small items in order to pay for room and board. While many tourists are turned off by the zoolike atmosphere, it is still an honor to be able to meet and support these unique, regal people.

ESSENTIALS

GETTING THERE   By Plane   Five daily Thai Airways flights connect Mae Hong Son to major routes via Chiang Mai (flight time: 45 minutes). During the July/August and November/December peak seasons, book in advance as flights fill up early. Also, be prepared for last minute flight cancellations. The valley sometimes fills with a cloud cover that blocks plane visibility. **Thai Airways'** office in Chiang Mai is at 240 Prapokklao Rd. (☎ 053/211-044), and in Mae Hong Son at 71 Singhanath-bamrung Rd. (053/611-297). The **Mae Hong Son Airport** (☎ 053/611-057) is in the town, toward the northeast.

By Bus   Three air-conditioned buses a day leave from Chiang Mai via Mae Sariang (trip time: 8 hours; 206B/$6.85); and four nonair-conditioned buses from Chiang Mai via Pai (trip time: 6 hours; 130B/$3.40). The **Chiang Mai Arcade Bus Terminal** is on Kaew Narawat Road, northeast of the old city across the Ping River

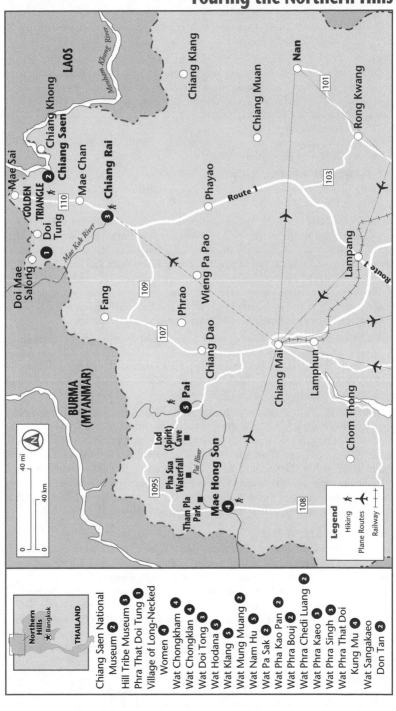

Legend

Hiking 🚶

Plane Routes ✈

Railway ━┼━

Chiang Saen National
Museum ②

Hill Tribe Museum ③

Phra That Doi Tung ①

Village of Long-Necked
Women ④

Wat Chongkham ④

Wat Chongklan ④

Wat Doi Tong ③

Wat Hodana ⑤

Wat Klang ⑤

Wat Mung Muang ②

Wat Nam Hu ⑤

Wat Pa Sak ②

Wat Pha Kao Pan ②

Wat Phra Bouj ②

Wat Phra Chedi Luang ②

Wat Phra Kaeo ③

Wat Phra Singh ③

Wat Phra That Doi
Kung Mu ④

Wat Sangakaeo
Don Tan ②

THAILAND

★ Bangkok

Northern
Hills

(☎ 053/242-664). The bus terminal in Mae Hong Son is on Khunlumprapas Road (the main street) 2 blocks north of the main intersection (☎ 053/611-318).

By Car   The 6-hour journey from Mae Hong Son is a fun mountain drive with spectacular views of rolling mountains, valleys carpeted with rice paddies, rural farm villages, and some nifty attractions, which are described in greater detail at the end of this section. The road is good quality, and safe driving, with places to stop for gas, food, toilets, and scenic points. Take Route 107 north from Chiang Mai to Route 1095 northwest through Pai.

A car with a driver can take you for 4,500B ($118.40). Call Mae **Hong Son Travel** at ☎ 053/611-621 for booking.

VISITOR INFORMATION   There is no TAT, but the **Tourist Police** (☎ 053/ 611-812), 1 Ratchathampitak Rd., 3 blocks east of the traffic light on the left, offers 24-hour assistance.

ORIENTATION   Mae Hong Son, or Amphur Muang (literally, capital city), is quite small, but contains three noteworthy landmarks: **Wat Phra That Doi Kung Mu,** on a hill at the west side of town; the **statue of King Singhanat Rajah** (the city's founder) on a small green at the town's center; and **Nong Chongkam Lake** to the east. Khunlumprapas, part of the Pai-Mae Sariang "highway" (Route 108) linking other provincial centers, is the town's main street and home to several travel agents, small hotels, and restaurants. Singhanat Bamrung Road, at the only traffic light, is the largest east-west street. The Night Market is one block east of this intersection.

GETTING AROUND   Walking is the best method of transport, but there are a few tuk-tuks parked outside the market for longer trips. A number of restaurants and guest houses rent 100cc motorbikes for day trips. Prices quoted ranged from 200B to 500B ($5.25 to $13.15) so be sure to shop around. Guest houses rent mountain bikes for 50B ($1.30) per day.

FAST FACTS   There are major **banks** along Khunlumprapas Road and Singhanat Bamrung Road with ATMs and currency exchanges. In addition, several banks open for each flight arrival at the airport. The **Sri Sangawan Hospital** is east of town on Singhanat Bamrung Road (☎ 053/611-378). The **post office** is opposite the King Singhanat Rajah statue (☎ 053/611-223). The **Overseas Call Office** is upstairs from the post office. I had a tough time finding an Internet cafe here, and was sent on a couple of wild goose chases, only to come up empty. I can only suspect that demand will see a few opening on main streets soon. Call the **Tourist Police** at ☎ 053/611-812.

WHAT TO SEE & DO

In town, there are many beautiful wats worth visiting. In the vicinity of Mae Hong Son, you can visit a village of long-necked Padung women, take a long-tail boat ride on the Pai River, or try an elephant ride in the nearby jungle.

Wat Chongklan and **Wat Chongkham** are reflected in the serene waters of Nong Chongkam Lake, in the heart of town. Their striking white chedis and dark teak viharn are the most telling elements of Burmese influence. Wat Chongklan was constructed from 1867 to 1871 as an offering to Burmese monks who made the long journey here to the funeral of Wat Chongkham's abbot. Inside are a series of folk-style **glass paintings** depicting the Buddha's life and a small collection of dusty Burmese wood carvings. The older Wat Chongkham (ca. 1827) was built by King Singhanat Rajah and his queen and is distinguished by gold-leaf columns supporting its viharn.

Wat Phra That Doi Kung Mu (also known as Wat Plai Doi) dominates the western hillside above the town, particularly at night, when the strings of lights rimming its two Mon pagodas are silhouetted against the dark forest. The oldest part (ca. 1860) of this compound was constructed by King Singhanat Rajah, and a 15-minute climb up its new naga staircase is rewarded by grand views of the mist-shrouded valley, blooming pink cassia trees, and Nong Chongkam Lake below. Each April, the national **Poy Sang Long Festival** honoring Prince Siddhartha's decision to become a monk is celebrated here by a parade of novices. Below Wat Phra That, there's a 40-foot-long **reclining Buddha** in Wat Phra Non.

There are two villages with **Padung** women in residence close to Mae Hong Son, and they can be visited in a day. **Rose Garden Tours,** 86/4 Khunlumprapas Rd. (☎ and fax **053/611-577**), has a half-day tour where you travel down the Pai River by long-tail boat to Nam Plong Dim village (800B/$21.05 per person). Their full-day trip takes you on a relaxing 2-hour bamboo raft to Huay Sua Tow village, and afterwards for a 1-hour elephant trek (1,200B/$31.60 per person). For short 1-day hill-tribe treks in the region, **Rose Garden Tours** (☎ **053/611-681**) has a couple of options, with stops at local natural attractions along Highway 1095 between Pai and Mae Hong Son. The first tour (700B/$18.40 per person) takes you to Meo and Shan villages, and a Kuomintang (KMT) village with stops at the **Pa Sua waterfall** and the **Fish Cave.** The second tour (also 700B/$18.40 per person) takes you to White Karen and Meo villages to the south of Mae Hong Son.

The Pai River originates in northern Burma and runs 180km (112 miles) down-stream through Pai and Mae Hong Son until it meets the Salween River in Burmese territory. During October and November, when the water is at its highest (30m wide by 7m deep/99 ft. by 23 ft. deep), rubber raft trips are a popular way to see the countryside. The best company for the trip is **Thai Adventure Rafting,** whose headquarters are in Pai, Rangsiyanon Road next to Chez Swan restaurant (☎ and fax **053/699-111,** www.activethailand.com/rafting), or visit their counter at the Mae Hong Son Airport. They'll be glad to arrange transportation from Mae Hong Song. See the section on Pai in this chapter for more details.

Mae Hong Son Off-Road Riding (☎ **053/611-537**) puts 10 years of experience to work in their exciting off-road motorbike trips through jungle paths. You can chose easy terrain to Pai and back again, or a more rugged trip with an overnight in a Karen Village. Bikes and safety attire are provided, and each group has a guide, mechanic, and spare motorcycle. Pay 3,500B ($92.10) per day for the trip.

WHERE TO STAY

Within the past decade, the first two grand hotels were built in Mae Hong Son to meet the influx of upscale tourists, overshadowing the pleasant but more modest accommodations that were available. The combination of luxury and landscape at the Rooks Holiday or Tara Imperial is a great experience if you can afford it, but the best value is found in the budget family-style guest houses clustering around Jong Kahm Lake, the base of Doi Kung Moo, or out of town.

Bai Yoke Chalet. 90 Khunlumprapas, Chong Kham, Amphur Muang, Mae Hong Son 58000. ☎ **053/611-536.** Fax 053/611-533. 40 units. A/C MINIBAR TV TEL. Low season 800B ($21.05) double. High season 1,330B ($35) double. Rates include breakfast. AE, MC, V. Mid-town across from post office.

This hotel offers decent, midsize rooms; though simple, they have some Thai style, with hardwood floors and private hot-water showers, and minibars. There's a pleasant second-floor terrace; rooms overlooking the back share access and are quieter. The coffee shop looks over the main street in town. The hotel is ideally situated, within walking distance to everything.

✪ **Fern Resort.** Contact Fern Travel Service, 87 Khunlumprapas Rd., Amphur Muang, 58000 Mae Hong Son. ☎ and fax **053/611-374.** 21 bungalows. Low season 975B ($25.65) bungalow with A/C; 760B ($20) bungalow with fan. High season 1,500B ($39.45) bungalow with A/C; 950B ($25) bungalow with fan. V, MC. 8km (5.4 miles) south of town.

Splendidly isolated on a hill with a rushing stream, beside the Mae Surin National Park, this newer resort combines harmony with nature and sufficient luxury. Tai Yai (Shan) style bungalows have *thong tueng* leaf roofs, glass windows and doors, simple but comfortable local-style furnishings, electric lights, and hot water in slate-tiled showers. The landscaping inspires relaxation, with bamboo irrigation gates sounding deep chimes with the water that trickles through them. Fern has its own clubhouse restaurant that offers local, Thai, and international cuisine. Experienced guides are available for nature treks.

Imperial Tara Mae Hong Son. 149 Moo 8, Tampon Pang Moo, Mae Hong Son 58000. ☎ **053/611-473.** Fax 053/611-252. 114 units. A/C MINIBAR TV TEL. Low season 2,884B ($75.90) double; from 4,944B ($130.10) suite. High season 3,296B ($86.75) double; from 5,650B ($148.70) suite. AE, DC, MC, V. 2km (1.2 miles) south of town.

Another deluxe hotel competing for the upscale traveler in Mae Hong Son. Although this place is about 2km (a little over a mile) out of town and deliberately rustic in style, the good taste, services, and upkeep mark it as one of Bangkok's Imperial chain of hotels. It's set on the edge of a teak forest and overlooks a lush garden with a stream running through it. The rooms are furnished in blond wood and wicker, with big wooden balconies, and the suites are positively enormous. There's a small fitness center, a medium-size free-form pool set into a wooden deck, and an open-air lobby restaurant with big round tables and a fine view. This place draws more Americans than other upscale resorts in the area—good or bad depending on your point of view. Also available is free airport transfer, tennis courts, and a gift shop.

Penporn Guesthouse. 6/1 Phadung Moi Tan, Amphur Muang, Mae Hong Son 58000. ☎ and fax **053/611-577.** 10 units. Low season 200B ($5.25) double. High season 300B ($7.90). Rates include tax and service. No credit cards. East from traffic signal, take fork to left, continue up to the left, find it on right.

This in-town lodge is more than a typical guest house; it's similar to a Spartan motel. Basic, bright rooms in an L-shaped wing surround a manicured lawn with potted flowers at the base of Doi Kung Moo Hill, off Khunlumprapas. Each is fan cooled and includes a private hot-water bathroom with shower. There's a simple rooftop breakfast terrace offering continental breakfast, plus open views of the mist-shrouded mountains.

Piya Guest House. 1/1 Khunlumprapas, Soi 3, Chong Kham, Amphur Muang, Mae Hong Son 58000. ☎ **053/611-260.** Fax 053/612-308. 14 units. 300B–450B ($7.90–$11.85) double; 600B ($15.80) bungalow with A/C. No credit cards. East side of Jong Kham Lake.

This is the best budget choice on beautiful Jong Kham Lake (easily the nicest part of town), and it's wise to book ahead in the busy season because the Piya usually has a waiting list. The hotel is a one-story wooden house with a garden courtyard; the airy rooms come with their own hot-water showers and toilets. The restaurant/bar/lobby needs major work, but the rooms are good for the price. Piya also runs a trekking service and rents out bikes and motorbikes at reasonable prices.

Rim Nam Klang Doi Resort. 108 Ban Huay Dua, Amphur Muang, Mae Hong Son 58000. ☎ **053/612-142.** Fax 053/612-086. 39 units. Low season 600B ($15.80) bungalow with A/C; 400B ($10.55) bungalow with fan. High season 750B ($19.75) bungalow with A/C; 500B ($13.15) bungalow with fan. V. 5km (3 miles) south of town on road to Huay Dua.

This small bungalow is a good-value in a rural setting. (Their minivan shuttles into town for 100B/$2.65 round-trip.) Many of the well-constructed bungalows have good river views; simple and cool in dark-wood tones. The small staff's English is lacking, but the resort grounds are lushly planted and attentively groomed. The better choices are the river-view bungalows with private hot-water showers. However, campers get the best deal because they can pitch their own tents or the resort's on the banks of the Pai for only 140B ($3.70) and have access to a toilet and cold-water shower.

Rooks Holiday. 114/5–7 Khunlumprapas Rd., Ching Kham, Amphur Muang, Mae Hong Son 58000. ☎ **053/612-212.** Fax 053/611524. 114 units. A/C MINIBAR TV TEL. Low season 1,212B ($31.90) double. High season 2,219B ($58.40). AE, DC, MC, V. 1½ km (1 mile) south of town.

Formerly part of the Holiday Inn chain, Rooks Holiday is a four-story deluxe facility that was once the toast of the town. Today, while the outside and public areas may not seem as impressive as they once were, the rooms are contemporary and well worth the money. Exceptional here are the balcony views of mountains towering above the beautifully landscaped grounds and two free-form swimming pools—they're especially ravishing in the morning, before the famous Mae Hong Son mists have blown away.

Prominent locals flock to the handsome, tile-floored dining room with more mountain views, which serves good Thai, Chinese, and Western fare at prices quite a bit higher than others in town. There's also a snooker club and a nightclub downstairs with local singers. They also have free airport transfer, in-house trekking services, an outdoor tennis court, and a pharmacy.

WHERE TO DINE

The local **Night Market** on Khunlumprapas is the busiest venue for budget travelers. Tiny tables are crowded with people sampling noodle soups, crisp-fried beef, dried squid, roast sausage, fish balls, and other snacks sold by various vendors. Prices run from 20B to 40B (53¢ to $1.05). Early risers (5:30 to 7am) will find it crowded with local merchants and vendors at breakfast.

Fern Restaurant and Bar. 87 Khunlumprapas Rd. ☎ **053/611-374.** Main courses 60B–120B ($1.60–$3.15). AE, MC, V. Daily 10:30am–2am (kitchen closes at 10pm). 1½ blocks south of traffic light, on left. THAI/CHINESE/INTERNATIONAL.

The biggest and best restaurant in town serves an especially wide variety of food for this part of the country—all of it well prepared and pleasantly served. The bar at the entrance has an inviting quality, and behind it an open-air deck stretches back toward another entertainment area with live music and a karaoke bar. If you come in the early evening, head for the rear left to get a view of Wat Phra That Doi Kung Mu.

Kai-Mook. 23 Udom Chaonitesh Rd. ☎ **053/612-092.** Main courses 50B–150B ($1.30–$3.95). No credit cards. Daily 11am–2pm and 5pm–3am. 1 block south from traffic light, turn left (east) and find it on right. THAI/CHINESE.

Kai-mook is a tin-roofed pavilion with more style than most: Overhead lights are shaded by straw farmer's hats, and Formica tables are interspersed between bamboo columns. The Thai and Chinese menu includes Kai-mook salad, a tasty blend of crispy fried squid, cashews, sausage, and onions, and a large selection of light and fresh stir-fried dishes.

EN ROUTE TO PAI

The **Tham Pla Park** is 17km (10½ miles) north of Mae Hong Son on Route 1095, the winding mountain road to Pai. This small landscaped park has been created around the Tham Pla, or fish cave. It's actually a grotto crowded with carp (legend says there are 10,000 of them) that mysteriously prefer it to the clear, flowing streams all around. There's a parking lot filled with young boys selling fish pellets (2B/5¢ per packet, but whoa! The carp wouldn't eat them!), a fancy visitors center (long closed), a Non-Formal Education Center with a Ping-Pong table, and a pretty promenade through the woods to the grotto.

There, under the watchful eyes of a religious shrine, are young girls selling papaya (6B/15¢ per packet) and hard-boiled eggs (12B/30¢ per packet)—both much preferred by the swollen carp—and candles and incense offerings for the shrine. The grotto, once unsuccessfully explored by Thai Navy divers, is said to be several meters deep and to extend for miles.

Ten km (6 miles) away in the park is the huge **Pha Sua Waterfall,** which tumbles over limestone cliffs in seven cataracts. The water is at its most powerful after the rainy season, in August and September. The Meo hill-tribe village of Mae Sou Yaa is beyond the park on a jeepable road, just a few kilometers from the Burmese border.

If you stop anywhere along the way, stop at the **Lod** or **Spirit Cave,** off Route 1095 (40km/24 miles northwest of Pai), about 8km (5 miles) north of the "highway" on a laterite road. This large, striking cave is filled with colorful stalagmites and stalactites, but more importantly, was discovered in the 1960s to be filled with **antique pottery** dating from the Ban Chiang culture. There are three caverns. The first is a lesson in natural cave architecture, while the second contains a prehistoric cave painting of a deer (which unfortunately has been largely blurred from curious fingers). The third cavern contains **prehistoric coffins** in the shape of canoes. A guide to all three caves is 100B ($2.65), with lantern rental. You'll have to give the canoe man an extra 200B ($5.25) to float you down the cave's river to the third cave. Or you can rent a lantern or bring a flashlight and explore on your own.

2 Pai

831km (516 miles) NW of Bangkok; 135km (84 miles) NW of Chiang Mai

Halfway between Chiang Mai and Mae Hong Son, the mountain road makes a winding descent into a large green valley carpeted with rice paddies and fruit groves. The mountains rise on all sides, and on warm afternoons, butterflies flit along the streets. Here you'll find a village called Pai, named after the river that runs through the valley. Pai is a speck of a place, a favorite for travelers who think Mae Hong Son is too overdeveloped. Pai's main roads (all four of them) are lined with homegrown guest houses, laid back restaurants and bars, local trekking companies, and some souvenir shops. Many people come here to raft down the Pai River, to trek to villages away from the Chiang Mai and Chiang Rai circuit, or to just hang around. Indeed, many who come for a few days find themselves sucked into the relaxed atmosphere and wake up a few weeks later to drag themselves away. In Pai, every day is a lazy Sunday.

One of the main attractions here, the Pai River, offers some of the best year-round river rafting in Thailand (but the best time is after the rainy season from August through to December), with nice rapids and stunning views of mountains and canyons. Trekking is also very good from here, with 2- and 3-day treks to Karen, Lahu, and Lisu villages, some of which see few outside travelers. You can also find a local map for hikes on your own to nearby waterfalls and caves. Or you can just stay in town sampling good food and enjoying the nightlife—both of which I think are better than in Mae Hong Son. Many of the business owners here are foreigners or bohemian Thais from Bangkok who come here for a better life, opening laid-back coffee shops and eateries and low budget bungalow operations, many of which are quite charming. If you're not exactly the backpacker type, Pai may not appeal to your tastes, but if you're in Thailand to do some serious unwinding, I recommend this village highly.

ESSENTIALS

GETTING THERE   By Bus   Four buses a day leave for Pai from Chiang Mai (trip time: 4 hours; 65B/$1.70). Four buses daily go to Pai from Mae Hong Son (trip time: 4 hours; 65B/$1.70). The **Chiang Mai Arcade Bus Terminal** is on Kaew Narawat Road, northeast of the old city across the Ping River (☎ **053/242-664**). The **bus terminal in Mae Hong Son** is on Khunlumprapas Road (the main street) 2 blocks north of the main intersection. All buses drop off and pick up at the "bus terminal" (more like a vacant lot) at one end of town. For bus information call ☎ **053/244-737.**

By Car   The scenic route is long, with steep, winding roads that make for some very pretty rural scenery: Take Route 107 north from Chiang Mai, then Route 1095 northwest to Pai.

A car with a driver can take you for 4,500B ($118.40). Call **Mae Hong Son Travel** at ☎ **053/611-318** for booking.

ORIENTATION & GETTING AROUND   Tiny Pai consists of four streets. Route 1095, or the Pai-Mae Hong Son Highway (colloquially known as Khetkelang Road), runs parallel to Rangsiyanon Road, which is the main drag for businesses. The bus terminal is at the northeast end of town at the crossroads of Rangsiyanon and Chaisongkram roads. Parallel to Chaisongkram is Raddamrong Road. Most of the guest houses and restaurants are in or around this central grid, with quite a few more bungalow resorts sprouting up in the countryside around the town. You can walk the town in 5 minutes. Some travelers like to rent a bicycle or motorcycle for day trips. Mountain bikes and motorcycles from guest houses or shops along the streets go for about 50B and 200B ($1.30 and $5.25).

FAST FACTS   You won't find TAT here, but what you will find are restaurateurs, bungalow owners, and travelers who can tell you more about the place than any authorized travel counter ever can. Pick up the *Detailed Map of Pai, Sop Pong and Mae Hong Son* published by the Pai Association for Travelers, on sale for 5B(15¢) at virtually every bungalow and eatery in town. There is one bank in Pai, on Rangsiyanon Road just next to Charlie House, with an ATM and money changing services on weekdays. The **Pai Hospital** (a tiny clinic; ☎ **053/699-211**) is 2 blocks west of the bus station. The **Town Police** is on Rangsiyanon Road (☎ **053/699-191**). The post office, where overseas calls can also be made, is about 1km (.62 mile) south of the police station. There are very few phones in town. A private telephone office is on Rangsiyanon in the center of town (☎ **053/699-024**). There's a small Internet cafe, appropriately named Sm@ll World, on Chaisongkram Road, just down and across the street from the bus terminal.

THINGS TO SEE & DO

No one comes to Pai because there's a lot to do. In the midst of relaxing, you can stroll around to the four small in-town wats. The principal one is **Wat Klang** next to the bus station, with several small pagodas surrounding a large one topped by a mondop. **Wat Hodana** and **Wat Nam Hu** are west of Route 1095; Nam Hu is known for its Chiang Saen–era Buddha, whose hollow head is filled with holy water. There's a **waterfall** about 7km (4.2 miles) west of town past the two wats, and a **hot spring** about 7km (4.2 miles) to the east, past the Pai High School.

The **Pai River** is perhaps the most exciting attraction. Overnight **rafting** trips take you through some nice rapids and scenic lazy spots, through canyons past walls of prehistoric fossilized lime and shell, and through a **wildlife sanctuary.** The pioneer of the rafting business, having routed out the territory some 10 years ago, Guy Gorias runs **Thai Adventure Rafting,** with regular trips year-round down the river. You'll begin from Pai, with a short van trip to the river, then 2 days to Mae Hong Son. From Pai the cost is 1,800B ($47.35) per person. All equipment is excellent quality imported from outside Thailand, and safety is emphasized. If you are in Mae Hong Son, his company will arrange a van to pick you up and rendezvous with the group at the river, at a cost of 1,900B ($50). Or, if you drive to Pai, they can arrange to deliver your car at the finish point (for a small extra charge), so you can continue your journey on to Mae Hong Son. Their Pai office is on Rangsiyanon Road next to Chez Swan restaurant (☎ and fax **053/699-111;** www.activethailand. com/rafting), or visit their counter at the Mae Hong Son Airport.

The Wild Planet, no. 9 Thonglor Soi 25, Sukhumvit 55, Prakanong, Bangkok (☎ **02/233-0977;** fax 02/712-8748; www.wild-planet.co.th), has the Pai rafting trip among their many adventure offerings. If you're planning other tours with them, you might want to throw this one in, too. Thai Adventure Rafting is their local operator, so you get the same trip as described above.

Small **trekking** companies, operated by locals, are at every guest house and on the main streets. The outfit with the best local reputation is at Duang Guesthouse. Pat, from a local Tai Yai village, takes you trekking for 3 days and 2 nights to Lisu, Karen, and Lahu villages in the hills around Pai for 1,200B ($31.60) per person. He's also put together a new 3-day/2-night trek to more remote villages—Karen, Lahu, and Tai Yai, with **bamboo rafting.** This trek, to areas not often visited, promises trekkers many quizzical stares from villagers (Pat got the giggles as he reminisced about recent treks). This trip is 1,500B ($39.45) per person. See him at **Duang Trekking** across from the bus terminal (☎ **053/699-101**).

Tiny Pai boasts quite a few traditional massage places. The best option is Mr. Jan's Herbal Sauna and Massage, where you'll get a Burmese-style massage which is much kinder and gentler than the rigorous Thai style. Ask around for directions to Mr. Jan's. It's on a narrow soi off Chaisongkram Road, and can be difficult to find, and there's no phone.

WHERE TO STAY

The previous edition of this book counted just over half a dozen guest houses in and around Pai. Today the number is closer to 40. You won't find a hotel (not five-star, four-star or any other star for that matter). Your choice for accommodations is limited to bungalow guest houses and resorts. Some of them are strictly budget—50B ($1.30) a night—backpacker dream shacks that aren't exactly comfortable. I've scouted around to find some pretty charming ones that are suitable for anyone and any budget.

Charlie's House. 9 Rungsiyanon Rd., Pai 58130, Mae Hong Son. ☎ **053/699-039.** 19 units. 200B ($5.25) double bungalow. No credit cards.

This small guest house is set in a nicely planted garden just off the main street, next to the Krung Thai Bank. Three fancy wooden bungalows, with the luxury of bedside lamps and hot-water showers, dominate the tranquil setting, but most rooms are very simple twin-bedded affairs in a block next to the clean communal toilets and showers. All rooms have fans and screened windows and are well maintained. This place is a very good value, with a new restaurant, a safe for valuables, and a more clean-cut crowd than most.

✪ **Pia on Pai.** 99 Moo 3 Viangtai, Pai, Mae Hong Son 58130. ☎ **053/699-539.** Fax 053/699-234. 35 units. 300B ($7.90) longhouse; 400B ($10.55) cottage; 500B ($13.15) riverside house. Cash only. 10-min. walk from bus terminal.

While the longhouse dormitory-style rooms and A-frame cottages are average standard, Pia's rooms in the riverside houses are my favorite choice in the whole town. The quaint wooden northern-style villas are connected by narrow boardwalks through gardens up to the Pai River. Inside, they have more space than average (for a bungalow) with wooden four poster beds, local wood carving crafts, and gobs of Thai country charm. Bathrooms are clean tile—a definite plus in comparison to other choices. One house even has adjoining rooms off a covered deck with a large wood opium bed and refrigerator for cocktail hour lounging—great for couples traveling together or families.

Thapai Spa Camping. Chiang Mai reservation office: 58/1 Patanachangpuak Road, Muang, Chiang Mai. ☎ **053/218-583.** Fax 053/219-610. Resort: 053/699-505, ext. 30. 20 units. 500B ($13.15) double; 700B ($18.40) double-sharing (for 4) or bungalow. No credit cards. Located 10-min. drive for Pai.

Don't let the name fool you—this is a small resort, not a campground. Located on the banks of the river, a 10-minute drive outside the town, the resort was built to take advantage of the small hot springs nearby. The highlight of this place—the free-form swimming pool filled with hot springs water— lets you enjoy the health benefits of a natural mineral soak without killing yourself (in the actual springs you can boil an egg). I liked Thapai's rooms, with walls made of local rock and masonry, large bathrooms, and a quaint garden courtyard, better than their bungalows. I also loved the rice paddies that fanned out from the resort's perimeter all the way to rising mountains in the distance. Unbelievable.

WHERE TO DINE

In addition to the suggestions below there are other eateries of note in town. **Pai Corner Bar** (no phone) on the corner of Rangsiyanon and Raddamrong roads, has fantastic sandwiches on crispy loaves—highly recommended. For a great selection of designer coffees and a laid-back breakfast atmosphere, head for **All About Coffee** (☎ 053/699-429) on Chiasongkram Road just across from Beebop. By the way, **Beebop** is the hottest nightspot in town, with an excellent house band, and a fun party crowd.

Thai Yai. Rangsiyanon Road, Pai. ☎ **053/699-093.** Main dishes 30B–120B (80¢–$3.15). No credit cards. Daily 7:30am–10:30pm. On main street, just south of Ratcharnrong Rd. WESTERN/THAI.

Thai Yai serves breakfast, lunch, and dinner, and there's always someone hanging out here, probably because the place serves up such terrific food and atmosphere at low prices. It's a clean, peaceful wooden room filled with picnic tables and plants, and there's a chessboard, music, and a small but excellent library to browse. On the walls you'll find information about projects that benefit the local hill-tribe people, including the ones that produce the raw materials for Thai Yai's excellent fresh-brewed coffee and whole-wheat bread.

Thairish. 26 Moo 4 Rangsiyanon Rd. ☎ **053/699-149.** Main dishes 30B–120B (80¢–$3.15). No credit cards. Daily 10am–2pm. 2 doors down from Thai Yai.

In a house that looks like a barn, Thairish is half Thai restaurant and half Irish pub, as its name suggests. Open late for beers, you'll hear Irish music in a fun and friendly atmosphere. The Thai and continental food is good, but when I was there, they were having a great Indian food party—fabulous curries and breads. If they've added these selections to the menu, you're in for a treat.

3 Chiang Rai

780km (485 miles) NE of Bangkok; 180km (112 miles) NE of Chiang Mai

Chiang Rai is Thailand's northernmost province; the mighty Mae Kok River (known to most readers as the Mekong of Vietnam fame) shares borders with Laos to the east and Burma to the west. The scenic Mae Kok River, which supports many hill-tribe villages along its banks, flows right through the provincial capital Amphur Muang, or Chiang Rai.

Chiang Rai is 1,885 feet above sea level in a fertile valley, and its cool refreshing climate, tree-lined riverbank, small Night Market, and easy-to-get-around layout lures travelers weary of traffic congestion and pollution in Chiang Mai. Although Chiang Rai has some decent hotels, good restaurants, and a convenient location to recommend it, the city already sees too many European tour groups, and I suggest that anyone seeking a really rural alternative to bustling Chiang Rai consider spending a few nights in Chiang Saen, the Golden Triangle, or Mae Hong Son.

ESSENTIALS

GETTING THERE   By Plane   Thai Airways has at least three flights daily from Bangkok to Chiang Rai (flying time: 85 minutes), and a daily flight from Chiang Mai (flying time: 40 minutes). Contact them in Bangkok at ☎ **02/232-8000,** or in Chiang Rai at 870 Phaholyothin Road (053/711-179).

The new **Angel Air** also flies from Bangkok to Chiang Rai daily. In Bangkok you can call them at ☎ **02/953-2260** weekdays and 02/535-6287 on weekends. Their agent in Chiang Rai is Hatsiam Tour at 2/1–2 Pratchasamphun Rd. (053/819-278).

The **Chiang Rai International Airport** (☎ **053/793-048**) is about 10km (6.2 miles) north of town. There's a bank exchange open daily 9am to 5pm and a gift shop. Taxis hover outside expectantly: Rates at the time of writing were 60B ($1.60) to town, 250B ($6.60) to Mae Chan, or 500B ($13.15) to Chiang Saen.

By Bus   Five air-conditioned buses leave daily from **Bangkok's Northern Bus Terminal** (☎ 02/272-5761) to Chiang Rai (trip time: 12 hours; price 412B/$10.85), but the two daily VIP buses have larger recliners for a more comfortable journey (640B/$16.85); 12 buses leave daily from Chiang Mai's **Arcade Bus Terminal** (☎ 053/242-664) (trip time: 3½ hours; 102B/$2.70). Chiang Rai's **Khon Song Bus Terminal** (☎ 053/711-369) couldn't be more conveniently located—on Phrasopsook Road off Phaholyothin Road near the Night Market just in the center of town. Tuk-tuks and samlors are easy to catch here for trips around town for 30B to 60B (80¢ to $1.60).

By Car   The fast, not particularly scenic, route from Bangkok is Highway 1 North, direct to Chiang Rai. A slow, scenic approach on blacktop mountain roads is Route 107 north from Chiang Mai to Fang, then Route 109 east to Highway 1.

By Boat   Long-tail boat taxis can be privately hired to ply the Mae Kok River between the village of Thaton and Chiang Rai (trip time: 3 or 4 hours; 1,200B/$31.60 per person). There's a daily bus from Chiang Mai at 12:30pm that goes directly to the boat pier (from the Chang Puak Bus Station on Chang Puak Road north of the north gate of the old city, ☎ 053/211-586) to connect with the Thaton boat taxi (160B/$4.20). You can take orange bus no. 1231 to Thaton town for 50B ($1.30) six times during the day (with morning buses), to arrange a whole day trip along the river with stops at interesting sites along the way. See "Things To See & Do" later in this section for more trip details. Songtao wait at the ferry in Chiang Rai to take you to town.

VISITOR INFORMATION   The **TAT** (☎ 053/744-674) is located at 448/16 Singhakai Rd., near Wat Phra Singh on the north side of town, and the Tourist Police are next door. The monthly *Welcome to Chiang Mai and Chiang Rai* is distributed free by most hotels, and has a good, reliable map of the town.

ORIENTATION   Chiang Rai is a small city, with most services grouped around the main north-south street, Paholyothin Road, until it turns right (east) at the Clock Tower, after which it's called Ratanaket. There are three noteworthy landmarks: the small clock tower in the city's center; the statue of King Mengrai (the city's founder) at the northeast corner of the city, on the superhighway to Mae Chan; and the Mae Kok River at the north edge of town. Singhakai Road is the main artery on the north side of town, parallel to the river. The bus station is on Prasopsuk Road, 1 block east of Paholyothin Road, near the Wiang Inn Hotel. The Night Market is on Paholyothin Road near the bus station.

GETTING AROUND   By Trishaw or Tuk-Tuk   You'll probably find walking the best method of transport. However, there are *samlors* (bicycle trishaws), parked outside the Night Market and on the banks of the Mae Kok River; they charge 10B to 30B (25¢ to 80¢) for in-town trips. During the day there are tuk-tuks, which charge 30B to 60B (80¢ to $1.60) for in-town trips.

By Bus   Frequent local buses are the easiest and cheapest way to get to nearby cities. All leave from the **bus station** (☎ 053/711-369) on Prasopsuk Road near the Wiang Inn Hotel.

By Motorcycle   Two local companies are recommended: **Soon Motorcycle,** 197/2 Trirath Rd. (☎ 053/714-068), and **Lek House,** 95 Thanalai Rd. (☎ 053/713337). Daily rates run about 550B ($14.45) for a 250cc motorcycle, 180B ($4.75) for a 100cc moped, and 15B (40¢) for a helmet.

By Car   **Avis** has a branch at the airport (☎ 053/793-827) and another at Dusit Island Resort Hotel (053/715-777), where self-drive vehicles cost from 1,800B ($47.35) for a Jeep to over 2,000B ($52.65) for a sedan, and cars with driver cost 6,300B ($165.80) per day, including insurance and 200km (120 miles) free. At **P. D. Tour & Car Rental Services,** 869/110 Pemawipat Rd. (☎ 053/712-829; fax 053/719-041), a Jeep goes for about 800B ($21.05) per day and a sedan for 1,200B ($31.60), not including gas.

FAST FACTS   This river valley and its surrounding areas have a mild climate similar to that of all northern Thailand, but the rainy season lasts longer here, usually April to July. Several bank exchanges are located on Paholyothin Road in the center of town. They are open daily 8:30am to 10pm. The **post office** is 2 blocks north of the Clock Tower on Uttarakit Road. There are plenty of **Internet** cafes, especially on the soi that leads off Paholyothin Road to Wiangcome Hotel, but the best one is **Chiang Rai Cyber Net** (☎ 053/752-513) just opposite form the hotel. Rates are 30B (80¢) per hour. The **Overbrook Hospital** (☎ 053/711-366) is on the north side of town at Singhakai and Trairat roads, west of the TAT. The **Tourist Police** (☎ 053/ 717-796) are next to the Tat on Singhakai Road.

A LOOK AT THE PAST

King Mengrai put Chiang Rai on the map in A.D. 1262. Born to the ruler of Chiang Saen's Yonnok Kingdom and a princess of Yunnan's Chiang Hung Kingdom, the ambitious Mengrai attacked his neighbors to the north and east as soon as he ascended to the Yonnok throne. To consolidate his conquests into the Lanna Kingdom, he established a new capital at the central city of Chiang Rai. With greater success in his imperial campaign, including the annexation of the Lamphun-based Nakorn Haripunchai Kingdom, he relocated the capital farther south to Chiang Mai. After 30 years as the center of power, Chiang Rai's position faded until it suffered under the hands of Burmese occupiers. In 1786 it became part of the Siam Kingdom and in 1910 was proclaimed an official province of Thailand by King Rama VI.

WHAT TO SEE & DO

In town, there are three historic wats and a small folk museum worth visiting. In the vicinity of Chiang Rai, you can visit hill-tribe villages, tour historic Chiang Saen, visit the scenic Golden Triangle, take a long-tail boat ride on the Mae Kok River, shop at the Mae Sai border, or explore the cool hillsides of Doi Mae Salong. You will probably be able to visit Burma (Myanmar) from Mae Sai and Laos from Chiang Khong.

Wat Phra Kaeo, on Trairat Road on the northwest side of town, is the best known of the northern wats because it once housed the Emerald Buddha now at Bangkok's royal Wat Phra Kaeo. Near its Lanna-style chapel is the chedi, which (according to legend) was struck by lightning in 1436 to reveal the precious green jasper Buddha. There is now a green jade replica of the image on display.

Wat Phra Singh is 2 blocks east of Wat Phra Kaeo. The restored wat is thought to date from the 15th century. Inside is a replica of the Phra Singh Buddha, a highly revered Theravada Buddhist image; the original was removed to Chiang Mai's Wat Phra Singh.

The Burmese-style **Wat Doi Tong** (Phra That Chomtong) sits atop a hill above the northwest side of town, up a steep staircase off Kaisornrasit Road, and offers an overview of the town and a panorama of the Mae Kok valley. It's said that King Mengrai himself chose the site for his new Lan Na capital from this very hill. The circle of columns at the top of the hill surrounds the city's new *lak muang* (city pillar), built to commemorate the 725th anniversary of the city and King Bhumibol's 60th birthday. It is often criticized for its failure to represent local style. (You can see the old wooden *lak muang* in the wihaan of the wat.)

The **Population and Community Development Association (PDA),** 620/25 Thanalai Rd., east of Wisetwang Road (☎ **053/719-167**), is a nongovernmental organization responsible for some of the most effective tribal development projects in the region. Through their family planning, waterworks, and agricultural projects, they have gotten to know their clients well. As part of their educational program, the top floor of the PDA offices has been turned into a small, but very interesting **Hill Tribe Museum.** With the help of international volunteers, a fascinating 20-minute slide show has been created to help visitors understand the different cultures of the nine major hill tribes. Its informative narration and the museum's well-labeled displays will teach you more, in less than an hour, than a day trip through the countryside. Children will enjoy touching many of the objects, making the tools work, and peeking into the model houses. There is a handicraft/clothing shop in front of the office where high-quality items for sale fund the PDA's work. Open daily 8:30am to 5pm; admission is a suggested contribution of 50B ($1.30) for the slide show.

Most of the **hill-tribe villages** within close range of Chiang Rai have become somewhat assimilated by the routine visits of group tours. If your time is too limited for a trek, several in-town travel agencies offer day trips to the countryside. Prices are based on a two-person minimum and decline as more people sign up; rates include transportation and a guide.

The best operation in Chiang Rai is **Golden Triangle Tours,** 590 Phaholyothin Rd. (☎ **053/711-339;** fax 053/713-963; e-mail: gotour@loxinfo.co.th). With about 20 different day and overnight trips, their experience has created offerings that are well in tune with what travelers seek in this area. For hill-tribe treks, they have day trips, and longer trips from 2 days and 1 night to 6 days and 5 nights. **Day trips** to surrounding villages include light trekking (1,300B/$34.20 per person for two or three people). If you include elephant trekking it's 1,700B ($44.75) per person for two or three people. Longer treks cost 3,200B ($84.20) per person (two to three people) for 2 days and 1 night, 4,200B ($110.55) per person for 3 days and 2 nights, and 7,500B ($197.37) per person for 6 days and 5 nights. You'll encounter numerous Akha, Hmong, Yao, Karen, or Lahu tribes, depending on the length of your trip.

Take a four-by-four over the **opium trail**—a 2-day excursion over newly cut roads connecting villages that are part of the Thai government's crop substitution project. In a tour designed to teach about the program and how it effects the hill-tribe way of life, you will see former opium villages with new schools and water systems, once only accessible by drug lord caravans. Learn about the struggles of integration into Thai society and the successes of the project while you learn about tribal peoples. The trip costs 5,300B ($139.45) per person (two to three people). Contact Golden Triangle Tours (☎ 053/711-339).

The **Mae Kok (Mekong) River** is a fascinating attraction here, not only for its historical significance, but also for its beautiful scenery on both the Thai and the Lao banks. You can hire a long-tail boat to zip you up and down the river, stopping at sites along the way. Charter boats begin at 7am, and can be booked at any time until 11pm. A full-day trip to Thathon and back costs 2,100B ($55.25) for boat hire. You'll have the option to stop at the Buddha cave, a temple within a cavern; an elephant camp, for trekking; a hot spring; and a riverside Lahu village. If you have limited time, you can hire a boat to view only one or two attractions from 300B to 700B ($7.90 to $18.40), depending on the stops you make. The ferry pier is beyond the bridge across from the Dusit Island Resort. Call **C. R. Harbour** (☎ 053/750-009) for information and taxi pickup.

Maesalong Tours, 882–4 Phaholyothin Rd. (☎ 053/712-515, fax 053/711-011), conducts half-day river cruises north of Chiang Saen, with a stop on the Lao side at the small riverside town of Muang Mom (1,520B/$40 per person). A full-day cruise includes additional stops at Stone Forest, with its picturesque natural rock formations, plus sand beaches and additional Lao villages (2,280B/$60 per person).

TOURS TO NEIGHBORING COUNTRIES

Many come to Chiang Rai in the hopes of crossing borders into the neighboring countries of **Burma (Myanmar)** and **Laos.** The areas of Burma that touch on Thailand's northern border are occupied primarily by the Shan people (relatives of the Tai Yai people of Thailand), who are infamous for their role in opium production and distribution, as well as for armed rebellions against the military junta that controls the country in which they live. Trekkers near the Burmese border are warned to take cautions against wandering too far into unknown territory—always travel with a guide who is familiar with Thai-Myanmar border positions. As for crossing the border at official sites, be prepared for disappointment. I've run into many travelers who were looking forward to crossing over at Mae Sai, a popular border crossing near Chiang Rai. But authorities are known to close the crossing here to internationals other than Thai and Burmese on a moment's notice. Even a visa from Bangkok will prove useless. A lot of people will try to tell you that crossing here is easy, but don't come with expectations. If you do wish to cross overland into Burma, and seek a more reliable gateway, see the sections on Mae Sot in chapter 9 or Ranong in chapter 7.

Laos is a different story. Friendly relations with Thailand, open doors to foreign visitors, and easy accessibility make this a far more practical trip from Thailand—and equally as fascinating. Laos has the lure that Thailand once had as a haven for back-packers seeking the adventure of remote destinations, contact with curious communi-ties, as well as gorgeous scenery and cultures. If you haven't procured a visa from the Laos consulate in Bangkok or your home country, numerous travel agents in Chiang Rai and Chiang Khong can get you one that is valid for 14 days of travel. It only takes a day and costs 1710B/$45.

For a do-it-yourself trip over the border, head for Chiang Khong along the Mae Kok River—"A Side Trip to Chiang Khong," later in this chapter has more details. For those with little time to travel or plan, several guided tours are organized in Chiang Rai—operators can take care of everything from visas to meals. **Golden Triangle Tours** (☎ **053/711-339**) has a day trip to the Laos border town, Houaixai, with a tour of the town; shopping; and visits to hill-tribe villages, cottage industries, and gems mines (4560B/$120 per person, two or three people).

Maesalong Tours, 882–4 Phaholyothin Rd. (☎ **053/712-505,** fax 053/711-011), coordinates longer trips to Laos. Cross the river at Chiang Khong, where you'll take a speedboat to Luang Prabang, an ancient capital with historic significance to both Laos and Thailand. Spend 2 days exploring the city's wats, museums, local markets, and surrounding natural beauty, and return by plane. The 3-day, 2-night trip costs $580 per person for two or three people.

Maesalong (☎ **053/712-515**) also has longer trips to the city of Kunming in Yunnan province, Southern China. A tour of this city, and Jing Hong, along the Mae Kok River in Laos, will reveal the origins of many Thai descendents, Chinese and Thai cultural ties, as well as the unique southern Chinese heritage. Cruise along the river to Chiang Saen, followed by a day tour of this towns' ruins and surrounding attractions. The 5-day, 4-night trip is 34960B/$920 per person for two to five people. They can also pare the trip down to 4 days and 3 nights for those with less time and spare cash.

WHERE TO STAY

This city of 40,000 has well over 2,000 hotel rooms, but group tours book most of these in the high season. The hotels listed are all within walking distance of the sights and shopping, with the exception of two very expensive choices, which are a 15-minute walk from the town center. You must add 7% government tax and 10% service charge to the rates quoted below unless otherwise noted. See "Tips on Accom-modations" in chapter 2, for more information.

VERY EXPENSIVE

✪ **Dusit Island Resort Hotel.** 1129 Kraisorasit Rd., Amphur Muang 57000, Chiang Rai. ☎ **053/715-777.** Fax 053/715-801. www.dusit.com. 271 units. A/C MINIBAR TV TEL. Low season 2,420B ($63.70) double; from 3,630B ($95.55) suite. High season 4,840B ($127.35) double; from 7,260B ($191.05) suite. AE, DC, MC, V. Over bridge at northwest corner of town.

Chiang Rai's best resort hotel occupies a large delta island in the Mae Kok River. It's sure to please those looking for international luxury and resort comforts, though at the expense of local flavor and homeyness.

The dramatic lobby is a soaring space of teak, marble, and glass, as grand as any in Thailand, with panoramic views of the Mae Kok. Rooms are luxuriously appointed in pastel cottons and teak trim. The Dusit Island's manicured grounds, pool, and other facilities create a resort ambience, but that shouldn't dissuade you from exploring the town. The hotel's most formal dining room is the semicircular Peak on the 10th floor, with sweeping views and a grand terrace overlooking the Mae Kok. The fine conti-nental fare will run $25 to $50 per person. Chinatown is a more casual Cantonese restaurant, with a large, tasty dim sum offering at lunch and excellent Chinese fare at dinner. The sunny coffee shop extends into an outdoor poolside terrace and makes for scenic dining. In the evening, there's the cozy Music Room bar and a new nightclub. An outdoor swimming pool, floodlit tennis courts, health club, and Yogi traditional Thai massage round out the resort's recreational facilities.

Rimkok Resort Hotel. 6 Moo 4, Tathorn Rd., Amphur Muang, 57100 Chiang Rai. ☎ **053/716-445.** Fax 053/715-859. 256 units. A/C MINIBAR TV TEL. 1,900B ($50) double; from 6,000B ($157.90) suite. AE, DC, MC, V. On north shore of Kok River, about 6km (3.7 miles) north of town center.

Though inconvenient, this riverside resort offers fine views. Well decorated and plush with first-class amenities, the rooms offer comforts rarely found in this town. The public spaces are also quite grand, thoroughly done over in Thai decor and arts and crafts, and lushly planted lawns open off large verandas. The Rimkok Resort has a free regular shuttle service to town, which is necessary as it's pretty far out. For meals, there's the attractive Saen Wee Coffee Shop and a poolside bar and terrace.

EXPENSIVE

Wangcome Hotel. 896/90 Penawibhata Rd., Chiang Rai Trade Center, Amphur Muang 57000, Chiang Rai. ☎ **053/711-800.** Fax 053/712-973. 234 units. A/C MINIBAR TV TEL. 1,500B–1,600B double ($39.45–$42.10); from 2,000B ($52.65) suite. AE, DC, MC, V. West off Paholyothin Rd.

The Wangcome is the best city hotel in town, plus it has a fabulous central location. Rooms are small but comfortable, detailed with Lanna Thai style, such as carved teak headboards. In the center of the hotel complex, rooms look out to the outdoor swimming pool. There's a lively coffee shop and a moody cocktail lounge, a popular rendezvous spot after the Night Market (across the street) closes.

Wiang Inn. 893 Paholyothin Rd., Amphur Muang 57000, Chiang Rai. ☎ **053/711-533.** Fax 053/711-877. 256 units. A/C MINIBAR TV TEL. 1,883B–2,354B ($49.55–$61.95) double; from 4,700B ($123.70) suite. AE, DC, MC, V. Center of town, south of bus station.

Wiang Inn offers full amenities, a helpful staff, several dining venues, a large pool, a reputable tour desk, and a convenient location, around the corner from the bus station and opposite the Night Market. Large rooms are trimmed in dark teak, with pale teak furniture and Thai artwork, including Lanna murals over the beds and ceramic vase table lamps. It's very well maintained, despite the steady stream of group tours, which makes an early booking advisable. Facilities are limited to a small pool and a massage center, but it is the best choice for a centrally located place to stay.

MODERATE

✪ **The Golden Triangle Inn.** 590 Paholyothin Rd., Amphur Muang 57000, Chiang Rai. ☎ 053/711-339. Fax 053/713-963. 39 units. A/C. 650B ($17.10) double. Rates include tax, service, and breakfast. MC, V. 2 blocks north of bus station.

A charming little hotel that offers comfort and lots of style and character, Golden Triangle is set in lush gardens—once inside you'd never believe bustling Chiang Rai is just beyond the front entrance. Large rooms have terra-cotta tiled floors, traditional-style furniture, and reproductions of Lanna artifacts and paintings. The owners and management are very down to earth and extremely helpful, and their operations are very well organized and professional. Their restaurant is excellent, and is reviewed separately in this chapter, as is their travel agency. My favorite pick for Chiang Rai.

INEXPENSIVE

Boonbundan Guesthouse. 1005/13 Jedyod Rd., Chiang Rai. ☎ **053/717-040.** Fax 053/712-914. 53 units. 100B–450B ($2.65–$11.85). No credit cards. South of Clock Tower.

This popular budget choice behind Wat Jedyod offers huge rooms with air-conditioning, private cold-water showers and toilets, and garden views at low prices. The smaller fan-cooled rooms, with shared hot-water shower and toilet, are an especially good value. There's an open pavilion restaurant crowded with budget travelers, a safe for valuables, and an inexpensive in-house trekking service.

White House Guesthouse. 789/7 Phaholyothin Rd., Amphur Muang 57000, Chiang Rai. ☎ **053/744-051.** 14 units. 150B ($3.95) double. Rates include tax and service. AE. Northeast edge of town, about 450 yards north of King Mengrai Statue.

This popular inn on the superhighway to Mae Sai isn't as noisy as its location may sound, and it's well run by an English-speaking staff. Fan-cooled rooms are pleasant, simple, and clean; they have private hot-water showers and toilets. The White House also has a small restaurant, rents vehicles, and runs treks at very reasonable prices.

YMCA International House. 70 Paholyothin Rd. Amphur Muang 57100, Chiang Rai. ☎ **053/713-785.** Fax 053/714-336. 24 units. From 400B ($10.55) double; dorm bed 90B ($2.35). 4¹/₂km (3 miles) north of center on the Superhighway.

Though the location isn't ideal, this modern hotel is an excellent value, and there's a swimming pool. Rooms are clean and comfortable, some with air-conditioning. There's an herbal sauna and Thai massage, and the Green Shop, selling health food, local herbal products, handicrafts, and organic snacks will appeal to the hippie in everybody.

WHERE TO DINE

There are several good restaurants in the heart of town, many of which serve northern Thai cuisine. Don't forget to try some of the pork and curry dishes and some local specialties: the huge *ching kong* catfish, caught in April to May; litchis, which ripen in June and July; and the sweet nanglai pineapple and pineapple wine, sold December to January.

Cabbages & Condoms. 620/25 Thanalai Road. ☎ **053/719-167.** Entrees 70B–200B ($1.85–$5.25). MC, V. Daily 10am–11pm. THAI.

Sister restaurant to Cabbages & Condoms in Bangkok, this northern branch was opened by the Population & Community Development Association to help support population control, AIDS awareness, and a host of rural development programs in the north. An extensive Thai menu, with local catfish specialties, is excellent. It's popular for tour groups, which also come for the exhibit upstairs (see "Things to See & Do" later in this section), but don't let that keep you away—it's good food for a good cause.

☺ Golden Triangle International Cafe. Golden Triangle Inn, 590 Phaholyothin Rd. ☎ **053/711-339.** Entrees from 80B–250B ($2.10–$6.60). V, MC. Daily 8am–10:30pm. THAI.

The decor, antique artifacts and photos, is an ode to old Chiang Rai. The owner grew up in the town, and loves it well. The best reason to eat here is for the menu, which is almost like a short book explaining Thai dinner menus, the various dishes that make up a meal, and describing the ingredients and preparation of each. The choose-your-own noodle dishes give you the chance to experiment with various tastes, and are prepared in quick and tasty fashion. Go for the regional treats, especially the curry sweetened with local litchies.

Islands Café. In the Dusit Island Resort Hotel, 1129 Kraisorasit Rd. ☎ **053/715-777.** Entrees 60B–300B ($1.60–$7.90). Daily 6am–11pm. INTERNATIONAL.

Overlooking the Kok River, this casual restaurant has excellent quality food and great selection. The lunch buffet is extensive and fresh and the atmosphere is cooling and relaxing. Like the rest of the resort's staff, waiters here provide excellent service.

The Night Market/Food Stalls. Trairat and Tanarai rds., northwest of Clock Tower.

Every night after 7pm, the cavernous, tin-roofed Municipal Market, south of the Rama Hotel comes alive with dozens of chrome-plated food stalls that serve steamed, grilled, and fried Thai treats. This is a fun sight (about a 10-minute walk northwest from the souvenir Night Market) but not as hygienic as most people would like.

SHOPPING

The recent influx of tourists has made Chiang Rai a magnet for hill-tribe clothing and crafts. You'll find many boutiques in the Night Market near the bus terminal off Phaholyothin Road, as well as some fine shops scattered around the city. Most are open daily from 8:30am to 10pm and accept credit cards. There's much less available than in Chiang Mai, but prices are reasonable.

Chiang Rai Handicrafts Center. 273 Moo 5, Paholyothin Rd. ☎ **053/713-355.** Open daily 8am to 6pm.

This is the largest of the hill-tribe shops, with a huge selection of well-finished merchandise, an adjoining factory, a good reputation for air-mail shipping, and a helpful sales staff that passes out hot tea to wilting shoppers. Aisle after aisle of newly made celadon and ceramics, textiles, pillow covers and table linens, carved woodwork, jewelry, and Thai handicrafts from other regions are sold at reasonable prices. The center is 4km (2.4 miles) north of town on the superhighway; call ahead for a free pickup.

Lily Handicraft Store. 869/85–86 Pisitsangoen Rd. ☎ **053/712-139.** Open daily 9am to 7pm. V.

Lily Tantanarat's shop is across from the Wangcome Hotel, and chock-full of local handicrafts. The array of clothing is particularly impressive, and much of it is made at a nearby factory—so that the prices are good and the fit is likely to be better than usual. There's a smaller branch on Phaholyothin Road near Silver Birch.

The Silver Birch. 891 Paholyothin Rd. ☎ **053/714-877.** Open from 10am to 10pm. No credit cards are accepted.

This popular shop near the Wiang Inn sells lovely old and new silver hill-tribe jewelry in addition to a wide variety of carved, unpainted wooden objects. The merchandise runs the gamut from tasteful flowers and bird mobiles, to sculptures of more dubious taste, like giant hands with male organs instead of fingers. There's a little table outside where drinks are served, and you can sit and watch the world go by on Paholyothin after making your purchases.

Sumalee's Handicraft Center. 879/7–8 Phaholyothin Rd. ☎ **053/752-273.**

Sumalee's is an interesting choice for handicrafts. While their specialty is in custom-order teak and rosewood furniture, they also have a good selection of smaller carved-wood items. They also carry silk and hemp fabrics.

CHIANG RAI AFTER DARK

Most visitors stroll through the Night Market and souvenir shop. It's really a miniversion of the more famous market in Chiang Mai. Shops clustered along Paholyothin Road near the Wiang Inn, and around the two lanes leading off it to the Wangcome Hotel, stay open until 10pm.

There's a small and rather tawdry nightlife district west and south of the Clock Tower along Punyodyana Road, a private lane with clubs named **Lobo, La Cantina, My Way, Mars Bar,** and **Butterfly.** You can also hit the disco or karaoke bar at the **Inn Come,** across from Little Duck on the superhighway, or have a draught beer and toss a few darts at the **Cellar Pub,** at the Dusit Island Resort.

A SIDE TRIP TO MAE SAI & THE BURMESE (MYANMAR) BORDER

Mae Sai, 60km (36 miles) due north of Chiang Mai, is Thailand's northern border crossing with Burma. A short concrete bridge leading to Tha Khi Lek spans the narrow stream separating the two countries. Normally hundreds of Thai and Burmese nationals, laden with goods to trade or sell, cross every day. However, the border is known to close at whim without prior notice, so don't count on a border crossing here as a definite feature of your vacation plans. If it is open during your visit, in addition to your passport, you will need three photos and $10 for the entry fee. You will probably be required to purchase $100 in local currency to spend in Burma—and the exchange rate will be substantially less on your return. Contact the TAT in Chiang Rai for more details.

Some people despise the crass commercialism of this ugly, newly built town. Dozens of girls in hill-tribe festival costumes and lipstick offer to pose for photographers (10B/25¢ per child, or 25B/65¢ for four children, per snapshot). More than 100 shops and stalls sell hill-tribe clothing, Burmese-made accessories and wood carvings, ruby and jade jewelry, *kalaga* (sequined Burmese tapestries), sandalwood, and herbal products. Shops are usually open daily 8am to 6pm. Bargain hard.

If you need to spend the night, the 32-room **Top North Hotel** (☎ 053/731-955), 305 Paholyothin Rd., is about 110 yards from the border post. Acceptable rooms with air-conditioning cost from 400B to 600B ($10.55–$15.80) (higher priced rooms have TV); Visa and MasterCard accepted. There are several small restaurants nearby.

Public buses leave every 15 minutes from Chiang Rai Bus Station (053/711-369); the 1½-hour trip costs 20B (50¢). Those with cars or motorbikes can take the Superhighway Route 110 north direct to Mae Sai or combine this with a side trip to Chiang Saen.

4 Chiang Saen & the Golden Triangle

935km (581 miles) NE of Bangkok; 239km (148 miles) NE of Chiang Mai

The small village of Chiang Saen has the sleepy, rural charm of Burma's ancient capital of Pagan. The single-lane road from Chiang Rai (59km/37 miles) follows the small Mae Nam Chan River past coconut groves and rice paddies guarded by water buffalo. Poinsettias and gladiola decorate thatched Lanna Thai houses with peaked rooflines that extend into Xs like buffalo horns. Deep irrigation ditches paralleling the road are often busy with women swinging fishing nets or sorting their catch in baskets balanced on inner tubes. Whole families in brightly patterned *lungi* (Burmese-style sarong) carefully tend fields of tobacco, strawberries, and pineapple.

Little Chiang Saen, the birthplace of expansionary King Mengrai, was abandoned for the new Lanna Thai capitals of Chiang Rai, then Chiang Mai, in the 13th century. With the Mae Khong River and the Laos border hemming in its growth, modern developers went elsewhere. Today, the slow rural pace, decaying regal wats, crumbling fort walls, and overgrown moat contribute greatly to its appeal. After visiting the excellent museum and local sites, most travelers head west along the Mae Khong to the Golden Triangle, the north's prime attraction.

Once upon a time, the Golden Triangle was the centerpoint of many illicit activities. The name was given to the area where Thailand, Laos, and Burma come together—a proximity that facilitated overland drug transportation of opium and heroin in its first steps toward international markets. Now cleaned up by Thai authorities, while some illegal activity goes on behind the scenes, the area is hardly filled with shady characters and titillating evidence of danger. Rather, Ban Sob Ruak, the Thai town at the junction, is a long and disappointing row of souvenir stalls. Still, if you stand at the crook of the river, you can look to the right to see Laos and to the left to see Burma. When the river is low, there's a sandbar in the river, that's apparently unclaimed by any authority.

ESSENTIALS

GETTING THERE   By Bus   Buses from Chiang Rai's Kohn Song Bus Terminal leave every 15 minutes from 6am to 6pm (trip time: 1½ hours; 20B (55¢). The bus drops you on Chiang Saen's main street. The museum and temples are walking distance, for convenient day trips, and songtao are across the street for trips to the Golden Triangle (about 10B/25¢).

By Car   Take the superhighway Route 110 north from Chiang Rai to Mae Chan, then Route 1016 Northeast to Chiang Saen.

VISITOR INFORMATION   There is no TAT, so make sure you talk to TAT in Chiang Rai before your trip. The staff at the few guest houses speak some English and try to be helpful.

ORIENTATION   Route 1016 is the village's main street, also called Paholyothin Road, which intersects after 500 meters (550 yd.) with the Mae Khong River. Along the river road, there are a few guest houses to the west, and an active produce, souvenir, and clothing market to the east.

GETTING AROUND   On Foot   There's so little traffic it's a pleasure to walk; all of the in-town sights are within 15 minutes' walk of each other.

By Bicycle & Motorcycle   It's a great bike ride (45 min.) from Chiang Saen to the prime nearby attraction, the Golden Triangle. The roads are well paved and pretty flat. **Chiang Saen House Rent Motor,** on the river road just east of the main street intersection, has good one-speed bicycles for 30B (80¢) per day and 100cc motorcycles (no insurance, no helmets) for 180B ($4.75) per day.

By Samlor   Motorized pedicabs hover by the bus stop in town to take you to the Golden Triangle for 60B ($1.60) one-way. Round-trip fares with waiting time are negotiable to about 250B ($6.60) for about 2 hours.

By Songao   Songtao (truck taxis) can be found on the main street across from the market; rides cost only 10B (25¢) to the Golden Triangle, or to nearby guest houses.

By Long-tail Boat   Long-tail boat captains down by the river offer Golden Triangle tours for about 350B ($9.21) per boat (seating eight) per half-hour. Many people enjoy the half-hour cruise, take a walk around the village of Sob Ruak after they've seen the Golden Triangle, and then continue on by bus.

FAST FACTS   There's a **Siam Commercial Bank** in the center of Phaholyothin Road, Route 1016, the main street, just close to the **bus stop, post** and **telegram office** (no overseas service and few local telephones), and the **police station.** The Chiang Saen National Museum are all on main street. There is a **currency exchange** booth at the Golden Triangle.

WHAT TO SEE & DO

Allow at least half a day to see all of Chiang Saen's historical sights before exploring the Golden Triangle. To help with orientation, make the museum your first stop. There's a good map about local historical sites on its second floor.

The **Chiang Saen National Museum,** 702 Paholyothin Rd. (☎ 053/777-102), houses a small but very fine collection of this region's historic and ethnographic products. The ground floor's main room has a collection of large bronze and stone Buddha images dating from the 15th- to 17th-century Lanna Kingdom. Pottery from Sukhothai-era kiln sites is displayed downstairs and on the balcony.

The handicrafts and cultural items of local hill tribes are fascinating, particularly the display of Nam Bat, an ingenious fishing tool. Burmese-style lacquer ware, Buddha images, and wood carvings scattered through the museum reinforce the similarities seen between Chiang Saen and its spiritual counterpart, Pagan. Allow an hour to go through the museum carefully. It's open Wednesday to Sunday 9am to 4pm, closed holidays; admission 30B (80¢).

Wat Pa Sak, the best preserved, is set in a landscaped historical park that contains a large, square-based stupa and six smaller chedis and temples. The park preserves what's left of the compound's 1,000 teak trees. The wat is said to have been constructed in 1295 by King Saen Phu to house relics of the Buddha, though some historians believe its ornate combination of Sukhothai and Pagan styles dates it later. The historical park is about 220 yards west of the Chiang Saen Gate (at the entrance to the village). It's open daily 8am to 5pm; admission 25B (65¢).

The area's oldest wat is still an active Buddhist monastery. Rising from a cluster of wooden dorms, **Wat Phra Chedi Luang** (or Jadeeloung) has a huge brick chedi that dominates the main street. The wat complex was established in 1331 under the reign of King Saen Phu and was rebuilt in 1515 by King Muang Kaeo. The old brick foundations, now supporting a very large, plaster seated Buddha flanked by smaller ones, are all that remain. Small bronze and stucco Buddhas excavated from the site are now in the museum. It's open daily from 8am to 5pm. Admission is free.

There are several other wats of note in and around the town. **Wat Mung Muang** is the 15th-century square-based stupa seen next to the post office. Above the bell-shaped chedi are four small stupas. Across the street, you can see the bell-shaped chedi from **Wat Phra Bouj.** It's rumored to have been built by the prince of Chiang Saen in 1346, though historians believe it's of the same period as Mung Muang. As you leave Chiang Saen on the river road, going northwest to the Golden Triangle, you'll pass **Wat Pha Kao Pan,** with some sculpted Buddha images tucked in niches and on its stupa, then the unrestored vihara mound of **Wat Sangakaeo Don Tan.** Both are thought to date from the 16th century.

THE GOLDEN TRIANGLE

The infamous Golden Triangle (12km/7½ miles northwest of Chiang Saen) is the point where Thailand, Burma, and Laos meet at the confluence of the broad, slow, and silted Mae Khong and Mae Ruak Rivers. They create Thailand's north border, separating it from overgrown jungle patches of Burma to the east and forested, hilly Laos to the west. The area's appeal as a vantage point over forbidden territories is quickly diminishing as there is now a legal crossing into Laos from nearby Chiang Khong.

Nonetheless, a "look" at the home of ethnic hill tribes and their legendary opium trade is still fascinating. Despite years of DEA-financed campaigns, the annual yield is still nearly 4,000 tons—about half of the heroin sold in the United States. The "surrender" of the notorious drug lord Khun Sa and his Muang Tai Army to the military dictators of Burma (Myanmar) effected little change—there were plenty of others waiting to take his place.

The appeal of this geopolitical phenomenon has created an entire village—Sob Ruak—of thatch souvenir stalls, cheap river-view soda and noodle shops, and very primitive guest houses. The **House of Opium,** 212 Moo 1 (☎ 053/784-062), is tiny and packed with visitors (if you see tour buses outside, go across the street and have a drink until they leave). Displays walk you through the opium process, from poppy cultivation, opium harvesting, drug production, and opium consumption. It makes a killing on camp appeal, but it is quite informative.

A SIDE TRIP TO CHIANG KHONG

From Chiang Saen you can travel downriver 70km (43 miles) to Chiang Khong, an official entry point into Laos. At the time of research, the only public transportation was a couple of songtao parked on the river road at the main intersection with Paholyothin Road in Chiang Saen. The more adventurous may want to follow the sometimes unpaved road along the river by private auto. You can also reach Chiang Khong from Chiang Rai by public bus; buses leave every hour between 5am and 6:45pm, and the 3-hour trip costs 39B ($1.03).

Chiang Khong's main street, Sai Klang Road, hugs the bank of the Mae Khong River and offers interesting views of river traffic, a couple of islands, and a French-built fort in Huaixai, Laos.

There are a few basic accommodations. I recommend the **Reuan Thai Sophapham** (☎ 053/791234), on the river north of Wat Phra Kaew, which has simple but clean rooms for 350B ($9.21) for a room with a fan, or from 500B to 600B ($13.15 to $15.80) for a double with air-conditioning (the higher-priced rooms have river views). The **Chiang Khong Hotel** (☎ 053/791182), a block farther north across the main street, has plain clean rooms with fans and hot showers for 150B to 200B ($3.95 to $5.25), or with air-conditioning for 250B to 350B ($6.60 to $9.21). There are several acceptable noodle shops along the main street, and **Rim Khong,** near the river down from the Damron Phusuk Hotel, offers some pretty good Thai food, with a small menu in English.

Unless you've acquired a proper tourist visa from a Lao Embassy in your home country, you'll have to get one in Thailand before you enter Laos. In Thailand, the embassies are located in Bangkok at 193 South Sathorn Rd. (☎ 02/539-667) and in Khon Kaen at 19/123 Nonthan Village, Phoathisan Road (☎ 043/223-698). The price for a 15-day tourist visa is 1,200B ($31.60). If you arrive without a visa, you can arrange to travel over for a day trip. For a price equivalent to $40, you'll be issued a day pass provided you have a current passport and a proper visa for reentry to Thailand. The price includes the cost of the ferry (only about 10B/25¢ anyway), and makes frequent trips all day long. Remember if you're only going for the day trip, the last ferry back to Thailand departs at 5pm. Check with the **TAT** in Chiang Rai (☎ 053/717-433) for the latest information before departing for Chiang Khong.

At the time of our research, only day trips to Laos were permitted; the border crossing fee was $10, and all foreigners were required to have a valid passport, three photos, and a valid Thai visa for reentry into Thailand. Check with the TAT in Chiang Rai (☎ 053/717433) for the latest information before departing for Chiang Khong.

WHERE TO STAY & DINE

There are a few tiny guest houses in Chiang Saen, and two fine resort hotels in the Golden Triangle area. I recommend the former to budget tourists who don't mind Spartan conditions, and the resorts to anyone who can afford them. The area is a very scenic, relaxing place—a good base for exploring all of the north.

The best restaurant ambience in tiny Chiang Saen is at the intersection of main street and the river road, with a large veranda overlooking the river. This is **Salathai,** known for its moderate prices and fine, simple Thai and Chinese fare geared to foreigners. There's also **Kaew-Varee,** a few doors up the street, with good food, a spotless venue, and a full menu of ice-cream selections.

For evening merrymaking, get on down to **Jang's Space,** in a little shop across from the Imperial Golden Triangle Resort. Have a beer while gazing out at Burma and Laos, and be entertained by the interesting characters who collect there.

Chiang Saen River Hill Hotel. 714 Moo 3 Tambol Viang, Chaeng Saen, Chang Rai. ☎ 053/650-826. Fax 053/650-830. 60 units. A/C TV. 800B–1,000B ($21.05–$26.30) double. No credit cards. 5-min. samlor ride from bus stop.

While the River Hill is a bit out of town, they have bicycle rentals for guests, and it's an easy peddle to the center of town. Guest rooms are quite interesting: Concrete block rooms with simple tile floors are dressed in northern finery, with wood carving details, and funky little Lanna-style seating arrangements—floor cushions around low *khan toke* tables under regal umbrellas! The large and colorful coffee shop (in shades of blue and aqua with little star lights from the ceiling) is open for breakfast, lunch, and dinner, with good selections and a relaxed and refreshing atmosphere.

Gin's Guest House. Chiang Saen. ☎ 053/650-847. 10 units, 1 bungalow. 300B ($7.90) double; 400B ($10.55) 4-person room. No credit cards. 1½ km from the bus station, on the road to the Golden Triangle.

This big, old two-story teak affair, with wide-plank floors and beautiful carved balconies and doors, is the most luxurious of the budget choices in Chiang Saen. The higher rates are for rooms with private hot-water bathroom and toilet. There's a porch that makes the most of the Mae Khong River view as well as a pleasant garden. Gin's lends bicycles at no charge for an hour, 15B (40¢) half day.

The Imperial Golden Triangle Resort. 222 Golden Triangle, Chiang Saen, 57150 Chiang Rai. ☎ 053/784-001. Fax 053/784-006. 73 units. A/C MINIBAR TV TEL. 3,500B–4,000B ($92.10–$105.25) double; from 7,000B ($184.20) suite. AE, MC, V. In Sob Ruak, 11km (7 miles) northwest of Chiang Saen.

This five-story hotel block looms over the west corner of tiny, souvenir-soaked Ban Sob Ruak. Modern, spacious guest rooms with pastel and rattan decor have large balconies, the more expensive rooms overlook the Golden Triangle. It's a fine, totally comfortable choice if you're passing through, but not nearly the tribal experience that the Le Meridien Baan Boran provides. There's a three-story, Lanna Thai–style restaurant, with multipeaked roofs, that serves northern Thai specialties and some continental cuisine and has an evening cocktail lounge. They also have a small outdoor pool.

✪ Le Meridien Baan Boran Hotel. Golden Triangle, Chiang Saen 57150, Chiang Rai. ☎ 800/225-5843 in the U.S., or 053/716-678. Fax 053/716-702. 110 units. A/C MINIBAR TV TEL. $100–$140 double; $250 suite. AE, DC, MC, V. Above river, 12km (7½ miles) northwest of Chiang Saen.

In stunning contrast to most new hotels, this one is a triumph of ethnic design. You'll never question whether you're in the scenic hill-tribe region because the Le Meridien Baan Boran's elegance and style depend on locally produced geometric and figurative weavings, carved teak panels, and pervasive views of the juncture of the Ruak and Mae Khong Rivers. On a hilltop just 2km (1.2 miles) west of the infamous Golden Triangle, the balconied rooms have splendid views. This oasis of comfort has attached rooms that are so spacious and private you'll feel like you're in your own bungalow. Tiled foyers lead to large bathrooms and bedrooms furnished in teak and traditionally patterned fabrics.

The **Yuan Lue Lau** is a lovely, casual dining pavilion with river views. Thai and continental set menus or main courses, snacks, and breakfast are served. Frequent barbecues and buffets are held on a lower, river-view terrace.

Appendix A:
Thailand in Depth

This appendix will introduce you to Thailand's history, its people, cultural traditions, and cuisine.

1 The Thai People

Although Bangkok at rush hour can feel packed with hordes, most of Thailand's 59 million people live in the countryside or in rural villages where they earn a living producing agricultural products, mostly rice.

For country folks who have trouble earning income, many relocate to Bangkok to find work. Population statistics for the capital put the number of residents at 6.7 million, but word on the street is that Bangkok has far surpassed the ten million mark. Bangkokians are divided between native Bangkok Thais (who hold a more prestigious position over their country cousins) and those who have settled here for jobs. Here you'll see a mix of middle-class university-educated professionals (most of whom are bilingual) mixed with up-country workers (who speak minimal English). It's an important distinction to Thais, who inherited a strict caste system from their Indian cultural ancestors. Today's Thai can meet a person, instantly size him up, and know precisely how to treat that person accordingly. Interestingly, as a foreigner, you are automatically awarded a position of stature, regardless of your social standing back home.

So, who exactly are the Thai people? It's hard to say. There really are no historically ethnic Thais. Today's Thai people (about 75% of the population) are a hodgepodge of waves of immigrants over the past ten or so centuries. "A Look at the Past," below, explains these waves in greater detail, but by in large the main bloodline is infused with indigenous people from the Bronze Age, southern Chinese tribes, Mons from Burma, Khmers from Cambodia, Malays, Arabs, and Europeans, plus more recent immigrants from China, Laos, Cambodia, and Burma. Although the central Thai people are a true melting pot, you'll find southern Thais have a closer ancestral affinity with Malays, while Thais in the north are more closely related to the Chinese hill tribes and Burmese people, and likewise in Isan in the northeast, where people trace their heritage to the Lao people. The remaining 25% are divided between Chinese (14%), and Indians, Malays, Karen, Khmer, and Mon (11%).

Statistics aside, the Thais are a warm and welcoming people. They take delight in any foreigner who takes an interest in their heritage, learns a little bit of the language, eats spicy food, and appreciates local customs. Above all, the Thai people have an incredible sense of humor. A light spirit and a big chuckle go a long way in Thailand. But to help you get by, I've provided some basic Thai etiquette—social norms throughout the country, Bangkok, and the rural parts included—that will put you in the good graces of most everyone.

ETIQUETTE   To the outsider, Thai customs can confuse and bewilder. While a lot of these social graces take time to pick up, even the most simple of gestures creates an enormous amount of goodwill.

Thais greet each other with a graceful bow called a *wai*. With hands pressed together, the higher they are held, the greater the show of respect. Younger people are always expected to *wai* an elder first, who will almost always return the gesture. Foreigners are somewhat exempt from this custom, as the cultural subtleties are difficult to grasp. In hotels, doormen, bellhops, and waitresses will frequently *wai* to you. Please do not feel compelled to return the greeting, a simple smile of acknowledgement is all that's necessary, or you'll be bowing all over town like a crazy person. In situations where a *wai* is appropriate (if you are meeting a business contact or a person of status), don't fret about the position of your hands. To keep them level to your chest is perfectly acceptable. Two exceptions—never *wai* to a child, and never expect a monk to *wai* back (they are removed from the custom).

One of the most important points of Thai etiquette you should remember is to always keep your wits about you. If you're prone to temper, aggravation, or frustration, it may sometimes be difficult for you to get by in this country. Anger and confrontational behavior are greeted here with blank stares. The Thais don't just think such outbursts are rude, they see it as an indication of a lesser-developed human being. The culturally sensitive Thais are not equipped to handle such in-your-face situations, and will do anything to spare themselves the embarrassment.

So what do you do if you encounter a frustrating situation? The Thai philosophy says, "*Mai pen rai,*" or, "Never mind." If it's a situation you can't control, like a traffic jam or a delayed flight—*mai pen rai*. If you find yourself in a truly frustrating situation, keep calm, try a little humor, and a nonconfrontational solution that will save face. The old "catching flies with honey" trick goes a long way in these parts.

The Thais hold two things sacred: their religion and their royal family. In temples, dress with respect—choose long pants or skirts with a neat shirt, and avoid sleeveless tops. Remove your shoes before entering temple buildings and give worshippers their space. Be mindful of your feet—sit with your legs curled beside you, never in front pointing at the Buddha image. While photographing images is allowed, do not climb on any image or pose near it in a way that can be seen as showing disrespect. Women should be especially cautious around monks, who are not allowed to touch members of the opposite gender. If a woman needs to hand something to the monk, she should either hand it to a man to give to the monk, or place the item on a saffron cloth laid in front of him. Never, ever, say anything critical or improper about the royal family, not even in jest.

To an outside observer, Thai society can seem very liberal, but in fact the opposite is true. You'll notice that, with some exceptions, the Thais dress very conservatively. If you're not sure what to wear, look around you. And while I've seen many tourists sunbathing topless at beach resorts, it is never accepted, merely tolerated. Thais are definitely not open to public displays of affection. While members of the same gender can hold hands and walk arm in arm, you'll never see a Thai couple acting this way. Some Thai women who date foreign men will bend the rules to compensate for cultural differences, and I have seen some mildly affectionate younger couples, but rarely so. Rule of thumb: As a couple, don't hold hands, touch each other, or kiss in public.

Here's the most innocent of insults, but one that most Westerners have a hard time getting used to: Don't use your feet to point at anything or to indicate anything ever. Especially do not point them at a person, or at a Buddha image. Buddhists believe the feet are the lowest part of the body—such gestures are unbelievably insulting.

In contrast, the head is considered the most sacred part of the body. Don't touch a Thai on the head, and avoid that friendly pat on the back or shoulders. Even barbers have to ask permission to touch a customer's crown.

2 A Look at the Past

THE EARLY PEOPLE Archaeologists believe that Thailand was a major thoroughfare for *Homo erectus* en route from Africa to China and other parts of Asia. The earliest evidence of prehistoric life lies in stone tools, dating back some 700,000 years from an excavation site around Lamphang in northern Thailand. Cave paintings, found throughout the country, are believed to originate as early as 2,000 B.C., with people dancing, dressed in feathers and kilts, with domesticated animals, popular regional fish such as dolphins (in the south) and catfish (in the north), and wild animals in hunting scenes and grassy patches that appear to be rice paddies. Human remains have been excavated at many exciting sites, the most famous of which, Ban Chiang, contained the first evidence of a Bronze Age in Thailand. Controversy over dating methods suggested that this area may have acquired metallurgy knowledge independent of the few other world centers who'd mastered the skill, but more accurate radiocarbon testing has put Thailand's Bronze Age at about 1500 to 1000 B.C., after China's. It is not known what eventually happened to these early inhabitants.

Modern civilization did not arrive in Thailand until about 1,000 years ago. There is archaeological evidence that points to an area in central and southern China as a cultural heartland for the descendents of many of the peoples of Southeast Asia. These people began to appear in northern Southeast Asia in the first millennium A.D., and continued to migrate south, east, and west in waves over the following 8 centuries, settling primarily in what is now Vietnam, Laos, Thailand, and Burma. These people, who are called *Tai,* became dispersed over a vast area of space, sharing a cultural and linguistic commonality. Their descendents are the core bloodline of the Thai people of today, the Shan of northern Burma, the Tai people of northern Laos, the Lu of Yunnan province in southern China, as well as groups in Vietnam, on the Chinese island of Hainan, and others in northeastern India. The total number of Tai people today is estimated at 70 million.

The **early Tais** lived in nuclear families with a dozen or two households forming an independently ruled *muang,* or village. They lived in raised houses in the lowlands, making a living from subsistence agriculture and gathering necessary items from the forest around them. In times of threat, either to economic stability or from outside aggression, many muang would collaborate and combine forces. The organization was usually lead by the strongest village or family. What developed were loosely structured feudal states where both lord and villager benefited—the lord from manpower and the villager from stability. The Tais expanded as ruling fathers sent sons out into the world to conquer or colonize neighboring areas, establishing new muang in farther regions.

THE DVARAVATI (MON) PERIOD From the 6th century, Southeast Asia underwent a gradual period of Indianization. Merchants and missionaries from India introduced Brahmanism and Buddhism to the region, as well as Indian political and social values, and art and architectural preferences. Many Tai groups adopted Buddhism, combining its doctrine with their own animistic beliefs. But the true significance of India's impact can be seen in the rise of two of the greatest Southeast Asian civilizations, the Mon and Khmer.

Historians have very little information about the **Mon civilization.** No one knows where these people came from, how far they reached, or where their capital was. What we do know is that around the 6th century A.D., the Mon were responsible for establishing Buddhism in central Thailand. Ancient Mon settlements lined the fringes of Thailand's central plains area, seemingly stretching as far west as Burma, north toward Chiang Mai, northeast to northern Laos and the Khorat Plateau, and east to Cambodia.

THE SRIVIJAYA EMPIRE In the southern peninsula, the **Srivijaya Empire,** based in Java, began to play an important role in cultural affairs. Before the 9th century A.D., port cities along southern shores had drawn traders from all over the region and beyond. However, the Srivijayas, who had assimilated their own unique brand of Buddhism from India, would have a lasting impression on these cities, linking them with other Southeast Asian lands and importing Buddhism and Buddhist art. While the empire never actually conquered and ruled the area, its cultural reign is still evident in Nakhon Si Thammarat, and in the southern arts of this period. Some historians argue that Chaiya, near Surat Thani, could have been capital of the empire for a time, but the claim is largely disputed. Srivijaya power, ground by endless warring with southern India, headed into decline and disappeared from Thailand by the 13th century.

THE KHMERS By the early 9th century A.D., the **Khmer Empire** had risen to power in Cambodia, spreading into surrounding areas. **Indravaraman** (877–89) saw the kingdom reach the Khorat Plateau in northeastern Thailand. **Suryavarman I** (1002–50) extended the kingdom to the Chao Phya Valley and north to Lamphun, driving out the Mons. **Suryavarman II** (1113–15?) pushed the kingdom even farther, forcing the Mons still deeper into Burma.

With each conquering reign, magnificent Khmer temples were constructed in outposts farther and farther from the Cambodian center of the empire. These early temples were built for the worship of Hindu deities. Brahmanism, having been brought to Cambodia with traders from southern India, influenced not only Khmer religion and temple design (with the distinct corncob shaped *prang,* or tower), but government administration and social order as well. Conquering or forcing villages into their control, the Khmers placed their own leaders in important centers and supplied them with Khmer administrative officers. The empire was extremely hierarchical, with the king as supreme power, ruling from his capital.

The populations of these outposts were largely Tai, and while the Khmers had the authority, Tais were blending in as laborers, slaves, and temple workers. Temple murals in Angkor show quite clearly the Khmer attitude toward what they called *Syam.* The mural shows a stiff orderly regiment of Khmer soldiers following Tais who were shoddy but fierce.

Angkor Wat, Cambodia's great ancient temple city, was built during the reign of **Suryavarman II.** It is believed the temples of Phimai and Phanom

Rung in Isan predated the Khmer's capital temple complex, influencing its style. But by this time the Khmer empire was already in decline. The last great Khmer ruler, **Jayavarman VII** (1181–1219), extended the empire to its farthest limits—north to Vientiane, west to Burma, and down the Malay peninsula. It was he who shifted Khmer ideology toward Buddhism, building temples in Khmer-style, but with a new purpose. His newfound Buddhism inspired him to build extensive highways (portions of which are still evident today), plus more than 100 rest houses for travelers and hospitals in the outer provinces. Jayavarman VII's death in 1220 marks Thailand's final break from Khmer rule. The last known Khmer settlement is at the sight of Wat Kamphaeng Laeng in Phetchaburi.

THE LANNA KINGDOM: THE NORTHERN TAIS   By 1000 A.D., the last of the Tai immigrants had traveled south from China to settle in northern Thailand. Several powerful centers of Tai power—Chiang Saen in northern Thailand, Chiang Hung in southern China, and Luang Prabang in Laos—were linked by a common heritage and the rule of extended families. In the region, muang grew stronger and better organized, but infighting remained a problem. In 1239, a leader was born in Chiang Saen who would conquer and unite the northern Tai villages and create a great kingdom. Born the son of the King of Chiang Saen and a southern Chinese princess, Mengrai ascended the throne in 1259, and established the first capital of the Lanna Kingdom at Chiang Rai in 1263. Conquering what remained of Mon and Khmer settlements in northern Thailand, he assimilated these peoples and cultures. After occupying Lamphun, he shifted his base of power to Chiang Mai in 1296.

Mengrai's Lanna Kingdom became an important empire in the north. Religiously, the Lanna Tais combined traditional animist beliefs with Mon Buddhism. Retaining Mon connections with Ceylon, the Lanna Kingdom saw the rise of a scholarly Buddhism, with strict adherence to orthodox Buddhist ways. Lanna kings were advised by a combination of monks and astrologers, ruling over a well-organized government bureaucracy. Citizens of Lanna enjoyed the benefits of infrastructure projects for transportation and irrigation; developed medicine and law; and heralded the arts through religious sculpture, sacred texts, and poetry. By and large the people were only mildly taxed, and were allowed a great deal of autonomy.

But a rising power threatened Lanna, as well as its neighbors. The Mongols, under the fierce expansionist leadership of Kublai Khan, forced their way into the region. Mengrai, forming strategic alliances with Shan leaders in Burma and two other Tai kingdoms to the south (one of which, the Sukhothai, would rise as the zenith of Thai culture), succeeded in keeping the Mongols at bay.

SUKHOTHAI: THE DAWN OF SIAMESE CIVILIZATION   While Mengrai was busy building Lanna, a small kingdom to the south was on the verge of stellar power. After the demise of first the Dvaravarti civilization, and later the Khmers, the Tai people who'd made their way into the Chao Phya valley found themselves in small disorganized vassal states. A tiny kingdom based in Sukhothai, would dwell in obscurity until the rise of founding father King Indraditya's second son, Rama. Single-handedly defeating an invasion from neighboring Mae Sot at the Burmese border, Rama proved himself a powerful force, immediately winning the respect of his people. Upon his coronation in 1279, Ramakhamghaeng, or "Rama the Bold," set the scene for what is recognized as the first truly Siamese civilization.

In response to the Khmer's tight grip, Ramakhamhaeng established himself as an accessible king. It is told he had a bell outside his palace for any subject to ring in the event of a grievance. The king himself would come to hear the dispute and would make a just ruling on the spot. He was seen as a fatherly and fair ruler who allowed his subjects immense freedoms. His kingdom expanded rapidly, it seems through voluntary subjugation, reaching as far west as Pegu in Burma, north to Luang Prabang, east to Vientiane, and south beyond Nakhon Si Thammarat to include portions of present-day Malaysia.

After centuries of diverse influences from outside powers, in Sukhothai, for the first time, we see an emerging culture that is uniquely **Siamese.** The people of the central plains had a heritage mixed with Tai, Mon, Khmer, and indigenous populations, with threads of India and China interwoven in their cultural tapestry. Ramakhamhaeng was a devout Buddhist, adopting the orthodox and scholarly Theravada Buddhism from missionaries from Nakhon Si Thammarat and Ceylon. A patron of the arts, the king commissioned many great Buddha images. While few sculptures from his reign remain today, those that do survive display gorgeous creativity. For the first time, physical features of the Buddha are Siamese in character. Images have graceful, sinuous limbs and robes, radiating flowing motion and delicate energy. Ramakhamhaeng initiated the many splendid architectural achievements of Sukhothai and nearby Si Satchanalai. In addition, he is credited with developing the modern Thai written language, derived from Khmer and Mon examples. Upon Ramakhamhaeng's death in 1298, he was succeeded by future kings who would devote their attentions to religion rather than affairs of the state. Sukhothai's brilliant spark faded almost as quickly at it had ignited.

AYUTTHAYA: SIAM ENTERS THE GLOBAL SCENE In the decades that followed, the central plains area found itself without firm leadership. Along came U Thong, born the son of a wealthy Chinese merchant family, he was also distantly related to the royals of Chiang Saen. Crowning himself Ramathibodi, he set up a capital at Ayutthaya, on the banks of the Lopburi River, and from here set out to conquer what was left of Khmer outposts, eventually swallowing the remains of Sukhothai. The new kingdom incorporated the strengths of its population—Tai military manpower and labor, Khmer bureaucratic sensibilities, and Chinese commercial talents—to create a strong empire. Ayutthaya differed quite greatly from its predecessor. Following Khmer models, the king rose above his subjects atop a huge pyramid-shaped administration. He was surrounded by a divine order of Buddhist monks and Brahman sanctities. During the early period of development, Ayutthaya rulers created strictly defined laws, caste systems, and labor units. Foreign traders from the region, China, Japan, and Arabia, were required to sell the first pick of their wares to the King for favorable prices. Leading trade this way, the kingdom was buttressed by great riches. Along the river, a huge fortified city was built—with temples that glittered as any in Sukhothai. This was the Kingdom of Siam that the first Europeans, the Portuguese, encountered in 1511.

But peace and prosperity would be disrupted with the coming of **Burmese invasion** forces that would take Chiang Mai (thus the Lanna Kingdom) in 1558 and finally Ayutthaya in 1569. The Lanna Kingdom that King Mengrai and his successors built would never regain its former glory. Fortunately Ayutthaya had a happier fate with the rise of one of the greatest leaders in Thai history. **Prince Naresuan,** born in 1555, was the son of the Tai King placed in Ayutthaya by the Burmese. Naresuan was directly descended from Sukhothai leaders, but his early battle accomplishments served to better distinguish him as a ruler. Having spent many years in Burmese captivity, he returned to Ayutthaya to raise armies to challenge Burmese rule. His small armies were inadequate against the Burmese, but in an historic battle scene, Naresuan, atop an elephant, challenged the Burmese crown prince and defeated him with a single blow.

With the Tais back in control, Ayutthaya continued through the following 2 centuries in grand style. Foreign traders—Portuguese, Dutch, Arab, Chinese, Japanese, and English—not only set up companies and missionaries, but were even encouraged to rise to some of the highest positions of power within the administration. Despite numerous internal conflicts over succession and struggles between foreign powers for court influence, the kingdom managed to proceed steadily. While its Southeast Asian neighbors were falling under colonial rule, the court of Siam was extremely successful in retaining its own sovereignty. It has the distinction of being the only Southeast Asian nation never to have been colonized, a point of great pride for Thais today.

The final demise of Ayutthaya would be two more **Burmese invasions.** The first, in 1760, was led by King Alaunghpaya, who would fail, retreating after he was shot by one of his own cannons. But 6 years later, two Burmese contingents, one from the north and one from the south, would besiege the city. The Burmese raped, pillaged, and plundered the kingdom—capturing fortunes and laborers for return to Burma. The Thai people still hold a bitter grudge against the Burmese for their horrible acts.

THE RISE OF BANGKOK: THE CHAKRI DYNASTY Interestingly, the Siamese did not hesitate to build another kingdom. The Burmese, leaving behind only small strongholds, left themselves open to a Siamese revival. Taksin, a provincial governor of Tak, in the central plains area, rose to power on military excellence, charisma, and a firm belief that he was divinely appointed to lead the land. Rather than build upon the ashes of Ayutthaya, Taskin rebuilt the capital at Thonburi, on the western bank of the Chao Phraya River, opposite present-day Bangkok. Within 3 years he'd reunited the lands under the previous kingdom, but his was a troubled rule. Taksin suffered from paranoia and his claims to divinity raised eyebrows in the monastic order and even within his own family. He had monks killed, and eventually his own wife and children. Regional powers were quick to get rid of him—he was swiftly kidnapped and while covered in a velvet sack was beaten to death with a sandalwood club and buried secretly in his own capital. These same regional powers turned to the brothers Chaophraya Chakri and Chaophraya Surasi, great army generals who'd recaptured the north from Burma, to lead the land. In 1782, Chaophraya Chakri ascended the throne as the first king of Thailand's present dynasty: the Chakri dynasty.

King Ramathibodi, as he was known, moved the capital across the river to Bangkok, where he built a Grand Palace, royal homes and administrative buildings, and great temples. The city was based upon a network of canals, with the river as the central channel for trade and commerce. Siam was now a true melting pot of cultures not limited to the Tai, Mon, and Khmer descendents of former powers, but including powerful Chinese, Arab, Indian, and European bloodlines. The king himself proved to be connected in some way to each major lineage. His early tasks were to reorganize the Buddhist monkhood under an orthodox Theravada Buddhist doctrine, reestablish the state ceremonies of Ayutthaya times without the emphasis of Brahman and animistic sensibility, and revise all laws based upon just and rational arguments. He also wrote the *Ramakien,* based upon the Indian Ramayana, a legend that has become a beloved Thai tale, and subject for many Thai classical arts.

While military threats continued to ensue from all directions, the kingdom continued to grow through a succession of kings from the new royal bloodline. Ramathibodi and his two successors expanded the kingdom to the borders of

The Ramakien: A Traditional Tale

The story of the *Ramakien* is a classic tale of morality from Hindu texts brought to Siam from India via Cambodia centuries ago when Hinduism reigned as the leading religion in Indochina. The Indo-Chinese cult of Vishnu made this tale, known as the Ramayana in India, a well-loved favorite, and over the years the characters and events took on their own unique Siamese traits.

The story is relayed in **temple murals** throughout the country.

The Ramakien:

Once upon a time there lived an evil demon king who ruled a dark land. King Tosakanth was too powerful to conquer, so his subjects remained enslaved.

The gods were concerned about the well-being of the people who lived on earth. Vishnu decided it was time to come to earth as a man and save everyone from Tosakanth. And so he incarnated himself as the great Rama, born into the world as prince of a great kingdom not far from the land of the demon king.

Rama grew to be a strong, brilliant, and handsome man who was loved by all in the land. One day Rama fell in love at first sight with the Princess Sita and she with him. Sita's father had promised that whoever may string the great Bow of Indra, a hard and stiff bow, would win his daughter's hand in marriage. Many suitors had tried and failed, but Prince Rama strung the great bow with ease, for he was a god. The two were married in a joyous ceremony.

Soon after, Rama's father decided that he was too old to rule the land, and announced that he would step down so Rama may rule. But the King had made a previous promise to another of his sons that he would be king. And so Rama went into exile with only his wife, the Bow of Indra, and two true arrows, Plaiwat and Promat. He declared that in 14 years time he would return to the kingdom having slain the evil Tosakanth, and would reclaim the throne. Another of his brothers, the brave and loyal Lakshman, was soon to join them.

present-day Thailand and beyond. Foreign relations in the modern sense were developed during this early era, with formal ties to European powers.

King Mongkut (1851–68) had a unique upbringing. As a monk he developed a scholarly character, which throughout his reign would show itself through his lean toward rational thinking and Western learning. With his son, **King Chulalongkorn** (1868–1910), he led Siam into the 20th century as an independent nation, establishing an effective civil service, formalizing global relations, and introducing industrialization-based economics. He united the royal line under the title Rama. Assigning the title Rama I to the dynasty's first king, Mongkut then became Rama IV, his son Rama V. As an aside, it was King Mongkut who hired Anna Leonowens (recall *The King and I*) as an English tutor for his children. Thai people want everyone to know that Mongkut was not the overbearing, pushover fop described in her account. Historians side with the Thais, for she is barely mentioned in court accounts—the story had its origins more in her imagination than in realty.

Meanwhile, word of Sita's immeasurable beauty reached Tosakanth in his kingdom. His love for beautiful women drove him into the forest where he found Rama and Lakshman, tricked them and kidnapped Sita, imprisoning her in his evil court.

Rama searched the forests with Lakshman for his wife. One day they encountered Hanuman, King of the monkey warriors. Hanuman volunteered to help Rama fight Tosakanth. On the way he met the beautiful Suwanna Malee, and fell in love. A princess from a distant land, Suwanna Malee vowed to enlist her father's armies for Rama's campaign. Hanuman traveled onward and found Sita unharmed in Tosakanth's court. He promised that he would return with Rama to free her.

Hanuman and Rama organized countless armies from many kingdoms for a great war with Tosakanth. They stormed the fortress and for days the armies fought the evil demon warriors. Finally Tosakanth challenged Rama to battle. Tosakanth, sensing his own weakness, drew a vial of poison from his breast and dipped the tip of his sword into the vial—a potion sure to kill Rama instantly. But Rama was forewarned of his trickery, and he drew the Bow of Indra and shot Tosakanth straight through the heart with the arrow Promat.

Tosakanth's miserable subjects were freed. The beautiful princess Sita was released and she and Rama were reunited. The following day, Rama ordered a trial by fire for Sita to prove her loyalty to him. She had been captive for 14 years, but the dying flames proved that she had successfully thwarted the evil king's advances and that she had remained true to Rama.

Armies returned to their homelands. Hanuman returned to Suwanna Malee's home, where they were married in a glorious ceremony. Rama returned to his kingdom exactly 14 years after his exile. His brother graciously gave up the throne. The entire kingdom and the lands beyond rejoiced.

The reign of **King Prajadhipok,** Rama VII (1925–35), saw the growth of the urban middle class, and the increasing discontent of a powerful elite. By the beginning of his reign, economic failings and bureaucratic bickering weakened the position of the monarchy, which was delivered its final blow by the Great Depression. To the credit of the king, he'd been pushing for a shift to constitutional monarchy, but in 1932, a group of midlevel officials beat him to the punch with a coup d'état. Prajadhipok eventually abdicated in 1935.

THAILAND IN THE 20TH CENTURY   Democracy had a shaky hold on Siam. Its original constitution, written in 1932, was more a tool for leaders to manipulate rather than a political blueprint to be adhered to. Over the following decades, government leadership changed hands fast and frequently, many times the result of hostile takeover. The military had constant influence, most likely the result of its ties to the common people as well as its strong unity. In 1939, the nation adopted the name "Thailand"—land of the free.

During World War II, democracy was stalled in the face of the Japanese invasion in 1941. Thailand gave up quickly, choosing alliance over conquer, even going so far as to declare war against the Allied powers. But at the war's end, no punitive measures were taken against Thailand, thanks to the Free Thai Movement organized by Ambassador Seni Pramoj in Washington, who had placed the declaration of war in his desk drawer rather than delivering it.

Thailand managed to stay out of direct involvement in the Vietnam War, however, it continues to suffer repercussions from the burden of refugees, as well as reap economic benefits from the infrastructure the U.S. military helped build. The United States pumped billions into the Thai economy, bringing riches to some and relative affluence to many but further impoverishing the poor, especially subsistence farmers, who were hit hard by the accompanying inflation. Communism became an increasingly attractive political philosophy to those ground down by burgeoning capitalism as well as to liberal-minded students and intellectuals, and a full-scale insurrection seemed imminent— which of course fueled further political repression by the military rulers.

In June 1973, thousands of Thai students demonstrated in the streets, demanding a new constitution and the return to democratic principles. Tensions grew until October when armed forces attacked a demonstration at Thammasat University in Bangkok, killing 69 students and wounding 800, paralyzing the capital with terror and revulsion.

The constitution was restored, a new government was elected, and democracy once again wobbled on. Many students, however, were not yet satisfied and continued to complain that the financial elite were still in control and were still resisting change. In 1976, student protests again broke out, and there was a replay of the grisly scene of 3 years before at Thammasat University. The army seized control to impose and maintain order, conveniently spiriting away some bodies and prisoners, and another brief experiment with democracy was at an end. Thanin Kraivichien was installed as prime minister of a new right-wing government, which suspended freedom of speech and the press, further polarizing Thai society.

In 1980, Prem Tinsulanonda was named Prime Minister, and during the following 8 years he managed to bring remarkable political and economic stability to Thailand. The Thai economy continued to grow steadily through the 1980s, fueled by Japanese investment and Chinese capital in flight from Hong Kong. Leadership since then has seen quite a few changes, including a military coup in 1991, and another student crackdown in 1992.

THAILAND TODAY

Every discussion of Thailand today begins with the economic crisis of 1997. On July 2, Thailand's economy was the first in the region to fall when it floated its currency; a move that caused the baht to devalue 20% in the week to follow. Other regional currencies fell like dominoes. The world watched as the economic scene unfolded, revealing a Southeast Asian legacy of suspicious government ties to industry, massive overseas borrowing, overbuilt property markets, and lax bank lending practices. Nations that once took pride in over 8% annual GDP growth rates stared down the barrel of growth rates in the negatives.

At first the military-led government sat on its hands, but in November 1997, Chuan Leekpai was elected into power to lead the country out of the crisis. Under his authority, Thailand accepted money and advice from the International Monetary Fund, began a revision of bank policies, and has tried to shake the shady ties between governing officials and big business. At the time of writing, economists report that the country is slated for a slow but steady recovery.

So what happened to the Chakri dynasty? King Bhimibol Adulyadej celebrated his sixth cycle birthday in 1998 (he turned 72). The king since 1946, he's seen the dynasty to the new millennium with dignity and noble grace. A compassionate man, while he has no real government power, he is believed by all to be the ultimate upholder of the will of the Thai people. He continues a proud cultural tradition that binds the national psyche to its past, present, and future.

THE BUDDHA IN THAILAND

Thai culture cannot be fully appreciated without some understanding of Buddhism, which is followed by 90% of the population. The Buddha was a great Indian sage who lived in the 6th century B.C. He was born Siddhartha Gautama, a prince who was carefully sheltered from the outside world. When he left the palace walls he encountered an old man, a sick man, a corpse, and a wandering monk. He concluded that all is suffering and resolved to search for relief from that suffering. Sensing that the pleasures of the physical world were impermanent and shallow, he shed his noble life and went into the forest to live as a solitary ascetic. But, nearing starvation, he was soon to realize this was not the path to happiness, so he turned instead to pure meditation. One night, while meditating under a Bodhi (fig) tree, with his mind pure he gained an intuitive insight into reality and a supernatural knowledge of the nature of the universe. His truth is the Dhamma—his doctrine, which he explained to his first five disciples at Deer Park in India—a sermon now known as "The Discourse on Setting into Motion the Wheel of the Law."

The highlights of his life include his temptation by Mara, the god of death, who sent demons to try to frighten him and have his beautiful daughters seduce him with voluptuous dancing; his protection by serpent king Mucalinda from raging floods that followed a 7-day storm; and his death and cremation. After his death two schools arose. The oldest and probably closest to the original is Theravada (Doctrine of the Elders), sometimes referred to less correctly as Hinayana (the Small Vehicle), which prevails in Sri Lanka, Burma, Thailand, and Cambodia, and Mahayana (the Large Vehicle), which is practiced in China, Korea, and Japan. In addition, Tibetan Buddhism and Zen Buddhism could be considered schools of their own.

The basic document is the **Pali canon,** which was recorded in writing in the 1st century A.D. The doctrine is essentially an ethical and psychological system in which no deity plays a role. It is a religion without a god, mystical in the sense that it strives for the intuitive realization of the oneness of the universe. It has no pope, no earthly authority, and no priests. It requires that individuals work out their own salvation as commanded by the Buddha himself, to "look within, thou art the Buddha," and in his final words, to "work out your own salvation with diligence." The open pagoda design of the temples reflects the openness and accessibility to all of the teaching that admits to no caste, no sex, no race superiority, and has no priest guarding the entrance to its portals. It is tolerant and seeks no converts.

What, you may ask, are the people doing who enter the temple and prostrate themselves before the Buddha, place their hands together in a gesture of worship, light incense, and make offerings of fruit and flowers? What role exactly does the Buddha image play and how did the image become so prevalent? At his death his disciples were distraught at the prospect of losing their great and beloved teacher, and they asked how they might remember him. Buddha granted them permission to make pilgrimages to the Great Events of his career and to gather his bodily relics and place them in stupas, or mounds, to remind them of his life and his teachings and to bring joy and contentment to their hearts. Stupas were built and the events of his life remembered by making symbolic representations of the elements of those events, and it was a short step from there to making representations of the Buddha himself. Buddha images were first produced about the beginning of the Christian era and have been reproduced by artists and artisans ever since. The images are honored in the same way that any great teacher is honored and revered in the Eastern tradition; they are not idols of worship but images that in their physical form radiate spirituality and convey the essence of Buddhist teachings. Flowers and fruits are offered by those who would pay their respects, and worshippers bow three times before the image—once for the Buddha himself, once for the sangha, and once for the dhamma.

Buddhism has one aim only: to abolish suffering. It proposes to do so by the purely human means of ridding oneself of the causes of suffering, which are desire, malice, and delusion. All Buddhists are expected to eliminate craving and ill will by exercising self-restraint and showing kindness to all creatures or "sentient beings," though only monks are able to participate directly in the struggle against delusion, which involves years of concentrated learning and discipline.

Other aspects of the philosophy include the law of *karma* whereby every action has effects and the energy of past action, good or evil, continues forever and is "reborn." (Some argue, though, that the Buddha took transmigration quite literally.) As a consequence *tam bun* (merit making) is taken very seriously. Merit can be gained by entering the monkhood (and most Thai males do so for a few days or months), helping in the construction of a monastery or a stupa, contributing to education, giving alms, or performing any act of kindness no matter how small.

When the monks go daily with their bowls from house to house, they are not begging, but are giving the people an opportunity to make merit; similarly the people selling caged birds, which people purchase and free, are allowing people to gain merit by freeing the birds. When making merit, it is the motive that is all important—the intention of the mind at the time of the action determines the karmic outcome, not the action itself. Buddhism calls for self-reliance; the individual embarks alone on the Noble Eightfold Path to Nirvana following the teachings that include the exhortations "to cease to do evil, learn to do good, cleanse your own heart."

Most Chinese and Vietnamese living in Thailand follow Mahayana Buddhism, and there are 34 such monasteries in the country.

Other religions and philosophies are also followed in Thailand including Islam, Christianity, Hinduism, and Sikhism. Sunni Islam is followed by more than two million Thais, mostly in the south. Most are of Malay origin and are descendants of the Muslim traders and missionaries who spread their teachings in the southern peninsula in the early 13th century. There are approximately 2,000 mosques in Thailand.

Christianity has been spread throughout Thailand since the 16th century by generations of Jesuit, Dominican, and Franciscan missionaries from Europe and Protestant missionaries from America. Even after centuries of evangelism, there are only a quarter of a million Christians living in the country. Yet Thais have accepted much that has come from the Christian missionaries, particularly ideas on education, health, and science.

3 The Language

Thai is derived principally from Mon, Khmer, Chinese, Pali, Sanskrit, and, increasingly, English. It is a tonal language, with distinctions based on inflection—low, mid, high, rising, or falling tones—rather than stress, which can elude most speakers of Western languages. Among students of Thai, there's a well-known sentence that can be composed of the word *mai* repeated with four variations of tone to say, "Doesn't the green wood burn?"

The grammar of Thai, however, is easily mastered, as there are no verb conjugations; one word says it for everyone. Verb tense indicators are easily learned, or you can stick with the present tense. One interesting aspect of the language that can be confusing to first-time visitors is that the polite words roughly corresponding to our sir and ma'am are not determined by the gender of the person addressed but by the gender of the speaker; females say *ka,* and males say *krup.*

The writing system is derived from Mon and Khmer, from southern Indian models, and is composed of 44 consonants (with only 21 distinct sounds) and 32 vowels (with 48 simple and diphthong possibilities). It reads from left to right, often without breaks between words. Few Westerners ever master it, and you should probably stick with trying to learn a few words of the spoken language.

Unfortunately there is no universal transliteration system—so that you will see the usual Thai greeting written in Roman letters as *sawatdee, sawaddi, sawasdee, sawusdi,* and so on, and the beach south of Pataya spelled Chomthien as well as Jomtien. Don't be afraid of getting lost in the different spellings. Derivations of most city names are close enough for anyone to figure out. The model most often used is more like French than English: *th* usually represents our *t* (as in Thailand); *t* represents our *d; ph* represents our *p; p* sounds more like our *b; kh* represents our *k; k* sounds like *g; r* often sounds like *l* or is not pronounced at all. (While, contrary to popular belief, there is an *r* in the alphabet, many Thais are lazy about pronouncing it, and you will hear the river called Chao Phya instead of Chao Phraya, especially by taxi drivers, who are mostly not from Bangkok.) Sometimes *r* is used merely to lengthen a vowel sound (Udon is often written Udorn), and *l* or *r* at the end of a word is pronounced more like our *n* (Ubon is often written Ubol). There is no *v* sound in Thai, and when you see it written, as in Sukhumvit, it should actually sound like our *w*—just the opposite of German. There is also an *ng*, which sounds like those letters in our word sing, used as an initial consonant and difficult for English speakers to hear and pronounce—though the distinction can be important: *noo* means rat or kid (informal for child), but *ngoo* means snake.

Most of the vowel sounds, however, will be familiar to those acquainted with the Romance languages—though the vowel sound in our word *see* may be written *ee* or *i,* that in our word "moon" may be *oo* or *u,* and that in our word *now* may be written *ow* or even *aew,* as well as the usual *ao.* Doubled vowels most often signify a simple lengthening of the sound, but *i* is usually pronounced as in "hit," and *ii* as in "meet."

Central Thai is the official written and spoken language of the country, and most Thais understand it, but there are three other major dialects: Northeastern-Thai, spoken in Isan, and closely related to Lao; Northern Thai, spoken in the northwest, from Tak Province to the Burmese border; and Southern Thai, spoken from Chumphon Province south to the Malaysian border. Each of these dialects also has several variations. The hill tribes in the North have their own distinct languages, most related to Burmese or Tibetan.

Just as in English, there are various degrees of formality, and words that are acceptable in certain contexts are impolite in others. The most common word for eat is *kin* (also written *gin*), usually *kin khao* ("eat rice"); *thaan* is more polite; *raprathaan* is reserved for royalty.

4 Thai Architecture 101

The Sukhothai period (13th–14th centuries) is regarded as the zenith of Thai culture, advancing major achievements in Thai art and architecture. One of the lasting legacies of the Sukhothai period is its sculpture, characterized by the graceful aquiline-nosed Buddha, either sitting in meditation or, more distinctively, walking sinuously. These Buddha images are considered some of the most beautiful representations ever produced. Sukhothai, the city, expanded and furthered the layout and decorative style of the Khmer capitals. With the inclusion of Chinese wooden building techniques and polychromatic schemes and Japanese-influenced carved flowing lines—the *wat,* or temple, with its murals, Buddhist sculpture, and spacious religious and administrative buildings, defined the first "pure" Thai Buddhist style. During this period came the mainstays of Thai wat architecture (in order of artistic importance): the *phra chedi* (stupa), *bot, wihaan, phra prang, mondop,* and *prasat,* all of which are explained further.

The dome-shaped *phra chedi*—usually called simply *chedi* and better known in the West as stupa—is the most venerated structure and an elaboration of the basic mound. Originally it enshrined relics of the Buddha—later of holy men and kings. A stupa consists of a dome (tumulus), constructed atop a round base (drum) and surmounted by a cubical chair representing the seated Buddha, over which is the *chatra* (umbrella) in one or several (usually nine) tiers. There are many different forms extant in Thailand: The tallest, oldest, and most sacred is the golden chedi of Nakhon Pathom (see chapter 6).

The *bot* (*ubosoth* or *uposatha*) is where the *bhikku* (monks) meditate and all ceremonies are performed. It consists of either one large nave or one nave with lateral aisles built on a rectangular plan where the Buddha image is enshrined. At the end of each ridge of the roof are graceful finials, called *chofa* (meaning "sky tassle"), which are reminiscent of animal horns but are thought to represent celestial geese or the Garuda (a mythological monster ridden by the god Shiva). The triangular gables are adorned with gilded wooden ornamentation and glass mosaics.

The *wihaan* (*vihara* or *viharn*) is a replica of the bot that is used to keep Buddha images.

The *phra prang,* which originated with the corner tower of the Khmer temple, is a new form of Thai stupa, elliptical in shape and also housing images of the Buddha.

The *mondop* may be made of wood or brick. On a square pillared base the pyramidal roof is formed by a series of receding stories, enriched with the same decoration tapering off in a pinnacle. It may serve to enshrine some holy object as at Saraburi, where it enshrines the footprint of the Lord Buddha, or it may serve as a kind of library and storeroom for religious ceremonial objects, as it does at Wat Phra Kaeo in Bangkok.

The *prasat* (castle) is a direct descendant of the Khmer temple, with its round-topped spire and Greek-cross layout. At the center is a square sanctuary with a domed *sikhara* and four porchlike antechambers that project from the main building, giving the whole a steplike contour. The *prasat* serves either as the royal throne hall or as a shrine for venerated objects, such as the *prasat* of

Wat Phra Kaeo in Bangkok, which enshrines the statues of the kings of the present dynasty.

Less important architectural structures include the *ho trai* or library housing palm-leaf books; the *sala,* an open pavilion used for resting; and the *ho rakhang,* the Thai belfry.

The Ayutthaya and Bangkok periods furthered the Sukhothai style, bringing refinements in materials and design. During the Ayutthaya period there was a Khmer revival; the Ayutthaya kings briefly flirted with Hinduism and built a number of neo-Khmer-style temples and edifices. The art and architecture evident in early Bangkok were directly inspired by the dominant styles of the former capital. After the destruction of Ayutthaya in the 18th century, the new leaders, having established their foothold in Thonburi, soon moved across the Chao Phraya to Bangkok and tried to copy many of the most distinctive buildings of Ayutthaya. This meant incorporating older Khmer (such as Wat Arun), Chinese, northern Thai, and, to a lesser degree, Western elements into contemporary wats, palaces, sculpture, and murals.

The last major influence in Thailand's architectural and artistic development was Western—and many would say that it is the single most important style today. Beginning with the opening up of the country to Europe during the later days of the Ayutthaya period, Jesuit missionaries and French merchants brought with them decidedly baroque fashions. Although the country was long reluctant in its relations with the West, European influences eventually became evident. Neoclassical elements were increasingly incorporated, notably in the Marble Wat in Bangkok, which was started by King Chulalongkorn in 1900 and designed by his half-brother, Prince Naris. A few decades later Art Deco became an important style, as can easily be seen today at Hualampong Station and along Ratchadamnoen Avenue, and the style is so prevalent that many writers use the term Thai Deco.

Today, much to the consternation of some leading Thai architects, anything goes, and you can see modernism, Greek revival, Bauhaus, sophisticated Chinese, and native Thai elements melded into eclectic designs that are often interesting and sometimes quite pleasing. Much of Bangkok, however, is almost indistinguishable from other fast-growing Asian capitals, such as Hong Kong and Singapore. Typical Thai wooden house blocks are cleared; klongs, filled in and replaced by wide thoroughfares; modern high-rise office and apartment complexes, hastily erected—in sharp contrast to the city's vibrant architectural treasures, which are fortunately being well preserved for visitors in search of something truly exotic.

5 Thailand's Exotic Bill of Fare: From Tiger Prawns to Pad Thai

Food is one of the true joys of traveling in Thailand. If you aren't familiar with Thai cooking, imagine the best of Chinese food ingredients and preparation combined with the sophistication of Indian spicing and topped off with red and green chili. The styles of cooking available in Bangkok run the gamut from mild northern *khan toke* to extremely spicy southern curries. In other words, you can find nearly any style of Thai (and international) cooking in the capital. Basic ingredients include a cornucopia of shellfish, fresh fruits, and vegetables—lime, asparagus, tamarind, bean sprouts, carrots, mushrooms (many different kinds), morning glory, spinach, and bamboo shoots—and spices, including basil, lemongrass, mint, chile, garlic, and coriander. Thai cooking also uses coconut milk, curry paste, peanuts, and a large variety of noodles and rice.

Among the dishes you'll find throughout the country are: *tom yum goong,* a Thai hot-and-sour shrimp soup; *satay,* charcoal-broiled chicken, beef, or pork strips skewered on a bamboo stick and dipped in a peanut-coconut curry sauce; spring rolls, similar to egg rolls but thinner and usually containing only vegetables; *larb,* a spicy chicken or ground-beef concoction with mint-and-lime flavoring; salads, made with nearly any ingredient as the prime flavor, but most have a dressing made with onion, chili pepper, lime juice, and fish sauce; *pad thai* ("Thai noodles"), rice noodles usually served with large shrimp, eggs, peanuts, fresh bean sprouts, lime, and a delicious sauce; *khao soi,* a northern curried soup served at small food stalls; a wide range of curries, flavored with coriander, chili, garlic, and fish sauce or coconut milk; spicy *tod man pla,* one of many fish dishes; sticky rice, served in the north and made from glutinous rice, prepared with vegetables and wrapped in a banana leaf; and Thai fried rice, a simple rice dish made with whatever the kitchen has on hand. ("American fried rice" usually means fried rice topped by an over-easy egg and sometimes accompanied by fried chicken.)

A word of caution: Thai palates relish incredibly spicy food, normally much hotter than is tolerated in even the most piquant Western cuisine. Protect your own palate with *"Mai phet, farang"* meaning "not spicy, foreigner." However, most Thai and Chinese food, particularly in the cheaper restaurants and food stalls, is cooked with lots of MSG (known locally as "Ajinomoto" because of the popular Japanese brand widely used), and it's almost impossible to avoid. If you want them to leave MSG out of your food, say *"Mai sai phong churot."*

Traditionally, Thai menus don't offer fancy desserts. The most you'll find are coconut milk–based sweets or a variety of fruit-flavored custards, but the local fruit is luscious enough for a perfect dessert. Familiar fruits are pineapple (served with salt to heighten the flavor), mangoes, bananas, guava, papaya, coconut, and watermelon, as well as the latest rage, apples grown in the royal orchards. Less familiar possibilities are durian, in season during June and July, which is a Thai favorite, but an acquired taste, as it smells like rotten onions; mangosteen, a purplish, hard-skinned fruit with delicate, whitish-pink segments that melt in the mouth, available April to September; jackfruit, which is large, yellow-brown with a thick, thorned skin that envelopes tangy-flavored flesh, available year-round; litchie; longan, a small, brown-skinned fruit with very sweet white flesh available July to October; tamarind, a spicy little fruit in a pod that you can eat fresh or candied; rambutan, which is small, red, and hairy, with transparent sweet flesh clustered round a woody seed, available May to July; and pomelo, similar to a grapefruit, but less juicy, available October to December. Some of these fruits are served as salads—the raw green papaya, for example, can be quite good.

The Thai family usually has an early breakfast of *khao tom,* a rice soup (made from leftovers) to which chicken, seafood, or meat may be added. Typically, it's served with a barely cooked egg floating on top and a variety of pickled vegetables, relishes, and spicy condiments to add flavor. It's widely available, even at the poshest hotels.

The Thais take eating very seriously, so businesspeople allow 2 to 3 hours for lunch. A formal business luncheon consists of several dishes, but most casual diners have a one-course rice, noodle, or curry dish. For two tourists, two hot dishes and perhaps a cold salad (mostly of the "not spicy" variety) are a satisfying way to sample new foods. Most restaurants throughout the country offer lunch from noon to 2pm; in fact, many close until 6 or 7pm before reopening for dinner.

Thais usually stop at one of the ubiquitous food stalls for a large bowl of noodle soup (served with meat, fish, or poultry), or dine at a department store food hall or market where they can buy snacks from many different vendors and have a seat. Snacking from street-side food stalls—some would claim the source of the best Thai food—is popular throughout the day. A note on etiquette: You won't see Thais walking down the street munching. Take a seat while you eat.

Dinner is the main meal, and consists of a soup (*gaeng jued*); curried dish (*gaeng ped*); steamed, fried, stir-fried, or grilled dish (*nueng, thod, paad,* or *yaang*); a side dish of salad or condiments (*krueang kiang*), steamed rice (*khao*), and some fruit (*polamai*). Two Thais dining out may share four or five dishes (typically balanced as sweet, salty, sour, bitter, and piquant), always helping themselves to a little portion at a time (so as not to appear gluttonous). Dishes are brought to the table as they're cooked and eaten in any order, family style. Use the serving spoon provided to put a little on your plate.

MEKONG & SANG THIP

You won't have a problem finding alcohol, as nearly every town in Thailand has an ample supply of bars, and liquor and beer are widely available in stores, restaurants, and hotels. Several fine varieties of beer are brewed in the country; the best known is Singha, and there's locally brewed Kloster (German) and Carlsberg (Danish) as well as imported Heineken. There isn't much in the way of Thai wine. Most wine is imported and often incredibly expensive—due in part to high import duties—but it's increasingly popular and readily available in Bangkok, Chiang Mai, and at the beach resorts, but not in the countryside, except in Western restaurants. Be warned that the storage of fine wines is sometimes not up to snuff, and you should consider the price and wine cellar conditions before splurging. Mekong and Sang Thip are two of the more popular local "whiskeys," even though they're actually rum (fermented from sugarcane). Thais will either buy a bottle or bring one to a restaurant where they can buy ice and mixers—usually cola or soda water. Waiters will keep the glasses full all the time. Be warned about doing shots in bars—while these "whiskeys" are incredibly inexpensive, sometimes they're laced with Red Bull, a locally produced caffeine and sugar injection that can push you over the edge.

Appendix B:
A Little Bit of Thai
to Help You Get By

Thai is a tonbal language, with distinctions based on inflection—low, mid, high, rising, or falling tone—rather than stress. There are five tonal markings:

low tone `
falling tone ^
middle tone (no marking)
rising tone ˇ
high tone ´

1 Basic Phrases & Vocabulary

Hello
Sawadee-krup (male)
Sawadee-ka (female)

How are you?
Sabai-dee r u?

I am fine
Sabai-dee

My name is . . .
P m chê . . . (male)
Deè-ch n chê . . . (female)

I come from . . .
P m/Deè-ch n ma jàk . . .

Do you speak English?
Khun pût pas angkrìt dâi m i?

I do not understand.
P m/Deè-ch n mâi khâo jai.

Excuse me.
Kh r tôd. (-krup, -ka)

Thank you.
Khòp khun. (-krup, -ka)

No; I do not want . . .
May âo . . .

Where is the toilet?
Hông sûam yù têe n i?

I need to see a doctor.
P m/Deè-ch n tôngkan m w.

Please call the police.
Chwây riâk tam-rùat dûay.

Never mind. No problem.
Mâi pen rai.

2 Getting Around

I want to go to . . .
Pôm/Deè-ch n yàk pai . . .

Where is the . . .
Yù têe n i . . .

taxi stand	**têe jòt rót téksêe**
bus terminal	**sat nee rót may**
train station	**sat nee rót fai**
airport	**san m bin**

boat jetty	**tâ rua**
bank	**tanakan**
TAT office	**tông tiâw pràtêt tai**
hospital	**rong payaban**

How much to . . . ?   What time does it depart?
Pai . . . tâo rai?   **Kèe mong jà àwk jàk têe nêe?**

3 In a Restaurant

coffee	**ca-fae**
tea	**naam-châ**
juice	**nám-kuá-la-m i**
bottled water	**nam kwât**
water	**naam**
wine	**wine**
bread	**ká-nom-pâng**
rice	**kâo**
chicken	**kài**
beef	**núa**
pork	**m o**
fish	**pla**
shrimp	**goông**
fruit	**kuá-la-m i**
dessert	**kong-wan**

I am a vegetarian.   Delicious!
P m/Deè-ch n kin jay.   **Ah-lòy!**

I don't like it spicy.   check
Mâi chôp pèt.   **chek-bin**

I like it spicy.
Chôp pèt.

4 Shopping

How much?   What is your best price?
Taô rai?   **Raka tàm sùt tâo rai?**

Expensive   Do you have a (smaller/larger) size?
Paeng   **Mee (lék kuà/yài kùa) née m i?**

Any discount?   Do you have another color?
Lót eèk dâi m i?   **Mee s e ùn m i?**

5 Numbers

one	**neung**	eleven	**sip-et**
two	**s ng**	twelve	**sip-s ng**
three	**sâm**	thirteen	**sip-s m**
four	**see**	twenty	**yee-sip**
five	**hah**	twenty-one	**yee-sip-et**
six	**hok**	one hundred	**neung-roi**
seven	**jed**	one thousand	**neung-pân**
eight	**pad**	one hundred thousand	**neung-s n**
nine	**gao**	one million	**neung-l n**
ten	**sip**		

A Little Bit of Thai

Index

Notes

FROMMER'S® COMPLETE TRAVEL GUIDES

FROMMER'S® DOLLAR-A-DAY GUIDES

Australia from $50 a Day
California from $60 a Day
Caribbean from $70 a Day
England from $70 a Day
Europe from $60 a Day
Florida from $60 a Day

Hawaii from $70 a Day
Ireland from $50 a Day
Israel from $45 a Day
Italy from $70 a Day
London from $85 a Day
New York from $80 a Day

New Zealand from $50 a Day
Paris from $85 a Day
San Francisco from $60 a Day
Washington, D.C.,
from $60 a Day

FROMMER'S® PORTABLE GUIDES

Acapulco, Ixtapa &
Zihuatanejo
Alaska Cruises & Ports of Call
Bahamas
Baja & Los Cabos
Berlin
California Wine Country
Charleston & Savannah
Chicago

Dublin
Hawaii: The Big Island
Las Vegas
London
Maine Coast
Maui
New Orleans
New York City
Paris

Puerto Vallarta, Manzanillo
& Guadalajara
San Diego
San Francisco
Sydney
Tampa & St. Petersburg
Venice
Washington, D.C.

FROMMER'S® NATIONAL PARK GUIDES

Family Vacations in the
National Parks
Grand Canyon

National Parks of the
American West
Rocky Mountain

Yellowstone & Grand Teton
Yosemite & Sequoia/
Kings Canyon
Zion & Bryce Canyon

FROMMER'S® GREAT OUTDOOR GUIDES

New England
Northern California

Southern California & Baja
Washington & Oregon

FROMMER'S® MEMORABLE WALKS

Chicago
London

New York
Paris

San Francisco
Washington D.C.

FROMMER'S® IRREVERENT GUIDES

Amsterdam
Boston
Chicago
Las Vegas

London
Los Angeles
Manhattan

New Orleans
Paris
San Francisco

Seattle & Portland
Vancouver
Walt Disney World
Washington, D.C.

FROMMER'S® BEST-LOVED DRIVING TOURS

America
Britain
California

Florida
France
Germany

Ireland
Italy
New England

Scotland
Spain
Western Europe

THE UNOFFICIAL GUIDES®

Bed & Breakfast in
New England
Bed & Breakfast in
the Northwest
Beyond Disney
Branson, Missouri
California with Kids
Chicago

Cruises
Disneyland
Florida with Kids
The Great Smoky &
Blue Ridge
Mountains
Inside Disney
Las Vegas

London
Miami & the Keys
Mini Las Vegas
Mini-Mickey
New Orleans
New York City
Paris
San Francisco

Skiing in the West
Walt Disney World
Walt Disney World
for Grown-ups
Walt Disney World
for Kids
Washington, D.C.

SPECIAL-INTEREST TITLES

Born to Shop: France
Born to Shop: Hong Kong
Born to Shop: Italy
Born to Shop: New York
Born to Shop: Paris
Frommer's Britain's Best Bike Rides
The Civil War Trust's Official Guide
to the Civil War Discovery Trail
Frommer's Caribbean Hideaways
Frommer's Europe's Greatest Driving Tours
Frommer's Food Lover's Companion to France
Frommer's Food Lover's Companion to Italy
Frommer's Gay & Lesbian Europe
Israel Past & Present
Monks' Guide to California

Monks' Guide to New York City
The Moon
New York City with Kids
Unforgettable Weekends
Outside Magazine's Guide
to Family Vacations
Places Rated Almanac
Retirement Places Rated
Road Atlas Britain
Road Atlas Europe
Washington, D.C., with Kids
Wonderful Weekends from Boston
Wonderful Weekends from New York City
Wonderful Weekends from San Francisco
Wonderful Weekends from Los Angeles

GET YOUR FREE TRIAL ISSUE!

FRESH. No-punches-pulled. Sometimes in your face. But ALWAYS crammed with hot tips, cool prices, and useful facts. That's every single issue of Arthur Frommer's BUDGET TRAVEL magazine.

Save 37% off the newsstand price! Call Today! 1-800-829-9121

ARTHUR FROMMER'S
BudgetTravel
vacations for real people
